**ORDNANCE SURVEY**

KU-356-835

STREET ATLAS
Oxfordshire

Contents

PHILIP'S

First edition published 1992
Second edition published 1994 by

Ordnance Survey	and	Philip's
Romsey Road		an imprint of Reed Consumer Books Limited
Maybush		Michelin House, 81 Fulham Road, London, SW3 6RB
Southampton SO16 4GU		and Auckland, Melbourne, Singapore and Toronto

ISBN 0-540-05986-2 (Philip's, hardback)
ISBN 0-540-05987-0 (Philip's, softback)
ISBN 0-319-00460-0 (Ordnance Survey, hardback)
ISBN 0-319-00461-9 (Ordnance Survey, softback)

To the best of the Publishers' knowledge, the information in this atlas was correct at the time of going to press. No responsibility can be accepted for any errors or their consequences.

The representation in this atlas of a road, track or path is no evidence of the existence of a right of way.

Printed and bound in Great Britain by
Butler & Tanner Ltd, Frome and London

Key to map symbols

Symbol	Description
⇌	**British Rail station**
⊖	**London transport station**
🚂	**Private railway station**
⬤	**Bus or coach station**
Ⓗ	**Heliport**
◆	**Police station** (may not be open 24 hours)
✚	**Hospital with casualty facilities** (may not be open 24 hours)
☐	**Post office**
+	**Place of worship**
▟	**Important building**
P	**Parking**
174	**Adjoining page indicator**
⨂	**No adjoining page**
═══	**Motorway or dual carriageway**
A27(T)	**Main or through road** (with Department of Transport number)
⊤	**Gate or obstruction to traffic** (restrictions may not apply at all times or to all vehicles)
- - - - -	**Footpath**
— — —	**Bridleway**
– – –	**Path**
═══	**Track**

The representation in this atlas of a road, track or path is no evidence of the existence of a right of way

Amb Sta	**Ambulance station**	LC	**Level crossing**
Coll	**College**	Liby	**Library**
FB	**Footbridge**	Mus	**Museum**
F Sta	**Fire station**	Sch	**School**
Hospl	**Hospital**	TH	**Town hall**

0	¼	½	¾	1mile
0	250m	500m	250m	1 Kilometre

The scale of the maps is 3½ inches to 1 mile (1:18103)

The small numbers around the edges of the maps
identify the 1 kilometre National Grid lines

Key to map pages

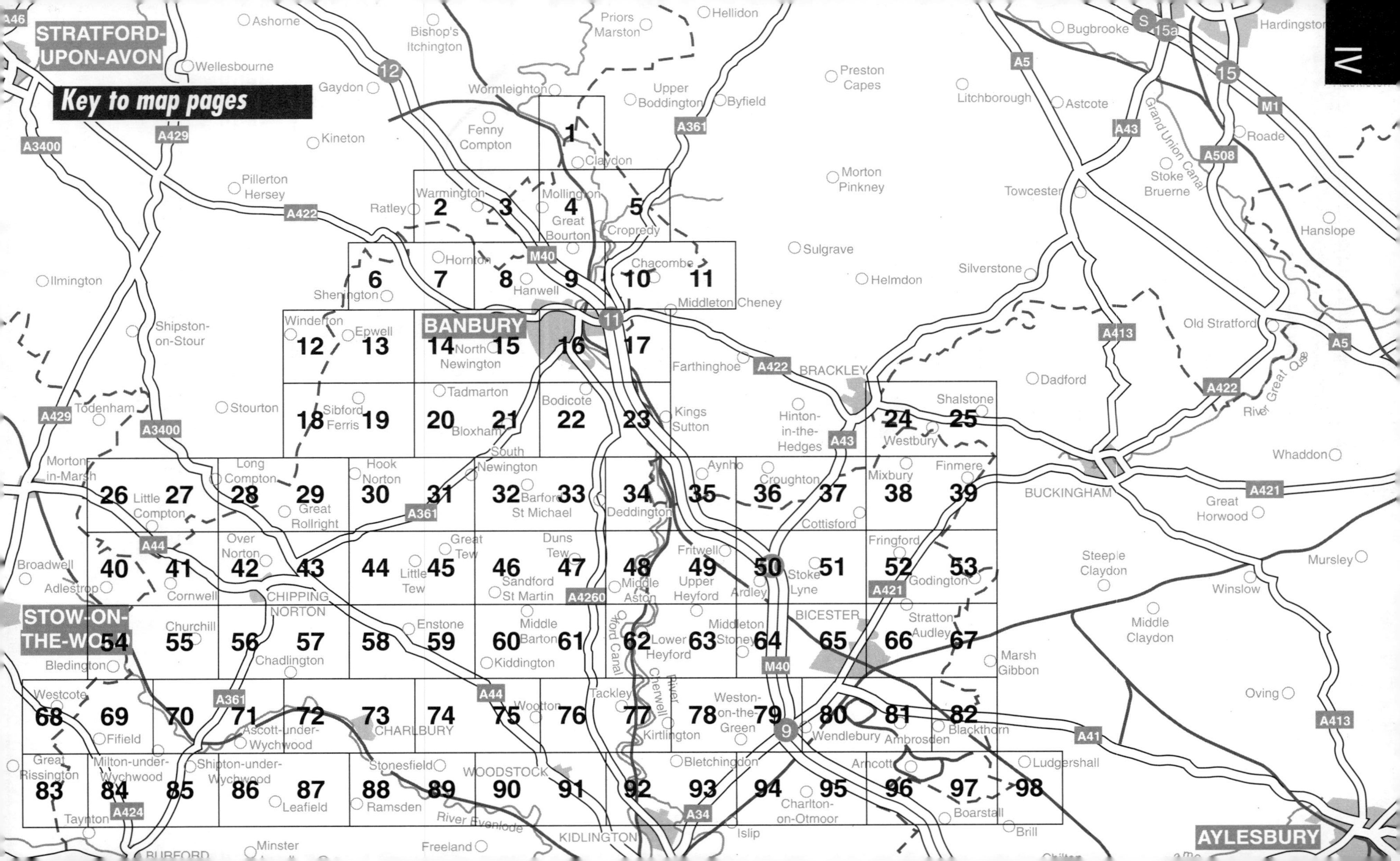
STRATFORD-UPON-AVON
BANBURY
BRACKLEY
BUCKINGHAM
BICESTER
CHIPPING NORTON
STOW-ON-THE-WOLD
CHARLBURY
WOODSTOCK
KIDLINGTON
AYLESBURY
BURFORD
Ashorne
Wellesbourne
Gaydon
Kineton
Bishop's Itchington
Wormleighton
Fenny Compton
Priors Marston
Hellidon
Upper Boddington
Byfield
Preston Capes
Litchborough
Astcote
Bugbrooke
Hardingstone
Roade
Stoke Bruerne
Grand Union Canal
Hanslope
Towcester
Silverstone
Morton Pinkney
Sulgrave
Helmdon
Old Stratford
River Great Ouse
Dadford
Whaddon
Great Horwood
Winslow
Mursley
Steeple Claydon
Middle Claydon
Oving
Pillerton Hersey
Ilmington
Shipston-on-Stour
Stourton
Todenham
Moreton-in-Marsh
Broadwell
Adlestrop
Bledington
Westcote
Great Rissington
Taynton
Minster
Freeland
Claydon
Warmington
Ratley
Mollington
Great Bourton
Cropredy
Hornton
Hanwell
Chacombe
Middleton Cheney
Shenington
Windetton
Epwell
North Newington
Farthinghoe
Sibford Ferris
Tadmarton
Bloxham
Bodicote
Kings Sutton
Hinton-in-the-Hedges
Shalstone
Westbury
Finmere
Mixbury
Aynho
Croughton
Cottisford
Long Compton
Little Compton
Great Rollright
Hook Norton
South Newington
Barford St Michael
Deddington
Over Norton
Cornwell
Great Tew
Little Tew
Duns Tew
Sandford St Martin
Middle Aston
Fritwell
Upper Heyford
Ardley
Stoke Lyne
Fringford
Godington
Churchill
Chadlington
Enstone
Middle Barton
Kiddington
Oxford Canal
Lower Heyford
Middleton Stoney
Stratton Audley
Marsh Gibbon
Fifield
Ascott-under-Wychwood
Wootton
Tackley
River Cherwell
Kirtlington
Weston-on-the-Green
Wendlebury
Ambrosden
Blackthorn
Milton-under-Wychwood
Shipton-under-Wychwood
Leafield
Stonesfield
Ramsden
River Evenlode
Bletchingdon
Islip
Charlton-on-Otmoor
Arncott
Boarstall
Ludgershall
Brill
M1
M40
A5
A43
A508
A413
A422
A421
A41
A361
A429
A3400
A44
A4260
A34
A424
A46
12
11
9
15
15a
S
1 2 3 4 5 6 7 8 9 10 11 12 13 14 15 16 17 18 19 20 21 22 23 24 25 26 27 28 29 30 31 32 33 34 35 36 37 38 39 40 41 42 43 44 45 46 47 48 49 50 51 52 53 54 55 56 57 58 59 60 61 62 63 64 65 66 67 68 69 70 71 72 73 74 75 76 77 78 79 80 81 82 83 84 85 86 87 88 89 90 91 92 93 94 95 96 97 98

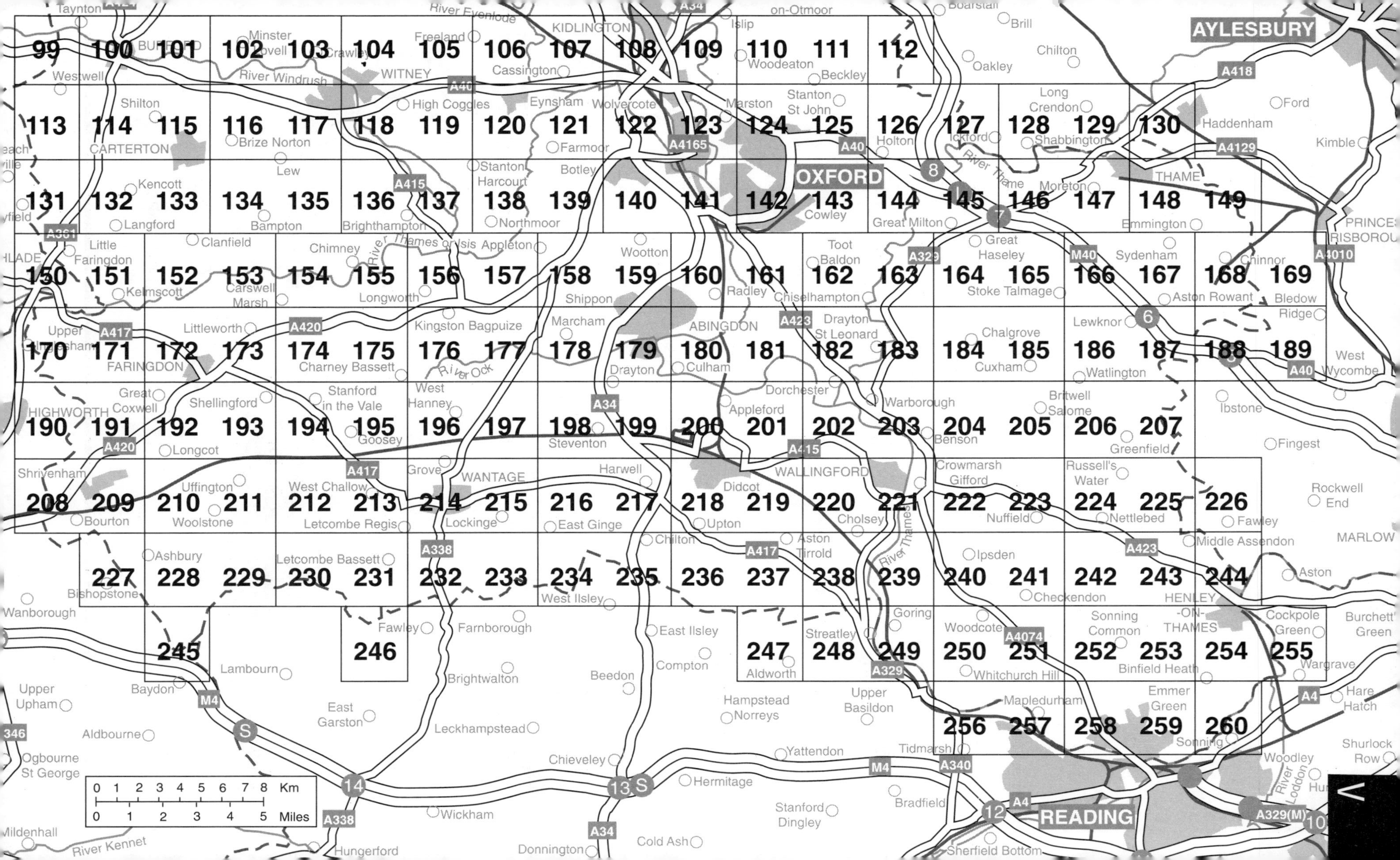
V
AYLESBURY
OXFORD
READING
WITNEY
KIDLINGTON
CARTERTON
THAME
PRINCES RISBOROUGH
ABINGDON
FARINGDON
HIGHWORTH
WANTAGE
WALLINGFORD
HENLEY-ON-THAMES
MARLOW
99 100 101 102 103 104 105 106 107 108 109 110 111 112
113 114 115 116 117 118 119 120 121 122 123 124 125 126 127 128 129 130
131 132 133 134 135 136 137 138 139 140 141 142 143 144 145 146 147 148 149
150 151 152 153 154 155 156 157 158 159 160 161 162 163 164 165 166 167 168 169
170 171 172 173 174 175 176 177 178 179 180 181 182 183 184 185 186 187 188 189
190 191 192 193 194 195 196 197 198 199 200 201 202 203 204 205 206 207
208 209 210 211 212 213 214 215 216 217 218 219 220 221 222 223 224 225 226
227 228 229 230 231 232 233 234 235 236 237 238 239 240 241 242 243 244
245 246 247 248 249 250 251 252 253 254 255
256 257 258 259 260
Taynton
River Evenlode
on-Otmoor
Islip
Brill
Oakley
Chilton
Westwell
Minster Lovell
Crawley
Freeland
River Windrush
Cassington
Woodeaton
Beckley
Shilton
High Coggles
Eynsham
Wolvercote
Marston
Stanton St John
Long Crendon
Ford
Haddenham
Kimble
Brize Norton
Farmoor
Holton
Ickford
Shabbington
Kencott
Lew
Stanton Harcourt
Botley
River Thame
Moreton
Langford
Bampton
Brighthampton
Northmoor
Cowley
Great Milton
Emmington
Little Faringdon
Clanfield
Chimney
River Thames or Isis
Appleton
Wootton
Toot Baldon
Great Haseley
Sydenham
Chinnor
Kelmscott
Carswell Marsh
Longworth
Shippon
Radley
Chiselhampton
Stoke Talmage
Aston Rowant
Bledow Ridge
Upper Inglesham
Littleworth
Kingston Bagpuize
Marcham
Drayton St Leonard
Lewknor
Chalgrove
Charney Bassett
River Ock
Drayton
Culham
Cuxham
Watlington
West Wycombe
Great Coxwell
Shellingford
Stanford in the Vale
West Hanney
Dorchester
Appleford
Warborough
Britwell Salome
Ibstone
Goosey
Steventon
Benson
Greenfield
Fingest
Longcot
Shrivenham
Uffington
West Challow
Grove
Harwell
Didcot
Crowmarsh Gifford
Russell's Water
Rockwell End
Bourton
Woolstone
Letcombe Regis
Lockinge
East Ginge
Upton
Cholsey
Nuffield
Nettlebed
Fawley
Ashbury
Letcombe Bassett
Chilton
Aston Tirrold
River Thames
Ipsden
Middle Assendon
Aston
Bishopstone
West Ilsley
Checkendon
Wanborough
Fawley
Farnborough
East Ilsley
Goring
Woodcote
Sonning Common
Cockpole Green
Burchett Green
Streatley
Lambourn
Compton
Aldworth
Whitchurch Hill
Binfield Heath
Wargrave
Brightwalton
Beedon
Upper Upham
Baydon
East Garston
Hampstead Norreys
Upper Basildon
Mapledurham
Emmer Green
Hare Hatch
Aldbourne
Leckhampstead
Yattendon
Tidmarsh
Sonning
Shurlock Row
Ogbourne St George
Chieveley
Woodley
River Loddon
Hermitage
Stanford Dingley
Bradfield
Wickham
Mildenhall
River Kennet
Hungerford
Donnington
Cold Ash
Sherfield Bottom
A40 A4165 A418 A4129 A4010 A415 A361 A329 M40 A423 A417 A420 A34 A338 A4074 A340 A4 A329(M) M4 A346
0 1 2 3 4 5 6 7 8 Km
0 1 2 3 4 5 Miles

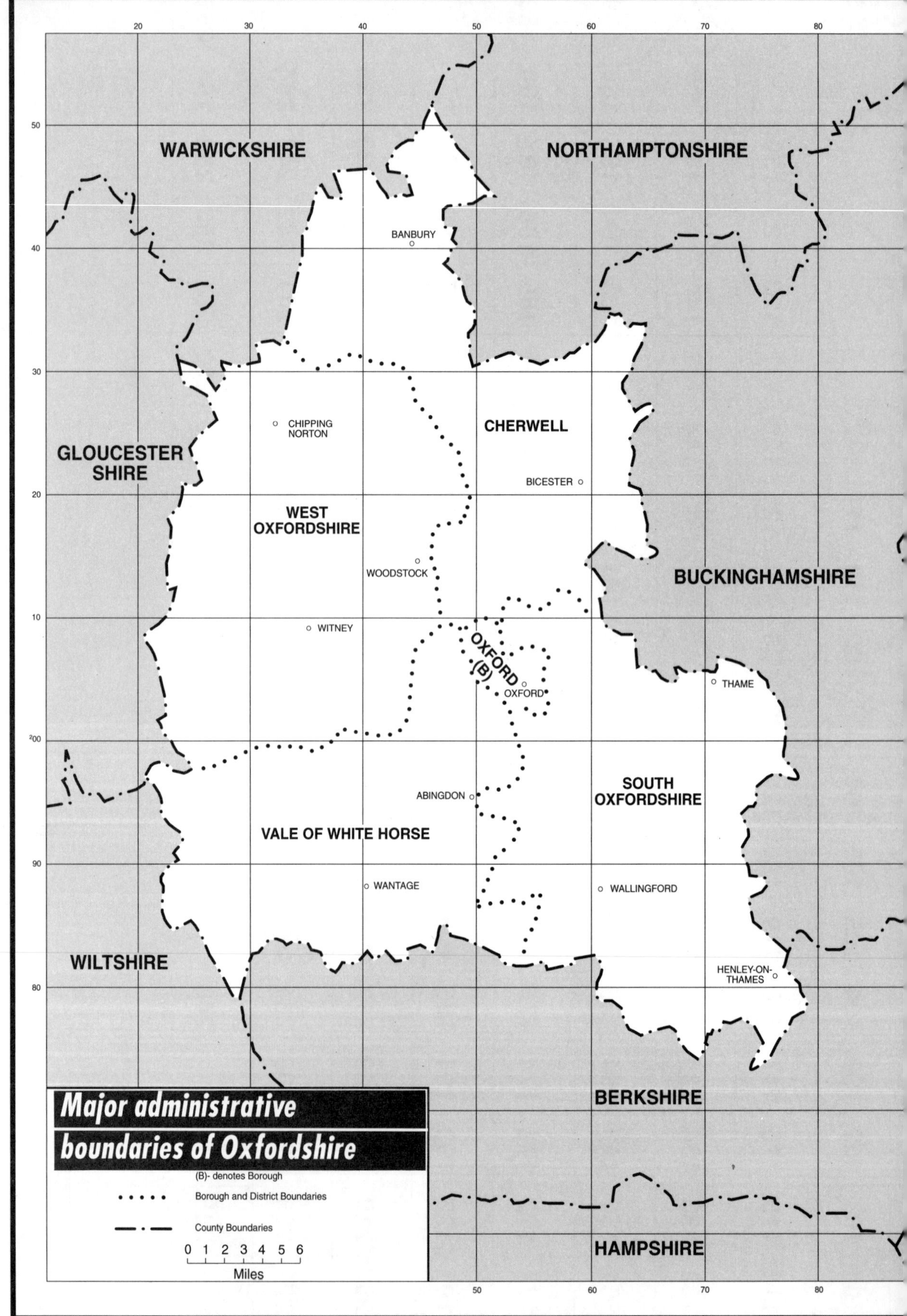

WARWICKSHIRE

NORTHAMPTONSHIRE

BANBURY ○

GLOUCESTER SHIRE

CHIPPING NORTON ○

CHERWELL

BICESTER ○

WEST OXFORDSHIRE

WOODSTOCK ○

WITNEY ○

BUCKINGHAMSHIRE

OXFORD (B) ○
OXFORD ○

THAME ○

VALE OF WHITE HORSE

ABINGDON ○

SOUTH OXFORDSHIRE

WANTAGE ○

WALLINGFORD ○

WILTSHIRE

HENLEY-ON-THAMES ○

BERKSHIRE

Major administrative boundaries of Oxfordshire

(B)- denotes Borough

• • • • •   Borough and District Boundaries

— ·· —   County Boundaries

0 1 2 3 4 5 6
Miles

HAMPSHIRE

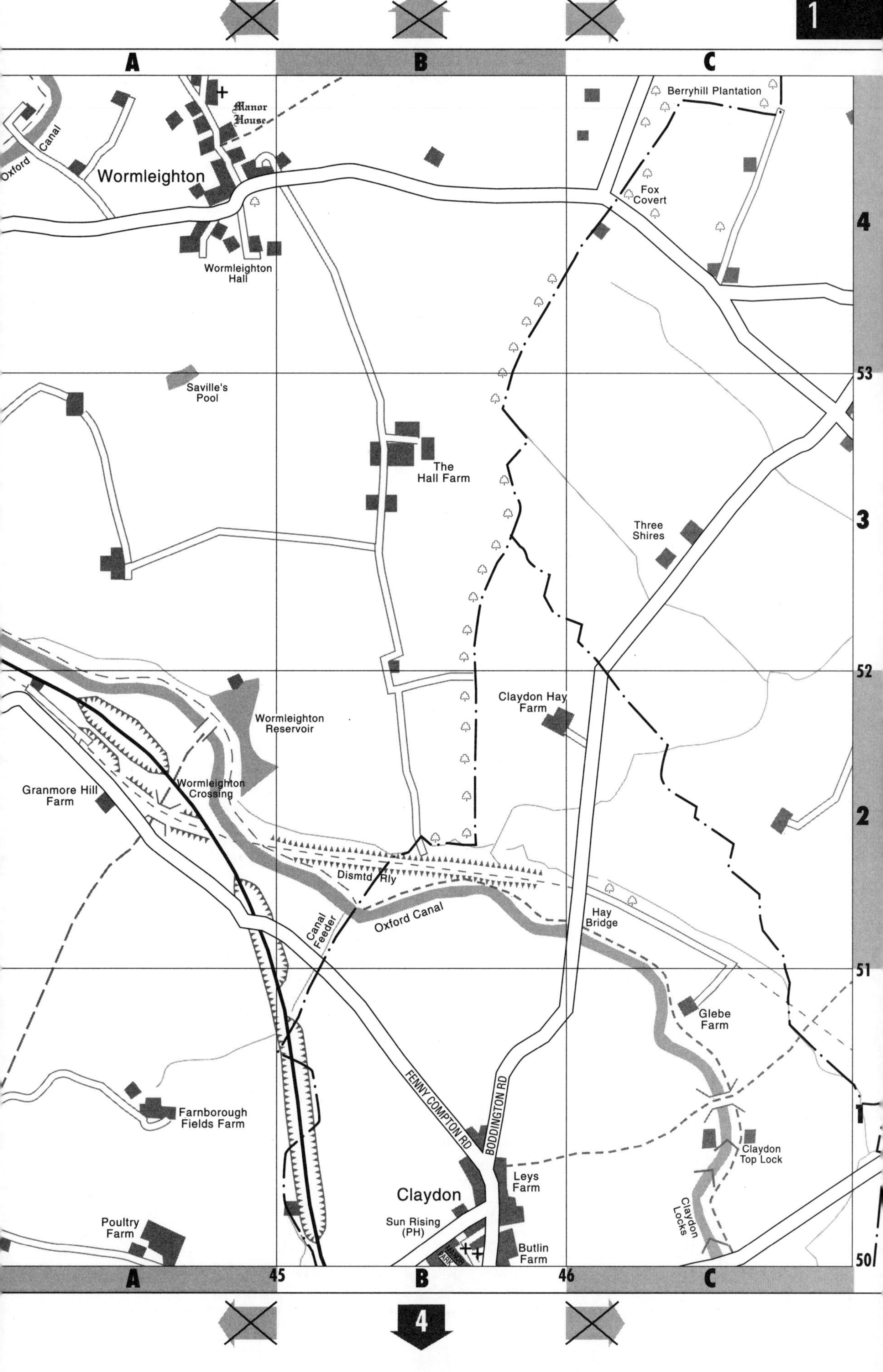
A
B
C
Manor House
Wormleighton
Oxford Canal
Wormleighton Hall
Berryhill Plantation
Fox Covert
Saville's Pool
The Hall Farm
Three Shires
Wormleighton Reservoir
Claydon Hay Farm
Granmore Hill Farm
Wormleighton Crossing
Dismtd Rly
Canal Feeder
Oxford Canal
Hay Bridge
Glebe Farm
Farnborough Fields Farm
FENNY COMPTON RD
BODDINGTON RD
Claydon Top Lock
Leys Farm
Claydon
Claydon Locks
Poultry Farm
Sun Rising (PH)
Butlin Farm
4
53
3
52
2
51
1
50
45
46
4

A   B   C

PARK CL

Knight's Farm

Avon Dassett

Yew Tree
Farm

B4400

M40

Burton Hill
Farm

4

Splash Leys
Farm

49

Glen Farm

Primrose Hill
Farm

B4086

3

Home Farm

Arlescote

Knowle
End

Wr
Twr

B4086

Camp Hill

Nadbury

Arlescote
Woods

B410

Edge Hill

48

CAMP LA

Nadbury
House

Cherry Tree
Farm

NEWT RD

2

Ratley

OLD RD

TOWNHILL

CHAPEL LA

Sch

Church
Farm

HIGH ST

PH

B4086

Motte &
Baileys

Manor
Farm

47

Manor
Farm

1

Bush Hill

Hornton Hill
Farm

46

38   A   39   B   40   C

4

D
E
F
AVON CARROW
Stonewold
Dassett Fields
Windmill Lodge
Farm
Sch
HEYDONS TERR
A423(T)
Sourland Pool
Butchers Arms
(PH)
Park
Lodge
Farnborough
4
Farnborough
Hall
The Rookery
Farnborough Park
Oak Hill
49
M40
Obelisk
Tile Barn
SOUTHAM RD
A423(T)
3
Markhamhole
Spinney
College
Farm
Mollington
Wood
Keepers
Cottage
48
SCHOOL LA
RECTORY CL
CHAPEL
ST
MOLLINGTON LA
PH
Warmington
1 ROUNDHILL RD
2 TINKERS LA
3 SCHOOL HILL
WHITEWAY
2
MAIN ST
MARCH RD
THE
PADDOCKS
THE HOLT
LOWER FARM
LA
THE
MEAD
Warmington
Wood
Deddington Hill
MARCH RD
Sch
47
BANBURY RD
Warmington
Fox Covert
The
Wobbly Wheel
(PH)
Angel
Piece
1
Valley Farm
B4100
M40
46
D
42
E
43
F

8

4

A B C

Farnborough Hill Farm

Claydon Crossing

MANOR PARK

Manor Farm

BIGNOLDS CL

Filter Bed

Claydon Locks

Farnborough Hill

Lawn Hill

Firs Farm

4

Priory
(remains of)

Clattercote

49

Oxford Canal

Towing Path

A423(T)

Clattercote
Reservoir

3

Oathill Farm

Cropredy Lawn

Lambert's Barn

48

Beecham's
Cottages

ROUNDHILL RD

SOUTHAM RD

Mollington

ROUNDHILL
RD

BLACKSMITHS
LA

CHURCH LA

THE HOLLOWAY

MAIN ST

CHESTNUT RD

ORCHARD
RISE

IVY LA

CLAYDON RD

2

Manor Farm

Mill Farm

OXHEY HILL

Cropredy Hill

Cemy

1 CREAMPOT
2 CREAMPOT
CRES

Oxhay Farm

CREAMPOT

ORCHARD
VIEW

CHAPEL LA

ORCHARD
LA

47

Cropredy

CUP AND
SAUCER PH

VICARAGE

1

STATION RD

River Che

Thickthorn Farm

A423(T)

Sch

46

44 A 45 B 46 C

D
E
F
Appletree
Appletree House
Appletree Farm
Appletree Farm
Highfield
Highfield Spinney
Works
Manor Farm
A361
BYFIELD RD
49
4
APPLETREE RD
THE CLOSE
CULWORTH RD
Chipping Warden
BANBURY RD
ALLENS ORCH
HOGG END
ARBURY BANKS
MILL LA
Arbury Banks
3
Rectory Farm
Varney's Lock
Highfurlong Brook
48
Broadmoor Lock
Broadmoor Bridge
Oxford Canal
Towing Path
Prescote Manor Farm
River Cherwell
The Mill House
Hay's Bridge
The Rookery
2
Wardington Gate Farm
Wardington Spinney
47
Prescote Manor
PH
Wardington House
Wardington
1
1644
Sewage Works
High Wardington Farm
Sch
THE GREENSWARD
Wardington Grange
A361
THORPE RD
46
D
48
E
49
F

A
B
C
Sun Rising
SUN RISING HILL
A422
Home Farm
Upton House
Sun Rising Covert
Sugarswell Cottages
Blackwell Wood
Spring Hill
Black Hut
Old Lodge Farm
Foxbury Barn
Sugarswell Farm
Temple Pool
Heath Wood
STRATFORD RD
SUGARSWELL LA
Shenington Hirons Covert
New Covert
Dairy
Sugarswell Farm
The Bungalow
Lodge Farm
Christmas Corner
Vehicle Proving Ground
Hill Barn
Rectory Farm
Manor Farm
Alkerto
STOCKING LA
KENHILL RD
PH
Hill Farm
Shenlow Hill
Mill Farm
MARSHALLS CL
Quarry Farm
Resr
Shenlow Farm
RATTLECOMBE RD
Shenington
Gliding Club
Mill Lane
Oxfordshire Circular Walks
4
45
3
44
2
43
1
42
35
36
37

13

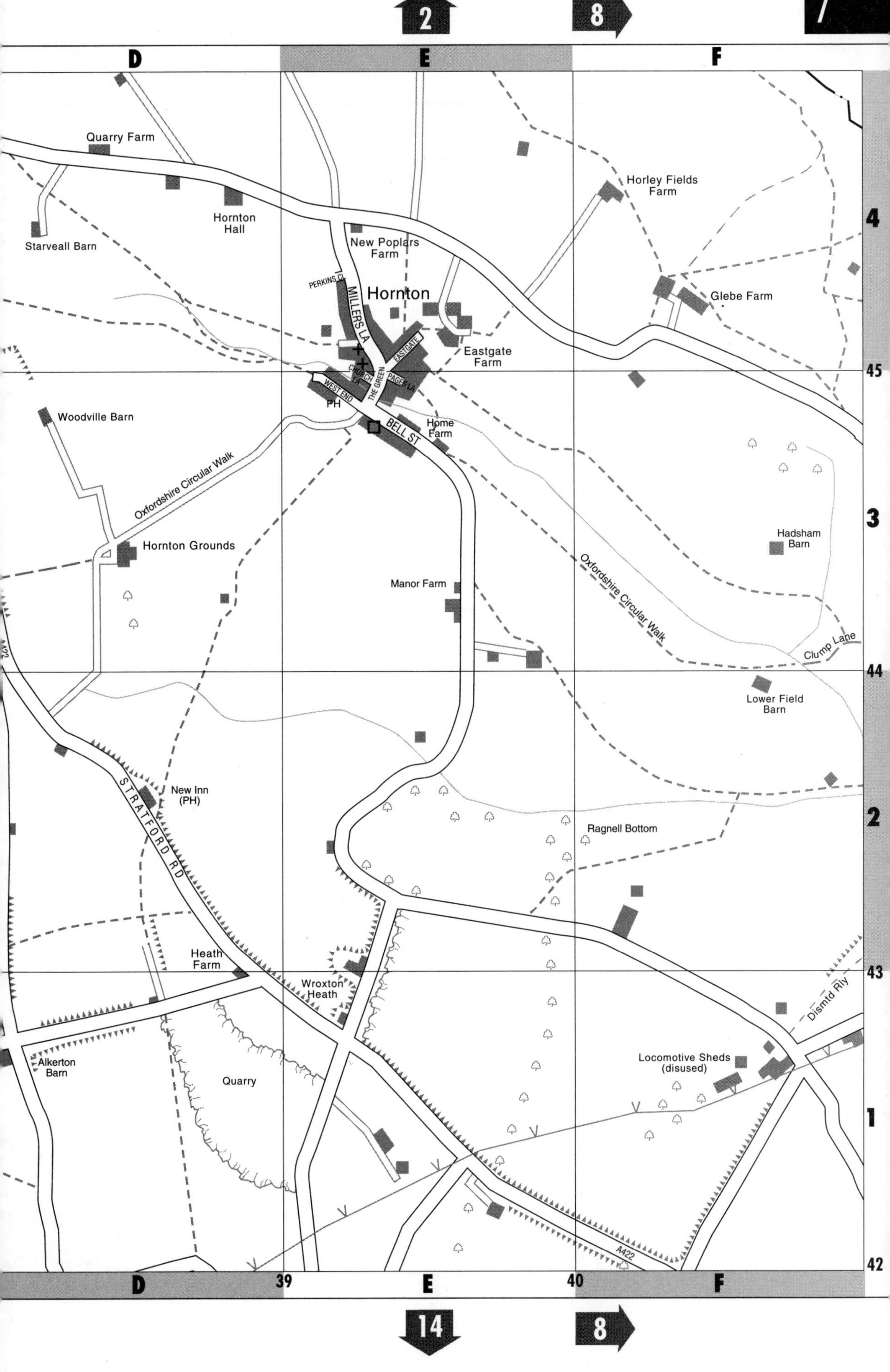

D   E   F

Quarry Farm

Hornton
Hall

Starveall Barn

4

New Poplars
Farm

Horley Fields
Farm

PERKINS CL

MILLERS LA

Hornton

Glebe Farm

EASTGATE

Eastgate
Farm

45

CHURCH LA

PAGETS LA

THE GREEN

WEST END

PH

BELL ST

Home
Farm

Woodville Barn

Oxfordshire Circular Walk

3

Hadsham
Barn

Hornton Grounds

Oxfordshire Circular Walk

Manor Farm

Clump Lane

44

Lower Field
Barn

STRATFORD RD

New Inn
(PH)

2

Ragnell Bottom

Heath
Farm

43

Dismtd Rly

Wroxton
Heath

Alkerton
Barn

Quarry

Locomotive Sheds
(disused)

1

A422

42

A
B
C

B4100

Slated
Barn

Slade
Barn

Laurel
Farm

MOLLINGTON RD

SHORT LA

MIDDLE LA

BAKEHOUSE LA

Bury Court
Farm

Shotteswell

4

45

Sor Brook

Hadsham House
Manor Farm

Water
Tower

3

Horley
House

Clump Lane

44

PH

LANE CL

GULLIVERS

Fish
Ponds

Bramhill
Park
Farm

Horley

Hanwell

MAIN ST

HANWELL CT

PARK CL

CHURCH LA

SACKVILLE CL

Hanwell
Castle

Fish
Ponds

2

Dismtd Rly

GULLIVERS LA

Park
Farm

WARWICK RD

43

Oxfordshire Circular Walk

Drayton
Lodge

Cemy

1

Lord's
Spinney

HORLEY PATH RD

B4100

HARDWICK PARK

HIGHLANDS

HORSHAM

CHEVIOT WAY

QUEEN'S CRES

A422

42

41
A
42
B
43
C

D | E | F

4

Great Bourton

Bourton House

Hillside House

STANWELL
MANOR CL
CHURCH LA
SWAN LA
THE STY

CROW LA

PH

THE GREEN

SCHOOL LA

THE CLOSE

SOUTH VIEW

A423(T)

Bourtonfields Farm

Slack Barn

Cemy

LC

Little Mill Crossing

Mill Lane

45

Littlegood Farm

Little Bourton

3

Old Manor Farm

Park Farm

SPRING LA

BUZZARDS CL

CHAPEL LA

UPLAND RISE

PH

Little Bourton House

44

Lock

River Cherwell

Fish Ponds

SOUTHAM RD

Hardwick Hill House

Oxford Canal

Towing Path

2

Cemy

Hardwick Hill

Hardwick Gorse

Hardwick Farm

43

1 GUERNSEY WAY
2 JERSEY DR
3 KERRY CL
4 AYRSHIRE CL
5 TROIKA CL
6 DURHAM MEWS
7 MONIQUE CT
8 BETTINA CRES
9 CHICHESTER WLK
10 AMBERLEY CT

Hanwell Fields

SYRINGA WLK

Hardwick

HIGHLANDS

HEREFORD WAY

FRENSHAM CL

DALE AVE

SILVIA

ERICA

MALLOW

JUNIPER

RISE

CONIFER

THE

GAME

THE HIGHLANDS

1 ACACIA WLK
2 AZALEA WLK
3 FORSYTHIA WLK
4 FUCHSIA WLK
5 THE WISTERIA
6 JAPONICA WLK
7 HYDRANGEA WLK
THE MAGNOLIAS

Dismtd Rly

Hardwick Lock

Hardwick

1

GLYNDEBOURNE PL

ALFRISTON

FERRERS

BANESBERIE CL

FORGE WAY

HEARTHWAY

LAVENDER CL

PEN WAY

BEAUMONT RD

BEAUMONT CL

A423(T)

Beaumont Ind Est

Works

Reservoir

Ind Est

WILDMERE RD

ACORN WAY

DAVENTRY RD

42

D | E | F

45 | 46

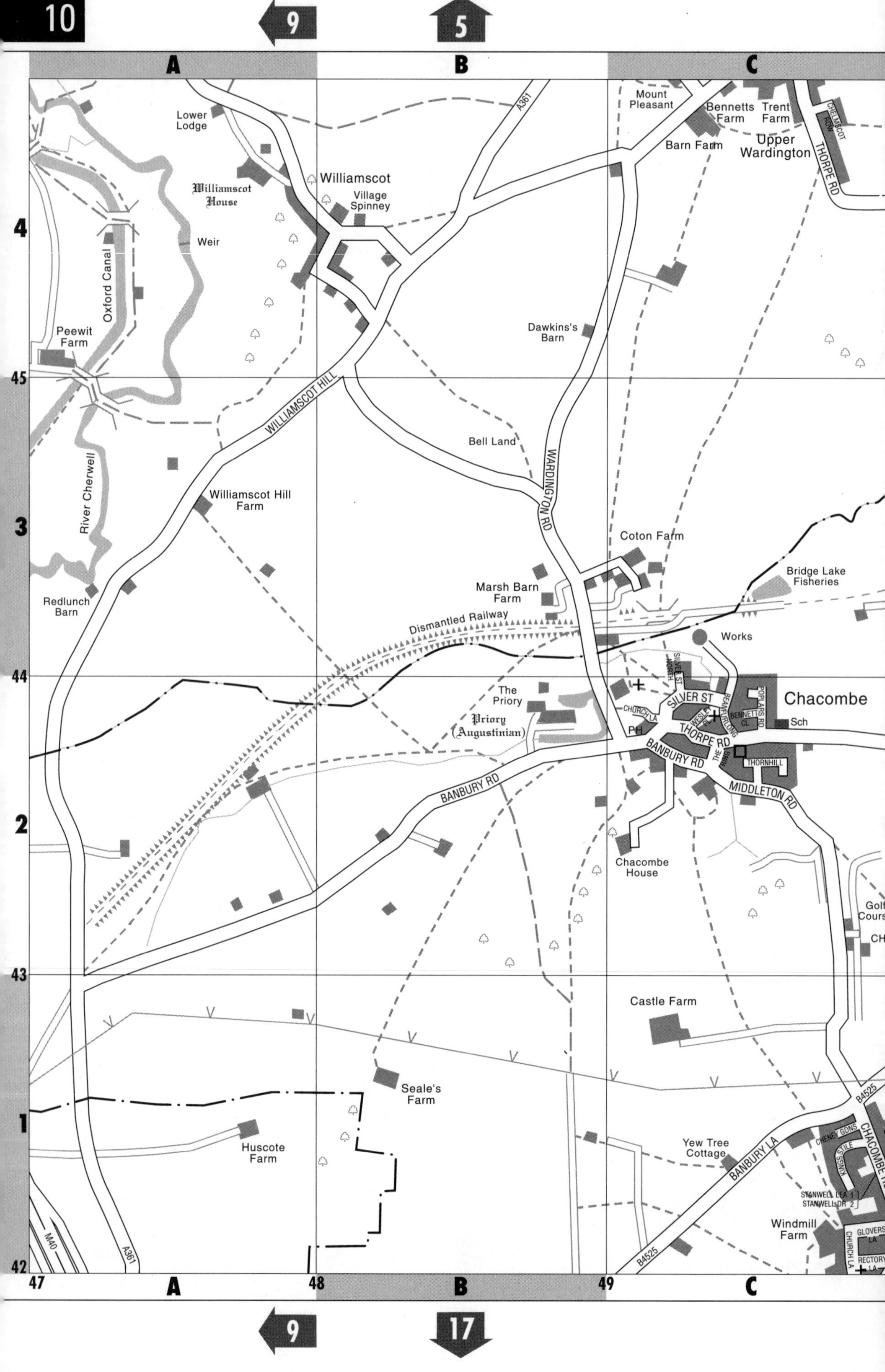
A
B
C
Mount Pleasant
Bennetts Farm
Trent Farm
Barn Farm
Upper Wardington
THORPE RD
CHELMSCOT ROW
Lower Lodge
A361
Williamscot
Williamscot House
Village Spinney
Weir
Oxford Canal
Peewit Farm
Dawkins's Barn
WILLIAMSCOT HILL
Bell Land
WARDINGTON RD
River Cherwell
Williamscot Hill Farm
Coton Farm
Bridge Lake Fisheries
Marsh Barn Farm
Redlunch Barn
Dismantled Railway
Works
The Priory
Priory (Augustinian)
Chacombe
SILVER ST
SILVER ST NORTH
CHURCH LA
POPLARS RD
BENNETTS CL
Sch
PH
THORPE RD
BANBURY RD
THE RING
THORNHILL
MIDDLETON RD
BANBURY RD
Chacombe House
Golf Cours
CH
Castle Farm
Seale's Farm
B4525
Huscote Farm
Yew Tree Cottage
BANBURY LA
CHENEY GDNS
KINGS STILE
CHACOMBE
STANWELL LEA
STANWELL DR
Windmill Farm
GLOVERS LA
CHURCH LA
RECTORY LA
M40
4
45
3
44
2
43
1
42
47
48
49

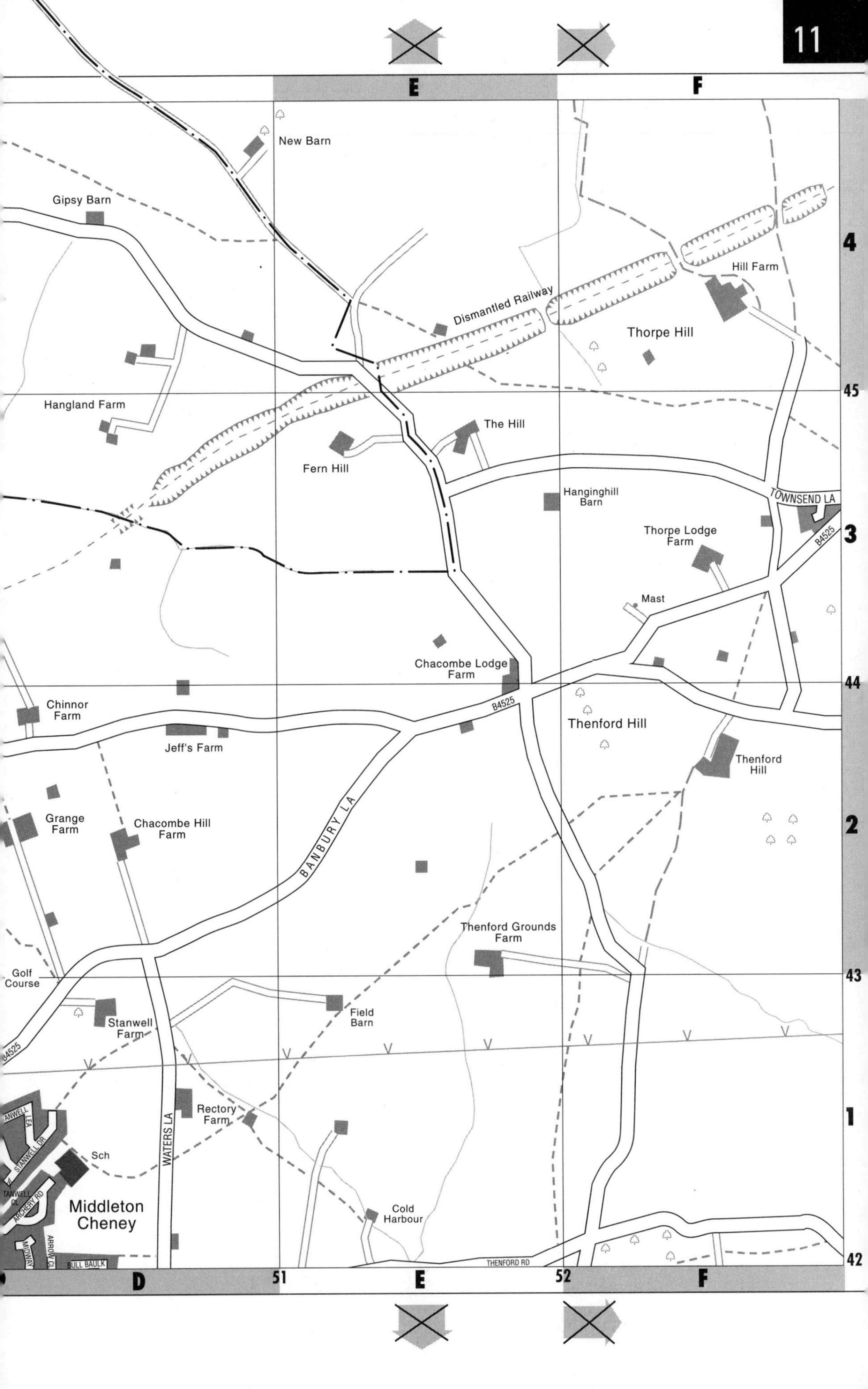
E
F
New Barn
Gipsy Barn
Dismantled Railway
Hill Farm
Thorpe Hill
Hangland Farm
The Hill
Fern Hill
Hanginghill Barn
TOWNSEND LA
Thorpe Lodge Farm
B4525
Mast
Chacombe Lodge Farm
Chinnor Farm
B4525
Thenford Hill
Jeff's Farm
Thenford Hill
Grange Farm
Chacombe Hill Farm
BANBURY LA
Thenford Grounds Farm
Golf Course
Stanwell Farm
Field Barn
B4525
Rectory Farm
WATERS LA
Sch
Middleton Cheney
Cold Harbour
THENFORD RD
BULL BAULK
D
51
E
52
F
4
45
3
44
2
43
1
42

A B C

Compton
Wynyates

Lady
Elizabeth's
Hill

Windertonroad
Spinney

Orchard
Hill

Compton
Wynyates

New
Meadow
Spinney

4

Comptn
Pike

Broomhill
Farm

Broom
Hill

Quarry
Farm

41

Birch
Wood

White
House

Winderton
Farm

Winderton

The
Warren

3

Alice Hyde's
Cottage

Hill
Barn

Mast

40

The
Brake

Sibford Heath
Farm

Sutton Brook

Hall Meadow
Farm

Sibford Heath

2

B4035

Gallow Hill
Farm

39

Gallow
Hill

B4035

HOLLOWAY HILL

Hill
Barn

Ryehill
Barn

1

Eddeneshill
Barn

Elmridge

HOLLOWAY LA

Hasty Leys
Farm

Ditchedge Lane

Beggars' Lane

38

Coombe
Slade Farm

32 A **33** B **34** C

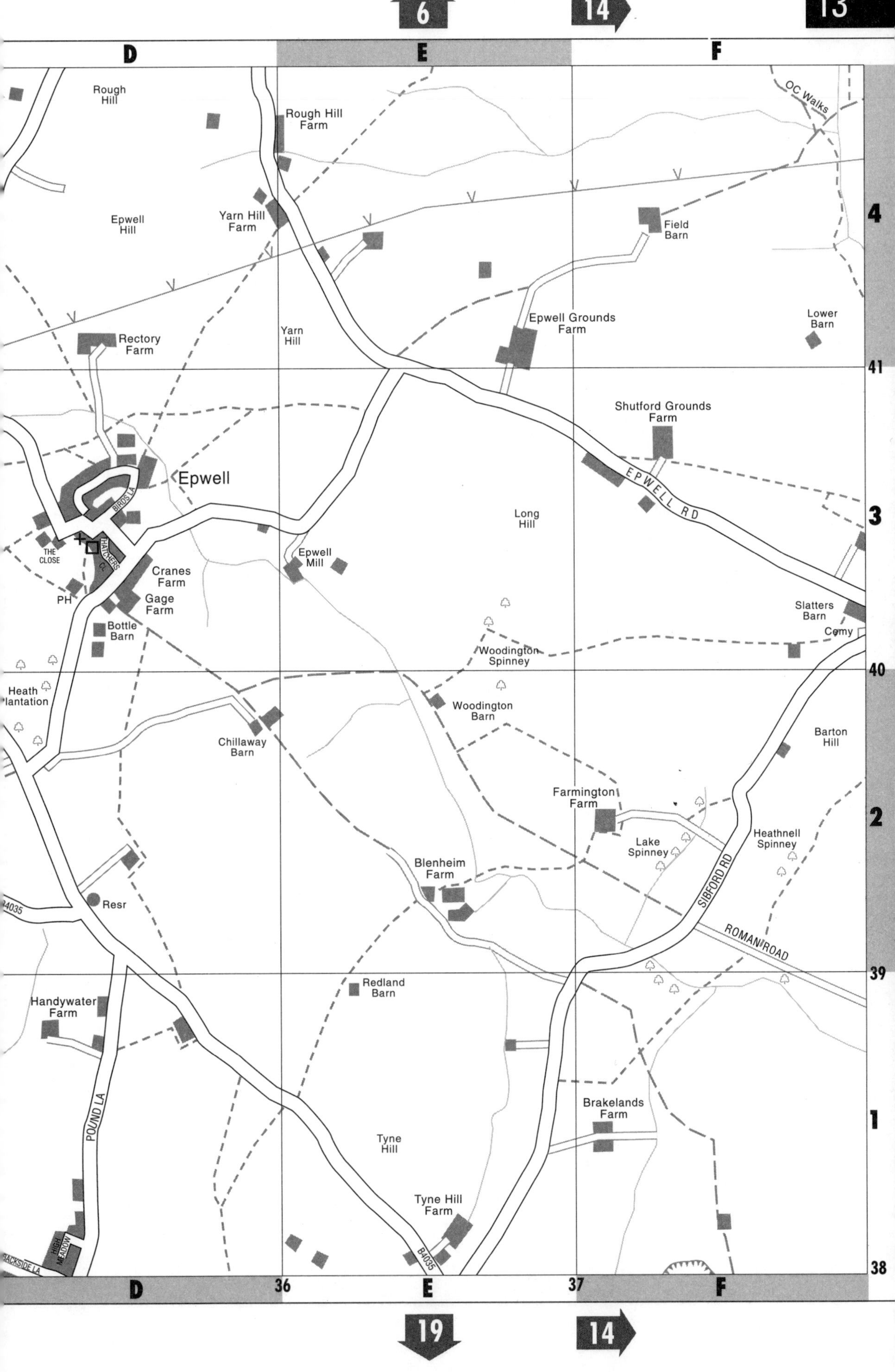

D
E
F

Rough Hill

Rough Hill Farm

OC Walks

Epwell Hill

Yarn Hill Farm

Yarn Hill

Field Barn

4

Epwell Grounds Farm

Lower Barn

Rectory Farm

41

Shutford Grounds Farm

Epwell

BIRDS LA

Long Hill

EPWELL RD

3

THE CLOSE

THATCHERS LA

Epwell Mill

Slatters Barn

Cemy

PH

Cranes Farm

Gage Farm

Bottle Barn

Woodington Spinney

40

Heath Plantation

Chillaway Barn

Woodington Barn

Barton Hill

Farmington Farm

Lake Spinney

Heathnell Spinney

2

Blenheim Farm

SIBFORD RD

B4035

Resr

ROMAN ROAD

39

Handywater Farm

Redland Barn

POUND LA

Brakelands Farm

1

Tyne Hill

Tyne Hill Farm

B4035

BRACKSIDE LA

HIGH MEADOW

38

D
E
F

36
37

13
7

A   B   C

Oxfordshire Circular Walk

Ash Farm
PH

Balscote

Alkerton Hill Farm

Manor House

Priory Farm

Guide Post

4

A422

STRATFORD RD

41

Sewage Works

Maidenhill Cottage

Padsdon Bottom

Castle Bank Enclosure

Balscote Mill

Shutford

PLOT RD

THE PLAIN RD

LOWER END

Beggars' Barn

Wroxton Mill

Tythe Farm

Claydonhill Covert

Clayd Hill

3

Cemy

COOK'S HILL

THE DAIRYGROUND

MALTHOUSE

LA

WEAVERS' ROW

WEST ST

HIGH ST

BANBURY RD

Five Ways

EPWELL RD

SIBFORD RD

PH

Manor House

Barton Hill Farm

Round Hill

Shutford Bridge

Claydon Hill Bungalow

SHUTFORD RD

40

Welshcroft Hill

Jester's Barn

Jester's Hill

Broughton Grounds Farm

2

Madmarston Hill

Langley Hill

39

Fort

ROMAN ROAD

Upper Lea Farm

Castle Brow

Earthwork

Sandfine Wood

SANDFINE RD

SWALCLIFFE LEA

SHUTFORD RD

1

Swalcliffe Mill

Swalcliffe Lea

Fulling Mill Far

Preedys Farm

38

38   A   39   B   40   C

13
20

D E F

A422

QUEEN'S CRES

Drayton

SUSSEX DR

B4100

BEDFORD
CL

ROMNEY RD

LANCHESTER
DR

Sch

Hotel

STRATFORD RD

HORLEY
PT RD

SILVER ST

+

MAIN ST

CHURCH ST

+

Wroxton
College

Wroxton
Abbey

Wroxton

Sch

LAMBITTS
GREEN

DARK LA

MILL LA

Abbey
Wood

MILL LA

RECTORY
GDNS

+

Park
Farm

STRATFORD RD

WARWICK RD

A422

4

TRINIT CHRITY CL

Sch

HILL VIEW
CRES

BERKELE CL

BRAMBER CL

Sch

LORD GREEN

THE
FAIRWAY

CHERRY
RD

Obelisk

41

Keeper's
Covert

CAERNARVON WAY

BRETCH HILL

MARLOWE CL

CHESTER WAY

French's
Buildings

Newington Grounds
Farm

French's
Covert

Sor Brook

Withycombe
Covert

Withycombe
Farm

CHERTSEY
GDNS

HARLECH CL

KENILWORTH
WAY

HIGHCLERE

3

40

SHUTFORD RD

MAIN ST

SCHOOL LA

Sch

THE POUND

PARK LA

PH

Park
Farm

North
Newington

North Newington
Mill

The
Bretch

Milestone
Farm

Bretch
Farm

BRIGGS
CL

DORCHESTER GR

DENBIGH CL

B4035

BROUGHTON RD

Crouch Hill
Farm

Crouch
Hill

2

BANBURY RD

Salt Way

Sewage
Works

Woadmill
Farm

Spring
Farm

Crouch
Farm

39

SANDFINE RD

Danver's
Cottage

MAIN RD

DANVERS LA

Broughton
Park

+

Broughton
Castle

PH

Broughton

DANVERS CL

Rectory
Farm

WYKHAM LA

BLOXHAM RD

1

Weir

B4035

Cross Road
Cottages

A361

38

D 42 E 43 F

15
9

A
B
C
4
41
3
40
2
39
1
38
44
45
46
BANBURY
Ruscote
Neithrop
Grimsbury
Calthorpe
Easington
Crouch Hill
Wykham Farm
Wykham Park Farm
Bodicote Lawn
Industrial Estate
Water Works
Holman Bridge
Wildmere Farm
Spiceball Country Park
Weir
Cemy
F Sta
Court
Hospl
Liby
Coll
Cross
Mus
Sch
Schs
Banbury Station
Cattle Market
Allot Gdns
Ind Est
Sewage Works
River Cherwell
Oxford Canal
Swing Bridge
Recn Gd
Playing Field
Salt Way
Offices
Dismtd Rly
WARWICK RD
RUSCOTE AVE
LONGELANDES WAY
SOUTHAM RD
CHERWELL ST
HENNEF WAY
MIDDLETON RD
CAUSEWAY
CASTLE ST
HIGH ST
BATH RD
ORCHARD WAY
WOODGREEN AVE
BROUGHTON RD
BRETCH HILL
QUEENSWAY
HIGHTOWN RD
HORTON VIEW
SPRINGFIELD AVE
OXFORD RD
BLOXHAM RD
GRANGE RD
BANKSIDE
WHITE POST RD
WYKHAM LA
BROAD GAP
A422
A423(T)
A361
A4260
B4100
B4035

Junction 11

A422

Overthorpe Hall (Sch)

BANBURY LA

B4525

BULL BAULK
CHURCH
QUEEN ST
HIGH ST
SCH
by

BLACKLOCKS HILL
Brinsall

WARKWORTH RD

Allot Gdns

BARRETT RD
THE MOORS DR

A422

MIDDLETON RD

ERMONT WAY

LOMBARD WAY

Nethercote

The Willows

Industrial Estate

Home Farm

Overthorpe

Longacre

ALTHAM GDNS

OVERTHORPE RD

The Bowling Green (PH)

Warkworth Farm

ASTROP RD

Warkworth House

Warkworth

Home Farm

Grove Lodge

Sewage Works

Warkworth Hall Farm

Dismantled Railway

Blackpits Farm

Farthinghoe Stream

Towing Path

River Cherwell

Swing Bridge

Oxford Canal

Grant's Lock

Sutton Lodge Farm

M40

A **B** **C**

Coombe Slade Farm

Rye Hill Farm

Smorel Hovel

The Colony

4

Smorel Brake

Ditchedge Lane

Haynes's Barn

Fisher's Coppice

Chinslade Barn

Round Hill

New Barn Farm

37

Lower Atchill

Gauthern's Barn

Chinslade Farm

Meadow Coppice

Cottage Barn Farm

Millhill Barn

Woodwa Farm

River Stour

College Barn

3

Traitor's Ford

Traitor's Ford Coppice

Temple Mills

Gibraltar Farm

Farnicombe

Sharps Hill

Leys Farm

36

New Barn

HOLLOWAY LA

ASCOTT HILL

TRAITOR'S FORD LA.

Fodge Farm

2

Cowpasture Farm

Six Ash Farm

Yew Tree Farm

35

Wyton's Piece

Lower Cowpasture

Sugarswell Farm

Cowpasture

Ascott Ho

Cowpastures

Ascott

Coleman's Elm Barn

1

Whichford

White's Barn

34

Oatley Hill Farm

32 **A** 33 **B** 34 **C**

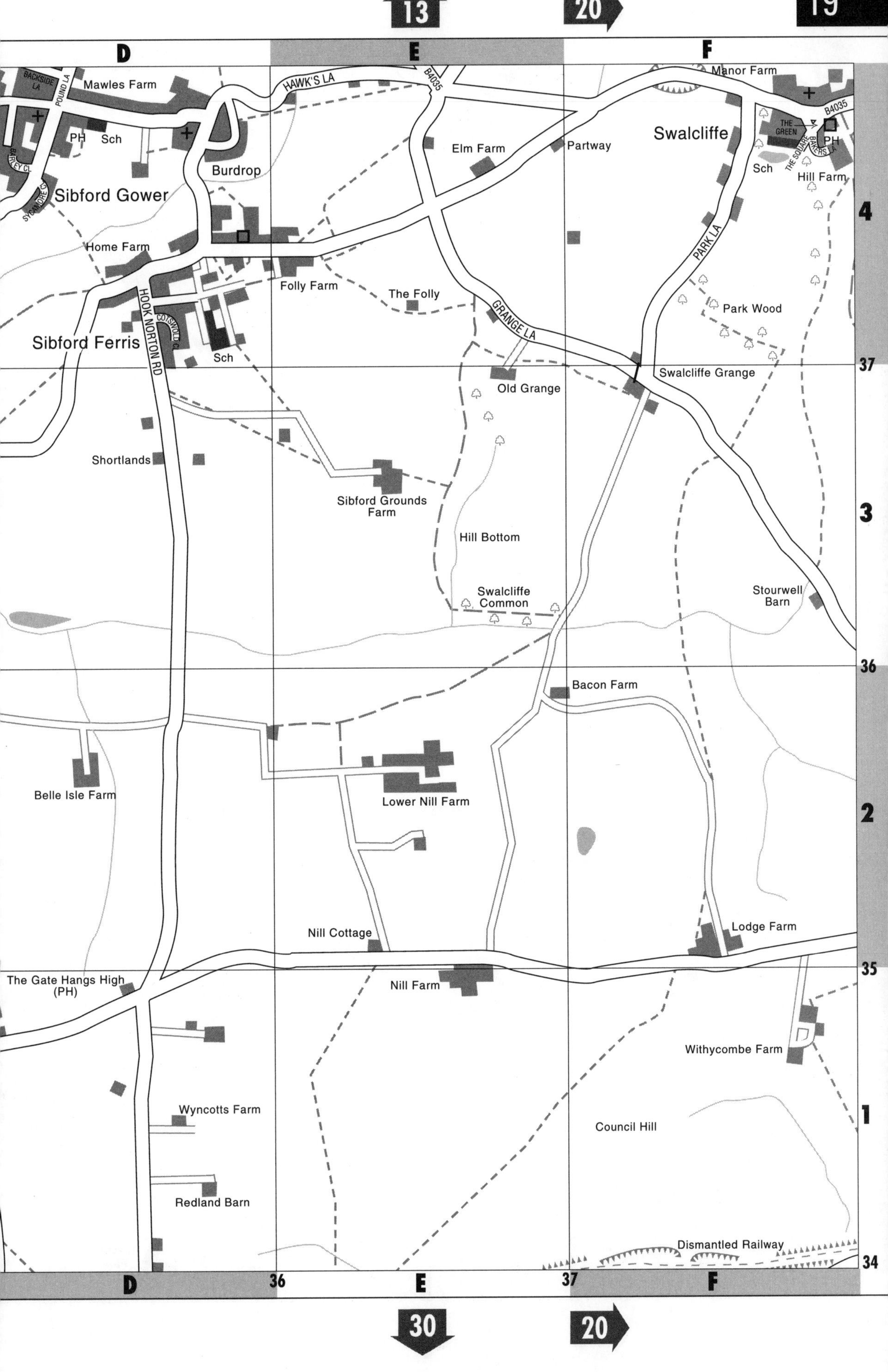
13
20
D
E
F
Mawles Farm
BACKSIDE LA
POUND LA
HAWK'S LA
B4035
Manor Farm
PH
Sch
Burdrop
Elm Farm
Partway
Swalcliffe
THE GREEN
B4035
PH
THE SQUARE
BAKERS LA
Sch
Hill Farm
Sibford Gower
SYCAMORE CL
Home Farm
PARK LA
Folly Farm
The Folly
Park Wood
HOOK NORTON RD
COTSWOLD CL
GRANGE LA
Sibford Ferris
Sch
Swalcliffe Grange
Old Grange
Shortlands
Sibford Grounds Farm
Hill Bottom
Swalcliffe Common
Stourwell Barn
Bacon Farm
Belle Isle Farm
Lower Nill Farm
Nill Cottage
Lodge Farm
The Gate Hangs High (PH)
Nill Farm
Withycombe Farm
Wyncotts Farm
Council Hill
Redland Barn
Dismantled Railway
4
37
3
36
2
35
1
34
D
36
E
37
F
30
20

19
14

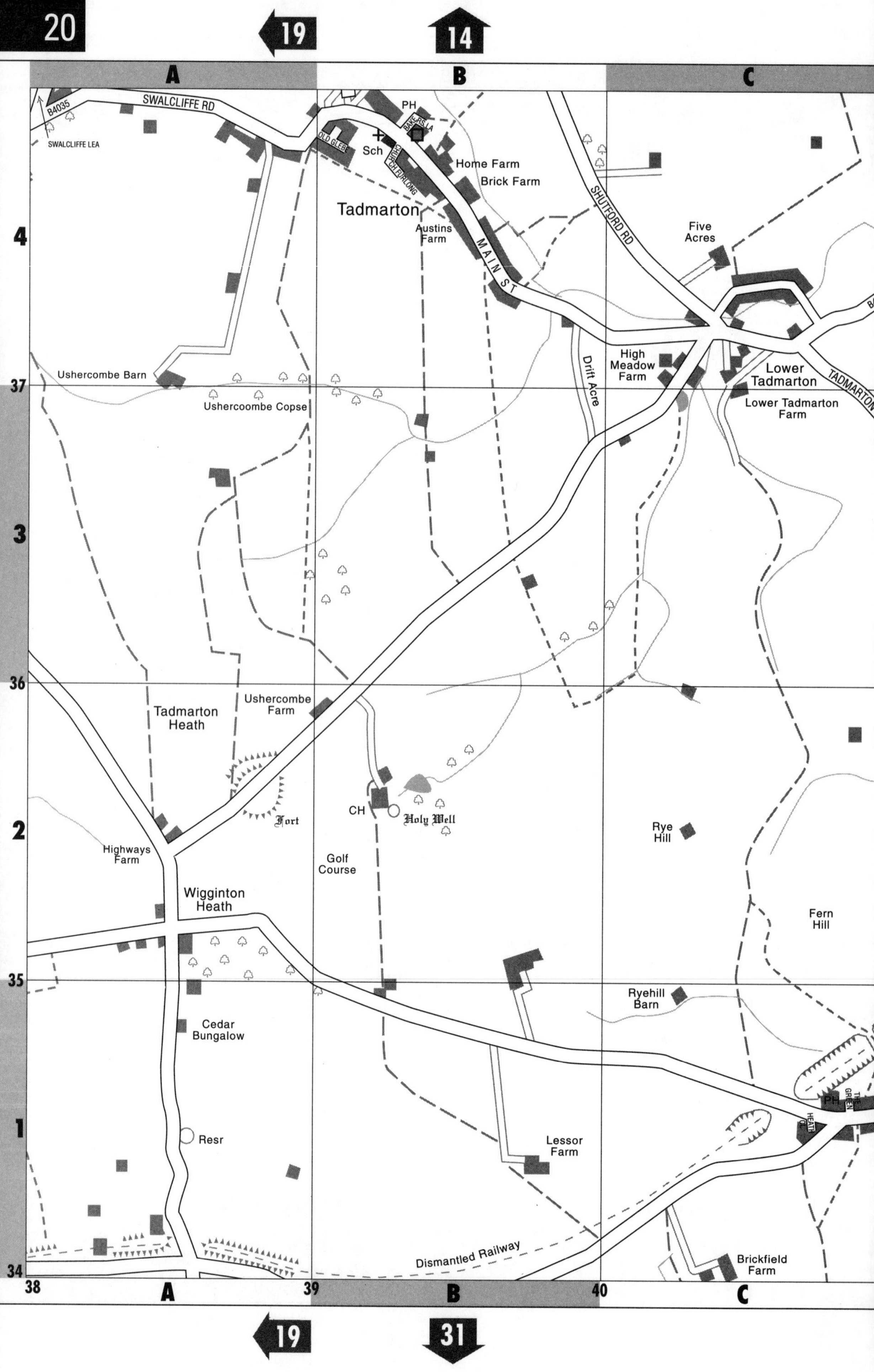
A
B
C
B4035
SWALCLIFFE RD
SWALCLIFFE LEA
PH
BAKERS LA
OLD GLEBE
Sch
CHURCH FURLONG
Home Farm
Brick Farm
Tadmarton
Austins Farm
MAIN ST
SHUTFORD RD
Five Acres
4
High Meadow Farm
Drift Acre
Lower Tadmarton
TADMARTON
Lower Tadmarton Farm
Ushercombe Barn
37
Ushercoombe Copse
3
36
Tadmarton Heath
Ushercombe Farm
Fort
CH
Holy Well
2
Highways Farm
Golf Course
Rye Hill
Wigginton Heath
Fern Hill
35
Ryehill Barn
Cedar Bungalow
PH
THE GREEN
HEATH CL
1
Resr
Lessor Farm
Dismantled Railway
Brickfield Farm
34
38
39
40
A
B
C

19
31

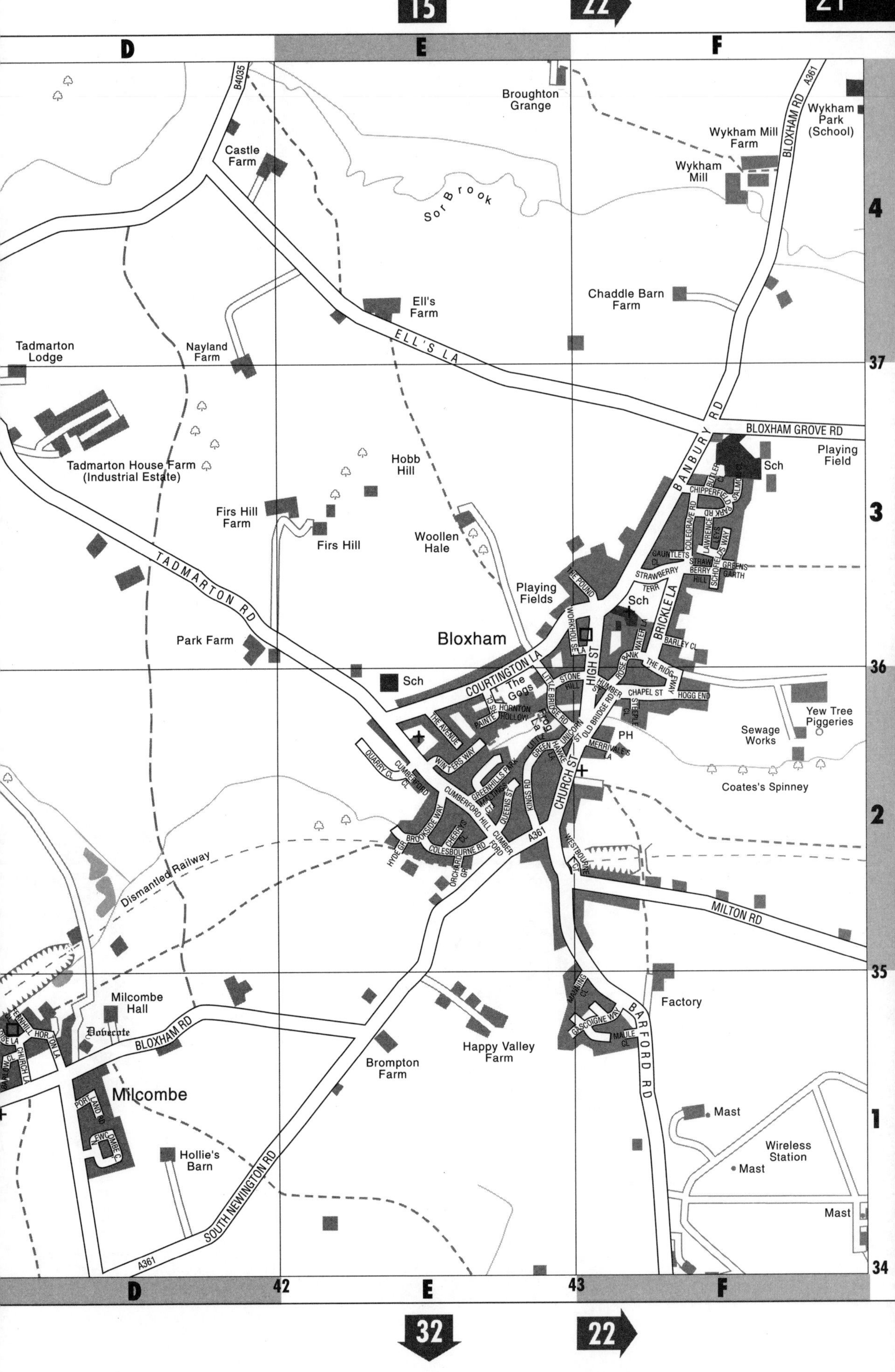

Broughton
Grange

Wykham Mill
Farm

Wykham
Park
(School)

Castle
Farm

Wykham
Mill

S o r B r o o k

Chaddle Barn
Farm

4

Ell's
Farm

ELL'S LA

Tadmarton
Lodge

Nayland
Farm

37

BLOXHAM GROVE RD

BANBURY RD

BLOXHAM RD

A361

Playing
Field

Sch

Tadmarton House Farm
(Industrial Estate)

Hobb
Hill

CHIPPERFIELD

BUTLER RD

SKILTS

COLESGROVE RD

LAWRENCE WAY

3

Firs Hill
Farm

Woollen
Hale

Playing
Fields

GAUNTLETS
CL

Strawberry
BERRY
HILL

STRAWBERRY

GREENS
GARTH

SCHOOL LA

Firs Hill

Park Farm

TADMARTON RD

Sch

Bloxham

COURTINGTON LA

WORKHOUSE LA

THE POUND

HIGH ST

Sch

BRICKLE LA

BARLEY CL

Strawberry
TERR

36

Sch

The Goggs

S HORNTON
HOLLOW

LITTLE BRIDGE RD

STONE
HILL

HUMBER

OLD BRIDGE RD

HOSE WATER

WATER LA

CHAPEL ST

HOGG END

THE RIDG

Yew Tree
Piggeries

THE AVENUE

WILKERSS WAY

QUARRY CL

CUMBERFORD

CUMBERFORD HILL

AINTES

GREENHILLS RD

GREEN LA

MILCOMBE

CHURCH ST

MERRIVALE'S

PH

Sewage
Works

2

Dismantled Railway

BROOKSIDE WAY

HYDE SE

COLESBOURNE RD

ORCHAR RD

GREE

QUEENS RD

KINGS RD

A361

CUMBER
FORD

WEST BOURNE

Coates's Spinney

MILTON RD

35

Milcombe
Hall

BLOXHAM RD

Factory

MANNING

GASCOIGNE WY

MAPLE
CL

BARFORD RD

Dovecote

Brompton
Farm

Happy Valley
Farm

KENNY

HORN LA

CHURCH LA

PORT LAND RD

LAMB C

Milcombe

Hollie's
Barn

SOUTH NEWINGTON RD

A361

Mast

Wireless
Station

Mast

1

Mast

34

21
16

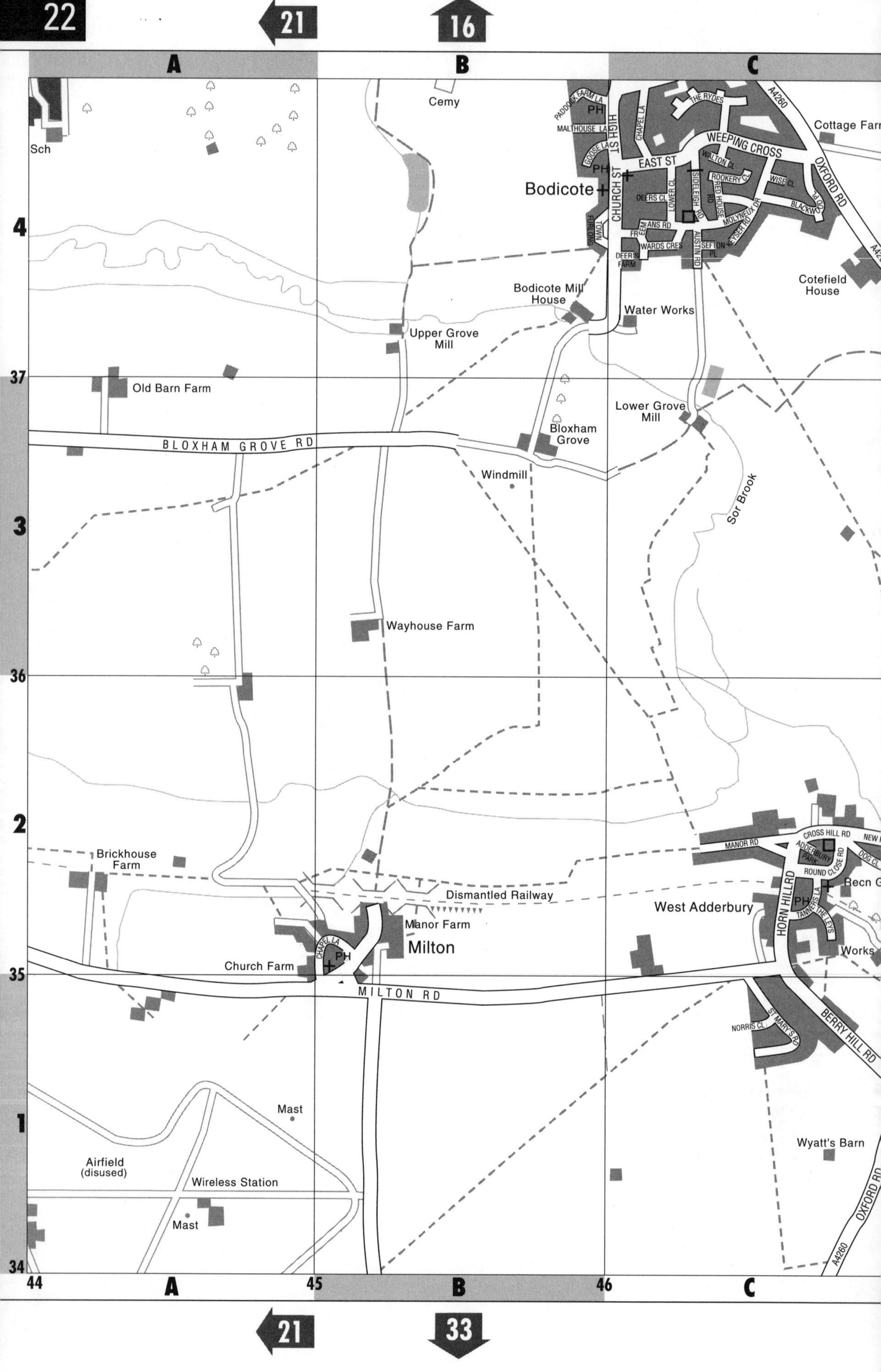
A
B
C
Cemy
Sch
PH
HIGH ST
CHAPEL LA
THE RYDES
A4260
Cottage Farm
PADDOCK FARM LA
MALTHOUSE LA
GOOSE LA
EAST ST
WEEPING CROSS
WALTON CL
OXFORD RD
Bodicote
CHURCH ST
ROOKERY CL
WISE CL
DEERS CL
LOWER CL
SIDELEIGH RD
RED HOUSE RD
MOLYNEUX DR
KEYSER RD
BLACKWOOD PL
TOWN FURLONG
FREEMANS RD
WARDS CRES
AUSTIN RD
SEFTON PL
DEER'S FARM
4
Bodicote Mill House
Water Works
Cotefield House
Upper Grove Mill
37
Old Barn Farm
Lower Grove Mill
Bloxham Grove
BLOXHAM GROVE RD
Windmill
3
Sor Brook
Wayhouse Farm
36
2
Brickhouse Farm
MANOR RD
CROSS HILL RD
ADDERBURY PARK
ROUND CLOSE RD
DOG CL
Dismantled Railway
HORN HILL RD
PH
Recn G
West Adderbury
TANNERS LA
THE LEYS
Manor Farm
CHAPEL LA
PH
Milton
Works
Church Farm
35
MILTON RD
NORRIS CL
ST MARY'S RD
BERRY HILL RD
1
Mast
Wyatt's Barn
Airfield (disused)
Wireless Station
OXFORD RD
A4260
Mast
34
44
45
46

21
33

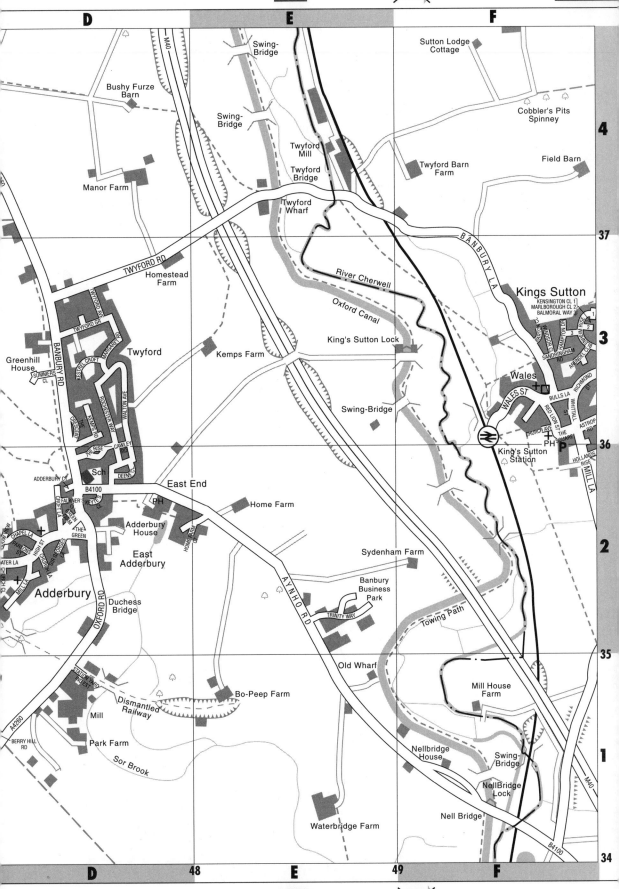

D E F

Swing-Bridge
Sutton Lodge Cottage
M40
Bushy Furze Barn
Swing-Bridge
Cobbler's Pits Spinney
Twyford Mill
Twyford Bridge
Twyford Barn Farm
Field Barn
Manor Farm
Twyford Wharf
BANBURY LA
TWYFORD RD
Homestead Farm
River Cherwell
Kings Sutton
KENSINGTON CL 1
MARLBOROUGH CL 2
BALMORAL WAY 3
Oxford Canal
TWYFORD AVE
TWYFORD GR
MARGARET RD
HAMPTON DR
WINDSOR CL
SANDRINGHAM RD
ARUNDEL CL
Twyford
King's Sutton Lock
Greenhill House
BANBURY RD
KESTREL CROFT
Kemps Farm
SUMMERS CL
Wales
WALES ST
BULLS LA
RICHMOND
ROCHESTER WAY
WALTON AVE
Swing-Bridge
RED LION ST
WHITTALL ST
THE CRESCENT
KEMPS RD
CHURCH AVE
THE SQUARE
ASTROP RD
THE RISE
CAWLEY RD
PH
King's Sutton Station
HOLLANDS RISE
MILL LA
Sch
ADDERBURY CT
DEENE CL
B4100
East End
FALKNER'S CL
KEYTE'S CL
PH
Home Farm
CROFT LA
GREEN FARM
THE GREEN
Adderbury House
HOME FARM CT
CHAPEL LA
PARSONS ST
HIGH ST
SIR GEORGES LA
CHURCH LA
East Adderbury
Sydenham Farm
MILL LA
Adderbury
AYNHO RD
Banbury Business Park
Duchess Bridge
OXFORD RD
TRINITY WAY
Towing Path
Old Wharf
STATION YARD IND EST
Bo-Peep Farm
Mill House Farm
Dismantled Railway
Mill
A4260
BERRY HILL RD
Park Farm
Nellbridge House
Swing-Bridge
Sor Brook
NellBridge Lock
M40
Nell Bridge
Waterbridge Farm
B4100

4 37 3 36 2 35 1 34

D 48 E 49 F

A   B   C

Burwell Farm

Turweston Manor
Turweston Fields

Oatleys Hall

Ash Furlong Lan

4

VALLEY CRES
VALLEY RISE
ST PETER'S
EGERTON CL
CHURCH
PEBBLE LA
OLD TOWN

MAIN ST
CHAPEL LA

Turweston

Oatleys Farm

Sch
Old Town

Brackley

1 CAESARS GATE
2 HADRIANS GATE
3 FLAVIUS GATE
4 REMUS GATE
5 ROMULUS WAY

37

WESTMINSTER CRES
BUCKINGHAM RD
WESTMINSTER CL
FARM RD
WILLOW RD
BOUNDARY RD
SHIRES RD

Glebe
Farm

Grove Farm

A422

Wks

3

COUNTY RD
BOROUGH RD
A43(T)

Hopcrafts Farm

Turweston Hill
Farm

Grovehill Farm

A422 BRACKLE

36

River Great Ouse

Dismantled Railway

Works
Westbury M

Dismantled Railway

2

Ash Beds

South Ground Covert

Evenley Mill Farm

Hill Ground
Spinney

35

1

Mixbury Hall
Farm

Mixbury Hall

Hollow Barn

Mossycorner La

Mossycorner
Spinney

Beaumont Castle
(remains of)

CHURCH Glebe Farm

34

59   A   60   B   61   C

Evershaw Copse

New Copse

Cow Pond Copse

Westbury Wild

Ash Furlong Lane

4

Treadwell Spinney

37

Shalstone Grounds Farm

Dust Houses

MAIN ST

Shalstone

3

Grass Drying Plant

Manor Farm

BIDDLESDEN RD

BRACKLEY RD

A422

Bear Bridge

36

Mill Farm

The Reindeer (PH)

Snowball Farm

MAIN ST

Doctor's Spinney

FULWELL RD

Westbury

ORCHARD PL

Huntsmill Farm

MILL LA

Sch

Hill Farm

2

Sewage Works

Fields Barn

35

River Great Ouse

Fulwell House

Dismantled Railway

Fulwell

Lower Barn

Bacon's House

1

Fulwell Cotts

Stonepit Spinney

34

D   63   E   64   F

A   B   C

Oak Coppice

Cooper's Coppice

4

Wolford Wood

Nethercote Bro

Rectory Farm

Barton Firs

Old Covert

Stanford Brook

Stanford Bridge

33

Hopyard Coppice

Hom Farm

Wolford Lodge

Gravels Barn

Barton House

Rainb Farr

3

Gravels Coppice

Barton-on-the-Heath

Four Shire House

Rectory Farm

A44

North Four Shire Stone Farm

32

Heath Farm

Brick Kiln Barn

Oakhouse Farm

2

Kitebrook Farm

Kitebrook

Brookend House

Kitebrook House

Salter's Well Farm

31

Kitebrook-End Farm

Resr

Middle Brookend Farm

The Bung

Rigside

1

Stuphill Covert

Tithe Barn

Grove Farm

Sewage Works

Inn

POOL SL COTTS

Little Compton

Chastleton Glebe

The Grove

Durham's Farm

BRE

30

23   A   24   B   25   C

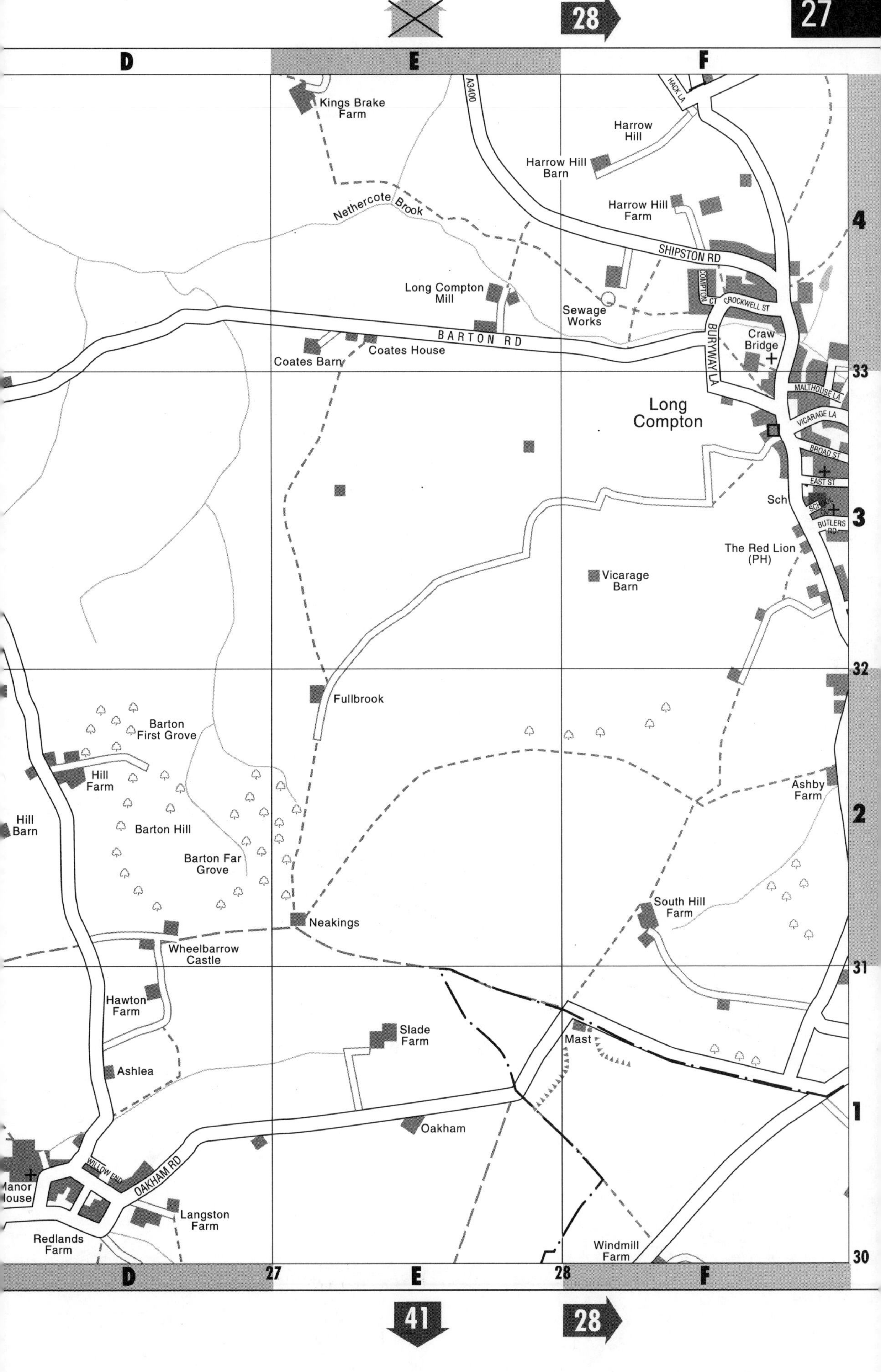

D   E   F

Kings Brake
Farm

Harrow
Hill

Harrow Hill
Barn

Harrow Hill
Farm

Nethercote Brook

SHIPSTON RD

4

Long Compton
Mill

Sewage
Works

A3400

COMPTON CT

CROCKWELL ST

BURYWAY LA

Craw
Bridge

BARTON RD

Coates House

Coates Barn

33

MALTHOUSE LA

VICARAGE LA

Long
Compton

BROAD ST

EAST ST

Sch

BUTLERS RD

3

Vicarage
Barn

The Red Lion
(PH)

32

Fullbrook

Barton
First Grove

Hill
Farm

Barton Hill

Hill
Barn

Barton Far
Grove

Ashby
Farm

2

South Hill
Farm

Neakings

Wheelbarrow
Castle

31

Hawton
Farm

Slade
Farm

Mast

Ashlea

1

Oakham

Manor
House

WILLOW END

OAKHAM RD

Langston
Farm

Redlands
Farm

Windmill
Farm

30

D   27   E   28   F

| | 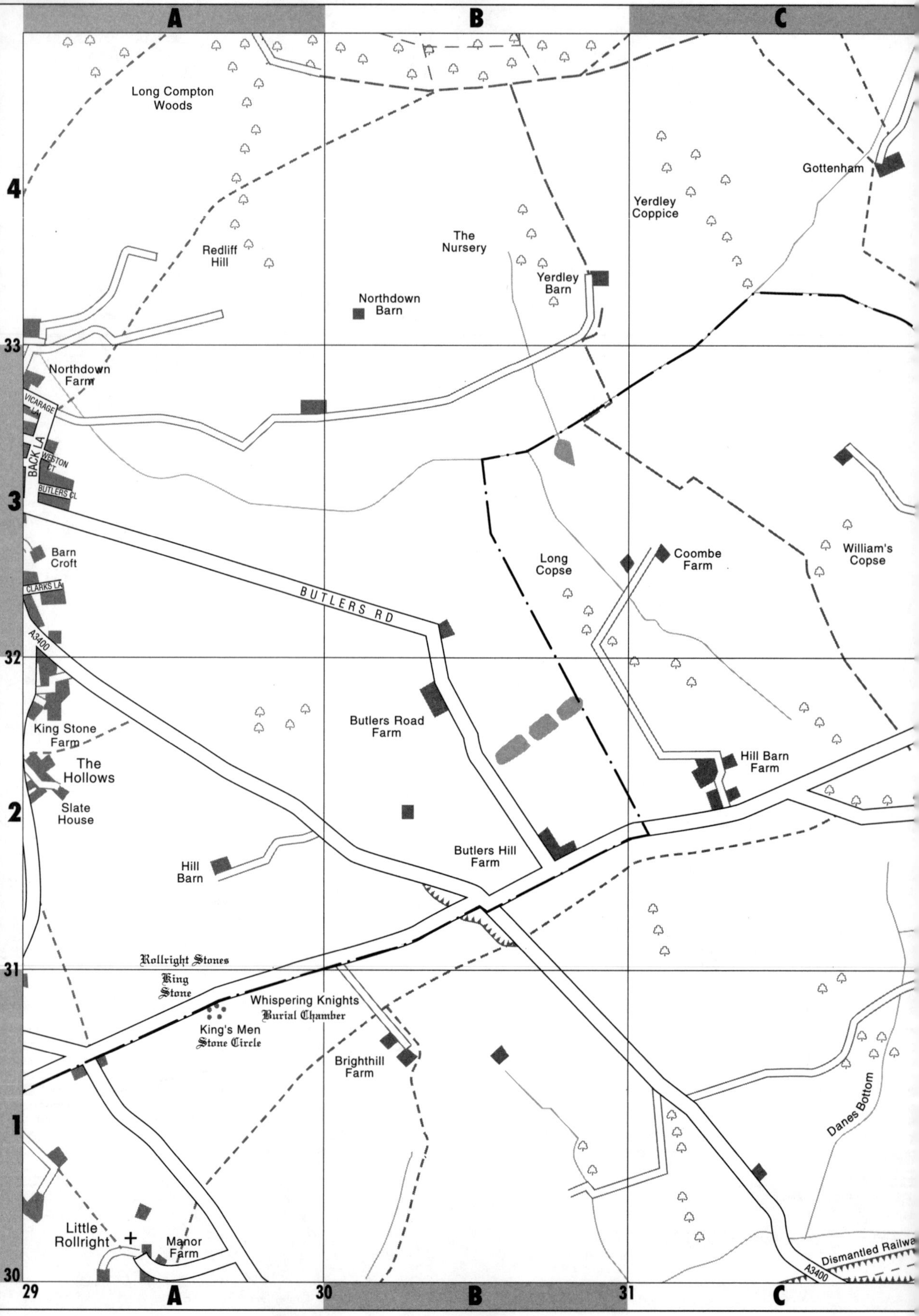 A | B | C |

Long Compton Woods

Redliff Hill

The Nursery

Yerdley Coppice

Gottenham

Northdown Barn

Yerdley Barn

Northdown Farm

VICARAGE LA
BACK LA
WESTON CT
BUTLERS CL

Barn Croft

CLARKS LA
A3400

BUTLERS RD

Long Copse

Coombe Farm

William's Copse

King Stone Farm

The Hollows

Slate House

Butlers Road Farm

Hill Barn Farm

Hill Barn

Butlers Hill Farm

Rollright Stones

King Stone

Whispering Knights Burial Chamber

King's Men Stone Circle

Brighthill Farm

Danes Bottom

Little Rollright

Manor Farm

Dismantled Railway
A3400

D
E
F

4

3

33

3

32

2

31

1

30

Whichford Hill Barn

TRAITOR'S FORD LA

Whichford Hill Farm

Mast

Wychford Lodge Farm

Court Farm

Berryfield Farm

Halfway Lane

Fanthill Farm

Brewery

BREWERY LA

Scotland End

Harwood House

Fanville Head Farm

on Grange Farm

Church End Farm

Church End

HILL RD

OLD CHOTOWELL RD

THE GREEN

STONE

SOUTH END

Great Rollright

Tyte End

or se

anor arm

Heath Farm Bungalow

Cardwell Farm

Heath Farm Cottages

Rollright Heath Farm

Duckpool Farm

Sewage Works

Limekiln Bungalow

Halt Farm

Dismantled Railway

River Swere

Walk Farm

Coldharbour Farm

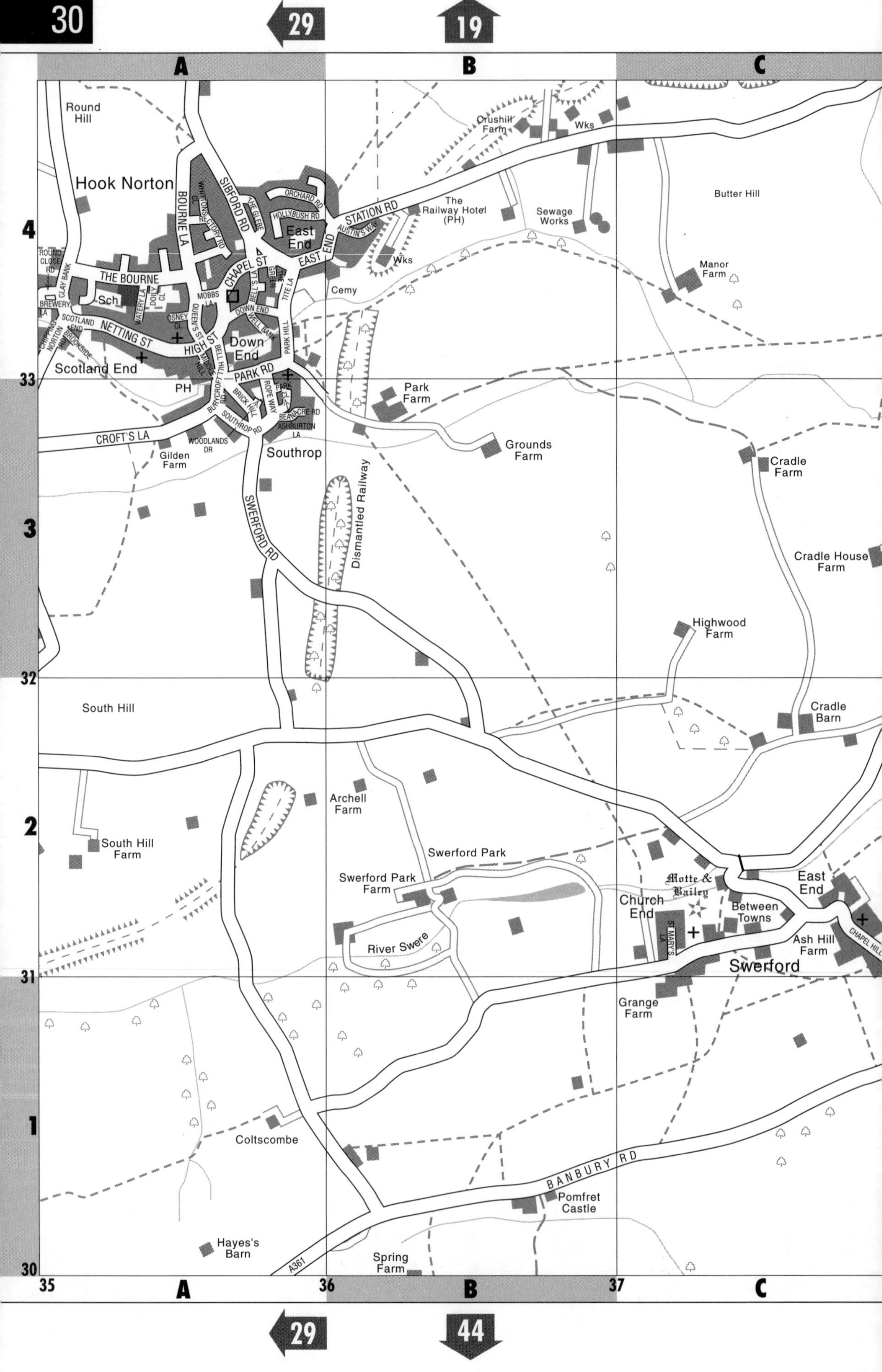

A B C

4

33

3

32

2

31

1

30

Round
Hill

Hook Norton

BOURNE LA
SIBFORD RD
THE GLEBE
ORCHARD RD
HOLLYBUSH RD
STATION RD
AUSTIN'S WK

East
End

EAST END
GREEN

ROUND
CLOSE
RD
CHAPEL ST
CLAY BANK
THE BOURNE
WHITTONS CLOSE
WHITTONS CROFT RD
Sch
MOBBS
BELL'S LA
DOLL'S
CL
TITE LA
Cemy
OSNEY
CL
BREWERY
CHIPPING
NORTON
SCOTLAND
END
BROOKSIDE
NETTING ST
WATER LA
QUEEN'S ST
HIGH ST
WALL BANK
DOWN END
Down
End
PARK HILL
WATERLA
BELL HILL
BRICK HILL
PARK HILL
Scotland End
PH
PARK RD
BURY LA
SOUTHROP RD
ROPE WAY
BEAUMONT RD
ASHBURTON LA
Southrop
CROFT'S LA
WOODLANDS
DR
Gilden
Farm

The
Railway Hotel
(PH)

Crushill
Farm
Wks

Wks

Sewage
Works

Butter Hill

Manor
Farm

Park
Farm

Grounds
Farm

Cradle
Farm

Cradle House
Farm

SWERFORD RD

Dismantled Railway

South Hill

Highwood
Farm

Cradle
Barn

South Hill
Farm

Archell
Farm

Swerford Park

Swerford Park
Farm

River Swere

Motte &
Bailey

Church
End

ST MARY'S LA

Between
Towns

East
End

CHAPEL HILL

Ash Hill
Farm

Swerford

Grange
Farm

Coltscombe

BANBURY RD

Pomfret
Castle

Hayes's
Barn

A361

Spring
Farm

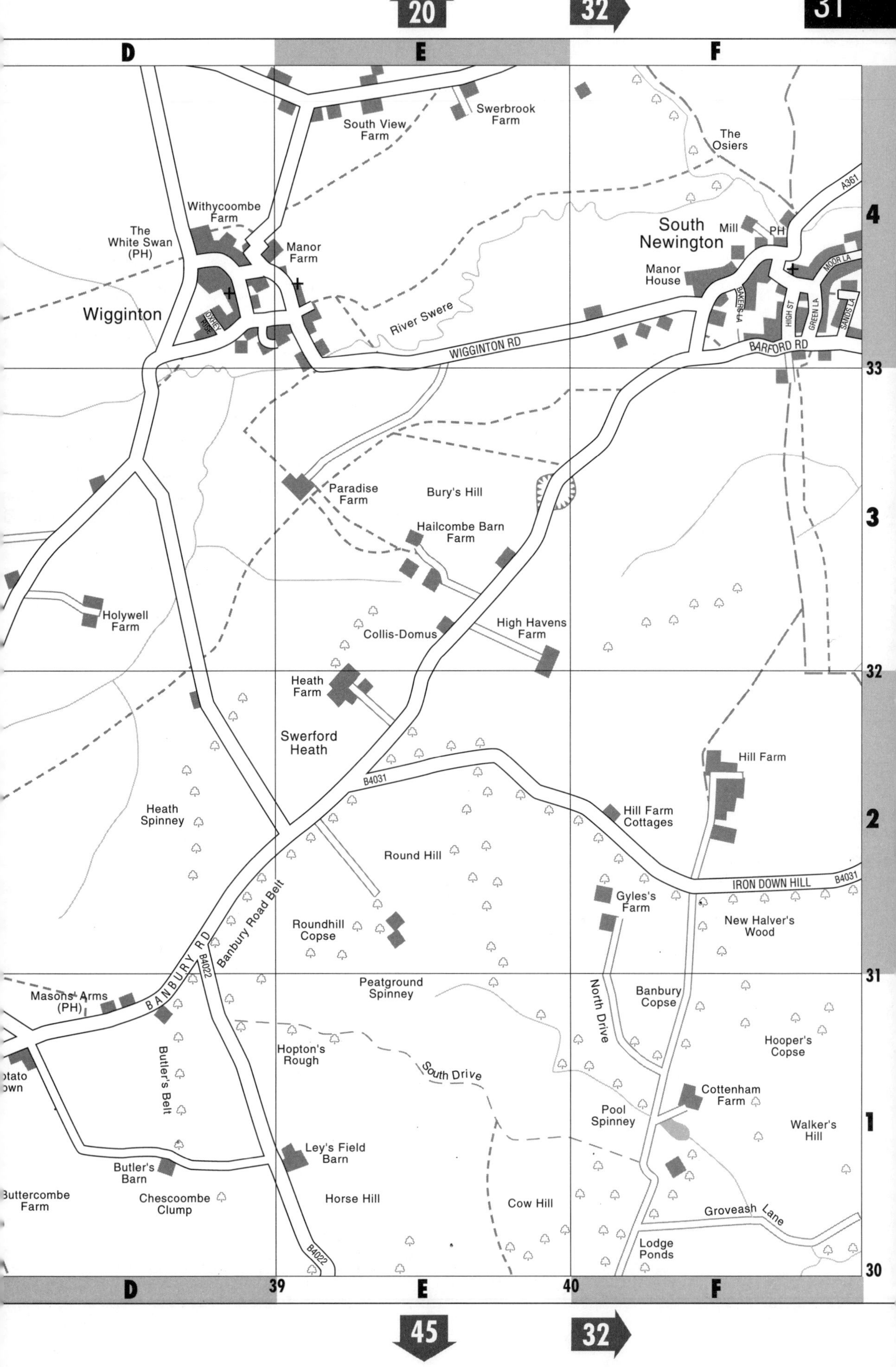
D
E
F
South View Farm
Swerbrook Farm
The Osiers
Withycoombe Farm
The White Swan (PH)
Manor Farm
Wigginton
OXHEY RISE
River Swere
WIGGINTON RD
South Newington
Mill
PH
A361
Manor House
MOOR LA
BAKERS LA
HIGH ST
GREEN LA
SANDS LA
BARFORD RD
4
33
Paradise Farm
Bury's Hill
Hailcombe Barn Farm
3
Holywell Farm
Collis-Domus
High Havens Farm
32
Heath Farm
Swerford Heath
Hill Farm
B4031
Heath Spinney
Hill Farm Cottages
2
Round Hill
IRON DOWN HILL
B4031
Gyles's Farm
Banbury Road Belt
New Halver's Wood
Roundhill Copse
BANBURY RD
B4022
31
Peatground Spinney
Masons' Arms (PH)
North Drive
Banbury Copse
Butler's Belt
Hooper's Copse
Hopton's Rough
South Drive
Cottenham Farm
Pool Spinney
Walker's Hill
1
Ley's Field Barn
Butler's Barn
Horse Hill
Cow Hill
Chescoombe Clump
Groveash Lane
Lodge Ponds
B4022
30
D
39
E
40
F

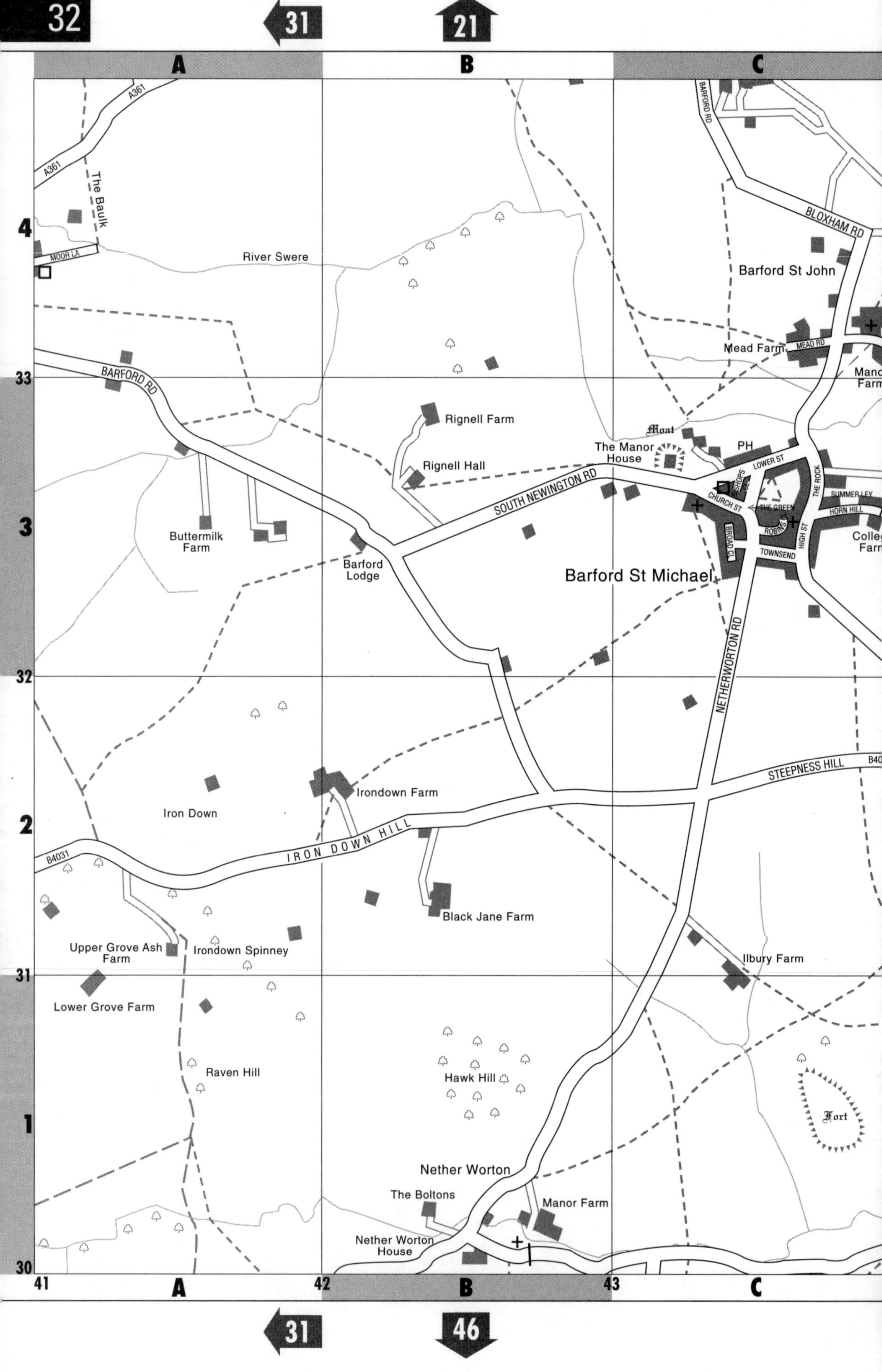

4

The Bauk
A361
A361

MOOR LA

River Swere

Barford St John

BLOXHAM RD
BARFORD RD

Mead Farm
MEAD RD

Manor
Farm

33

BARFORD RD

Rignell Farm

Rignell Hall

Moat

The Manor House

PH
LOWER ST

SHOPS

CHURCH ST

THE GREEN

ROBINS

SUMMER LEY

HORN HILL

THE ROCK

3

Buttermilk Farm

Barford Lodge

SOUTH NEWINGTON RD

HIGH ST

BRIDGE RD

TOWNSEND

College Farm

Barford St Michael

NETHERWORTON RD

32

STEEPNESS HILL
B40

2

Iron Down

B4031

Irondown Farm

IRON DOWN HILL

Black Jane Farm

Ilbury Farm

31

Upper Grove Ash Farm

Irondown Spinney

Lower Grove Farm

Raven Hill

Hawk Hill

Fort

1

Nether Worton

The Boltons

Manor Farm

Nether Worton House

30

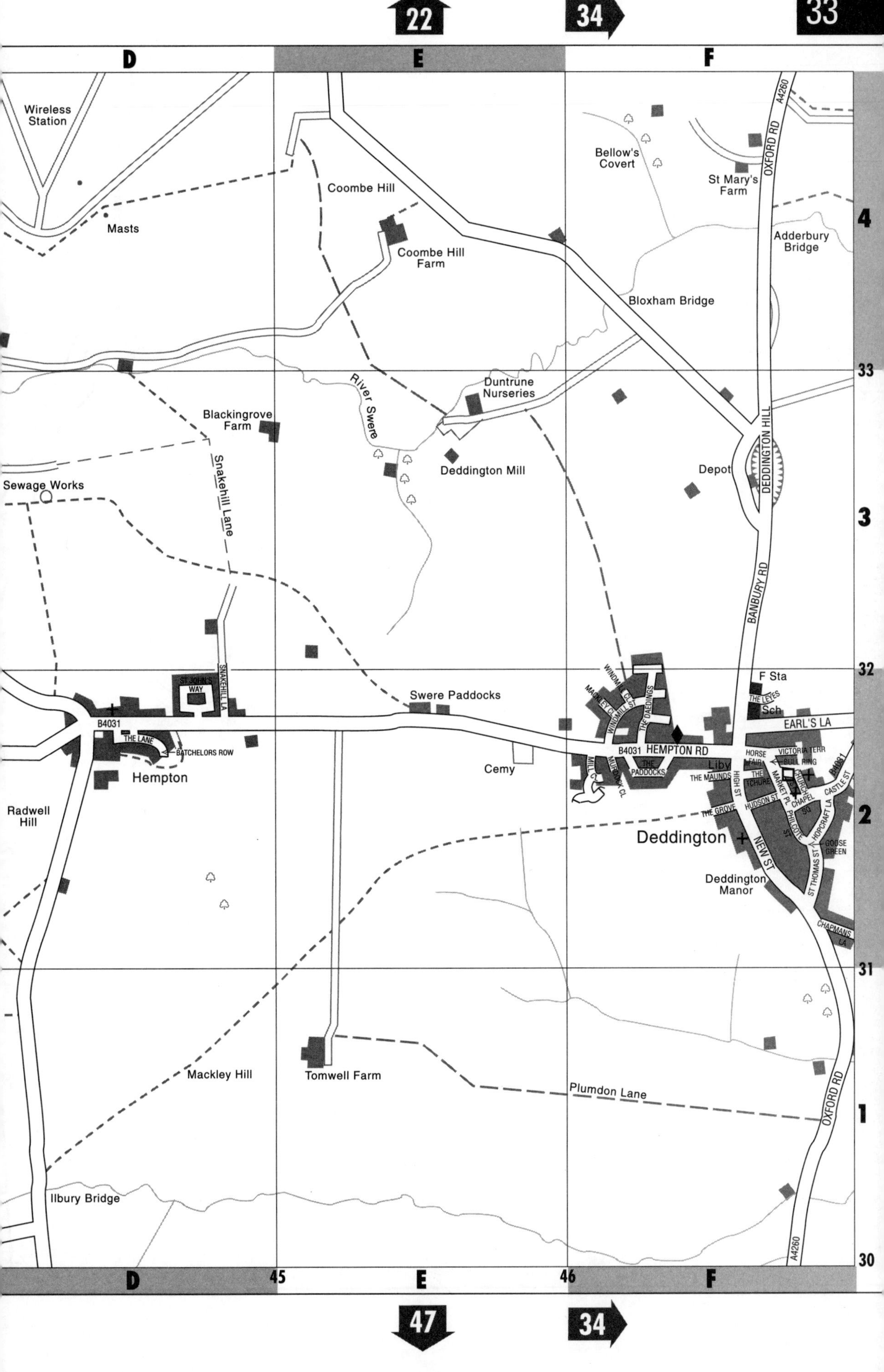
D
E
F
Wireless Station
Masts
Coombe Hill
Coombe Hill Farm
Bellow's Covert
St Mary's Farm
OXFORD RD
A4260
Adderbury Bridge
Bloxham Bridge
4
33
Duntrune Nurseries
River Swere
Blackingrove Farm
Deddington Mill
Depot
DEDDINGTON HILL
Sewage Works
Snakehill Lane
3
BANBURY RD
32
F Sta
THE LEYES
Sch
EARL'S LA
WINDMILL CL
MACKLEY CL
WINDMILL ST
THE DAEDINGS
Swere Paddocks
ST JOHN'S WAY
SNAKEHILL LA
B4031
THE LANE
BATCHELORS ROW
Hempton
B4031 HEMPTON RD
Cemy
MILL CL
MURDOCK CL
THE PADDOCKS
Liby
THE MAUNDS
HIGH ST
HORSE FAIR
VICTORIA TERR
BULL RING
THE TCHURE
MARKET PL
CHURCH ST
CHAPEL SQ
HUDSON ST
THE GROVE
PHILCOTE ST
HOPCRAFT LA
CASTLE ST
B4031
Radwell Hill
2
Deddington
NEW ST
GOOSE GREEN
Deddington Manor
ST THOMAS ST
CHAPMANS LA
31
Mackley Hill
Tomwell Farm
Plumdon Lane
OXFORD RD
1
Ilbury Bridge
A4260
30

33
23

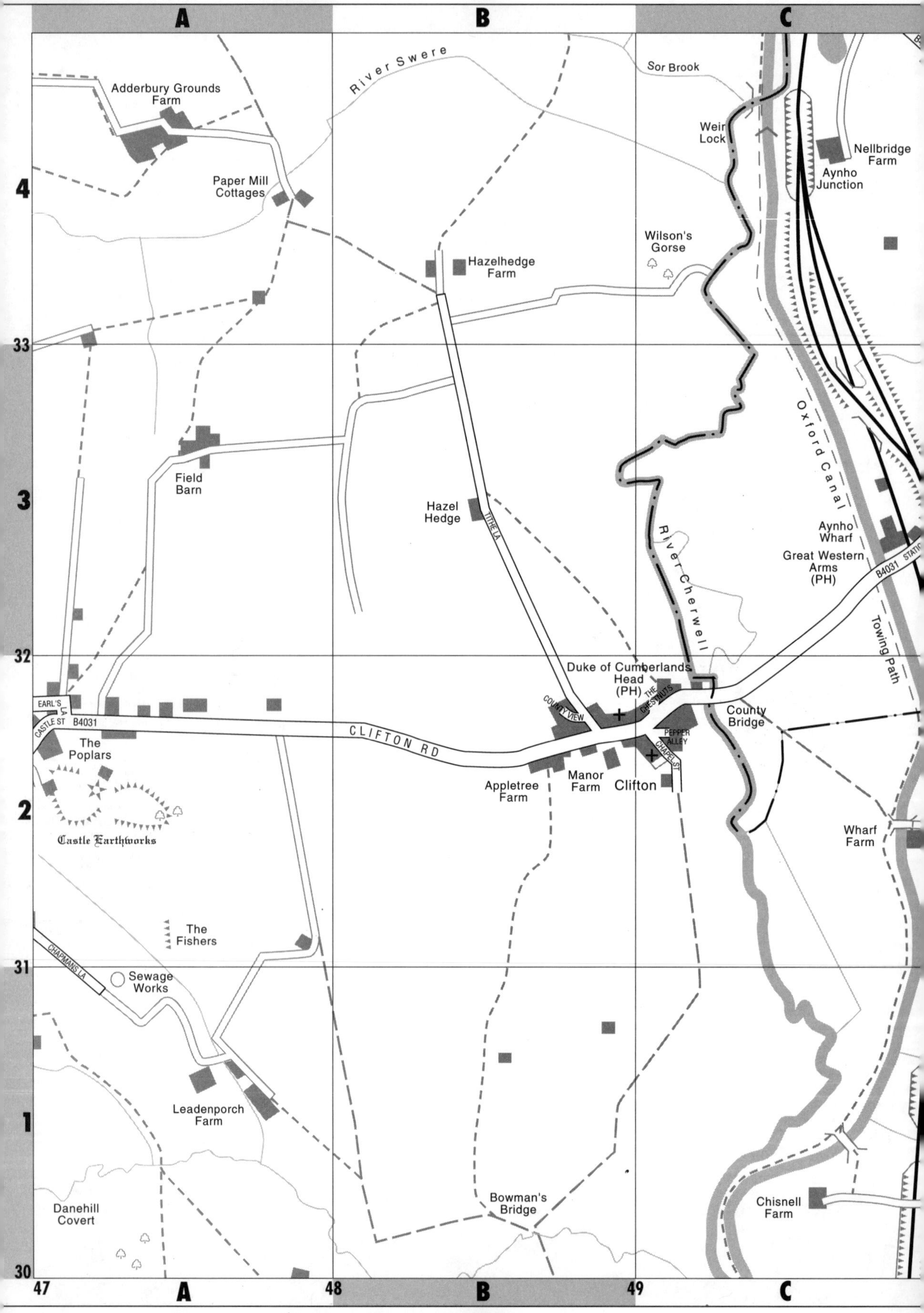

A **B** **C**

River Swere

Sor Brook

Adderbury Grounds Farm

Weir Lock

Nellbridge Farm

Aynho Junction

4

Paper Mill Cottages

Wilson's Gorse

Hazelhedge Farm

33

Oxford Canal

Field Barn

Hazel Hedge

River Cherwell

3

Aynho Wharf

Great Western Arms (PH)

B4031 STATION

Towing Path

32

Duke of Cumberlands Head (PH)

County View

THE CHESTNUTS

County Bridge

EARL'S LA

CASTLE ST

B4031

CLIFTON RD

The Poplars

Appletree Farm

Manor Farm

Clifton

PEPPER ALLEY

CHAPEL ST

2

Castle Earthworks

Wharf Farm

The Fishers

CHAPMANS LA

31

Sewage Works

Leadenporch Farm

1

Danehill Covert

Bowman's Bridge

Chisnell Farm

30

47 **A** 48 **B** 49 **C**

33
48

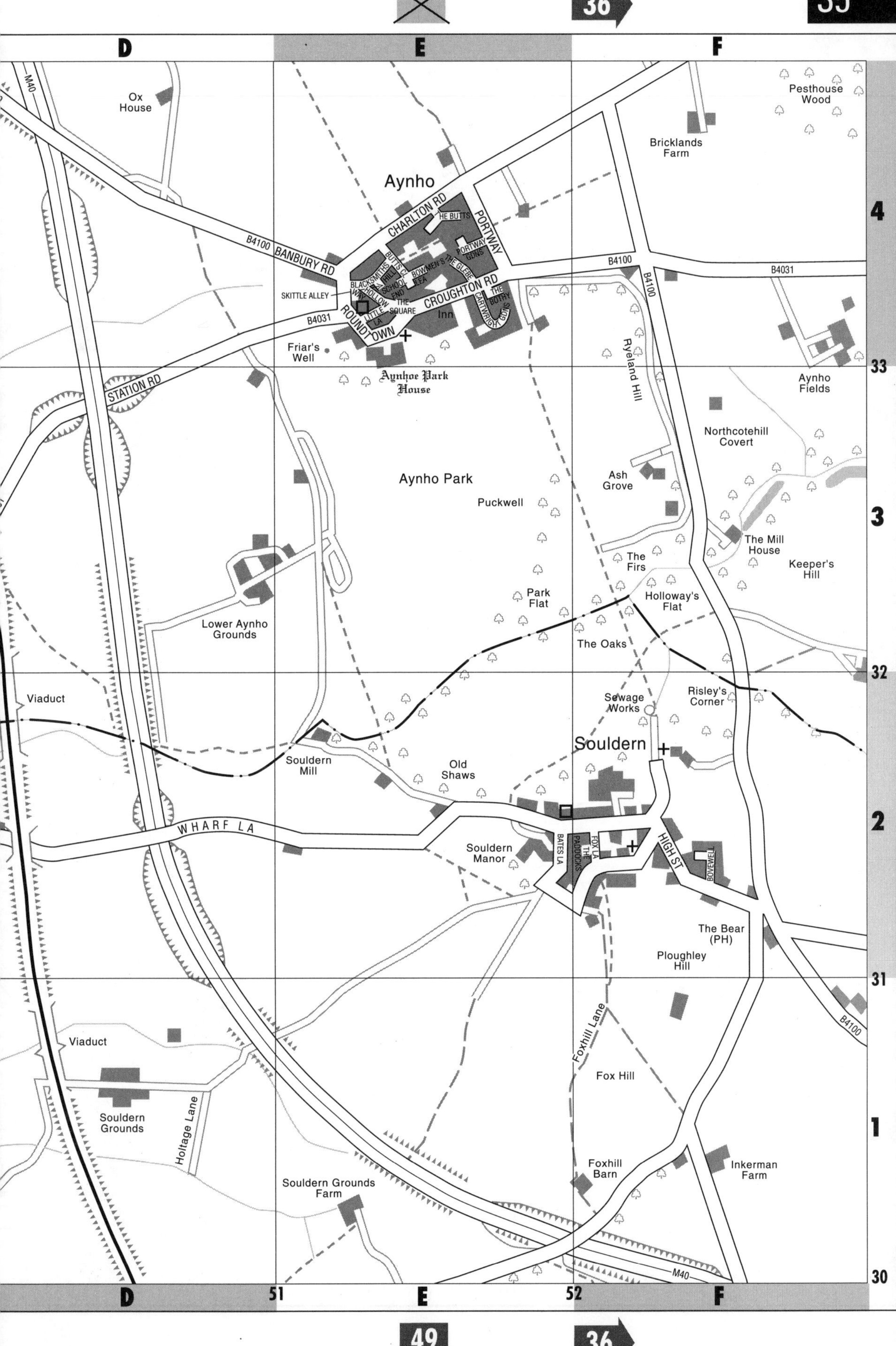
M40
Ox House
Aynho
Pesthouse Wood
Bricklands Farm
CHARLTON RD
THE BUTTS
PORTWAY
PORTWAY GDNS
BANBURY RD
B4100
B4031
BUTTS CL
BOWMEN'S LEA
THE GLEBE
BLACKSMITHS HILL
HOLLOW WAY
SCHOOL END
SKITTLE ALLEY
LITTLE LA
THE SQUARE
CROUGHTON RD
THE BOTHY
CARTWRIGHT GDNS
ROUNDTOWN
Inn
Friar's Well
Aynhoe Park House
STATION RD
Ryeland Hill
Aynho Fields
Northcotehill Covert
Aynho Park
Ash Grove
Puckwell
The Mill House
The Firs
Keeper's Hill
Park Flat
Holloway's Flat
Lower Aynho Grounds
The Oaks
Viaduct
Sewage Works
Risley's Corner
Souldern
Souldern Mill
Old Shaws
WHARF LA
Souldern Manor
BATES LA
FOX LA
THE PADDOCKS
HIGH ST
BOYEWELL
The Bear (PH)
Ploughley Hill
Foxhill Lane
Viaduct
Fox Hill
Souldern Grounds
Holtage Lane
Foxhill Barn
Inkerman Farm
Souldern Grounds Farm
4
3
2
1
33
32
31
30

Warren Farm

Home Farm

Cemy

Sch

The Moors

Blackbird (PH)

WHEELER'S RISE

HIGH ST

YEW TREE RISE

PARK END

BRACKLEY RD

BLENHEIM

B4031

The Green

MILL LA

CHAPEL RD

CHURCH LA

Croughton

PORTWAY CRES

PORTWAY DR

PORTWAY

Ford

Sewage Works

Park Farm

SIXTH ST

FIFTH AVE

FIFTH ST

SIXTH ST

SECOND

FOURTH AVE

Schs

Old Down Covert

Old Down Pond

Padbury's Bottom

Smanhill Covert

New Buildings

FOURTH ST

ANDREWS AVE

THIRD

SECOND

FIRST ST

Masts

Middle Covert

Upper Aynho Grounds

Ockley Brook

Pimlico Farm

Crook's Firs

Thriftwood House

Tower Farm

Roundhill Farm

Low Rook

B4100

Horwell Corner

Tumulus

Round Hill

Wr Twr

Oxford Lodge

Park Farm

Hermitage Belt

B4100

Horwell Farm

A43(T)

Sharmans Pit

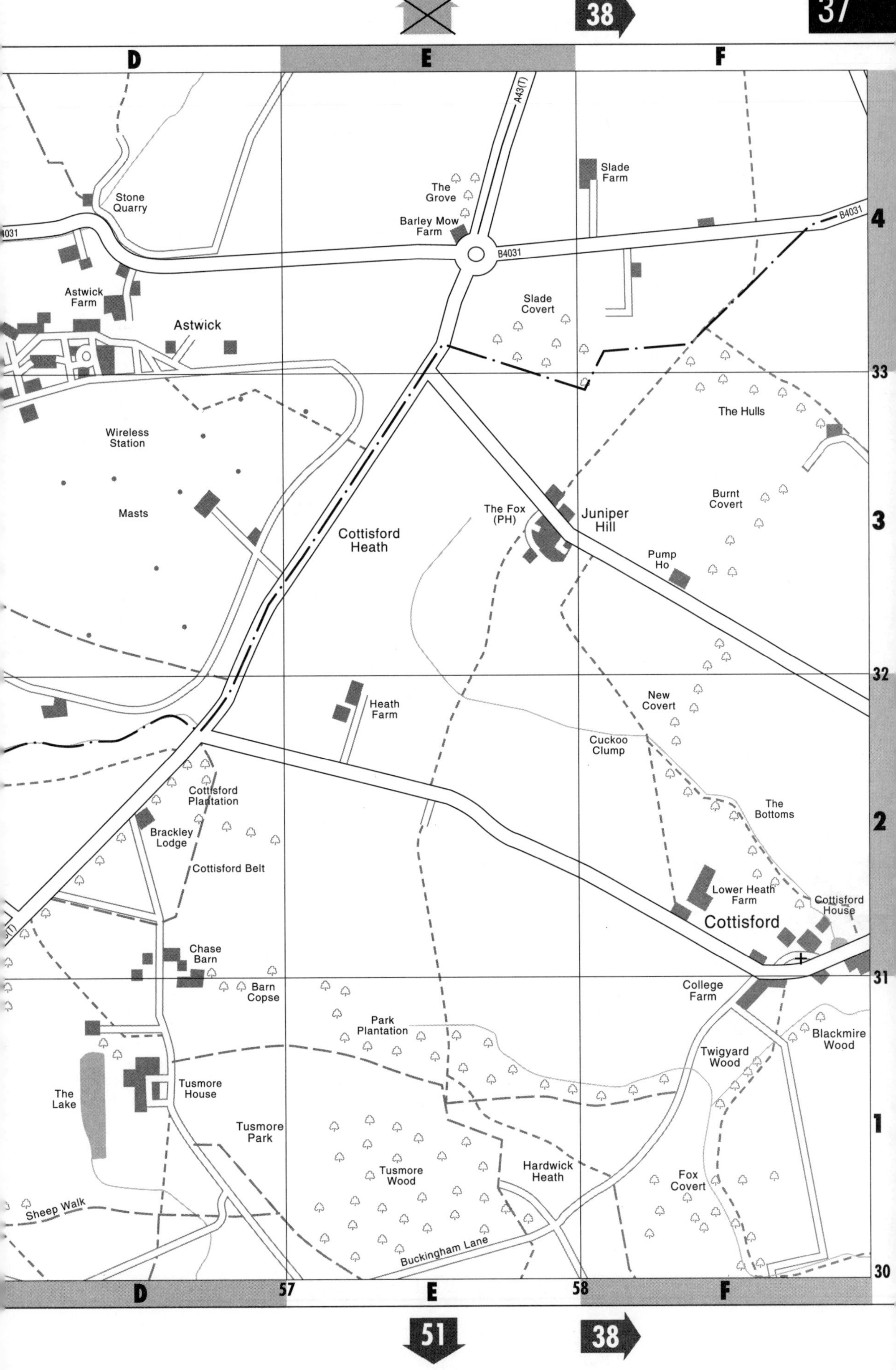

38

D   E   F

Stone Quarry

The Grove

Slade Farm

Barley Mow Farm

B4031

B4031

4031

Astwick Farm

Astwick

Slade Covert

4

The Hulls

33

Wireless Station

Masts

Cottisford Heath

The Fox (PH)

Juniper Hill

Burnt Covert

Pump Ho

3

New Covert

32

Heath Farm

Cuckoo Clump

The Bottoms

2

Cottisford Plantation

Brackley Lodge

Cottisford Belt

Lower Heath Farm

Cottisford House

Cottisford

Chase Barn

Barn Copse

College Farm

31

Park Plantation

Twigyard Wood

Blackmire Wood

The Lake

Tusmore House

Tusmore Park

Hardwick Heath

Fox Covert

1

Tusmore Wood

Sheep Walk

Buckingham Lane

30

D   57   E   58   F

51   38

37
24

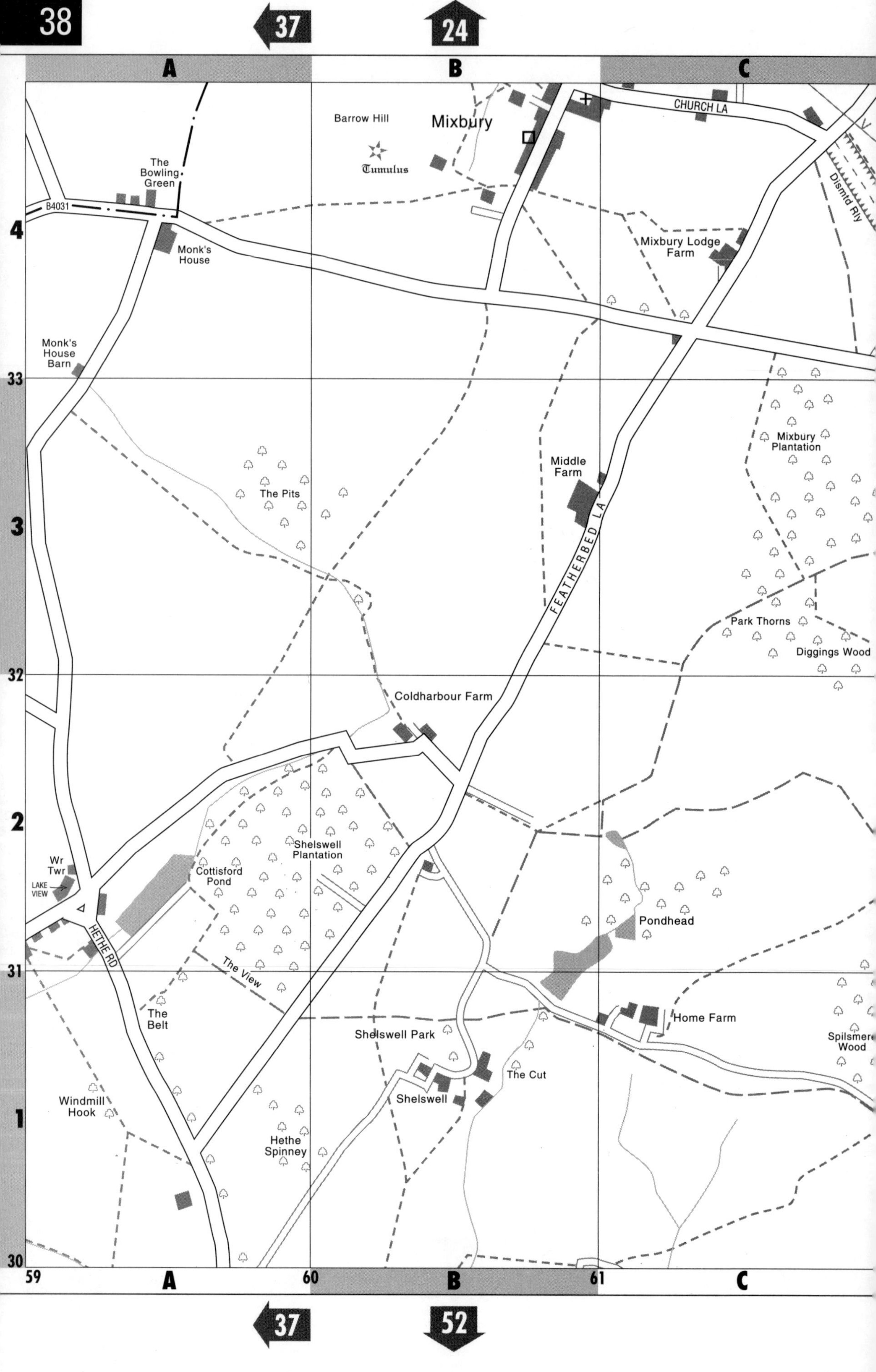
A
B
C
Barrow Hill
Mixbury
Tumulus
CHURCH LA
The Bowling Green
B4031
Monk's House
Dismtd Rly
Mixbury Lodge Farm
Monk's House Barn
Mixbury Plantation
Middle Farm
The Pits
FEATHERBED LA
Park Thorns
Diggings Wood
Coldharbour Farm
Shelswell Plantation
Wr Twr
LAKE VIEW
Cottisford Pond
HETHE RD
Pondhead
The View
The Belt
Home Farm
Shelswell Park
Spilsmere Wood
The Cut
Shelswell
Windmill Hook
Hethe Spinney
4
33
3
32
2
31
1
30
59
60
61
A
B
C

37
52

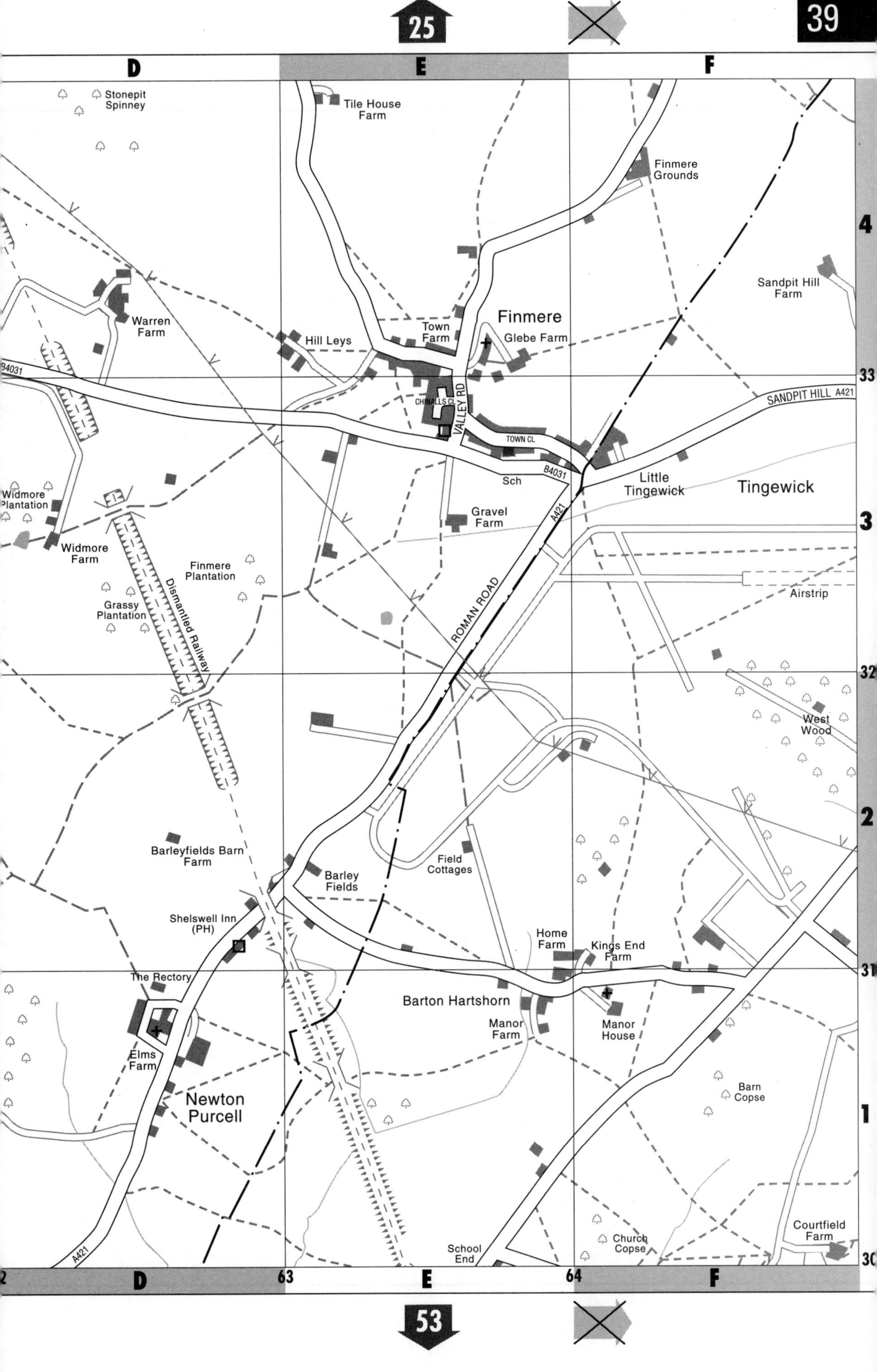

D   E   F

Stonepit
Spinney

Tile House
Farm

Finmere
Grounds

4

Sandpit Hill
Farm

Warren
Farm

Town
Farm

Finmere

Hill Leys

Glebe Farm

33

CHINALLS CL

VALLEY RD

SANDPIT HILL A421

Widmore
Plantation

TOWN CL

Sch

B4031

Little
Tingewick

Tingewick

Widmore
Farm

Gravel
Farm

A421

3

Finmere
Plantation

Dismantled Railway

Grassy
Plantation

ROMAN ROAD

Airstrip

32

West
Wood

Barleyfields Barn
Farm

2

Barley
Fields

Field
Cottages

Shelswell Inn
(PH)

Home
Farm

Kings End
Farm

31

The Rectory

Barton Hartshorn

Elms
Farm

Manor
Farm

Manor
House

Barn
Copse

Newton
Purcell

1

Church
Copse

Courtfield
Farm

A421

School
End

30

2   D   63   E   64   F

26

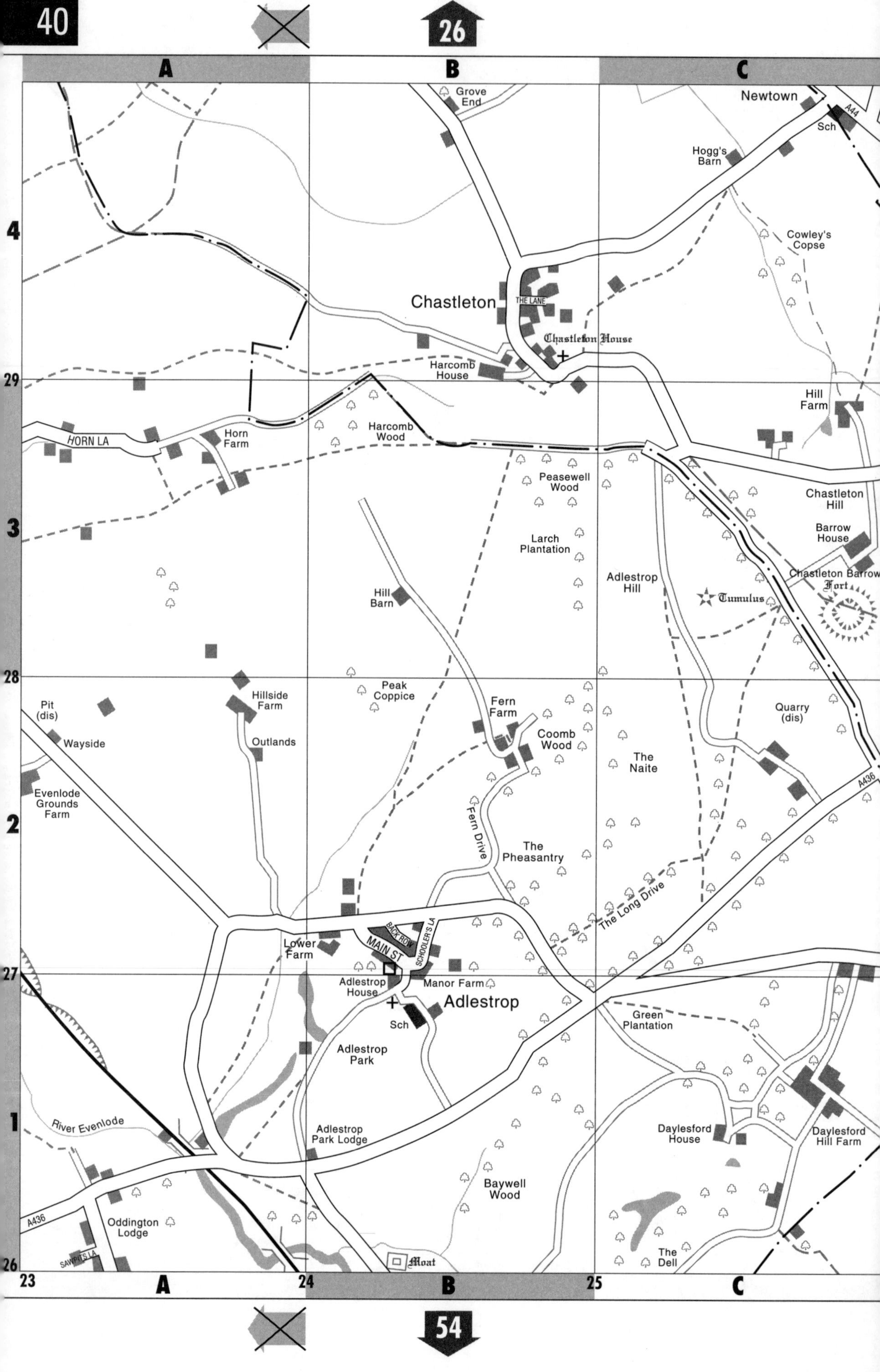

A
B
C
Grove End
Newtown
Sch
A44
Hogg's Barn
Cowley's Copse
4
Chastleton
THE LANE
Chastleton House
Harcomb House
29
Hill Farm
HORN LA
Horn Farm
Harcomb Wood
Peasewell Wood
Chastleton Hill
3
Larch Plantation
Barrow House
Adlestrop Hill
Chastleton Barrow Fort
Tumulus
Hill Barn
28
Pit (dis)
Hillside Farm
Peak Coppice
Fern Farm
Quarry (dis)
Wayside
Outlands
Coomb Wood
The Naite
Evenlode Grounds Farm
A436
2
Fern Drive
The Pheasantry
The Long Drive
BACK ROW
SCHOOLER'S LA
Lower Farm
MAIN ST
27
Adlestrop House
Manor Farm
Adlestrop
Sch
Green Plantation
Adlestrop Park
1
River Evenlode
Adlestrop Park Lodge
Daylesford House
Daylesford Hill Farm
Baywell Wood
A436
Oddington Lodge
SAWPITS LA
The Dell
Moat
26
23
24
25

54

D
E
F

Pump
House

Twin Brook
Farm

Hillside

4

Quarry
(dis)

Hirons Hill
Farm

GREYGOOSE LA

Cross Hands
(PH)

29

Springhill
Farm

Burnt Hill

A436

A44

Tumulus

Chastleton
Hill

Hollis Hill
Farm

3

Salford

Rushy
Bottom

PHELPS

Fisher's
Barn

Greathouse
Barn

Manor
Farm

Sch

CHAPEL LA

COOKS LA

ROSES LA

28

Cornwell
Holt

LOWER END

ORCHARD CL

Park
Farm

A44

2

Manor
Farm

Cornwell

Glebe
Farm

Cornwell
Manor

27

Top
Farm

Mill
Copse

Whitequarry
Hill

Swailsford
Bridge

1

Sch

Kingham
Hill Farm

26

D
27
E
28
F

Pond Bay

Manor Farm

Choicehill Farm

LIttle Meadows

Dismantled Railway

A3400

B402?

Over Norto Hous

Over Norto Park

Choicehill RD

Home Farm

RADBONE HILL

MAIN ST

Over Norton

CHARHILL CT

CLEEVES CNR

Firs Farm

Rectory Farm

Larches Farm

The Cleeves

CLEEVES AVE

Castle Earthworks

OVER NORTON RD

PARK RD

MARLBOROUGH RD

BANBURY RD

CROMW PARK

CHALFORD

B4026

Hospl

A44

BANBURY RD CROSSING

Hospl

LONDON RD

Salford Mill

Elmsfield Farm

Church LA

CHURCH ST

SPRING ST

PORTLAND PL

SUMMERTON Schs

Rock Hill

Bridge Field

DISTON'S LA

MARKET ST

FINSBURY

HIGH ST

SHEPARD WAY

COOPER DR

ROWELL WAY

ALBION ST

1 WHITEHOUSE LA
2 VICTORIA PL
3 KING'S HEAD MEWS
4 HILL LAWN CT

HORSE FAIR

Cemy

NEW ST A44

TH

ALBION P

CATTLE MKT

WARDS RD

W Tw

Nuholme

Industrial Estate

STATION RD

NEW ST A44

DUNSTAN AVE

WITHERS WAY

WEST ST

Sch

FOX CL

HITCHMAN DR

BURFORD RD

F Sta

Tan Far

WORCESTER RD

KENCEL LA

TOLYA LA

TOYLA

COMMON LA

Indl Est

Chipping Norton Common

LEWIS RD

CROSSLEYS RD

WEBB CRES

JOHNSTON'S WAY

WILLIAM BLISS AVE

PEARCE DR

MILLVIEW

WEST END

A361

A361

CHIPPING NORTON

Sch

Cornwell Hill Farm

Sewage Works

THE LEYS

CROSSLEY'S RD

ALFRED TERR

THE GREEN

ALFRED Sch

B4450

COTSWOLD CRES BUNGALOWS

COTSWOLD TERR

Allot Gdns

Westend Farm

PARADISE TERR

LORDS PIECE RD

TILSLEY RD

ALD GO

HAILEY AVE

MARSHALL

WINTERBUSH RD

COTSWOLD CRES

A361

B4026

Meads Farm

CHURCHILL RD

KORNISH RD

HAILEY RD

HAILIS RD

HAILEY CRES

Westfield Farm

BURFORD RD

B4450

4

29

3

28

2

27

1

26

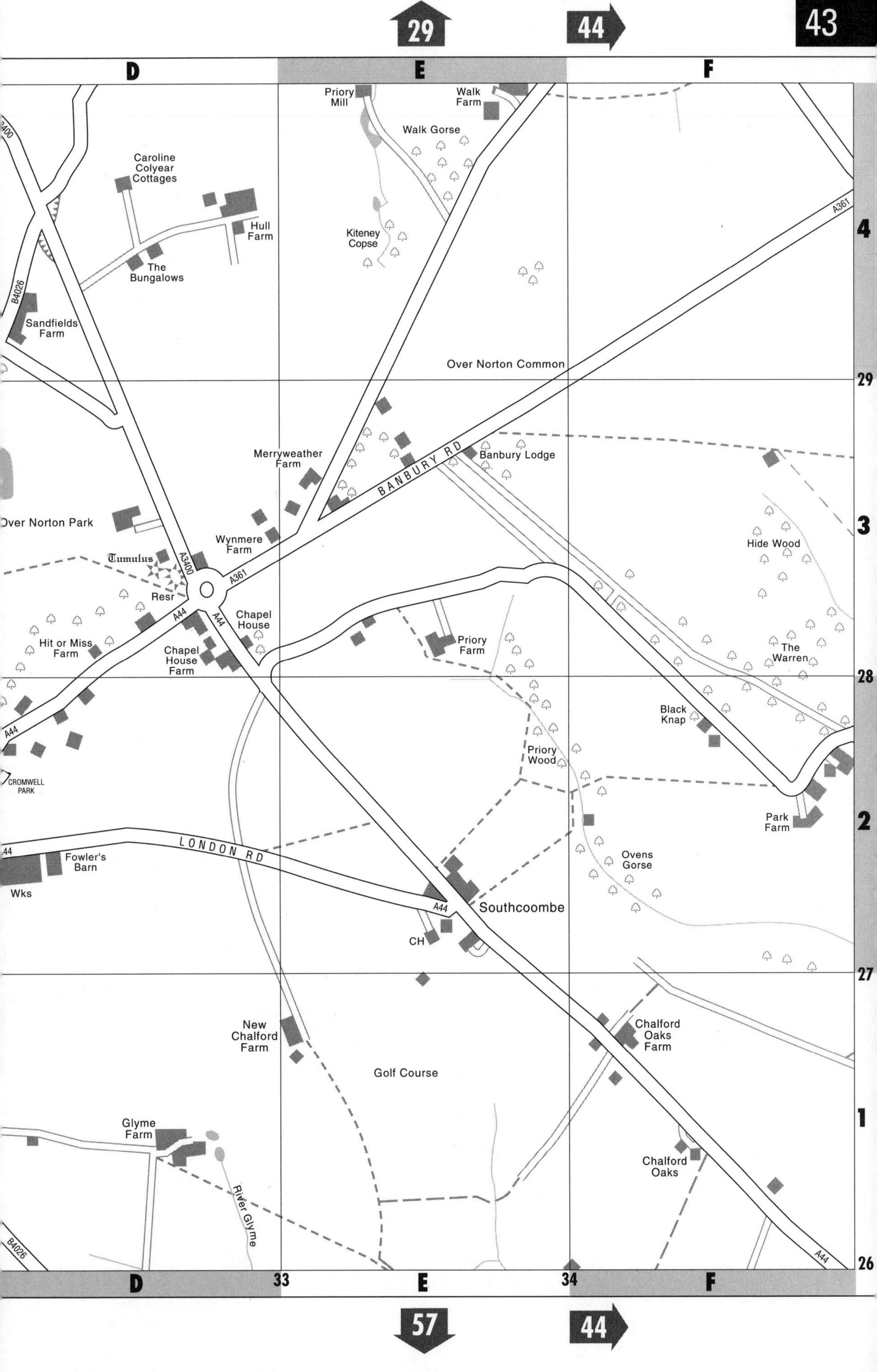

D
E
F

Priory Mill
Walk Farm
Walk Gorse
Caroline Colyear Cottages
Hull Farm
Kiteney Copse
The Bungalows
Sandfields Farm
4
Over Norton Common
29
A361
Merryweather Farm
Banbury Lodge
BANBURY RD
Over Norton Park
Hide Wood
3
Wynmere Farm
A3400
Tumulus
A361
Resr
Chapel House
Priory Farm
The Warren
Hit or Miss Farm
A44
Chapel House Farm
Black Knap
28
CROMWELL PARK
Priory Wood
LONDON RD
Park Farm
2
A44
Fowler's Barn
Ovens Gorse
Wks
A44
Southcoombe
CH
27
New Chalford Farm
Chalford Oaks Farm
Golf Course
1
Glyme Farm
Chalford Oaks
River Glyme
B4026
A44
26

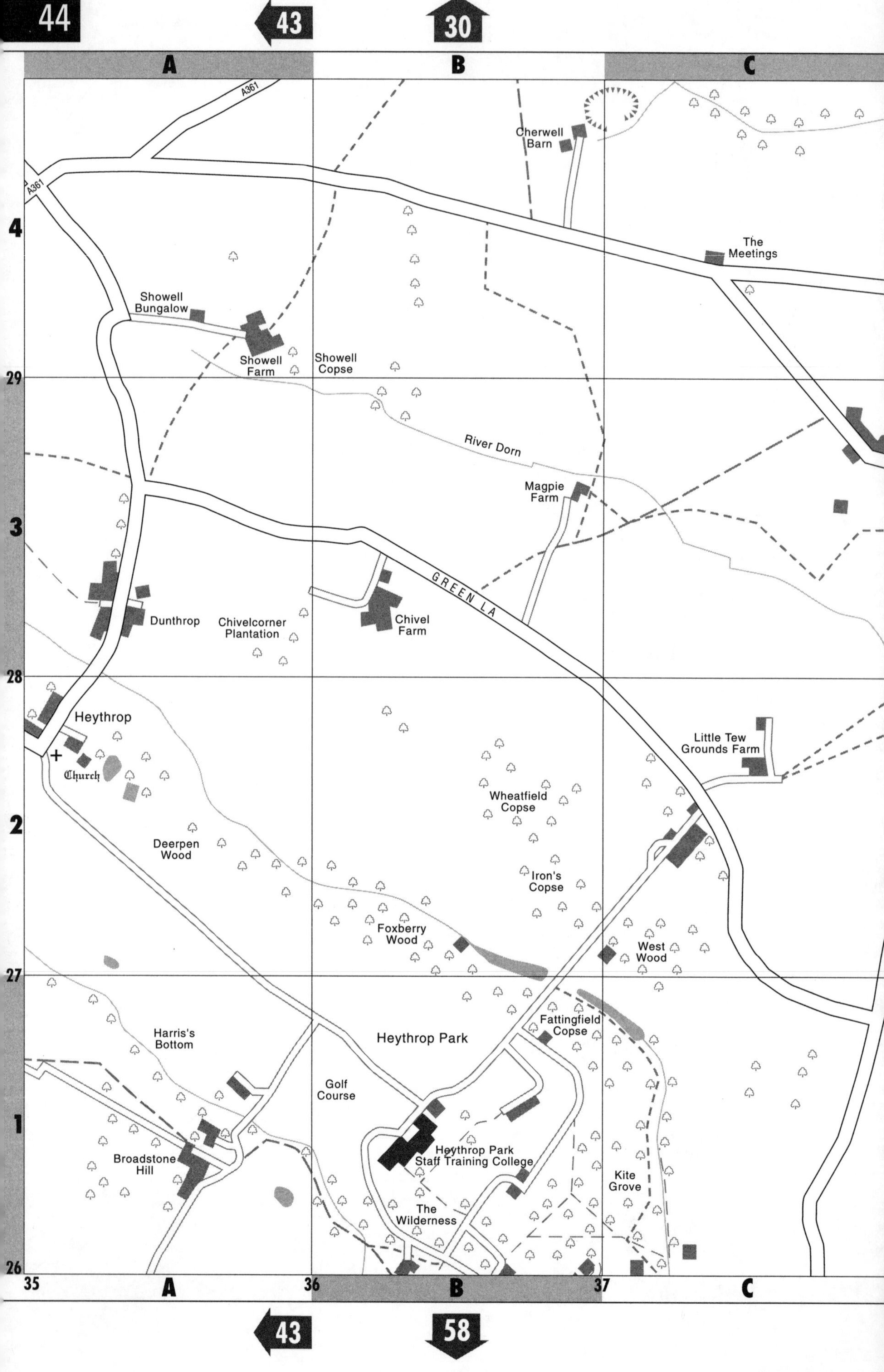

A   B   C

A361

A361

4

Cherwell
Barn

The
Meetings

Showell
Bungalow

Showell
Farm

Showell
Copse

29

River Dorn

Magpie
Farm

3

GREEN LA

Dunthrop

Chivelcorner
Plantation

Chivel
Farm

28

Heythrop

Little Tew
Grounds Farm

+

Church

Wheatfield
Copse

2

Deerpen
Wood

Iron's
Copse

Foxberry
Wood

West
Wood

27

Harris's
Bottom

Heythrop Park

Fattingfield
Copse

Golf
Course

1

Broadstone
Hill

Heythrop Park
Staff Training College

Kite
Grove

The
Wilderness

26

35   A   36   B   37   C

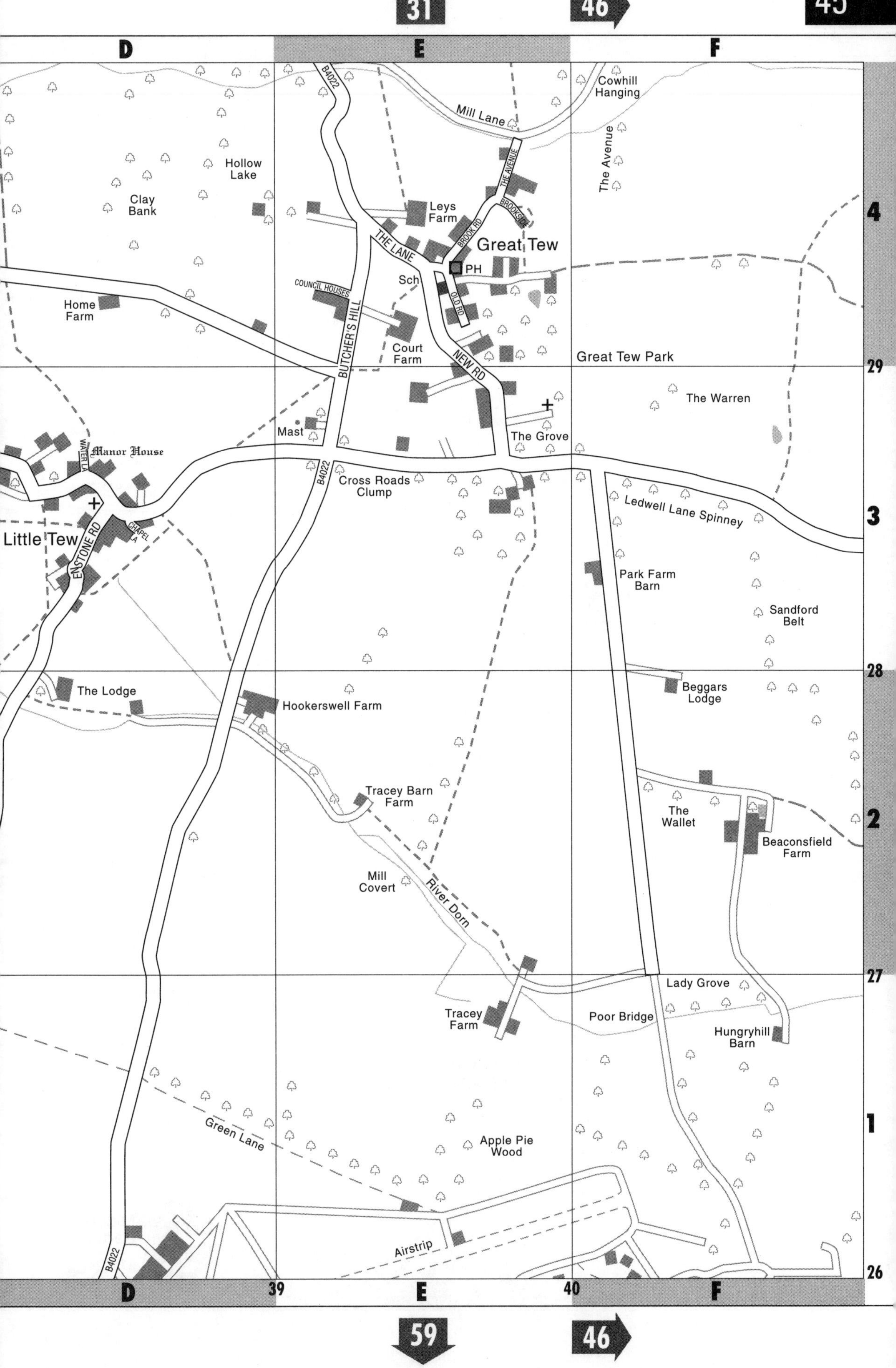

D
E
F

Cowhill
Hanging

Mill Lane

The Avenue

Hollow
Lake

Clay
Bank

Leys
Farm

THE AVENUE

BROOK RD

BROOKSIDE

Great Tew

4

THE LANE

B4022

Home
Farm

COUNCIL HOUSES

Sch

PH

OLD RD

Great Tew Park

29

BUTCHER'S HILL

Court
Farm

NEW RD

The Warren

Mast

The Grove

Manor House

Cross Roads
Clump

Ledwell Lane Spinney

3

WATER LA

B4022

Little Tew

CHAPEL LA

ENSTONE RD

Park Farm
Barn

Sandford
Belt

28

The Lodge

Hookerswell Farm

Beggars
Lodge

Tracey Barn
Farm

The
Wallet

Beaconsfield
Farm

2

Mill
Covert

River Dorn

Lady Grove

27

Tracey
Farm

Poor Bridge

Hungryhill
Barn

Green Lane

Apple Pie
Wood

1

B4022

Airstrip

26

D
39
E
40
F

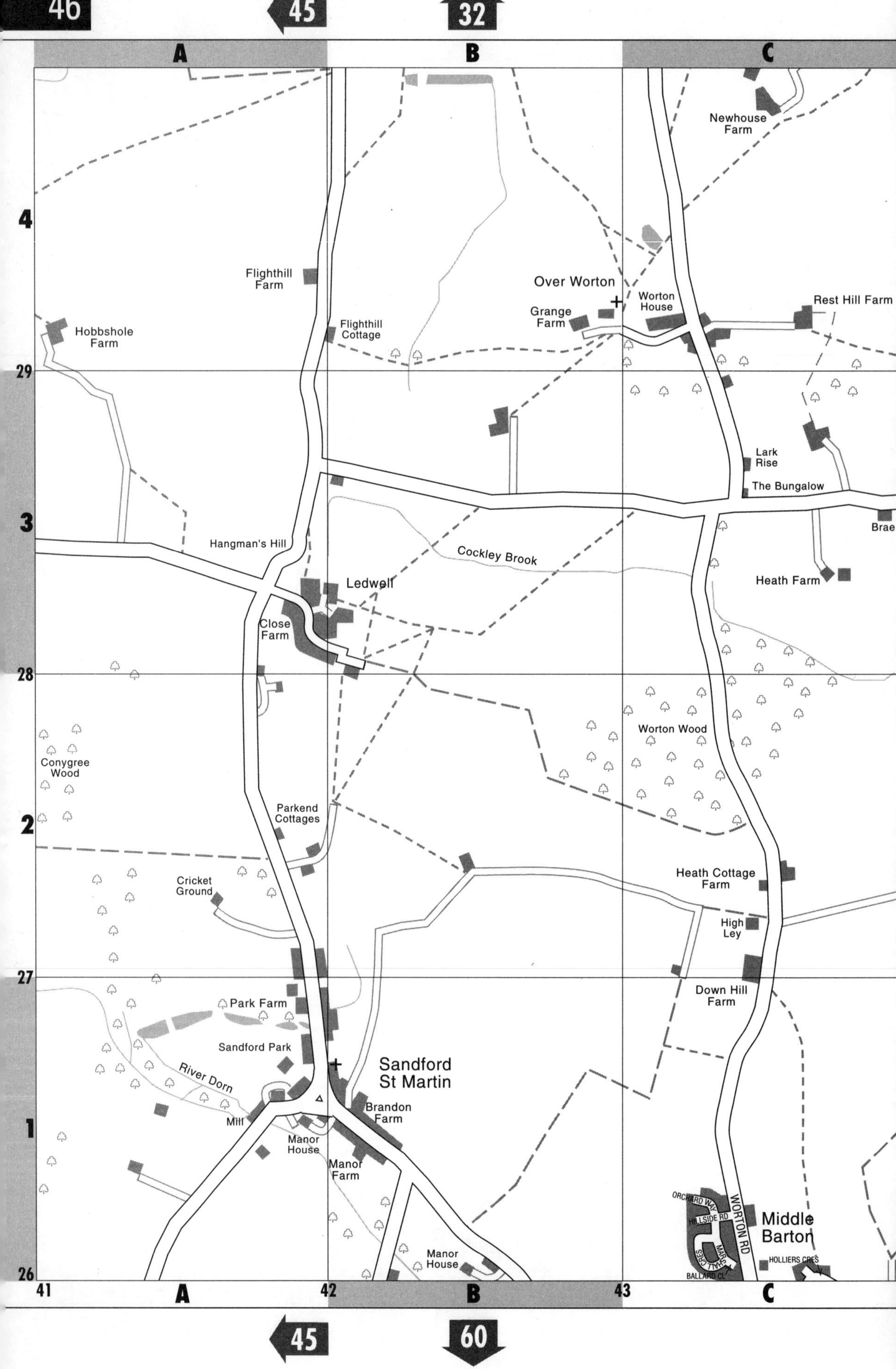

45
32

A   **B**   **C**

4

Newhouse Farm

Flighthill Farm

Flighthill Cottage

Over Worton

Worton House

Grange Farm

Rest Hill Farm

Hobbshole Farm

29

Lark Rise

The Bungalow

3

Hangman's Hill

Cockley Brook

Brae

Ledwell

Heath Farm

Close Farm

28

Worton Wood

Conygree Wood

Parkend Cottages

2

Heath Cottage Farm

Cricket Ground

High Ley

27

Down Hill Farm

Park Farm

Sandford Park

River Dorn

Sandford St Martin

Mill

Brandon Farm

1

Manor House

Manor Farm

ORCHARD WAY

WORTON RD

HILLSIDE RD

BRYNY CT

Middle Barton

Manor House

HOLLIERS CRES

BALLARD CT

26

41   **A**   **42**   **B**   **43**   **C**

45
60

D E F

4

Hill Farm

Dane Hill

Lower Farm

Common Barn
Farm

Pumping
Station

29

Duns Tew

Manor
Farm

Manor
House

HILL FARM LA

DASHWOOD RISE

3

The Nurseries

SPRING
FARM

PH

GLEBE CT

OXFORD RD

A4260

Resr

28

Cockley Brook

Blue Barn
Farm

Warren
Farm

Seagrave's
Covert

2

Sand Quarries

Horsehay
Farm

Greenacres

27

Brasenose
Farm

Brasenose
Cottage

1

Sycamore
Farm

A4260

Westfield
Farm

26

47 34

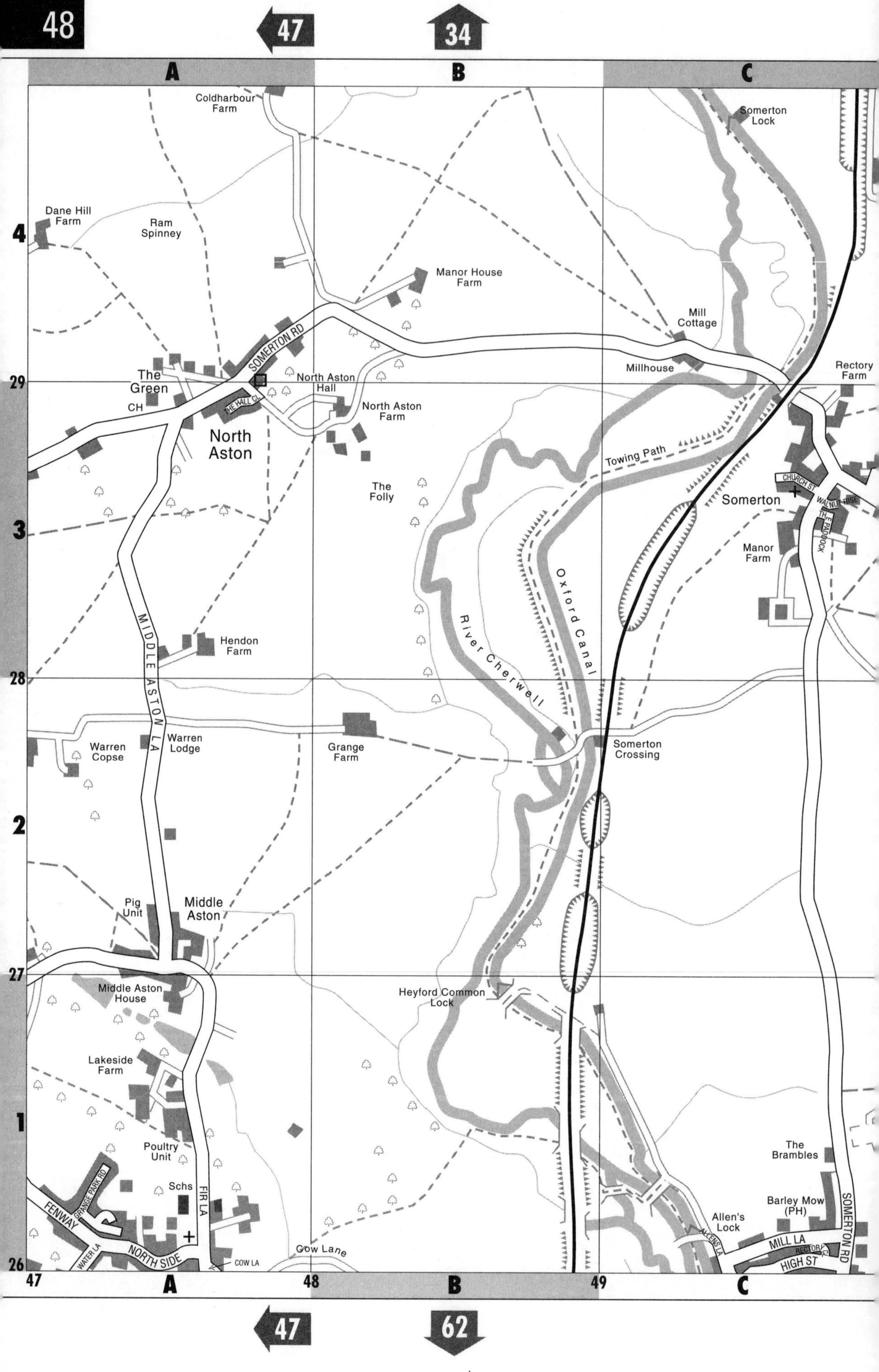

A   B   C

Coldharbour Farm

Dane Hill Farm

Ram Spinney

4

Manor House Farm

Somerton Lock

Mill Cottage

SOMERTON RD

North Aston Hall

Millhouse

Rectory Farm

29

The Green

CH

North Aston

THE HALL CL

North Aston Farm

Towing Path

Somerton

CHURCH ST

WALNUT RISE

THE PADDOCK

The Folly

River Cherwell

Oxford Canal

Manor Farm

3

Hendon Farm

28

Warren Copse

Warren Lodge

MIDDLE ASTON LA

Grange Farm

Somerton Crossing

2

Pig Unit

Middle Aston

27

Middle Aston House

Heyford Common Lock

Lakeside Farm

The Brambles

1

Barley Mow (PH)

Poultry Unit

Schs

FIR LA

Allen's Lock

RECTORY LA

MILL LA

SOMERTON RD

FENWAY

GRANGE PARK RD

WATER LA

NORTH SIDE

COW LA

Cow Lane

HIGH ST

26

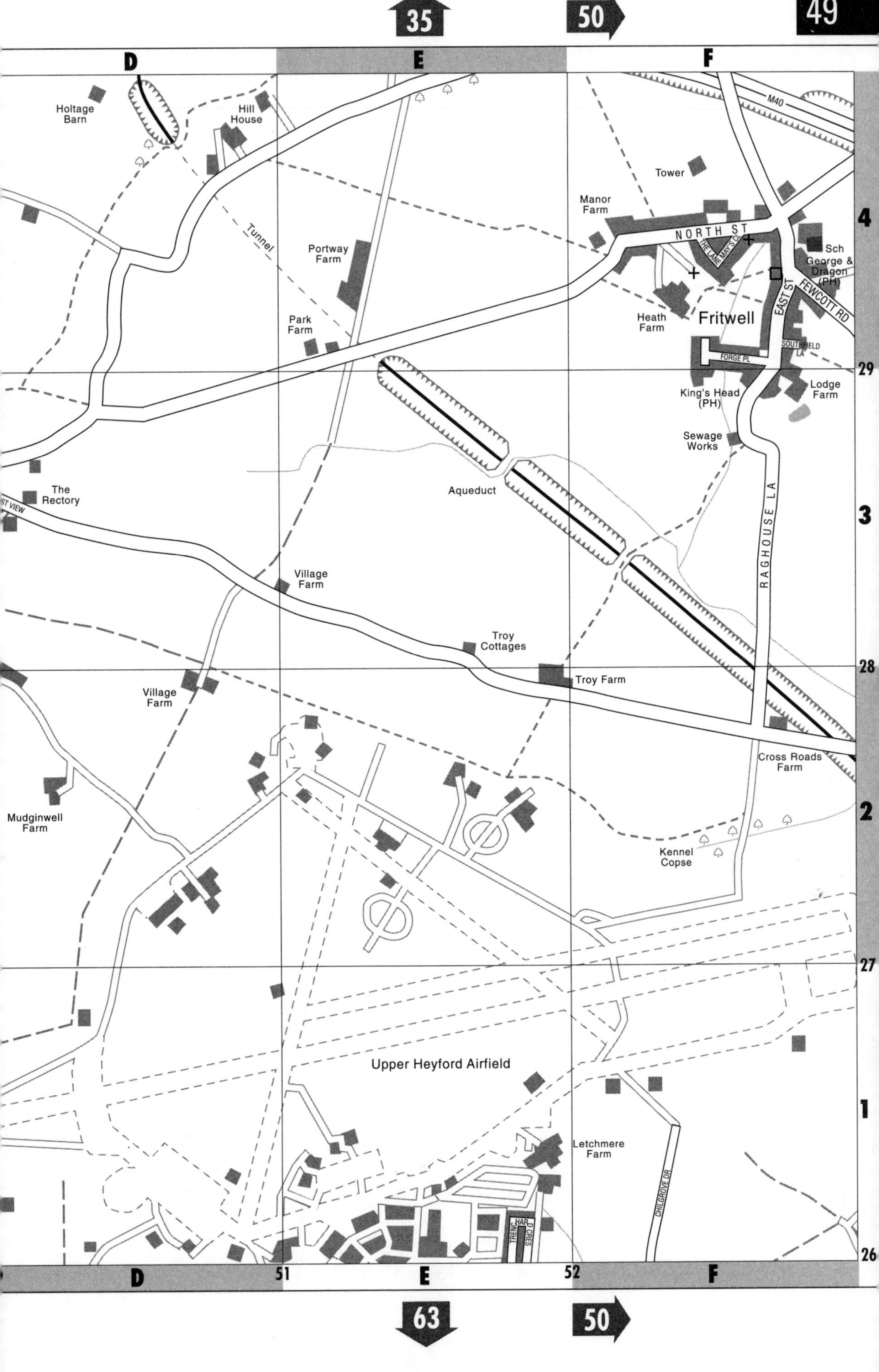

D E F

Holtage
Barn

Hill
House

Tunnel

Portway
Farm

Park
Farm

M40

Tower

Manor
Farm

NORTH ST

FIVE LANE ENDS

Sch
George &
Dragon
(PH)

Heath
Farm

Fritwell

EAST ST

FEWCOTT RD

SOUTHFIELD LA

FORGE PL

4

29

King's Head
(PH)

Lodge
Farm

Sewage
Works

RAGHOUSE LA

EAST VIEW

The
Rectory

Aqueduct

Village
Farm

Troy
Cottages

Troy Farm

3

28

Village
Farm

Mudginwell
Farm

Cross Roads
Farm

Kennel
Copse

2

27

Upper Heyford Airfield

Letchmere
Farm

CHILGROVE RD

TRENCHARD CRES

1

26

D 51 E 52 F

49
36

A   B   C

Horwell

B4100

M40

Green
Farm

Park Farm Belt

A43

4

Baynards Green
Farm

Medkre

Baynard's
Green

A43

Baynard
House

29

Lone
Barn

3

A43

Fewcott

Sewage
Works

Sycamore
Grove

Manor
Farm

Fewcott
Farm

28

FRITWELL RD

B430

Stoke
Wood

WATER LA

PLOUGHLEY
CL

PADDOCK RD

RUSSET RD

ARDLEY RD

Woodbine
Cottage

ORCHARD RD

KEEYS CL

SOMERTON RD

Ardley

2

Ardley
Wood

PH

Kilby's
Barn

Earthwork

Manor
Farm

CHURCH RD

STATION RD

27

Kilby's
Copse

Nevilles
Farm

1

Ashgrove
Farm

Digging
Copse

Woodlands
Farm

B430

Ardley Fields
Farm

M40

26
53   A   54   B   55   C

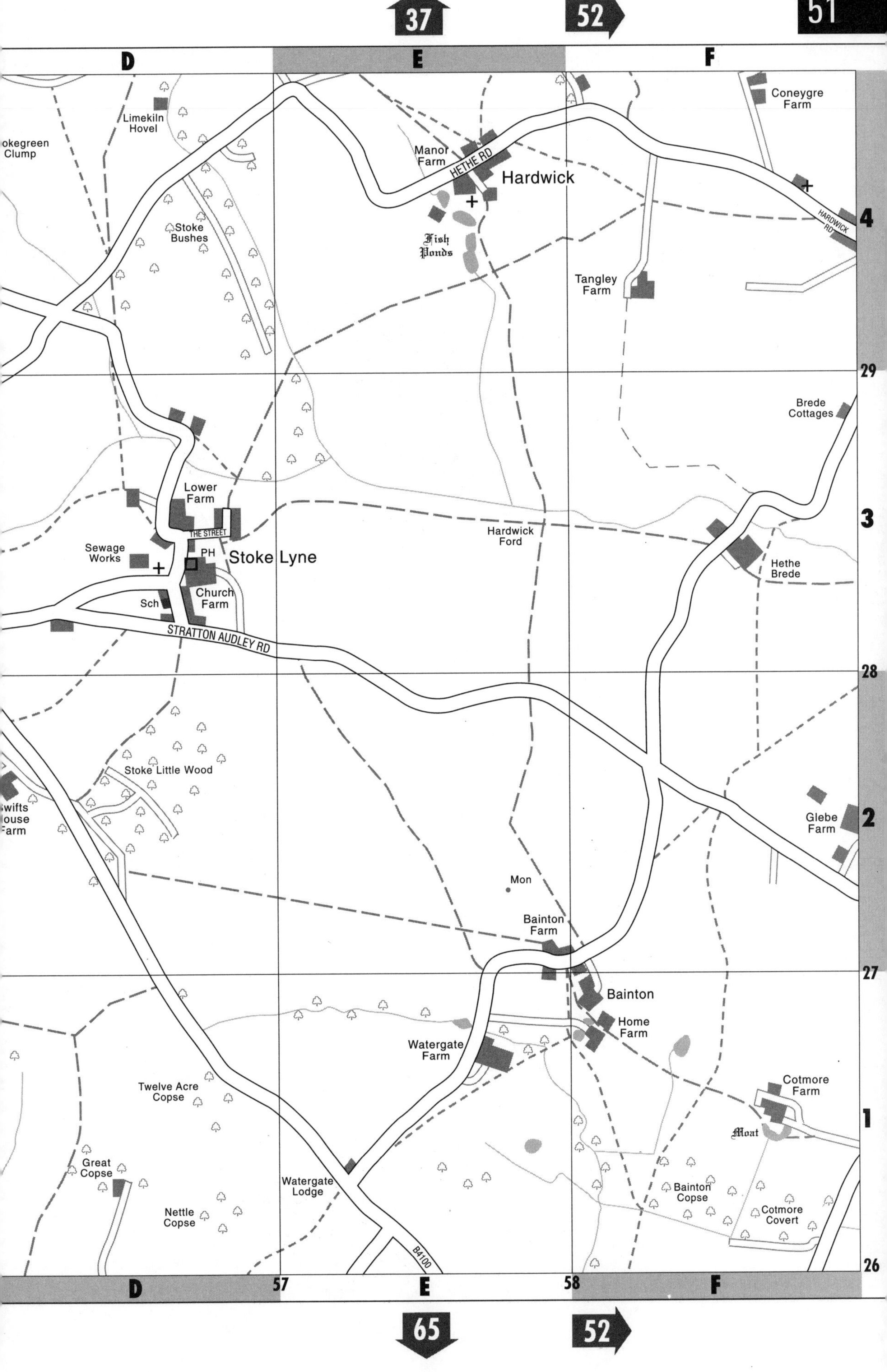
D
E
F
Limekiln Hovel
okegreen Clump
Stoke Bushes
Manor Farm
HETHE RD
Hardwick
Fish Ponds
Coneygre Farm
HARDWICK RD
Tangley Farm
4
29
Brede Cottages
Lower Farm
THE STREET
Sewage Works
PH
Stoke Lyne
Church Farm
Sch
STRATTON AUDLEY RD
Hardwick Ford
Hethe Brede
3
28
Stoke Little Wood
wifts ouse arm
Glebe Farm
2
Mon
Bainton Farm
27
Bainton
Home Farm
Watergate Farm
Cotmore Farm
Moat
1
Twelve Acre Copse
Great Copse
Nettle Copse
Watergate Lodge
Bainton Copse
Cotmore Covert
B4100
26
57
58

51
38
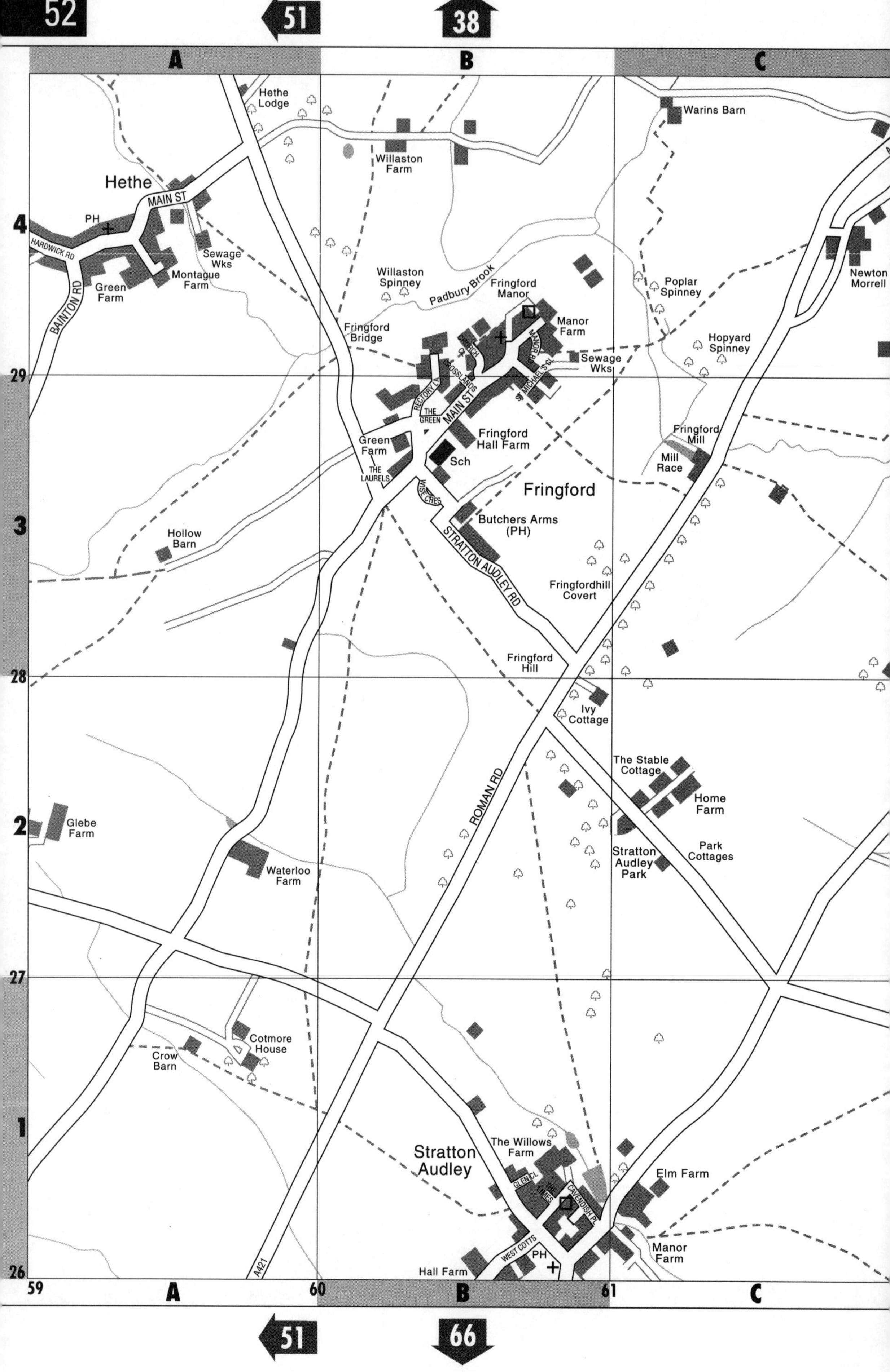
A
B
C
4
3
2
1
29
28
27
26
59
60
61
Hethe Lodge
Hethe
MAIN ST
PH
HARDWICK RD
BAINTON RD
Green Farm
Montague Farm
Sewage Wks
Willaston Farm
Warins Barn
Willaston Spinney
Padbury Brook
Fringford Manor
Manor Farm
CHURCH CL
MANOR RD
CROSSLANDS
ST MICHAEL'S CL
Sewage Wks
Fringford Bridge
RECTORY LA
THE GREEN
MAIN ST
Poplar Spinney
Hopyard Spinney
Newton Morrell
Green Farm
THE LAURELS
Fringford Hall Farm
Sch
WISE CRES
Fringford
Fringford Mill
Mill Race
Butchers Arms (PH)
Hollow Barn
STRATTON AUDLEY RD
Fringfordhill Covert
Fringford Hill
Ivy Cottage
The Stable Cottage
Home Farm
ROMAN RD
Glebe Farm
Stratton Audley Park
Park Cottages
Waterloo Farm
Cotmore House
Crow Barn
The Willows Farm
Stratton Audley
GLEN CL
THE LIMES
CAVENDISH PL
Elm Farm
WEST COTTS
PH
Hall Farm
Manor Farm
A421
51
66

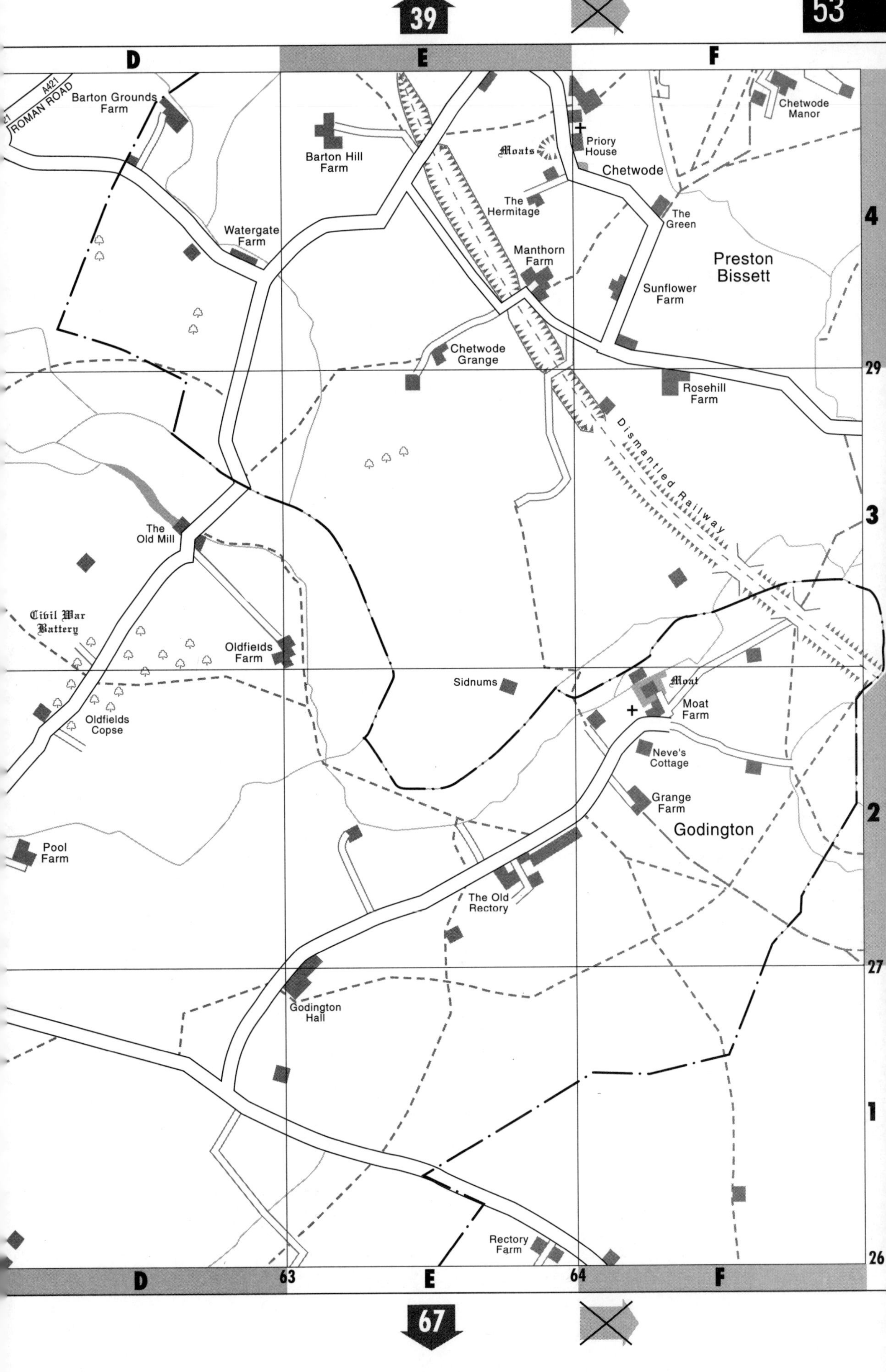

D   E   F

ROMAN ROAD
A421

Barton Grounds Farm

Barton Hill Farm

Moats

Priory House

Chetwode Manor

Chetwode

The Hermitage

The Green

4

Watergate Farm

Manthorn Farm

Preston Bissett

Sunflower Farm

Chetwode Grange

29

Rosehill Farm

Dismantled Railway

3

The Old Mill

Civil War Battery

Oldfields Farm

Sidnums

Moat

Moat Farm

Neve's Cottage

Oldfields Copse

Grange Farm

Godington

2

Pool Farm

The Old Rectory

27

Godington Hall

1

Rectory Farm

26

D   63   E   64   F

A **B** **C**

Lower Oddington

CHURCH PL

Oddington House

CHURCH RD

The Dell

Daylesford

Daylesford New Farm

4

New Barn

Lower Oddington Ashes

25

Bledington Heath

River Evenlode

3

Moat

Bledington Grounds

WEST END

MANOR FARM CL

COZENS LA

CHURCH

College Farm

24

ORCHARD WAY

B4450

NEW RD

Hotel

FIELD RD

STATION RD

2

Pebbly Hill

Dismantled Railway

Pebbly Hill Farm

Mickland's Hill

23

Industrial Park

STOW RD

CHAPEL LA

Banks Farm

MAIN ST

Hotel

Kingham Sta

B4450

PH

Village Farm

CHURCH RD

Little OLD FORGE Lane

CHURCH LA

OLD BURFORD RD

JACKSON RD

FIRS CL

NEW RD

Sewage Works

Sch

Kingham Sta

Bledington Mill Farm

Manor Farm

1

Pebbly Hill Barn

Oxfordshire Way

Bledington

Westcote Brook

22

Westcote Brook

23 **A** **24** **B** **25** **C**

D
E
F
Slade Farm
Warden's House
Lower Kingham Hill Cottages
Churchill Grounds Farm
Churchill Grounds Cottages
B4450
Churchill Mill
Sarsden Halt
BESBURY LA
Church
Grange Farm
Churchill Crossing
Mount Farm
Sch
CHURCHILL RD
The Caravan
SIDINGS RD
HASTINGS HILL
B4450
Hill View
Meadow Place
KINGHAM RD
Churchill
Churchill Farm
Sch
PH
CHURCH ST
CHAPEL LA
Kingham
ORCHARD WAY
HACKERS LA
Mount Farm
JUNCTION RD
The Mount
The Lodge
Dismantled Railway
Home Farm
York Cottage
Sarsden
Sarsden House
Sars Brook
Rynehill Farm
B4450
Churchill Heath Farm
Churchill Heath Bungalow
Lower Buildings
4
25
3
24
2
23
1
22
27
28

55
42

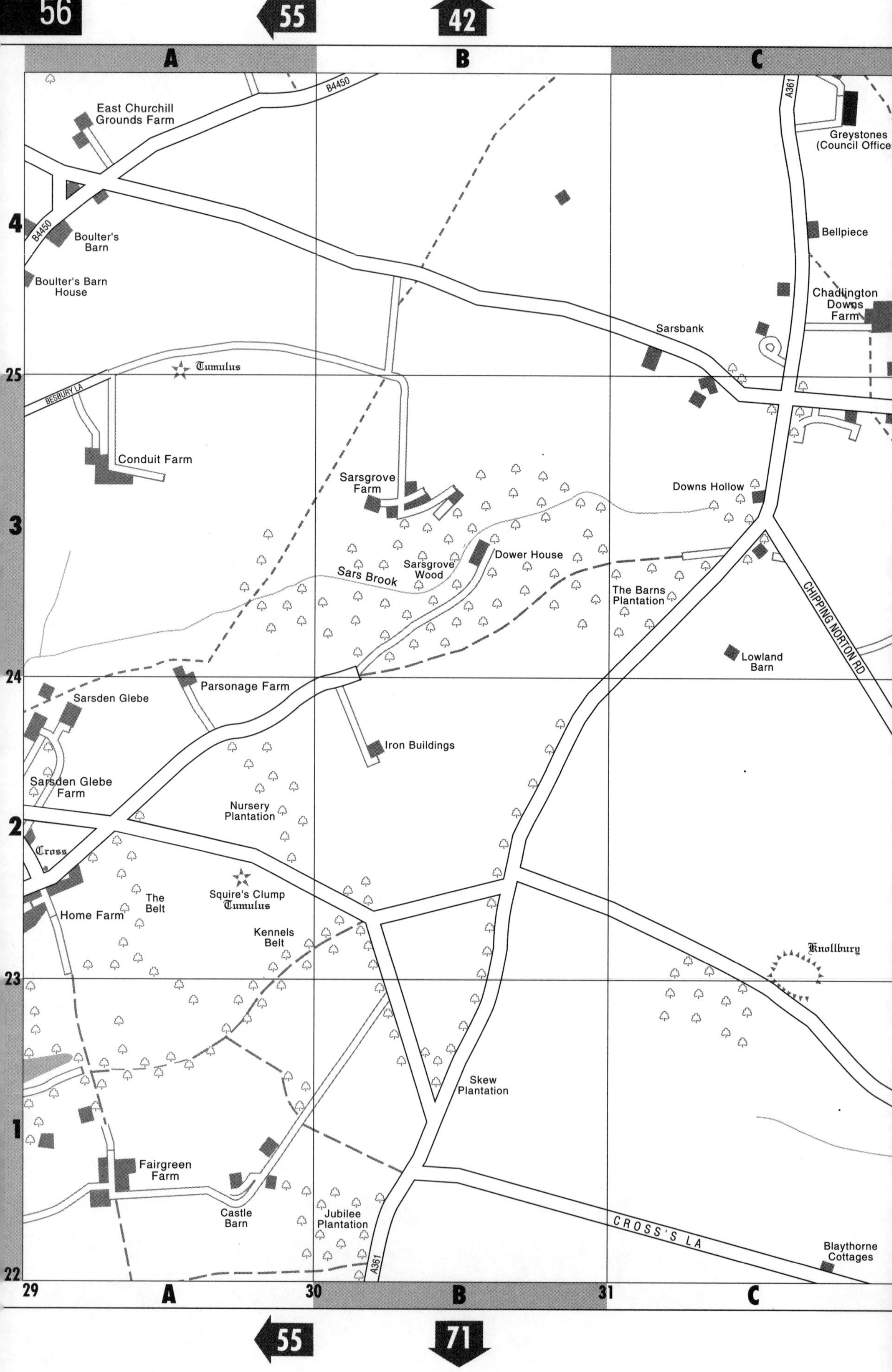
A
B
C
B4450
East Churchill Grounds Farm
A361
Greystones (Council Office
Boulter's Barn
Boulter's Barn House
Bellpiece
Chadlington Downs Farm
Sarsbank
Tumulus
BESBURY LA
Conduit Farm
Sarsgrove Farm
Downs Hollow
Dower House
Sarsgrove Wood
Sars Brook
The Barns Plantation
CHIPPING NORTON RD
Lowland Barn
Parsonage Farm
Sarsden Glebe
Iron Buildings
Sarsden Glebe Farm
Nursery Plantation
Cross
Squire's Clump
Tumulus
The Belt
Home Farm
Kennels Belt
Knollbury
Skew Plantation
Fairgreen Farm
Castle Barn
Jubilee Plantation
CROSS'S LA
Blaythorne Cottages
A361
4
25
3
24
2
23
1
22
29
30
31

55
71

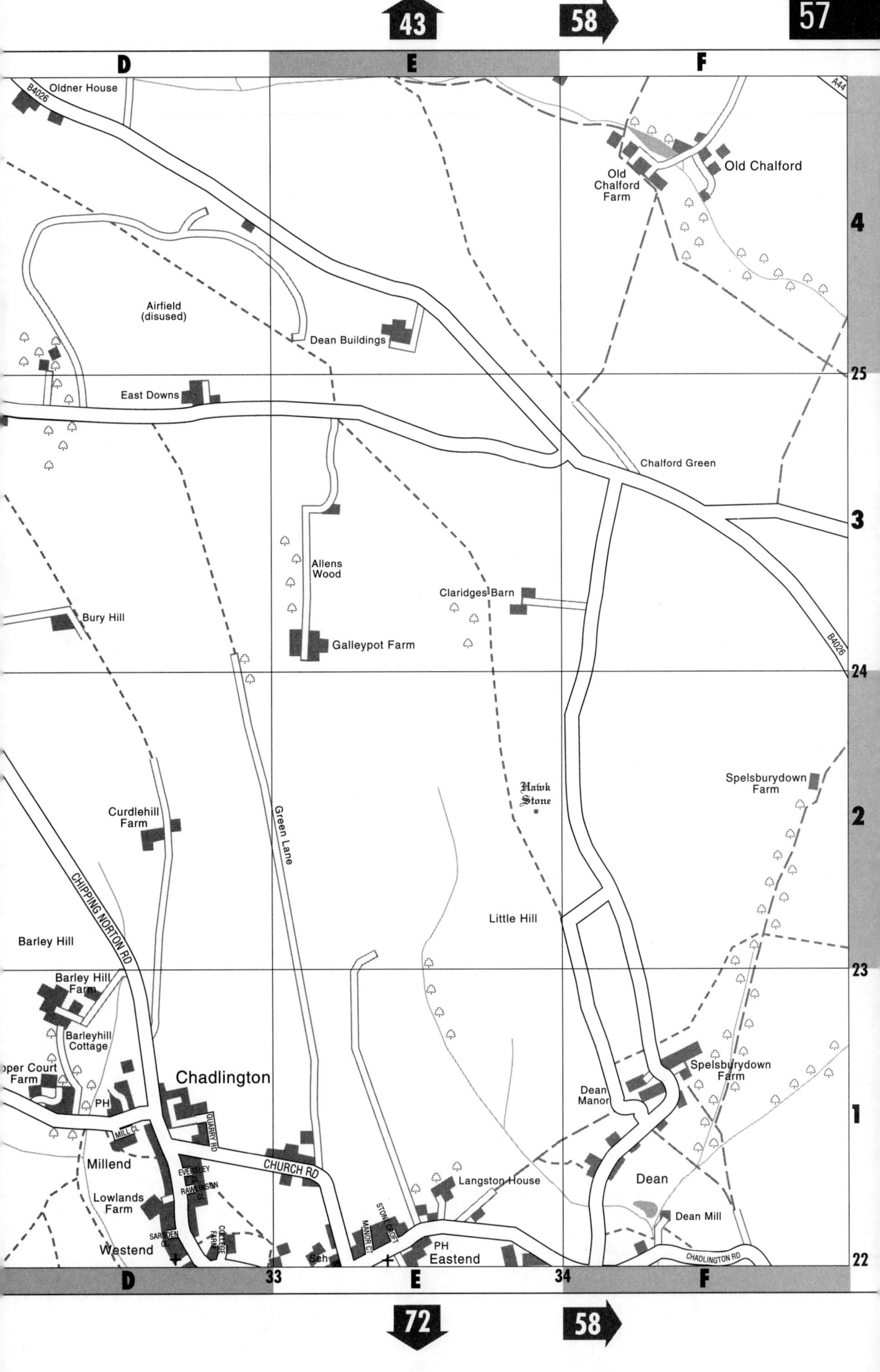

B4026
Oldner House

4

Airfield
(disused)

Dean Buildings

Old
Chalford
Farm

Old Chalford

25

East Downs

Chalford Green

3

Allens
Wood

Claridges Barn

Bury Hill

Galleypot Farm

24

Curdlehill
Farm

Hawk
Stone

Spelsburydown
Farm

2

CHIPPING NORTON RD

Green Lane

Little Hill

Barley Hill

23

Barley Hill
Farm

Barleyhill
Cottage

pper Court
Farm

Spelsburydown
Farm

Chadlington

PH

Dean
Manor

1

MILL CL

QUARRY RD

Dean

Millend

CHURCH RD

Langston House

Lowlands
Farm

EVERSLEY CL
RAWLINSON CL

STONE OFT

MANOR CL

Dean Mill

Westend

SARDEN CL
COLLEGE FARM

Sch

PH
Eastend

CHADLINGTON RD

22

A44

B4026

A
B
C

Leys Farm

Broadstone Plantation

Long
Firs

4

Manor Farm

Sewage
Works

Church
Enstone

PH

Medieval Village
(site of)

B4

25

Stone
Farm

Lidstone

Lidstone Bottom

Quarry
(dis)

Stoney
Bridge

Bicester Rd

PH

River Glyme

B4030

Enstone

Hill Farm

CHAPEL LA

Oxford Rd

Nea
Ensto

3

LITCHFI
ELL CL

Sch

WOODFORD CL

CLEVELE

Litchfield Farm

THE SPINNEYS

24

PH

B4026

QUARRY
CL

B4

Hoar Stone
Burial Chamber

Enstone
Firs

2

Fulwell Farm

Fulwell

23

Fulwell Brake
North

Henley Knapp

The Warren

Resr

Henel Buildings

1

Henel

Taston

David's Plantation

Lau
Corr

Cross

Middle Farm
Plantation

TASTON RD

B4022

B4026

22

35
A
36
B
37
C

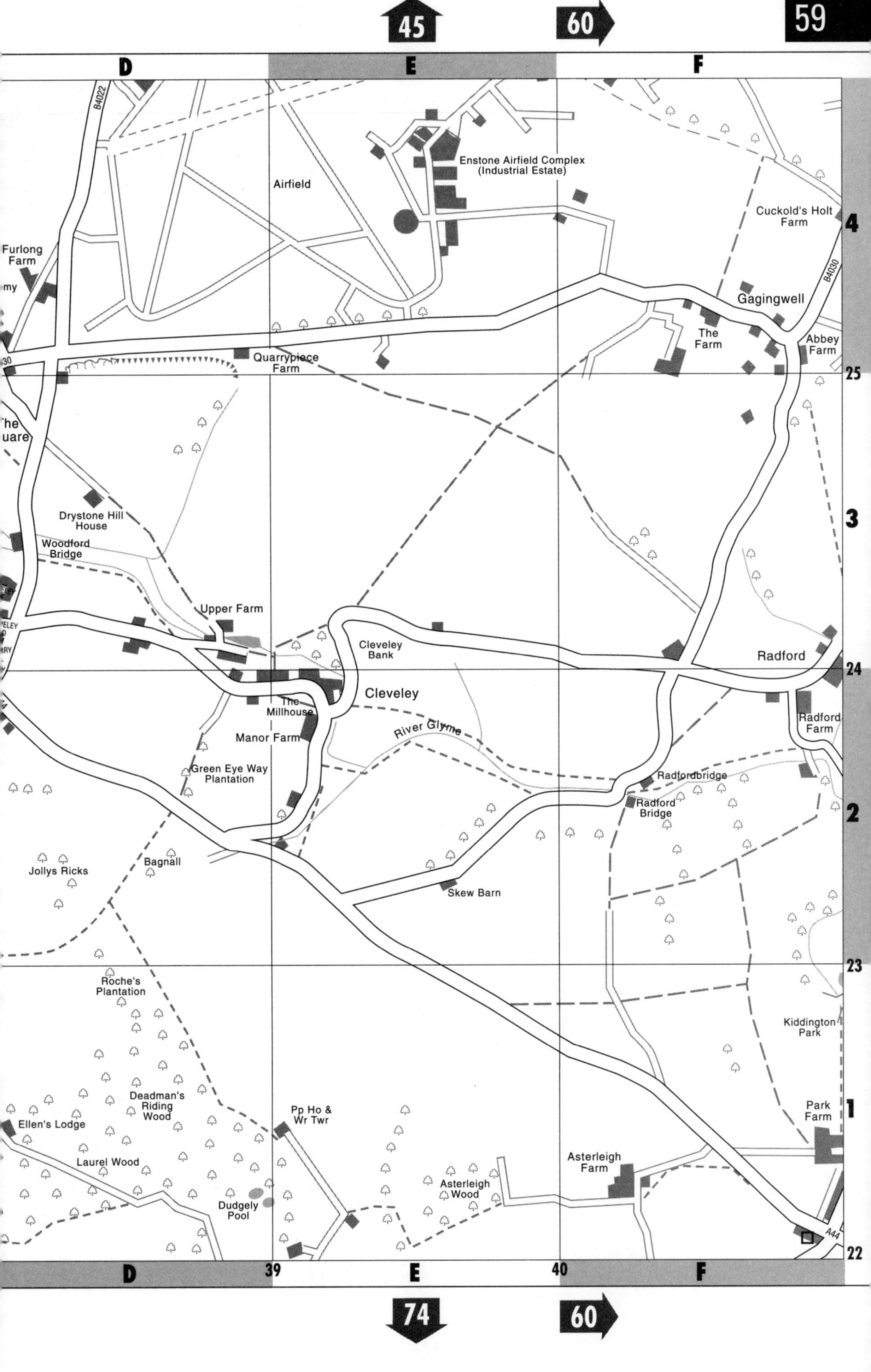

D
E
F

B4022

Airfield

Enstone Airfield Complex
(Industrial Estate)

Cuckold's Holt
Farm

Furlong
Farm

my

Gagingwell

B4030

The
Farm

Abbey
Farm

30

Quarrypiece
Farm

4

25

he
uare

Drystone Hill
House

3

Woodford
Bridge

Upper Farm

Cleveley
Bank

Radford

24

ELEY
D
RY

Cleveley

The
Millhouse

River Glyme

Radford
Farm

Manor Farm

Radfordbridge

2

Green Eye Way
Plantation

Radford
Bridge

Jollys Ricks

Bagnall

Skew Barn

23

Roche's
Plantation

Kiddington
Park

Deadman's
Riding
Wood

Pp Ho &
Wr Twr

Park
Farm

1

Ellen's Lodge

Asterleigh
Farm

Laurel Wood

Asterleigh
Wood

Dudgely
Pool

A44

22

D
39
E
40
F

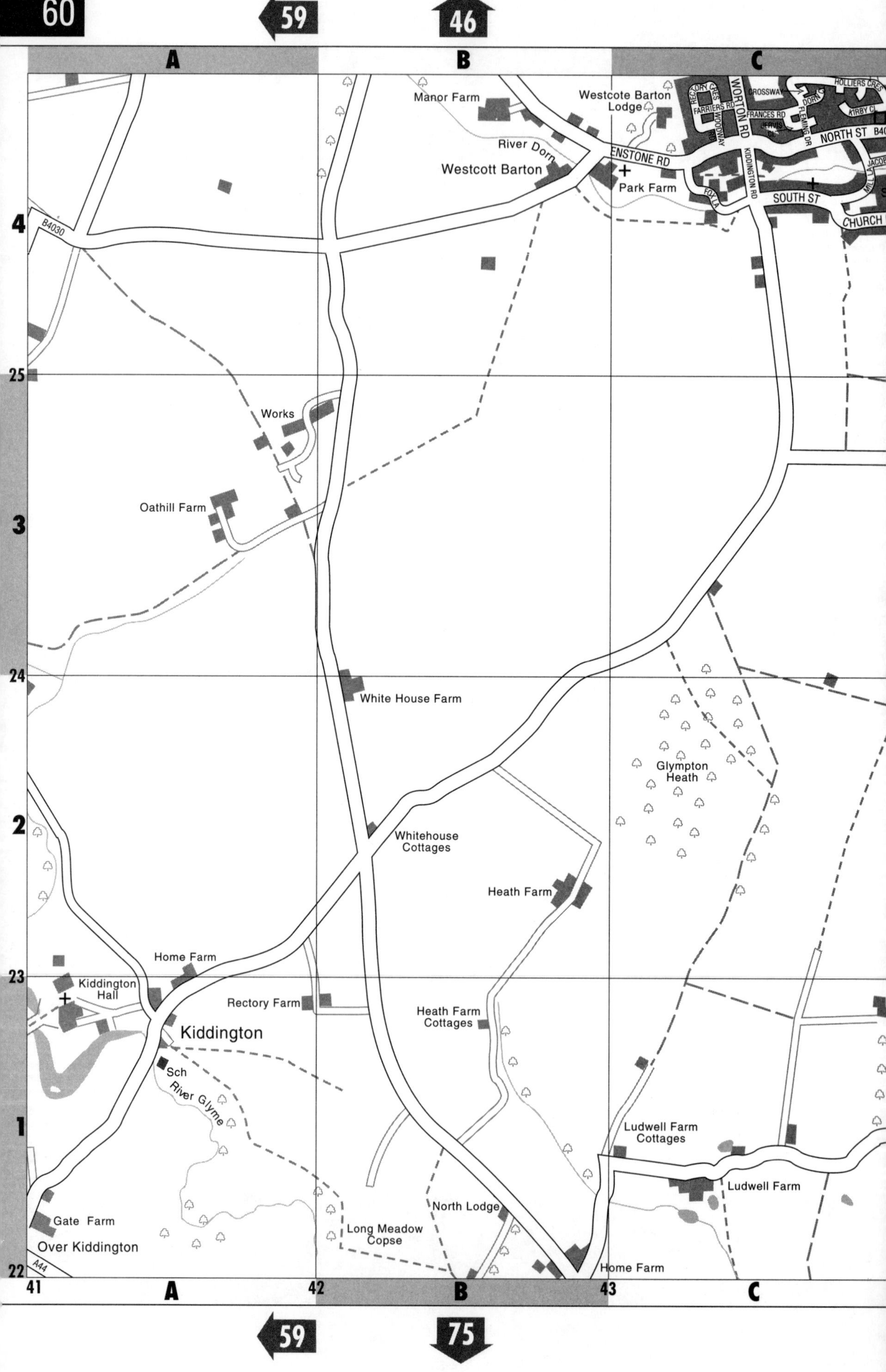

A

B

C

4

25

Works

Oathill Farm

3

24

White House Farm

2

Whitehouse
Cottages

Heath Farm

Home Farm

23

Kiddington
Hall

Rectory Farm

Kiddington

Heath Farm
Cottages

Sch

River Glyme

1

Ludwell Farm
Cottages

Ludwell Farm

Gate Farm

Over Kiddington

22

Long Meadow
Copse

North Lodge

Home Farm

Manor Farm

River Dorn

Westcott Barton

Westcote Barton
Lodge

WORTON RD

CORN CRES
FARRIERS RD
WOODWAY

CROSSWAY

FRANCES RD

HOLLIERS CRES

KIRBY CL

NORTH ST B4

ENSTONE RD

Park Farm

KIDDINGTON RD

SOUTH ST

CHURCH

Glympton
Heath

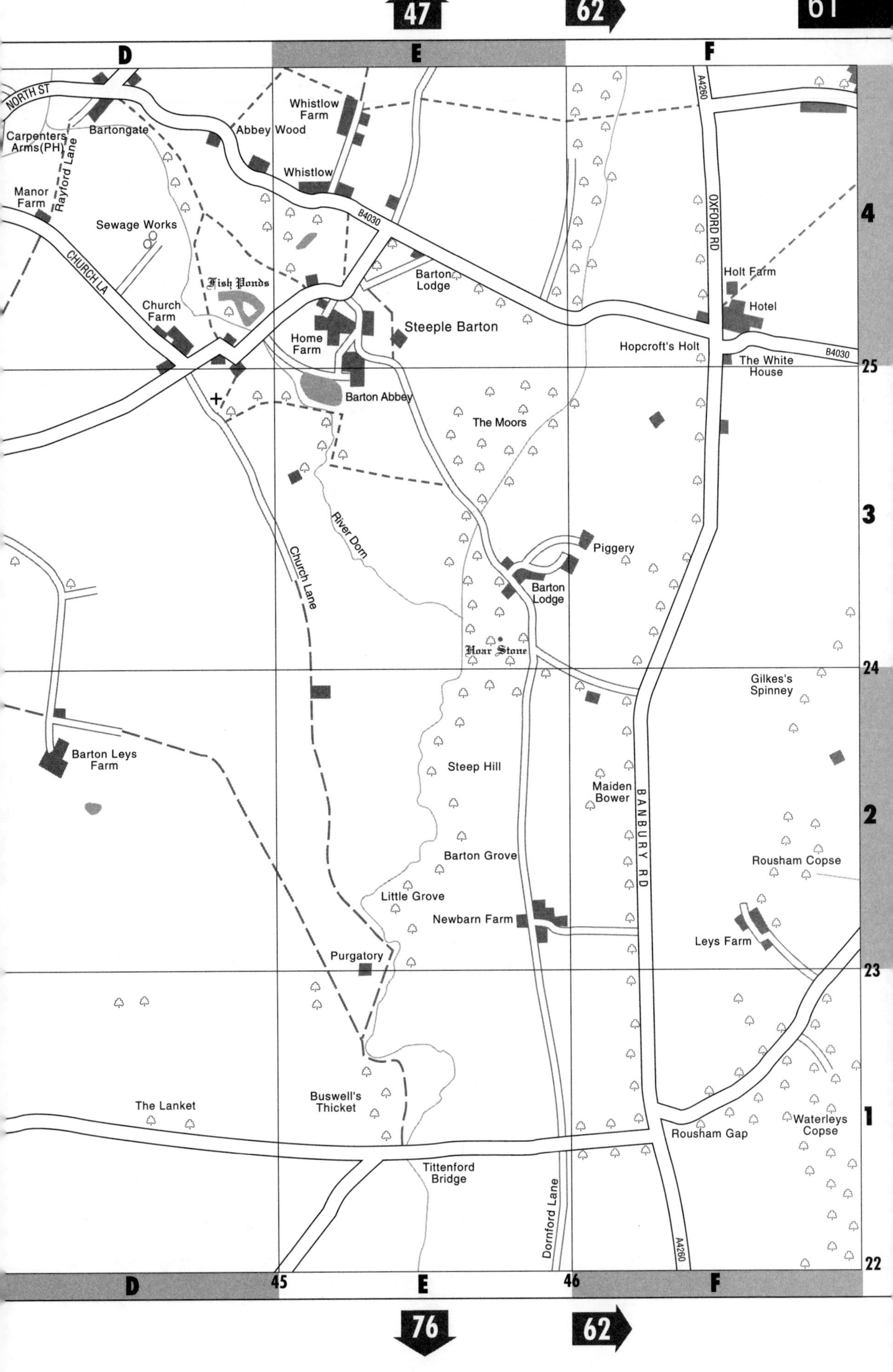
D
E
F
NORTH ST
Bartongate
Carpenters Arms(PH)
Rayford Lane
Manor Farm
Sewage Works
CHURCH LA
Church Farm
Fish Ponds
Abbey Wood
Whistlow Farm
Whistlow
B4030
Barton Lodge
Home Farm
Steeple Barton
Barton Abbey
The Moors
A4260
OXFORD RD
Holt Farm
Hotel
Hopcroft's Holt
The White House
B4030
River Dorn
Church Lane
Piggery
Barton Lodge
Hoar Stone
Gilkes's Spinney
Barton Leys Farm
Steep Hill
Maiden Bower
BANBURY RD
Barton Grove
Rousham Copse
Little Grove
Newbarn Farm
Leys Farm
Purgatory
The Lanket
Buswell's Thicket
Rousham Gap
Waterleys Copse
Tittenford Bridge
Dornford Lane
A4260
4
25
3
24
2
23
1
22
45
46

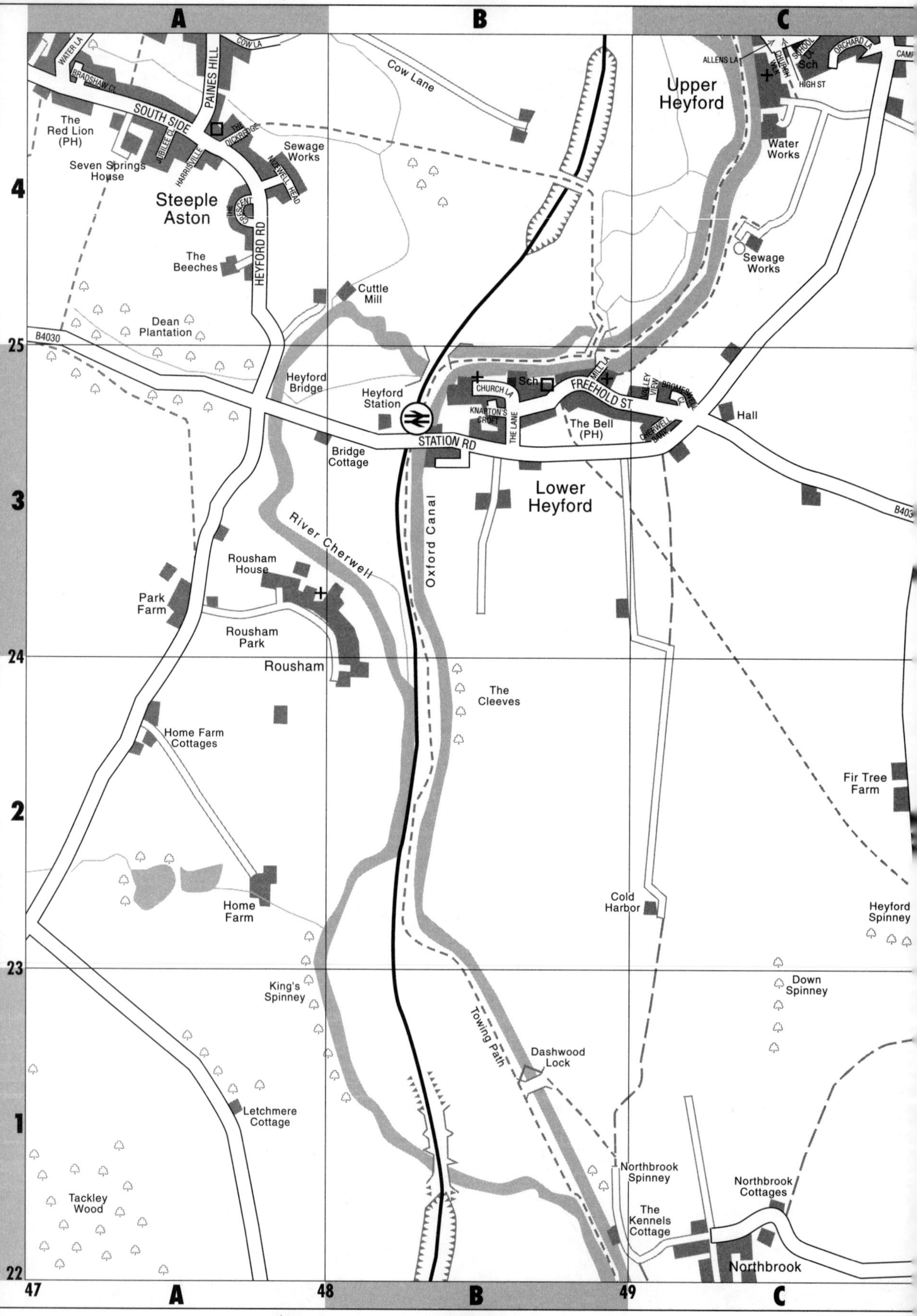

A   B   C

4

Water La
Bradshaw Ct
SOUTH SIDE
PAINES HILL
COW LA
Cow Lane

The Red Lion (PH)
JUBILEE CL
THE DICKREDGES
HARRISVILLE
NUFFNELL ROAD

Seven Springs House

Steeple Aston

Sewage Works

Upper Heyford
ALLENS LA
CHURCH
School
Sch
HIGH ST
ORCHARD LA
CAMP

Water Works

THE CRESCENT
HEYFORD RD

The Beeches

Cuttle Mill

Sewage Works

25

B4030
Dean Plantation

Heyford Bridge

Heyford Station

CHURCH LA
Sch
KNAPTON'S CROFT
THE LANE
MILL LA
FREEHOLD ST
VALLEY VIEW
BROMES PL
CHERWELL BANK
Hall

The Bell (PH)

3

River Cherwell

Oxford Canal

STATION RD

Bridge Cottage

Lower Heyford

B403

Rousham House

Park Farm

Rousham Park

Rousham

The Cleeves

Fir Tree Farm

24

Home Farm Cottages

2

Home Farm

Cold Harbor

Heyford Spinney

23

King's Spinney

Down Spinney

Letchmere Cottage

Towing Path

Dashwood Lock

Northbrook Spinney

Northbrook Cottages

1

Tackley Wood

The Kennels Cottage

Northbrook

22

47   A   48   B   49   C

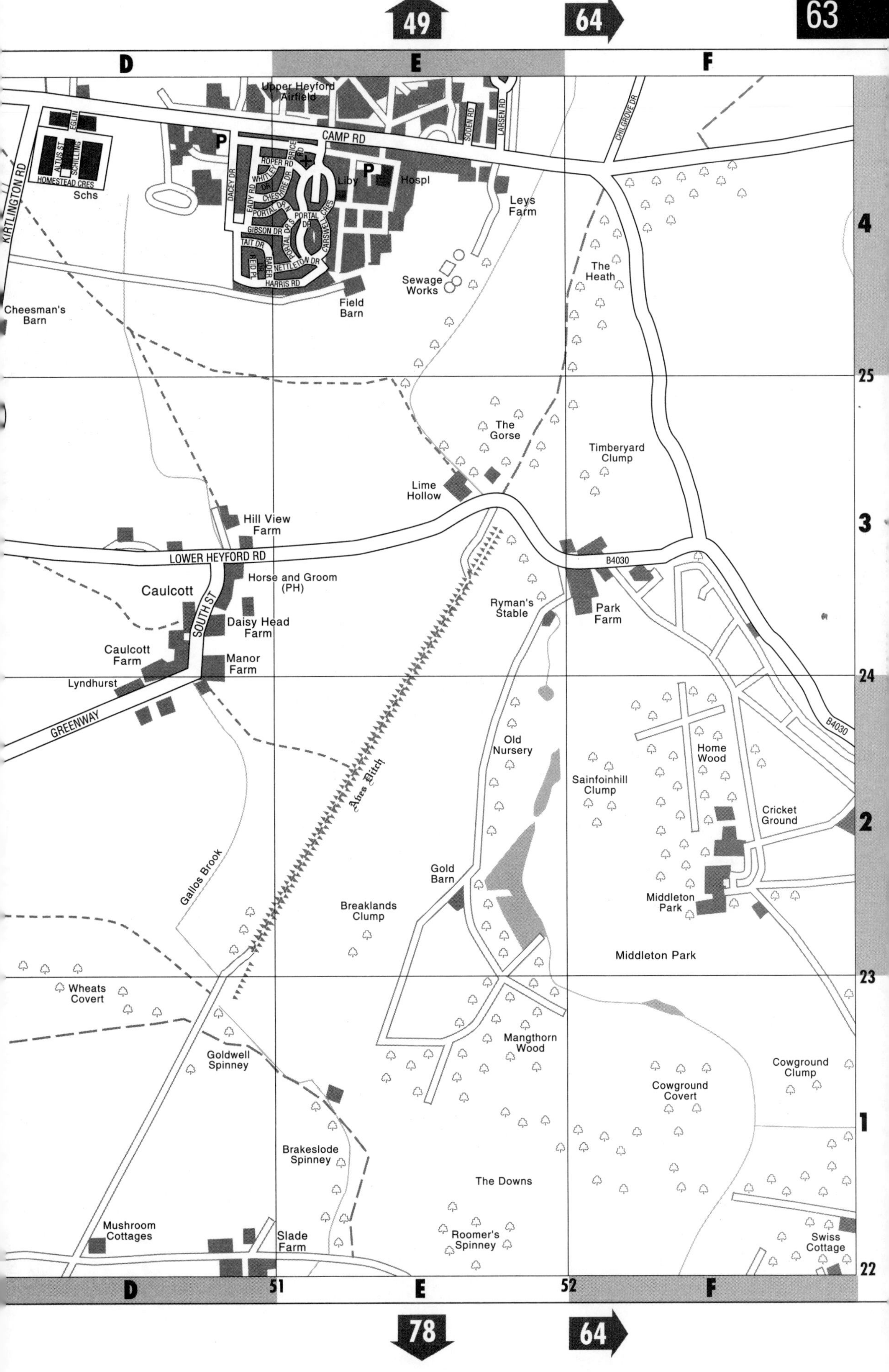

D
E
F

Upper Heyford Airfield

ALUSS ST
SCHILLENS
LEGLIN
HOMESTEAD CRES
KIRTLINGTON RD

P

CAMP RD

DACRE DR
ROPER RD
PRICE RD
WHITE DR
FAIRY RD
CHESHIRE DR
PORTAL DR
GIBSON DR
PORTAL DR
PORTAL CRES
CARSWELL CRES
TAIT DR
BOYLE RD
NETTLETON DR
HARRIS RD

P

Liby
Hospl

Leys Farm

CHILGROVE DR
SODEN RD
LARSEN RD

4

Schs

Cheesman's Barn

Sewage Works

Field Barn

The Heath

25

The Gorse

Timberyard Clump

Lime Hollow

Hill View Farm

LOWER HEYFORD RD

3

B4030

Caulcott

Horse and Groom (PH)

SOUTH ST

Daisy Head Farm

Ryman's Stable

Park Farm

Caulcott Farm

Manor Farm

Lyndhurst

GREENWAY

24

B4030

Old Nursery

Home Wood

Gallos Brook

Sainfoinhill Clump

Cricket Ground

2

Alne Ditch

Gold Barn

Middleton Park

Breaklands Clump

Middleton Park

23

Wheats Covert

Mangthorn Wood

Cowground Clump

Goldwell Spinney

Cowground Covert

1

Brakeslode Spinney

The Downs

Mushroom Cottages

Slade Farm

Roomer's Spinney

Swiss Cottage

22

63
50

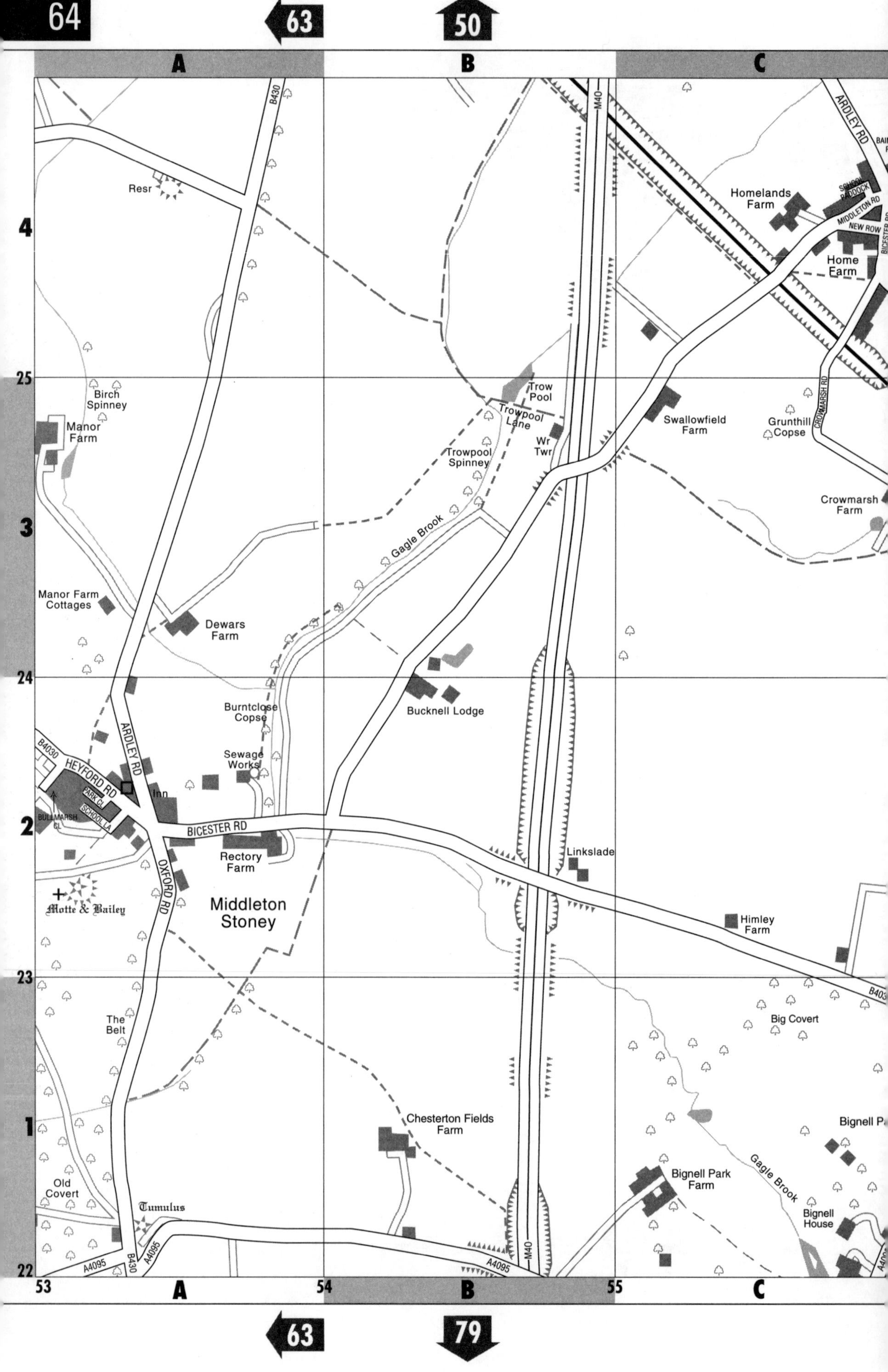
A
B
C
4
3
2
1
25
24
23
22
53
54
55
B430
Resr
M40
ARDLEY RD
Homelands Farm
SCHOOL PADDOCK
MIDDLETON RD
NEW ROW
BICESTER RD
Home Farm
Birch Spinney
Manor Farm
Trow Pool
Trowpool Lane
Wr Twr
Swallowfield Farm
Grunthill Copse
CROWMARSH RD
Trowpool Spinney
Crowmarsh Farm
Gagle Brook
Manor Farm Cottages
Dewars Farm
Bucknell Lodge
Burntclose Copse
Sewage Works
ARDLEY RD
B4030
HEYFORD RD
PARK CL
SCHOOL LA
BULLMARSH CL
Inn
BICESTER RD
Rectory Farm
Linkslade
OXFORD RD
Motte & Bailey
Middleton Stoney
Himley Farm
B4030
Big Covert
The Belt
Chesterton Fields Farm
Bignell P
Old Covert
Bignell Park Farm
Gagle Brook
Bignell House
Tumulus
A4095
B430
A4095
A4095
M40

63
79

51
66
D
E
F
Manor Farm
BAINTON RD
Lower Farm
Bucknell Manor Farm
Bucknell
B4100
Lodge
Caversfield House
Caversfield
Home Farm
BICESTER RD
Hawkwell Farm
Aldershot Farm
Lord's Farm
Oxford Lodge
Bricknells Farm
Slade Farm
Gowell Farm
Himley Farm
BICESTER
Woodfield
BANBURY RD
ROMAN ROAD
BUCKINGHAM RD
CHURCHILL RD
BUCKNELL RD
SHAKESPEARE DR
Highfield
Bicester North Station
Coll
Schs
Sch
Cattle Market
LAUNTON RD
Garth Park
MIDDLETON STONEY RD
A4095
King's End
Hospl
Cemy
Liby
Bicester Crossing
QUEENS AVE
NORTH ST
SHEEP ST
MANORSFIELD RD
LONDON RD
Whitelands Farm
SKIMMINGDISH LA
4
25
3
24
2
23
1
22
D
57
E
58
F
80
66

65
52

A
B
C
Fringford Lodge
A421
Hall
Moat
Dymock's Farm
West Farm
Sewage Works
The Kennels
Brashfield House
Quarry
FAIRHAVEN RD
WOODCOTE RD
ROMAN ROAD
MONTGOMERY RD
RALI CT
GRIFFITHS GDNS
THOMPSON DR
HARMON CL
TURNPIKE RD
Airfield
SKIMMINGDISH LA
A421
Field Barn
SKIMMINGDISH RD
WARWICK CT
Schs
SHACKLETON CL
LANCASTER CL
WELLINGTON CL
ANSON WAY
CHURCHILL RD
STERLING CL
FAIRFORD WAY
TURNBERRY CL
LYNEHAM RD
SPITFIRE CL
BENSON CL
SCAMPTON CL
TELFORD RD
WEDGWOOD RD
LAUNTON RD
JARVIS LA
MURDOCK RD
GRANVILLE WAY
LC
CHARBRIDGE LA
Ind Est
Manor Farm
BICESTER RD
Sch
THE SPINNEY
SHERWOOD CL
ANCIL AVE
SKINNER RD
SYCAMORE RD
BLENHEIM DR
Grange Farm
STATION RD
Folly Cottage
LC
THE POPLARS
PH
THE GREEN
Launton
PH
WEST END CL
WEST END
CHESTNUT CL
BLACKTHORN RD
Tubb's Crossing
Bicester Fields Farm
HERON DR
OSPREY CL
BESSEMER CL
FALLOWFIELDS
4
25
3
24
2
23
1
22
59
60
61

65
81

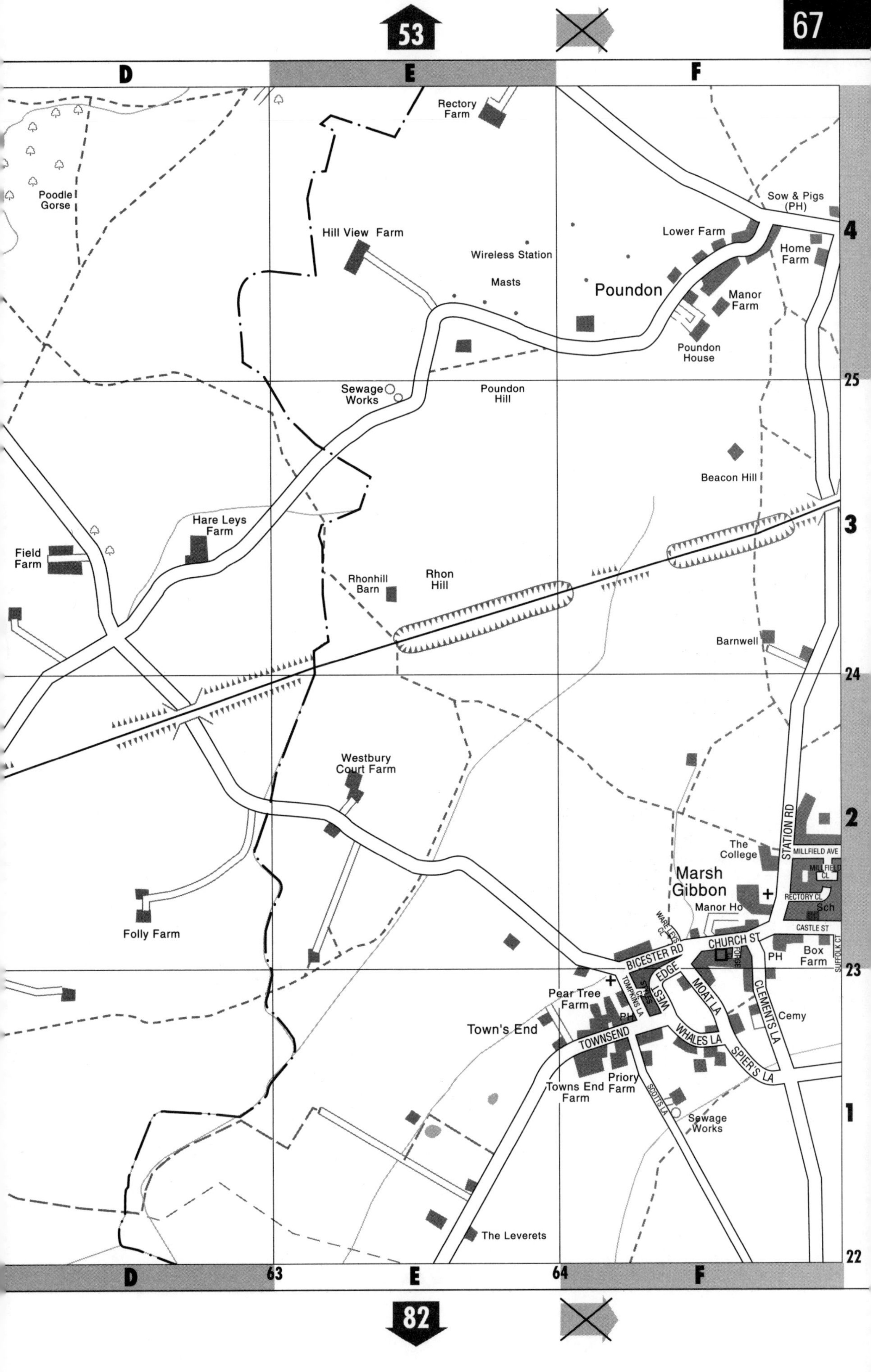

D

Poodle
Gorse

Rectory
Farm

Hill View Farm

Wireless Station

Masts

Sow & Pigs
(PH)

Lower Farm

Home
Farm

Poundon

Manor
Farm

4

Poundon
House

25

Sewage
Works

Poundon
Hill

Hare Leys
Farm

Beacon Hill

3

Field
Farm

Rhonhill
Barn

Rhon
Hill

Barnwell

24

Westbury
Court Farm

2

STATION RD

The
College

Millfield Ave

MILLFIELD
CL

Marsh
Gibbon

RECTORY CL

Sch

Folly Farm

Manor Ho

CASTLE ST

SUFFOLK CT

WARE LEYS CL

CHURCH ST

CLEMENTS LA

PH

Box
Farm

23

BICESTER RD

WEST EDGE

Pear Tree
Farm

TOMPKINS LA

Cemy

Town's End

PH

MOAT LA

WHALES LA

SPIER'S LA

TOWNSEND

Priory
Farm

Towns End
Farm

SPIER'S LA

Sewage
Works

1

The Leverets

22

D
63
E
64
F

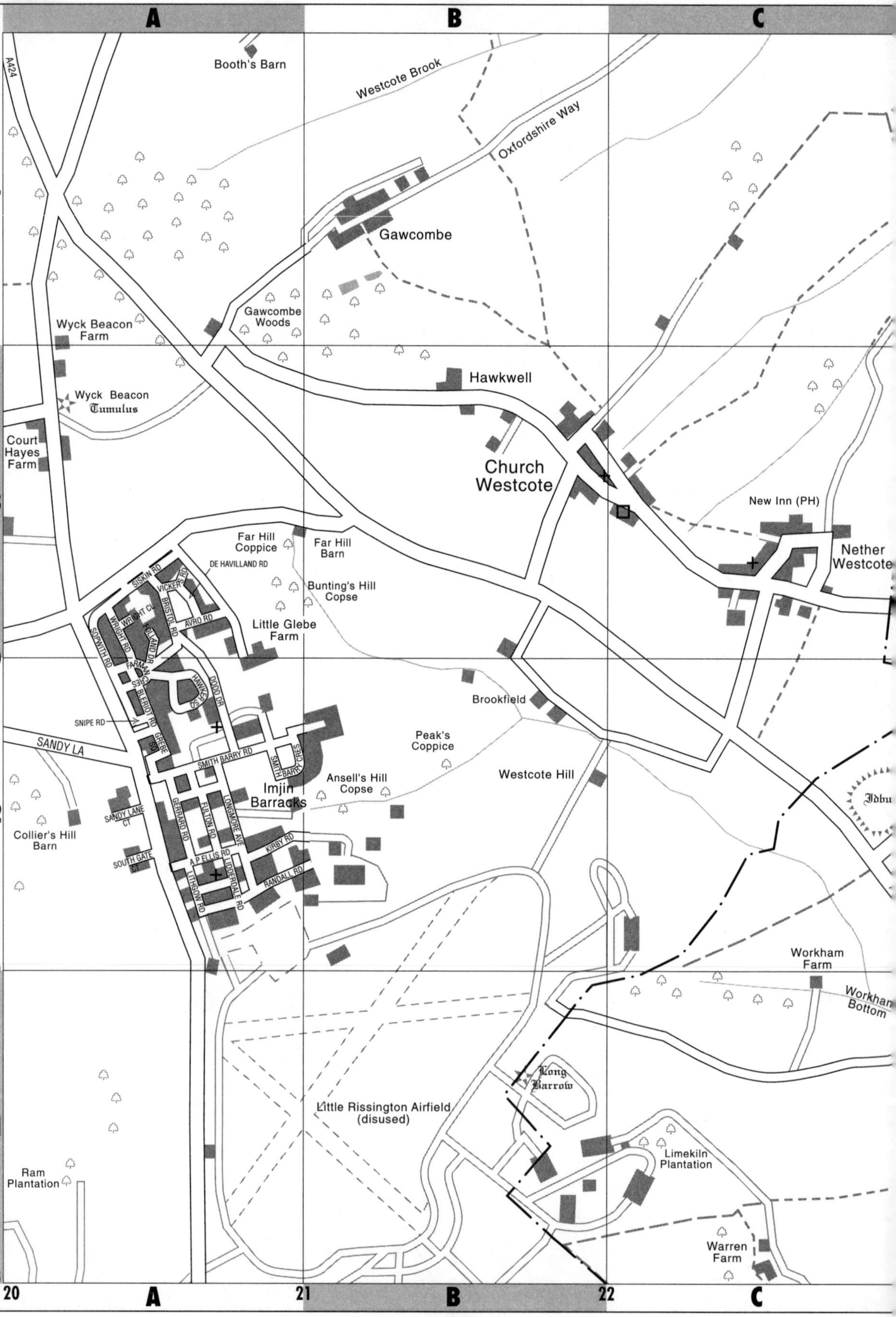

	A	B	C

Booth's Barn

Westcote Brook

Oxfordshire Way

4

Gawcombe

Gawcombe Woods

Wyck Beacon Farm

21

Hawkwell

Wyck Beacon Tumulus

Court Hayes Farm

Church Westcote

New Inn (PH)

3

Far Hill Coppice

Far Hill Barn

Nether Westcote

DE HAVILLAND RD

SISKIN RD

VICKER RD

Bunting's Hill Copse

WRIGHT CL

BRISTOL RD

Little Glebe Farm

OXFORD RD

AVRO RD

20

SOPWITH RD

FARMAN

HAWKER CL

TEDDER RD

Brookfield

SNIPE RD

BLENHEIM RD

FOKKER DR

Peak's Coppice

Westcote Hill

SANDY LA

GRIEVE

GERRARD RD

SMITH BARRY RD

SMITH BARRY

Idbu

Imjin Barracks

Ansell's Hill Copse

2

SANDY LANE CT

FULTON RD

Workham Farm

Collier's Hill Barn

SOUTH GATE CT

A P ELLIS RD

KIRBY RD

LONGMORE AVE

LONGMORE RD

Workham Bottom

LITHGOW RD

RANDALL RD

19

Long Barrow

1

Little Rissington Airfield (disused)

Limekiln Plantation

Ram Plantation

Warren Farm

18

20	A	21	B	22	C

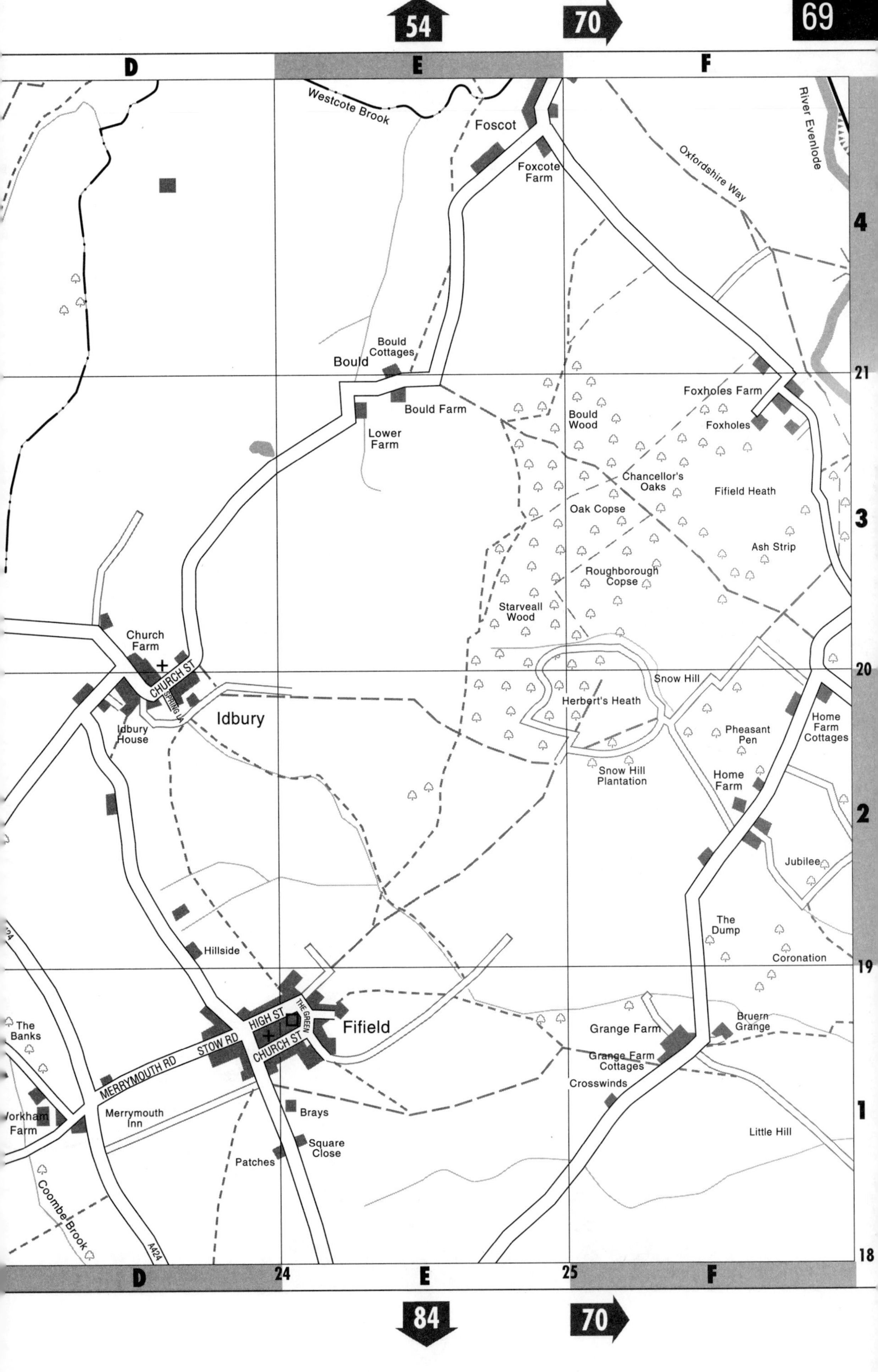

54
70

D   E   F

Westcote Brook

Foscot

River Evenlode

Foxcote Farm

Oxfordshire Way

4

Bould Cottages

Bould

21

Foxholes Farm

Bould Farm

Bould Wood

Foxholes

Lower Farm

Chancellor's Oaks

Fifield Heath

Oak Copse

Ash Strip

3

Roughborough Copse

Church Farm

Starveall Wood

CHURCH ST

Snow Hill

20

Idbury

Herbert's Heath

Idbury House

Pheasant Pen

Home Farm Cottages

Snow Hill Plantation

Home Farm

2

Jubilee

The Dump

Hillside

Coronation

19

The Banks

Fifield

HIGH ST

THE GREEN

CHURCH ST

Grange Farm

Bruern Grange

STOW RD

MERRYMOUTH RD

Grange Farm Cottages

Crosswinds

Workham Farm

Merrymouth Inn

Brays

1

Square Close

Little Hill

Patches

Coombe Brook

A424

18

D   24   E   25   F

84
70

69
55

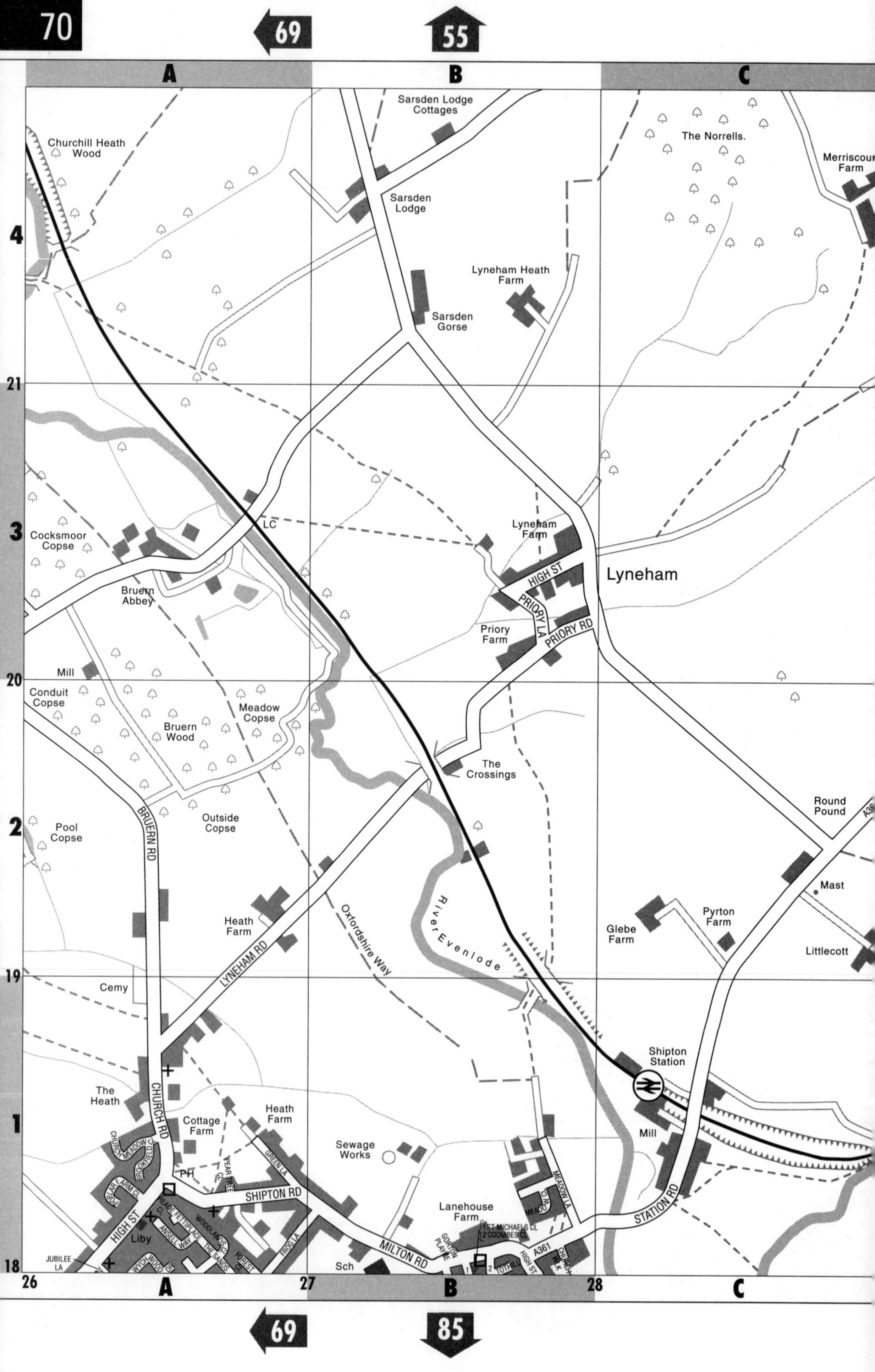
A
B
C
Sarsden Lodge Cottages
Churchill Heath Wood
The Norrells.
Merriscourt Farm
Sarsden Lodge
Lyneham Heath Farm
Sarsden Gorse
4
21
3
Cocksmoor Copse
LC
Lyneham Farm
HIGH ST
Lyneham
Bruern Abbey
PRIORY LA
PRIORY RD
Priory Farm
Mill
20
Conduit Copse
Meadow Copse
Bruern Wood
The Crossings
Round Pound
2
Pool Copse
BRUERN RD
Outside Copse
Mast
River Evenlode
Oxfordshire Way
Heath Farm
LYNEHAM RD
Glebe Farm
Pyrton Farm
Littlecott
19
Cemy
Shipton Station
The Heath
CHURCH RD
Cottage Farm
Heath Farm
1
Mill
Sewage Works
PH
SHIPTON RD
GREEN LA
MEADOW LA
Lanehouse Farm
STATION RD
MILTON RD
HIGH ST
Liby
1 ST MICHAELS CL
2 COOMBES CL
A361
JUBILEE LA
Sch
18
26
27
28
A
B
C

69
85

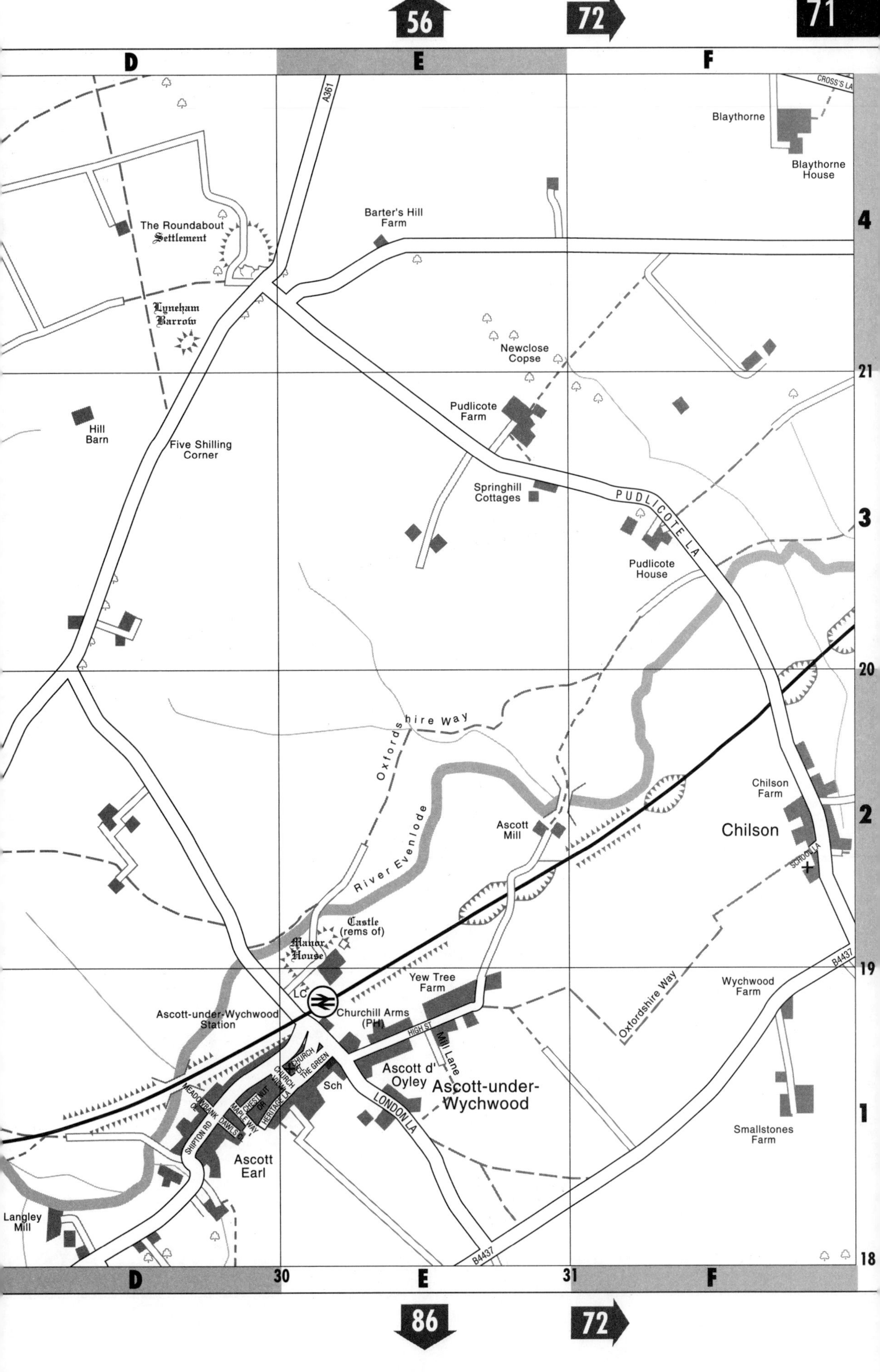

D   E   F

4

Blaythorne

Blaythorne
House

CROSS'S LA

The Roundabout
Settlement

Barter's Hill
Farm

Lyneham
Barrow

Newclose
Copse

21

Hill
Barn

Five Shilling
Corner

Pudlicote
Farm

Springhill
Cottages

PUDLICOTE LA

3

Pudlicote
House

20

Oxfordshire Way

Chilson
Farm

River Evenlode

Ascott
Mill

Chilson

2

SCHOOL LA

Castle
(rems of)

Manor
House

Yew Tree
Farm

LC

Ascott-under-Wychwood
Station

Churchill Arms
(PH)

Oxfordshire Way

Wychwood
Farm

B4437

19

HIGH ST

Ascott d'
Oyley

Ascott-under-
Wychwood

MEADOW BANK
CHURCH
PRIEST MTT DR
HEDGEHOG LA
THE GREEN
DAVIES WAY
CHURCH
Sch

Mill Lane

LONDON LA

1

Smallstones
Farm

SHIPTON RD

Ascott
Earl

Langley
Mill

B4437

18

D   30   E   31   F

A **B** **C**

CROSS'S LA

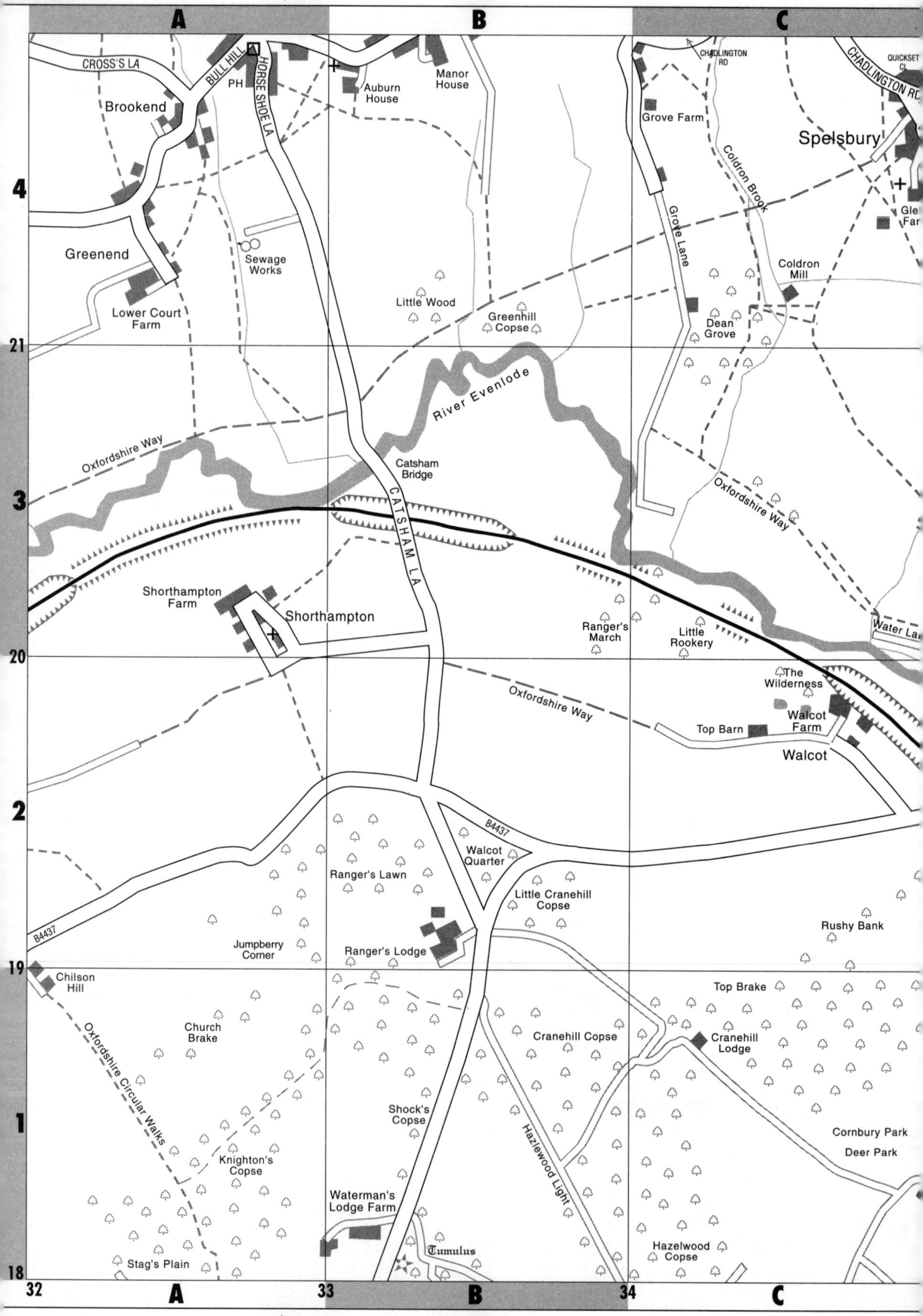

Brookend

BULL HILL

HORSE SHOE LA

PH

Auburn House

Manor House

CHADLINGTON RD

QUICKSET CL

CHADLINGTON RD

Grove Farm

Spelsbury

Coldron Brook

Grove Lane

4

Gle Far

Greenend

Sewage Works

Coldron Mill

Lower Court Farm

Little Wood

Greenhill Copse

Dean Grove

21

River Evenlode

Oxfordshire Way

Oxfordshire Way

Catsham Bridge

3

CATSHAM LA

Shorthampton Farm

Shorthampton

Ranger's March

Little Rookery

Water La

Water La

The Wilderness

20

Oxfordshire Way

Top Barn

Walcot Farm

Walcot

2

B4437

Walcot Quarter

Ranger's Lawn

Little Cranehill Copse

Rushy Bank

B4437

Jumpberry Corner

Ranger's Lodge

Top Brake

19

Chilson Hill

Cranehill Lodge

Oxfordshire Circular Walks

Church Brake

Cranehill Copse

Shock's Copse

Hazelwood Light

Cornbury Park

1

Deer Park

Knighton's Copse

Waterman's Lodge Farm

Hazelwood Copse

Stag's Plain

Tumulus

18

32 **A** **33** **B** **34** **C**

D
E
F

TASTON RD

Taston

Lower Farm

B4022

Shilcott Wood
Shilcott Light

New Park

4

Coathouse Farm

Taston Brook

Harry Fowlers

Norman's Grove

Model Brake North

Conygree Farm

Banbury Hill Farm

21

Wayhill

BANBURY HILL

Pintle Stripe

Clarke's Bottom

Hundley Way

Pintle Barn

3

Bobwell Farm

DITCHLEY RD

Spelsbury Villas

KENDAL PIECE

JEFFERSONS PIECE

Water Lane

B4026

20

NINE ACRES CL

THE SHEET

RAMPERS

NINE ACRES LA

EVENLODE CT

POUND HILL

CHARTWELL DR

B4022

Dyer's Hill Bridge

COTSWOLD VIEW

THAMES ST

PH
Mus
Lib

ENSTONE RD

WYCHWOOD PADDOCKS

WYCHWOOD CL

Dyer's Hill

DYER'S HILL

MARKET ST

BROWN'S LA

POOL'S LA

CRAWBOROUGH RD

Sch

Charlbury

B4437

FOREST RD

Charlbury Station

CHURCHILL

THE ALLEY

CHURCH ST

BALL'S LA

FISHER'S LA

SANDFORD RISE

SANDFORD HILL CL

HANOVER CL

2

SHEEP ST

TANNERS CT

DANGERS HILL

SANDFORD PARK

PARK ST

HIXETWOOD

WOODCROFT DR

Woody Lane

MARLBOROUGH PL

GRAMMAR SCHOOL HILL

LEES HTS

Lee's Rest

Sewage Works

COLLINSONS ROW

STURT RD

LITTLE LEES

FIRE
Sta

HIGHNES CL

19

River Evenlode

The Lodge

Tumulus

STURT CL

B4437

North Lodge

B4437

WOODSTOCK RD

STONESFIELD LA

Lower Park

Bevis Farm

1

Battery

Oxfordshire Way

Cornbury House

Tumulus

B4022

18

D
36
E
37
F

| | A | B | C |

Old Grubbs

Dog Kennel Wood

Timber Yard Cottages

Ballhall Bottom

Pump Copse

Grimsdyk Farm

New Park

Kiddington Lodge

Kiddington Drive

Grim's Ditch

4

The Lower House

Round Clump

Ditchley

Kiddington Lodge Plantation

Ditchley Park

21

Grim's Ditch

Little Park

Big Park

Out Wood

Little Park Plantation

Model Farm

3

Model Farm Plantation

Hopyard Close

Rushy Bottom

Bottom Wood

Spurnell's Well (Pump House)

Devils Pool

Tumulus

Tumulus

Dustfield Farm

20

Kingswood Brake

Wood Farm

Ash Copse

Lodge Farm

Devil's Pool

Harry's Plantation

Kingswood Bottom

Kingswood Lane

Kingswood Farm

2

B443

Sheer's Copse

Newbarn Farm

19

King's Wood

B4437

STONESFIELD RIDING

1

Callow Farm

Hill Barn Farm

18

| 38 | A | 39 | B | 40 | C |

60
76

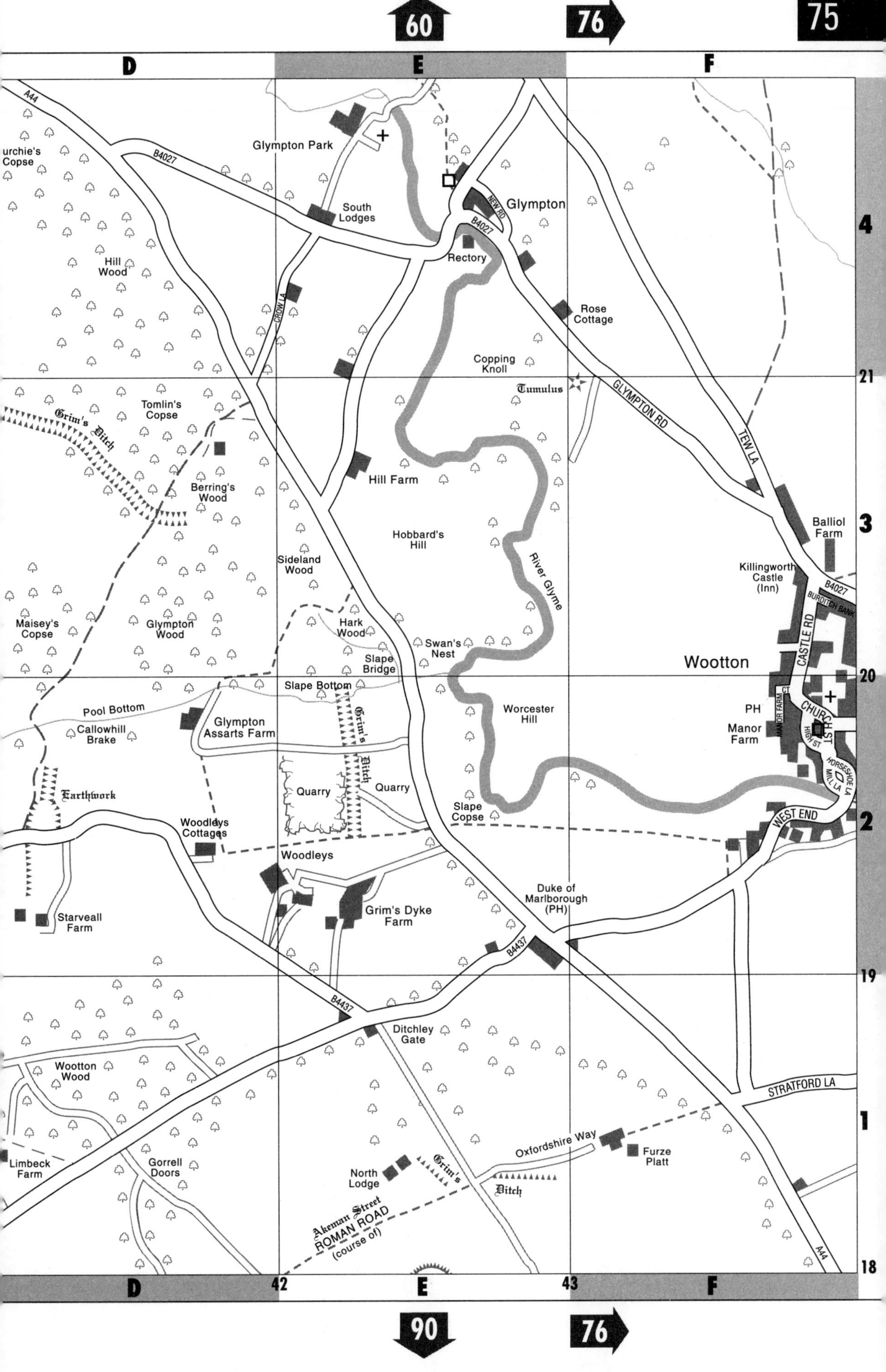
D
E
F
Glympton Park
South Lodges
Glympton
Rectory
Rose Cottage
Copping Knoll
Tumulus
GLYMPTON RD
TEW LA
Hill Wood
urchie's Copse
Tomlin's Copse
Grim's Ditch
Berring's Wood
Hill Farm
Hobbard's Hill
Sideland Wood
River Glyme
Balliol Farm
Killingworth Castle (Inn)
B4027
BURDITCH BANK
CASTLE RD
Wootton
Maisey's Copse
Glympton Wood
Hark Wood
Swan's Nest
Slape Bridge
Slape Bottom
Pool Bottom
Callowhill Brake
Glympton Assarts Farm
Worcester Hill
PH
Manor Farm
MANOR FARM CT
CHURCH ST
HIGH ST
HORSESHOE LA
MILL LA
Earthwork
Quarry
Quarry
Slape Copse
WEST END
Woodleys Cottages
Woodleys
Starveall Farm
Grim's Dyke Farm
Duke of Marlborough (PH)
B4437
Ditchley Gate
Wootton Wood
STRATFORD LA
Oxfordshire Way
Furze Platt
Limbeck Farm
Gorrell Doors
North Lodge
Grim's Ditch
Akeman Street
ROMAN ROAD (course of)
A44
CROW LA
NEW RD
4
21
3
20
2
19
1
18
42
43

90
76

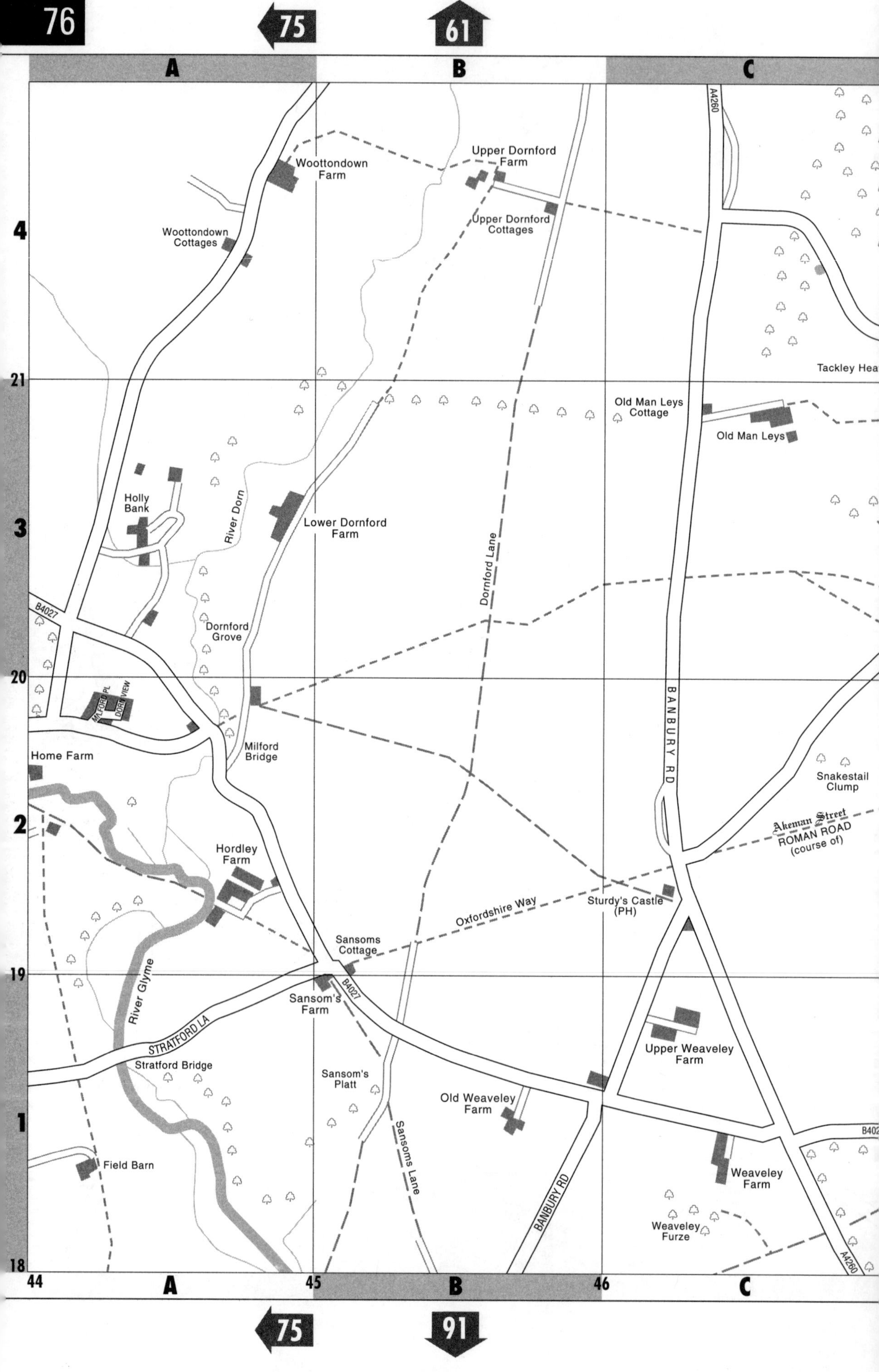

A

B

C

4

Woottondown Farm

Upper Dornford Farm

Upper Dornford Cottages

Tackley Heat

Woottondown Cottages

21

Old Man Leys Cottage

Old Man Leys

River Dorn

Holly Bank

3

Lower Dornford Farm

Dornford Lane

Dornford Grove

B4027

20

Banbury Rd

MAPLE PL

DORN VIEW

Milford Bridge

Snakestail Clump

Home Farm

Akeman Street

ROMAN ROAD (course of)

2

Hordley Farm

Oxfordshire Way

Sturdy's Castle (PH)

Sansoms Cottage

River Glyme

19

Sansom's Farm

B4027

STRATFORD LA

Stratford Bridge

Sansom's Platt

Upper Weaveley Farm

Sansoms Lane

Old Weaveley Farm

1

BANBURY RD

B402

Field Barn

Weaveley Farm

A4260

Weaveley Furze

18

44

A

45

B

46

C

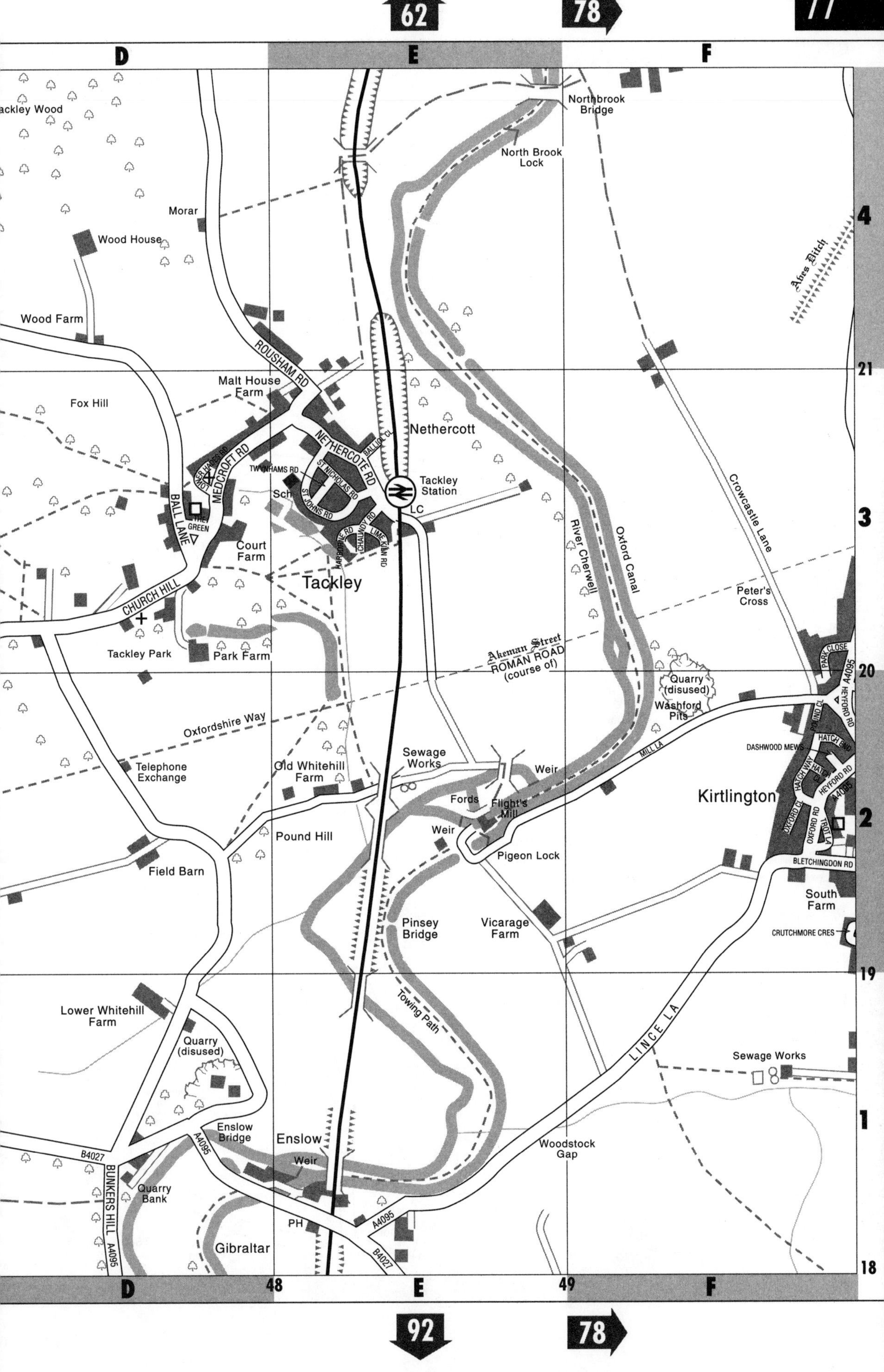

D
E
F

4

Tackley Wood

Morar

Wood House

North Brook
Lock

Northbrook
Bridge

Ams Ditch

21

Wood Farm

ROUSHAM RD

Malt House
Farm

Fox Hill

NETHERCOTE RD

MEDCROFT RD

Nethercott

BALLIOL CL

TWYNHAMS RD

ST NICHOLAS RD

ST JOHNS RD

BALL LANE

ABEL ASH

GREEN

Sch

Tackley Station

LC

River Cherwell

Oxford Canal

Crowcastle Lane

3

Court
Farm

HARDEN RD

HAMMOND RD

LIME KILN RD

Tackley

Peter's
Cross

CHURCH HILL

Tackley Park

Park Farm

Akeman Street
ROMAN ROAD
(course of)

Quarry
(disused)
Washford
Pits

PARK CLOSE

A4095

20

Oxfordshire Way

Telephone
Exchange

Old Whitehill
Farm

Sewage
Works

Weir

HEYFORD RD

DASHWOOD MEWS

HATCH

HATCHWAY

HEYFORD RD

POUND CL

OXFORD RD

A4095

MILL LA

Kirtlington

2

Fords

Flight's
Mill

Pound Hill

Weir

Pigeon Lock

BLETCHINGDON RD

Field Barn

CRUTCHMORE CRES

South
Farm

Vicarage
Farm

Pinsey
Bridge

19

Lower Whitehill
Farm

Towing Path

LINCE LA

Sewage Works

Quarry
(disused)

1

B4027

Enslow
Bridge

Enslow

A4095

BUNKERS HILL A4095

Quarry
Bank

Weir

PH

A4095

Woodstock
Gap

Gibraltar

B4027

18

D
E
F

77
63

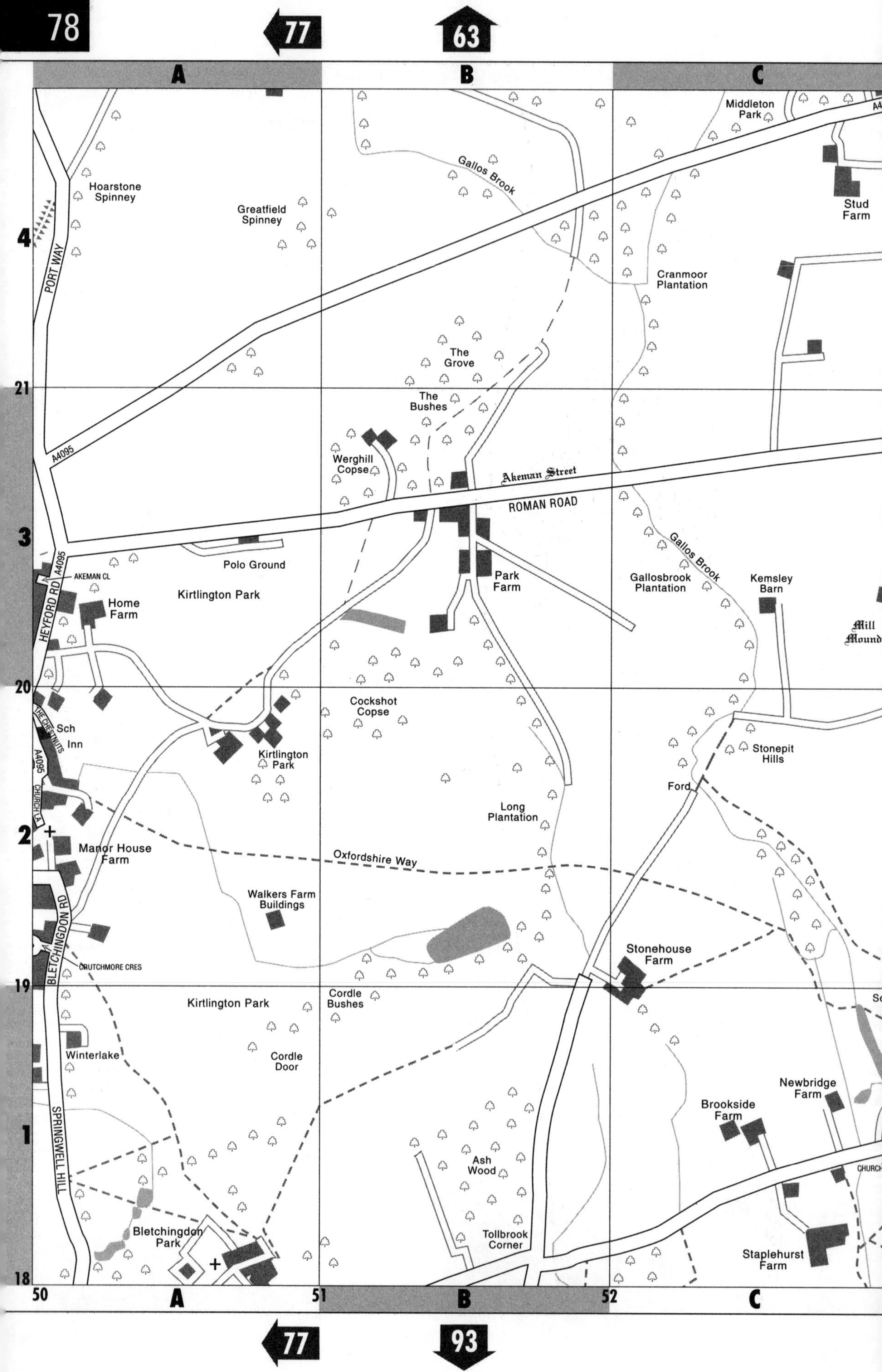
A
B
C
Middleton Park
Hoarstone Spinney
Greatfield Spinney
Gallos Brook
Stud Farm
PORT WAY
Cranmoor Plantation
The Grove
The Bushes
A4095
Werghill Copse
Akeman Street
ROMAN ROAD
Polo Ground
A4095
AKEMAN CL
HEYFORD RD
Kirtlington Park
Home Farm
Park Farm
Gallos Brook
Gallosbrook Plantation
Kemsley Barn
Mill Mound
Cockshot Copse
THE CHESTNUTS
Sch
Inn
Kirtlington Park
Stonepit Hills
A4095
CHURCH LA
Ford
Long Plantation
Manor House Farm
Oxfordshire Way
Walkers Farm Buildings
BLETCHINGDON RD
Stonehouse Farm
CRUTCHMORE CRES
Cordle Bushes
Kirtlington Park
Winterlake
Cordle Door
Newbridge Farm
Brookside Farm
SPRINGWELL HILL
Ash Wood
CHURCH
Bletchingdon Park
Tollbrook Corner
Staplehurst Farm
4
21
3
20
2
19
1
18
50
51
52
A
B
C

77
93

B4095
B430
Stud Farm
Cottages
Simms
Farm
Doctor's
Barn
M40
A4095
Chesterton
Belt
BIGNELL VIEW
A4095
ALCHESTER RD
Sch
Vicarage
Farm
Tanora
Cottage
ORCHARD RISE
4

Spring Well
Farm
CH
Golf
Course
FORTESCUE DR
ASH

Chesterton

GREEN LA
THE
GREEN

21

Greystone
Court
3

Airfield
Little
Chesterton
Grange
Farm

New Barn
Farm
20

Middieleys
Spinney
A41(T)
CHURCH LA

Great
Spinney
MEADOW
VIEW
2

Ebenoe
Manor
Farm

Southfield
Farm
A34(T)
A41(T)

NORTH LA
PH
19
Fox
Covert
M40

WEST LA
BUS AVE

Village
Farm
CHURCH RD
Weston-on-the-Green
1
URCH LA

Hotel
Weston Park
Farm

Knowle
Farm
Manor
Farm
Wormough
Copse
KNOWLE LA
B430
A34(T)
18

A
B
C
Recn Grd
MCKAY TRADING ESTATE
Bicester Town Station
B4100
The Talisman Business Centre
TALISMAN RD
LONDON RD
PINGLE DR
A41(T)
A421
OXFORD RD A41(T)
Foxey Leys Copse
Home Farm
Gagle Brook
ALCHESTER RD
1 CHESTNUT CL
2 FORTESCUE DR
GREEN LA
The Red Cow (PH)
Chesterton Lodge
ROMAN ROAD
Langford Park Farm
Rodney House
Works
Wendlebury Farm
Lodge Farm
Promised Land Farm
Bowler's Copse
LCs
Graven Hill
Depot
CIRCULAR RD
Gravenhill Wood
LC
LANGFORD LA
Alchester
ROMAN TOWN
(site of)
RECTORY CL
CHURCH LA
Red Lion (PH)
Elm Tree Farm
ST GILES CL
FARRIER'S MEAD
Wendlebury
College Farm
Langford Lane
Merton Grounds
ROMAN ROAD
(course of)
M40
Astle
Bridg
Cotta
4
21
3
20
2
19
1
18
56
57
58

D
E
F
OSPREY CL
SHEARWATER DR
PEREGRINE WAY
SWALLOW CL
MERLIN WAY
AVOCET WAY
KINGFISHER WAY
WRETCHWICK WAY
RAVENCROFT
KESTREL WAY
NEUNKIRCHEN WAY
SEELSCHEID WAY
Middle Wretchwick Farm
Little Wretchwick Farm
Blackthorn Hill
A41(T)
LC
PIONEER RD
CIRCULAR RD
Akeman Street
ROMAN ROAD
Wretchwick Farm
Mill House Farm
Stone Pits Farm
Hill Farm
B4011
WEST HAWTHORN RD
OAK LA
ASH LA
EAST HAWTHORN RD
LANGTON AVE
ALLECTUS AVE
ERMINGTON CL
GLEBE CL
QUINTAN AVE
AKEMAN AVE
Sch
Willow End
SYCAMORE RD
ALDER DR
WILLOW RD
ELM CL
BIRCH RD
ELM LA
LABURNUM CL
MERTON RD
PARK RISE
OLD ARNCOTT RD
PLOUGHLEY RD
HOME FARM CL
PH
Ambrosden
Rose and Crown (PH)
LOWER RD
THAME RD
Pound Farm
Home Farm
Arncott Bridge
River Ray
Manor Farm
Jasper's Copse
Astley Bridge Farm
Brook Farm
Lower Arncott
The Tally-Ho (PH)
4
3
2
1
21
20
19
18
60
61

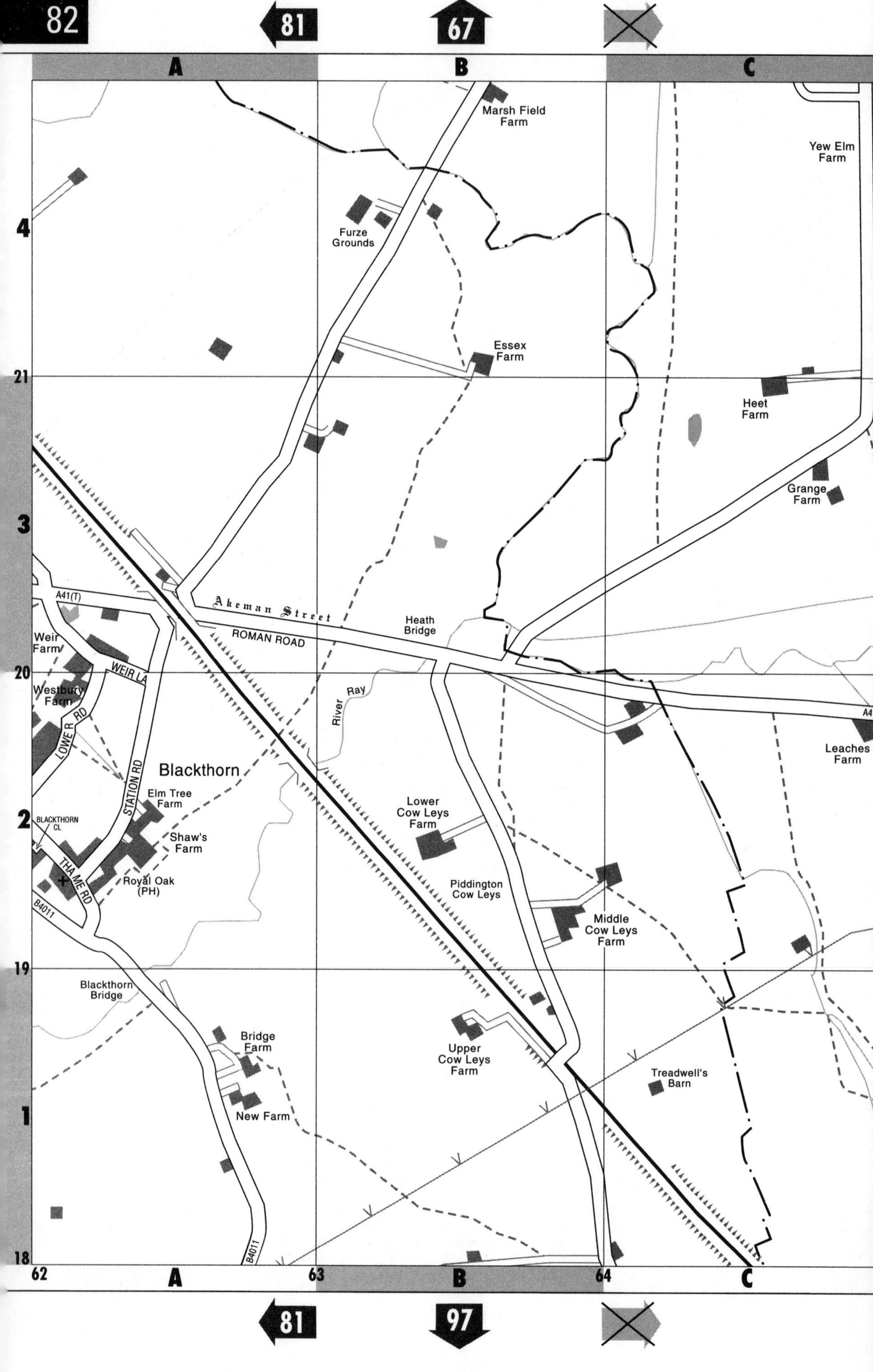

A B C

Marsh Field
Farm

Yew Elm
Farm

Furze
Grounds

4

Essex
Farm

21

Heet
Farm

Grange
Farm

3

Akeman Street

ROMAN ROAD

Heath
Bridge

Weir
Farm

A41(T)

WEIR LA

20

River Ray

A4

Westbury
Farm

LOWER RD

Leaches
Farm

Blackthorn

STATION RD

Elm Tree
Farm

Lower
Cow Leys
Farm

BLACKTHORN
CL

2

Shaw's
Farm

Piddington
Cow Leys

Middle
Cow Leys
Farm

THAME RD

Royal Oak
(PH)

B4011

19

Blackthorn
Bridge

Bridge
Farm

Upper
Cow Leys
Farm

Treadwell's
Barn

1

New Farm

18

62 A 63 B 64 C

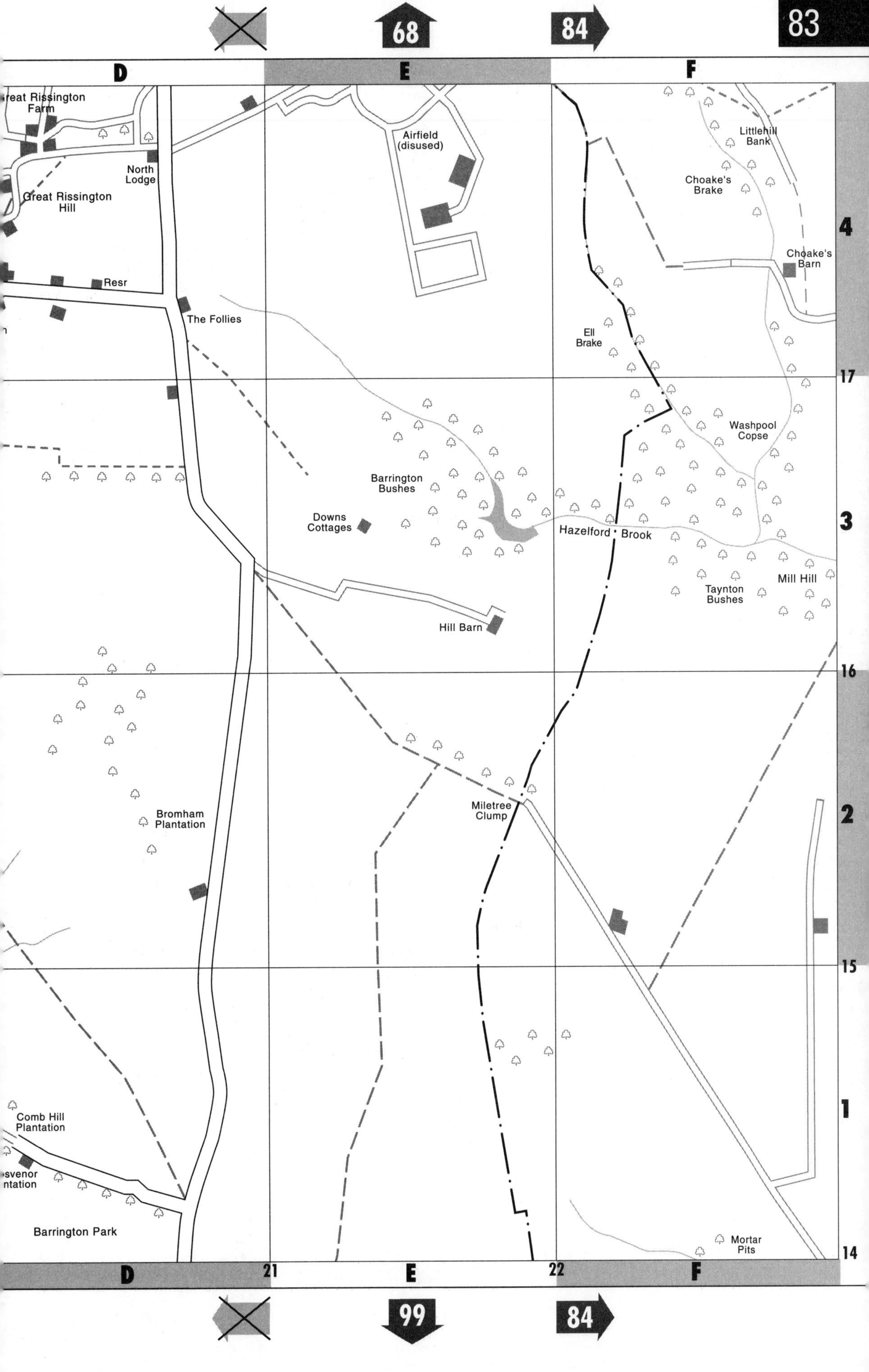

68

84

D E F

Great Rissington Farm

Airfield (disused)

Littlehill Bank

Choake's Brake

North Lodge

Great Rissington Hill

4

Choake's Barn

Resr

The Follies

Ell Brake

17

Washpool Copse

Barrington Bushes

Downs Cottages

Hazelford Brook

3

Mill Hill

Taynton Bushes

Hill Barn

16

Bromham Plantation

Miletree Clump

2

15

Comb Hill Plantation

1

svenor ntation

Barrington Park

Mortar Pits

14

D E F

21

99

22

84

83
69

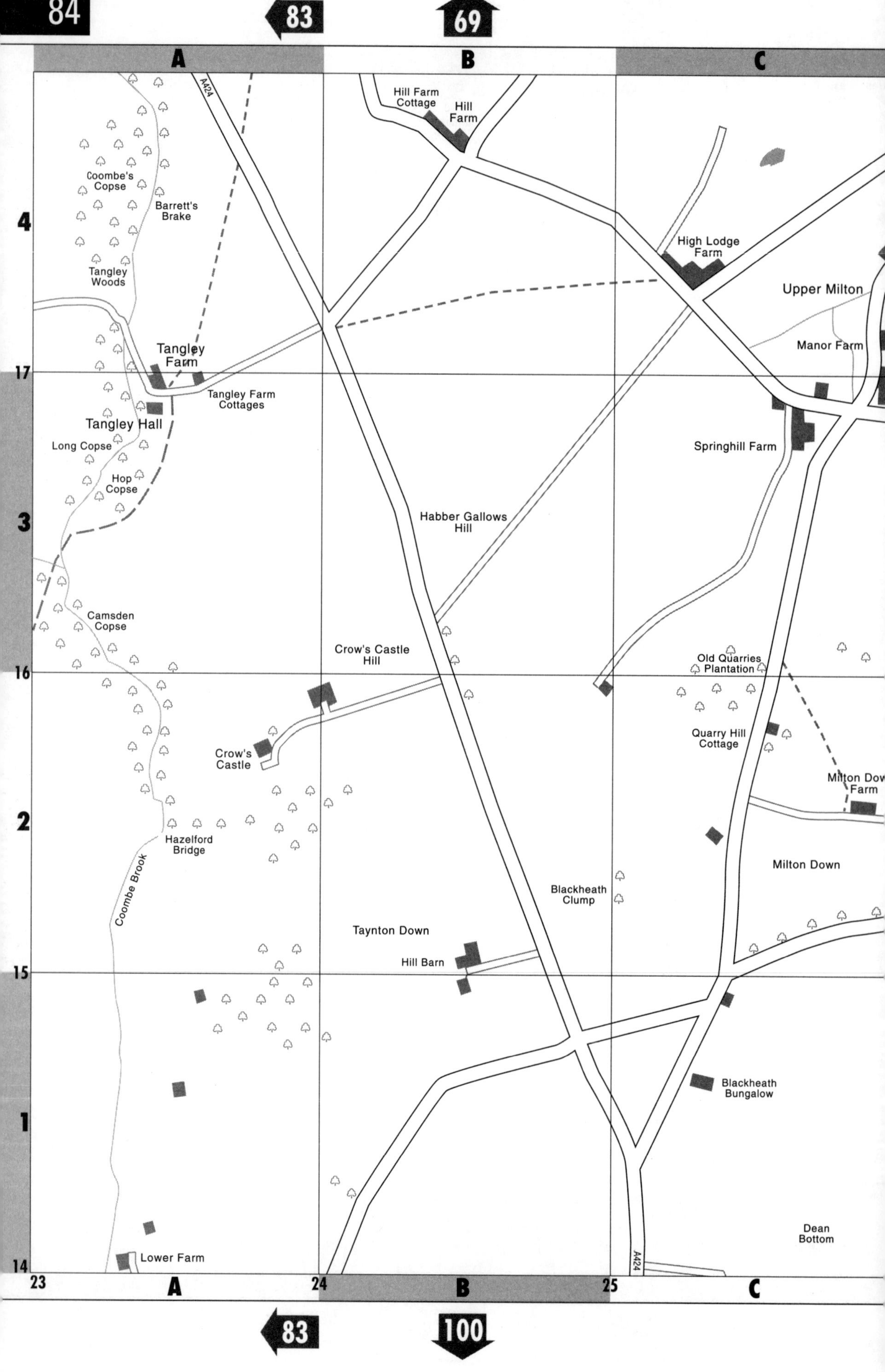
A
B
C
4
17
3
16
2
15
1
14
23
24
25
A424
Hill Farm Cottage
Hill Farm
Coombe's Copse
Barrett's Brake
Tangley Woods
High Lodge Farm
Upper Milton
Manor Farm
Tangley Farm
Tangley Farm Cottages
Tangley Hall
Long Copse
Hop Copse
Springhill Farm
Habber Gallows Hill
Camsden Copse
Crow's Castle Hill
Old Quarries Plantation
Crow's Castle
Quarry Hill Cottage
Milton Down Farm
Hazelford Bridge
Coombe Brook
Milton Down
Blackheath Clump
Taynton Down
Hill Barn
Blackheath Bungalow
Dean Bottom
Lower Farm
A424

83
100

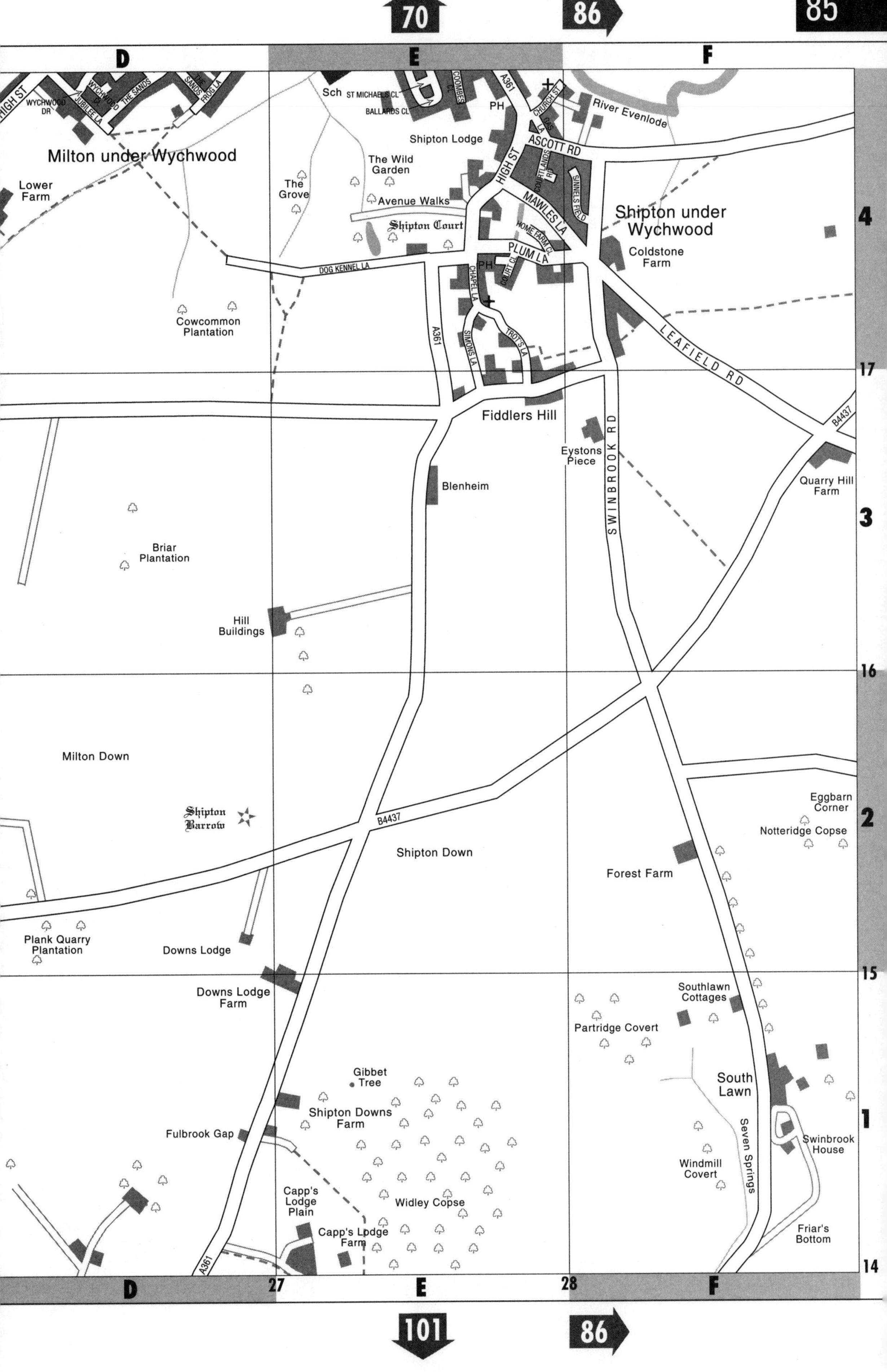

D
E
F

Milton under Wychwood

HIGH ST
WYCHWOOD DR
JUBILEE LA
THE SANDS
SANDS PRICE LA

Sch
ST MICHAELS CL
BALLARDS CL
St Michaels Cl
COOMBES
A361
PH
River Evenlode
Shipton Lodge
ASCOTT RD
FOUR ROWLANDS RD
CHURCH ST
SINNELS FIELD

The Wild Garden

Lower Farm

The Grove

Avenue Walks

MAWLES LA

Shipton Court

HOME FARM
HIGH ST

Shipton under Wychwood

Coldstone Farm

PLUM LA

4

Cowcommon Plantation

DOG KENNEL LA

CHAPEL LA
PH
DR PINE RD
A361
SIMONS LA
TROTS LA

LEAFIELD RD

17

Fiddlers Hill

Eystons Piece

SWINBROOK RD

B4437

Blenheim

Quarry Hill Farm

3

Briar Plantation

Hill Buildings

16

Milton Down

Shipton Barrow

Eggbarn Corner
Notteridge Copse

2

B4437

Shipton Down

Forest Farm

Plank Quarry Plantation

Downs Lodge

15

Downs Lodge Farm

Southlawn Cottages

Partridge Covert

South Lawn

1

Gibbet Tree

Shipton Downs Farm

Fulbrook Gap

Windmill Covert

Seven Springs

Swinbrook House

A361

Capp's Lodge Plain

Widley Copse

Capp's Lodge Farm

Friar's Bottom

14

D
27
E
28
F

A | B | C

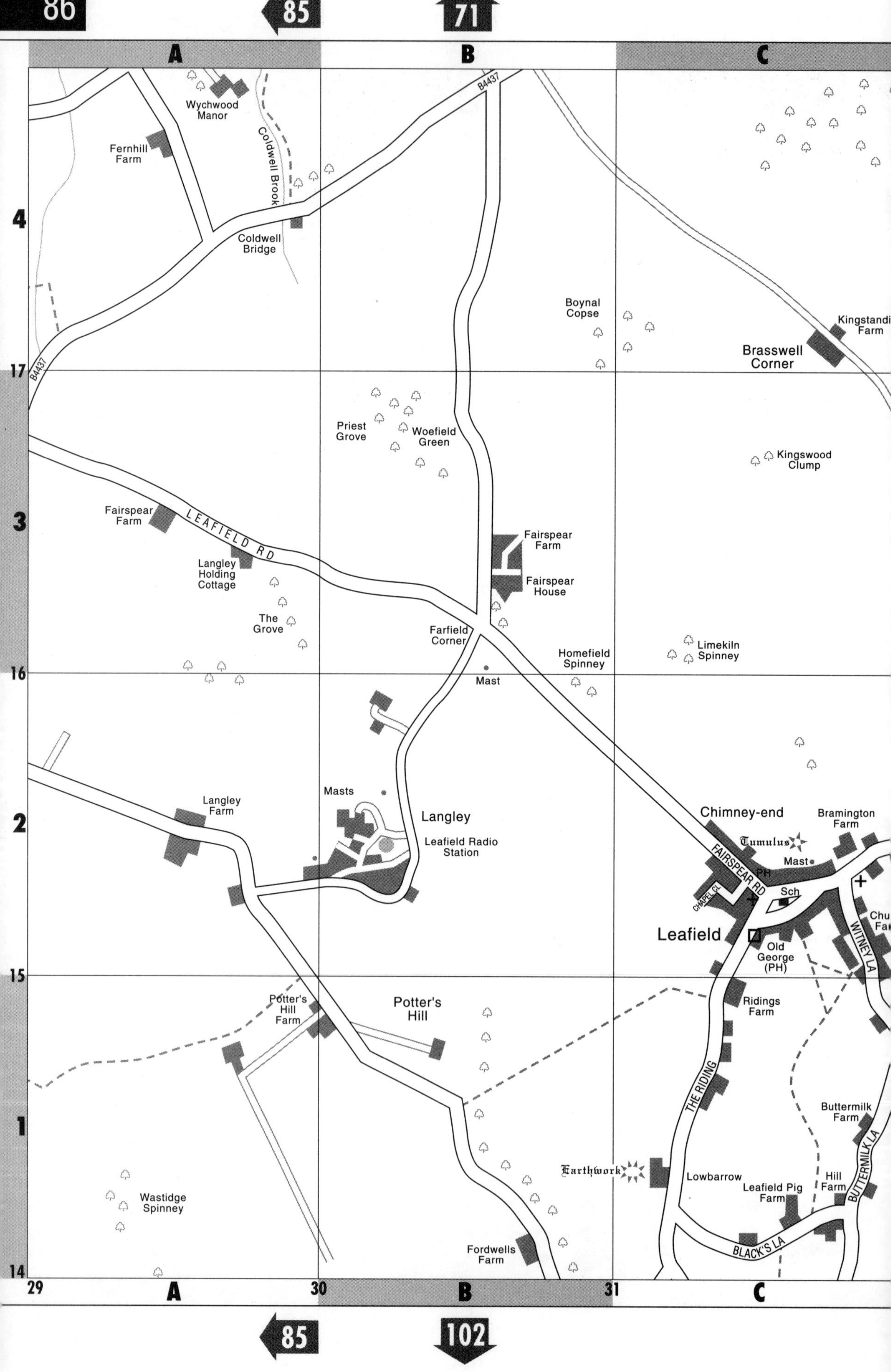

Wychwood Manor

Fernhill Farm

Coldwell Brook

Coldwell Bridge

B4437

B4437

4

Boynal Copse

Brasswell Corner

Kingstandi Farm

17

Priest Grove

Woefield Green

Kingswood Clump

Fairspear Farm

LEAFIELD RD

Langley Holding Cottage

The Grove

Fairspear Farm

Fairspear House

3

Farfield Corner

Homefield Spinney

Limekiln Spinney

16

Mast

Langley Farm

Masts

Langley

Leafield Radio Station

Chimney-end

Bramington Farm

Tumulus

Mast

FAIRSPEAR RD

CHAPEL CL

Sch

Chu Fa

WITNEY LA

2

Leafield

Old George (PH)

15

Potter's Hill Farm

Potter's Hill

Ridings Farm

THE RIDING

Buttermilk Farm

BUTTERMILK LA

1

Earthwork

Lowbarrow

Leafield Pig Farm

Hill Farm

Wastidge Spinney

BLACK'S LA

Fordwells Farm

14

29 | A | 30 | B | 31 | C

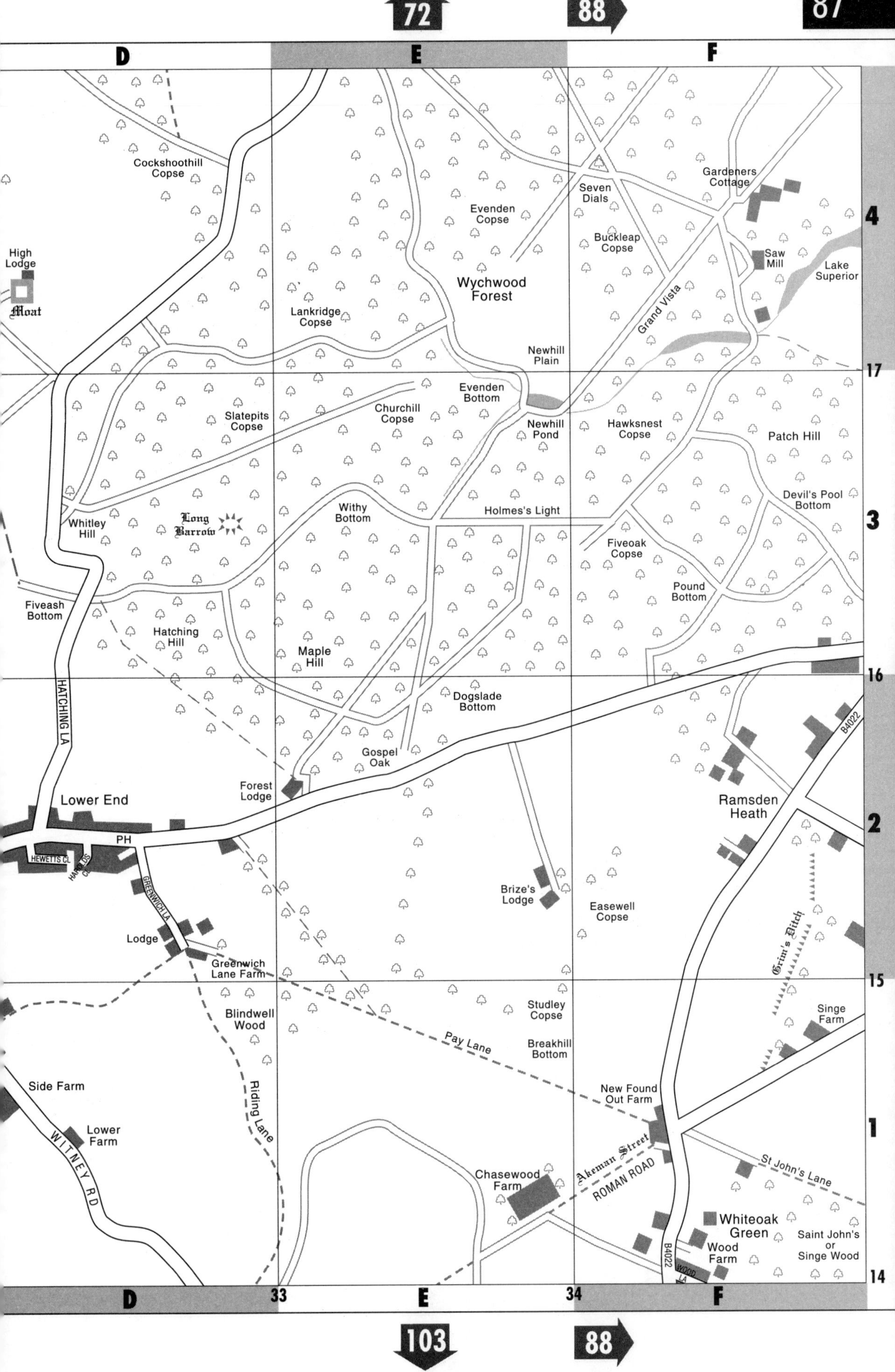

4

Cockshoothill Copse

Evenden Copse

Seven Dials

Gardeners Cottage

Buckleap Copse

Wychwood Forest

Saw Mill

Lake Superior

High Lodge

Moat

Lankridge Copse

Newhill Plain

Grand Vista

17

Slatepits Copse

Churchill Copse

Evenden Bottom

Newhill Pond

Hawksnest Copse

Patch Hill

Devil's Pool Bottom

3

Whitley Hill

Long Barrow

Withy Bottom

Holmes's Light

Fiveoak Copse

Fiveash Bottom

Hatching Hill

Maple Hill

Pound Bottom

16

HATCHING LA

Dogslade Bottom

B4022

Gospel Oak

Lower End

Forest Lodge

Ramsden Heath

2

PH

HEWETIS CL

HAWTHORN CL

GREENWICH LA

Brize's Lodge

Easewell Copse

Grim's Ditch

Lodge

Greenwich Lane Farm

15

Blindwell Wood

Studley Copse

Singe Farm

Riding Lane

Pay Lane

Breakhill Bottom

Side Farm

New Found Out Farm

1

Lower Farm

WITNEY RD

Akeman Street

St John's Lane

Chasewood Farm

ROMAN ROAD

Whiteoak Green

Wood Farm

Saint John's or Singe Wood

B4022

WOOD LA

14

87
73

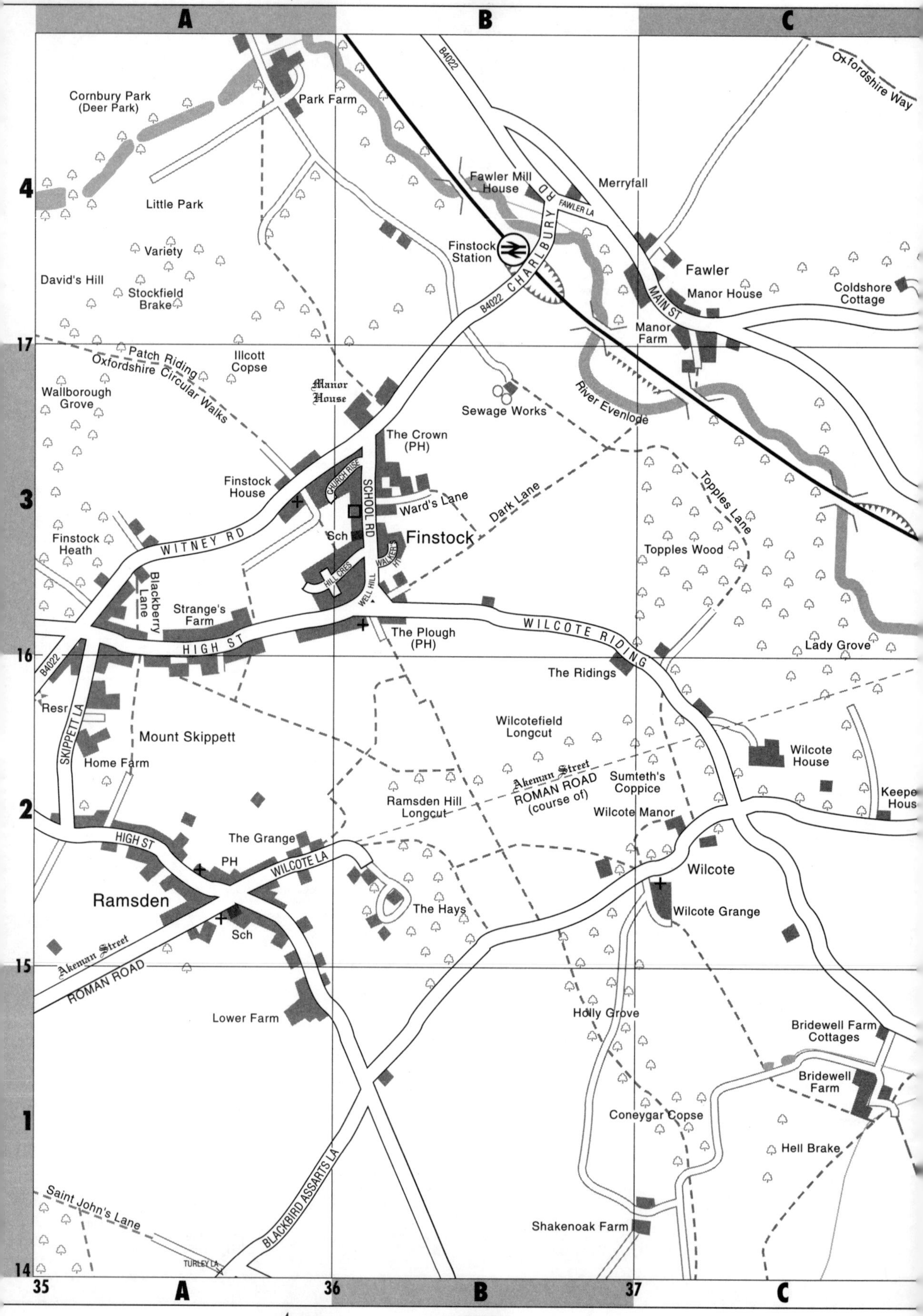

A B C

4

Cornbury Park
(Deer Park)

Park Farm

B4022

Fawler Mill
House

Merryfall

FAWLER LA

Little Park

Finstock Station

Fawler

Variety

Manor House

Coldshore Cottage

David's Hill

Stockfield Brake

CHARLBURY RD

MAIN ST

Manor House

B4022

Manor Farm

17

Patch Riding

Oxfordshire Circular Walks

Illcott Copse

Manor House

Sewage Works

River Evenlode

Wallborough Grove

The Crown (PH)

3

Finstock House

CHURCH RISE

SCHOOL RD

Ward's Lane

Dark Lane

Topples Lane

Sch

Finstock

Topples Wood

Finstock Heath

WITNEY RD

HILL CRES

TILL HILL

WALKER RI

Strange's Farm

Blackberry Lane

The Plough (PH)

WILCOTE RIDING

Lady Grove

16

HIGH ST

B4022

The Ridings

Resr

SKIPPETT LA

Mount Skippett

Wilcotefield Longcut

Wilcote House

Home Farm

Akeman Street
ROMAN ROAD
(course of)

Sumteth's Coppice

Keepe Hous

2

HIGH ST

The Grange

Ramsden Hill Longcut

Wilcote Manor

PH

WILCOTE LA

Wilcote

Ramsden

The Hays

Wilcote Grange

Akeman Street

Sch

ROMAN ROAD

15

Lower Farm

Holly Grove

Bridewell Farm Cottages

Bridewell Farm

1

BLACKBIRD ASSARTS LA

Coneygar Copse

Hell Brake

Saint John's Lane

Shakenoak Farm

TURLEY LA

14

35 A 36 B 37 C

Oxfordshire Way

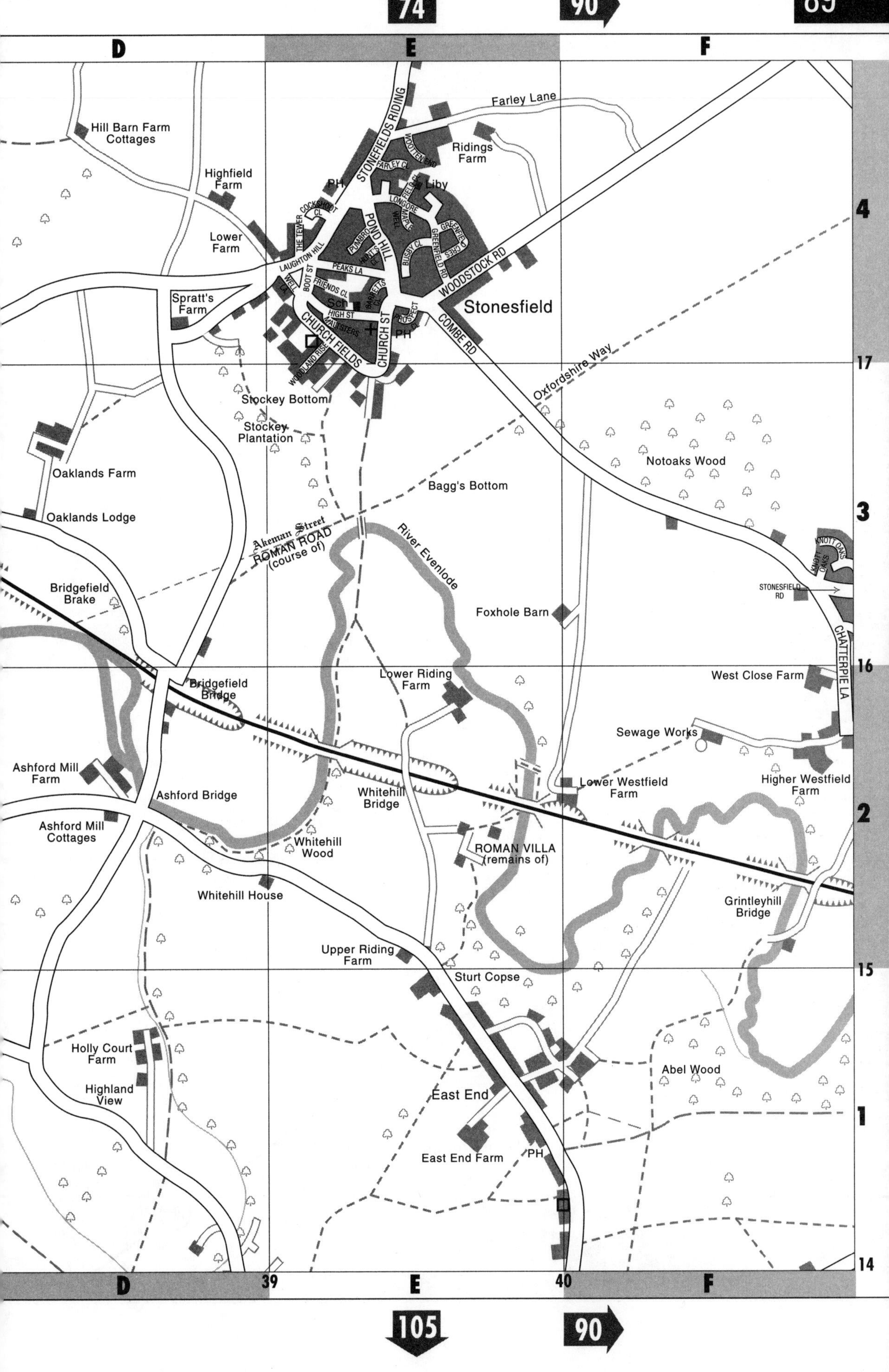
D
E
F
Hill Barn Farm Cottages
Highfield Farm
Lower Farm
Spratt's Farm
Farley Lane
Ridings Farm
STONEFIELDS RIDING
PH
Liby
POND HILL
WOODSTOCK RD
Stonesfield
COMBE RD
CHURCH ST
CHURCH FIELDS
Sch
PH
Oxfordshire Way
Stockey Bottom
Stockey Plantation
Oaklands Farm
Oaklands Lodge
Bagg's Bottom
Notoaks Wood
Akeman Street
ROMAN ROAD (course of)
River Evenlode
Bridgefield Brake
Foxhole Barn
STONESFIELD RD
CHATTERPIE LA
West Close Farm
Bridgefield Bridge
Lower Riding Farm
Sewage Works
Ashford Mill Farm
Ashford Bridge
Whitehill Bridge
Lower Westfield Farm
Higher Westfield Farm
Ashford Mill Cottages
Whitehill Wood
ROMAN VILLA (remains of)
Whitehill House
Grintleyhill Bridge
Upper Riding Farm
Sturt Copse
Holly Court Farm
Highland View
East End
Abel Wood
East End Farm
PH
4
17
3
16
2
15
1
14
39
40

89
75
A
B
C
Littleworth Farm
Oxfordshire Way
Akeman Street
ROMAN ROAD (course of)
Stonefield Steps
The Big Clump
Mapleton Pond
Akeman Street Farm
Park Farm
Great Park
Column of Victory
Fourteen Acre Clump
Long Firs
Square Firs
SQUARE FIRS
AKEMAN ST
Blenheim Park
Fair Rosamund's Well
Grand Bridge
KNOTT OAKS
STONESFIELD RD
Combe
Foxhole Farm
CHATTERPIE LA
ORCHARD CL
PH
COMBE GATE
New Park
PARK RD
Manor Farm
The Lake
WEST END
Sch
ROBIN HILL
Combe Lodge
High Park
Resr
Peagle Wood
Wedgehook Wood
BOLTON'S LA
Boltons Farm
East End
High Lodge
Combe Cliff
Dog Kennel Hill
Combe Station
Combe Mill
River Evenlode
Waterfall
Millwood Farm
MILLWOOD END
BROOK WAY
ABELWOOD RD
EVENLODE DR
MILLWOOD VALE
MYRTLE CL
Myrtle Farm
Long Hanborough
PARK LA
Long House
Long Hanborough Bridge
PH
Sch
MAIN RD
WASTIE'S ORCH
LODGE RD
LOWER RD
WITNEY RD
A4095
HURDESWELL
NEW RD
CHURCHILL WAY
GLYME WAY
CHURCH RD
ROOSEVELT RD
RILEY CL
BECKETTS CL
Motel
Hanborough Station
Mus
4
17
3
16
2
15
1
14
41
42
43
89
106

D E F

4

A4260

Old
Woodstock

River Glyme

Green Lane

Cemy

Sewage
Works

VANBRUGH CL

CLERMONT
RISE

MANOR
RD

WESTLAND
WAY
FARM END

Manor
Farm
PH

MARLBOROUGH CRES

UPPER
BROOK HILL

Mus

THE CAUSEWAY

OXFORD ST

BROOK HILL

GREEN LA

GLYME RD

CHURCHILL LA

PEAR TREE CT

UNION ST

HENSINGTON RD

THE QUADRANGLE

GREEN CT

Hensington
Farm

BANBURY RD

Sansoms Lane

The
Retreat

Hensington

Sch

Shipton Slade
Farm

Dismantled Railway

Shipton Slade
Cottages

17

A4095

1 CHAUCER'S LA
2 BROWN'S LA
3 MARKET PL

HARRISON'S LA

PARK ST

TH

HIGH ST

Liby

NEW RD

PARK ST

RESIDENT WAY

CAMPBELLS CL

FLEMINGS RD

RYE GRASS

Sch

GLOUCESTER ST

PLANE TREE
WAY

Sch

RECTORY LA

COCKPIT CL

CADOGAN

PARK

THE CRESCENT

THE CRESCENT

PRINCES RIDE

HEDGE END

Perdiswell
Farm

SHIPTON RD

UPPER CAMPSFIELD RD

3

Upper
Campsfield
Farm

P

Home
Lodge

WOODSTOCK

CHURCHILL'S
GATE

Firs
Farm

Queen
Pool

Blenheim
Palace

Temple
of Diana

Blenheim
Park

The
Cowyards

OXFORD RD

16

Lower Park

Campsfield
Wood

A44

A4095

Oxford
Airport

2

Middle
Lodge

BLADON RD

Bladon
Bridge

River Glyme

Home
Farm

GROVE RD

HOMESTEAD RD

ORCHARD FIELD LA

WOODSTOCK RD

Campsfield

15

Bladon
Lodge

PARK CL

PH Sch

PARK ST

Bladon

LANGFORD LA

The
Lince

P

CHURCH ST

THE GREEN

Rectory
Farm

LAMB LA

MANOR RD

HEATH LA

Withy
Clump

Lince
Bridge

MAIN RD

A44

WOODSTOCK RD E

1

Thatch
Cottage

Rowel Brook

Burleigh
House

Bladon Heath

14

D E F

91
77

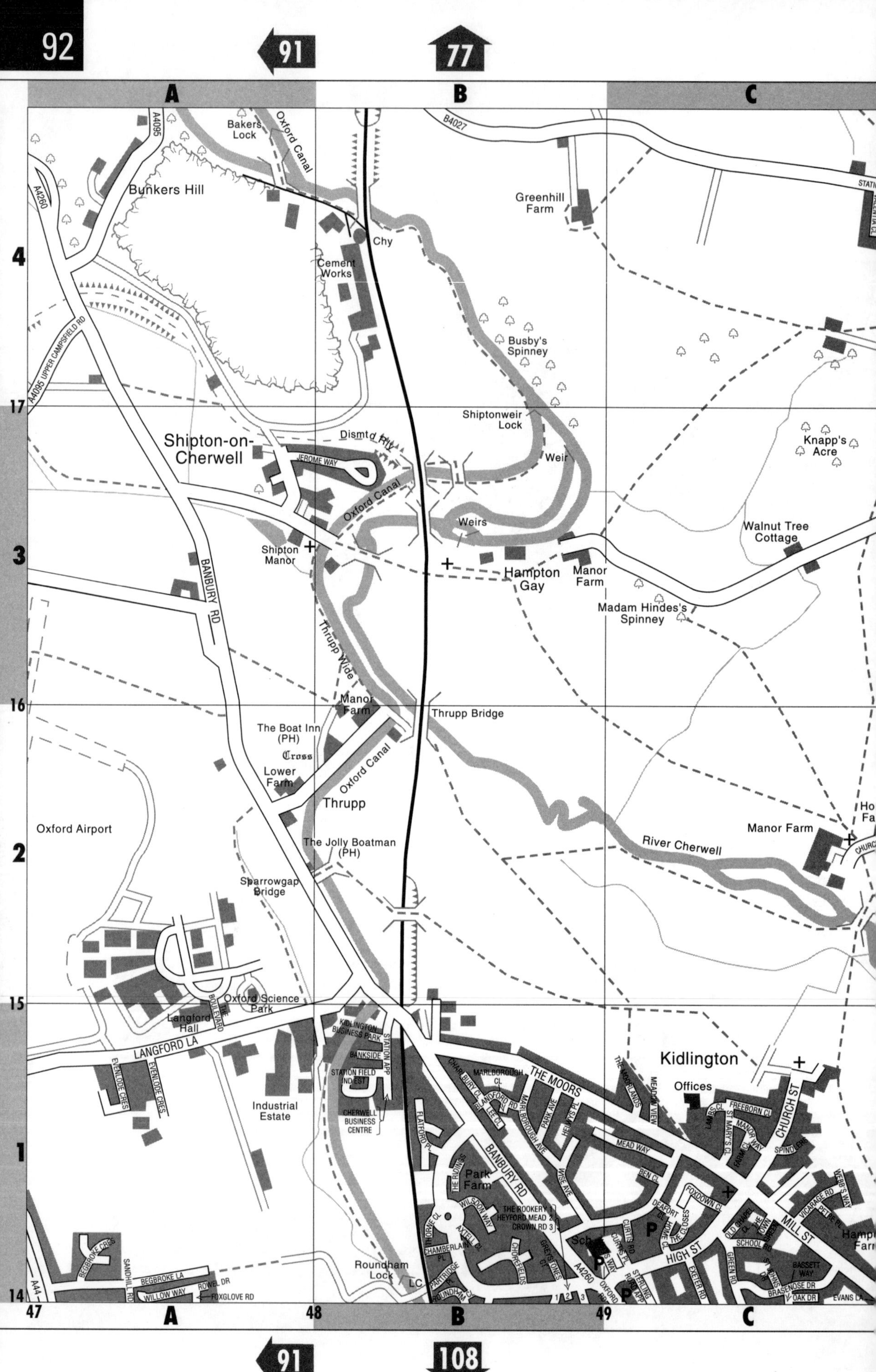
A
B
C
4
17
3
16
2
15
1
14
47
48
49
Bakers Lock
Oxford Canal
Bunkers Hill
Chy
Cement Works
Greenhill Farm
B4027
A4095
A4260
A4095 UPPER CAMPSFIELD RD
Busby's Spinney
Shiptonweir Lock
Knapp's Acre
Shipton-on-Cherwell
JEROME WAY
Dismtd Rly
Weir
Weirs
Shipton Manor
Hampton Gay
Manor Farm
Walnut Tree Cottage
Madam Hindes's Spinney
BANBURY RD
Thrupp Wide
Manor Farm
Thrupp Bridge
The Boat Inn (PH)
Cross
Lower Farm
Thrupp
Oxford Airport
River Cherwell
Manor Farm
The Jolly Boatman (PH)
Sparrowgap Bridge
Oxford Science Park
Langford Hall
THE BOULEVARD
LANGFORD LA
KIDLINGTON BUSINESS PARK
BANKSIDE
STATION APP
STATION FIELD IND EST
CHERWELL BUSINESS CENTRE
Industrial Estate
EVENLODE CRES
Kidlington
Offices
THE MOORS
MARLBOROUGH CL
LANGFORD RD
MARLBOROUGH AVE
PARK AVE
HELWYS PL
THE MOORLANDS
MEADOW VIEW
MEAD WAY
BEN CL
FREEBORN CL
LAMBS CL
ST MARY'S CL
MANOR WAY
CHURCH ST
FARM CL
SPINDLERS
FLATFORD PL
Park Farm
THE RIDINGS
WILSON WAY
THE ROOKERY 1
HEYFORD MEAD 2
CROWN RD 3
WISE AVE
FOXDOWN CL
VICARAGE RD
WEBB'S WAY
MILL ST
THOMAS CL
AXTELL CL
CHAMBERLAIN PL
CHOREFIELDS
GREYSTONES CT
CURTIS RD
THE CLOSES
HIGH ST
SCHOOL RD
SCHOOL
GREEN RD
EXETER RD
BASSETT WAY
BRASENOSE DR
OAK DR
EVANS LA
PARTRIDGE PL
Roundham Lock
LC
BEGBROKE CRES
SANDHILL RD
BEGBROKE LA
WILLOW WAY
ROWEL DR
FOXGLOVE RD
A44
A4260
OXFORD RD
STERLING ROAD APP
Sch

91
108

D
E
F
Bletchingdon Park
Park Farm
Church End
NEW RD
CAUSEWAY
PH
Sch
Bletchingdon
ISLIP RD
Manor Farm
Home Farm
OXFORD RD
Walker's Copse
Grove Farm
Black Leys
Pinchgate Lane
Dolly's Barn
College Farm
Diamond Farm
B4027
Heathfield House
Heathfield Farm
A34(T)
The Lodge
Frogsnest Farm
Heathfield Cottages
Model Farm
BLETCHINGDON RD
Hampton Poyle
Bell Inn (PH)
OXFORD RD
Brick Kiln Farm
Hampton Gorse
Field Barn Farm
Chipping Farm
River Cherwell
Weir
Weir
WATERMEAD
BICESTER RD
A34(T)
BLETCHINGDON RD
Islip Station
Manor Farm
Sch
KIDLINGTON RD
CHURCH CL
B4027
HIGH ST
MIDDLE WAY
NORTH ST
MIDDLE ST
CHURCH SQ
KING'S HEAD LA
LOWER ST
THE RISE
CHURCH LA
THE WALK
4
17
3
16
2
15
1
14
51
52

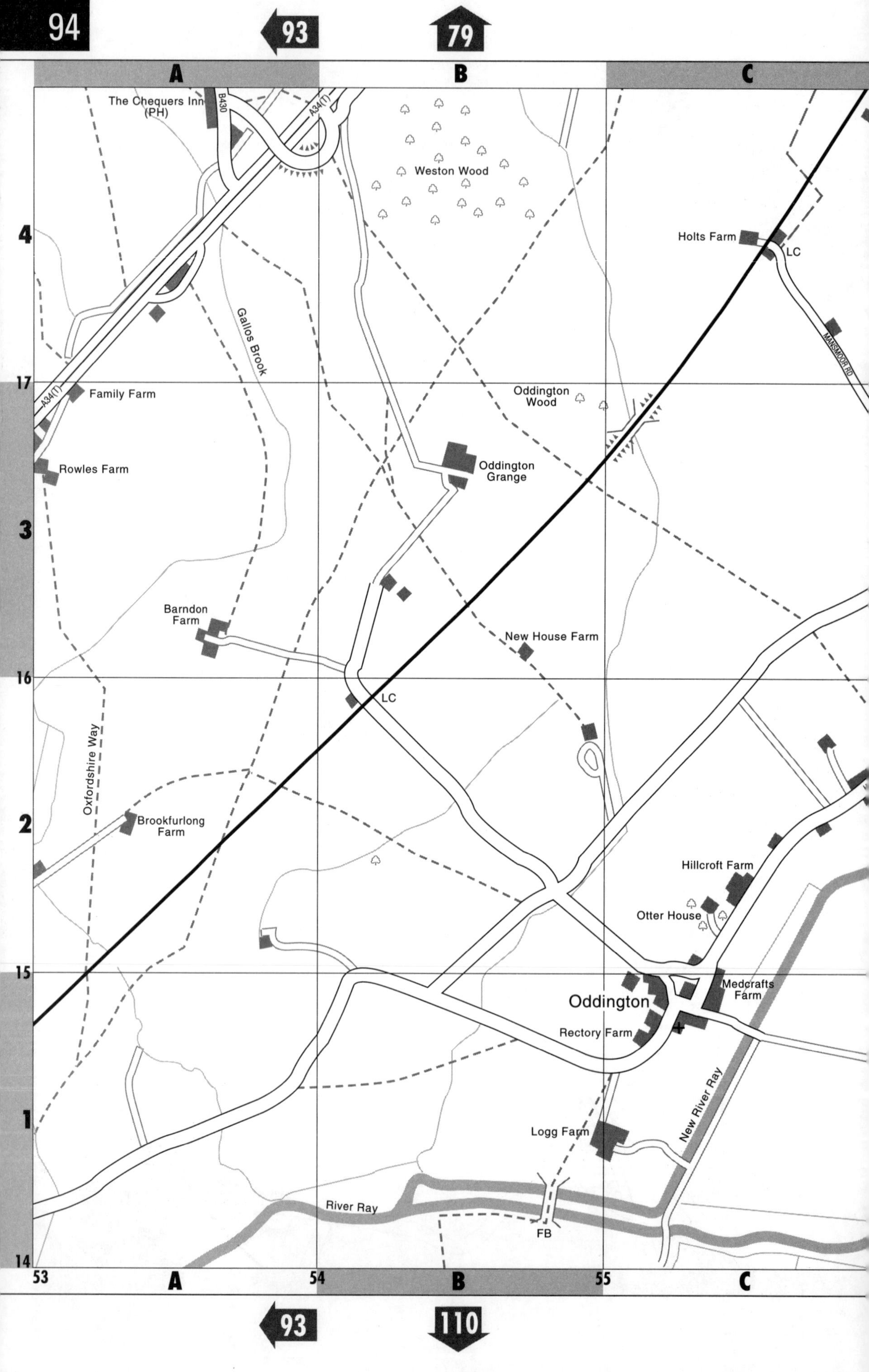

A   B   C

The Chequers Inn
(PH)

B430

A34(T)

Weston Wood

Holts Farm   LC

HARDMOOR RD

4

Gallos Brook

A34(T)

17

Family Farm

Oddington
Wood

Oddington
Grange

Rowles Farm

3

Barndon
Farm

New House Farm

Oxfordshire Way

16

LC

Brookfurlong
Farm

Hillcroft Farm

2

Otter House

Medcrafts
Farm

15

Oddington

Rectory Farm

New River Ray

1

Logg Farm

River Ray

FB

14

53   A   54   B   55   C

D E F

Sewage Works

West End
Farm

PH

Merton

River Ray

17

Street Hill

ROMAN ROAD
(course of)

3

NEWGATE RD

M40

Fencott Bridge

Bridge House
Farm

The
Homestead

Mill Lane

Bull's
Lane

Pound Lane

Wks

MILL LA.

Fencott

CHURCH VIEW

Sch

Manor Farm

16

FENCOTT RD

Murcott

EW POND LA

THE BROADWAY

Moor Lands

Field Lane

HIGH ST

Charlton-on-Otmoor

Fiveacres

PH

SMITH LA

New River Ray

PH

Pigeonhouse
Farm

2

OTMOOR LA

PIGEONHOUSE LA

15

1

Ot Moor

Danger Area

14

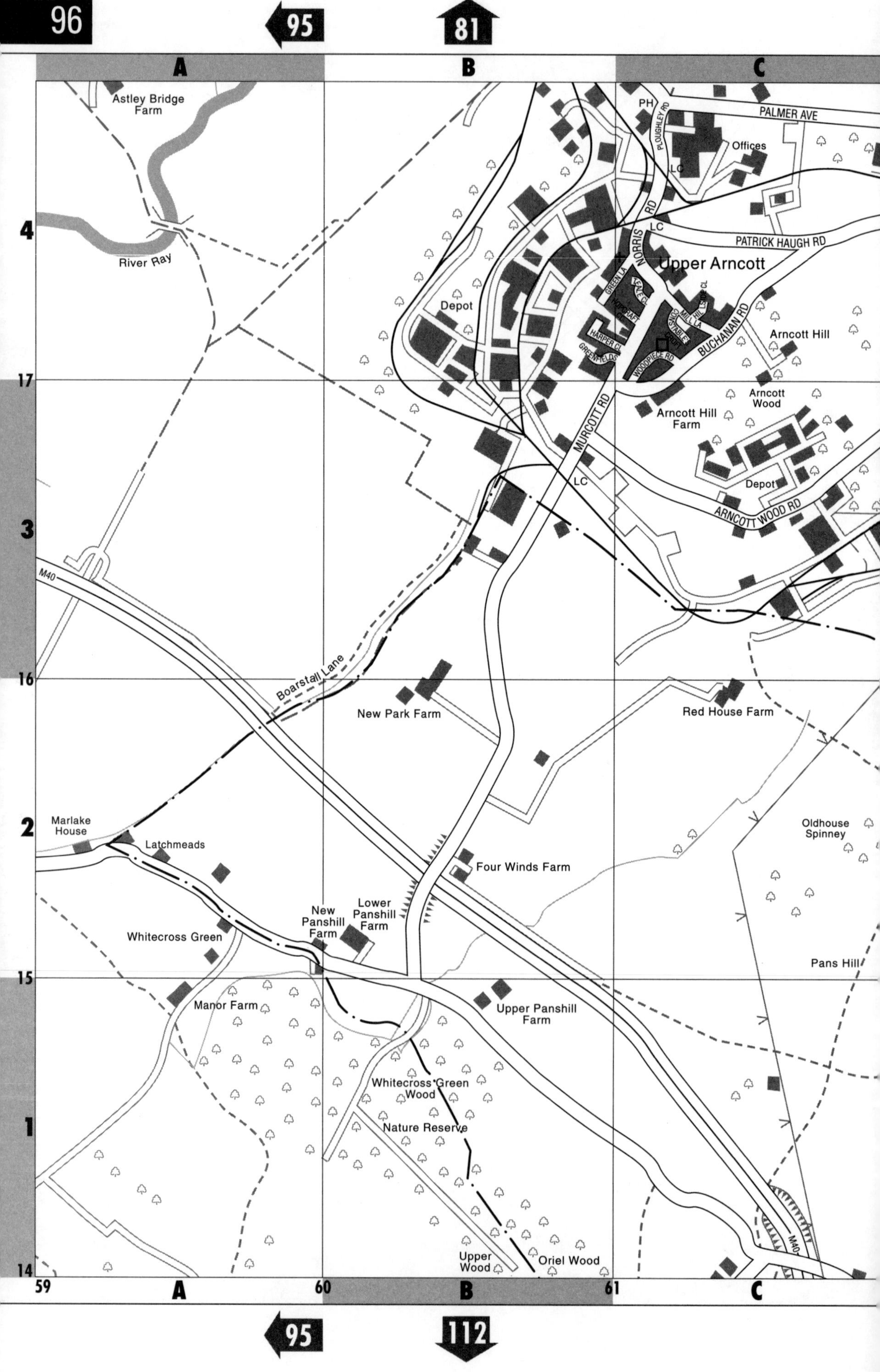

A   B   C

Astley Bridge
Farm

River Ray

PLOUGHLEY RD
PALMER AVE
Offices
LC
LC
PATRICK HAUGH RD

4

NORRIS RD
Upper Arncott

Depot

PH

GREEN LA
TAYLOR CL

MIRRI LA
INGLE ST CL

BUCHANAN RD

Arncott Hill

Arncott
Wood

HARPER CL
GREENFIELDS
WOODRIDGE RD

Arncott Hill
Farm

Depot

17

MURCOTT RD
LC

ARNCOTT WOOD RD

3

M40

Boarstall Lane

16

New Park Farm

Red House Farm

2

Marlake
House
Latchmeads

Oldhouse
Spinney

Four Winds Farm

Whitecross Green

New
Panshill
Farm

Lower
Panshill
Farm

Pans Hill

15

Manor Farm

Upper Panshill
Farm

Whitecross Green
Wood

Nature Reserve

1

M40

Upper
Wood   Oriel Wood

14

D E F

Sports Ground

PALMER AVE

B4011

Depot

Rookery Farm

LOWER END

LC

WIDNELL LA

ARNCOTT RD

Ludgershall RD

Piddington

4

PATRICK HAUGH RD

LC

Seven Stars (PH)

EASTBROOK CL

Laurell Farm

17

HM Prison

Lower Farm

THAME RD

VICARAGE LA

LC

Depot

Hill Farm

LC

3

Piddington Wood

Chilling Place Stud

Clue-Hills Farm

Piddington Gate

B4011

16

Little Wood

Corble Farm

Muswellhill Farm

2

Oakcroft Farm

Muswell Hill

Boarstall Decoy

Decoy Pond

Nature Reserve

15

Muswell Hill Farm House

Manor Farm

Middle Farm

1

Tower Farm

Village Farm

Boarstall

Touchbridge

Tower

Moat

Moat

B4011

Spar Green

14

A   B   C

Nursery

Kings Farm

PIDDINGTON RD

D'Oyley's Farm

BICESTER RD

Rookery Farm

The Green

DUCK LA

Bridge Farm

Ludgershall

Bull & Butcher (PH)

SOLTERS CL

BROOK CL

SALTERS LA

Manor Farm

Tittershall Wood

4

WHITE HART

HIGH ST

Ludgershall Farm

Glebe Farm

CHURCH LA

Sch

BRILL RD

Moat

WOTTON END

17

KINGSWOOD LA

The Lake

Clearfields Farm

3

Long Wood

The Warre

Poletrees Farm

Lapland Farm

16

The Warre

Fivearch Bridge

Fivearch Wood

Grenville's Wood

Rushbeds Wood (Nature Reserve)

2

Lawn Farm

Tramway Farm

Rid's Hill

15

Brillbury Hall Farm

Coldharbour Farm

Springfield Farm

Brill Common

1

North Hill

Dorton Park Farm

TRAMHILL

Chinkwell Wood

Dorton

WINDMILL ST

Brill

Windmill

TEMPLE ST

HIGHLAND CL

Brook Farm

PH

Sch

Sta

Court

14

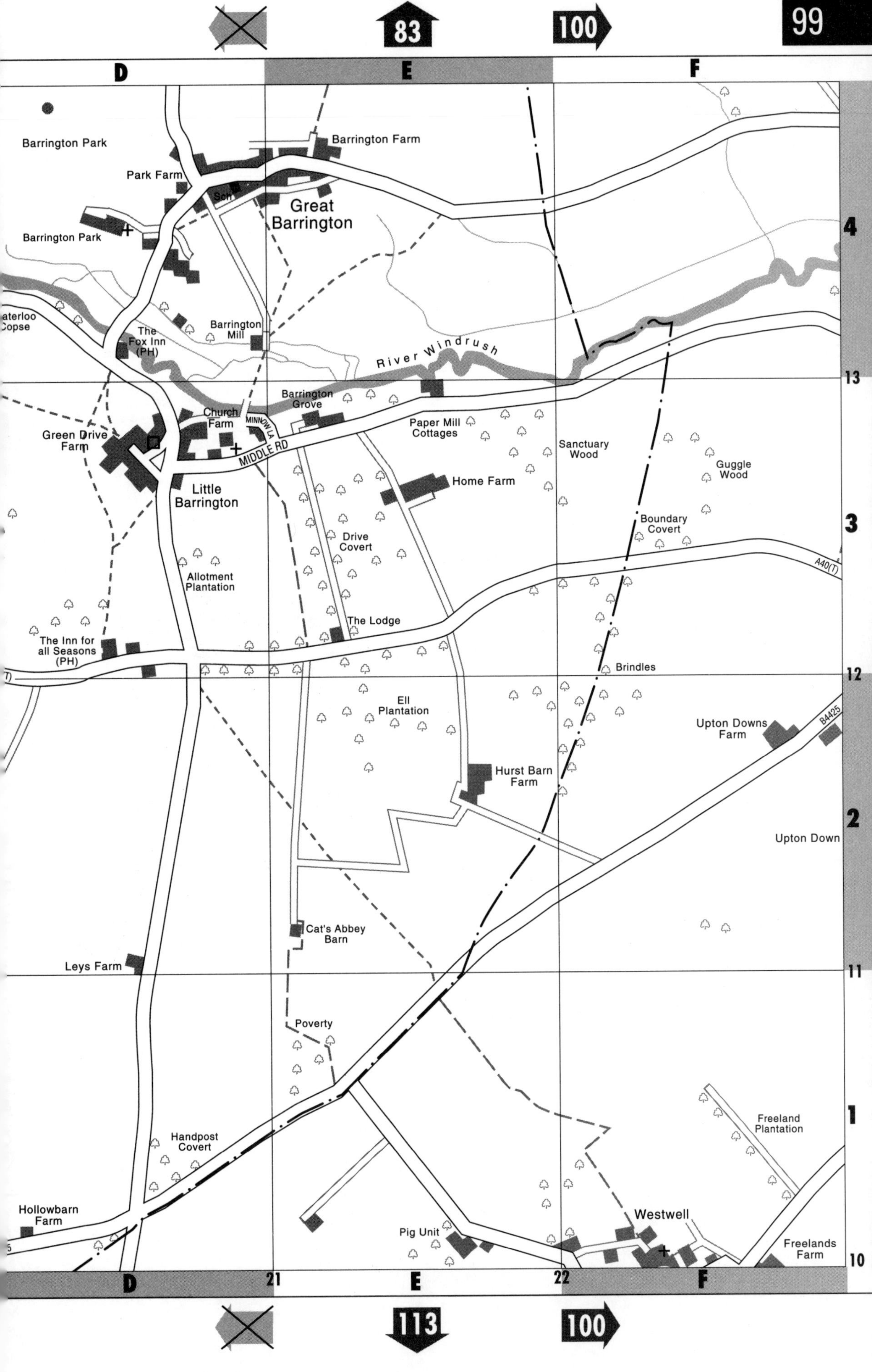

83   100

D   E   F

Barrington Park

Park Farm

Barrington Farm

Barrington Park

Great
Barrington

Sch

4

Waterloo
Copse

The
Fox Inn
(PH)

Barrington
Mill

River Windrush

13

Green Drive
Farm

Church
Farm

Barrington
Grove

MIDDLE RD

MINNOW LA

Paper Mill
Cottages

Sanctuary
Wood

Guggle
Wood

Little
Barrington

Home Farm

Boundary
Covert

3

Drive
Covert

Allotment
Plantation

A40(T)

The Inn for
all Seasons
(PH)

The Lodge

Brindles

12

Ell
Plantation

Upton Downs
Farm

B4425

Hurst Barn
Farm

2

Upton Down

Leys Farm

Cat's Abbey
Barn

11

Poverty

Freeland
Plantation

1

Handpost
Covert

Hollowbarn
Farm

Pig Unit

Westwell

Freelands
Farm

10

D   21   E   22   F

113   100

99
84

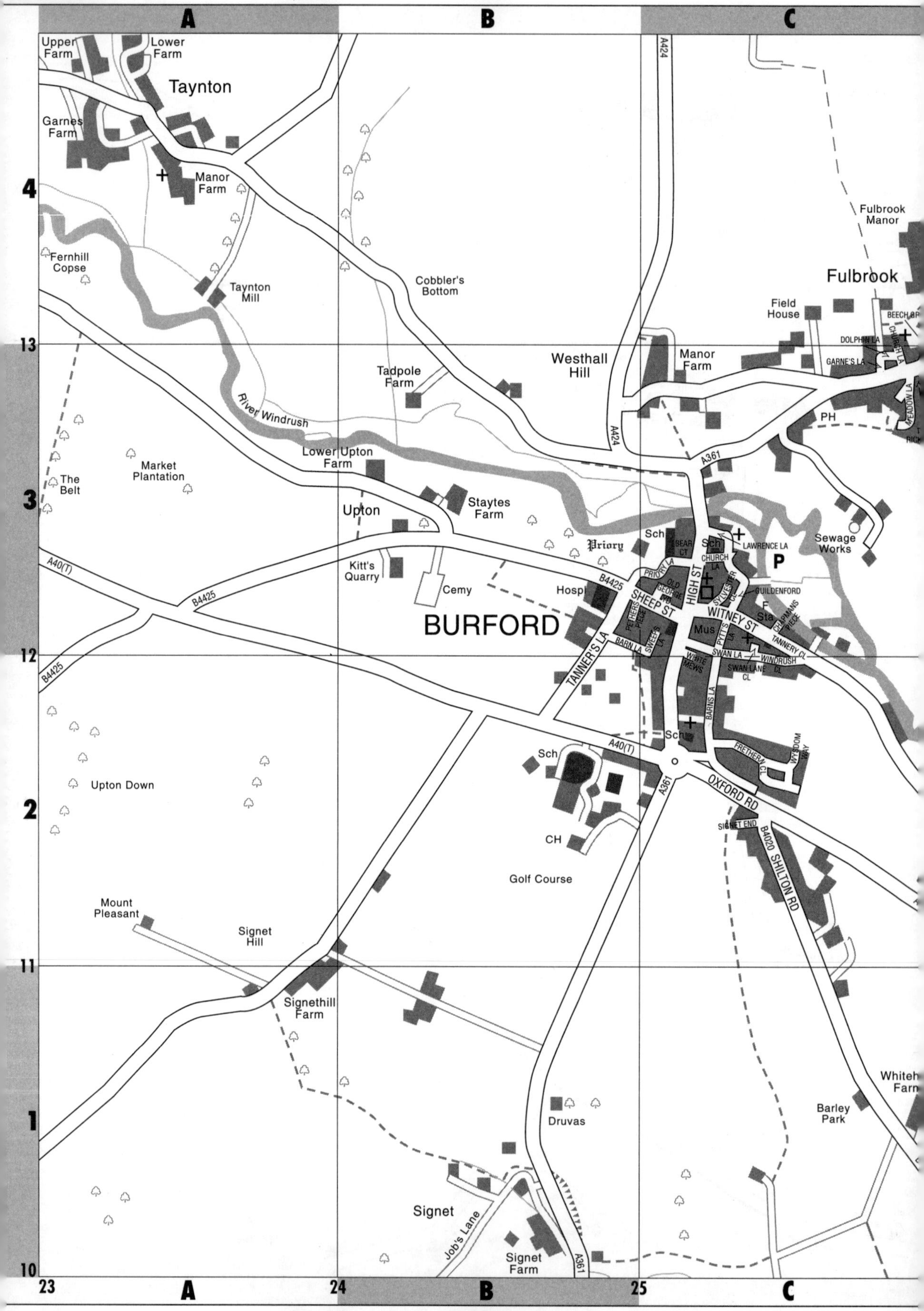
A
B
C
Upper Farm
Lower Farm
Taynton
Garnes Farm
Manor Farm
Fernhill Copse
Taynton Mill
Cobbler's Bottom
Fulbrook Manor
Fulbrook
Field House
Westhall Hill
Manor Farm
Tadpole Farm
River Windrush
PH
A424
A361
Lower Upton Farm
Market Plantation
The Belt
Upton
Staytes Farm
Kitt's Quarry
Cemy
Priory
Sch
Hospl
BURFORD
HIGH ST
SHEEP ST
WITNEY ST
LAWRENCE LA
GUILDENFORD
Sewage Works
P
Mus
F Sta
SWAN LA
WINDRUSH CL
TANNER'S LA
BARN LA
BARNS LA
A40(T)
B4425
OXFORD RD
SIGNET END
B4020 SHILTON RD
FRETHERNE CL
WYSDOM WAY
Upton Down
Sch
CH
Golf Course
Mount Pleasant
Signet Hill
Signethill Farm
Druvas
Barley Park
Signet
Job's Lane
Signet Farm
4
13
3
12
2
11
1
10
23
24
25

99
114

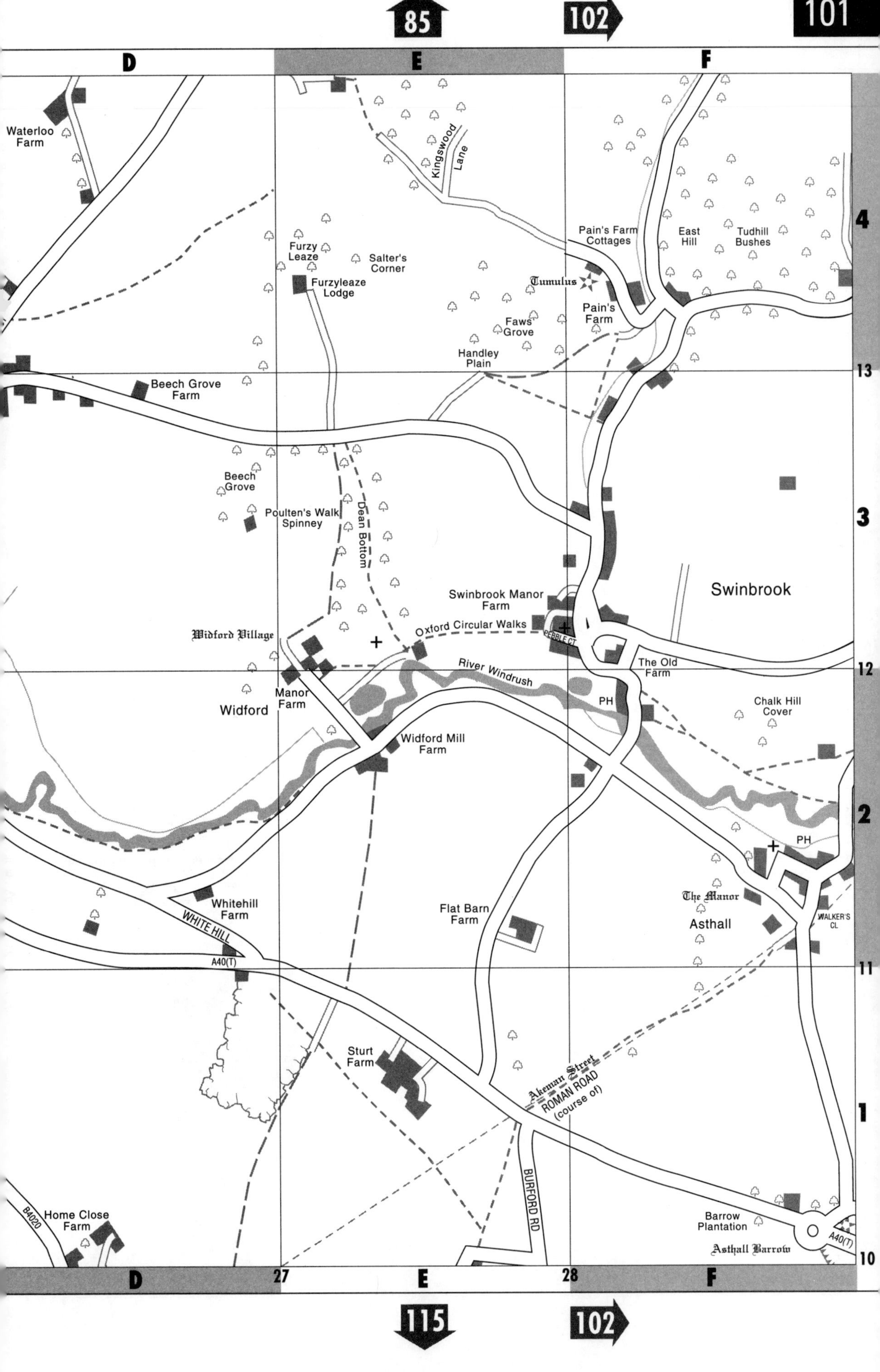

D   E   F

Waterloo Farm

Kingswood Lane

Furzy Leaze

Salter's Corner

Furzyleaze Lodge

Pain's Farm Cottages

East Hill

Tudhill Bushes

4

Tumulus

Pain's Farm

Faws Grove

Handley Plain

Beech Grove Farm

13

Beech Grove

Poulten's Walk Spinney

Dean Bottom

Swinbrook Manor Farm

Swinbrook

3

Widford Village

Oxford Circular Walks

PEBBLE CT

The Old Farm

River Windrush

Chalk Hill Cover

12

Widford

Manor Farm

PH

Widford Mill Farm

The Manor

PH

2

Whitehill Farm

WHITE HILL

Flat Barn Farm

Asthall

WALKER'S CL

A40(T)

11

Sturt Farm

Akeman Street
ROMAN ROAD
(course of)

1

Home Close Farm

B4020

BURFORD RD

Barrow Plantation

Asthall Barrow

A40(T)

10

D   27   E   28   F

A B C

4

Hens Grove

Roustage

Tumuli

Fordwells

Lovegrove
Holding

BUTTERMILK LA

Home Farm

Field
Assarts

MINSTER RIDING

Bockett's
Corner

Stockley Copse

Wisdom's Bottom

13

College Farm
Asthall Leigh

Olde Farm

Pool's
Bottom

Wisdom's
Copse

The
Grove

Postern
Bottom

Standridge
Copse

3

Holywell
Barn

Pinnocks
Farm

Akeman Street
ROMAN ROAD
(course of)

Bangry
Bottom

MINSTER RIDING

NINETY CUT HILL

Worsham Turn
Cottage

Worsham
Turn

Shorthazel
Bottom

12

Quarry
(dis)

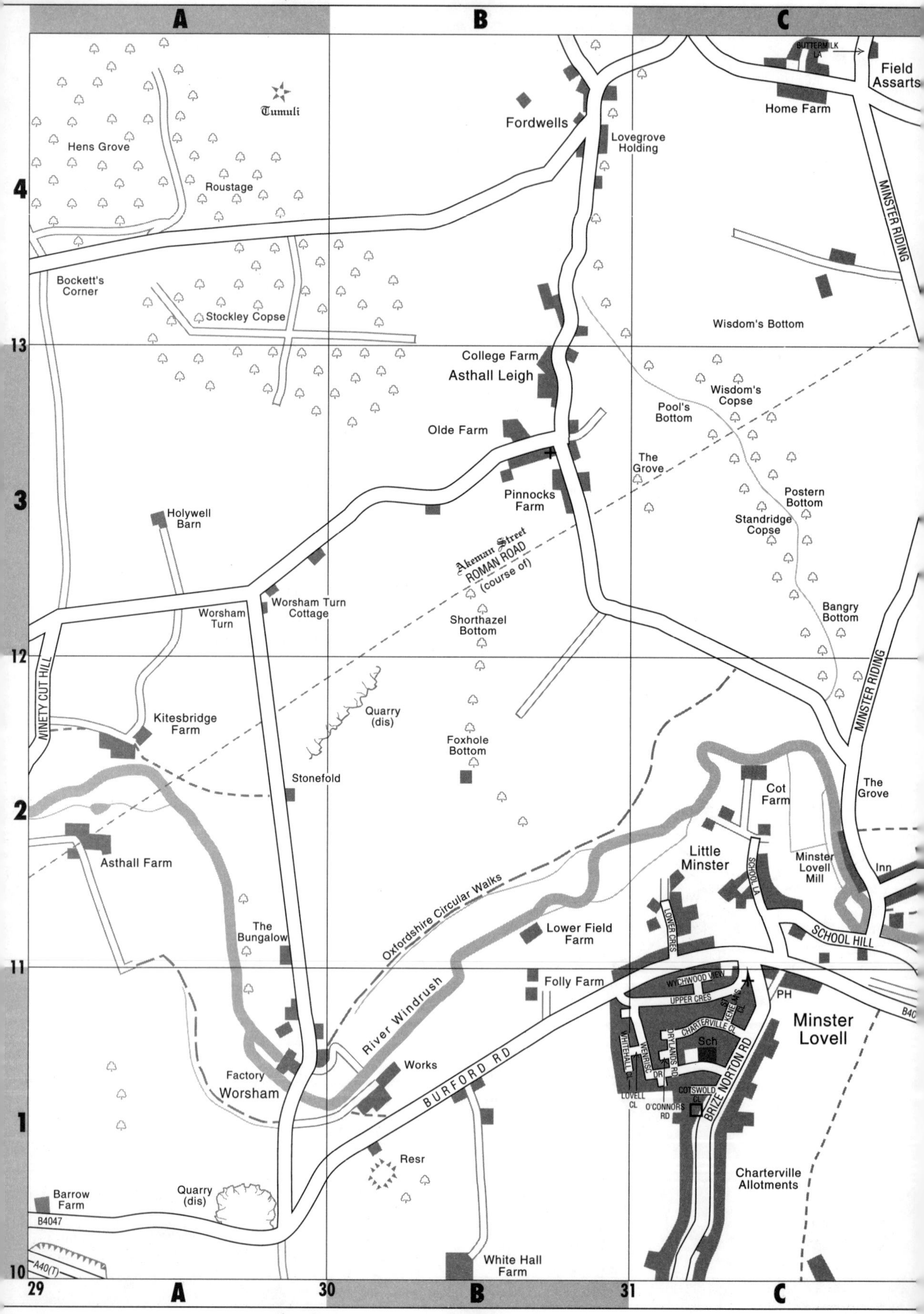

Foxhole
Bottom

Kitesbridge
Farm

Stonefold

Cot
Farm

The
Grove

2

Asthall Farm

The
Bungalow

Oxfordshire Circular Walks

Lower Field
Farm

Little
Minster

Minster
Lovell
Mill

Inn

SCHOOL LA

SCHOOL HILL

11

River Windrush

Folly Farm

LOWER CRES

WYCHWOOD MEWS
UPPER CRES

PH

B4047

Minster
Lovell

Factory
Worsham

Works

BURFORD RD

WHITEHILL CL
WELROSE
DR
DRYLANDS RD

CHARTERVILLE CL

ST KENELMS
BRIZE NORTON RD
COTSWOLD

Sch

1

LOVELL
CL
O'CONNORS
RD

Charterville
Allotments

Barrow
Farm

Quarry
(dis)

Resr

B4047

10

A40(T)

White Hall
Farm

29 A 30 B 31 C

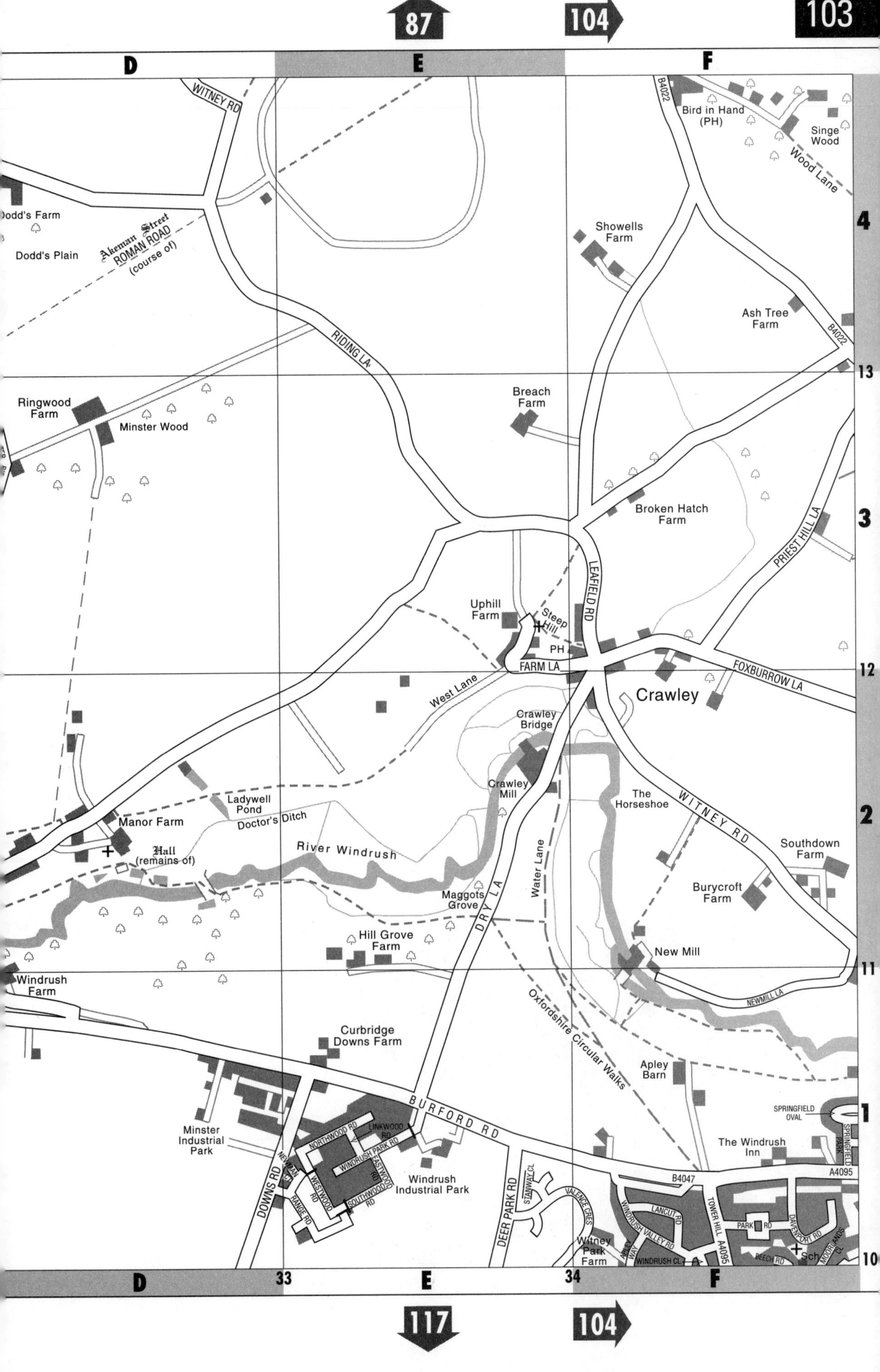

WITNEY RD

Bird in Hand (PH)

Singe Wood

Wood Lane

Dodd's Farm

Akeman Street ROMAN ROAD (course of)

Dodd's Plain

Showells Farm

4

Ash Tree Farm

B4022

RIDING LA.

13

Ringwood Farm

Minster Wood

Breach Farm

Broken Hatch Farm

PRIEST HILL LA.

3

Uphill Farm

Steep Hill

PH

LEAFIELD RD

Crawley

FOXBURROW LA.

12

FARM LA.

West Lane

Crawley Bridge

Crawley Mill

The Horseshoe

WITNEY RD

Southdown Farm

2

Ladywell Pond

Doctor's Ditch

Water Lane

Burycroft Farm

Manor Farm

Hall (remains of)

River Windrush

Maggots Grove

DRY LA.

New Mill

11

Hill Grove Farm

NEWMILL LA.

Windrush Farm

Oxfordshire Circular Walks

Curbridge Downs Farm

Apley Barn

Springfield Oval

1

BURFORD RD

Minster Industrial Park

NORTHWOOD RD

LINKWOOD RD

EASTWOOD RD

WINDRUSH PARK RD

The Windrush Inn

SPRINGFIELD PARK

DOWNS RD

NEW WAY

WESTWOOD RD

RANGE RD

SOUTHWOOD RD

Windrush Industrial Park

DEER PARK RD

STANWAY CL

VALENCE CRES

B4047

A4095

Witney Park Farm

WINDRUSH VALLEY RD

LANGUT RD

TOWER HILL

PARK RD

DAVENPORT RD

BEECH RD

A4095

MOOR CL

Sch

WINDRUSH CL

10

A B C

Turley Farm

TURLEY LA

Gigley Farm

The Bungalow

North Leigh Lane

Delly End

DELLY R

WHITINGS LA

4

Common Leys Farm

Hickrall

Taylor's Copse

HATFIELD PITS LA

Breach Lane

The Hydes

NEW YATT LA

New Yatt

New Yatt Farm

Manor House

Breach Farm

Keepers Cottage

Business Centre

KILE Lane

GREEN L

13

DELLY HILL B4022

GIBRALLS LA

Middletown

Sch PH

Job's Copse

PH

Home Farm

Moorland Farm

NEW RD

HENRY'S

Hailey

Spicers Lane

Heath Holm Farm

CHURCH LA

Poffley End

3

CHAPEL LA

POFFLEY END LA

SWANHALL LA

Swanhall Farm

Witheridge Farm

Witheridge Cross

Water Lane

12

FOXBURROW LA

FOX CL

University Farm

Downhill Farm

Osney Hill Farm

A40

DOWNHILL LA

Highcroft Farm

Merryfield Farm

The Bungalow

2

MILKING LA

Sch

Middlefield Farm

Sch

Cogges Wood

SCHOFIELD AVE

HOYLES RD

HAILEY RD

EASTFIELD RD

TANNER RD

NEW YATT RD

TARRANT AVE

11

WITNEY RD

WESTFIELD

TAPHOUSE AVE

CHESTNUT CL

VINER CL

WOODSTOCK RD

CRAWLEY RD

B4022

FARMERS CL

FARMERS CL

SYCAMORE

MADLEY CL

EARLY RD

BAKERS PIECE

WEST END

PIE CRESCENT

Sch

Northfield Farm

SPRINGFIELD OVAL

River Windrush

Wks

WOODGREEN HILL

WOODLANDS RD

Madley Brook

SPRINGFIELD PARK

Mills

WEST END NORTH

WOODGREEN

Woodgreen

WITNEY

BURFORD RD A4095

MILL ST

RIVERSIDE RD

HIGH ST

BRIDGE ST

NEWLAND

NEWLANDS MILL

Newland

MOOR AVE

DARK CL

PUCK LA

GLOUCESTER PL

THE OLD COACHYARD

THE WILLOWS

WREN WAY

B4022

COURTS GDNS

Sch

MOORLAND RD

Hospl

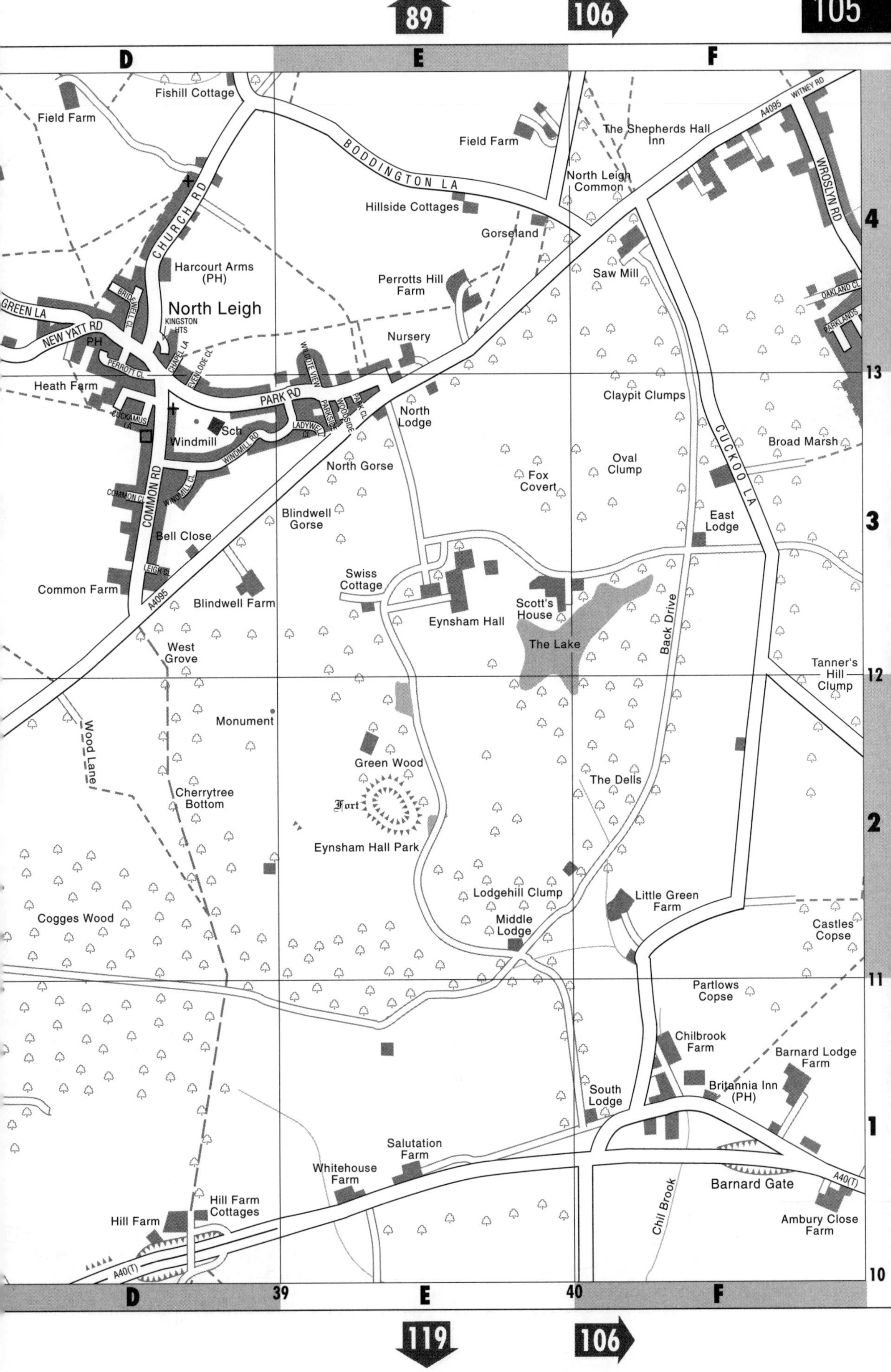

D
E
F

Fishill Cottage
Field Farm
Field Farm
BODDINGTON LA
The Shepherds Hall Inn
North Leigh Common
A4095
WITNEY RD
WROSLYN RD
Hillside Cottages
Gorseland
North Leigh Common
4
Harcourt Arms (PH)
Perrotts Hill Farm
Saw Mill
OAKLAND CL
CHURCH RD
GREEN LA
North Leigh
PARKLANDS
NEW YATT RD
PH
KINGSTON HTS
Nursery
13
Heath Farm
PARK RD
North Lodge
Claypit Clumps
Broad Marsh
Windmill
Sch
North Gorse
Fox Covert
Oval Clump
North Lodge
CUCKOO LA
3
Blindwell Gorse
East Lodge
Bell Close
LEIGH CL
A4095
Common Farm
Blindwell Farm
Swiss Cottage
Eynsham Hall
Scott's House
The Lake
Back Drive
West Grove
Tanner's Hill Clump
12
Wood Lane
Monument
Cherrytree Bottom
Green Wood
The Dells
Fort
2
Eynsham Hall Park
Lodgehill Clump
Little Green Farm
Castles Copse
Cogges Wood
Middle Lodge
Partlows Copse
11
Chilbrook Farm
Barnard Lodge Farm
South Lodge
Britannia Inn (PH)
1
Salutation Farm
Whitehouse Farm
Chil Brook
Barnard Gate
A40(T)
Hill Farm Cottages
Hill Farm
Ambury Close Farm
A40(T)
10

D
39
E
40
F

105
90

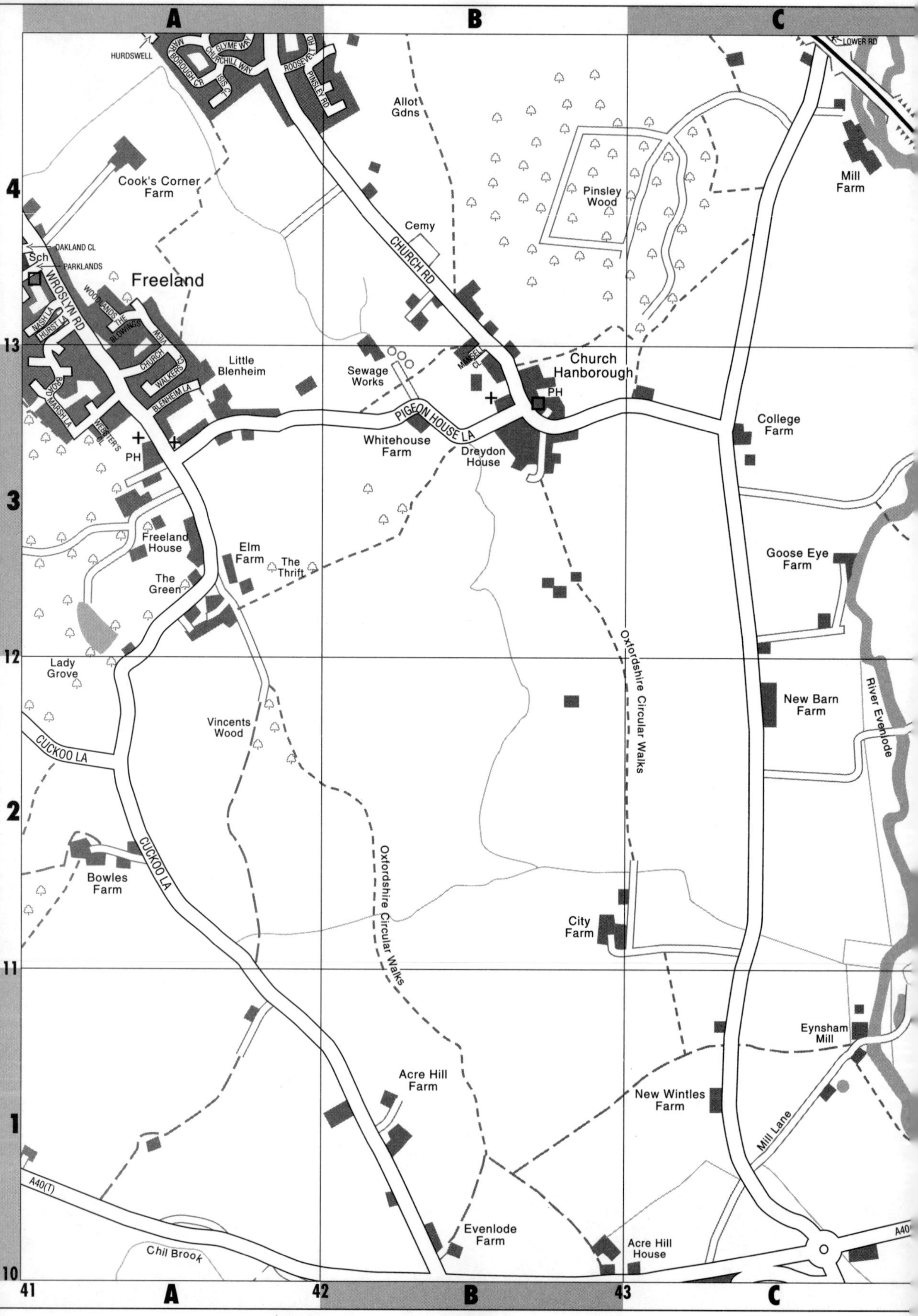

A   B   C

HURDSWELL

GLYME WAY
CHURCHILL WAY
ROOSEVELT RD
PINSLEY RD

Allot
Gdns

Pinsley Wood

Mill
Farm

LOWER RD

Cook's Corner
Farm

4

Cemy

CHURCH RD

OAKLAND CL
Sch
PARKLANDS

WROSLYN RD
WOODLANDS
HURST CL
BLOWINGS

Freeland

13

Little
Blenheim

Sewage
Works

MURSELL
CL

Church
Hanborough

PH

College
Farm

CHURCH
WALKER'S
BLENHEIM LA
PEETER'S
MARSH LA

PH

PIGEON HOUSE LA

Whitehouse
Farm

Dreydon
House

3

Freeland
House

Elm
Farm

The
Thrift

Goose Eye
Farm

The
Green

Oxfordshire Circular Walks

12

Lady
Grove

New Barn
Farm

River Evenlode

Vincents
Wood

CUCKOO LA

2

Oxfordshire Circular Walks

Bowles
Farm

CUCKOO LA

City
Farm

11

Acre Hill
Farm

Eynsham
Mill

New Wintles
Farm

1

MILL LANE

A40(T)

Evenlode
Farm

Acre Hill
House

A40

Chil Brook

10

41   A   42   B   43   C

105
120

Reservoir
Bladon Heath
Round Castle
Burleigh Lodge
Burleigh Wood
Worton Heath
Hall Farm
Priory
ST MICHAEL'S LA
SPRING HILL RD
Dolton Lane
Begbroke Wood
Burleigh Farm
River Evenlode
Spring Hill
Frogwelldown Lane
Works
Purwell Farm
Jericho Farm
CASSINGTON RD
YARNTON RD
Rectory Farm
Worton
The Elms
ELMS RD
THE TENNIS
BELL CL
BELL LA
LYNTON LA
ORCHARD CL
THE GREEN
Cassington
Sch
ST PETER'S CL
CHURCH LA
HOLLOW FURLONG
Manor Farm
POUND LA
EYNSHAM RD
MANOR CL
MARLBOROUGH DR
HORSEMERE LA
Dismantled Railway
A40(T)
Marlborough Pool
Works
Durham Lane
Wharf Farm
River Thames or Isis
Oxfordshire Circular Walk
4
13
3
12
2
11
1
10
45
46

A
B
C
Begbroke
Rowel Brook
Parker's Farm
Begbroke Hill
SANDY LA
Sandy Lane Crossing
Yarnton
College Farm
Yarnton House
Sch
Little Blenheim
Frogwelldown Lane
Hill Farm
The Red Lion (PH)
The Grapes Inn (PH)
Yarnton Lane Crossing
Sewage Works
Kidlington Green Lock
Towing Path
Oxford Canal
Garden City
Stratfield Farm
Stratfield Brake
Stonehouse Farm
Ickworth
WOODSTOCK RD
CASSINGTON RD
Manor House
Mead Farm
Kingsbridge Brook
Frieze Farm
Swing-Bridge
Loop Farm
Dismtd Rly
Peartree Hill
Peartree Hill Roundabout
Motel
Golf Course
Service Area
Oxey Mead
Duke's Lock
Red Barn Farm Cottage
King's Weir
Pixey Mead
Yarnton or West Mead
River Thames or Isis
Oxfordshire Circular Walks
King's Lock
Weir
WESTERN BY-PASS RD
NORTHERN BY-PASS RD
Hotel
Manor Farm
A40(T)
A44
A4260
A44(T)
A34(T)
BICESTER RD
OXFORD RD
YARNTON RD
YARNTON LA
EVANS LA
Schs
Gosford
Liby
1 FERNHILL CL
2 MORRELL CL
3 BELGROVE CL
1 WOODSTOCK RD E
2 WOODSTOCK RD W
RUTTEN LA
4
3
2
1
13
12
11
10
47
48
49

93
110

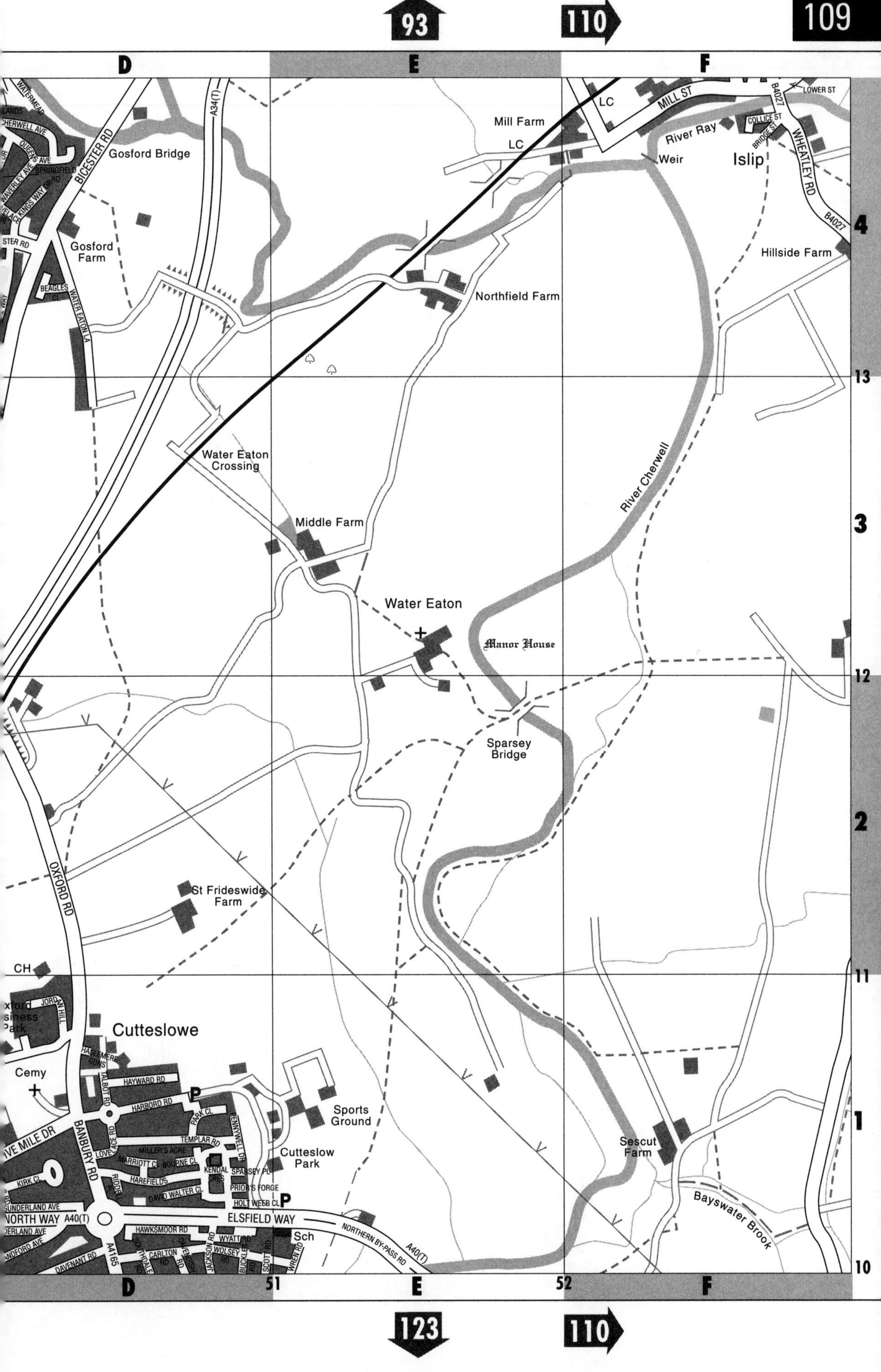
D
E
F
Mill Farm
LC
MILL ST
LOWER ST
B4027
COLLICE ST
BRIDGE ST
WHEATLEY RD
River Ray
Weir
Islip
Gosford Bridge
BICESTER RD
A34(T)
Gosford Farm
Hillside Farm
Northfield Farm
WATER EATON LA
BEAGLES CL
13
Water Eaton Crossing
Middle Farm
River Cherwell
3
Water Eaton
Manor House
12
Sparsey Bridge
2
OXFORD RD
St Frideswide Farm
CH
11
Cutteslowe
Cemy
HAYWARD RD
HARBORD RD
TALBOT RD
PARK CL
TEMPLAR RD
PENNYWELL DR
Sports Ground
Cutteslow Park
1
Sescut Farm
BANBURY RD
FIVE MILE DR
MILLER'S ACRE
MARRIOTT CL
BOURNE CL
HAREFIELDS
DAVID WALTER CL
KENDAL CRES
SPARSEY PL
PRIOR'S FORGE
HOLT WEEB CL
SUNDERLAND AVE
NORTH WAY
A40(T)
ELSFIELD WAY
HAWKSMOOR RD
WYATT RD
NORTHERN BY-PASS RD
Sch
Bayswater Brook
A4165
CARLTON RD
JACKSON RD
WOLSEY RD
SCOTT RD
WREN RD
DAVENANT RD
10
51
52

123
110

109
94

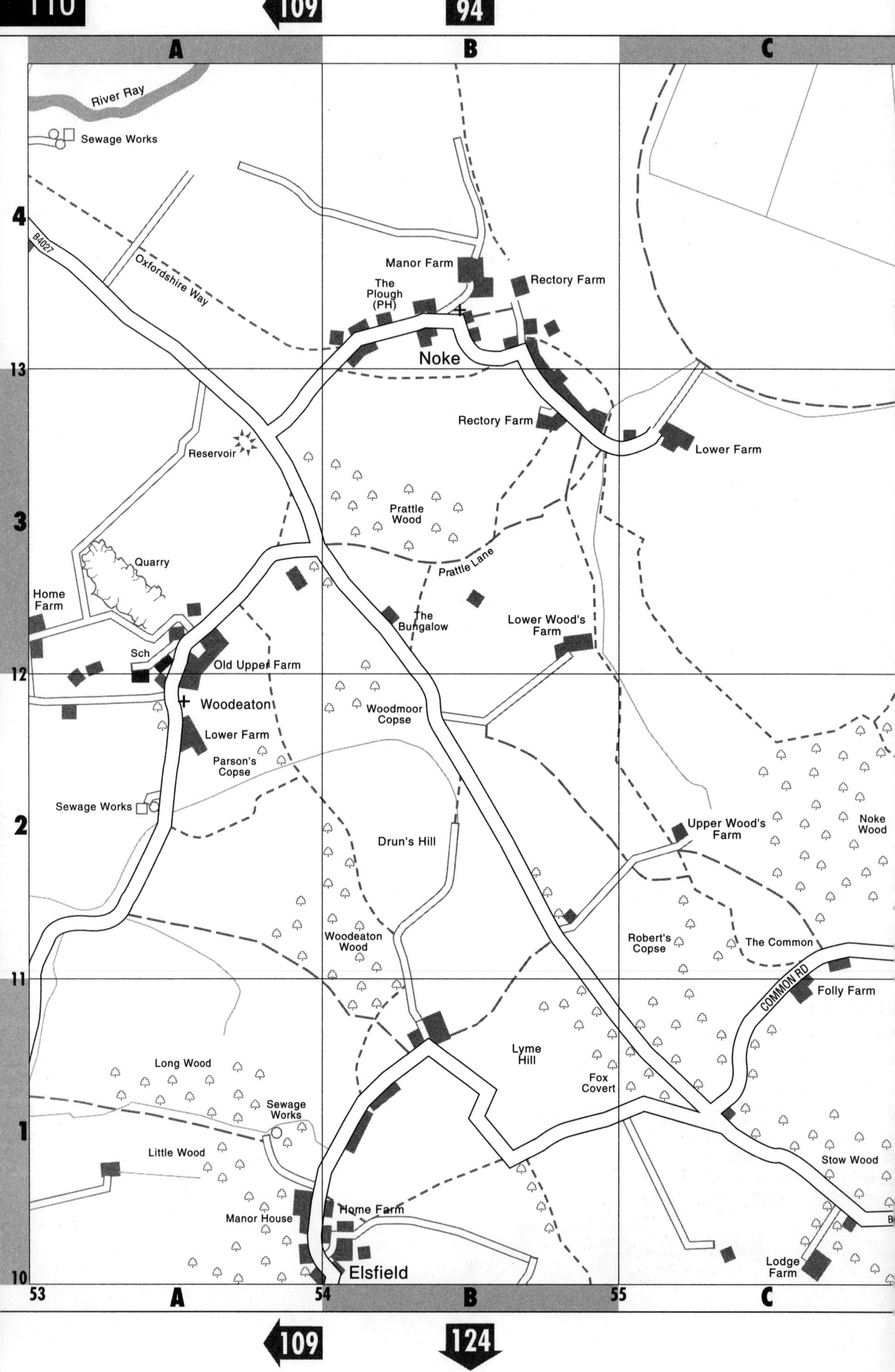
A
B
C
River Ray
Sewage Works
4
B4027
Oxfordshire Way
Manor Farm
The Plough (PH)
Rectory Farm
Noke
13
Rectory Farm
Lower Farm
Reservoir
3
Prattle Wood
Quarry
Prattle Lane
Home Farm
The Bungalow
Lower Wood's Farm
Sch
Old Upper Farm
12
Woodeaton
Woodmoor Copse
Lower Farm
Parson's Copse
Sewage Works
2
Upper Wood's Farm
Noke Wood
Drun's Hill
Woodeaton Wood
Robert's Copse
The Common
11
COMMON RD
Folly Farm
Lyme Hill
Long Wood
Fox Covert
Sewage Works
1
Little Wood
Stow Wood
Home Farm
Manor House
Lodge Farm
Elsfield
10
53
54
55

109
124

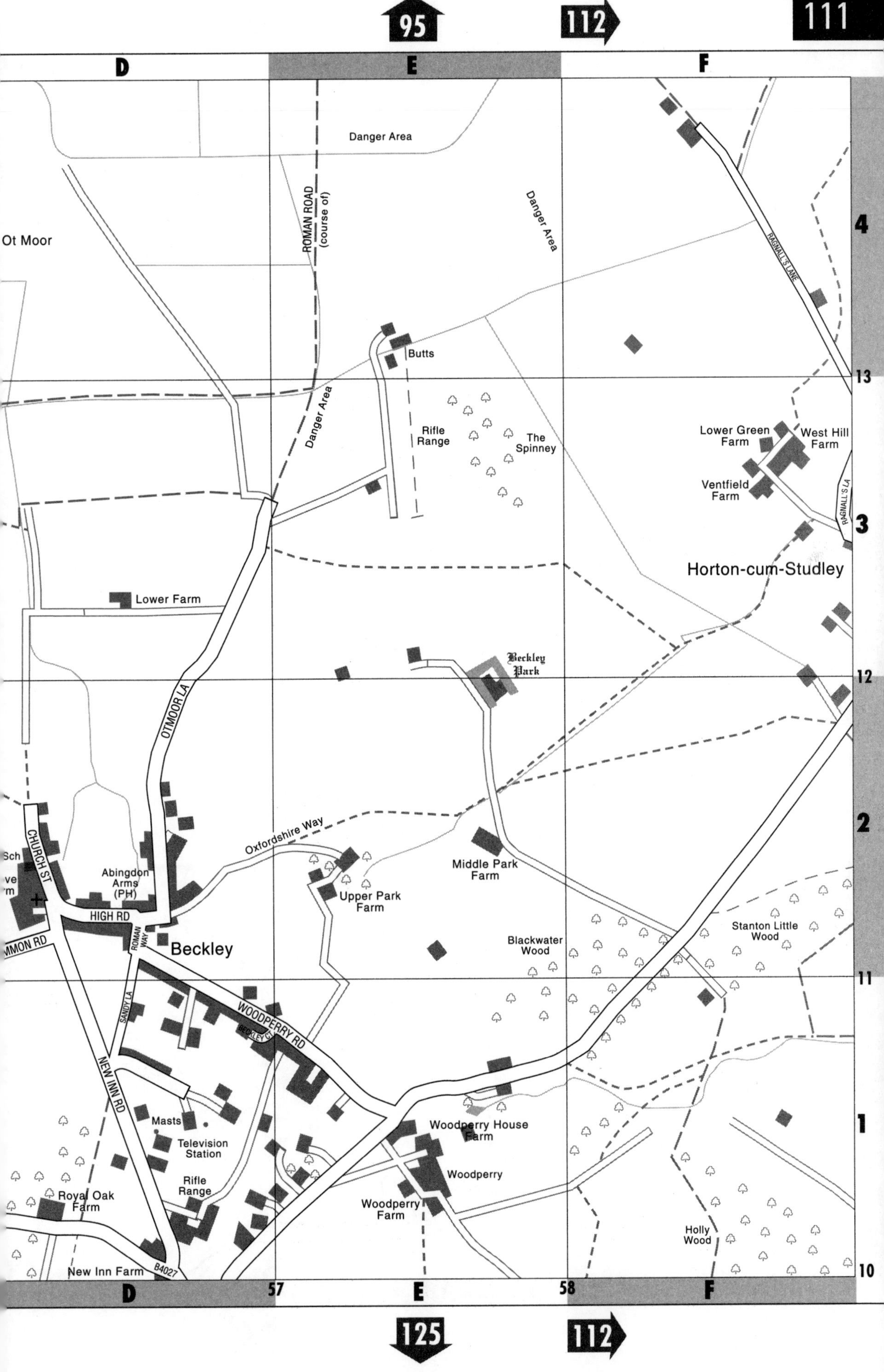

D
E
F

4

Ot Moor

Danger Area

ROMAN ROAD (course of)

Danger Area

RAGNALL'S LANE

13

Butts

Rifle Range

The Spinney

Lower Green Farm

West Hill Farm

Ventfield Farm

RAGNALL'S LA

3

Horton-cum-Studley

Danger Area

Lower Farm

Beckley Park

12

OTMOOR LA

2

Sch

Oxfordshire Way

Middle Park Farm

Stanton Little Wood

ve m

CHURCH ST

Abingdon Arms (PH)

Upper Park Farm

Blackwater Wood

+

HIGH RD

ROMAN WAY

MMON RD

Beckley

11

SANDY LA

WOODPERRY RD

BECKLEY

1

NEW INN RD

Masts

Television Station

Woodperry House Farm

Rifle Range

Woodperry

Royal Oak Farm

Woodperry Farm

Holly Wood

New Inn Farm

B4027

10

D
57
E
58
F

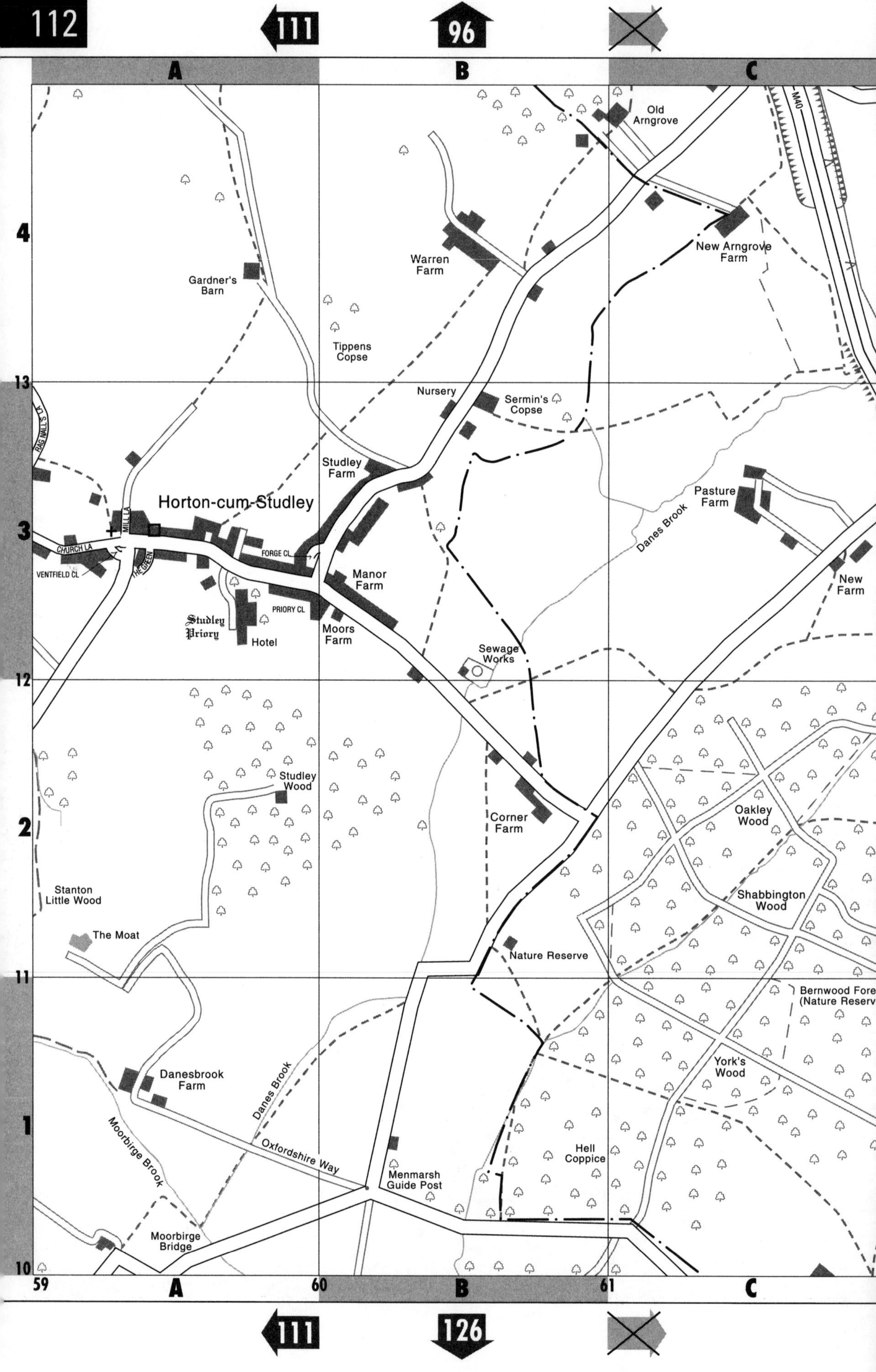

A   **B**   **C**

4

Old Arngrove

Gardner's Barn

Warren Farm

New Arngrove Farm

Tippens Copse

13

Nursery

Sermin's Copse

Studley Farm

Pasture Farm

Horton-cum-Studley

Danes Brook

3

RAG HALL'S CT.

CHURCH LA

MILL LA

THE GREEN

VENTFIELD CL.

FORGE CL.

Manor Farm

New Farm

Studley Priory

PRIORY CL.

Hotel

Moors Farm

Sewage Works

12

Studley Wood

Corner Farm

Oakley Wood

2

Shabbington Wood

Stanton Little Wood

The Moat

Nature Reserve

11

Bernwood Forest (Nature Reserve)

York's Wood

Danesbrook Farm

Danes Brook

Moorbirge Brook

Oxfordshire Way

1

Hell Coppice

Menmarsh Guide Post

Moorbirge Bridge

10

59   **A**   **60**   **B**   **61**   **C**

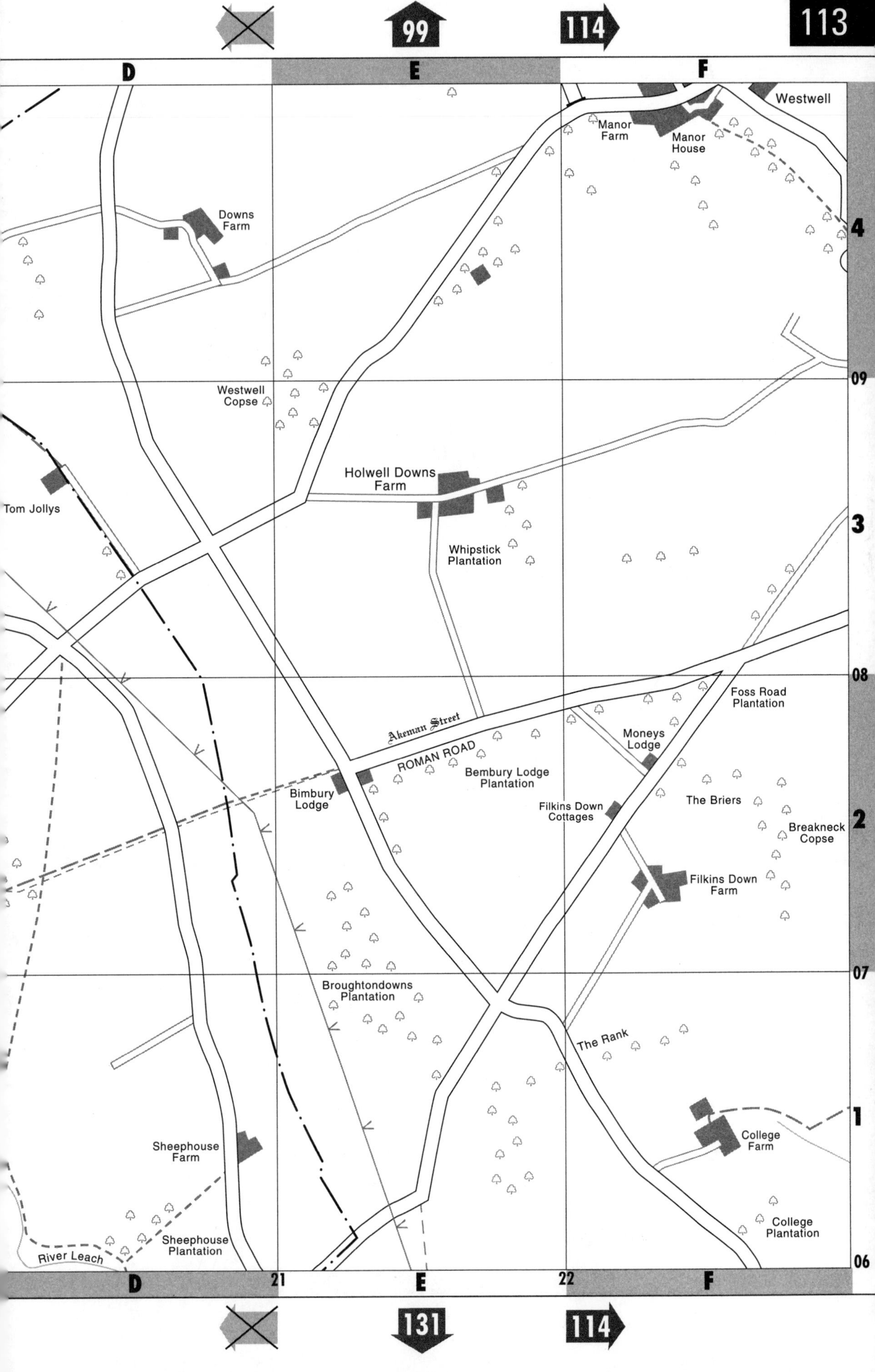

D E F

Westwell

Manor
Farm

Manor
House

4

Downs
Farm

09

Westwell
Copse

Holwell Downs
Farm

Tom Jollys

3

Whipstick
Plantation

08

Foss Road
Plantation

Akeman Street

ROMAN ROAD

Moneys
Lodge

Bembury Lodge
Plantation

Bimbury
Lodge

The Briers

Filkins Down
Cottages

Breakneck
Copse

2

Filkins Down
Farm

Broughtondowns
Plantation

07

The Rank

1

Sheephouse
Farm

College
Farm

River Leach

Sheephouse
Plantation

College
Plantation

06

D 21 E 22 F

	A	B	C

4

Job's Lane

A361

Tansley's
Buildings

Shill Brook

Sturt
Copse

Mount Zi
Bottom

Manor
Farm

Holwell
Plantation

Upper Glissard's
Plantation

Porters
Buildings

Akeman Street
ROMAN ROAD
(course of)

Shilton Downs
Farm

Holwell

Hospital
(disused)

09

Old Pits
Plantation

Groveground
Plantation

Glissard's
Wood

Caravan
Park

Lower Glissard's
Plantation

Hen and Chicken
Wood

3

P

Woodside
Farm

THE COTTAGES

Bradwell Grove
(Wild Life Park)

Aston Copse

Fishpond
Copse

Westfie
Farm

The Kennels

08

Home
Farm

Bradwell Grove
Wood

South
Lodge

Manor Dairy
Farm

Works

Bradwell Grove
Park

Scrubs
Farm

2

07

Furze
Ground

Sewage Works

Pumphouse
Plantation

1

Hill
Plantation

Kencot Hill
Farm

Furzey Hall
Farm

A361

06

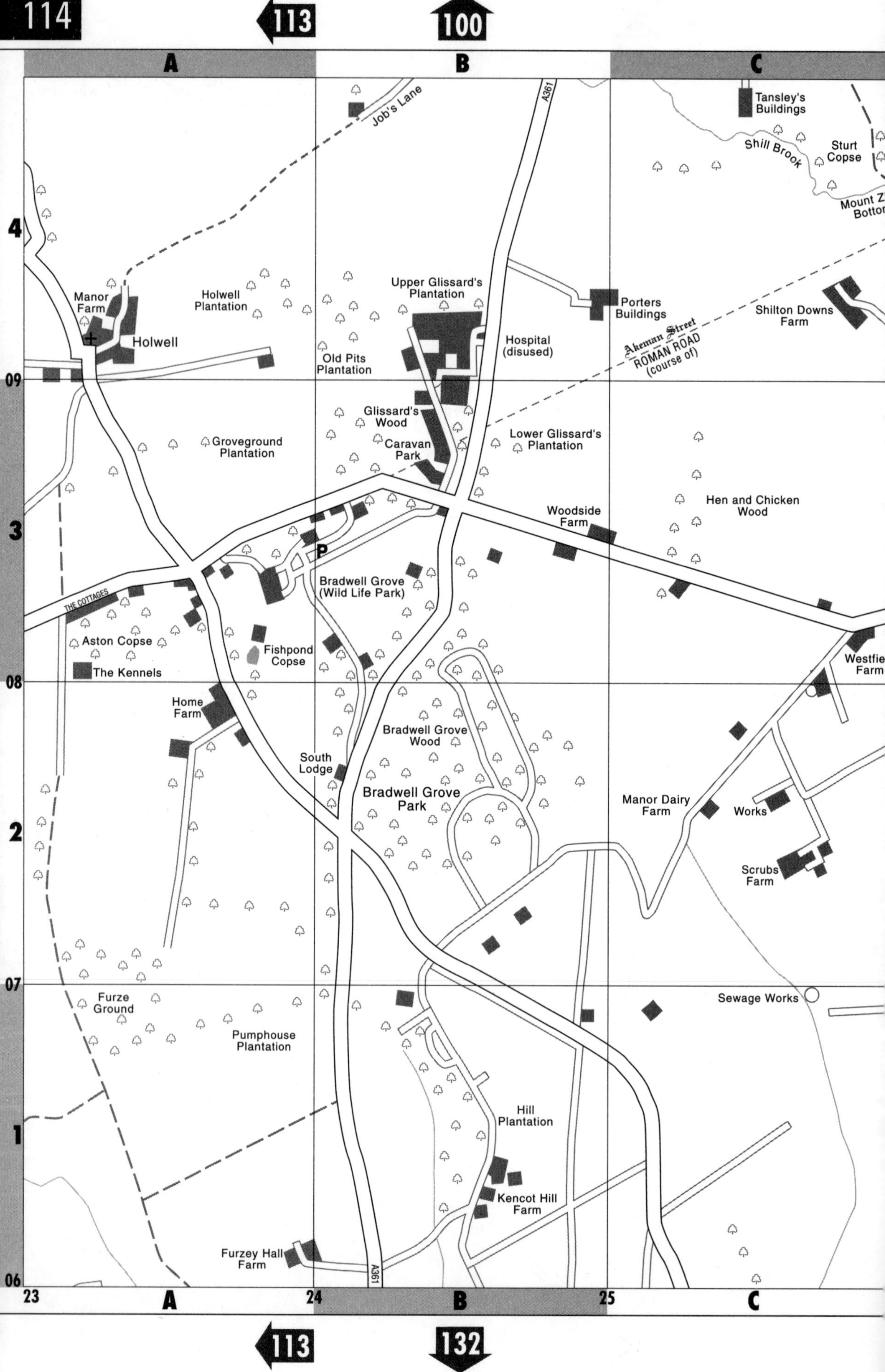

D E F

4

Home Close Farm

Akeman Street
ROMAN ROAD
(course of)

Stonelands

Lingermans

Macaroni Barn

BURFORD RD

09

Well Head

Johnsons Farm

Lodge Plantation

Kilkenny Farm

Glebe Farm

PH

KILKENNY LA

3

West End

LADBURY LA

esland

CHURCH

Shilton

MANOR RD

GARNER RD

STONELEIGH

SHILLBROOK AVE

WYCHWOOD RD

BURLWIN RD

SWINBROOK RD

LOVATT CL

STRATHMORE CL

GLENMORE RD

HEATHER CL

BRACKEN CL

Shill Brook

SHILTON RD

LIPSCOMBE PL

BRIZEWOOD

BEVERLEY CRES

YORK RD

08

CONNOLLY CL
SHILDEALE
COTSWOLD WAY
HILL VIEW
DOVE COT
DOVETREES

NORTHWOOD CRES

YATESBURY RD

TANGMERE AVE

PITREAVIE AVE

UPWOOD DR

BRITANNIA CL

DIDHAM

Carterton

Alvescot Downs Farm Cottages

Alvescot Downs Farm

Coll

ROBINSON CL

B4020

BURFORD RD

NORTHOLT RD

LYNHAM

KENLEY

INNSWORTH

GAYDON

DUXFORD

ELY

P

WEST OXON IND PARK

2

Alvescot Down

UPAVON WAY

STIRLING CL

CARR AVE

SOMMA

MERLIN CL

RESTREE CL

LUPIN CL

PINCHCROFT

ROCK RD

ROCK RD

POULTNEY PL

SYCAMORE CL

ST JOHNS

FELTWELL CL

STANMORE CRES

Sch

SELLWOOD DR

HUMPHRIES

BRIZE NORTON RD

BOVINGDON

CARTERTON RD

07

Field Farm

UPAVON WAY

SOMMA

WHIMBREL

ARUNDEL CL

BRONZENS DR

HOME CL

LAWTON CL

ARKELL AVE

CARTERS CL

PHILCOTE CL

ROSE CL

Sch

ALVESCOT RD

KINGHAM DR

BUTLERS DR

P

FEEL

CHURCH VIEW

AMER RD

CRANWELL AVE

DAVIS RD

WYCOMBE WAY

HALTON RD

NETHERTON RD

Sch

HASTINGS DR

ANDOVER

Brize Norton Airfield

1

Kenn's Farm

Shill Bridge

B4020

LAVENDER PL

EDGEWO

MINTY CL

OSLER CL

INKS

FROGNELL

HAYWARD

P

HOLLOWAY RD

FROGNELL

ASHFIELD RD

WATTONS RD

MILESTONE RD

BLACK BOURTON RD

MAPLE

CAMP RD

QUEENS RD

ANSON AVE

Sch

DEVON PL

Carterton South Ind Est

06

HAWTHORN GR

CORBETT RD

THE MAPLES

MAYFIELD CL

OAKFIELD RD

CLARKSTON RD

MILESTONE RD

BELLE TERR

CLANE TERR

WHITTINGTON PL

D 27 E 28 F

115
102

A
B
C
4
3
2
1
09
08
07
06
29
30
31
A40(T)
Oxfordshire Circular Walks
BRIZE NORTON RD
Bushey Ground Farm
Nurseries
Bushey Ground
Grove Farm
Grove Farm Cottages
Well
CASWELL LA
Rabbit's Piece Copse
Grange Farm
BURFORD RD
MINSTER RD
Astrop Cottages
WITNEY RD
Mason's Arms (PH)
Astrop Farm
Wilbro Farm
CHAPEL HILL
Manor Farm
Abingdon Lane
Round Copse
MANOR RD
Brize Norton
Ten Acre Copse
Huck's Copse
CARTERTON RD
DALBIGNY MEAD
MOAT CL
SQUIRES CL
PH
Sch
THE FOSSEWAY
SOUTH MERE
STATION RD
THE CHESTNUTS
HONEYHAM CL
Norton Ditch
Upper Haddon Farm
Sewage Works
Highmoor Brook
Brize Norton Airfield
The Copse
Tumulus
The Plantation
Dismantled Railway
Lew Gorse

115
134

D
E
F
Sewage Works
Witney Town Football Club
Peashell Farm
Oxfordshire Circular Walks
Colwell Brook
DEER PARK RD
Sch
Cemy
TOWER HILL
CURBRIDGE RD
DUCKLINGTON LA
THORNEY LEYS
A40(T)
Ind Est
PH
Charity Farm
Manor Farm
Curbridge
WELL LA
A4095
Caswell Farm
Black Moat
Duttons Farm
BAMPTON RD
Glebe Farm
Dismantled Railway
Abingdon Lane
Coursehill Farm
Davis's Copse
Moulden's Wood
Sewage Works
Barleypark Farm
Hill View
Lew
Morgans Farm
Lew House
Manor Farm
Lower Farm
Elm Bank Ditch
Barleypark Wood
4
09
3
08
2
07
1
06
33
34

A
B
C
WELCH WAY
HIGH ST
CORN ST
WITAN WAY
Ducklington
Cogges
Newland
OXFORD HILL
Gibbets Close Farm
Clementsfield Farm
Shores Green
Cogges Hill
High Cogges Farm
High Cogges
Lindsey Farm
Spring Hill
Springhill Farm
Dismantled Railway
STANTON HARCOURT RD
STATION LA
Industrial Estates
Recn Gd
A40(T)
Hotel
The Moors
Emma's Dike
WITNEY RD
Windrush Farm
Church End
River Windrush
Mill
Coggess Bridge Cottage
STANDLAKE RD
ASTON RD
Clealings
Sherald's Copse
Home Farm
Cokethorpe Park
Fishhouse Plantation
Fish House
Gill Mill
Berryham Plantation
Ford
Boys Wood
Hardwick
A415
Sch
09
08
07
06
35
36
37
4
3
2
1

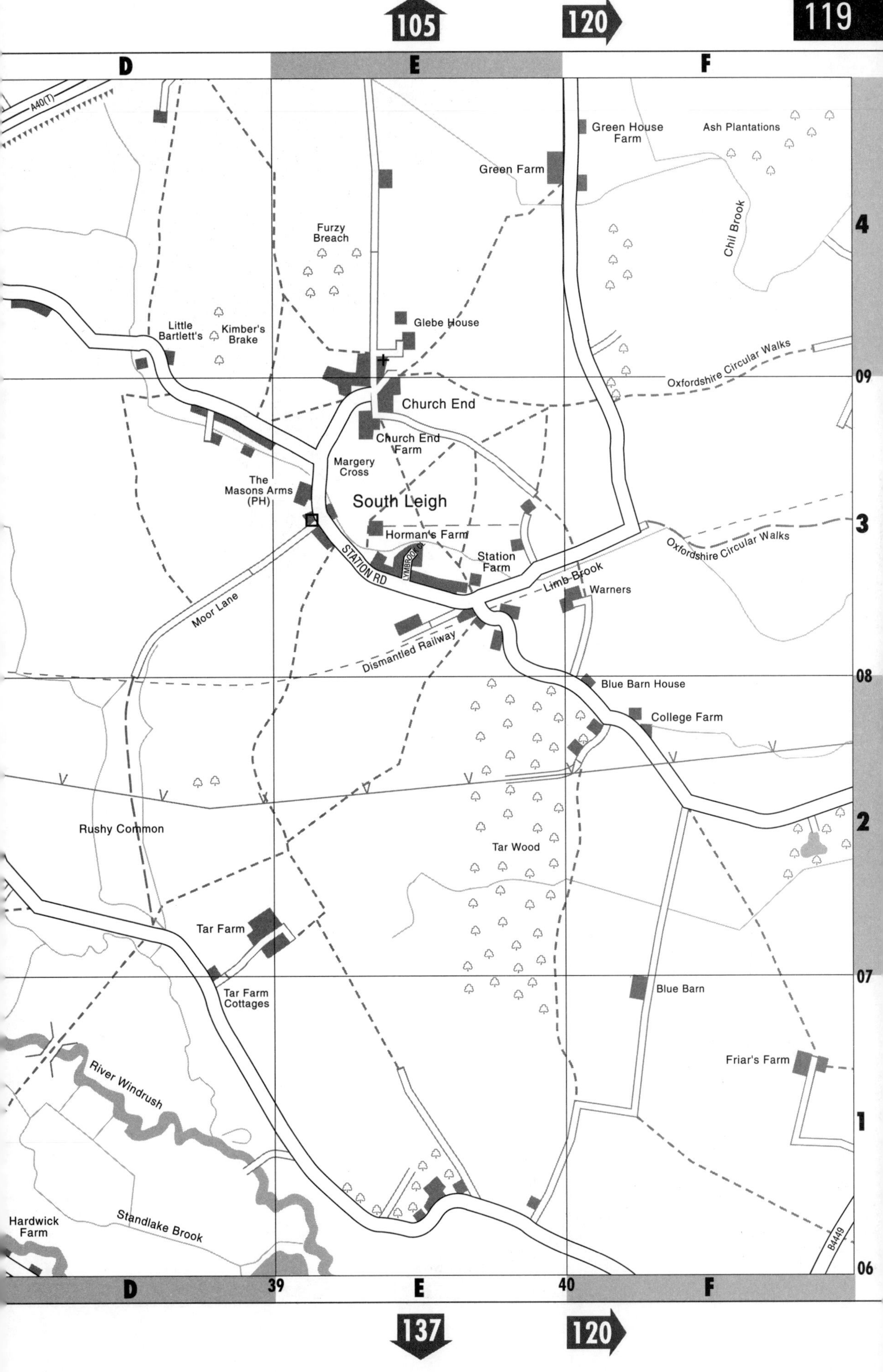

D E F

4

Green House Farm
Ash Plantations
Green Farm
Chil Brook

Furzy Breach

Little Bartlett's
Kimber's Brake
Glebe House

Oxfordshire Circular Walks

09

Church End

Church End Farm

Margery Cross

The Masons Arms (PH)
South Leigh

Horman's Farm
Station Farm

Limb Brook
Warners

Oxfordshire Circular Walks

3

STATION RD

Moor Lane

Dismantled Railway

Blue Barn House

08

College Farm

Rushy Common

Tar Wood

2

Tar Farm

07

Tar Farm Cottages

Blue Barn

River Windrush

Friar's Farm

1

Hardwick Farm
Standlake Brook

06

119

106

A   B   C

Chil Brook

PH

A40(T)

Cox's Barn
Farm

OLD WITNEY RD

OLD WITNEY RD

FRUITLANDS

ILGARSLEY RD

DUNCAN
CL

SPRAGACKLA
STRATFORD DR

GREEN'S RD

MARLBOROUGH PL

MARLBOROUGH
RD

HANBOROUGH CL

WYNHAM WAY

DONNINGTON
CLOSE CL

B4449

SHAKESPEARE

FALSTAFF CL

ST JOHN ST

HELL
CL

EVANS
RD

LOPES
RD

QUEEN'S ST

BEECH RD

MILLWOOD

HANBOROUGH RD

WYNHAM
CL

Sch

HAWTHORN
RD

4

Twelve Acre Farm

WITNEY RD

Sch

NEWLAND ST

MILL ST

CASSINGTON

Paddock
Close

CHILBRIDGE RD

THORNBURY RD

CLOVER PL

ACRE END ST

BACK LA

NEWLAND
ST

QUEENS
ST

HIGH ST

TANNER LA

THE ORCHARD

P

Lby

OXFORD RD

THE SQUARE

BITTERELL

B4449

Litchfield
Farm

Chil Brook

MERTON CL

BLANKSTONE
CL

STATION RD

SWAN ST

ABBEY

LOMBARD
ST

HANDS
ST

THE
SQUARE

ABBEY PL

THE
ORCHARD

Eynsham

09

Abbey
Farm

Oxfordshire Circular Walks

Dismtd Rly

Dismtd Rly

F Sta

SASH
PARK

B4449

B4449

B404

Southfield
Cottages

Lower Farm

Southfield
Barn

OVERCHURCH CLOSE

PINKHILL LA

Oxfordshire Circular Walks

3

08

Foxley Farm

Limb Brook

Bell Bridge

2

The Bungalow

Pinkhill
Farm

07

University Cottages

Nicholls'
Farm

Sutton
Farm

Sutton
Green

River Thames or Isis

Towing Path

we

1

Beaumont
House

SUTTON LA

Cox's
Farm

B4449

Sutton

BURR CT

Lower
Farm

FOXLEY RW

The Fox
(PH)

Boat

Sewage Works

06

41   42   43

A   B   C

119

138

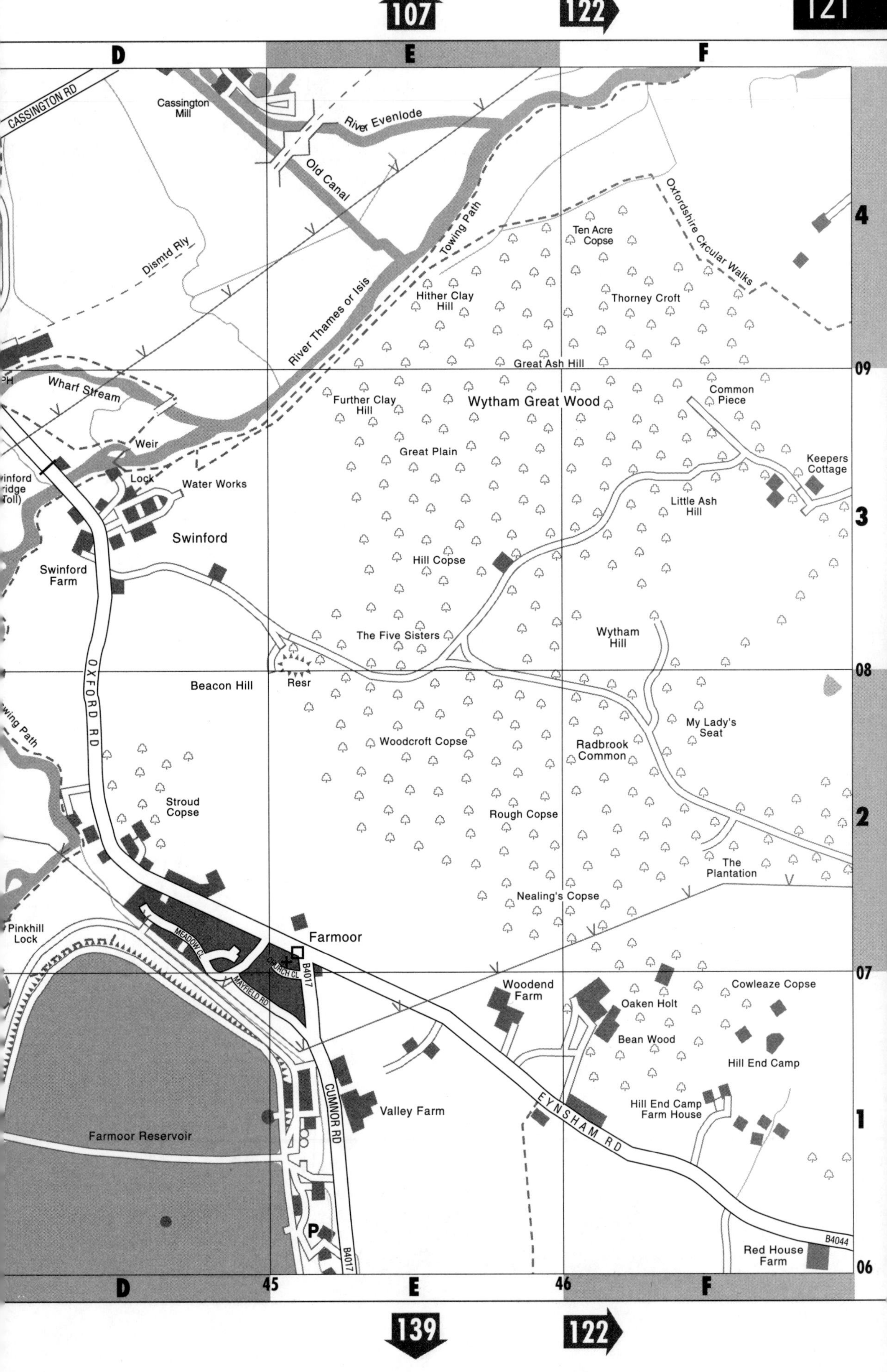

107
122
D
E
F
CASSINGTON RD
Cassington Mill
River Evenlode
Old Canal
Oxfordshire Circular Walks
Towing Path
Ten Acre Copse
Dismtd Rly
Hither Clay Hill
Thorney Croft
River Thames or Isis
Great Ash Hill
Wharf Stream
Further Clay Hill
Wytham Great Wood
Common Piece
Great Plain
Weir
Keepers Cottage
Lock
Water Works
Little Ash Hill
Swinford
Swinford Farm
Hill Copse
The Five Sisters
Wytham Hill
Beacon Hill
Resr
OXFORD RD
My Lady's Seat
Woodcroft Copse
Radbrook Common
Stroud Copse
Rough Copse
The Plantation
Nealing's Copse
Pinkhill Lock
Farmoor
MEADOW CL
CHURCH CL
MAYFIELD RD
B4017
Woodend Farm
Cowleaze Copse
Oaken Holt
Bean Wood
Hill End Camp
CUMMOR RD
Valley Farm
EYNSHAM RD
Hill End Camp Farm House
Farmoor Reservoir
P
B4044
Red House Farm
4
09
3
08
2
07
1
06
45
46
139

121
108

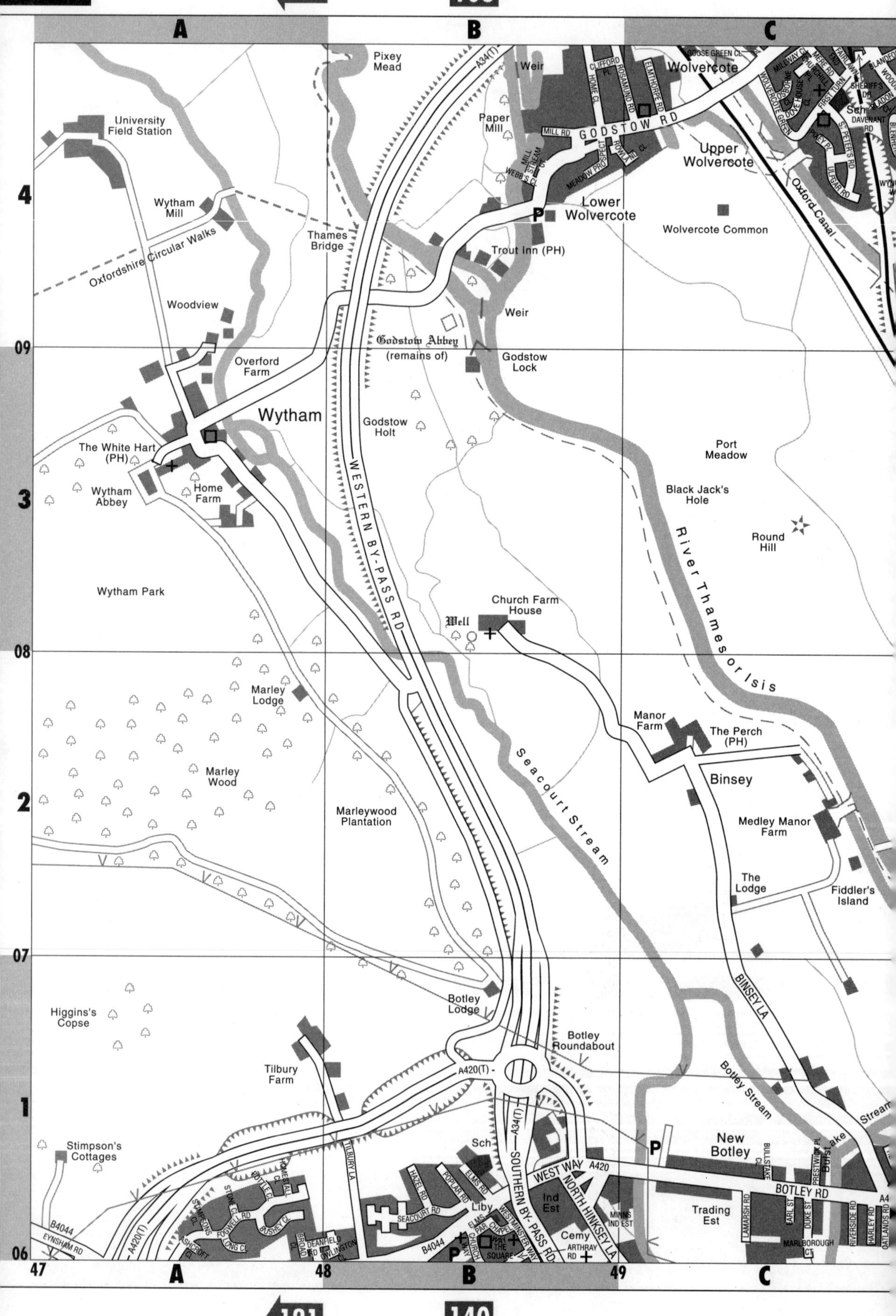
A
B
C
4
3
2
1
09
08
07
06
47
48
49
Pixey Mead
A34(T)
Weir
Wolvercote
GODSTOW RD
University Field Station
Paper Mill
Upper Wolvercote
Wytham Mill
Lower Wolvercote
Wolvercote Common
Oxford Canal
Oxfordshire Circular Walks
Thames Bridge
Trout Inn (PH)
Woodview
Weir
Godstow Abbey (remains of)
Godstow Lock
Overford Farm
Wytham
Godstow Holt
The White Hart (PH)
Port Meadow
Wytham Abbey
Home Farm
Black Jack's Hole
WESTERN BY-PASS RD
River Thames or Isis
Round Hill
Wytham Park
Church Farm House
Well
Marley Lodge
Manor Farm
The Perch (PH)
Binsey
Marley Wood
Seacourt Stream
Marleywood Plantation
Medley Manor Farm
The Lodge
Fiddler's Island
BINSEY LA
Higgins's Copse
Botley Lodge
Botley Roundabout
Tilbury Farm
A420(T)
Botley Stream
Stimpson's Cottages
Sch
New Botley
WEST WAY
A420
NORTH HINKSEY LA
SOUTHERN BY-PASS RD
BOTLEY RD
Ind Est
Trading Est
Liby
Cemy
B4044
EYNSHAM RD
TILBURY LA
SEACOURT RD

121
140

109
124

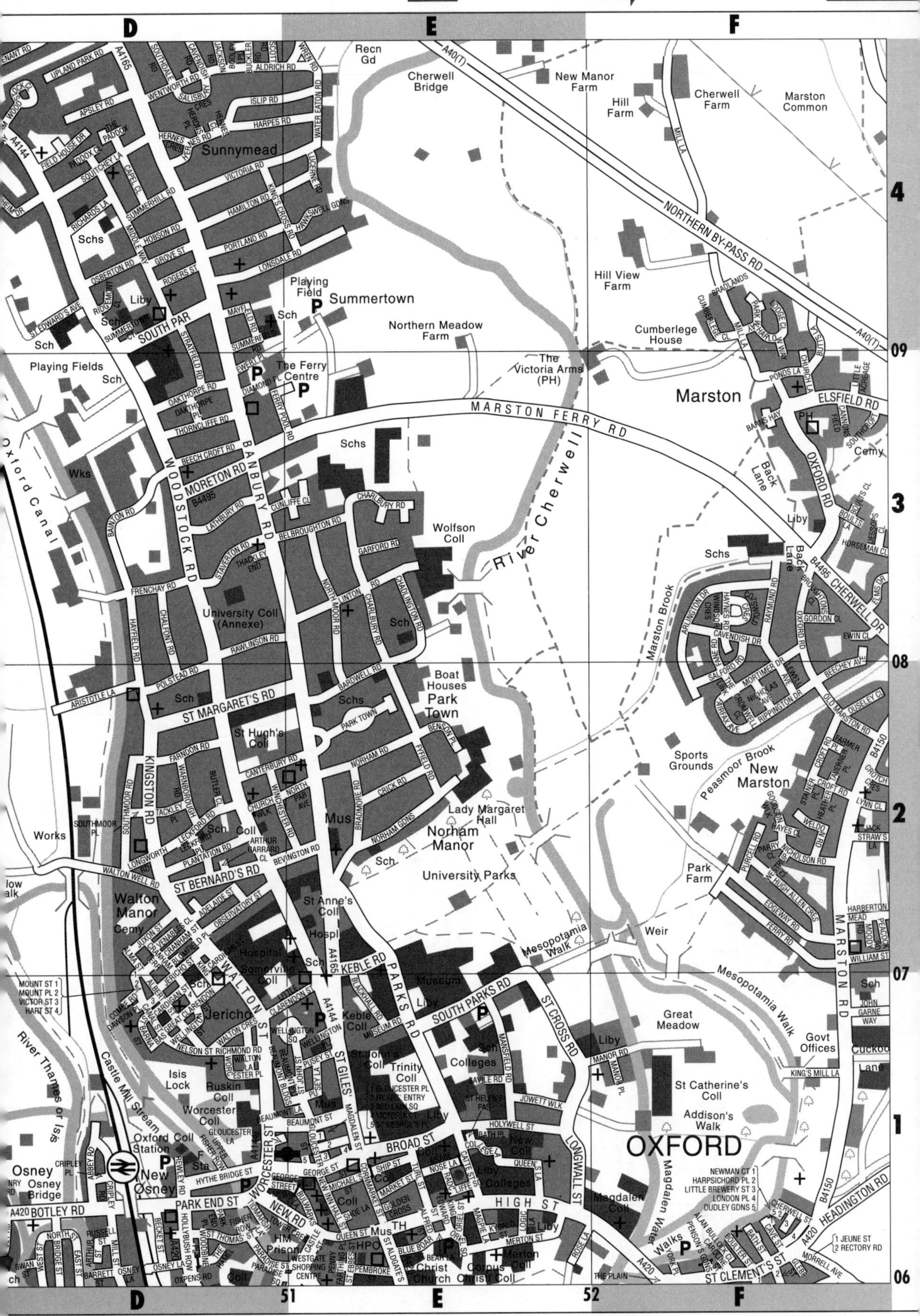
D
E
F
4
09
3
08
2
07
1
06
51
52
Recn Gd
Cherwell Bridge
New Manor Farm
Hill Farm
Cherwell Farm
Marston Common
Sunnymead
NORTHERN BY-PASS RD
Hill View Farm
Playing Field
Summertown
Northern Meadow Farm
Cumberlege House
Playing Fields
The Ferry Centre
The Victoria Arms (PH)
Marston
MARSTON FERRY RD
Oxford Canal
Wks
Schs
River Cherwell
Wolfson Coll
Back Lane
University Coll (Annexe)
Marston Brook
Boat Houses
Park Town
St Hugh's Coll
ST MARGARET'S RD
WOODSTOCK RD
BANBURY RD
Sports Grounds
Peasmoor Brook
New Marston
Lady Margaret Hall
Norham Manor
University Parks
Works
KINGSTON RD
ST BERNARD'S RD
Walton Manor
Park Farm
St Anne's Coll
Hospital
Somerville Coll
Mesopotamia Walk
Weir
Museum
Keble Coll
Jericho
WALTON ST
Great Meadow
Govt Offices
River Thames or Isis
Castle Mill Stream
Isis Lock
Ruskin Coll
Worcester Coll
Trinity Coll
Colleges
St Catherine's Coll
Addison's Walk
Oxford Station
Osney
New Osney
Osney Bridge
BOTLEY RD
PARK END ST
HM Prison
BROAD ST
HIGH ST
New Coll
OXFORD
Magdalen Coll
Magdalen Water Walks
Christ Church
Corpus Christi Coll
Merton Coll
ST CLEMENT'S ST
HEADINGTON RD
MARSTON RD
ST GILES'
PARKS RD
LONGWALL ST
ST CROSS RD
SOUTH PARKS RD
KEBLE RD
Cuckoo Lane
NEWMAN CT 1
HARPSICHORD PL 2
LITTLE BREWERY ST 3
LONDON PL 4
DUDLEY GDNS 5
1 JEUNE ST
2 RECTORY RD
MOUNT ST 1
MOUNT PL 2
VICTOR ST 3
HART ST 4
1 GLOUCESTER PL
2 FRIARS' ENTRY
3 RED LION SQ
4 VICTORIA CT
5 ST GEORGE'S PL

141
124

A   B   C

Pennywell
Wood
Church
Farm
Hill
Farm
Vicarage

Wadley Hill

Sidlings
Copse

Field Barn
Cottage

Wick
Copse

B4150
A40(T)

ELSFIELD RD

Football Gd

Wick
Farm

Crem
Stowford
Farm

Bayswater Brook

Lower
Farm

Alesworth Gr 1
Broadhead Pl 2

MARSH LA

Sch

BORROWMEAD RD

NORTHERN BY-PASS RD

Sch

High Cross Way

COPSE LA

Headington
Coll

Barton

NORTH WAY

B4495
B4150

Cemy

DUNSTAN RD

ST ANDREW'S RD

A40(T)

Headington
Hill

HEADLEY WAY

Hospl

P

Sch

P

OSLER RD

OLD HIGH ST

Liby

A420

A4142

Sch

Sch

LONDON RD
B4495

St LEONARD'S RD

Headington
Quarry

QUARRY RD

Coll

Cuckoo Lane

HEADINGTON RD

GIPSY LA

P

B4495

WINDMILL RD

Schs

EASTERN BY-PASS RD

Gov
Offices

Cuckoo Lane

Coll

Sch

Resrs

Sch

All Saints RD

Hospl

OLD RD

Shotover
Trading Esta

CHENEY LA

WARNEFORD LA

New
Headington

THE SLADE
B4495

Schs

A4142

Resr

MORRELL AVE

Hospl

Hospls

Hospl

53   A   54   B   55   C

D
E
F

New Inn Farm

B4027

ROMAN ROAD (course of)

BAYSWATER RD

Stanton House

POUND LA

MILL ST

SILVER BIRCHES

Mill Farm

Sewage Works

Kennels

Rectory Farm

COCKS LA

Stanton St John

Stanton Great Wood

4

HILLCRAFT RD

COURTFIELD RD

PH

PH

Sch

Recn Gd

09

Shepherd's Pit

Ashen Copse

Breach Farm

3

Bayswater Mill

Minchin Court Farm

STANTON RD

BOXGATE END LA

Sewage Works

Bayswater Farm

1 HUMFREY RD
2 MALFORD RD
3 CLAYMOND RD

Vent Farm

08

BAGSWATER FARM RD

Sandhills

HILL VIEW

DEER BUSH AVE

Sch

MILTON CRES

BOWELL RD

RANGER

WHEATLEY RD

ROBERTS CL

Manor Farm

Cemy

Forest Hill

B4027

HAZEL WOOD AVE

BURDELL AVE

PURSELL

The Vicarage

2

Sch

LONDON RD

P

Red Hill Farm

GROVELANDS RD

RINGWOOD RD

Nielsen House

Thornhill Farm

Swilly

Red Hill

Risinghurst

Lodge

07

KILN LA

A40(T)

Pointed Covert

Shotover House

OLD RD

Monk's Wood

Thorn Hill

Obelisk

1

Monk's Farm

Shotover Hill

Forest Farm

The Spinney

Home Farm

P

Shotover Plain

Ochre Pits

06

D
57
E
58
F

125
112

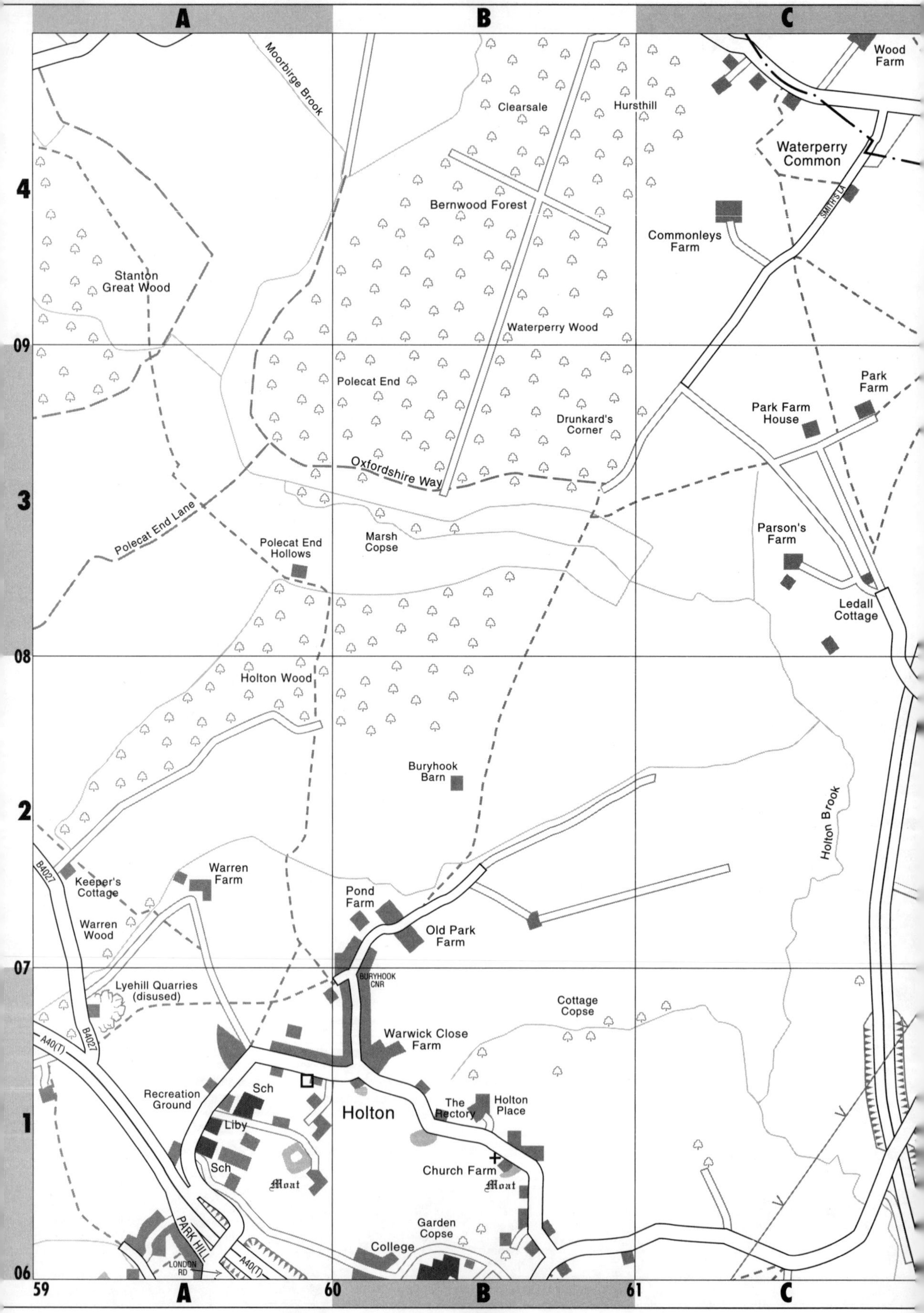

A B C

Moorbrige Brook

4

Clearsale   Hursthill

Stanton
Great Wood

Bernwood Forest

Waterperry Wood

Waterperry
Common

Wood
Farm

Commonleys
Farm

09

Polecat End

Drunkard's
Corner

Park
Farm

Park Farm
House

3

Oxfordshire Way

Polecat End Lane

Marsh
Copse

Polecat End
Hollows

Parson's
Farm

Ledall
Cottage

08

Holton Wood

Buryhook
Barn

Holton Brook

2

B4027

Keeper's
Cottage

Warren
Farm

Warren
Wood

Pond
Farm

Old Park
Farm

07

Lyehill Quarries
(disused)

BURYHOOK
CNR

Cottage
Copse

A40(T)

B4027

Warwick Close
Farm

Recreation
Ground

Sch

Holton

The
Rectory

Holton
Place

1

Liby

Sch

Moat

Church Farm

Moat

PARK HILL

Garden
Copse

College

A40(T)

LONDON
RD

06

59   A   60   B   61   C

125
144

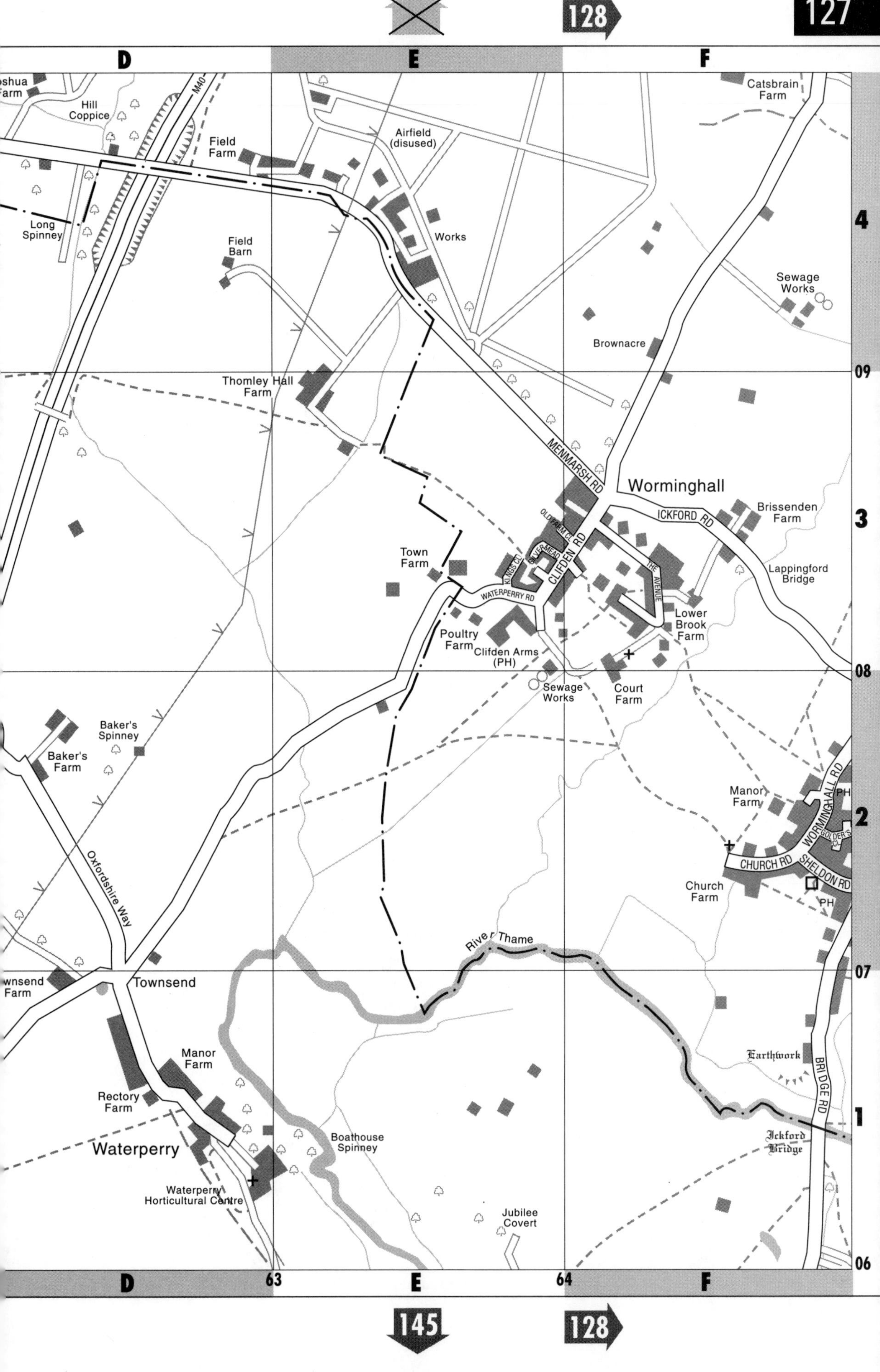

128

D   **E**   **F**

Catsbrain
Farm

Joshua
Farm

Hill
Coppice

Field
Farm

Airfield
(disused)

4

Long
Spinney

Field
Barn

Works

Sewage
Works

Brownacre

09

Thomley Hall
Farm

MENMARSH RD

Worminghall

3

ICKFORD RD

Brissenden
Farm

Town
Farm

OLD FARM RD

KINGS CL

CLIFDEN RD

WATERPERRY RD

THE AVENUE

Lappingford
Bridge

Poultry
Farm

Lower
Brook
Farm

Clifden Arms
(PH)

08

Sewage
Works

Court
Farm

Baker's
Spinney

Baker's
Farm

Manor
Farm

BOLDER'S

WORMINGHALL RD

PH

2

CHURCH RD

SHELDON RD

Church
Farm

PH

Oxfordshire Way

River Thame

07

Townsend

Townsend
Farm

Earthwork

BRIDGE RD

Manor
Farm

Rectory
Farm

Boathouse
Spinney

Ickford
Bridge

1

Waterperry

Waterperry
Horticultural Centre

Jubilee
Covert

06

D   63   **E**   64   **F**

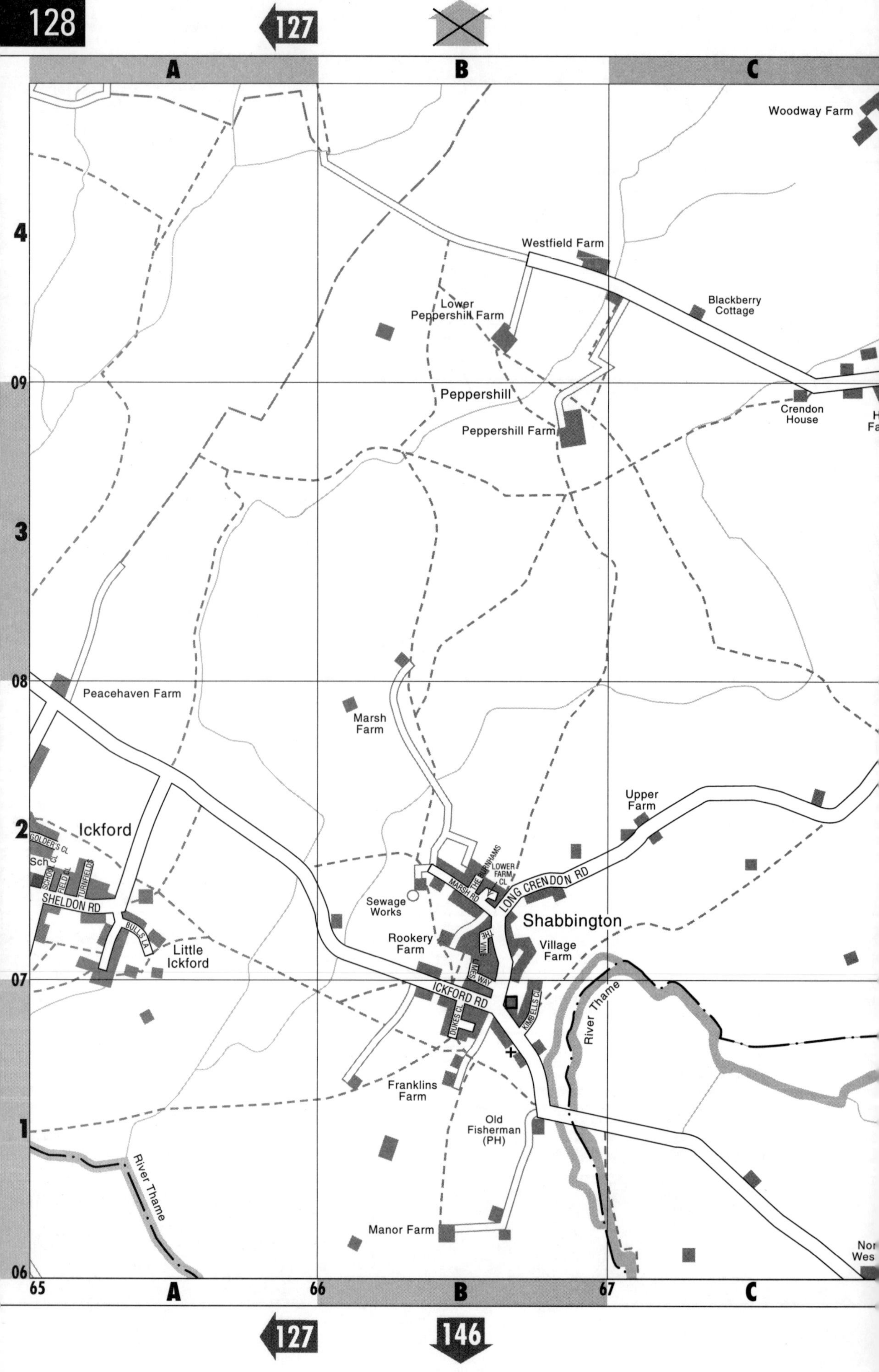

A

B

C

4

Woodway Farm

Westfield Farm

Lower
Peppershill Farm

Blackberry
Cottage

09

Peppershill

Crendon
House

H
Fa
Wes

Peppershill Farm

3

08

Peacehaven Farm

Marsh
Farm

Upper
Farm

2

Ickford

BOLGER'S CL

Sch

THE GREEN

TUNWELLS

SHELDON RD

BULL'S LA

Little
Ickford

Sewage
Works

MARSH RD

THE BURNHAMS

LOWER
FARM
CL

LONG CRENDON RD

Shabbington

Rookery
Farm

THE VINE

Village
Farm

ICKFORD RD

07

LONG WAY

DUKE'S CL

KIMBELL'S CL

River Thame

Franklins
Farm

Old
Fisherman
(PH)

1

River Thame

Manor Farm

Nor
Wes

06

65

A

66

B

67

C

The Nursery Bungalow

Glebe Farm

Notley Gate

School

CHEARSLEY RD

Manor Farm

Larch Plantation

Lower End

Northend Farm

CARTERS LA

CHILTON RD

OLD WINDMILL WAY

Church End

Cop Hill

Long Crendon

PH

BICESTER RD

SANDY LA

HIGH ST

NEEDLEMAKERS

CHURCH GREEN

Redding's Farm

Liby
THE SQUARE

Harroell

FROGMORE LA

BILLWELL

B4011

The Manor

Sewage Works

Drake's Farm

Long Crendon Industrial Estate

MEADOW VIEW

FIELD END

marsh Farm

Shabbington Fields

Mottymead

THAME RD

Lopemede Farm

Clacken Arches

AYLESBURY RD

A418

Mead Farm

07

B4011

A418

A4129

River Thame

Thame Bridge

B4445

A4129

The Prebendal

PRIESTEND

CHURCH RD

AYLESBURY RD

College

HIGH ST

BELL LA

NORTH ST

B4445

Sch

A   B   C

4

Cheardsley Rd

Long Mead
Copse

Dovecote

Notley
Farm

Home
Copse

Notley
Abbey
(remains of)

River Thame

Dad Brook

Yolsum
Plantation

Roundhill
Farm

A418

Aylesbury and
Thame Airport

09

Crosse's
Covert

AYLESBURY RD

Haddenham

WINDMILL RD

THE B

LONG PICKINS

WATER LANE FLD

LANXEY CL

YEW HILL CL

DOVECOTE CL

DOVECOTE

BRUERN WAY

MARRIOTT'S LA

MARRIOTT'S CL

MARRIOTT'S
WAY

WYKEHAM WAY

WYKEHAM GATE

GREENWAY

3

P

Haddenham
and Thame
Parkway

THAME RD

Fowlers Field

SHEEPCOTE

Allot
Gdns

SOUTH END

CROFT
COURTYARD

TOWNSIDE

THE DRIVE

POTTS

LC

SLAVE HILL

STATION RD

WHITECROSS
RD

Diggs

08

A418

Scotsgrove
Farm

Grove End
Farm

Scotsgrove
House

A418   SCOTSGROVE HILL

MILL LA

Scotsgrove
Mill

Dogkennel
Covert

Tythrop Park
Farm

Decoy
Pond

Long
Covert

Tythro
Hous

07

Sewage
Works

MOOREND LA

Tythro
Lodge

1

A4129

1 RUSHALL RD
2 RUPERT WAY
3 SEDGEMOOR DR
4 DUNBAR DR
5 CHARLES DR
6 ROUNDHEAD DR

7 STUART WAY
8 CAVANDISH WLK
9 PENNINGTON PL
10 PELHAM RD
11 GLENHAM RD

CAVALIER RD

HAMILTON
RD

GRENVILLE WAY

ASTLEY RISE

A4129

BERKELEY
RD

SHIPTON
RD

CLARENDON
DR

MARSTON DR

BLAK

OVERTON DR

ONSLOW DR

Pilmoor
Arch

KINGSEY RD

WINDMILL RD

Sch

CROMWELL AVE

A4129

Pumping Station
(dis)

06

71   72   73

A   B   C

D   E   F

LOCOMBE HILL

4

Eastleach
Turville

+

Oxleaze
Farm

The
Cottages

Field Barn

Sch

+   Eastleach Martin

THE
BOURNE

Coate
Farm

05

Kings Hay

Oxleaze
Common

The Pills

3

Coate Mill

Shire
Gate

Broadwell Brook

The
Bungalow

Greenhill
Barn

04

Coate
Farm

Baxter's
Farm

Fyfield

PH

Sch

2

+   Manor House

Langford
Downs Farm

A361

Manor Farm

River Leach

Southrop

03

Langford
Downs
House

Rottonborough
Copse

1

Common Barn
Farm

Furzy Knoll
Plantation

A361

02

D   21   E   22   F

131
114

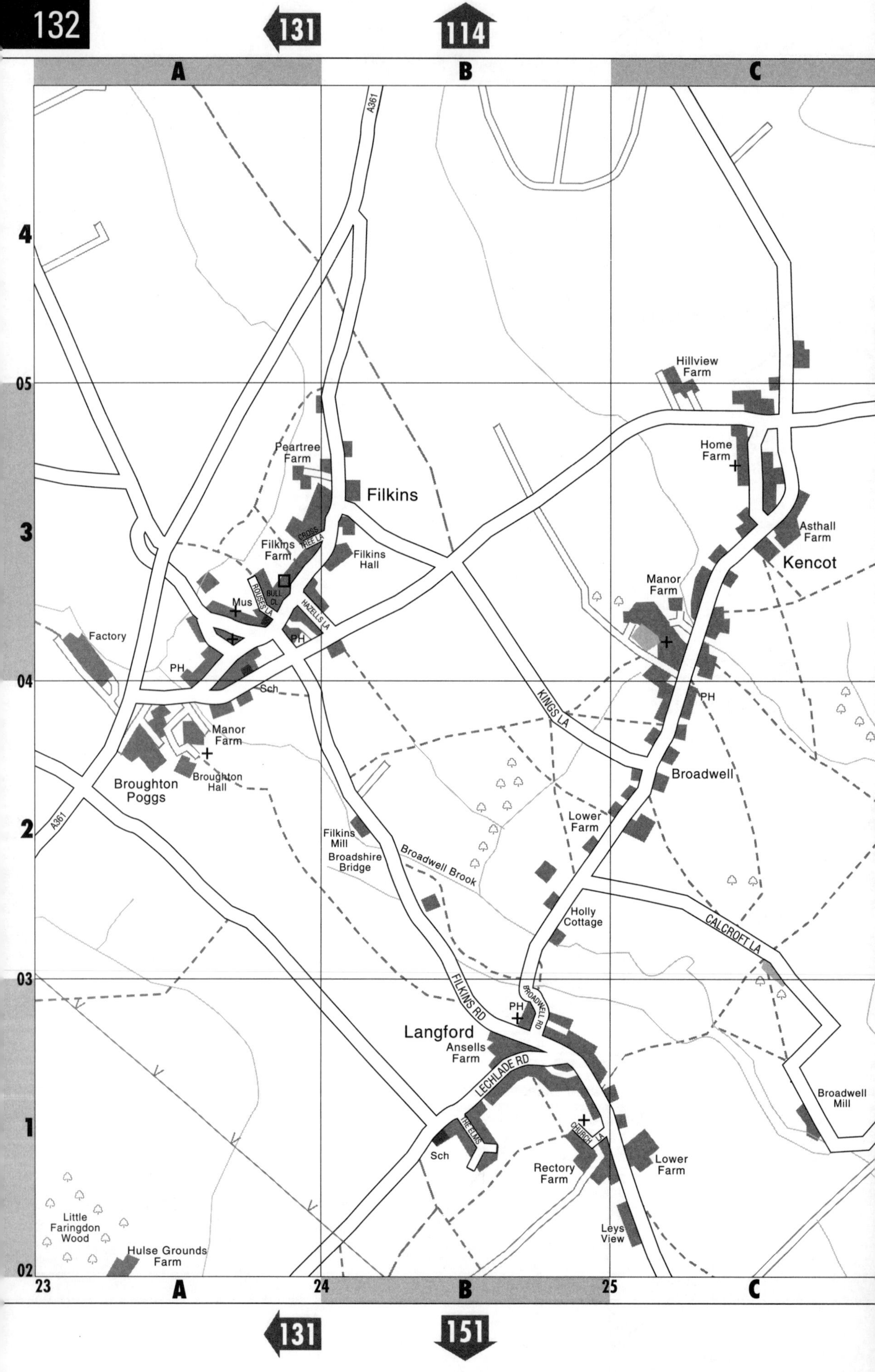
A
B
C
A361
Filkins
Peartree Farm
Filkins Farm
CROSS TREE LA
Filkins Hall
BULL CL
ROUSES LA
HAZELLS LA
Mus
PH
Factory
Sch
Manor Farm
Broughton Hall
Broughton Poggs
Hillview Farm
Home Farm
Asthall Farm
Kencot
Manor Farm
PH
KINGS LA
Broadwell
Lower Farm
Holly Cottage
CALCROFT LA
Filkins Mill
Broadshire Bridge
Broadwell Brook
FILKINS RD
BROADWELL RD
PH
Langford
Ansells Farm
LECHLADE RD
THE ELMS
Sch
CHURCH LA
Rectory Farm
Lower Farm
Leys View
Broadwell Mill
Little Faringdon Wood
Hulse Grounds Farm
4
05
3
04
2
03
1
02
23
24
25

131
151

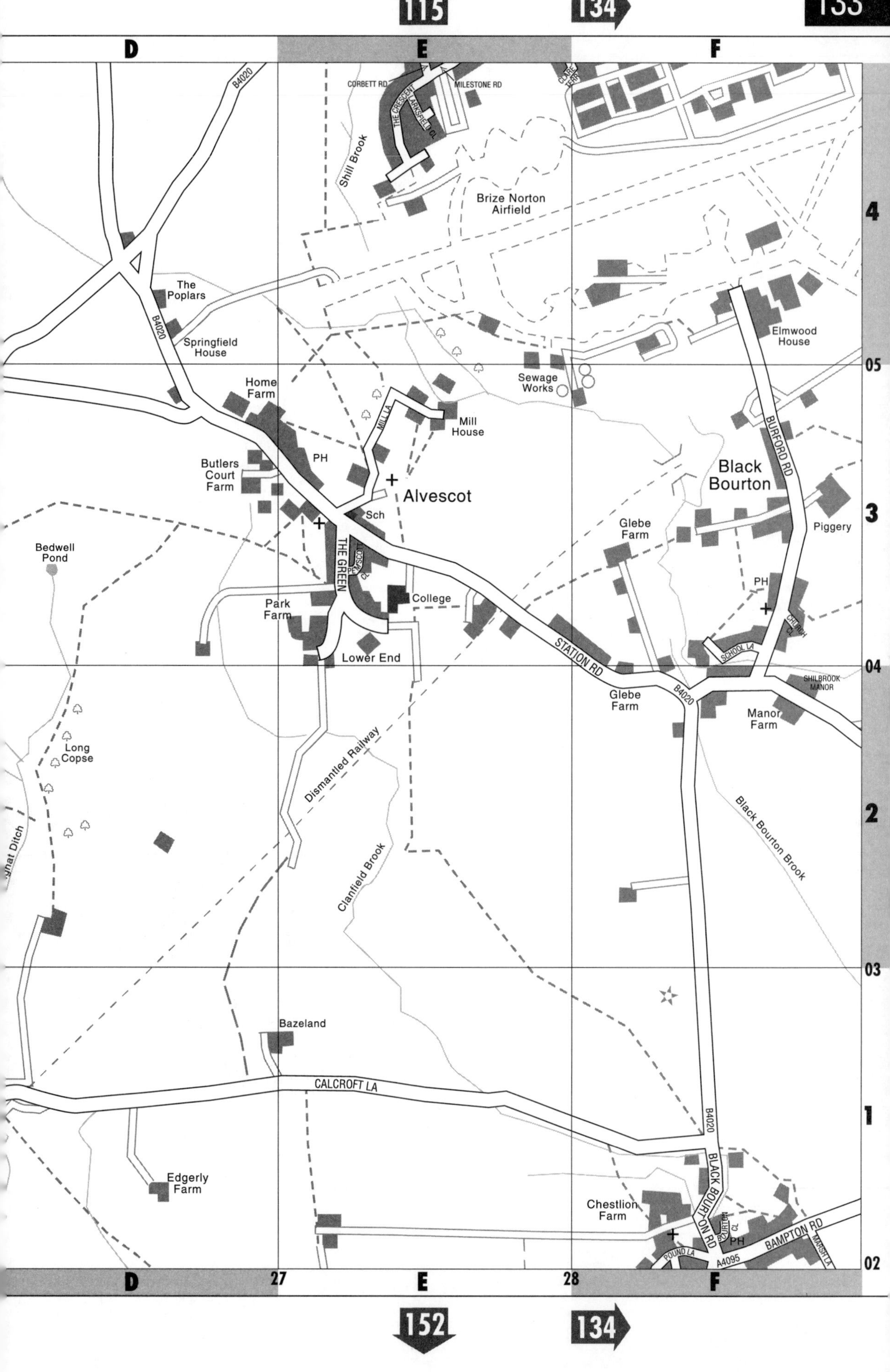

D
E
F

CORBETT RD
MILESTONE RD
THE CRESCENT
RUSSELL CL
CLANE TERR

Shill Brook

Brize Norton
Airfield

4

The
Poplars

B4020

Springfield
House

Elmwood
House

05

Home
Farm

MILL LA

Mill
House

Sewage
Works

Burford RD

Butlers
Court
Farm

PH

Black
Bourton

Piggery

3

Bedwell
Pond

Alvescot

Sch

Glebe
Farm

THE GREEN

CROSS RD

PH

College

Park
Farm

CHURCH RD

SCHOOL LA

SHILBROOK
MANOR

Lower End

Station RD

04

Glebe
Farm

B4020

Manor
Farm

Long
Copse

Dismantled Railway

Black Bourton Brook

2

gnat Ditch

Clanfield Brook

03

Bazeland

CALCROFT LA

1

B4020

Edgerly
Farm

BLACK BOURTON RD

Chestlion
Farm

PH

BAMPTON RD

POUND LA

A4095

MONASTERY

02

A   B   C

4

Dismantled Railway

Ven Bridge

Lower Haddon Farm

Piggery

A4095

Lew Heath House

Wind Pum

05

3

Garson's Copse

Deanery Farm

STATION RD

Hobbs Buildings

Mill Farm

Highmoor Brook

The Plantation

The Windmill   Bampton

04

Field Cottage

Shill Brook

Sch

Cemy

F Sta

BLUELANDS
LANDEL'S
NEW RD
THE LANES
BUSHY ROW
POCOCKS
THE PIECES

2

CHURCH VIEW
BROAD ST
CHEAPSIDE

Liby

CHURCH ST
CHURCH VIEW
ROSEMARY
GREEN ST
LAMB LA
B4449

HIGH ST

ASTON
BUCKL

Ham Court

Sch
PH
BRIDGE ST
A4095
BELL LA

The Grange

03

Cowleaze Corner

Shill Brook

Weald Manor

MILL GREEN

WEALD ST

Weald Manor Farm

Blackhouse Farm

1

Weald Farm

A4095
Black Bourton Brook

Weald

Glebe Farm

02

29   A   30   B   31   C

117 136

D   E   F

4

Rushy
Butts

Claywell
Hill

Ditcham
Wood

Elm Bank Ditch

Newhouse
Farm

University
Farm

Lew
Lodge

05

Newhouse
Farm Cottages

Mount Owen
Farm

Far
Horizons

3

Coalpit
Farm

Cote Ditch

04

White
Owl
Farm

2

CALAIS DENE

North Street
Farm

Aston Ditch

Aston

MOUNT OWEN RD

MERCURY CL

BACK LA

KILN CL

NORTH ST

Sch

COTE RD

B4449

TALBOT
FIELDS

B4449

GREENACRES

Home
Farm

FOXWOOD

FOXWOOD

THE
SQUARE

Kingsway
Farm

LAUNDRY LA

HIGH ST

WOODBRIDGE
CL

03

B4449

BAMPTON RD

SOUTHLANDS

STATION RD

PRIORY CL

WOODBRIDGE
CL

MANOR
RD

SAXEL CL

BULL ST

BULL LA

Bull Inn
(PH)

Lower
Farm

Sewage
Works

Westmoor Lane

BUCKLAND RD

Shill Brook

HAM LA

1

02

D   33   E   34   F

135
118

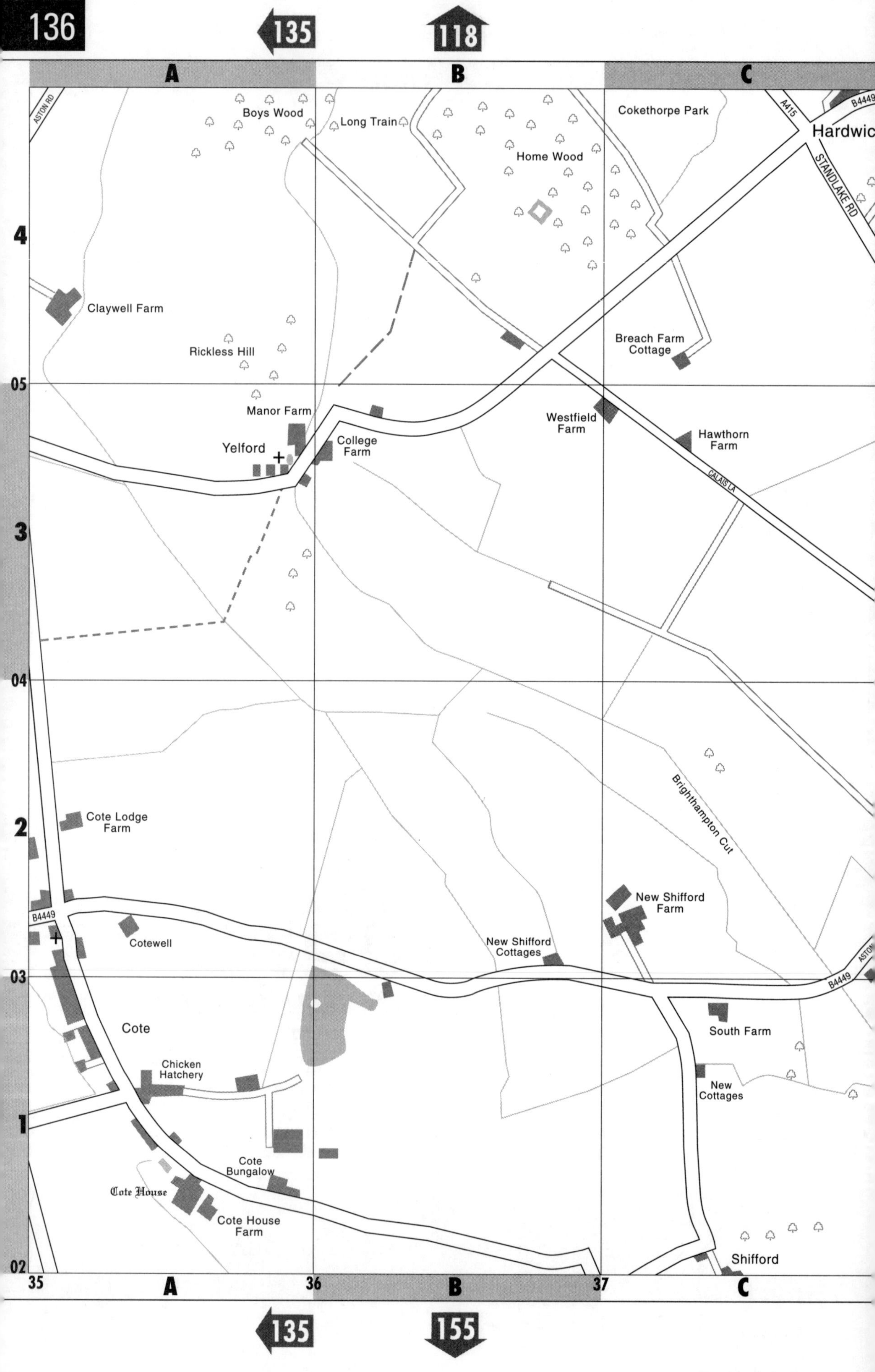
A
B
C
ASTON RD
Boys Wood
Long Train
Home Wood
Cokethorpe Park
A415
B4449
Hardwic
STANDLAKE RD
4
Claywell Farm
Rickless Hill
Breach Farm Cottage
05
Manor Farm
Westfield Farm
Hawthorn Farm
Yelford
College Farm
CALAIS LA
3
04
Brighthampton Cut
2
Cote Lodge Farm
New Shifford Farm
B4449
Cotewell
New Shifford Cottages
ASTON
B4449
03
South Farm
Cote
Chicken Hatchery
New Cottages
1
Cote Bungalow
Cote House
Cote House Farm
Shifford
02
35
36
37
A
B
C

135
155

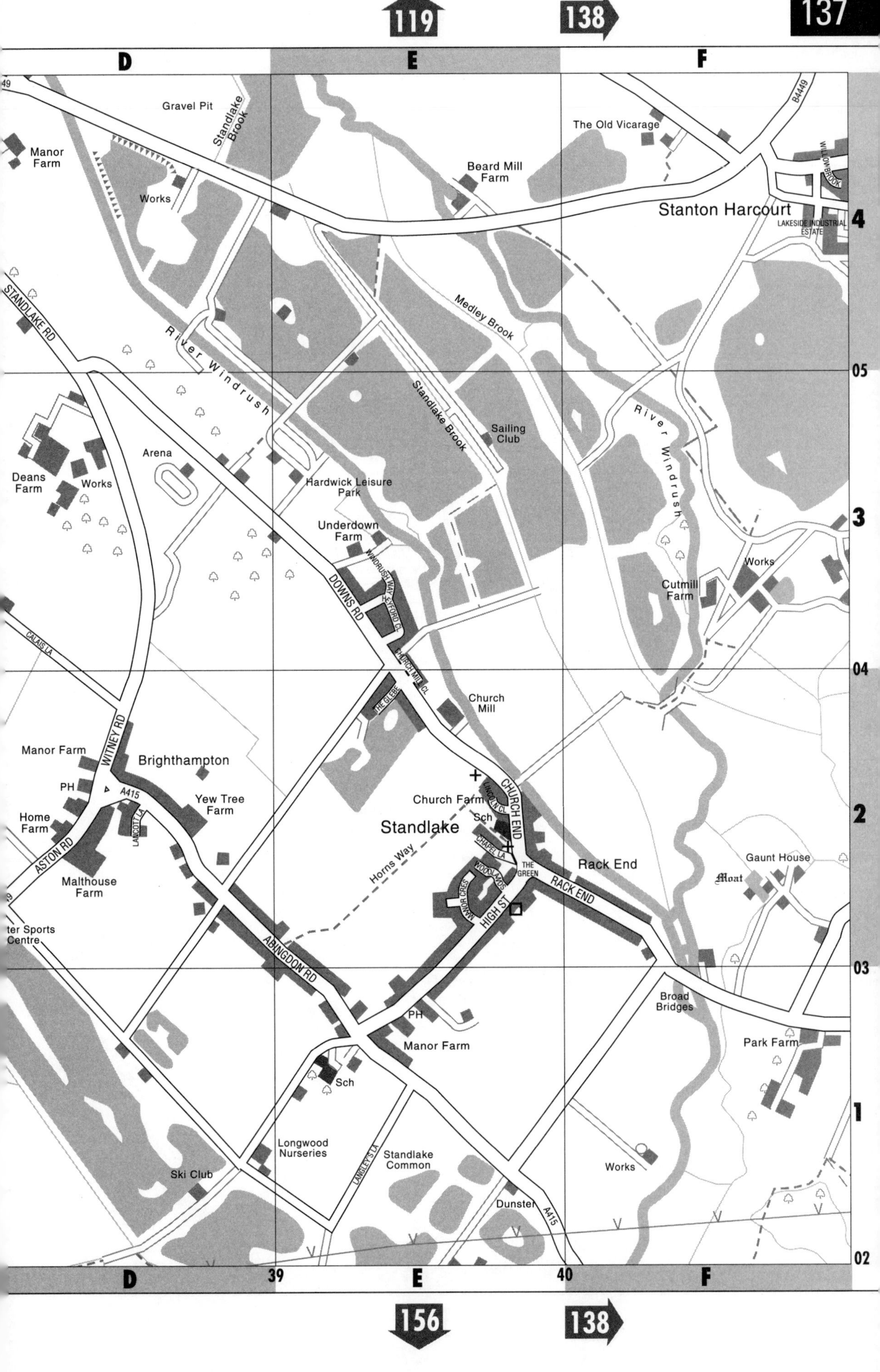
119
138
D
E
F
Gravel Pit
Standlake Brook
Manor Farm
Works
Beard Mill Farm
The Old Vicarage
B4449
Stanton Harcourt
WILLOW BROOK
LAKESIDE INDUSTRIAL ESTATE
4
STANDLAKE RD
River Windrush
Medley Brook
05
Standlake Brook
Sailing Club
River Windrush
Arena
Deans Farm
Works
Hardwick Leisure Park
Underdown Farm
3
WINDRUSH WAY
HEYFORD CL
DOWNS RD
Works
Cutmill Farm
CALAIS LA
CHURCH MILL CL
THE GLEBE
Church Mill
04
Manor Farm
WITNEY RD
Brighthampton
PH
A415
Yew Tree Farm
Home Farm
LANCOTT LA
ASTON RD
Church Farm
LINCOLN CL
CHURCH END
Sch
Standlake
2
CHAPEL LA
Horns Way
WOODLANDS
THE GREEN
Rack End
RACK END
Gaunt House
Moat
Malthouse Farm
MANOR CRES
HIGH ST
ter Sports Centre
ABINGDON RD
03
Broad Bridges
PH
Manor Farm
Park Farm
Sch
1
Longwood Nurseries
Standlake Common
LANGLEY'S LA
Works
Ski Club
Dunster
A415
02
D
39
E
40
F
156
138

137
120

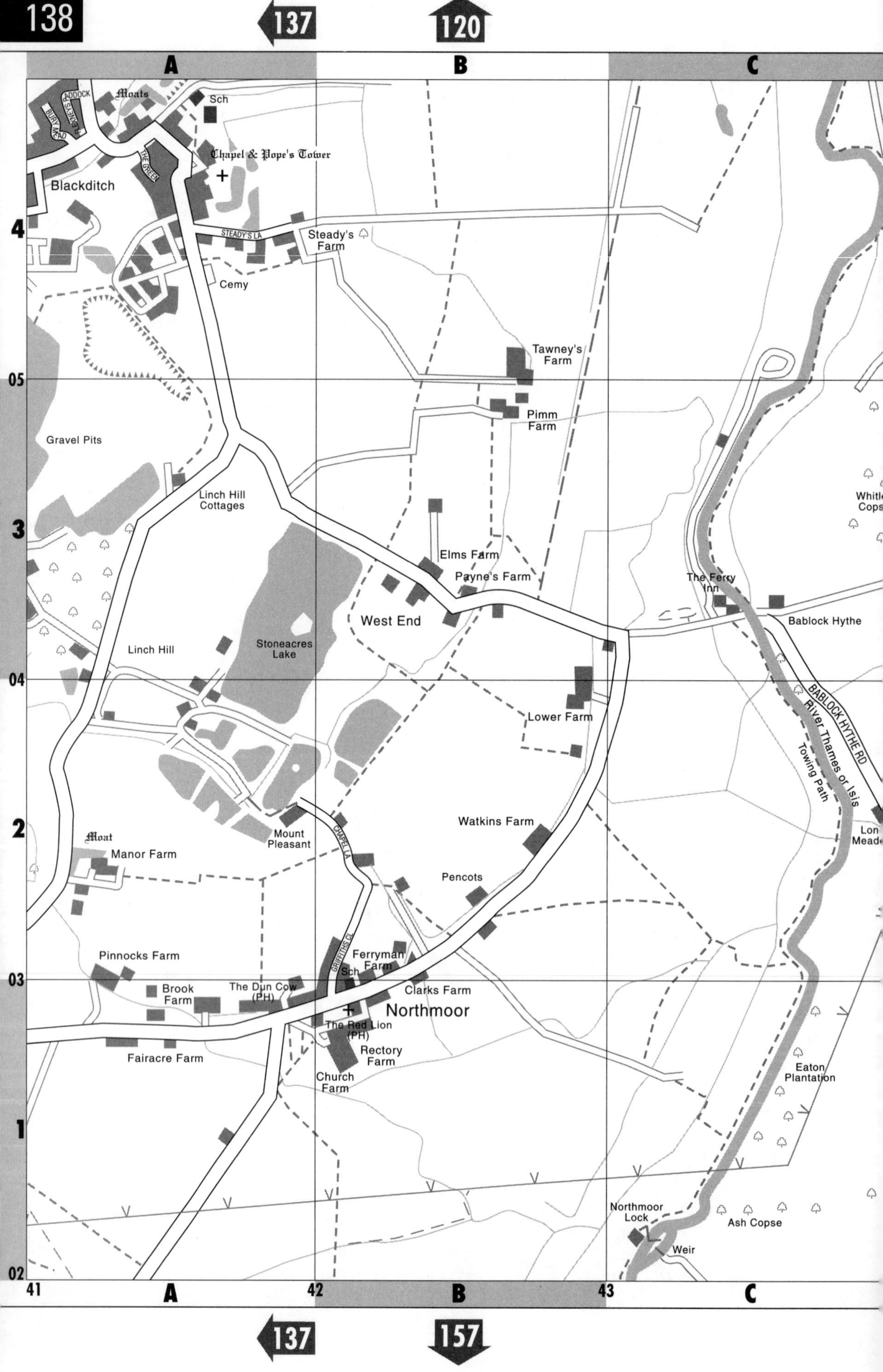
A
B
C
Moats
Sch
Chapel & Pope's Tower
Blackditch
THE GREEN
STEADY'S LA
Steady's Farm
Cemy
Tawney's Farm
Pimm Farm
Gravel Pits
Linch Hill Cottages
Elms Farm
Payne's Farm
The Ferry Inn
Bablock Hythe
West End
Stoneacres Lake
Linch Hill
Lower Farm
BABLOCK HYTHE RD
River Thames or Isis
Towing Path
Watkins Farm
Mount Pleasant
CHAPEL LA
Moat
Manor Farm
Pencots
Pinnocks Farm
GRIFFITHS CL
Ferryman Farm
Sch
Brook Farm
The Dun Cow (PH)
Clarks Farm
Northmoor
The Red Lion (PH)
Rectory Farm
Fairacre Farm
Church Farm
Eaton Plantation
Northmoor Lock
Ash Copse
Weir
4
05
3
04
2
03
1
02
41
42
43

137
157

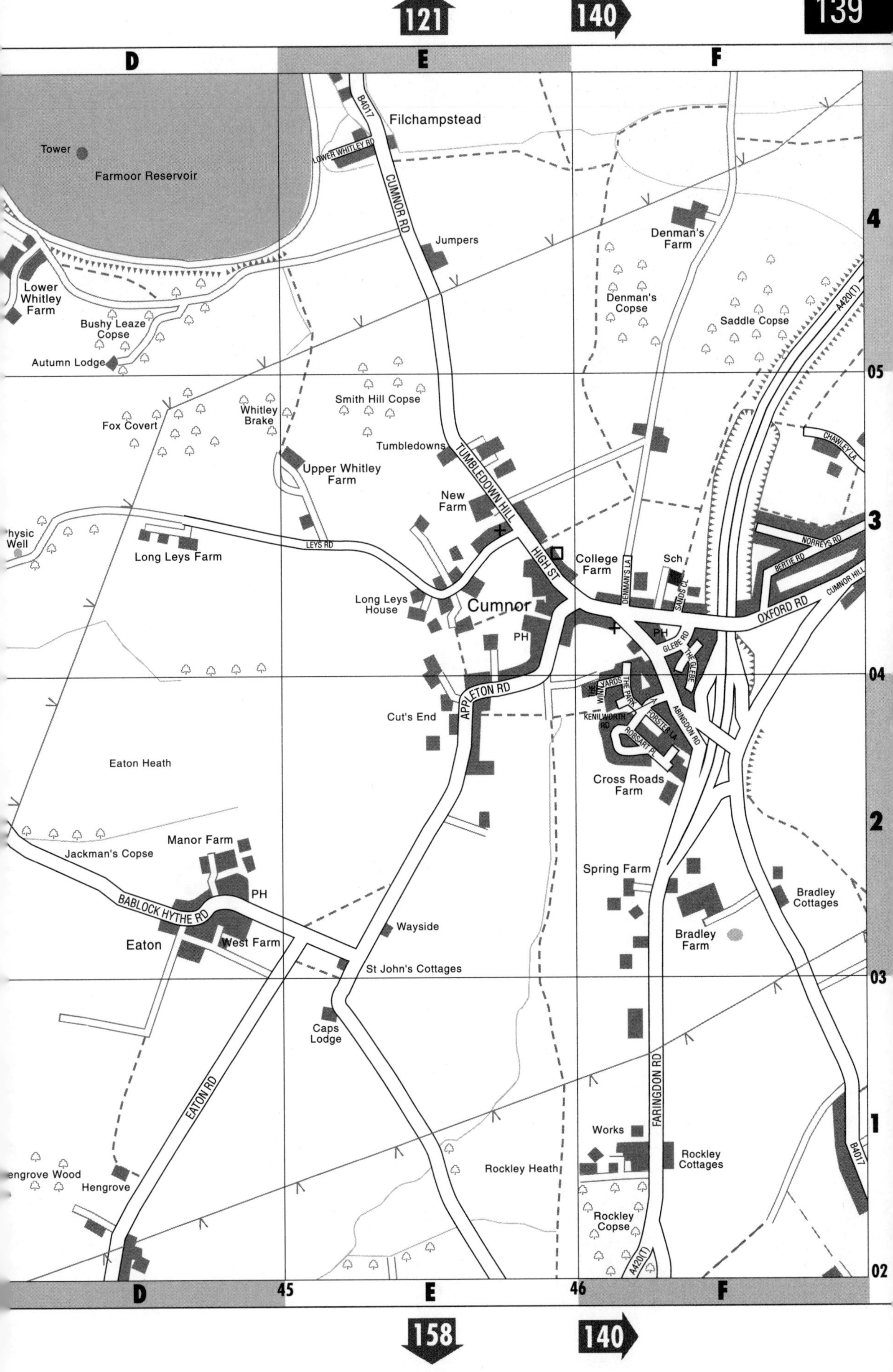

4

Tower
Farmoor Reservoir

Filchampstead

Denman's Farm

Jumpers

Denman's Copse

Saddle Copse

Lower Whitley Farm

Bushy Leaze Copse

Autumn Lodge

05

Smith Hill Copse

Whitley Brake

Fox Covert

Tumbledowns

Upper Whitley Farm

New Farm

College Farm

Sch

3

hysic Well

Long Leys Farm

LEYS RD

Long Leys House

Cumnor

HIGH ST

TUMBLEDOWN HILL

DENMAN'S LA

SANDS CL

NORREYS RD

BERTIE RD

OXFORD RD

CUMNOR HILL

CHAWLEY LA

PH

PH

GLEBE RD

THE GLEBE

04

APPLETON RD

Cut's End

THE WINDY ARDS

THE PARK

FOXSTER LA

KENILWORTH RD

ROBSART PL

ABINGDON RD

Eaton Heath

Cross Roads Farm

2

Jackman's Copse

Manor Farm

Spring Farm

Bradley Cottages

BABLOCK HYTHE RD

PH

Bradley Farm

Eaton

West Farm

Wayside

St John's Cottages

03

EATON RD

Caps Lodge

FARINGDON RD

1

Works

Rockley Cottages

B4017

A420(T)

engrove Wood

Hengrove

Rockley Heath

Rockley Copse

02

139
122

A B C

EYNSHAM RD B4044 B4044 FOGWELL RD GRANGE CT ROSE GDNS WEST WAY ARTHRAY RD PAUL'S CRES FINMORE RD A34(T) STANLEY CL YARNELL'S RD FERRY HINKSEY RD New Botley

Nobles Farm Cottages ORCHARD RD A420(T) NOBLES CL PINNOCKS WAY THIRD ACRE RISE EVELYN CL CONIFER CL SPRINGFIELD HURST RISE RD CUMNOR RISE RD MONTAGU RD COPE CL Botley MAPLE CL THE GARTH NORTH HINKSEY LA SOUTHERN BY-PASS RD Bulstake Stream

Dean Court QUEENS CL PINNOCK'S WAY DEAN COURT RD STUBBLE CL DENTON CL BROWNING CL SONGERS CL HUTCHCOMB RD HAWTHORN CL CRABTREE RD CROZIER CL WESTMINSTER WAY Sch

4

Hid's Copse CUMNOR HILL STANVILLE RD TOYNBEE CL CHESTNUT RD CEDAR RD BEECH RD LABURNUM RD YARNELL'S HILL SWEETMANS RD BOSSOM CL RALEIGH PARK RD PH Hinksey Stream NORTH HINKSEY LA

HID'S COPSE RD ARNOLD'S WAY SYCAMORE RD LIME RD Sch Raleigh Park North Hinksey Village The Fold

DELAMARE WAY HALLS CL Cumnor Hill

05

Chawley Long Copse COLERIDGE DR HIDE DOWN COTSWOLD RD TURNPIKE RD CLOVER CL Dene House Coll Water Tower HARCOURT HILL VERNON AVE STANTON RD GROSVENOR RD Harcourt Hill A34(T)

CHAWLEY LA NORREYS RD HURST LA Playing Field

3

Hurst Hill

04

Powder Hill Copse

Hen Wood

2

Chiswell Farm

Chiswell House (Priory)

Whitebarn Youlbury Wood Circular Walks Oxfordshire Birch Copse CHILSWELL LA

Resr Mast

03

Henwood Farm Youlbury Pond Pickett's Heath Farm Chiswell Farm Cottages

Upper Youlbury Heath West Gardens

1

SANDY LA Boars Hill RED COPSE

RIDGEWAY Wootton Close Jarn Mound BEDWELLS HEATH Yatscombe Copse HENWOOD DR WHITE HILL LA Oxford Preservation Trust

Mayo's Farm Old Boars Hill FOXCOMBE RD HAMELS LA CUMNOR RD B4017 White Hill Farm ORCHARD LA JARN WAY Ripon Hall BERKELEY RD BRUMCOMBE LA

02

47 A 48 B 49 C

139
159

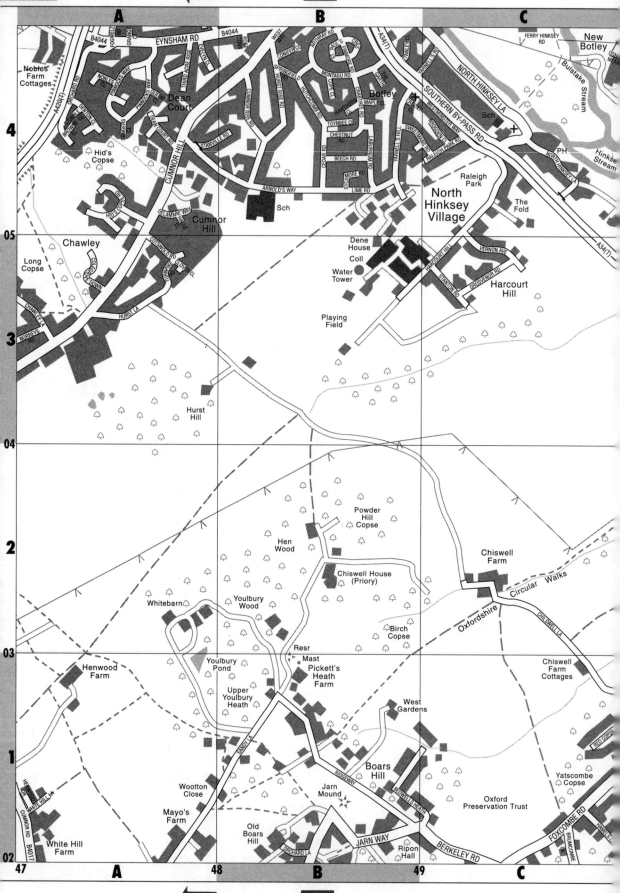

123
142

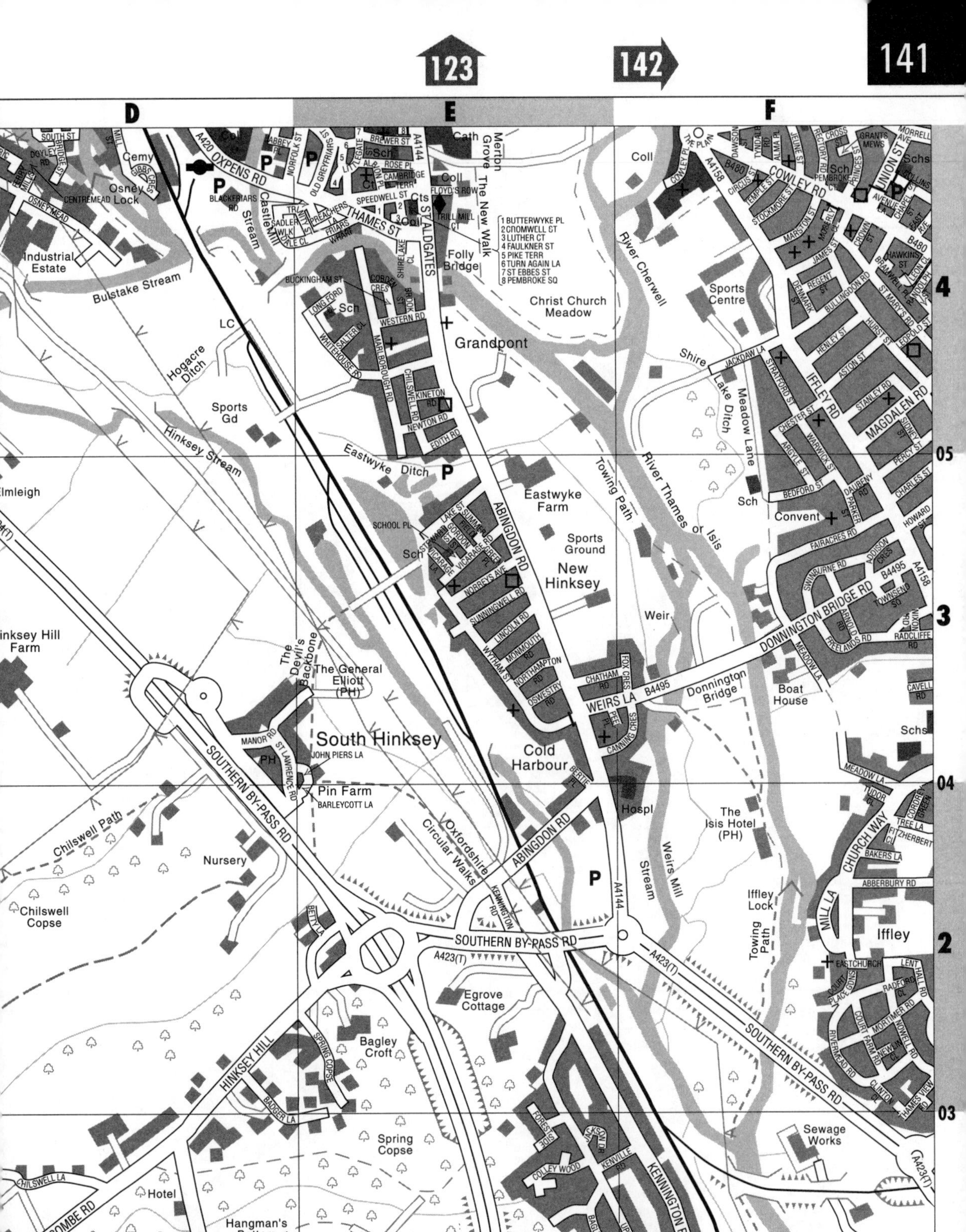
D
E
F
4
05
3
04
2
03
1
02
51
52
1 BUTTERWYKE PL
2 CROMWELL ST
3 LUTHER CT
4 FAULKNER ST
5 PIKE TERR
6 TURN AGAIN LA
7 ST EBBES ST
8 PEMBROKE SQ
Osney Lock
Cemy
Industrial Estate
Bulstake Stream
A420 OXPENS RD
Castle Mill Stream
THAMES ST
ST ALDGATES
A4144
Cath
Coll
Merton Grove
The New Walk
Folly Bridge
Christ Church Meadow
Grandpont
River Cherwell
Sports Centre
COWLEY RD
B480
IFFLEY RD
MAGDALEN RD
UNION ST
Schs
Sch
Shire Lake Ditch
Meadow Lane
Hogacre Ditch
Sports Gd
Hinksey Stream
Eastwyke Ditch
Eastwyke Farm
Sports Ground
New Hinksey
Towing Path
River Thames or Isis
ABINGDON RD
Convent
DONNINGTON BRIDGE RD
Weir
Elmleigh
Hinksey Hill Farm
The Devil's Backbone
The General Elliott (PH)
South Hinksey
Cold Harbour
WEIRS LA
B4495
Donnington Bridge
Boat House
Hospl
The Isis Hotel (PH)
Weirs Mill Stream
Pin Farm
Chilswell Path
Nursery
Chilswell Copse
Oxfordshire Circular Walks
SOUTHERN BY-PASS RD
A423(T)
A4144
Iffley Lock
Iffley
CHURCH WAY
Towing Path
Egrove Cottage
Bagley Croft
HINKSEY HILL
Spring Copse
Sewage Works
KENNINGTON RD
Hotel
FOXCOMBE RD
OXFORD RD
Hangman's Bottom
Middle Hill
West Wood
Bagley Wood
Cow Hall Bottom
Colley's Ladder East
Under Woods
A34(T)
Rose Island
Liby
BAGLEY WOOD RD
THE AVENUE
Kennington

160
142

141

124

A B C

Morrell Ave, Collins St, East Ave, Tawney St, Parsons Pl, Stone St, Hospital, Hill Top Rd, Divinity Rd, Minster Rd, Warneford Rd, Randolph St, Bartlemas Rd, Southfield Rd, Southfield Pk, CH, B480, Green St, Leopold St, Conv, Bartlemas Cl, Sports Gd, Herbert Cl, Belvedere Rd, Magdalen Rd, Whitson Pl, Essex St, Leys Pl, Kenilworth Ave, Barracks La, Sch, Cowley Rd, Hertford St, Ridgefield Rd, Cumberland Rd, Don Stuart Pl, Glanville Rd, Percy St, Barnet St, Charles St, Howard St, Cricket Rd, Saunders Rd, Westfield Cl, Gillians Way, Shelley Rd, Milton Rd, Catherine St, Allot Gdns, Boundary Brook Rd, Quarry Rd, Morris Cres, Pipkin Way, Georgeville Cl, A4158, 1 Radcliffe Rd, Iffley Rd, Florence Park, Hendred St, Littlehay Rd, Edmund Rd, Maidcroft Rd, Rymers La, Cornwallis Rd, Cornwallis Cl, Lytton Rd, Florence Park Rd, Outram Rd, Campbell Rd, Cavell Rd, Henley Ave, Iffley Turn, Church Way, B4495, Church Cowley Rd, Eleanor Cl, Cemy, Aubrey Ct, Wootten Dr, Bay Tree Cl, Tree La, Ellesmere Rd, Stone Quarry La, Bears Hedge, Courtland Rd, Annesley Rd, Villiers La, Rose Hill, Abberbury Rd, Abberbury Ave, Hunsdon Rd, 1 Sheepway Ct, 2 West View, Romney Rd, Spencer Cres, Lenthall Rd, Dashwood Rd, Ashhurst Way, Fiennes Rd, Jersey Rd, St Martin's Rd, Asquith Rd, Desborough Cres, Lambourn Rd, Nowell Rd, Wynbush Rd, Danvers Rd, Cottesmore Rd, Devereux Pl, Pattison Pl, Williamson Way, A4142

Oxford Rd, A4158, Bury Cres, Kelburne Rd, Hilsborough Rd, Mayfair Rd, Fairlie Rd, Rose Hill, Eastern Ave, Newman Rd, Cardinal Cl, Church Hill Rd, Beauchamp Pl, Beauchamp La, Wykeham Cres, Crowell Rd, Hampden Rd, The Grates, Lewin Cl, Gaisford Rd, Pulker Cl, Compass Cl, Littlemore Rd, Cowley Rd, Bartholomew Rd, Rahere Rd, Van-Dieman's La, Orchard Way, Bodley Rd, Addison Dr, Sheldon Way, Long La, Herschel Cres, Recn Gd, Hardings, Champion Way, Elm Tree Cl, Longwall, Milvery Way, Swinbourne Rd, M'boro Cl, Giles Rd, Giles Cl, College La, Upton Cl, Northfield Cl, Alice Smith Sq, St Nicholas Rd, Grange Rd, Vicarage Cl, St Mary's Cl, Priory Rd, Redmoor Ct, Carpenter Cl, Minchery Rd, Schs, Littlemore, Lanham Way, Kempson Cres, Thomson Terr, Brocklesby Rd, Gwyneth Rd, Chapel La, Railway La, Dudgeon Dr, Morrell Cres, Pheasant Wlk, Heyford Hill La, Yeftly Dr, Broadhurst Gdns, Sandford Rd, Hospital, A423(T), Oxford Science Park, Grenoble Rd, Sewage Works, Littlemore Brook, Minchery Farm, Minchery Farm Cottages

Hospital, Boundary Brook, Golf Course, Barracks La, Cowley Marsh, Marsh Rd, Lenfield Rd, Barracks La, Turner Cl, Crescent Cl, Crescent Rd, Temple Rd, Salesian Gdns, Junction Rd, Schs, Temple Cowley, Garland Cl, Oxford Rd, Temple Rd, Silkdale Cl, Salegate La, Liby, Clive Rd, Havelock Rd, Cleveland Dr, Gerard Pl, Lawrence Rd, John Allen Centre, Between Towns Rd, Pound Way, Banjo Rd, The Oval, Upper Barr, Knolles Rd, St Luke's Rd, Coleridge Cl, Napier Rd, Phipps Rd, Bailey Rd, Boswell Rd, Frederick Rd, Liddell Rd, Dodgson Rd, Chillingworth, Barns Rd, Burgan Cl, Lockheart Cres, Kersington Cres, Amory Cl, Sch, Bampton Cl, Sandy La W, Peter's Way, Ledgers Cl, Spring La, Broadfields, Ind Est, Playing Field, B4495, B480

Heath Cl, Warren Cres, Peat Moors, B4495, Wood Farm Rd, Atkyns Rd, Nuffield Rd, Chillingworth Cres, 1 Bracegirdle Rd, Open Magdalen, Holland Pl, Pauling Rd, Peppercorn Ave, Leiden Rd, 1 Abbots Wood (W), 2 Abbots Wood (E), Broad Oak, The Slade, Benson Rd, Dene Rd, Binnaminta Rd, Bulan Rd, Glebelands, Fairview, Lye Valley, Coverley Rd, Town Furze, Nott Furze, Three Fields Rd, Stubbs Ave, Long Cl, Pickett Ave, Mascall Ave, Horspath Driftway, F Sta, Hospital, Hollow Way, James Wolfe Rd, Kennedy Cl, Lambton Cl, Hayter Cl, Fletcher Rd, Yeats Cl, Cranmer Rd, Burton Pl, Fairfax Rd, Rupert Rd, Ridley Rd, Brasenose Driftway, Coruna Cres, Crauford Rd, Horspath Rd, Marshall Rd, Wilkins Rd, White Rd, Sunnyside, Bleache Pl, Paget Rd, Fanshawe Pl, Normandy Cres, Oliver Rd, Fern Hill Rd, Burbush Rd, Cowley, Garsington Rd, A4142, Eastern By-Pass Rd, Works, Stadium, Ashville Way, Harrow Rd, Watlington Rd, Sandy La, Tucker Rd, Adenham Rd, Longlands Rd, Druce Way, Jourdain Rd, Balfour Rd, Kent Cl, Allin Cl, Wingate Cl, Furlong Cl, Playing Field, Moorbank, Sampit Rd, Bray Cl, Haldane Rd, Poulton Pl, Warburg Cres, Wesley Cl, Cuddesdon Way, Blackbird Leys Rd, Linnet Cl, Kestrel Cres, Brambling Way, Mallard Cl, Merlin Rd, Willow Way, Whitethorn Way, Overmead Green, Birchfield Cl, Blackbird Leys Rd, Peregrine Rd, Monks Cl, Nuthatch Cl, Knights Rd, Spindleberry Cl, Sch, Northfield Brook, Blackbird Leys Farm

A4142, The Ridings, Fourth Ave, Seventh Ave, Eighth Ave, First Ave, Brasenose Wood, Ninth Ave, Brasenose Farm, Peterley Rd, Pony Rd, Industrial Estate, Oxford Rd, Roman Way, Works, County Trading Est, 1 Prunus Cl, 2 Pine Cl, Oxford Rd, B480, Comfrey Rd, Erica Cl, Sorrel Rd, Briar Way, Pegasus Ct, Juniper Dr, Woodruff Cl, Park, Blackbird Leys, 1 Jasmine Cl, 2 Timothy Way, 3 Rest Harrow, 4 Starwort Path, 5 Periwinkle Pl, Field Ave, Clematis Pl, Harebell Rd, Pegasus Rd, Thrift Pl, Cranberry Rd, Samphire Rd, Windale Ave, Andromeda Cl, Angelica Cl, Bulrush Rd, Clover Pl, Flaxfield Rd, Gentian Rd, 1 Strawberry Path, 2 Butterworth Pl, Shepards Hill, Greenfinch Cl, Blacksmiths Meadow, Jane Seaman

4 05 3 04 2 03 1 02

53 54 55

A B C

141

161

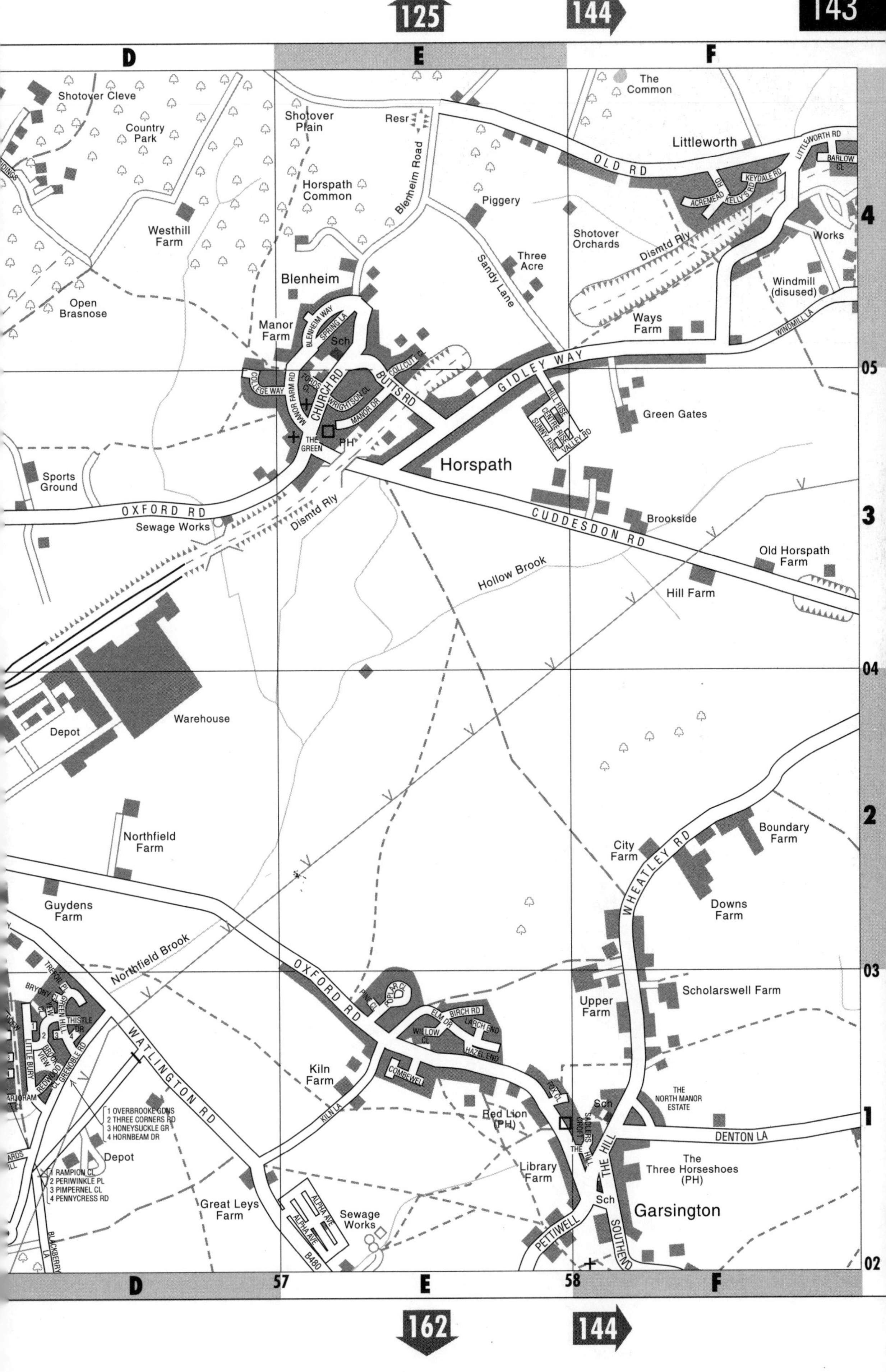
D
E
F
Shotover Cleve
Country Park
Westhill Farm
Open Brasnose
Shotover Plain
Resr
Horspath Common
Blenheim Road
Blenheim
Manor Farm
Sch
The Common
Littleworth
OLD RD
Piggery
Shotover Orchards
Dismtd Rly
Three Acre
Sandy Lane
Works
Windmill (disused)
Ways Farm
GIDLEY WAY
Green Gates
Horspath
PH
Sports Ground
OXFORD RD
Sewage Works
Brookside
CUDDESDON RD
Old Horspath Farm
Hollow Brook
Hill Farm
Warehouse
Depot
Northfield Farm
City Farm
WHEATLEY RD
Boundary Farm
Guydens Farm
Downs Farm
Northfield Brook
Scholarswell Farm
Upper Farm
WATLINGTON RD
Kiln Farm
Red Lion (PH)
Sch
THE NORTH MANOR ESTATE
DENTON LA
1 OVERBROOKE GDNS
2 THREE CORNERS RD
3 HONEYSUCKLE GR
4 HORNBEAM DR
Depot
1 RAMPION CL
2 PERIWINKLE PL
3 PIMPERNEL CL
4 PENNYCRESS RD
Library Farm
The Three Horseshoes (PH)
Great Leys Farm
Sewage Works
Sch
Garsington
PETTIWELL
SOUTHEND
THE HILL
4
05
3
04
2
03
1
02
57
58

A B C

Sch
WESTFIELD
RD
BLENHEIM LA
KILN LA
TEMPLE RD
ST MARYS CL
THE GLEBE
Coll
Holton Mill
LITTLEWORTH RD
CHURCH RD
HOLLOWAY RD
Sch
P
HIGH ST
BARLOW CL
STATION RD
HATHAWAYS
SIMONS CL
FARM CLOSE
Sch
ANGER CL
CAMBRIDGE RISE
OLD LONDON RD
Wheatley
FARM CLS
Sch
CROWN RD
LONDON RD
F Sta
HOWE CL
KIMBER CL
BERRY CL
ORCHARD RD
BEECH RD
MAY TRIANGLE
JACKIES LA
CULLUM RD
MILLER RD
THE AVENUE
ROMAN RD
4
KELHAM HALL DR
ELM CL
HILARY LA
CLYTON CRES

WINDMILL LA
The Plough
(PH)
Wheatley
Bridge
Dismantled
Railway
Sewage
Works
A40(T)
Bridge House
(PH)
A418

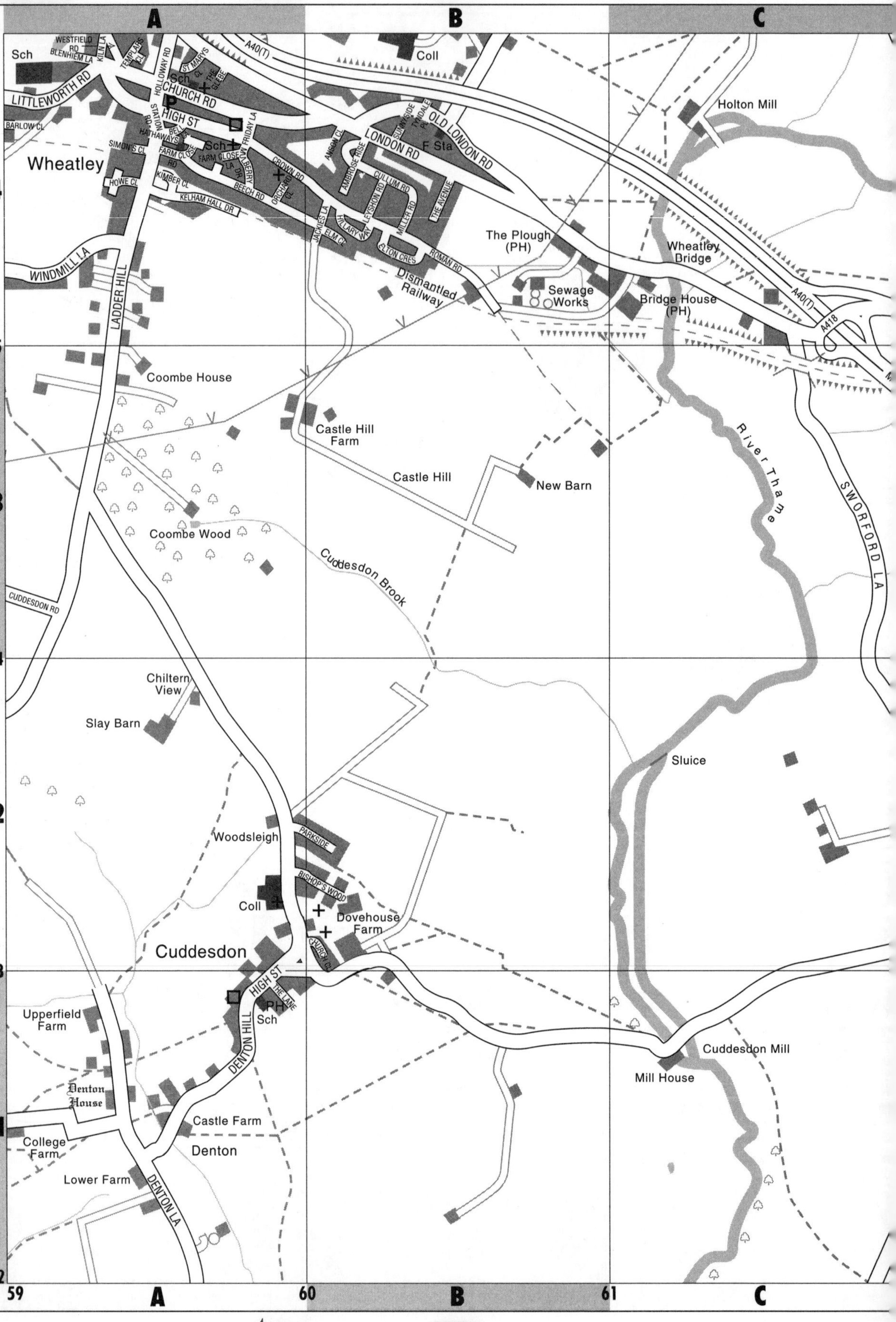

05

LADDER HILL
Coombe House
Castle Hill
Farm
New Barn
River Thame
SWORFORD LA

3
Castle Hill
Coombe Wood
Cuddesdon Brook

CUDDESDON RD

04

Chiltern
View
Slay Barn
Sluice

2
Woodsleigh
PARKSIDE
BISHOPS WOOD
Coll
Dovehouse
Farm
CHURCH CL

Cuddesdon

03
HIGH ST
THE LANE
Upperfield
Farm
DENTON HILL
PH
Sch
Cuddesdon Mill
Mill House

Denton
House
Castle Farm
College
Farm
1
Denton

Lower Farm
DENTON LA

02

59 A 60 B 61 C

D
E
F
Manor Farm
Draycot
Albury Farm
Waterstock House
Stockwell Lane
Waterstock
Bow Bridge
Home Farm
Oxfordshire Way
ICKFORD RD
NORTH CL
BROOKSIDE CL
Waterstock Mill
River Thame
The Fox (PH)
Tiddington
Hyde Spinney
A418
ALBURY VIEW
OXFORD RD
Lower Farm
Walter's Farm
Chilworth House
Dismantled Railway
Holloway Farm
M40
Sandylane Farm
SANDY LA
Lower Chilworth Farm
LONDON RD
Camp Corner
Chilworth Farm
Trindalls Farm
Branscrouch
OLD LONDON RD
SWORFORD LA
CHILWORTH RD
Sewage Works
Heath Farm
Tripps Farm
LOWER END
POTT'S CL
Orpwoods Farm
Sch
A329
Kings Head (PH)
HIGH ST
PEGSWELL LA
Sch
FULLERS FIELD
GREEN HITCHINGS
Mount Pleasant Farm
THAME RD
OXEN PIECE
Green Ways
Great Milton
CHURCH RD
THE FORTIES
The Views
LYCH GATE LA
Mill House
Milton Common
Windmill (disused)
Romeyns Court
Manor Farm
Haseley Estate
Glebe Farm
A329
4
05
3
04
2
03
1
02
63
64

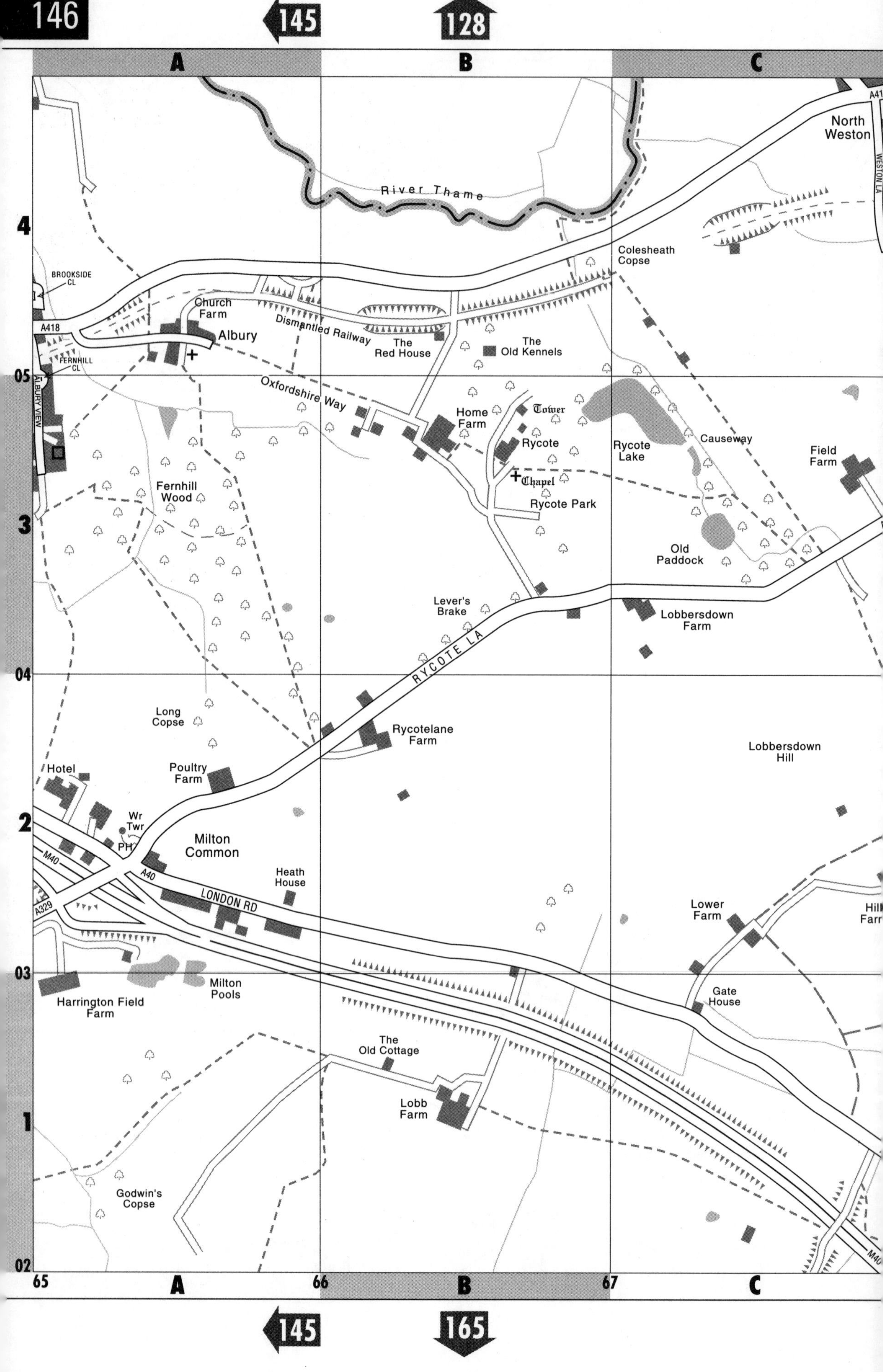

A   B   C

North Weston

A41

WESTON LA

River Thame

4

Colesheath Copse

BROOKSIDE CL

A418

Church Farm

Albury

Dismantled Railway

The Red House

The Old Kennels

FERNHILL CL

05

ALBURY VIEW

Oxfordshire Way

Home Farm

Tower

Rycote

Rycote Lake

Causeway

Field Farm

Fernhill Wood

Chapel

Rycote Park

Old Paddock

3

Lever's Brake

Lobbersdown Farm

RYCOTE LA

04

Long Copse

Rycotelane Farm

Lobbersdown Hill

Hotel

Poultry Farm

Wr Twr
PH

Milton Common

Heath House

Lower Farm

Hill Farm

2

M40

A40

LONDON RD

A329

03

Harrington Field Farm

Milton Pools

Gate House

The Old Cottage

Lobb Farm

1

Godwin's Copse

M40

02

65   A   66   B   67   C

D
E
F

OXFORD RD
A418
BEECH RD
SYCAMORE DR
CHESTNUT AVE
MANOR AVE
Sch
Sch
Sch
POPLAR CRES

BROOK LA
MITCHELL CL
SPRING PATH
HIGH ST
TH MARKET
BUTTERM
NORTH ST
LEA ST
KINGS
WELLINGTON ST

THAME

HAMILTON RD
LINCOLN LN
P
UPPER HIGH ST
P
ANDREW CT
EAST ST

Recn
Gd
F Sta

SHARMAN BEER CT
SOUTHERN RD
ROOKS LA
BELMONT
MEWS
GOODSONS
IND MEWS

PARK ST

MORETON LA
HOLLIERS CL
NELSON ST
ELMS RD
PEARCE

Liby

COOMBE HILL CRES
CONDUIT HILL
AROUND LA
WINDMILL RD
WATERS
Recn
Gd

4

Manor
Farm

Dismantled Railway

RYCOTE LA

Depot

Works

Abbey
Farm

A329

VAN DIEMAN'S RD
HAMPDEN AVE

Depot 88

Batesleys
Farm

05

Moreton
Farm

Greys
Mead
B4012

3

THE FURLONGS
Elmtree
Farm

PH

Leys
Farm

Chestnut
Farm

Meadowbrook
Farm

Cuttle Brook

Moreton

04

Parkgrange
Farm

obersdown-hill
Farm

Thame
Park

2

Moreton
Gap

Oxfordshire Way

Moretonfield
Farm

Moretongap
Wood

Lodges
Musgrave's
Covert

03

Osierbed
Wood

Horsenden Hill
Judd's Lane

Spencer's
Farm

Tetsworth
Common

Sewage
Works

1

Fox
Covert

Upper
Atlington
Wood

HIGH ST
A40

B4012

02

D
69
E
70
F

147
130

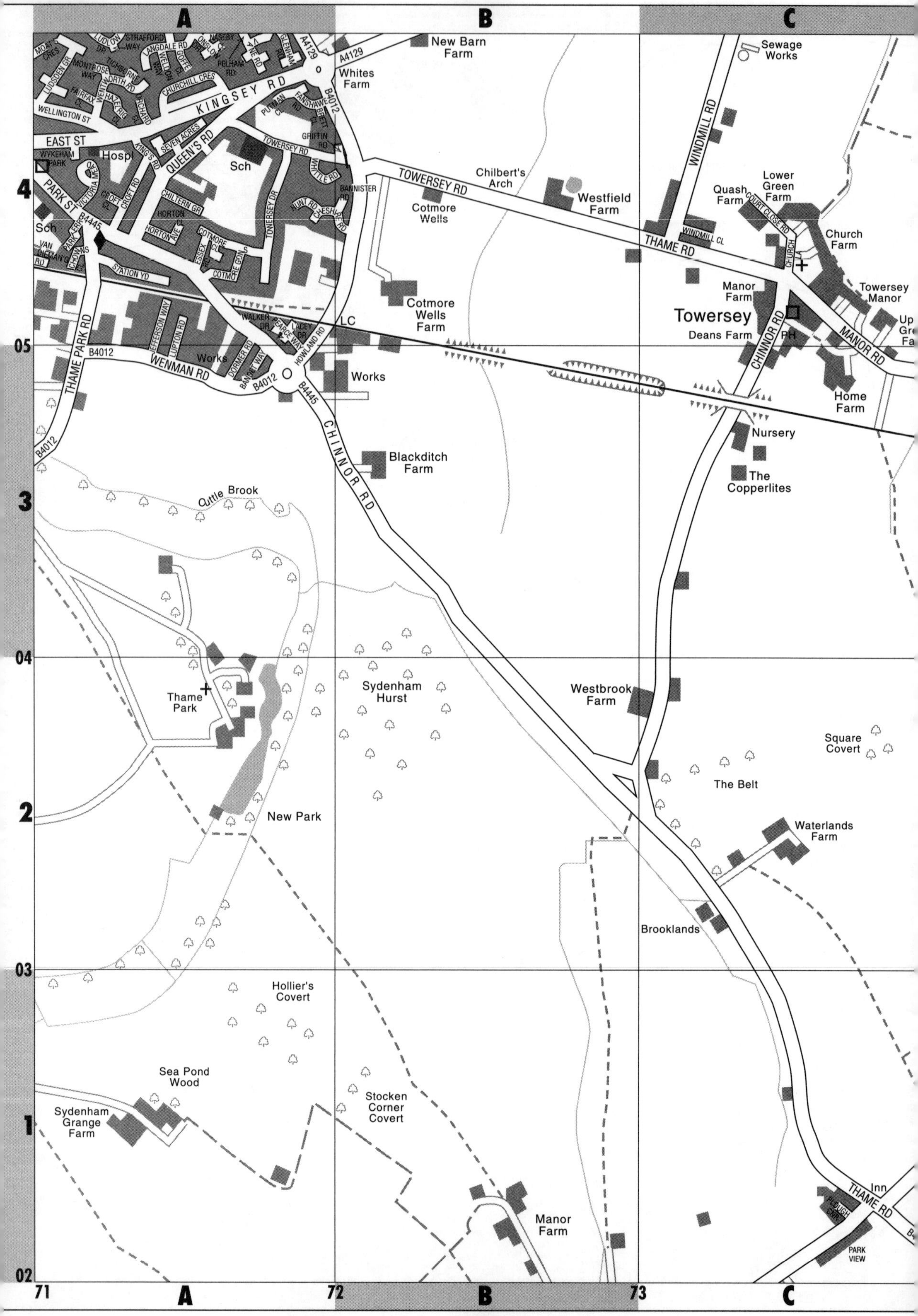

A

B

C

MOT CRES
STRAFFORD WAY
NASEBY RD
LANGDALE RD
GLENTHAM
A4129
New Barn Farm
A4129
Whites Farm
Sewage Works

LUSTED GDN
MONTROSE WAY
NORTH RD
RICHARD
CHURCHILL CRES
PELHAM RD
WINDMILL RD

WELLINGTON ST
KINGSEY RD
B4012
FANSHAWE RD

EAST ST
QUEEN'S RD
GRIFFIN RD
TOWERSEY RD
Chilbert's Arch
Westfield Farm
Quash Farm
Lower Green Farm
Church Farm

Hospl
Wykeham Park
Sch
TOWERSEY RD
THAME RD
WINDMILL CL
CL
Towersey Manor

4
Sch
B4445
CHILTERN GR
HORTON
NNT RD
CHESHAM RD
BANNISTER
Cotmore Wells
Manor Farm
Towersey Manor

Sch
VAN DIEMAN'S RD
ESSEX RD
COTMORE
STATION YD
Cotmore Wells Farm
Towersey
Deans Farm
PH
Up Gre Fa

05
THAME PARK RD
B4012
WENMAN RD
Works
B4012
HOWLAND RD
LC
Works
CHINNOR RD
MANOR RD
Home Farm

B4012
JEFFERSON WAY
UPTON RD
LADEY
B4445
Blackditch Farm
Nursery
The Copperlites

3
Cuttle Brook
CHINNOR RD

04
Thame Park
Sydenham Hurst
Westbrook Farm
Square Covert

2
New Park
The Belt
Waterlands Farm

Brooklands

03
Hollier's Covert

Sea Pond Wood
Stocken Corner Covert
THAME RD
Inn

1
Sydenham Grange Farm
PLOUGH
PARK VIEW

02
71
72
73

A
B
C

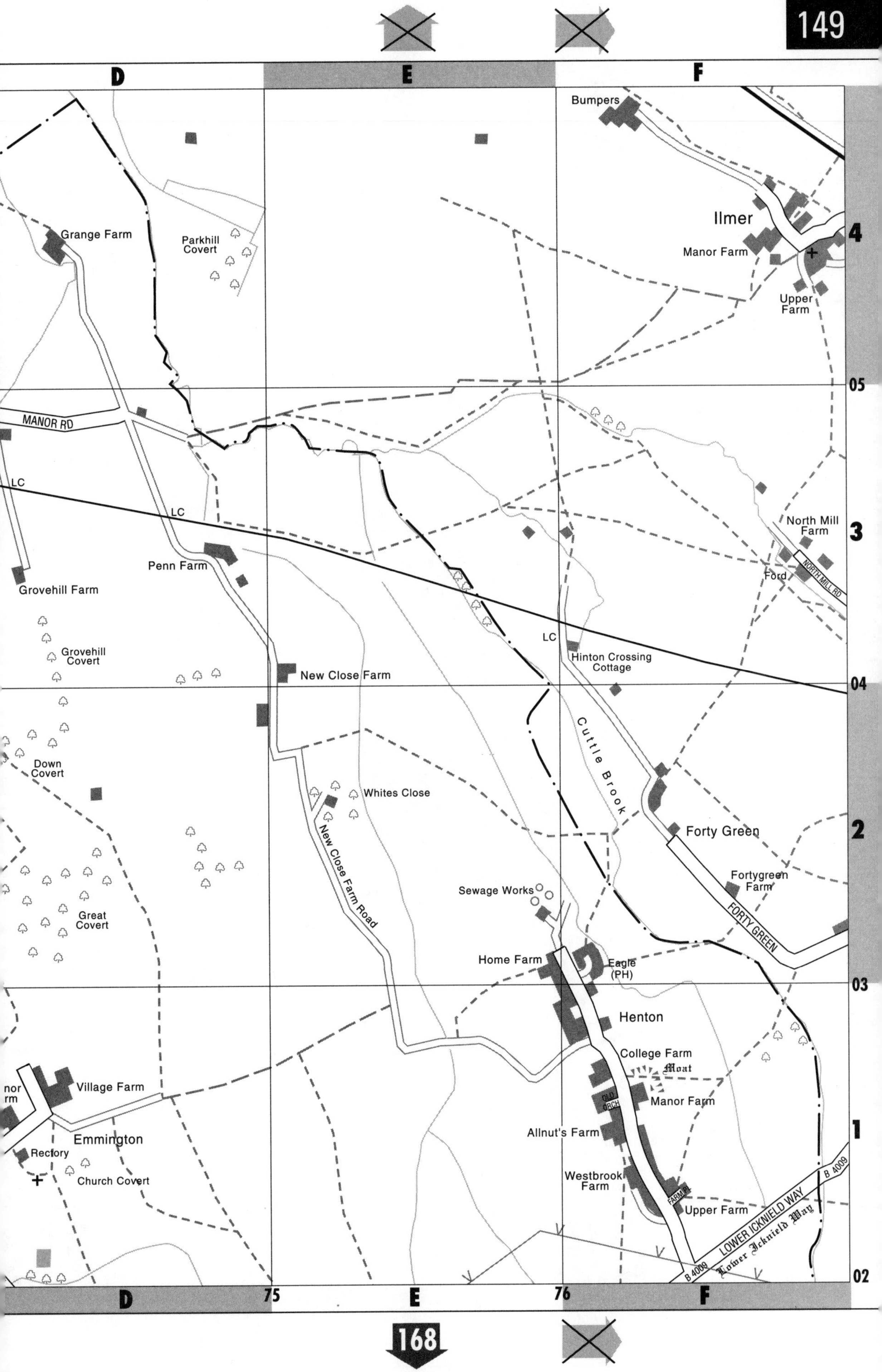

D   E   F

Bumpers

Ilmer

4

Manor Farm

Upper
Farm

Grange Farm

Parkhill
Covert

05

MANOR RD

LC

North Mill
Farm

LC

3

Grovehill Farm

Penn Farm

Ford

NORTH MILL RD

Grovehill
Covert

New Close Farm

LC

Hinton Crossing
Cottage

04

Down
Covert

Whites Close

Cuttle Brook

New Close Farm Road

Forty Green

2

Great
Covert

Fortygreen
Farm

FORTY GREEN

Sewage Works

Home Farm

Eagle
(PH)

03

Henton

College Farm
Moat

Village Farm

OLD
RECH

Manor Farm

nor
rm

Allnut's Farm

1

Emmington

Westbrook
Farm

Rectory

FARM

Church Covert

Upper Farm

LOWER ICKNIELD WAY

Lower Icknield Way

B 4009

B 4009

02

D 75 E 76 F

131

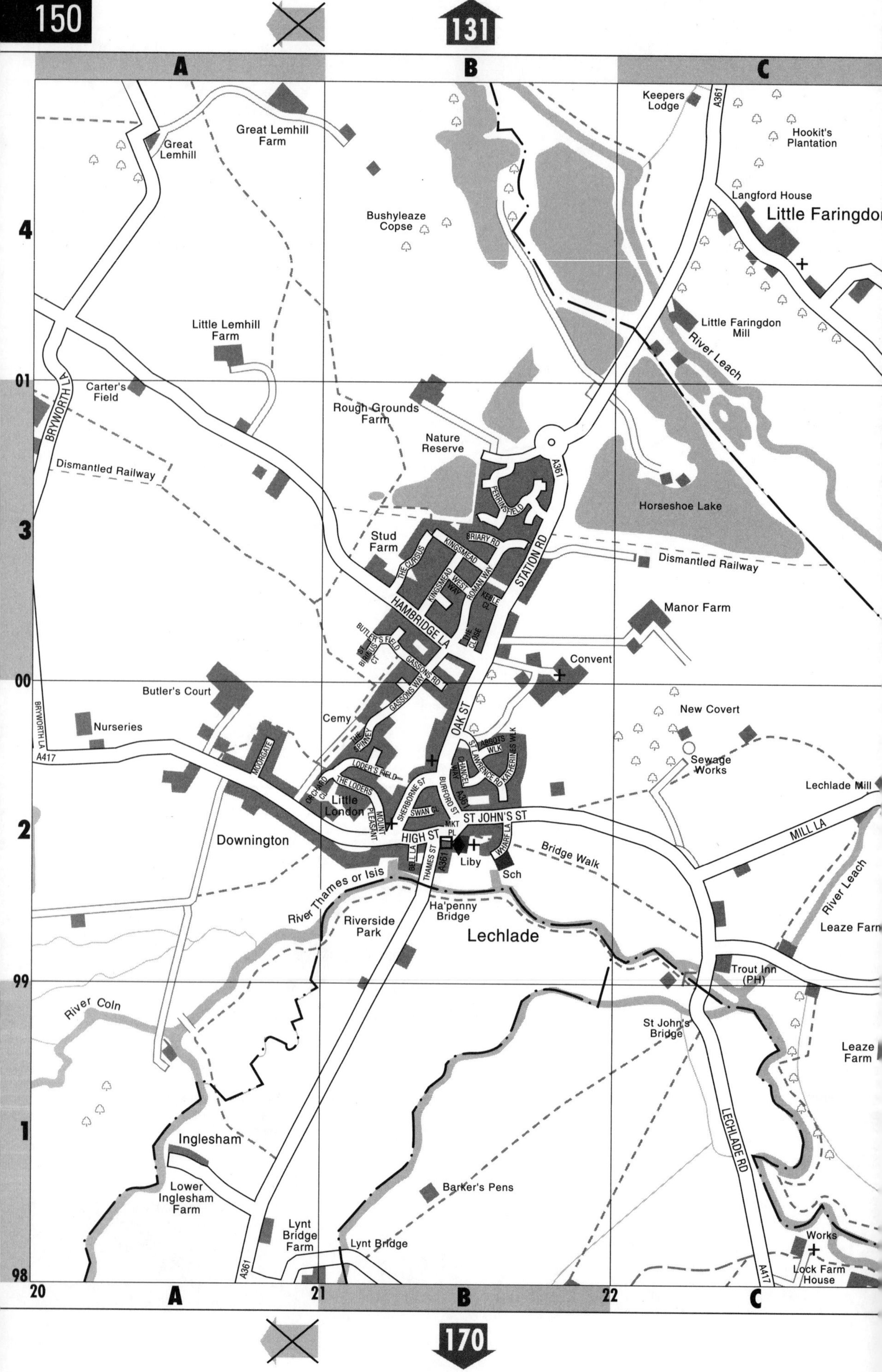
A
B
C
4
01
3
00
2
99
1
98
20
21
22
Great Lemhill
Great Lemhill Farm
Keepers Lodge
A361
Hookit's Plantation
Langford House
Little Faringdon
Bushyleaze Copse
Little Faringdon Mill
River Leach
Little Lemhill Farm
BRYWORTH LA
Carter's Field
Rough Grounds Farm
Nature Reserve
Dismantled Railway
PERRINSFIELD
Horseshoe Lake
Stud Farm
BRIARY RD
KINGSMEAD
THE CURSUS
STATION RD
Dismantled Railway
WEST WAY
ROMAN WAY
KEBLE CL
HAMBRIDGE LA
Manor Farm
BUTLER'S FIELD
ST BIRINUS CT
THE CLOSE
GASSONS RD
GASSONS WAY
Convent
Butler's Court
BRYWORTH LA
Nurseries
Cemy
New Covert
OAK ST
ABBOTS WLK
KATHERINES WLK
THE SPINNEY
A417
MOORGATE
LODER'S FIELD
CHANCEL WAY
ST LAWRENCE RD
Sewage Works
Lechlade Mill
ORCHARD CL
THE LODERS
SHERBORNE ST
BURFORD ST
A361
Little London
MOUNT PLEASANT
SWAN CL
ST JOHN'S ST
MILL LA
Downington
HIGH ST
MKT PL
WHARF LA
Bridge Walk
BELL LA
THAMES ST
Liby
Sch
River Thames or Isis
River Leach
Ha'penny Bridge
Riverside Park
Lechlade
Leaze Farm
Trout Inn (PH)
River Coln
St John's Bridge
Leaze Farm
Inglesham
LECHLADE RD
Lower Inglesham Farm
Barker's Pens
Lynt Bridge Farm
Lynt Bridge
Works
Lock Farm House
A417

170

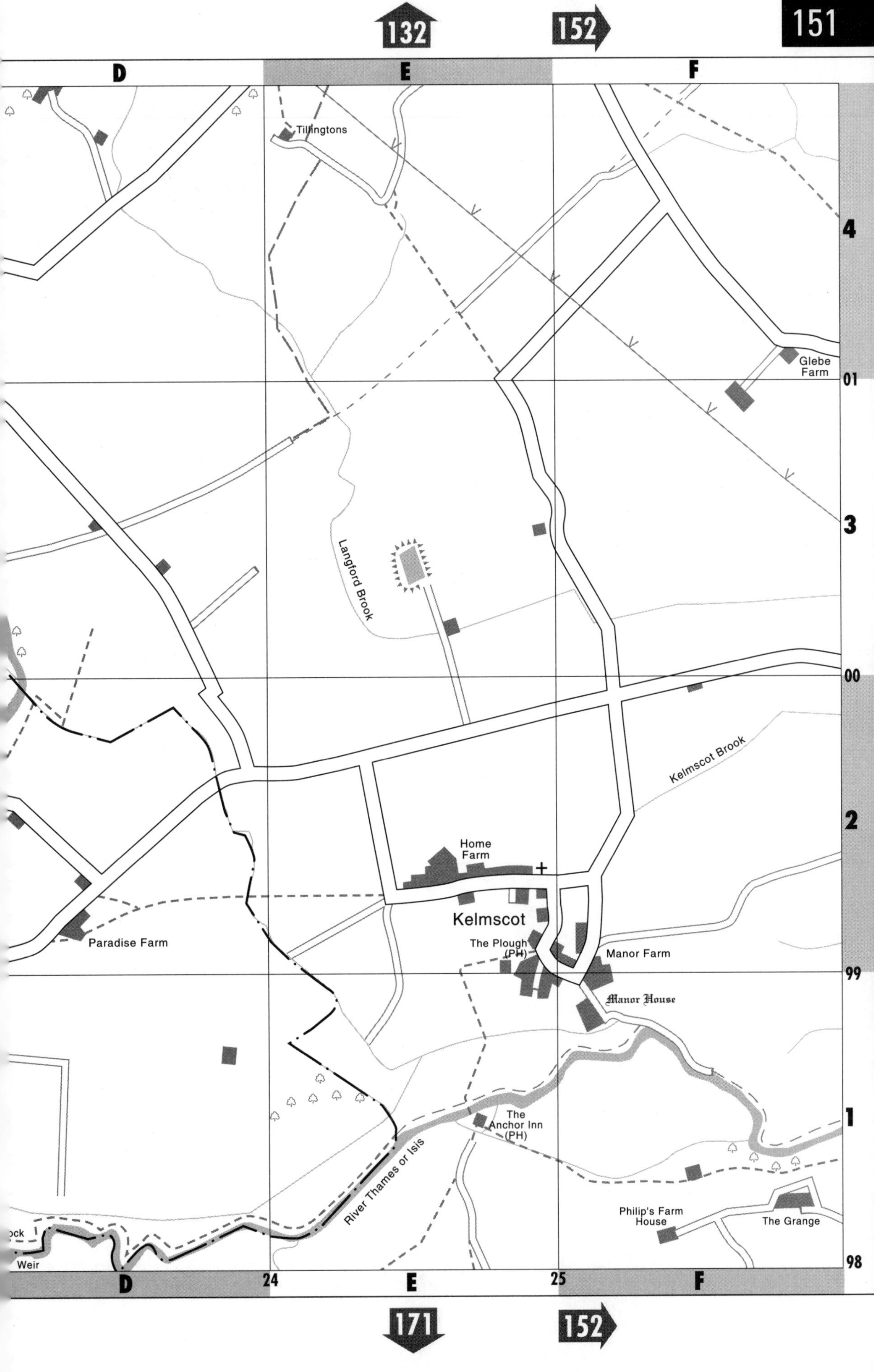

Tillingtons

Glebe Farm

4

01

Langford Brook

3

00

Kelmscot Brook

2

Home Farm

Kelmscot

The Plough (PH)

Manor Farm

99

Paradise Farm

Manor House

The Anchor Inn (PH)

1

River Thames or Isis

Philip's Farm House

The Grange

98

Weir

151
133

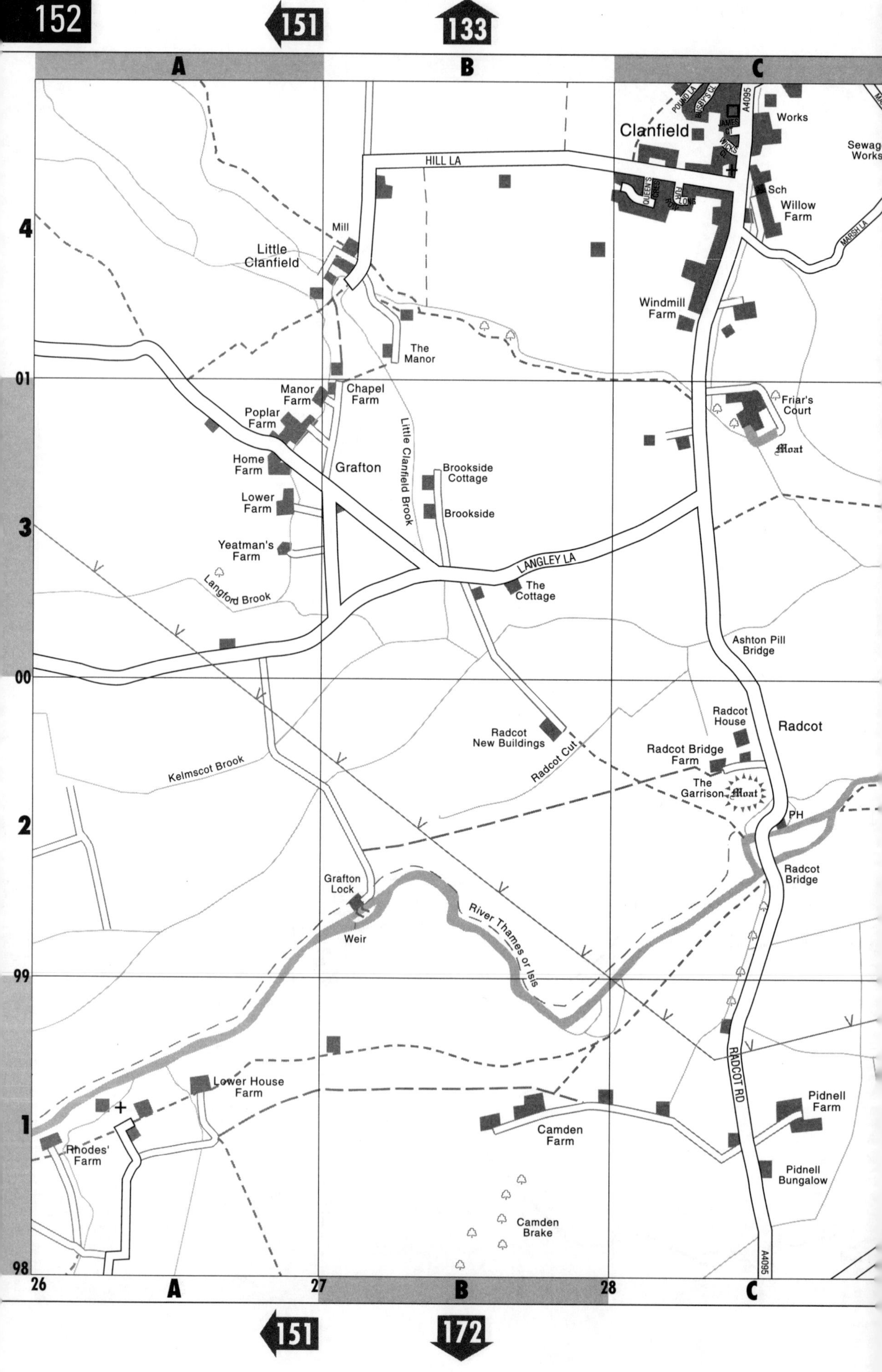
A
B
C
Clanfield
POUND LA
BUSBY'S CL
JAMES CT
WICKS CL
A4095
Works
Sewage Works
HILL LA
QUEEN'S CRES
FUR LONG ROW
Sch
Willow Farm
MARSH LA
Mill
Little Clanfield
Windmill Farm
The Manor
Manor Farm
Chapel Farm
Poplar Farm
Friar's Court
Moat
Home Farm
Grafton
Little Clanfield Brook
Brookside Cottage
Lower Farm
Brookside
Yeatman's Farm
LANGLEY LA
Langford Brook
The Cottage
Ashton Pill Bridge
Radcot House
Radcot
Radcot New Buildings
Radcot Bridge Farm
Kelmscot Brook
Radcot Cut
The Garrison
PH
Radcot Bridge
Grafton Lock
Weir
River Thames or Isis
RADCOT RD
Lower House Farm
Pidnell Farm
Rhodes' Farm
Camden Farm
Pidnell Bungalow
Camden Brake
A4095
4
01
3
00
2
99
1
98
26
27
28

151
172

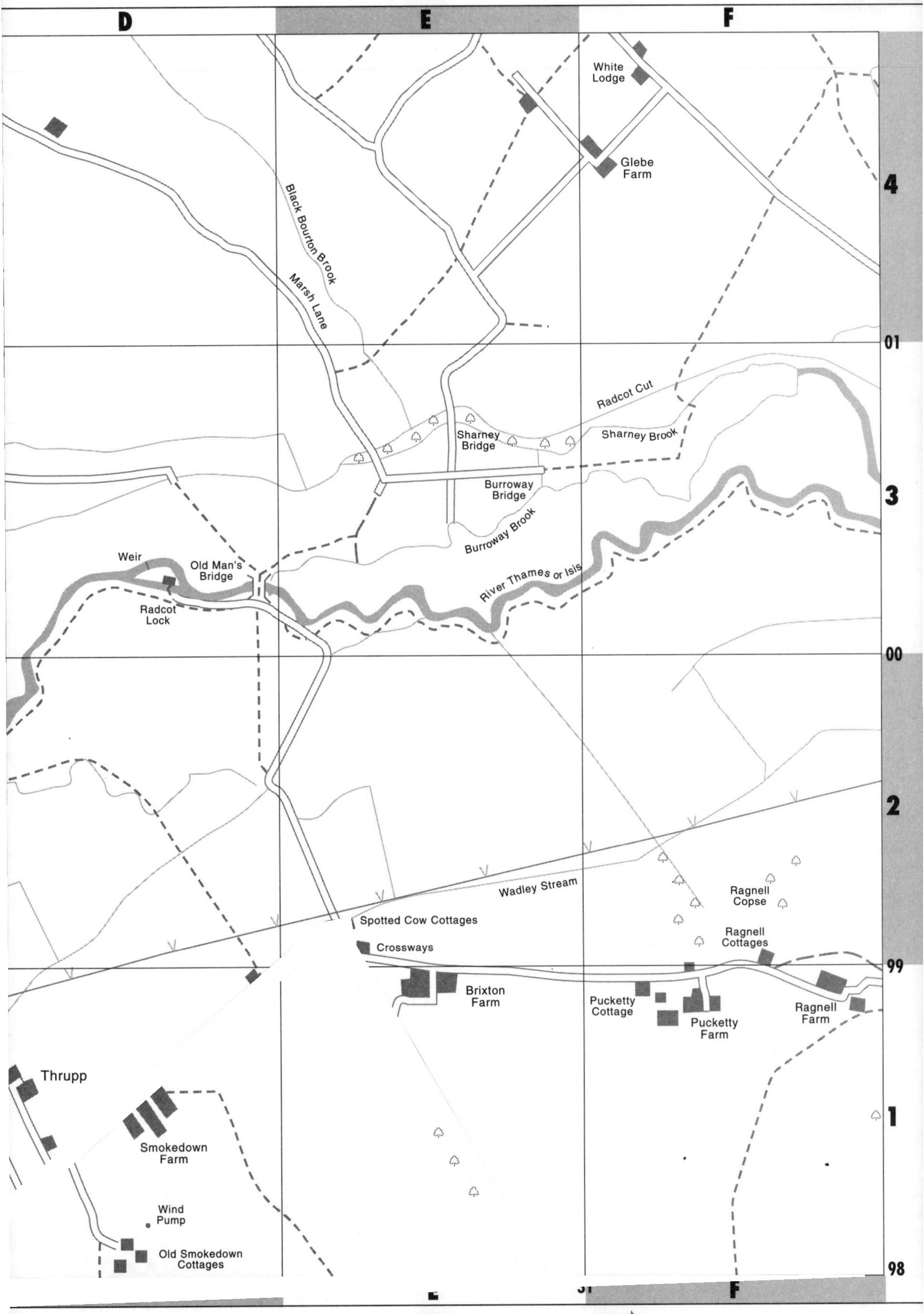

D E F

White
Lodge

Glebe
Farm

4

Black Bourton Brook

Marsh Lane

01

Radcot Cut

Sharney
Bridge

Sharney Brook

Burroway
Bridge

3

Burroway Brook

Weir

Old Man's
Bridge

River Thames or Isis

Radcot
Lock

00

2

Wadley Stream

Ragnell
Copse

Spotted Cow Cottages

Ragnell
Cottages

Crossways

99

Brixton
Farm

Pucketty
Cottage

Ragnell
Farm

Pucketty
Farm

Thrupp

1

Smokedown
Farm

Wind
Pump

Old Smokedown
Cottages

98

E F

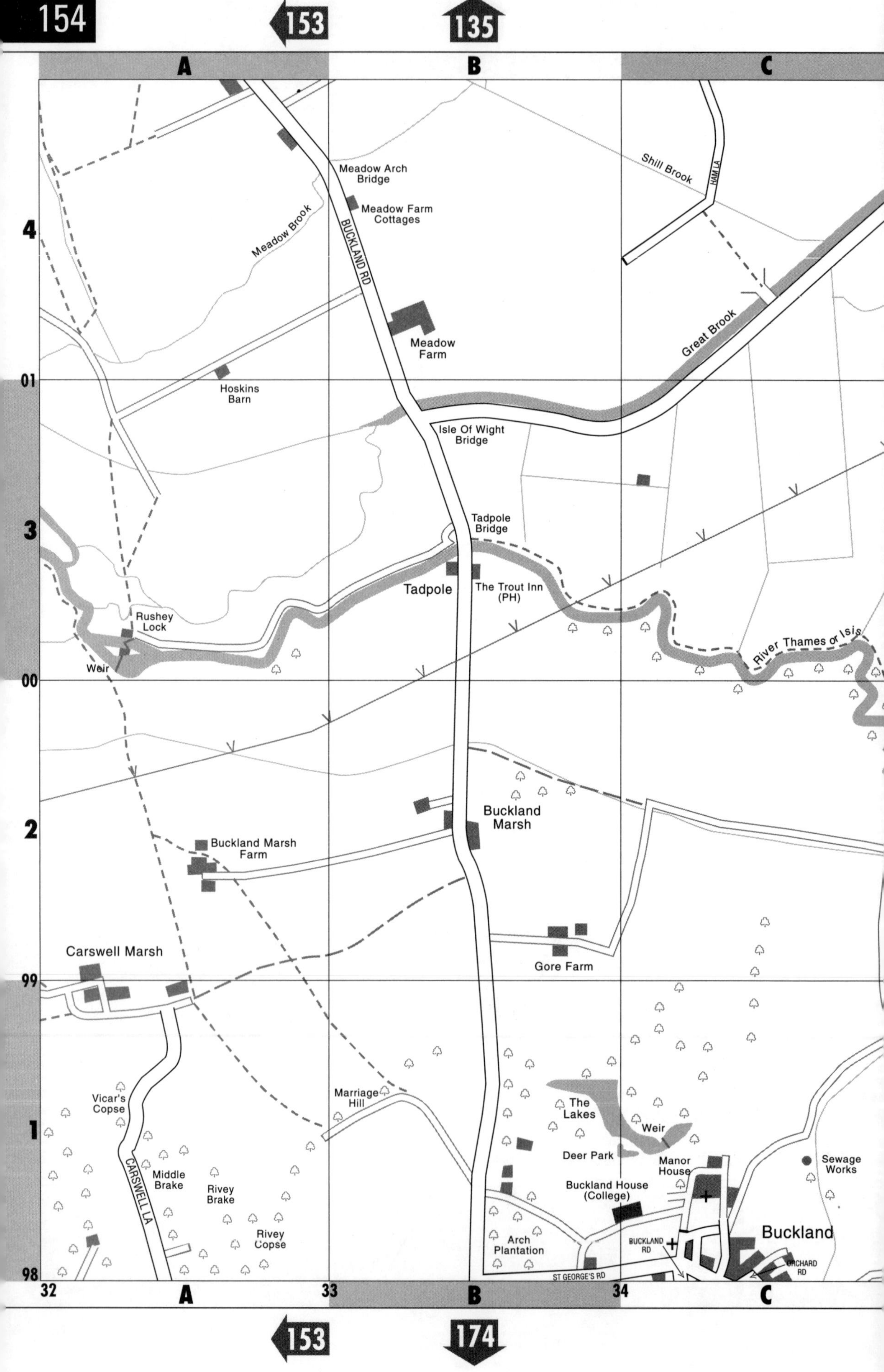

A   B   C

4

Shill Brook

HAM LA

Meadow Arch
Bridge

Meadow Farm
Cottages

Meadow Brook

BUCKLAND RD

Meadow
Farm

Great Brook

01

Hoskins
Barn

Isle Of Wight
Bridge

Tadpole
Bridge

3

Tadpole

The Trout Inn
(PH)

Rushey
Lock

River Thames or Isis

Weir

00

2

Buckland Marsh
Farm

Buckland
Marsh

Carswell Marsh

Gore Farm

99

Vicar's
Copse

Marriage
Hill

The
Lakes

Weir

1

CARSWELL LA

Middle
Brake

Rivey
Brake

Deer Park

Manor
House

Sewage
Works

Buckland House
(College)

Buckland

Rivey
Copse

Arch
Plantation

BUCKLAND
RD

ORCHARD
RD

98

ST GEORGE'S RD

32   A   33   B   34   C

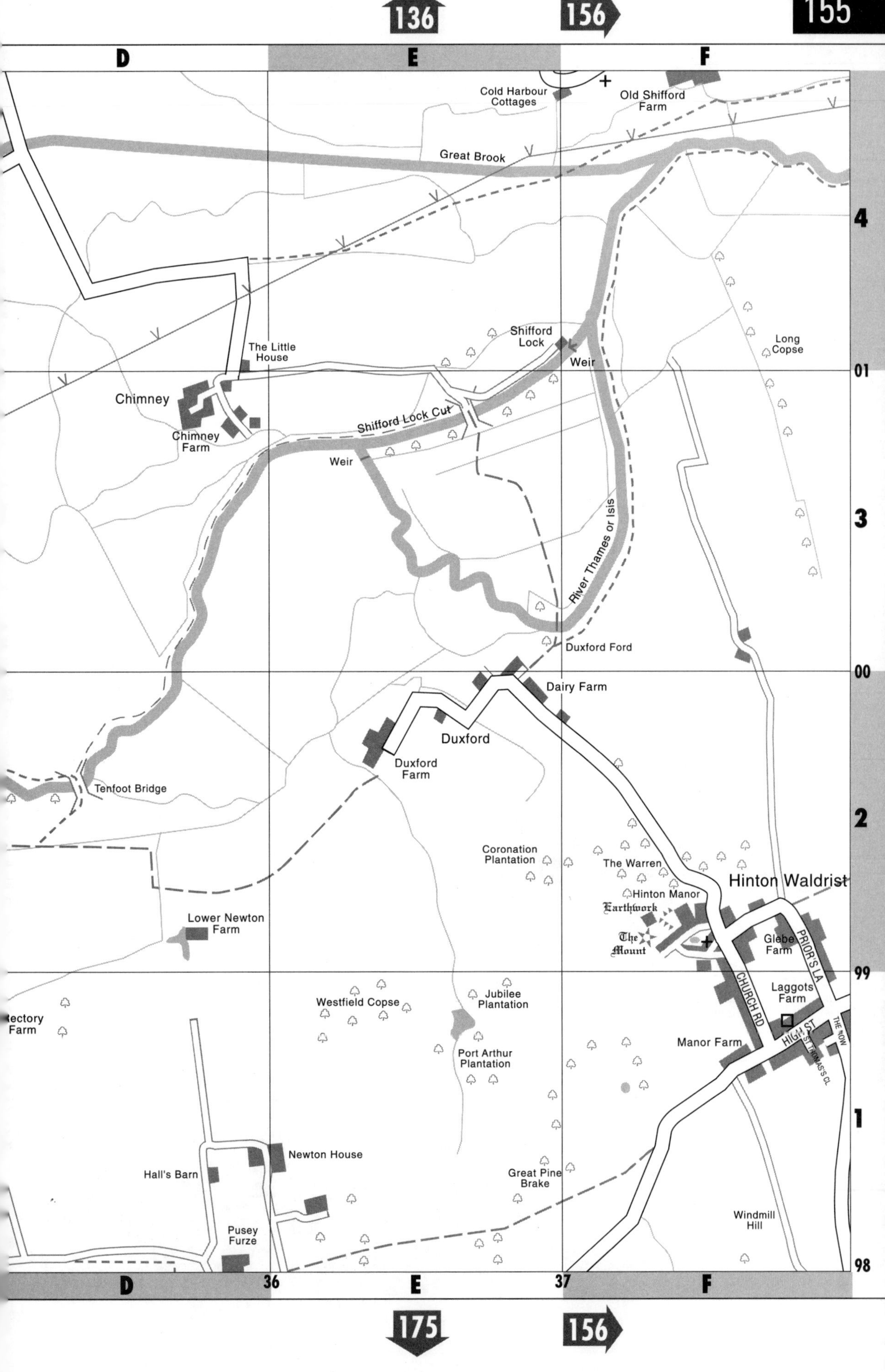

D E F

Cold Harbour Cottages

Old Shifford Farm

Great Brook

4

The Little House

Shifford Lock

Long Copse

Weir

01

Chimney

Shifford Lock Cut

Chimney Farm

Weir

River Thames or Isis

3

Duxford Ford

00

Dairy Farm

Duxford

Tenfoot Bridge

Duxford Farm

2

Coronation Plantation

The Warren

Hinton Waldrist

Hinton Manor

Lower Newton Farm

Earthwork

The Mount

Glebe Farm

PRIOR'S LA

99

Rectory Farm

Westfield Copse

Jubilee Plantation

Laggots Farm

CHURCH RD

Manor Farm

HIGH ST

ST THOMAS'S CL

THE ROW

Port Arthur Plantation

1

Hall's Barn

Newton House

Great Pine Brake

Windmill Hill

Pusey Furze

98

D 36 E 37 F

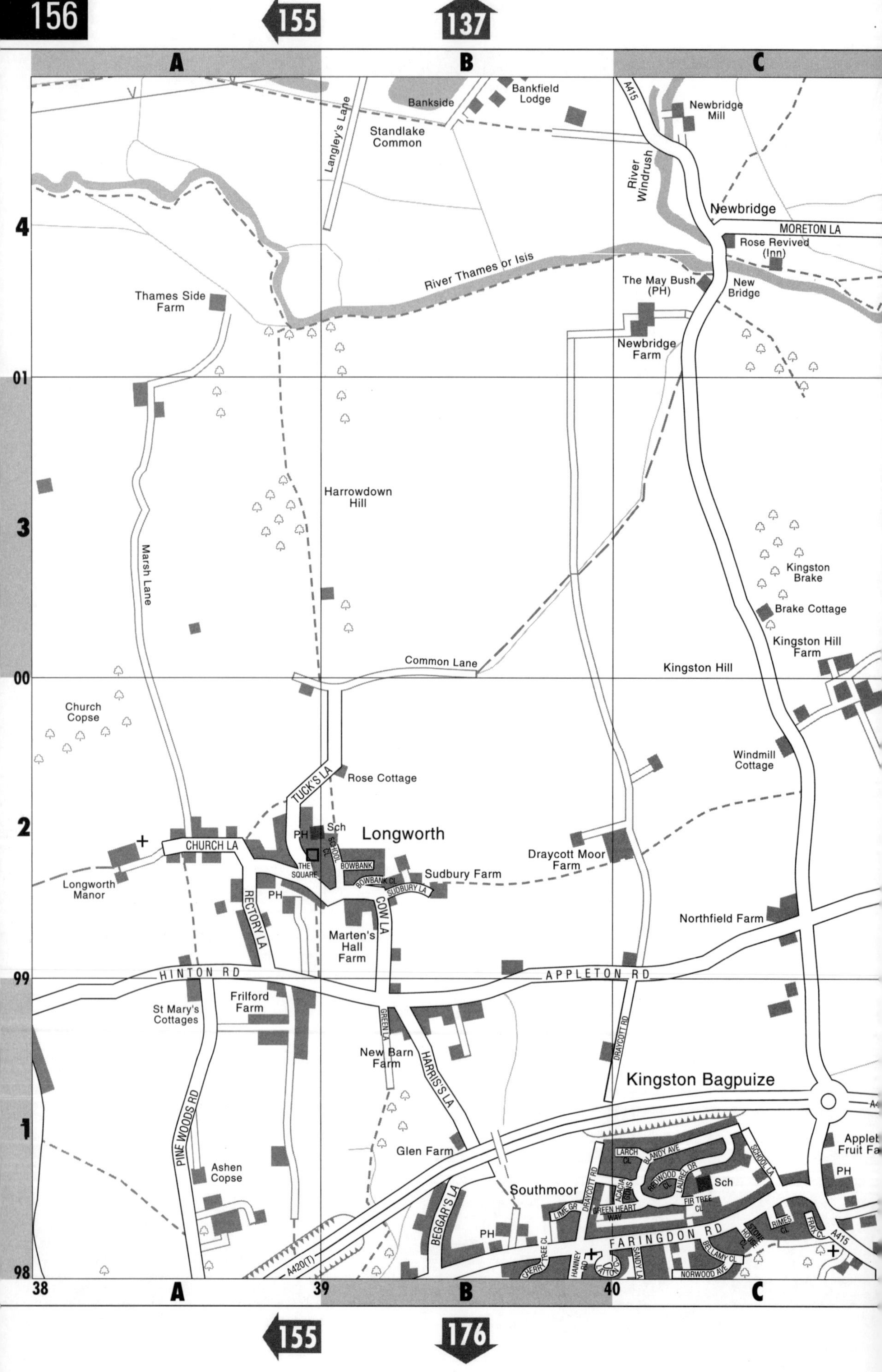

155
137

A   B   C

4

Bankfield
Lodge
Bankside
Standlake
Common
Langley's Lane

A415
Newbridge
Mill

River
Windrush

Newbridge

MORETON LA
Rose Revived
(Inn)

Thames Side
Farm

River Thames or Isis

The May Bush
(PH)

New
Bridge

Newbridge
Farm

01

Harrowdown
Hill

Kingston
Brake

Brake Cottage

3

Marsh Lane

Kingston Hill
Farm

Common Lane

Kingston Hill

00

Church
Copse

Windmill
Cottage

Rose Cottage

2

TUCK'S LA

Sch
PH
Longworth
SCHOOL PL

Draycott Moor
Farm

THE
SQUARE
BOWBANK

CHURCH LA

BOWBANK CL

Sudbury Farm

SUDBURY LA

Longworth
Manor

PH

Northfield Farm

RECTORY LA

COW LA

Marten's
Hall
Farm

99

HINTON RD

APPLETON RD

St Mary's
Cottages

Frilford
Farm

GREEN LA

New Barn
Farm

DRAYCOTT RD

HARRIS'S LA

Kingston Bagpuize

A4

1

PINE WOODS RD

Glen Farm

Applet
Fruit Fa

LARCH
CL

SANDY AVE
Sch
PH

Ashen
Copse

BEGGAR'S LA

Southmoor

GREEN HEART
WAY

FIR TREE
CL

SCHOOL LA

STONE

RIMES
CL

A415

PH

FARINGDON RD

A420(T)

BELLAMY CL

NORWOOD AVE

98

38   A   39   B   40   C

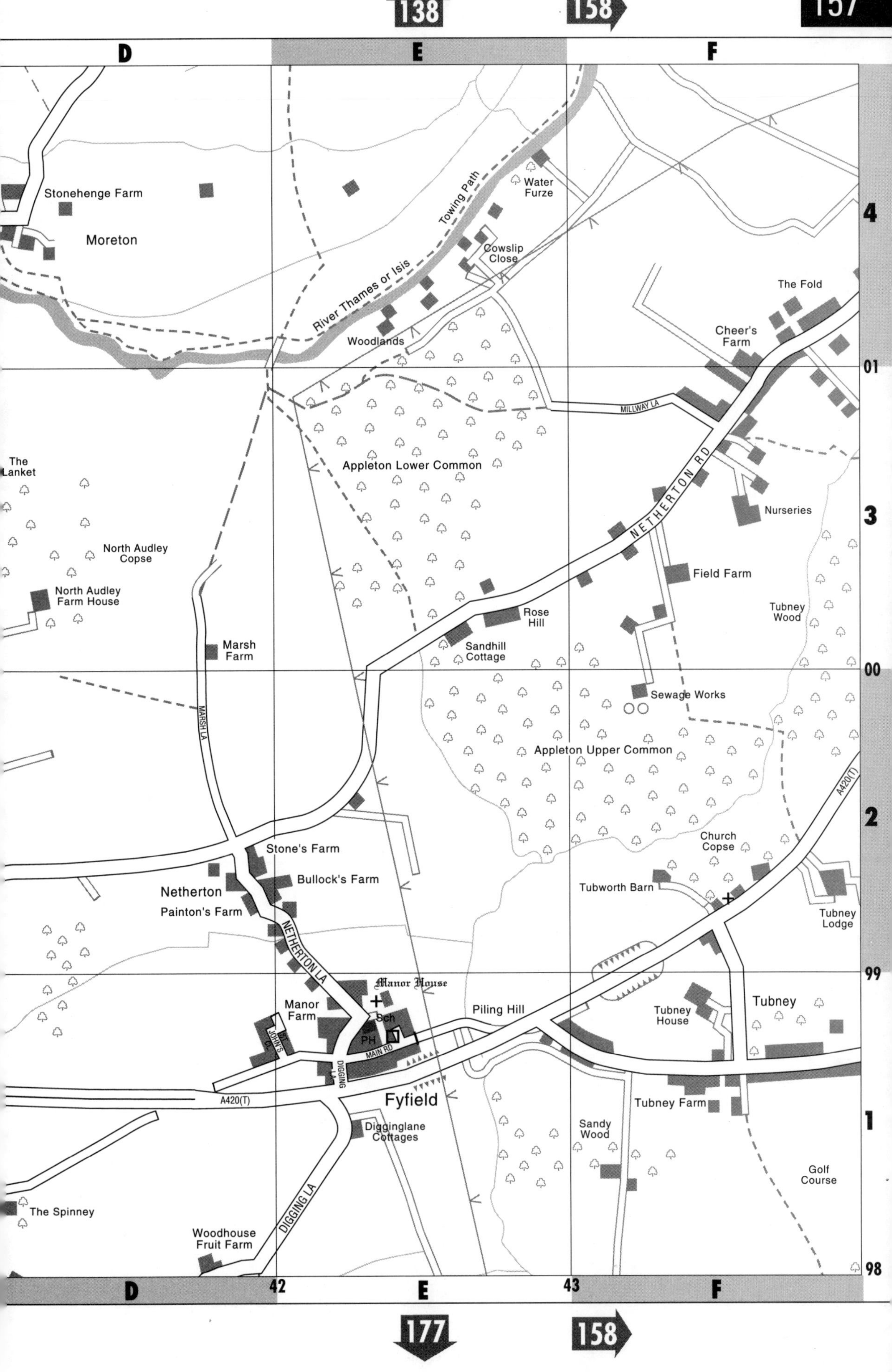

D   E   F

4

Stonehenge Farm

Moreton

Water
Furze

Towing Path

Cowslip
Close

River Thames or Isis

01

Woodlands

The Fold

Cheer's
Farm

MILLWAY LA

Appleton Lower Common

The
Lanket

NETHERTON RD

Nurseries

3

North Audley
Copse

Field Farm

Tubney
Wood

North Audley
Farm House

Rose
Hill

Marsh
Farm

Sandhill
Cottage

00

Sewage Works

MARSH LA

Appleton Upper Common

A420(T)

2

Stone's Farm

Church
Copse

Bullock's Farm

Tubworth Barn

Tubney
Lodge

Netherton

Painton's Farm

NETHERTON LA

99

Manor House

Tubney

DIGGING

Manor
Farm

Sch

Piling Hill

Tubney
House

PH

MAIN RD

A420(T)

Fyfield

Digginglane
Cottages

Sandy
Wood

Tubney Farm

1

DIGGING LA

The Spinney

Golf
Course

Woodhouse
Fruit Farm

98

← 157
↑ 139

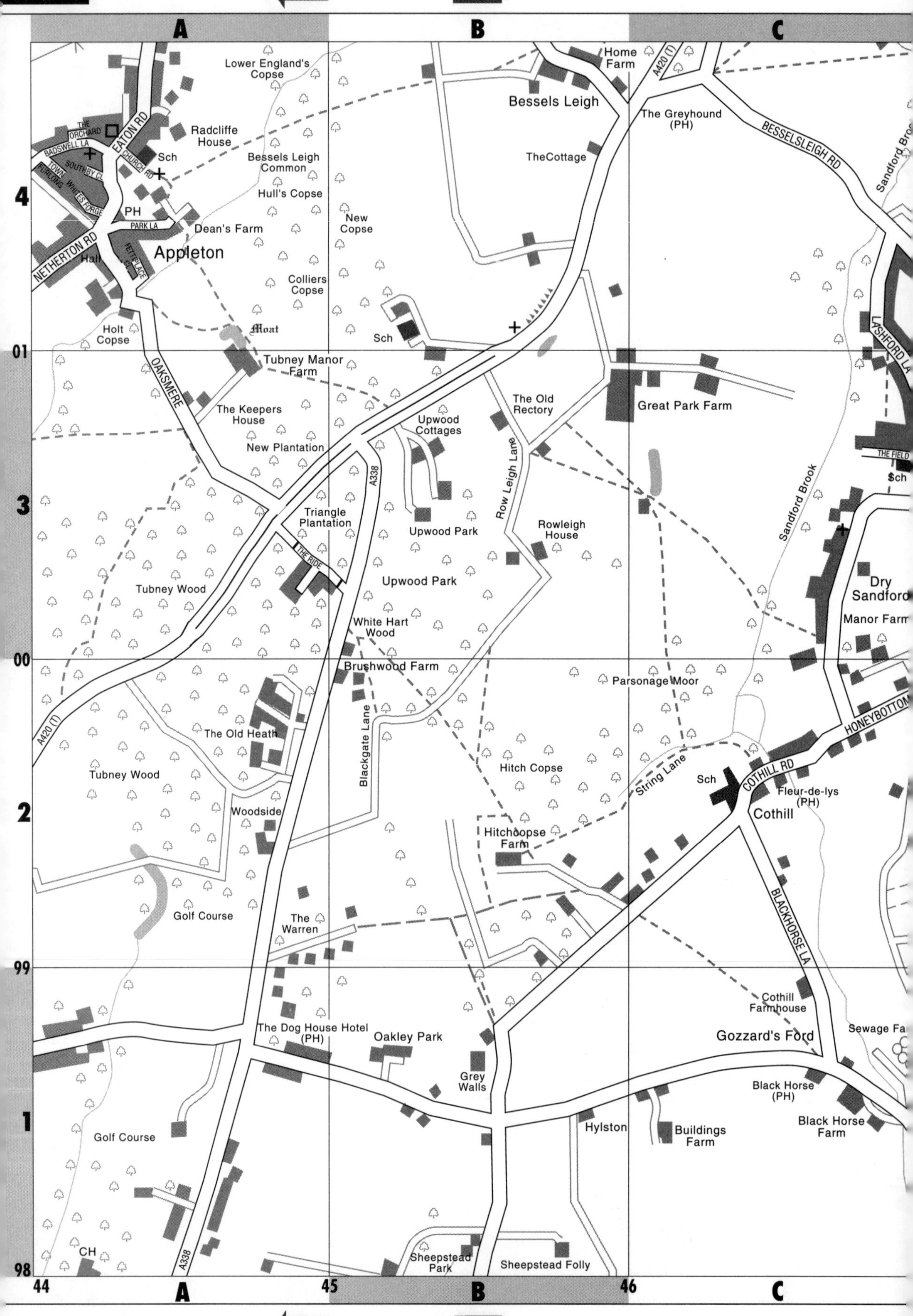

A   B   C

Lower England's Copse

Home Farm

Bessels Leigh

The Greyhound (PH)

BESSELSLEIGH RD

Sandford Brook

A420 (T)

EATON RD

THE ORCHARD

BADSWELL LA

SOUTHBY CL

TOWN FURLONG

WHITES FORGE

CHURCH RD

Sch

PARK LA

PH

Radcliffe House

Bessels Leigh Common

TheCottage

Hull's Copse

New Copse

Dean's Farm

Appleton

Hall

PETT PLACE

NETHERTON RD

Colliers Copse

4

Holt Copse

Moat

Sch

Tubney Manor Farm

The Old Rectory

Great Park Farm

LASHFORD LA

THE FIELD

Sch

OAKSMERE

The Keepers House

New Plantation

Upwood Cottages

Row Leigh Lane

01

A338

THE RIDE

Triangle Plantation

Upwood Park

Rowleigh House

Sandford Brook

Dry Sandford

3

Tubney Wood

Upwood Park

Manor Farm

White Hart Wood

Brushwood Farm

Parsonage Moor

00

A420 (T)

The Old Heath

Blackgate Lane

HONEYBOTTOM

COTHILL RD

String Lane

Sch

Fleur-de-lys (PH)

Tubney Wood

Hitch Copse

Cothill

Woodside

2

Hitchcopse Farm

BLACKHORSE LA

Golf Course

The Warren

99

The Dog House Hotel (PH)

Oakley Park

Cothill Farmhouse

Sewage Fa

Gozzard's Ford

Grey Walls

Black Horse (PH)

1

Golf Course

Hylston

Buildings Farm

Black Horse Farm

CH

A338

Sheepstead Park

Sheepstead Folly

98

44   A   45   B   46   C

← 157
↓ 178

D
E
F
Old Boars Hill
Blackthorn
Foxcombe Hill
Duckling's Copse
Wooton Village
Middle Farm
The Fox Inn (PH)
Wootton
Manor Farm
Tommy's Farm
Broom Hill Copse
Community Centre
Copse View
Blagrove Copse
Church Farm
Sunningwell
White House Farm
Blagrove Farm
Oxfordshire Circular Walks
Pen Lane
Starveall Farm
Abingdon Airfield
Long Furlong Farm
Dunmore Farm
Williams Farm
Wildmoor Brook
Wildmoor
Schs
Stowford House
Shippon
Manor Farm
FOX LA
CUMNOR RD
LAMBOROUGH HILL
HONEYBOTTOM LA
WHITE CROSS
SUNNINGWELL RD
FOXCOMBE RD
BRUMCOMBE LA
QUARRY RD
LONG TOW
CHOLSWELL RD
FARINGDON RD
BARROW RD
WOOTTON RD
DUNMORE RD
NORTHCOURT RD
A34(T)
B4017
4
01
3
00
2
99
1
98
48
49

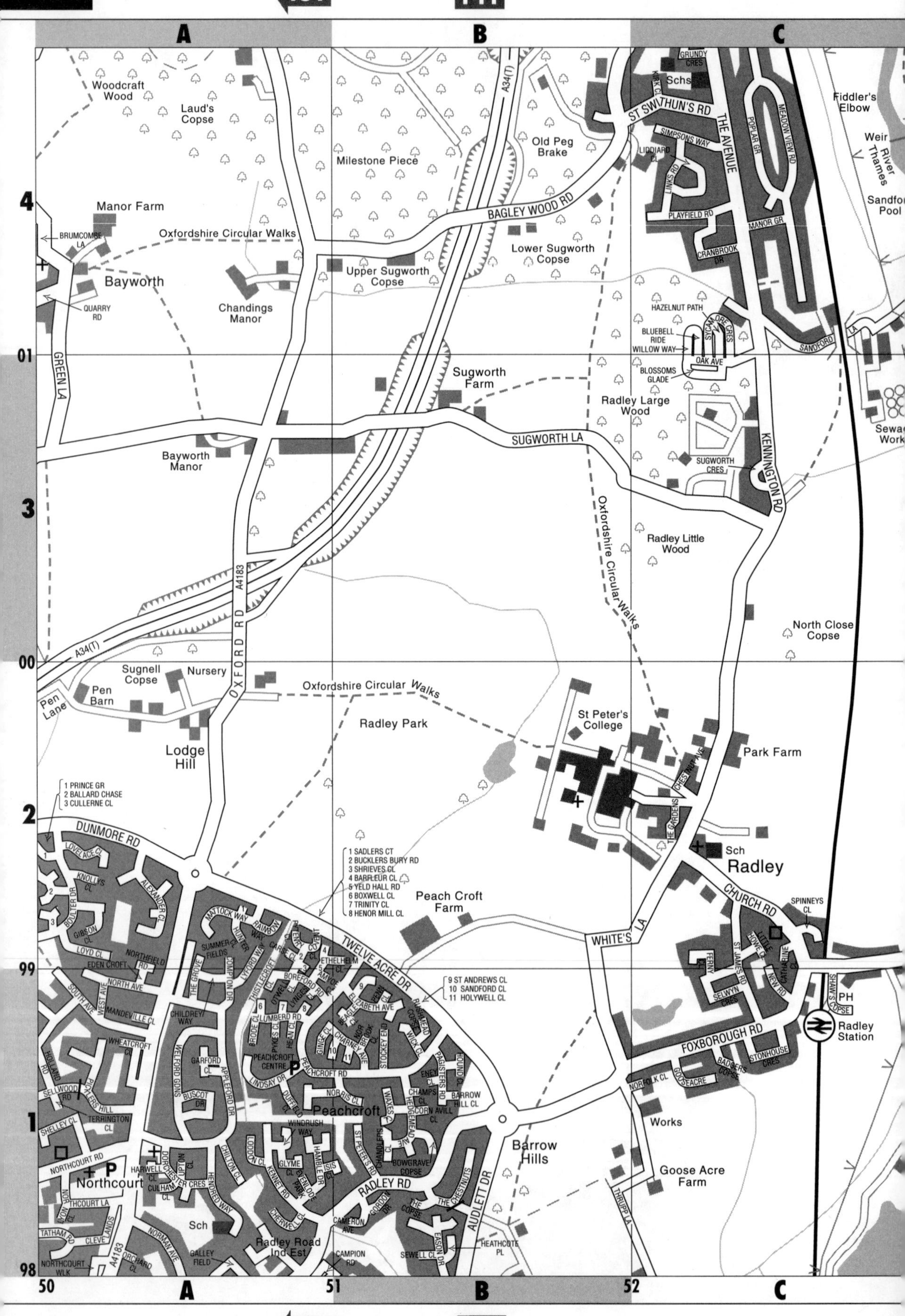

A   B   C

Woodcraft Wood

Laud's Copse

Milestone Piece

Old Peg Brake

A34(T)

St SWITHUN'S RD

SIMPSONS WAY

LIDDIARD

GRUNDY CRES

Schs

THE AVENUE

POPLAR GR

MEADOW VIEW RD

LINKS RD

Fiddler's Elbow

Weir

River Thames

Sandfo Pool

4

Manor Farm

BRUMCOMBE LA

Oxfordshire Circular Walks

BAGLEY WOOD RD

Lower Sugworth Copse

PLAYFIELD RD

CRANBROOK DR

MANOR GR

Bayworth

QUARRY RD

Upper Sugworth Copse

Chandings Manor

HAZELNUT PATH

BLUEBELL RIDE

WILLOW WAY

SCAMOR CRES

OAK AVE

BLOSSOMS GLADE

SANDFORD

LA

01

GREEN LA

Sugworth Farm

SUGWORTH LA

Radley Large Wood

Sugworth Cres

KENNINGTON RD

Sewa Work

Bayworth Manor

Radley Little Wood

3

OXFORD RD A4183

Oxfordshire Circular Walks

North Close Copse

00

A34(T)

Sugnell Copse

Nursery

Oxfordshire Circular Walks

St Peter's College

Park Farm

Pen Lane

Pen Barn

Radley Park

Lodge Hill

1 PRINCE GR
2 BALLARD CHASE
3 CULLERNE CL

THE GARDENS

CRES WAY AVE

Sch

Radley

2

DUNMORE RD

LOVELACE CL

KNOLLYS CL

ALEXANDER CL

MANTOCK WAY

RAILWAY

1 SADLERS CT
2 BUCKLERS BURY RD
3 SHRIEVES CL
4 BARFLEUR CL
5 YELD HALL RD
6 BOXWELL CL
7 TRINITY CL
8 HENOR MILL CL

Peach Croft Farm

SPINNEYS CL

BOATER CL

GIBSON CL

SUMMER FIELDS

COMMON RD

THISTLE DOWNS

ETHELHELM

BOREFORD RD

CATHERINE

LITTLE CL

PRIORY

ST JAMES RD

SELWYN CRES

LOYD CL

EDEN CROFT

NORTHFIELD CL

THE GROVE

GARE

COVENT

ELIZABETH AVE

CHILTERN

RD

WHITE'S LA

CHURCH RD

FERRY

SHAWS CL

PH

99

SOUTH AVE

NORTH AVE

MANDEVILLE CL

CHILDREY WAY

WELFORD GDNS

GARFORD CL

PEACHCROFT CENTRE

LINDSAY DR

PEACHCROFT RD

NORRIS RD

CHARNEY AVE

COPSE HILL RD

RAGLAN RD

COPSE

9 ST ANDREWS CL
10 SANDFORD CL
11 HOLYWELL CL

NORFOLK CL

GOOSEACRE

STONHOUSE CRES

BADGERS COPSE

Radley Station

SELLWOOD RD

PETERS HILL

SHELLEY CL

TERRINGTON CL

WHEATCROFT

BISCOT DR

NORB'S CL

CHAMPS CL

ACORN CL

WAXES CL

BARROW HILL CL

FOXBOROUGH RD

Works

1

SHELLEY CL

NORTHCOURT RD

HARWELL CL

DOUGLAS

CULHAM CRES

HENORS WAY

PEACHCROFT

WINDRUSH WAY

GLYME CL

HAMBLE DR

ST PETER'S WAY

BOWGRAVE COPSE

ENEY CL

CORN AVILL CL

AUDLETT DR

Barrow Hills

Goose Acre Farm

P

Northcourt

TATHAM RD

CLEVE

NORTHCOURT LA

NORTHCOURT WLK

A4183

ORCHARD CL

Sch

NORMAN AVE

CHILTON CL

MERKIN CL

GALLEY FIELD

Radley Road Ind Est

CAMERON AVE

CAMPION RD

SEWELL CL

RADLEY RD

THE CHESTNUTS

THE COPSE

EASTER CT

HEATHCOTE PL

THORPE LA

98

50   A   51   B   52   C

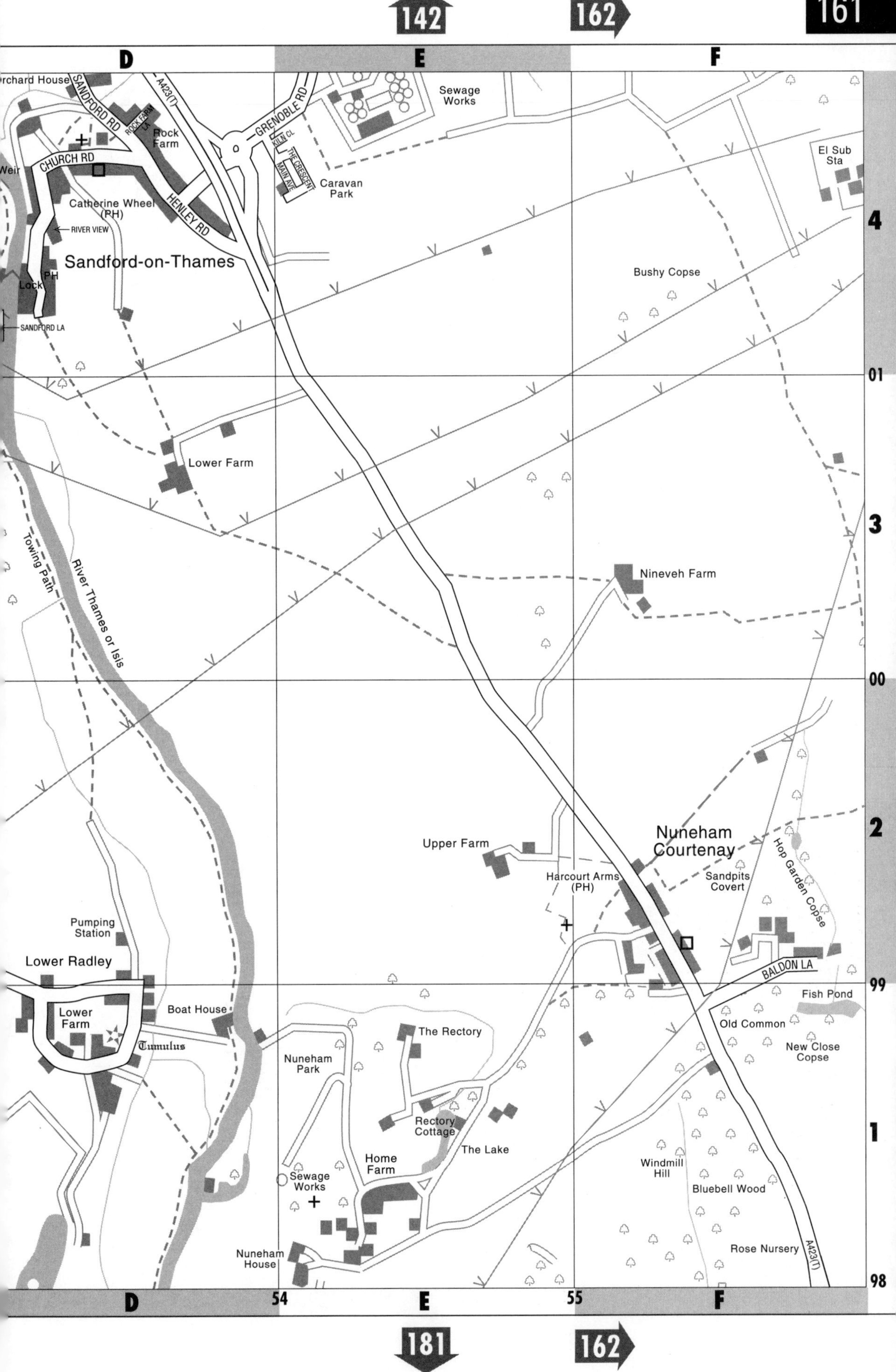

D | E | F

Orchard House
SANDFORD RD
A423(T)
ROCK FARM
Rock Farm
GRENOBLE RD
KILN CL
FIELD CRESCENT
MAIN AV
Caravan Park
Sewage Works
El Sub Sta

CHURCH RD
Weir
Catherine Wheel (PH)
HENLEY RD
RIVER VIEW
Sandford-on-Thames
PH
Lock
SANDFORD LA

4

Bushy Copse

01

Towing Path
River Thames or Isis

Lower Farm

3

Nineveh Farm

00

Upper Farm

Nuneham Courtenay

2

Harcourt Arms (PH)
Sandpits Covert
Hop Garden Copse

Pumping Station

Lower Radley

BALDON LA

Fish Pond

99

Lower Farm
Boat House
Tumulus

The Rectory
Old Common
New Close Copse

Nuneham Park

Rectory Cottage
The Lake

1

Home Farm
Windmill Hill
Bluebell Wood

Sewage Works

Nuneham House

Rose Nursery
A423(T)

98

D | E | F
54 | 55

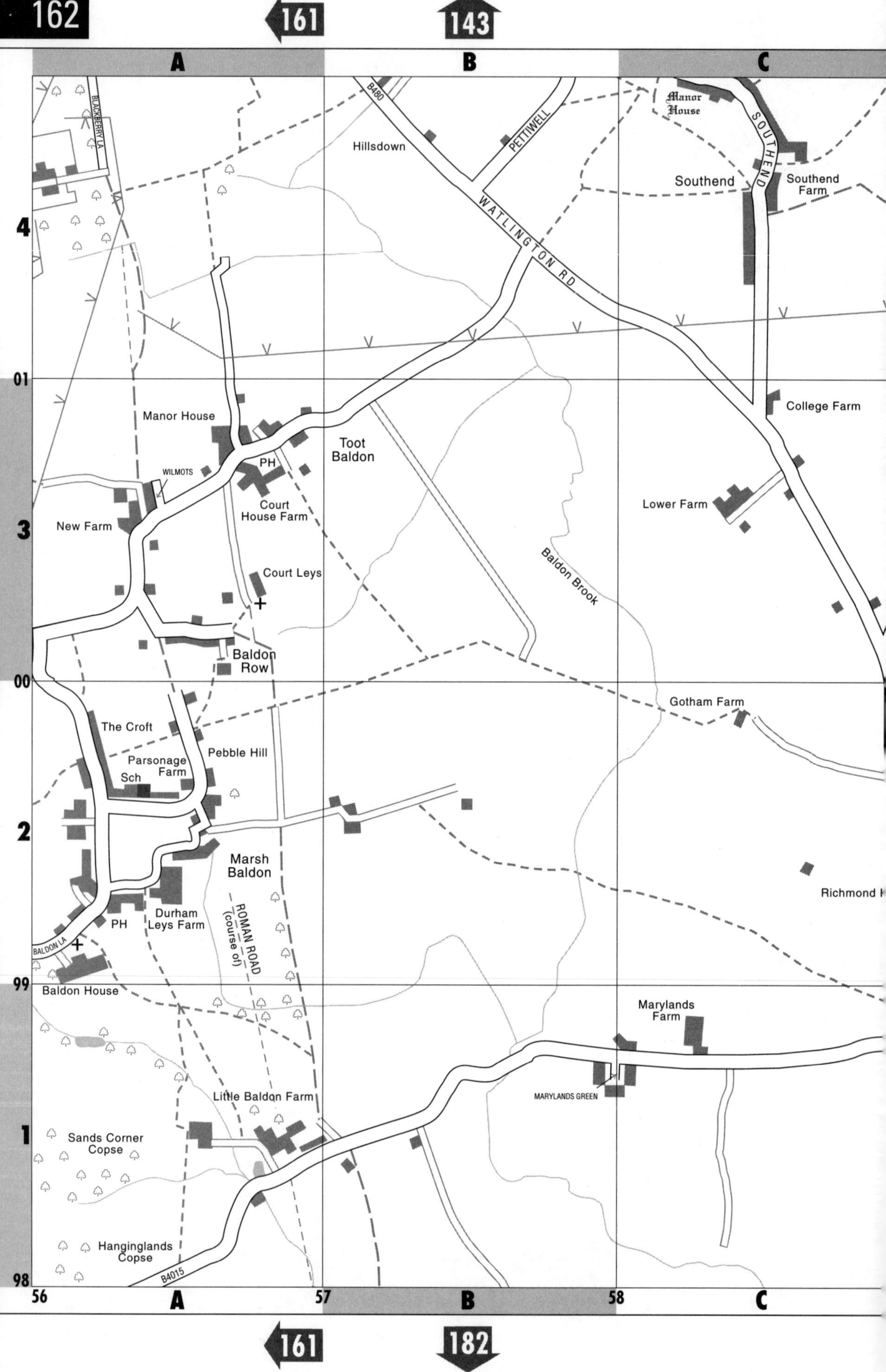

A B C

BLACKBERRY LA

4

Hillsdown

B480

PETTIWELL

WATLINGTON RD

Manor House

Southend

Southend Farm

01

Manor House

WILMOTS

PH

Toot Baldon

College Farm

New Farm

Court House Farm

Lower Farm

3

Court Leys

Baldon Brook

Baldon Row

00

The Croft

Gotham Farm

Parsonage Farm

Pebble Hill

Sch

2

Marsh Baldon

Richmond H

PH

Durham Leys Farm

ROMAN ROAD (course of)

BALDON LA

99

Baldon House

Marylands Farm

Little Baldon Farm

MARYLANDS GREEN

1

Sands Corner Copse

Hanginglands Copse

B4015

98

56 A 57 B 58 C

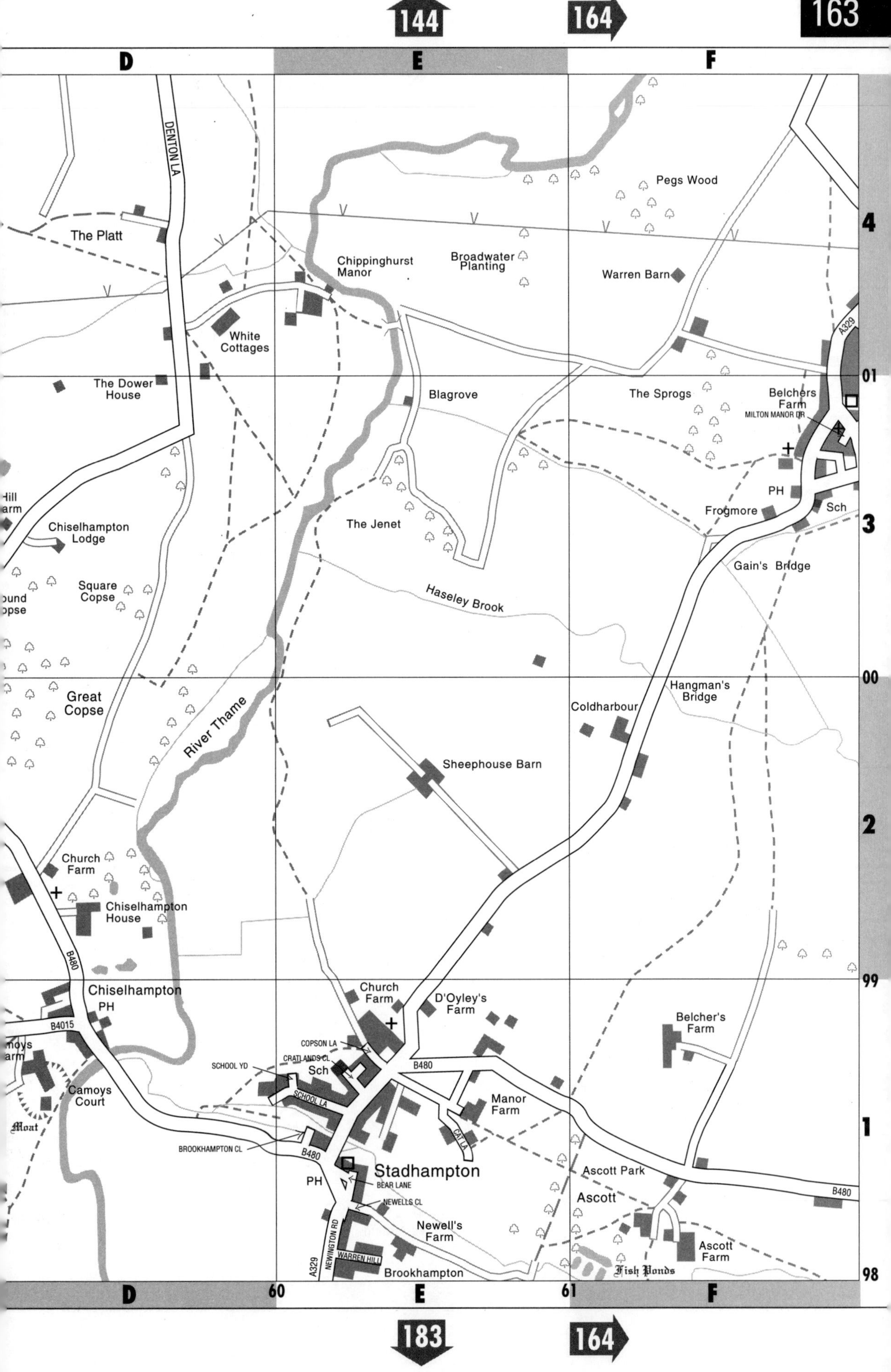
144
164
D
E
F
4
3
2
1
01
00
99
98
60
61
DENTON LA
The Platt
Chippinghurst Manor
Broadwater Planting
Pegs Wood
Warren Barn
White Cottages
The Dower House
Blagrove
The Sprogs
Belchers Farm
MILTON MANOR DR
A329
PH
Frogmore
Sch
Chiselhampton Lodge
The Jenet
Gain's Bridge
Square Copse
Haseley Brook
Great Copse
Hangman's Bridge
Coldharbour
River Thame
Sheephouse Barn
Church Farm
Chiselhampton House
B480
Chiselhampton
PH
B4015
Camoys Court
Moat
Church Farm
D'Oyley's Farm
Belcher's Farm
COPSON LA
CRATLANDS CL
SCHOOL YD
Sch
SCHOOL LA
B480
Manor Farm
CAT LA
BROOKHAMPTON CL
B480
Stadhampton
PH
BEAR LANE
NEWELLS CL
Ascott Park
Ascott
B480
Newell's Farm
Ascott Farm
NEWINGTON RD
WARREN HILL
A329
Brookhampton
Fish Ponds
183
164

163
145

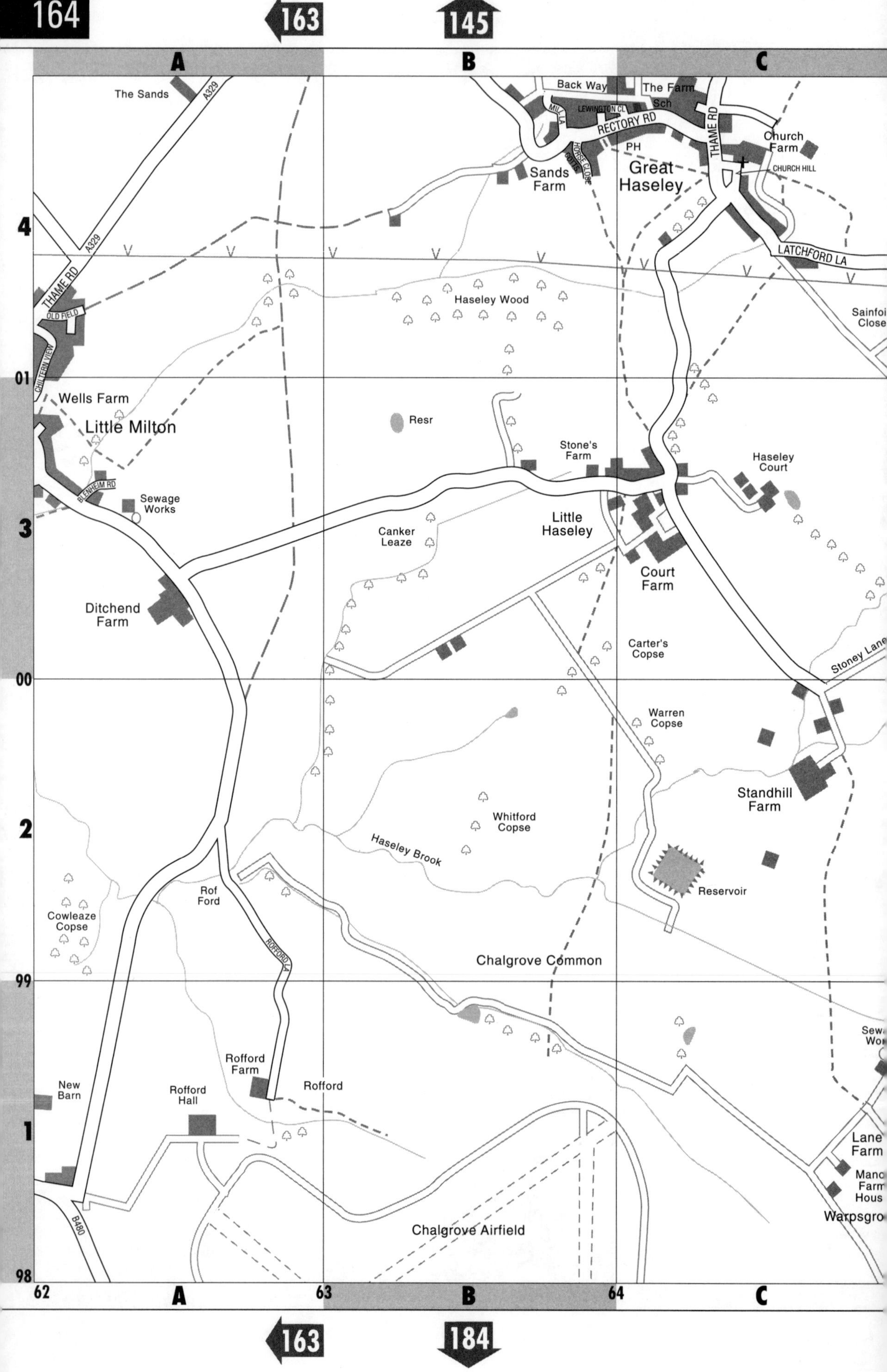

A
B
C
The Sands
A329
Back Way
The Farm
Sch
LEWINGTON CL
MILL LA
RECTORY RD
THAME RD
Church Farm
PH
HORSE CLOSE
COTTS
Sands Farm
Great Haseley
CHURCH HILL
LATCHFORD LA
4
THAME RD
OLD FIELD
Haseley Wood
Sainfoi Close
CHILTERN VIEW
01
Wells Farm
Little Milton
Resr
Stone's Farm
Haseley Court
BLENHEIM RD
Sewage Works
Little Haseley
3
Canker Leaze
Court Farm
Ditchend Farm
Carter's Copse
Stoney Lane
00
Warren Copse
Standhill Farm
2
Whitford Copse
Haseley Brook
Reservoir
Rof Ford
Cowleaze Copse
ROFFORD LA
Chalgrove Common
99
Rofford Farm
Rofford
New Barn
Rofford Hall
1
Lane Farm
Mano Farm Hous
Warpsgro
B480
Chalgrove Airfield
98
62
63
64

163
184

D
E
F
M40
Manor Farm
Goldpits Farm
Jointer's Farm
Latchford House
LATCHFORD LA
Latchford Farm
Latchford
Oxhouse Farm
Latchford Copse
Haseley Brook
01
Sheepbridge Copse
Peggs Farm
Cornwell Copse
3
4
Stoke Grange
The Island
00
Poppets Hill
Oxfordshire Way
2
Poppets Hill Farm
Stoke Talmage
Manor Farm
Stoney Lane
99
North Farm
Clare
1
Clare Copse
South Farm
98
D
66
E
67
F

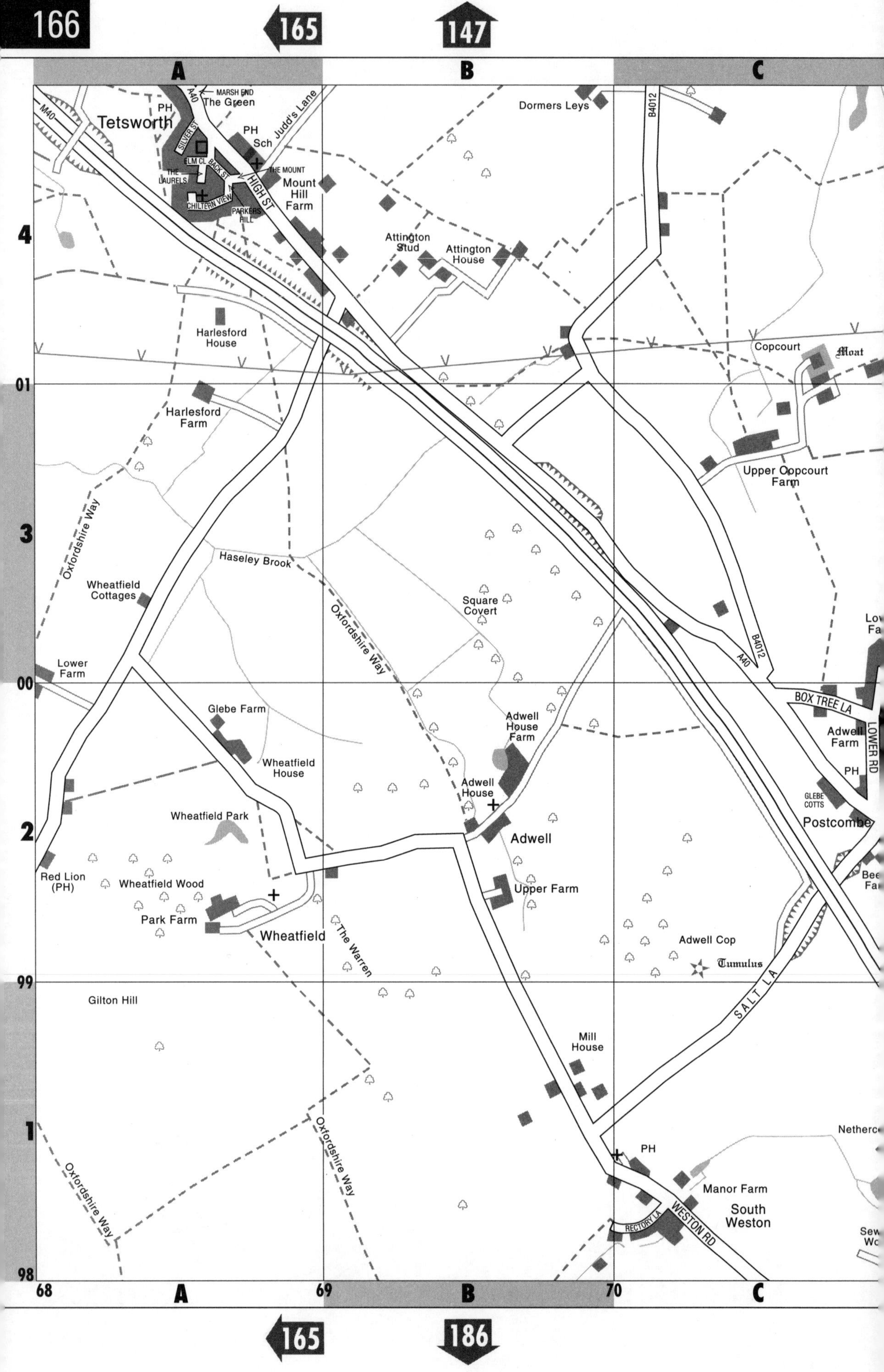

A   B   C

MARSH END
The Green
Judd's Lane
Dormers Leys
B4012
PH
Tetsworth
SILVERS
PH Sch
ELM CL
BACK ST
THE MOUNT
THE LAURELS
CHILTERN VIEW
PARKERS HILL
HIGH ST
Mount Hill Farm
Attington Stud
Attington House
A40

4

Harlesford House
Copcourt
Moat

01

Harlesford Farm
Upper Copcourt Farm

Oxfordshire Way

3

Haseley Brook
Square Covert
B4012
A40

Wheatfield Cottages
Oxfordshire Way

Lower Farm
Lo. Fa

00

Glebe Farm
Adwell House Farm
BOX TREE LA
Adwell Farm
LOWER RD

Wheatfield House
Adwell House
PH
GLEBE COTTS

Wheatfield Park
Adwell
Postcombe

2

Red Lion (PH)
Wheatfield Wood
Upper Farm
Bee Fa

Park Farm
Wheatfield
The Warren
Adwell Cop
Tumulus
SALT LA

99

Gilton Hill

Mill House

1

Oxfordshire Way
Oxfordshire Way
PH
Netherc

Manor Farm
South Weston
Sew Wo

RECTORY LA
WESTON RD

98

68   A   69   B   70   C

D E F

Prospect Hill

Vears Farm

Croton Farm

SYDENHAM OR

Ryder's Farm

The Slades

PH

Sydenham

PH Musgrive Farm

HOLLIERS CL

Vic

4

Sewell's Lane

V V V

Kingston Stert

Manor Farm

Nursery

01

Chalford

Upper Chalford Farm

Kingston Stert Farm

nheim arm

3

00

Lower Icknield Way

Moat Manor

BAKER'S PIECE

PLECH TRE RISE

Lower Farm

STERT RD

BROOK ST

OLD CROFT CL

PH

B4009

HIGH ST

PARK LA

2

CHALFORD RD

Town Farm

Kingston Blount

Kingston House

Sch

SCHOOL LA

Aston Park Stud

THE GREEN

PLOWDEN PARK

Home Farm

CHURCH LA

99

ASTON PARK

Hope Lodge

Aston Rowant

The Croft

CHINNOR RD

Woodway Farm

Woodway Cottages

1

Dismantled Railway

Ridgeway

BUTTS WAY

B4009

M40

Swan's Way

Sheepbrook House

Hotel

A40

98

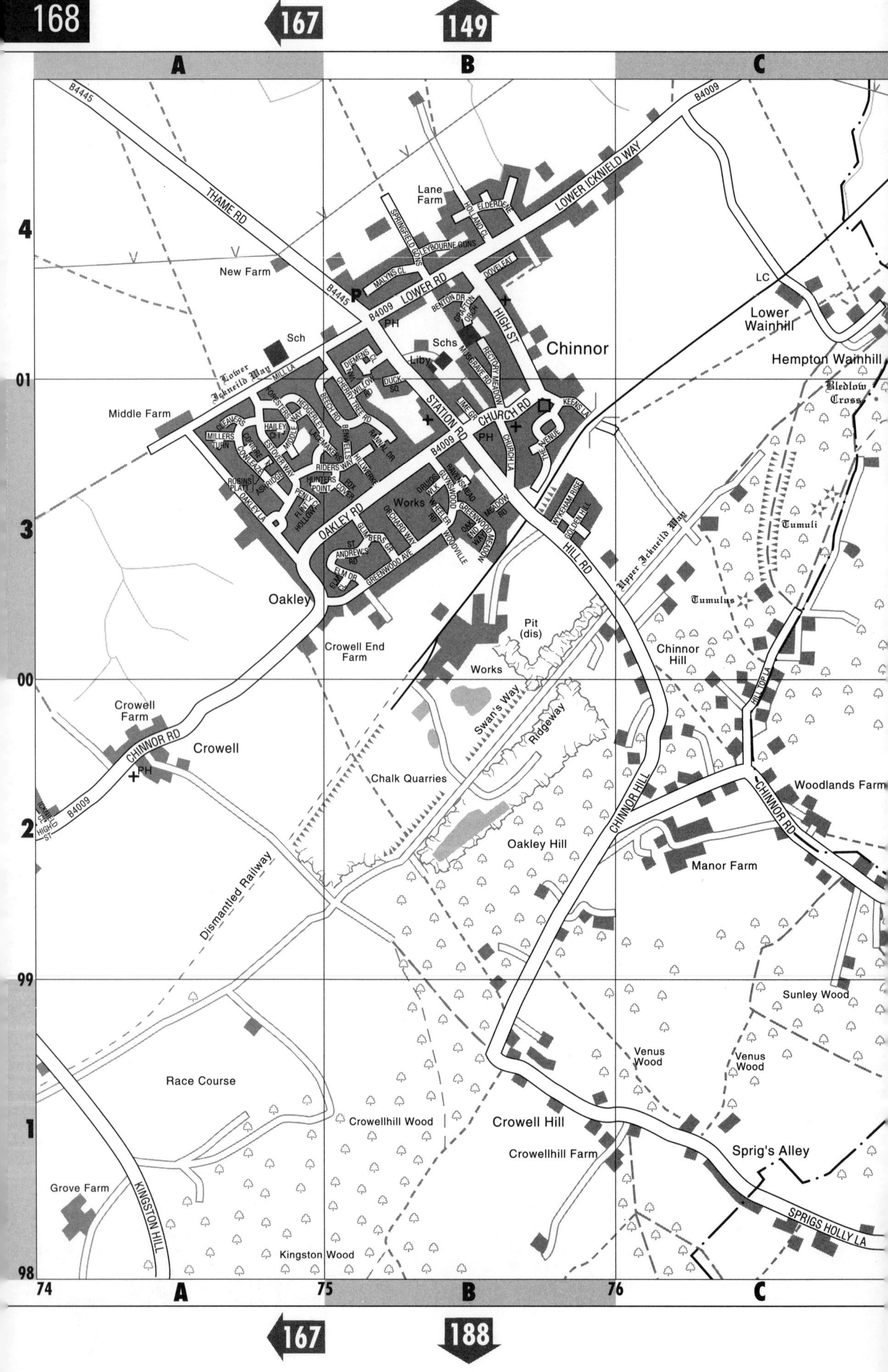

A   B   C

4

B4445
THAME RD
New Farm
B4445
Lower Icknield Way
Middle Farm
Oakley
Lane Farm
HOLLAND DR
ELDERDENE
SPRINGFIELD GDNS
GLEYBOURNE GDNS
MALTIS CL
DOVELEAT
LOWER RD
BENTON DR
SPAFFORD
HIGH ST
Sch
Libry
B4009
PH
Schs
DIEMENS
LOWER ICKNIELD WAY
LC
Chinnor
Lower Wainhill
Hempton Wainhill
Bledlow Cross

01

MILL LA
FOREST RISE
GREEN LA
CHURN RISE RD
BIRCHILEY MEAD
HILLY VIEW
TANNAL DR
Lower Icknield Way
DUCK SQ
STATION RD
MINERVA RD
RECTORY MEADOW
CHURCH RD
CHURCH LA
KEANS LA
PH
Tumuli
Tumulus

3

MILLERS TURN
HAILEY
CROFT
STONEY WAY
CONY CROFT
PENY'S CT
HUNTERS POINT
RIDERS WAY
BOX
WEAVERS
ASH RIDGE
ROBINS PLAT
OAKLEY LA
FLY HOLLOW
OAKLEY RD
CLIMBERS WAY
ORCHARD WAY
GREENWOOD AVE
ELM DR
St ANDREW'S RD
Works
BARR'S MEAD
OAKWOOD
GREENWOOD
WLK
WHEELER
WOODVILLE
OAK MEADOW
DANKS
WYKEHAM RISE
BIGNELL HILL
HILL RD
Upper Icknield Way
Chinnor Hill

Crowell End Farm
Pit (dis)
Works
Woodlands Farm

00

Crowell Farm
CHINNOR RD
Crowell
PH
B4009
LOWER HIGH ST
Swan's Way
Ridgeway
Chalk Quarries
CHINNOR HILL
CHINNOR RD
Manor Farm

99

Dismantled Railway
Oakley Hill
Sunley Wood
Venus Wood
Venus Wood

1

Race Course
Crowellhill Wood
Crowell Hill
Crowellhill Farm
Sprig's Alley

Grove Farm
KINGSTON HILL
Kingston Wood
SPRIGS HOLLY LA

98

74   A   75   B   76   C

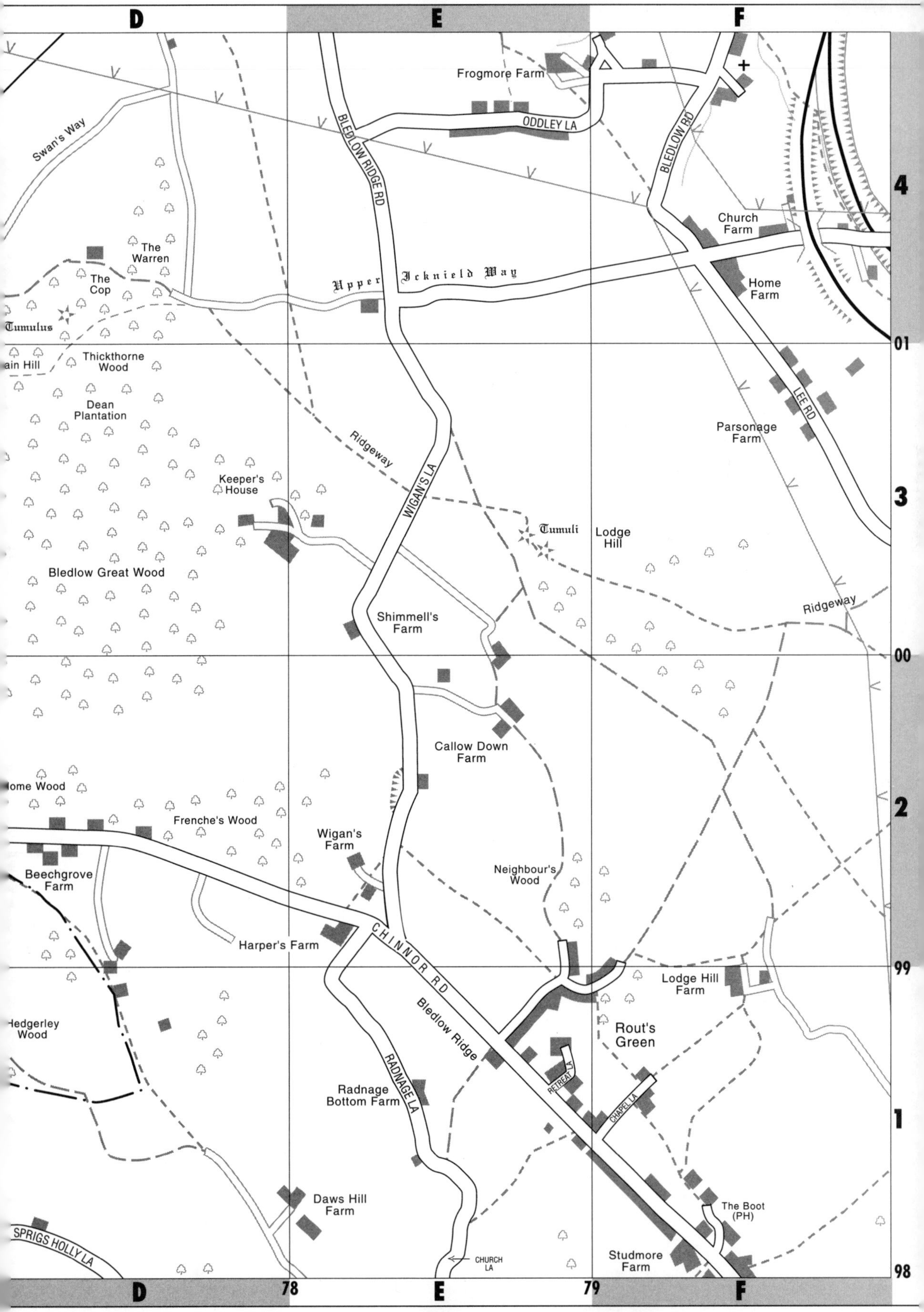

D **E** **F**

Frogmore Farm

ODDLEY LA

BLEDLOW RD

+

BLEDLOW RIDGE RD

4

Church Farm

Home Farm

Swan's Way

The Warren

The Cop

Upper Icknield Way

Tumulus

LEE RD

ain Hill

Thickthorne Wood

Dean Plantation

Ridgeway

Parsonage Farm

3

Keeper's House

WIGAN'S LA

Tumuli

Lodge Hill

Bledlow Great Wood

Shimmell's Farm

Ridgeway

00

Callow Down Farm

ome Wood

Frenche's Wood

Wigan's Farm

Neighbour's Wood

2

Beechgrove Farm

Harper's Farm

CHINNOR RD

Lodge Hill Farm

99

Hedgerley Wood

Bledlow Ridge

Rout's Green

RADNAGE LA

RETREAT

CHAPEL LA

Radnage Bottom Farm

1

Daws Hill Farm

The Boot (PH)

SPRIGS HOLLY LA

CHURCH LA

Studmore Farm

98

D 78 **E** 79 **F**

189

A **B** **C**

4

River Thames or Isis

Weir

Buscot Wick

Buscot Wick
Farm

Weston
Cottages

The
Rectory

LECHLADE RD

A417

A361

97

Weston
Farm

Upper
Inglesham

3

Manor
Farm

Lynt
Farm

LYNT RD

Snowswick
Cottages

Broadlea
Farm

SNOWSWICK LA

96

River Cole

Snowswick
Farm

Snowswick
Copse

2

College
Farm

Pennysw
Farm

95

1

Worsall
Farm

LECHLADE RD

Roundhill
Farm

A361

94

20 **A** **21** **B** **22** **C**

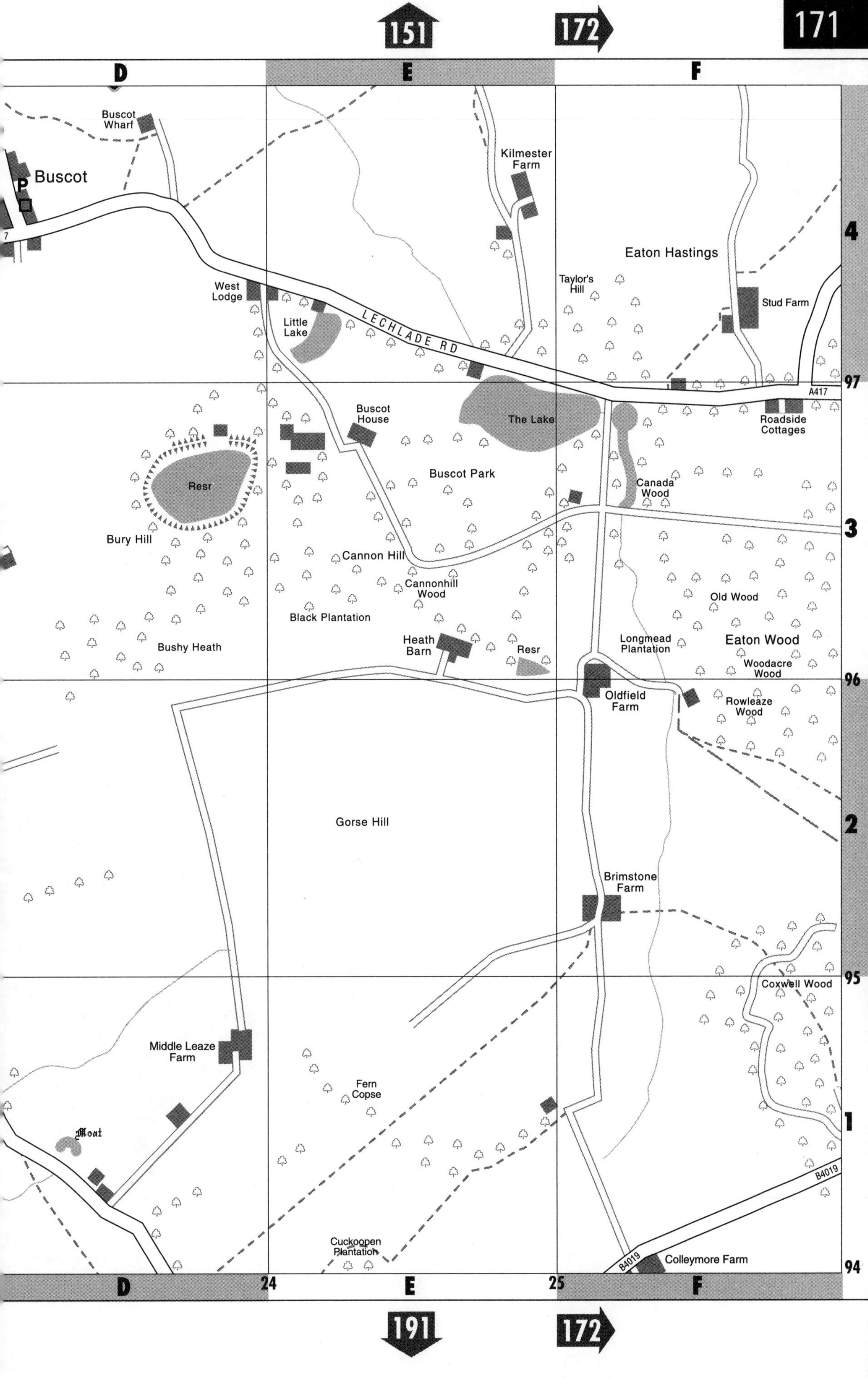

Buscot Wharf

Buscot

P

7

Kilmester Farm

Eaton Hastings

Taylor's Hill

Stud Farm

4

West Lodge

LECHLADE RD

Little Lake

A417

97

Buscot House

The Lake

Roadside Cottages

Resr

Buscot Park

Canada Wood

Bury Hill

Cannon Hill

Old Wood

3

Cannonhill Wood

Black Plantation

Eaton Wood

Bushy Heath

Heath Barn

Resr

Longmead Plantation

Woodacre Wood

Oldfield Farm

Rowleaze Wood

96

Gorse Hill

2

Brimstone Farm

Coxwell Wood

95

Middle Leaze Farm

Fern Copse

1

Moat

B4019

Cuckoopen Plantation

B4019

Colleymore Farm

94

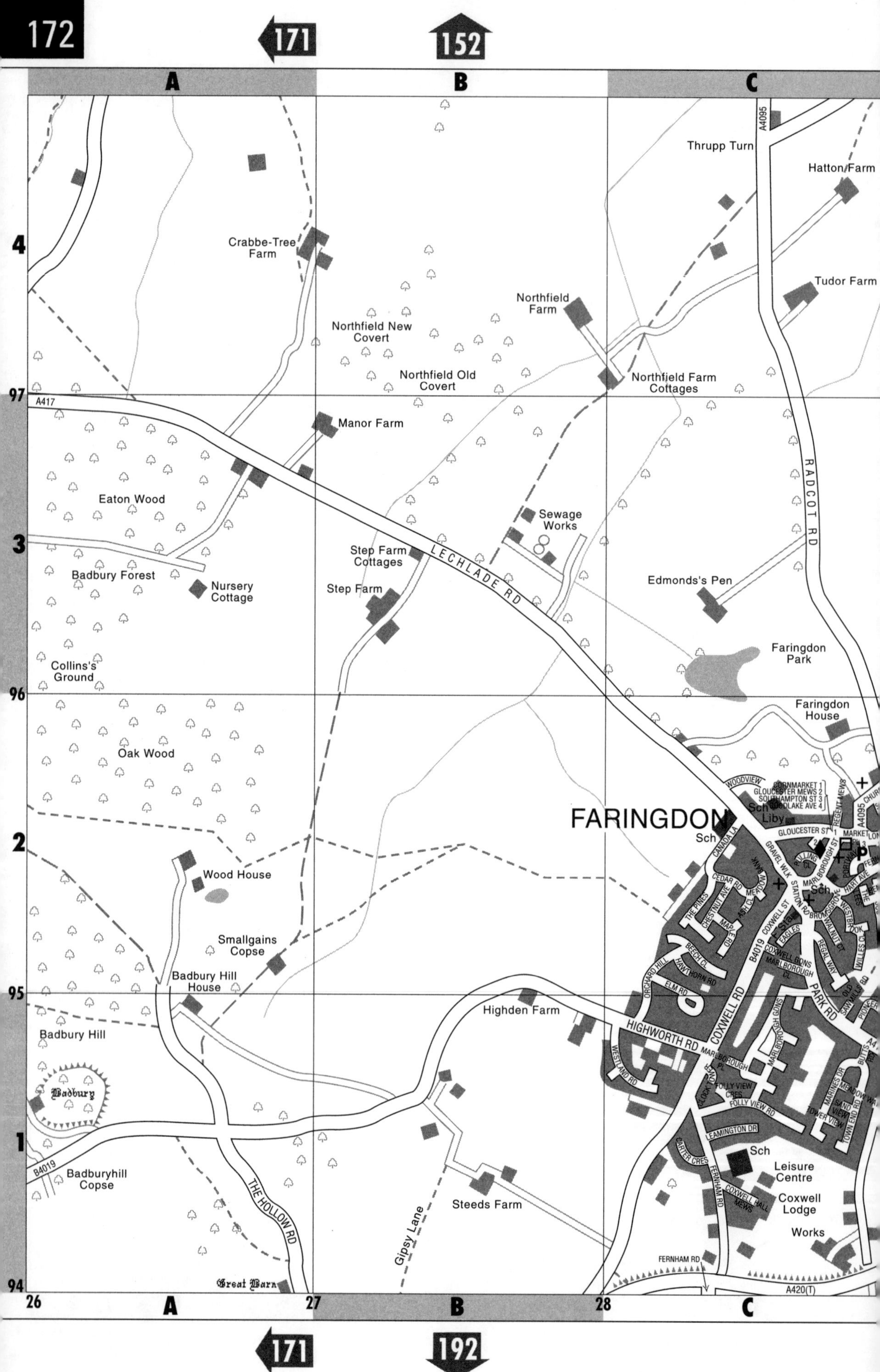

A   B   C

4

Thrupp Turn

Hatton Farm

Crabbe-Tree
Farm

Tudor Farm

Northfield
Farm

Northfield New
Covert

Northfield Old
Covert

Northfield Farm
Cottages

97

A417

Manor Farm

Sewage
Works

Eaton Wood

Step Farm
Cottages

LECHLADE RD

3

Badbury Forest

Nursery
Cottage

Step Farm

Edmonds's Pen

Faringdon
Park

Collins's
Ground

96

Faringdon
House

Oak Wood

RADCOT RD

A4095

FARINGDON

2

Wood House

Smallgains
Copse

95

Badbury Hill
House

Highden Farm

HIGHWORTH RD

COXWELL RD

PARK RD

Badbury Hill

Badbury

1

Badburyhill
Copse

B4019

THE HOLLOW RD

Steeds Farm

Gipsy Lane

Leisure
Centre

Coxwell
Lodge

Works

FERNHAM RD

94

Great Barn

A420(T)

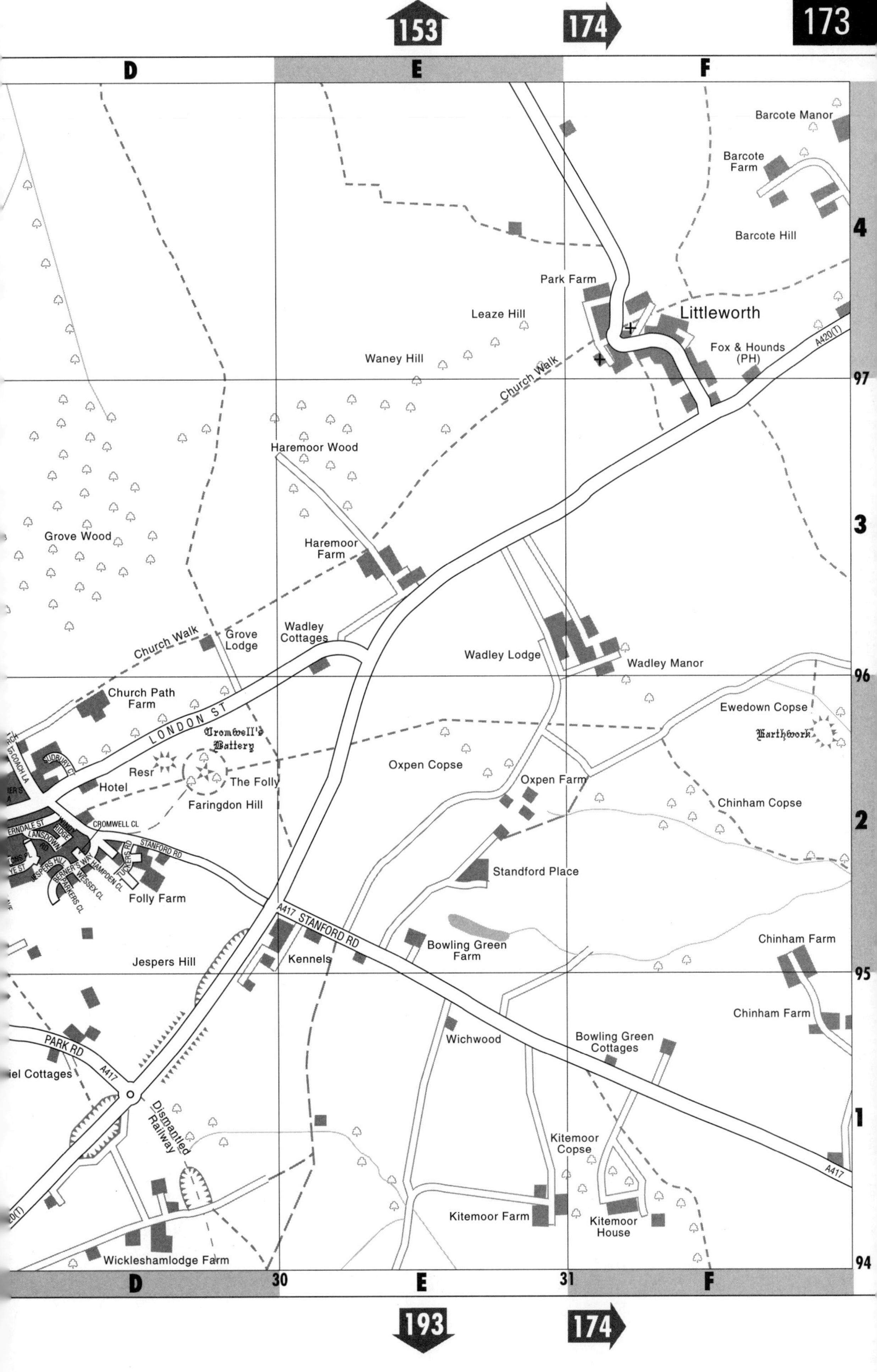

D   E   F

Barcote Manor

Barcote Farm

Barcote Hill

4

Park Farm

Leaze Hill

Littleworth

Waney Hill

Fox & Hounds (PH)

A420(T)

Church Walk

97

Haremoor Wood

Grove Wood

3

Haremoor Farm

Church Walk

Grove Lodge

Wadley Cottages

Wadley Lodge

Wadley Manor

96

Ewedown Copse

Church Path Farm

LONDON ST

Cromwell's Battery

Earthwork

Resr

Oxpen Copse

Oxpen Farm

Chinham Copse

Hotel

The Folly

Faringdon Hill

2

CROMWELL CL

FERNDALE ST
LANSDOWN
RIDGE
YE ST

JESPERS HILL

STANFORD RD

BUNKERS WK
HAMPDEN CL
ESSEX CL

BUNKERS CL

Standford Place

Chinham Farm

Folly Farm

A417 STANFORD RD

Jespers Hill

Kennels

Bowling Green Farm

95

Chinham Farm

PARK RD

iel Cottages

A417

Wichwood

Bowling Green Cottages

Dismantled Railway

1

Kitemoor Copse

A417

Kitemoor Farm

Kitemoor House

Wickleshamlodge Farm

94

D   30   E   31   F

173
154

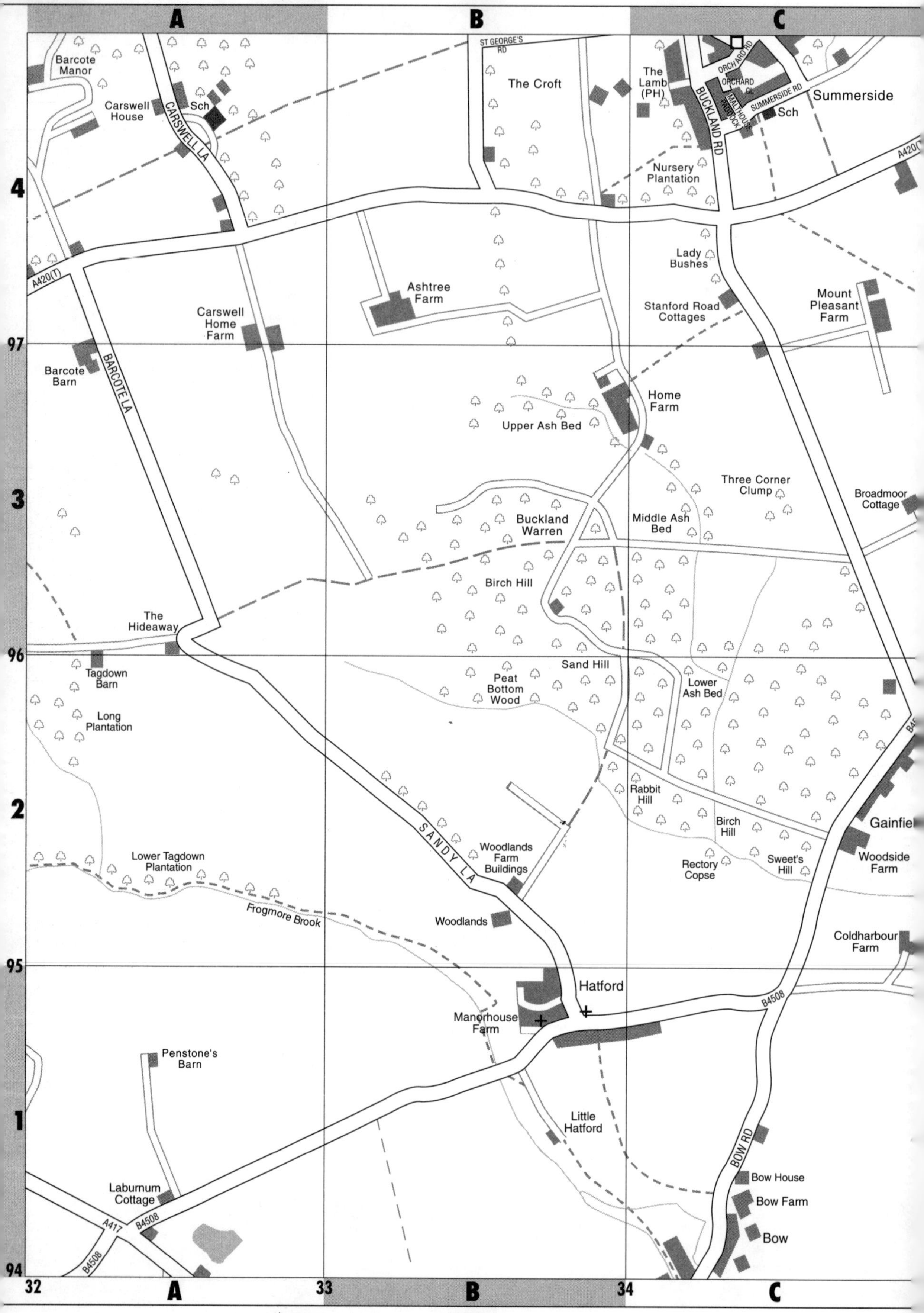

A **B** **C**

Barcote Manor

Carswell House

Sch

CARSWELL LA

The Croft

ST GEORGE'S RD

The Lamb (PH)

ORCHARD RD

ORCHARD CL

MALTHOUSE PADDOCK

BUCKLAND RD

SUMMERSIDE RD

Sch

Summerside

A420(T)

4

A420(T)

Nursery Plantation

Lady Bushes

Carswell Home Farm

Ashtree Farm

Stanford Road Cottages

Mount Pleasant Farm

97

Barcote Barn

BARCOTE LA

Home Farm

Upper Ash Bed

Three Corner Clump

Broadmoor Cottage

3

Buckland Warren

Middle Ash Bed

Birch Hill

The Hideaway

96

Tagdown Barn

Sand Hill

Peat Bottom Wood

Lower Ash Bed

Long Plantation

SANDY LA

Rabbit Hill

Birch Hill

Gainfiel

2

Lower Tagdown Plantation

Woodlands Farm Buildings

Rectory Copse

Sweet's Hill

Woodside Farm

Frogmore Brook

Woodlands

Coldharbour Farm

95

Hatford

B4508

Manorhouse Farm

Penstone's Barn

Little Hatford

BOW RD

1

Laburnum Cottage

A417

B4508

Bow House

Bow Farm

Bow

B4508

94

A **B** **C**

32 33 34

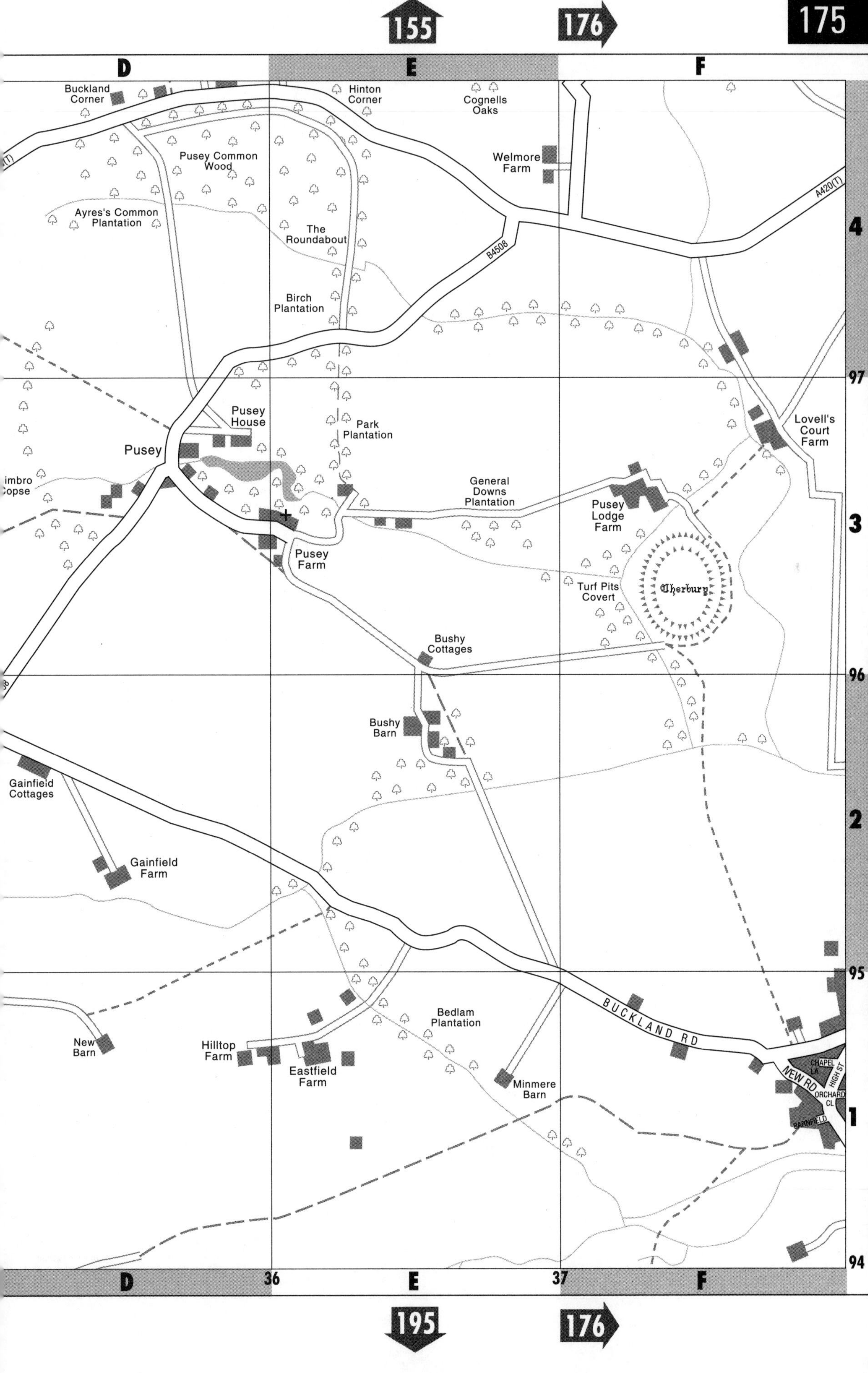
D
E
F
Buckland Corner
Hinton Corner
Cognells Oaks
Welmore Farm
Pusey Common Wood
Ayres's Common Plantation
The Roundabout
A420(T)
B4508
Birch Plantation
4
97
Pusey House
Park Plantation
Lovell's Court Farm
Pusey
imbro
Copse
General Downs Plantation
Pusey Lodge Farm
3
Pusey Farm
Turf Pits Covert
Cherbury
Bushy Cottages
96
Bushy Barn
Gainfield Cottages
2
Gainfield Farm
95
Bedlam Plantation
BUCKLAND RD
New Barn
Hilltop Farm
Eastfield Farm
Minmere Barn
CHAPEL LA
HIGH ST
NEW RD
ORCHARD CL
BARNFIELD
1
94
D
36
E
37
F

175
156

A
B
C

String Copse
PINE WOODS RD
Middle Barn
CHERRY TREE CL
HAYES AVE
STONEHILL LA
SANDY LA
Blenheim Farm
Kingston Bagpuize House
SPRING HILL
A420(T)
BULLOCKSPITS LA
Lamb and Flag (PH)
A420(T)
Nursery
Sewage Works
Race Farm
RECTORY LA

4

Lower Lodge Farm
Bullockspits Farm
New House
HANNEY RD

97
Newhouse Farm
Plantation Bar
Swannybr Farm

Hunters Moon
Newhouse Cover

3
Cherbury Cottages

Cherbury House
Sheephouse Farm
Stanborough Covert

96

Ock Bridge

2
River Ock

LONGWORTH RD

95
Chaldwick's Barn

Northfield Farm
Manor Farm
THE GREEN
Charney Bassett
Lyford Bridge
Lyford Grange

Charney Wick
ORCHARD CL

1
Lyford Manor
THE GREEN
Lyford
Manor Farm

Poplars Farm

Gallows Bridge

94

175
196

D
E
F
A415
DIGGING LA
Denys Farm
Resrs
Pickwick Farm
Collin's Farm
Frilford
Dry Leys
Hamfield Barn
A415
Comberley
Manor Farm
Fyfield Wick
A338
River Ock
Millets Farm
Noah's Ark (PH)
Garford
Sch
College Farm
Garford Field
Nor Brook
Venn Mill
Childrey Brook
Common Barn
ROMAN ROAD
Letcombe Brook
A338
4
97
3
96
2
95
1
94
42
43
D
E
F

177
158

A **B** **C**

CH
Golf Course

Sheepstead Farm

Sherwood

Sheepstead House

Sheepstead Park

West Down Lane

Cow Lane

4

A338

Peat Moor Lane

Sch

Peads and Barnett's Farm

Fish Ponds

FORD LA

A415

KINGS AVE

CHANGE WAY

HOWARD CORNISH RD

HYDE COPSE

THE FAIRWAY

DUFFIELD PL

FETTIPLACE RD

HAINES CT

HANSON CL

97

A338

A415

Denman College

THE GAP

TOWER CL

ORCHARD WAY

HARLAND RD

Sch

Hyde Farm Nurseries

MARCHAM RD

Cemy

NEW RD

ALL SAINTS

PARK SIDE

CHURCH ST

NORTH ST

SWEET BRIAR

Marcham

PH

Sandford Brook

3

Kiln Copse

FRILFORD RD

PACKHORSE LA

PRIORY LA

Marcham Priory

Manor Farm

MILL RD

96

Meadow Farm House

2

Nor Brook

River Ock

Marcham Mill

Childrey Brook

Weirs

95

Landmead Farm

1

94

44 **A** 45 **B** 46 **C**

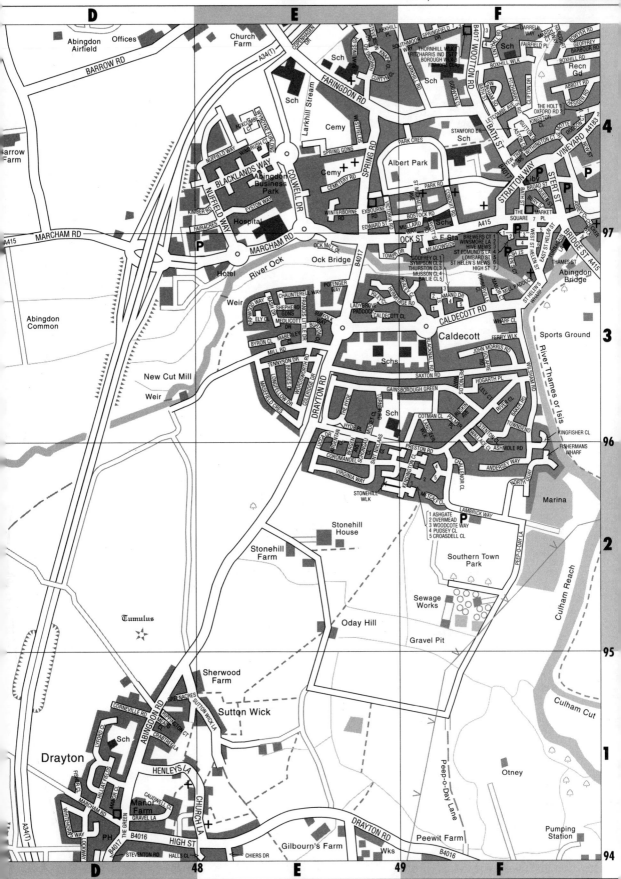

D E F

Abingdon Airfield
Offices
BARROW RD

Church Farm

Sch
COPENHAGEN DR
FARINGDON RD
Larkhill Stream

Sch
Sch
Sch
Sch

LARKHILL PL
SPRINGFIELD DR
SOUTHMOOR WAY
THORNHILL WLK
FITZHARRIS IND EST
BOROUGH WLK
FITZROO CSA

B4017 WOOTTON RD
DARRELL WAY
MARSH RD
FAIRFIELD PL
BOWYER RD
GEOFFREY
BARBOUR RD

Sch
Recn Gd

barrow Farm
BLACKLANDS WAY
NUFFIELD WAY
WINRUSH DR

Cemy
SPRING GDNS
PARK CRES

Albert Park
STANFORD DR
Sch
BATH ST

THE HOLT
OXFORD RD
KINGSTON CL

A4183
ABBOTT RD

4

Abingdon Business Park
Cemy
CEMETERY RD

PARK RD
ST MICHAELS AVE
CONDUIT RD

STRATTON WAY
STERT ST
VINEYARD

97

KIMBER RD
FAIRACRES
Hospital
MARCHAM RD
EYSTON WAY

WINTERBORNE RD
EXBOURNE RD
VICTORIA RD
EDWARD ST
MULLARD WAY
BOSTOCK RD

Schs
THE SQUARE
THE MARKET PL
BURY'S
BRIDGE ST
A415

MARCHAM RD
A415
P
COLWELL DR

Hotel
River Ock
Ock Bridge

OCK MILL CL
B4017
TOWER DR
OCK ST

F Sta
MEADOWSIDE
GODFREY CL 1
SYMPSON CL 2
THURSTON CL 3
MUSSON CL 4
BAILIE CL 5

BREWERS CT 1
WINSMORE LA 2
HIVE MEWS 3
ST EDMUND'S LA 4
LOMBARD ST 5
ST HELEN'S MEWS 6
HIGH ST 7

THAMES ST
Abingdon Bridge

Weir
BREWOOD WAY
NASH DR
ELY CL
SHEPHERD GDNS
FRANCIS LITTLE DR
CHAUNTERELL WAY
SUFFOLK WAY
BURY WAY

POTENGER WAY
LADYGROVE PADDOCK
CALDECOTT CL
HERMITAGE RD
RAVEL CL

ST HELEN'S WHARF

3

New Cut Mill
Weir
BYRON CL
MABERLEY CL
MEDLICOTT DR

MILL RD
TENNYSON DR
BRIDGES
WORDSWORTH R
COLERIDGE DR
DRAYTON RD

AMAND DR

CALDECOTT RD
Caldecott
WHARF CL
Sports Ground
River Thames or Isis

MASEFIELD CRES
LOWER FIELD

THE HYDE
HYDE CL
MID CRES
TURNERS RD
SINY NICKAS
Sch
SAXTON RD

GAINSBOROUGH GREEN
PRESTON RD
COTMAN CL
LANE SEEN
PALMER ROW
JOHN MORRIS RD
REYNOLDS WAY
HOGARTH PL
WILSHAM RD
STEVENTON RD
TOWNSEND
ELY CL
RILEY CL
BAKER CL

KINGFISHER CL
FISHERMANS WHARF

96

LUCCA DR
ROBERTSON
BERGEN
SCHONGAU
COROMANDEL
Virginia Way
STONEHILL WLK

METCALF CL
KENSINGTON CL
WALLACE CL
ASHMOLE RD
CAVENNOR CL
NORTH QUAY
ANDERSEY WAY

Marina

1 ASHGATE
2 OVERMEAD
3 WOODCOTE WAY
4 PUDSEY CL
5 CROASDELL CL

LAMBRICK WAY
P

2

Stonehill House
Stonehill Farm

Southern Town Park
PEEP-O-DAY LA
Culham Reach

Tumulus

Oday Hill

Sewage Works
Gravel Pit

95

Sherwood Farm

Culham Cut

CORNEVILLE RD
ABINGDON RD
GREENACRES
CHIPPINGTON MEADS
CHIPPINGTON CT
SUTTON WICK LA
Sutton Wick

1

IVYFORD CL
Sch
CRABTREE LA
Drayton
HENLEYS LA
CHURCH LA

Peep-o-Day Lane
Otney

FISH CL
HILLAT FIELDS
MANOR CL
CAUDWELL CL
Manor Farm
GRAVEL LA
THE GREEN
B4016
HIGH ST

DRAYTON RD
Peewit Farm
B4016

Pumping Station

A34(T)
WHITEHORN'S WAY
LOCKWAY
PH
STEVENTON RD
MARCHAM RD
HALLS CL
CHIERS DR
Gilbourn's Farm
Wks

94

D 48 E 49 F

A B C

BOWYER RD
JOHN MASON RD
A4183
WARWICK CL
NORTHCOURT WLK
NORMAN AVE
GALLEY FIELD
BOXHILL RD
OX CL
SWINBURNE RD
GEOFFREY BARBOUR RD
OXFORD RD
ST JOHN'S RD
RADLEY RD
Sch
Schs
ABBOTT RD
GRUNDY CL
SAFFRON CT
CAMPION CL
PURSLANE
DAISY BANK
RAMSONS WAY
FENNEL WAY
DENTON CL
KENT CL
LEVERY CL
GARDINER CL
EASON DR
Wick Hall
Home Farm
THRUPP LA
HADLAND RD
MINSHULL
NYATT RD
FERGUSON PL
THE WARREN
WELLESBOURNE
READE AVE
HERMAN CL
DUNLAS CL
FIENES RD
LEE AVE
HOBBS CL
AUDLETT DR
CLARENDON CL
MORTON CL
HART CL
SHERWOOD AVE
CURTIS AVE
KEMPSTER CL
BARTON LA
JACKMAN CL
THAMES VIEW
THAMES VIEW IND PARK
ABBEY CENTRE
THE QUADRANT
NAPIER RD
ABINGDON
Barton Lane
Gravel Pit
Science Park
Dismantled Railway
Thrupp House
Abbey Stream
Weir
Lock
ABBEY CL

4

97
Rye Farm
Weirs
Lock Wood
River Thames or Isis
A415
P
Andersey Island
3
Back Water
Causeway
Culham Brake
Warren Farm
The Warren
High Lodge
96
Culham Bridge
Sloven Copse
Thame Lane
Colmoor Farm
The Knoll
The Toot
P
THAME LA
THE BURYCROFT
Schola Europaea
2
Mushroom Farm
ABINGDON RD
Culham Station
PH
STATION RD
Culham House
The Wagon and Horses (PH)
TOLLGATE RD
THE GLEBE
Sch
HIGH ST
Zouch Farm
95
The Lion (PH)
Culham
P
Manor Farm
Manor House
Culham Cut
Culham Lock
Sutton Bridge
River Thames or Isis
Sutton Pools
1
ABINGDON RD
Weir
APPLEFORD RD
PH
Works
Manor House
CHURCH ST
ALL SAINTS LA
B4016
P
CHURCHMERE RD
B4016
94

50 A 51 B 52 C

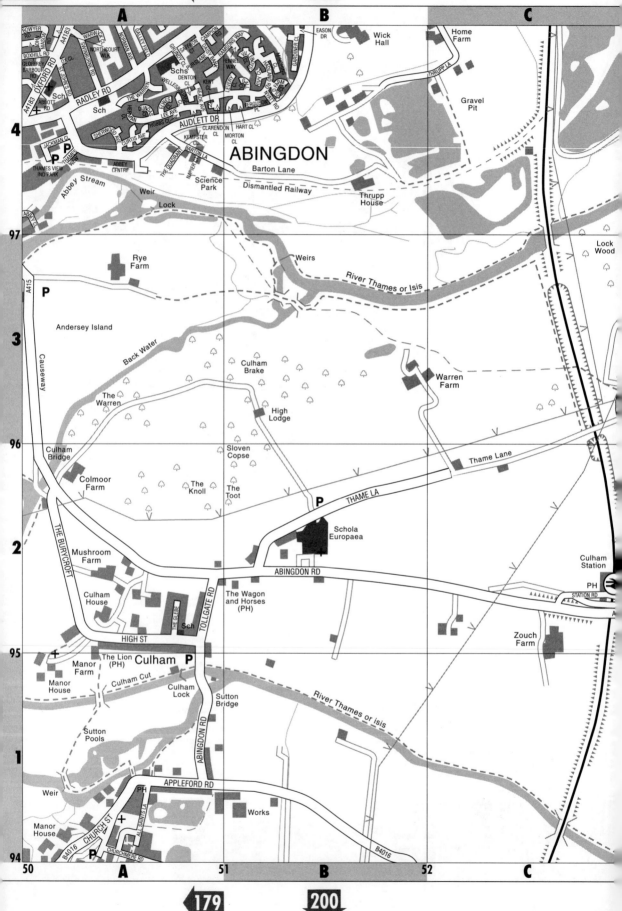

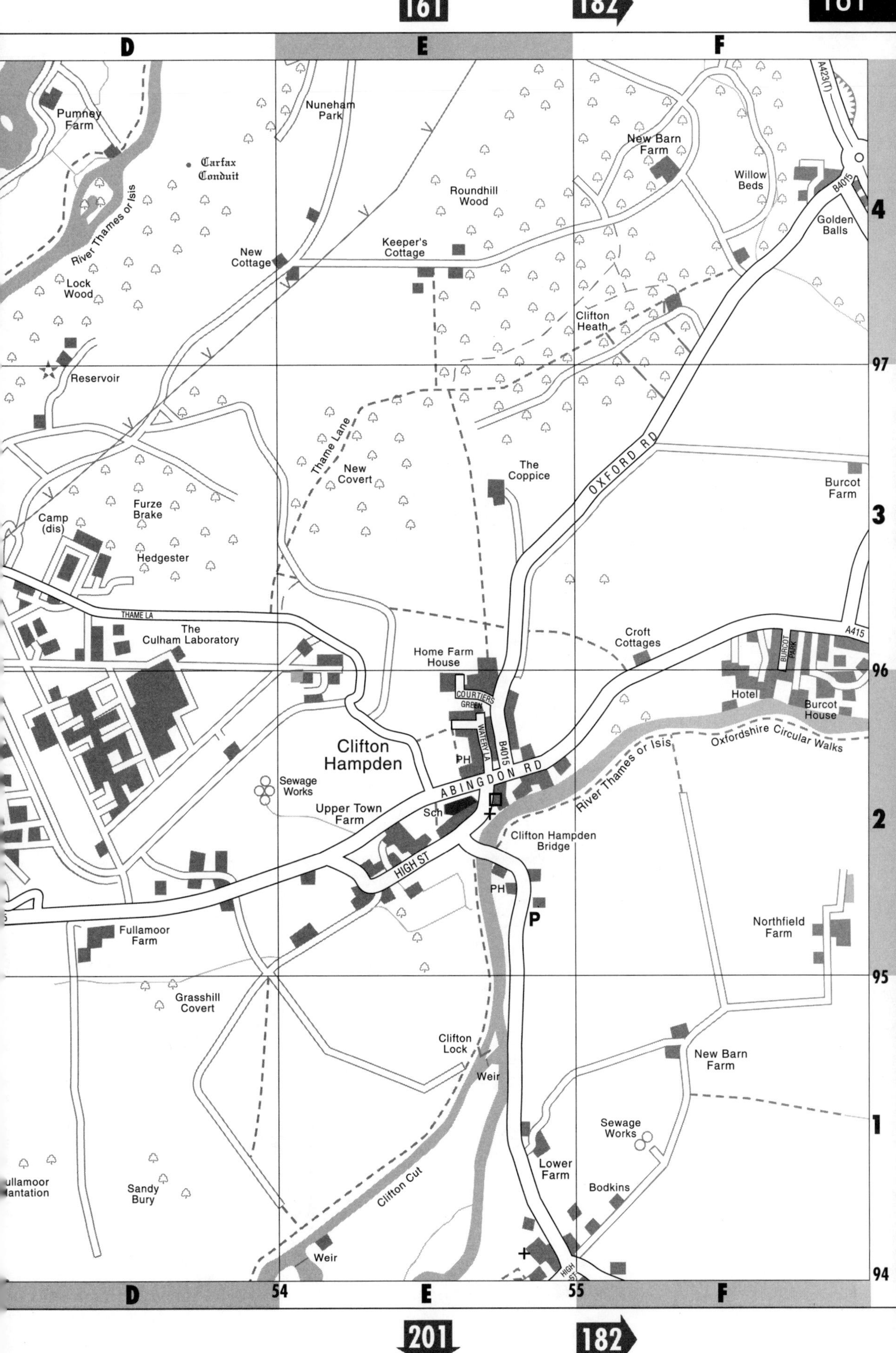
D
E
F
Pumney Farm
Carfax Conduit
River Thames or Isis
Lock Wood
Reservoir
Nuneham Park
New Cottage
Roundhill Wood
Keeper's Cottage
New Barn Farm
Willow Beds
A423(T)
B4015
Golden Balls
Clifton Heath
97
Thame Lane
New Covert
The Coppice
OXFORD RD
Burcot Farm
Camp (dis)
Furze Brake
Hedgester
3
THAME LA
The Culham Laboratory
Home Farm House
Croft Cottages
A415
BURCOT PARK
96
Hotel
Burcot House
COURTIERS GREEN
WATERY LA
B4015
Clifton Hampden
PH
ABINGDON RD
River Thames or Isis
Oxfordshire Circular Walks
Sewage Works
Upper Town Farm
Sch
Clifton Hampden Bridge
2
HIGH ST
PH
P
Fullamoor Farm
Northfield Farm
95
Grasshill Covert
Clifton Lock
Weir
New Barn Farm
1
Sewage Works
Lower Farm
Bodkins
ullamoor
lantation
Sandy Bury
Clifton Cut
Weir
HIGH ST
94
4
54
55

A B C

Baldon Brook

B4015

Golden Balls

ROMAN ROAD
(course of)

A423(T)

97

The Copse

Burcot Farm

RUSSELL JACKSON CL
BARRINGTON CL
PRITCHARD CL
TOWER RD
PINE DR

CRUTCH FURLONG
CHERWELL RD
EVENLODE DR
GLYME DR
COLNE DR

3

WESTFIELD
LAY AVE
OCK DR

Berinsfield

GREEN FURLONG
CONCLE
LEACH RD

SHOWELL
WHARTONS ROW RD
BULLINGDON AVE
WEY RD

Schs

CHILTERN CL

Mount Farm

Works

A415 BALFOUR COTTS

96 A415 ABINGDON RD
WINDRUSH RD
OGDEN AVE
KENNET CL

DORCHESTER RD

Burcot PH

BURCOT LA

Wally
Corner

2

Weir

DRAYTON RD

Oxfordshire Circular Walks

River Thames or Isis

ABINGDON RD

95

Queenford Farm

Queenford
Bridge

River Thame

OXFORD RD

THE MEWS

PH

DRAYTON RD

Bishop's
Court

Cemy
HERRINGCOT

PARK LANE

QUEENS

MARTIN'S LA
JEMMETTS
CL
CROWN
LA

MANOR FARM RD

Sch

1

Dorchester
ROMAN TOWN

HIGH ST
BEECHCROFT

MALTHOUSE
LA

Weir

Abbey Bridge

PH
ROTTEN ROW
BRIDGE END
WATLING LA

Mus

A423(T)

Overy
Farm

Overy

94

56 A 57 B 58 C

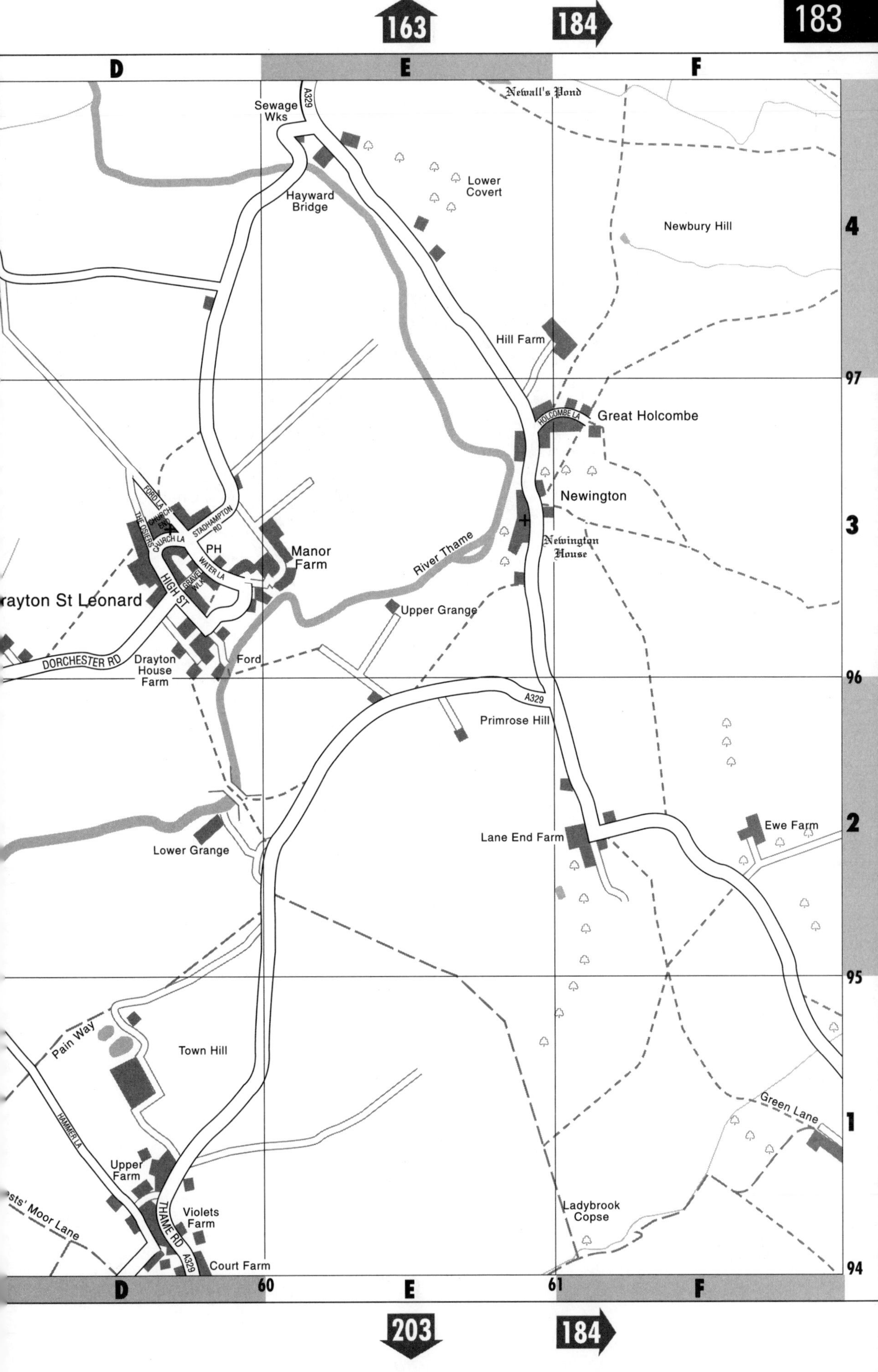

D

E

F

Newall's Pond

Sewage Wks

A329

Hayward Bridge

Lower Covert

Newbury Hill

4

Hill Farm

97

Holcombe La

Great Holcombe

Newington

3

River Thame

Newington House

PH

Manor Farm

Church La

Stadhampton Rd

Water La

Water Wlk

The Crofts

Drayton St Leonard

HIGH ST

Upper Grange

Dorchester Rd

Ford

Drayton House Farm

96

Primrose Hill

A329

Lower Grange

Lane End Farm

Ewe Farm

2

95

Pain Way

Town Hill

Green Lane

Hammer La

1

Upper Farm

Ladybrook Copse

Thame Rd

ests' Moor Lane

Violets Farm

A329

Court Farm

94

D

60

E

61

F

183
164

A
B
C
B480
Chalgrove Airfield
Hitchcox Poultry Farm
Chalgrove Field
Newberry Hill
4
1643
The Lamb (PH)
Moat
HIGH ST
Fox Covert
97
Manor Farm
Mill House
Langley Hall
Little Holcombe Covert
Langley Field Farm
Hampden's Monument
MONUMENT RD
Chalgrove
CROMWELL CL
Sch
CHURCH LA
Church Farm
BERRICK RD
MILL LA
3
Chalgrove Farm
96
Hares Leap
Southfield Barn
Cadwell Lane
Hollandstide House
Cadwell Covert
Cadwell Farm
2
95
Whitehouse Farm
Lonesome Farm
Manor Farm
Rumbolds Lane
1
Berrick Prior
Green Lane
Hollandtide Bottom
PH
Ivyhouse Farm
Berrick Salome
94
62
63
64

183
204

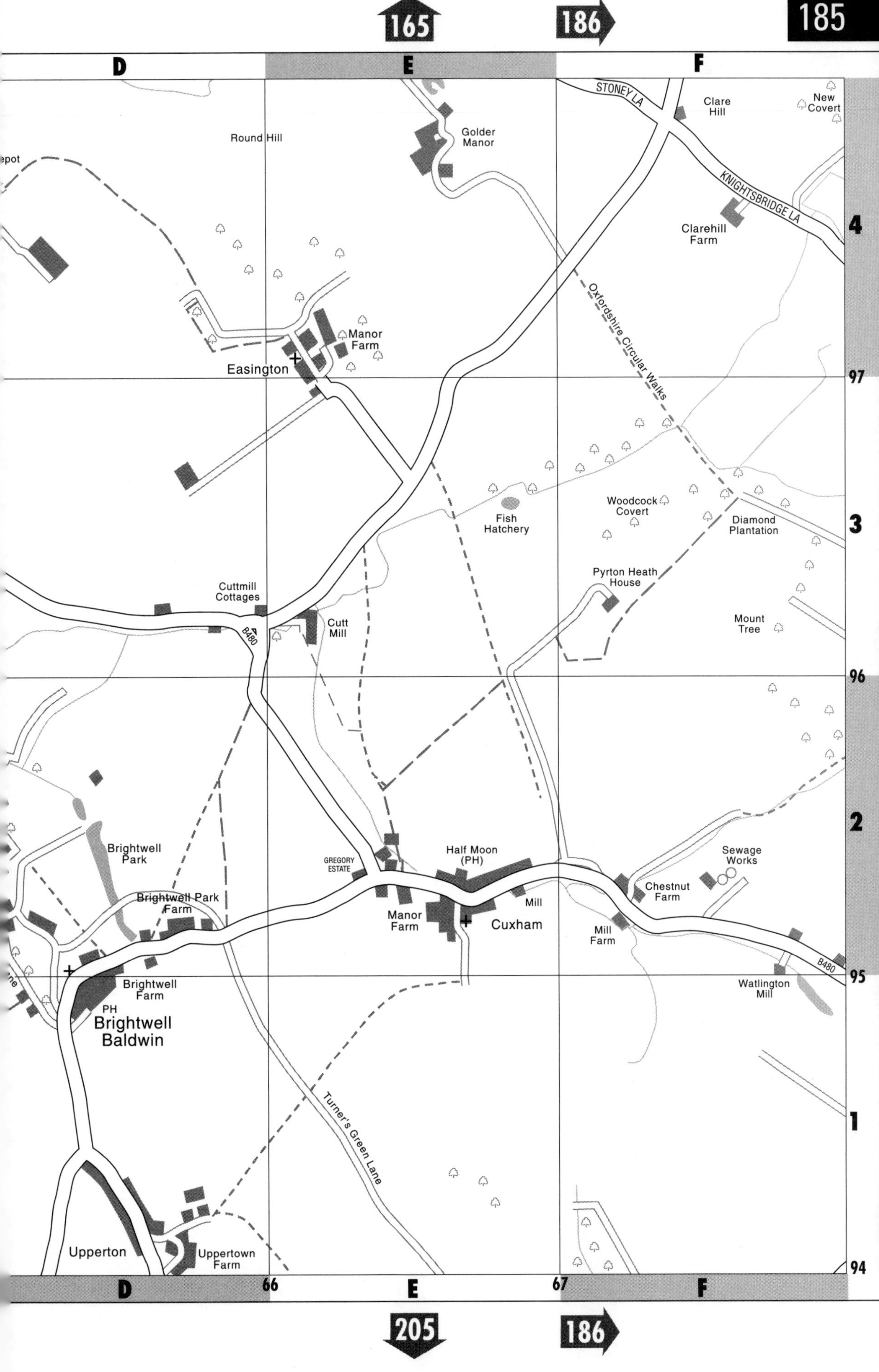

D   E   F

STONEY LA
Clare Hill
New Covert
KNIGHTSBRIDGE LA
Clarehill Farm
4

Round Hill
Golder Manor

Manor Farm
Easington
97

Oxfordshire Circular Walks

Fish Hatchery
Woodcock Covert
Diamond Plantation
3

Pyrton Heath House
Mount Tree

Cuttmill Cottages
B480
Cutt Mill
96

Brightwell Park
Half Moon (PH)
Sewage Works
2

GREGORY ESTATE
Chestnut Farm
Brightwell Park Farm
Manor Farm
Mill
Cuxham
Mill Farm
B480
95

Brightwell Farm
Watlington Mill
PH
Brightwell Baldwin

Turner's Green Lane
1

Upperton
Uppertown Farm
94

D   66   E   67   F

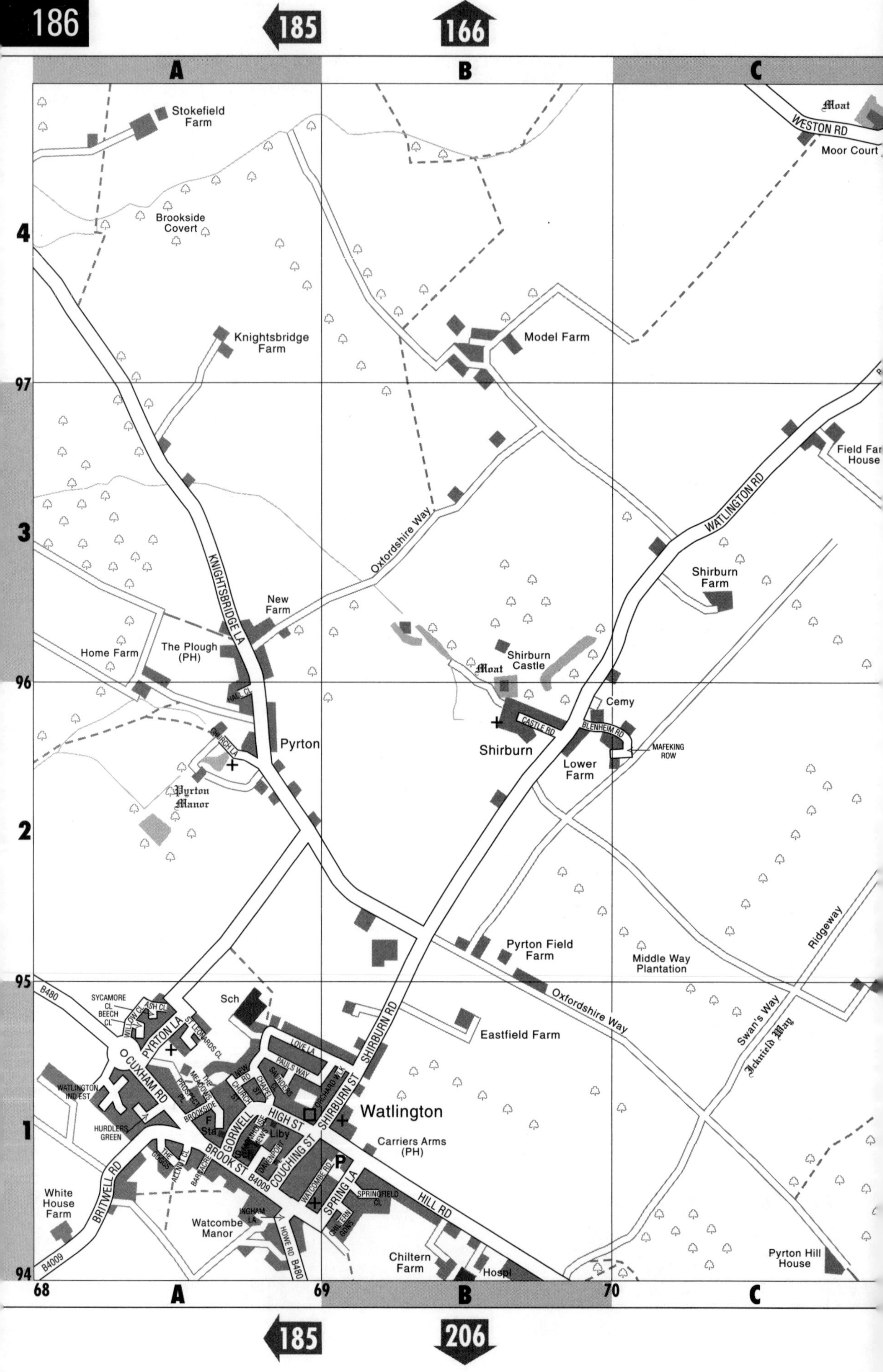

A **B** **C**

Moat
WESTON RD
Moor Court

Stokefield Farm

Brookside Covert

4

Model Farm

Knightsbridge Farm

Field Farm House

97

WATLINGTON RD

Oxfordshire Way

Shirburn Farm

3

New Farm

Home Farm

The Plough (PH)

KNIGHTSBRIDGE LA

Moat

Shirburn Castle

Cemy

96

HALL CL

CHURCH LA

Pyrton

CASTLE RD

BLENHEIM RD

Shirburn

MAFEKING ROW

Lower Farm

Pyrton Manor

2

Ridgeway

Pyrton Field Farm

Middle Way Plantation

95

B480

SYCAMORE CL
BEECH CL
ASH CL

Sch

Oxfordshire Way

Swan's Way

Icknield Way

WILLOW CL
PYRTON LA
ST LEONARDS CL
LOVE LA
PAULS WAY
SAUNDERS
Eastfield Farm

CUXHAM RD

WATLINGTON IND EST

Watlington

HURDLERS Green

BROOKSIDE

CORNWELL

HIGH ST
SHIRBURN ST
SHIRBURN RD
Liby

1

Sta

Carriers Arms (PH)

BROOK ST

COUCHING ST

B4009

SPRING LA
SPRINGFIELD CL

HILL RD

White House Farm

BRITWELL RD

INGHAM LA

Watcombe Manor

HOME RD B480

Chiltern Farm

Hospl

Pyrton Hill House

94

B4009

68 **A** **69** **B** **70** **C**

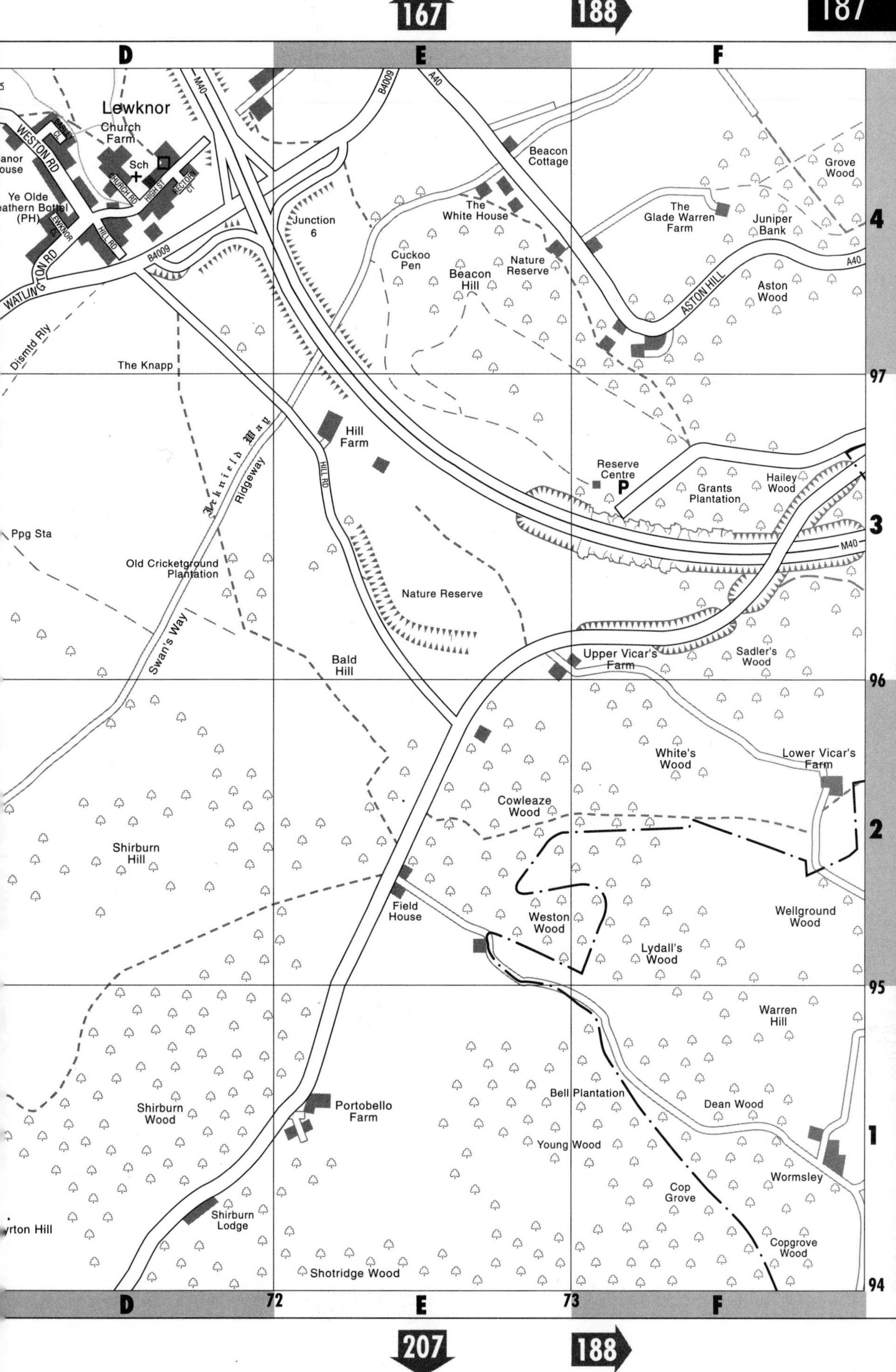
D
E
F
Lewknor
Church Farm
Sch
WESTON RD
Manor House
Ye Olde Leathern Bottel (PH)
CHURCH RD
HIGH ST
RECTORY CT
LEWKNOR CL
HILL RD
WATLINGTON RD
B4009
M40
A40
Junction 6
Beacon Cottage
The White House
Cuckoo Pen
Beacon Hill
Nature Reserve
The Glade Warren Farm
Juniper Bank
Grove Wood
ASTON HILL
Aston Wood
Dismtd Rly
The Knapp
Hill Farm
Icknield Way
Ridgeway
Reserve Centre
P
Grants Plantation
Hailey Wood
Ppg Sta
Old Cricketground Plantation
Nature Reserve
Swan's Way
Bald Hill
Upper Vicar's Farm
Sadler's Wood
White's Wood
Lower Vicar's Farm
Cowleaze Wood
Shirburn Hill
Field House
Weston Wood
Lydall's Wood
Wellground Wood
Warren Hill
Bell Plantation
Dean Wood
Shirburn Wood
Portobello Farm
Young Wood
Wormsley
Cop Grove
Copgrove Wood
Shirburn Lodge
Shotridge Wood
Pyrton Hill
4
97
3
96
2
95
1
94
72
73

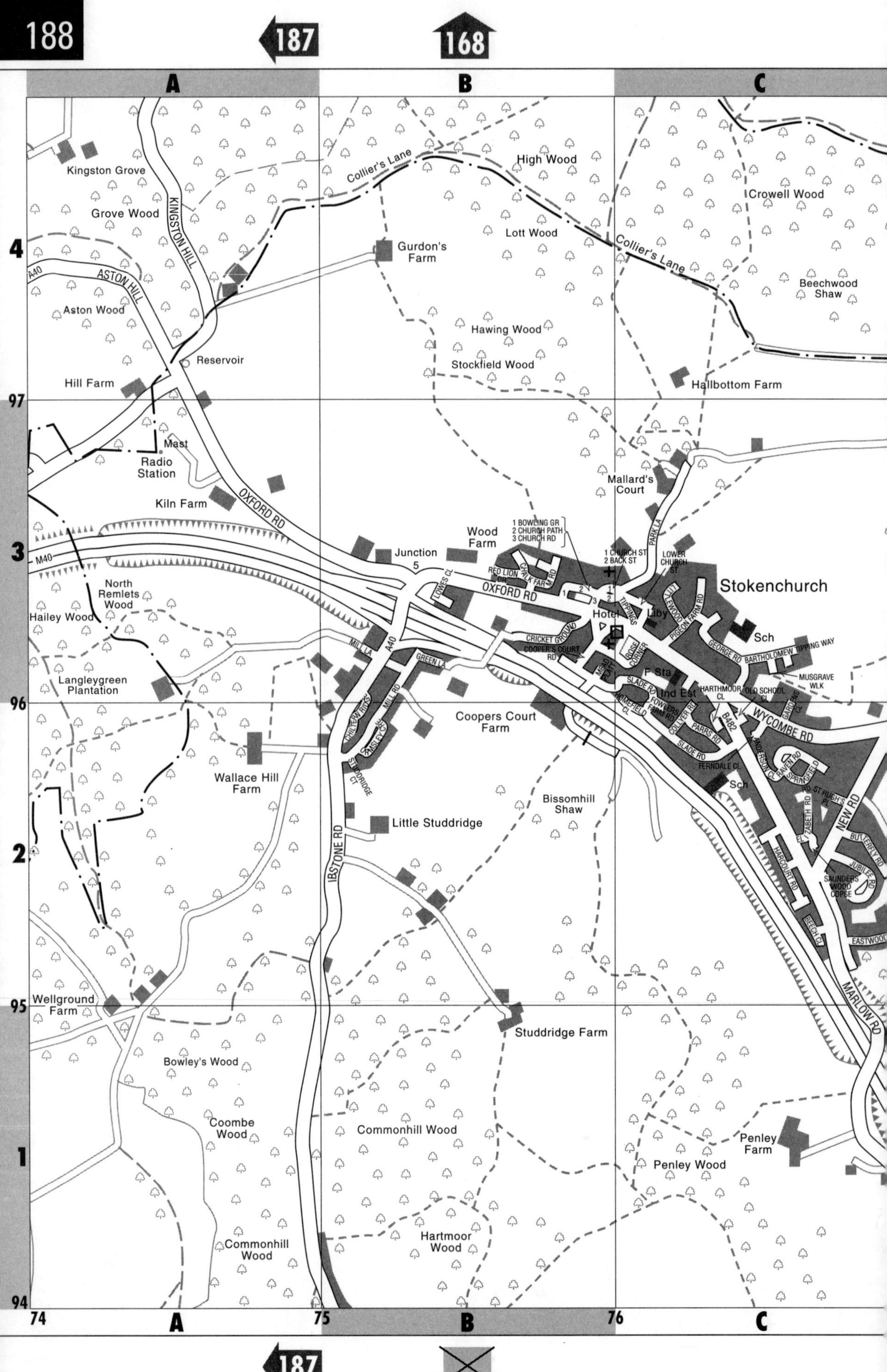

A **B** **C**

Kingston Grove

Grove Wood

KINGSTON HILL

Collier's Lane

High Wood

Lott Wood

Crowell Wood

4

A40

ASTON HILL

Gurdon's Farm

Collier's Lane

Beechwood Shaw

Aston Wood

Hawing Wood

Reservoir

Stockfield Wood

Hill Farm

Hallbottom Farm

97

Mast

Radio Station

OXFORD RD

Mallard's Court

Kiln Farm

Wood Farm

1 BOWLING GR
2 CHURCH PATH
3 CHURCH RD

PARK LA

1 CHURCH ST
2 BACK ST

LOWER CHURCH ST

3

M40

Junction 5

CLOWES CL

OAK FARM

RED LION LA

OXFORD RD

2
1
2 3

Hotel

UPPINGS

Stokenchurch

Lby

PIGEON FARM RD

North Remlets Wood

Hailey Wood

CRICKET GROUND

COOPERS COURT RD

Sch

GEORGE RD
BARTHOLOMEW

SPRING WAY

OPTING WAY

F Sta

Ind Est

HARTHMOOR CL

OLD SCHOOL

MUSGRAVE WLK

96

Langleygreen Plantation

MILL LA

A40

GREEN LA

Coopers Court Farm

HOLMEFIELD

SLADE RD
FOWLER RD

PARRS RD

SLADE RD

FERNDALE CL

WYCOMBE RD

B482

Wallace Hill Farm

CHILTERN RISE

MILL RD

RASKEL'S

ST BRIDGE CT

Bissomhill Shaw

Sch

NEW RD

ELIZABETH RD

HARROW HILL RD

MARLOW RD

2

IBSTONE RD

Little Studdridge

BUTTERFLY RD

JUBILEE RD

SAUNDERS WOOD COPSE

BEECH RD

EASTWOOD

95

Wellground Farm

Studdridge Farm

Bowley's Wood

Penley Farm

1

Coombe Wood

Commonhill Wood

Penley Wood

Hartmoor Wood

Commonhill Wood

94

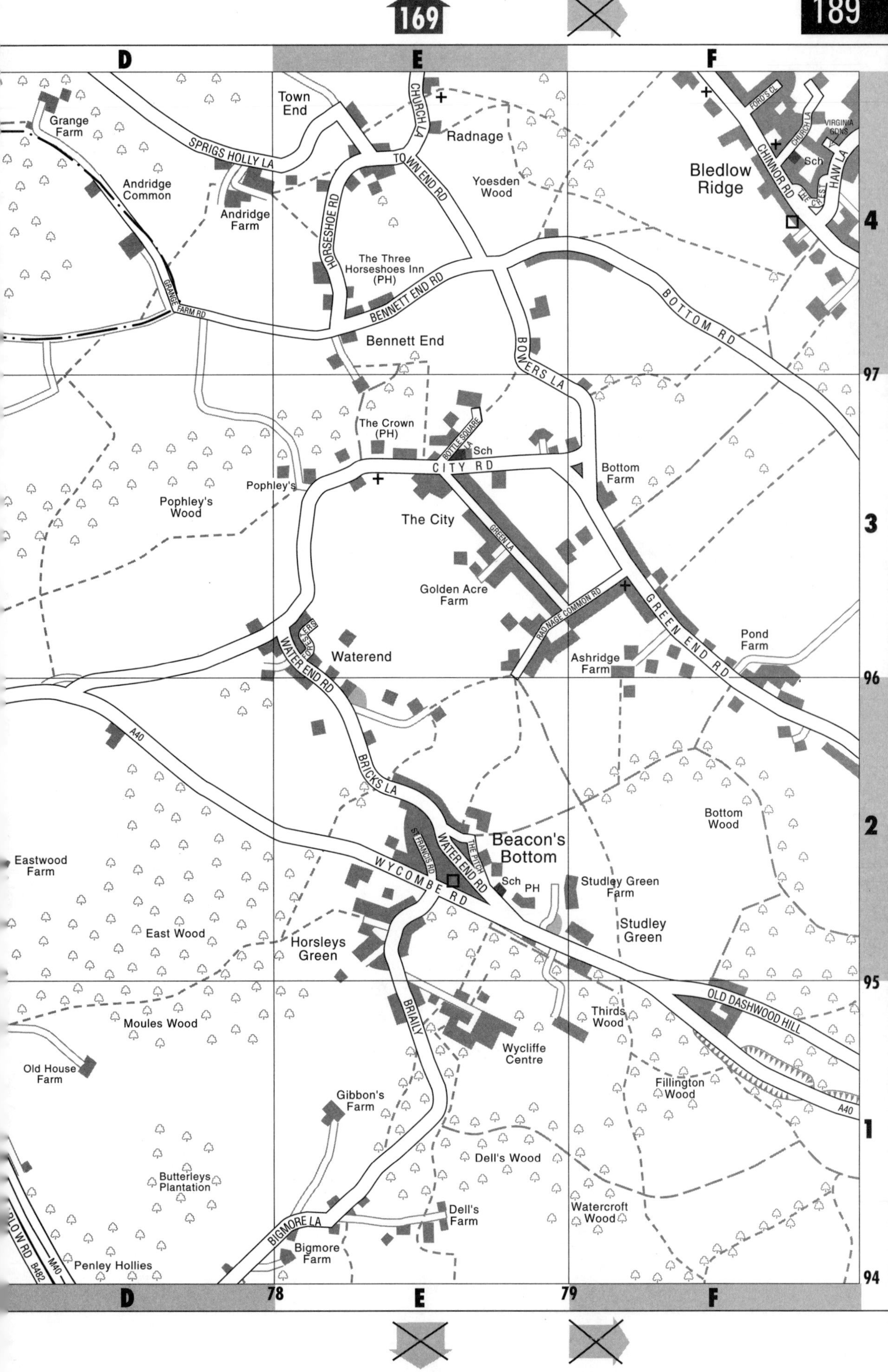

D · E · F

4 · 3 · 2 · 1

97 · 96 · 95 · 94

Grange Farm
SPRIGS HOLLY LA
Town End
CHURCH LA
Radnage
Yoesden Wood
Bledlow Ridge
FORD'S CL
VIRGINIA GDNS
CHINNOR RD
CHURCH LA
HAW LA
CREST
Sch
Andridge Common
Andridge Farm
HORSESHOE RD
TOWN END RD
The Three Horseshoes Inn (PH)
BENNETT END RD
Bennett End
GRANGE FARM RD
BOWERS LA
BOTTOM RD
The Crown (PH)
BOTTLE SQUARE
LA
Sch
CITY RD
Bottom Farm
Pophley's
Pophley's Wood
The City
GREEN LA
RADNAGE COMMON RD
Golden Acre Farm
GREEN END RD
Bottom Farm
Ashridge Farm
Pond Farm
FRS
WATER END RD
Waterend
A40
BRICKS LA
Bottom Wood
Eastwood Farm
St FRANCIS RD
WATER END RD
THE HIGH
Beacon's Bottom
Sch
PH
Studley Green Farm
Studley Green
WYCOMBE RD
East Wood
Horsleys Green
Wycliffe Centre
Thirds Wood
OLD DASHWOOD HILL
Moules Wood
BRIARLY
A40
Old House Farm
Gibbon's Farm
Fillington Wood
Butterleys Plantation
OW RD
B482
M40
BIGMORE LA
Dell's Wood
Dell's Farm
Watercroft Wood
Penley Hollies
Bigmore Farm

A	B	C

4

A361

BLACKWORTH

EDENCROFT

LANE FURLONG

FOLLY WAY

SEALEY DR

FOLLY
CL

Sch

KNOWLANDS RD

KNOWLANDS WAY

KNOWLANDS

SPA CL

ROUNDHILLS MEAD

Lower
Barn

Common
Farm

Wickstead
Farm

Ragla
Woo

River Cole

BA

93

GROVE HILL

WESTROP

FOLLY CL

LECHLADE RD

QUEENS AVE

THE CHILTERNS

THE DOWNES

BIDDEL
SPRINGS

SPA CL

BIDDEL
SPRINGS

HIGHWORTH

Eastrop
Farm

Fresden
Wood

Starveall
Barn

DOWNS
VIEW

CHERRY ORCHARD

ORANGE CL

PRIORY GREEN

THE MEWS

VICARAGE

STATION
RD

ST
MICHAEL'S
AVE

SHEEP
ST

THE WILLOWS

EASTROP

Fresde
Farm

3

CRICKLADE
RD

THE ELMS

SWINDON
ST

HIGH ST

BLUNSDON

BREWERY ST

B4019

KINGS AVE

PARK AVE

Sch

THE GREEN

B4000

STONEFIELD DR

A361

SWINDON RD

Schs

Eastrop
Grange

92

The
Buildings

Highmoor
Copse

River
Cole

2

SHRIVENHAM RD

Wrag
Farm

Round
Robin
Farm

Round
Robin
Wood

Folly
Plantation

Friars Hill

91

B4508

B4000

Coombes
Copse

River Cole

HIGHWORTH RD

Sevenhampton

Bellingham
Farm

Earthworks

New
Covert

Little
Coombes
Copse

Friars
Farm

Swan's Nest
Copse

1

The
Rookery

BELLINGHAM LA

Sevenhampton
Farm

HOVES LA

Thorny
Copse

Homegrown
Copse

B4000

90

A	B	C

| 20 | 21 | 22 |

D E F

4

93

3

92

2

91

1

90

Coleshill

CHURCH LA

SCHOOL LA

PH

B4019

Colleymore
Farm

Long
Shrubbery

Home
Farm

Coleshill Bridge

Coleshill Park

Flamborough
Wood

Ashen
Copse
Farm

Ashen
Copse

Ashencopse
Cottage

Fresden
Barn

River Cole

Waterloo
Copse

Vinthill
Withy
Bed

Tellhard's
Copse

Waterloo
Lodge

Grove
Copse

Strattenborough
Castle Farm

Watchfield Common
Wood
(Nature Reserve)

Pea Pits
Copse

Tithe
Farm

A420(T)

Southdown
Farm

tmill
dge

Westmill
Farm

MAJORS RD

B4508

B4508

B4508

BOWER GREEN

BOWER GRE

MAJORS RD

Pennyhooks Brook

SHRIVENHAM HUNDRED

STAR LA

PH

MEADOW RD

FARINGDON RD

BARRINGTON AVE

Pennyhooks
Farm

Pennyhooks
Lane

A420(T)

Ratcoombe
Copse

Golf
Course

OXFORD SQ

CHAPEL HILL

HIGH ST

BARRING... RD

Sch

FOLLY CRES

HILL RD

WELLINGTON

Watchfield

Bower Brook

Royal Military
College of Science

D 24 E 25 F

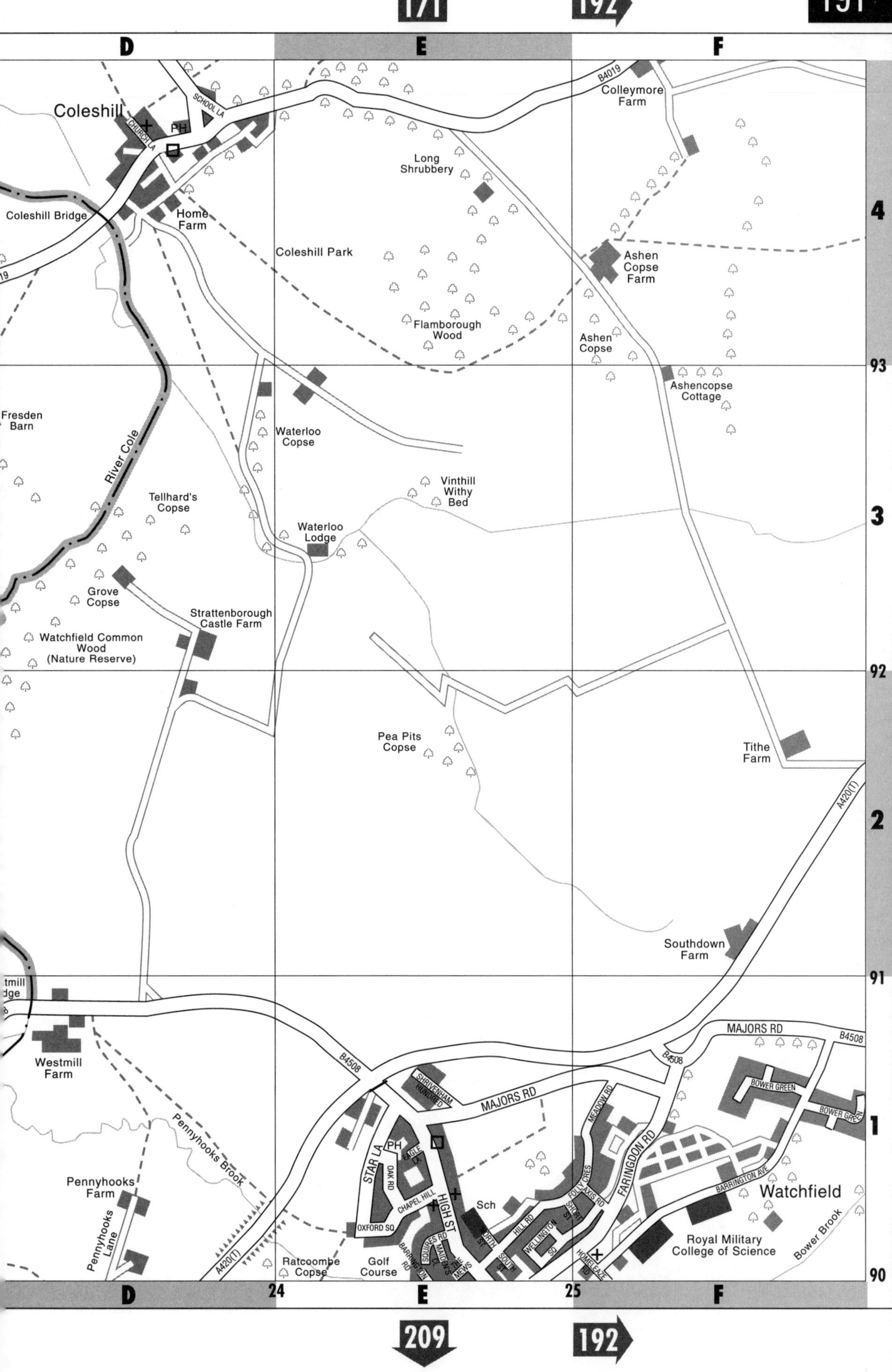

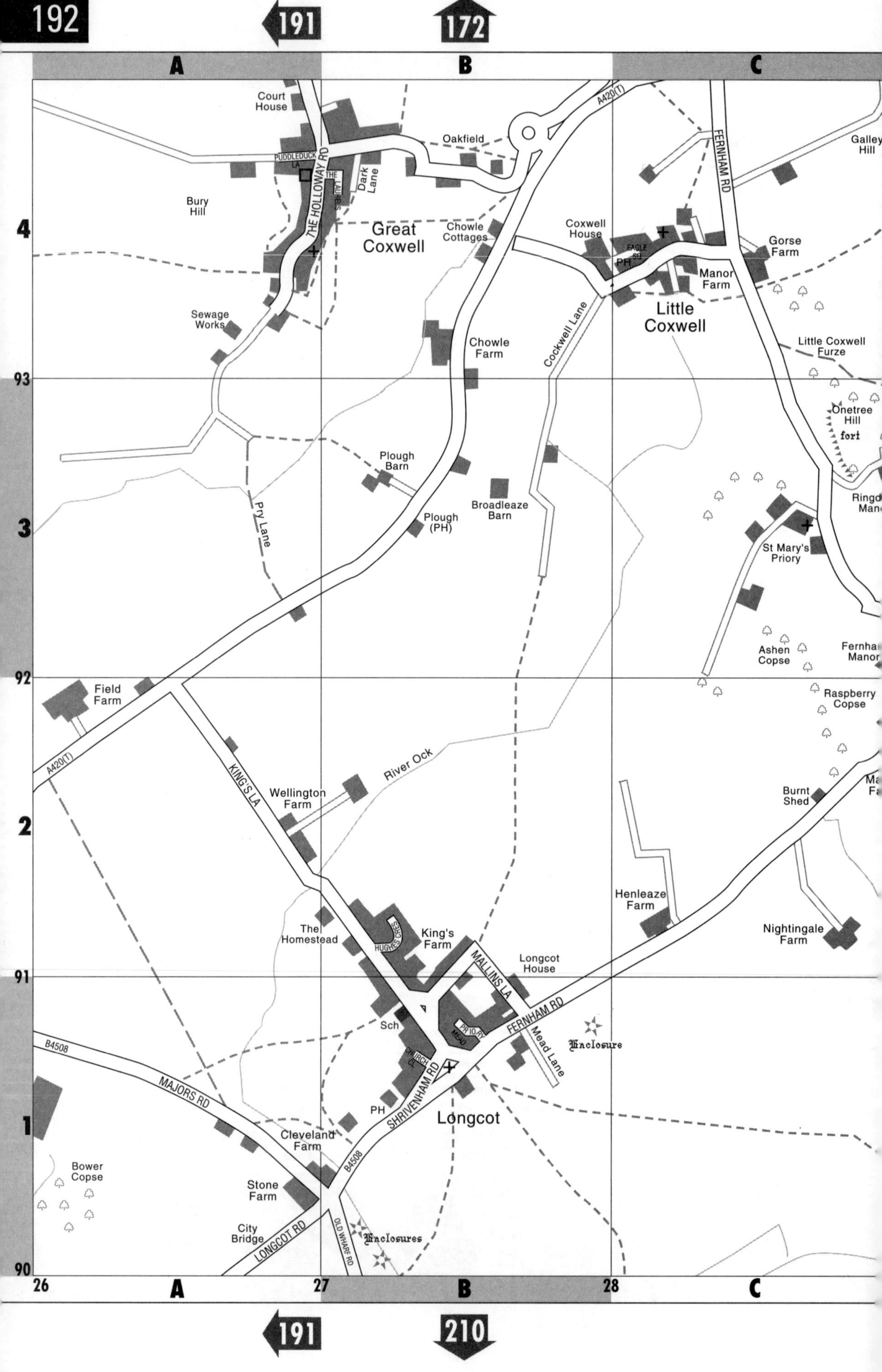

191
172

A B C

4

93

3

92

2

91

1

90

26 A 27 B 28 C

Court House
Oakfield
PUDDLEDUCK LA
THE
THE LAWNS
Dark Lane
Bury Hill
Great Coxwell
Chowle Cottages
Coxwell House
EAGLE St PH
Gorse Farm
Manor Farm
Little Coxwell
Sewage Works
Chowle Farm
Cockwell Lane
Little Coxwell Furze
Onetree Hill fort
Pry Lane
Plough Barn
Broadleaze Barn
Ringd Man
Plough (PH)
St Mary's Priory
Ashen Copse
Fernha Manor
Field Farm
Raspberry Copse
A420(T)
King's LA
Wellington Farm
River Ock
Burnt Shed
Ma Fa
The Homestead
HUGHE
King's Farm
Longcot House
Henleaze Farm
Nightingale Farm
MALLINS LA
B4508
Sch
Enclosure
MEAD
FERNHAM RD
Mead Lane
MAJORS RD
SHRIVENHAM RD
PH
Longcot
Bower Copse
Cleveland Farm
B4508
Stone Farm
City Bridge
LONGCOT RD
OLD WHARF RD
Enclosures

191
210

D E F

Cole's Pits

Dismantled Railway

Wickwood Farm

Chaslins Copse

Home Farm

B4508

CASTLE CRES

CHURCH ST

Sch

4

Wickwood Copse

Lyde Copse

Little Newbury Farm

93

Ashen Copse

FERNHAM RD

Field Barn

3

South Farm House

Sands Farm

Hill Pond

Belia's Coppice

Fernham Farm

ELMSIDE
CHAPEL LA

B4508

Ford

Bagmore Brook
Ford

92

4508
CHURCH LA
PH
HIGH ST
THE GREEN
BAKERS SQ

Fernham

Long Lane

Dismantled Railway

Spencer Farm

Manor Farm

Hyde Farm

2

Barrowbush Barn

Barrowbush Hill

Middle Green Farm

Cottage Lane

Gains Bridge

91

Alfred's Hill

Moor Mill Farm

Baulking Green

Church Farm

Baulking

Forty's Farm

BAULKING LA

1

River Ock

Oldland Copse

Vicarage Farm

90

D 30 E 31 F

193
174

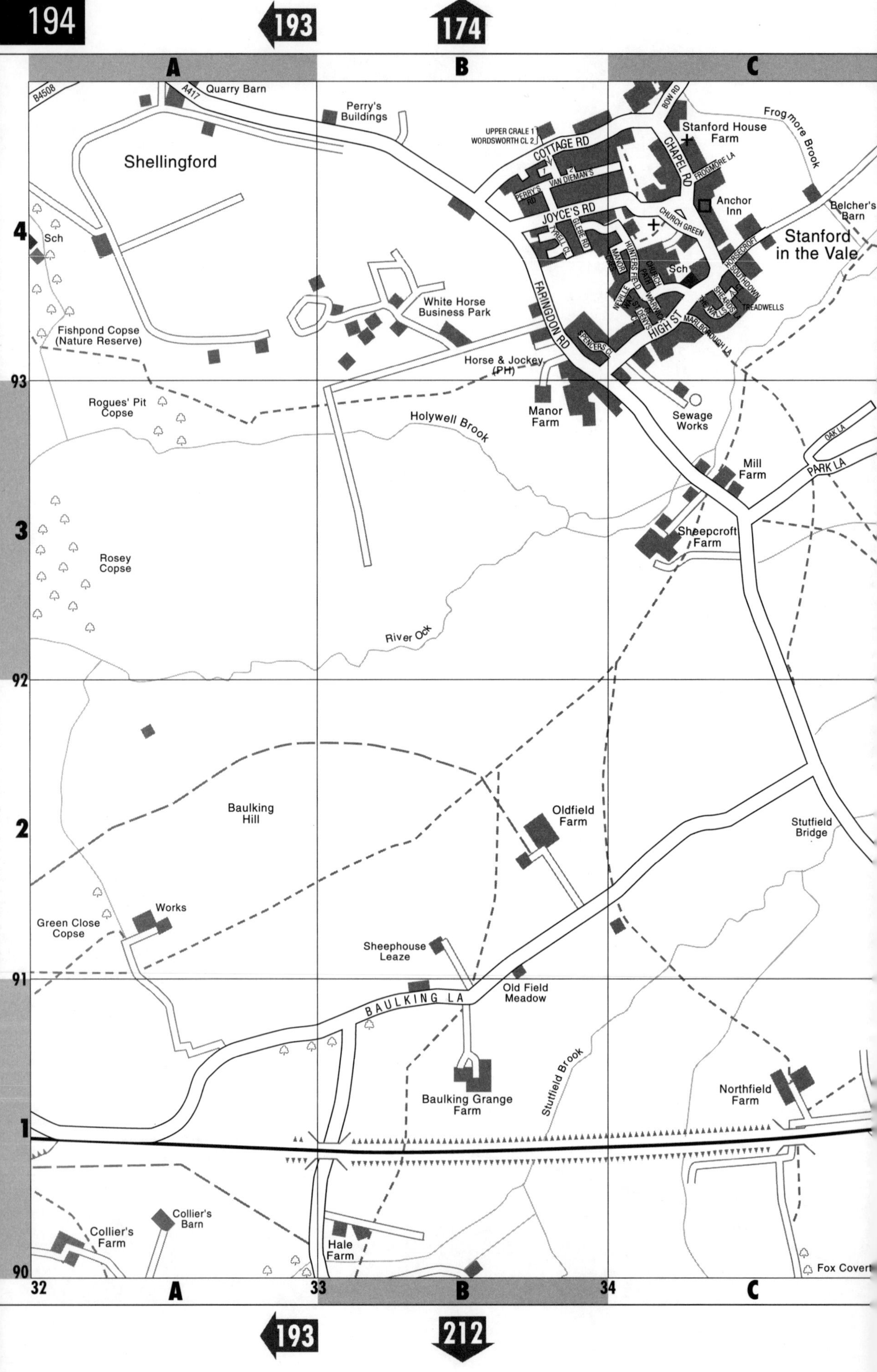

A B C

Quarry Barn
B4508
A417
Perry's Buildings

Shellingford

UPPER CRALE 1
WORDSWORTH CL 2
COTTAGE RD
VAN DIEMAN'S
Stanford House Farm
Frogmore Brook
CHAPEL RD
FROGMORE LA
BOW RD

Sch

PERRY'S RD
JOYCE'S RD
GLEBE RD
CHURCH GREEN
Anchor Inn
Belcher's Barn

4

TYRELL PL
HUNTERS FIELD
MANOR RD
HORSECROFT
MOURNDOWN
Stanford in the Vale

Fishpond Copse
(Nature Reserve)
White Horse Business Park
FARINGDON RD
Sch
THE WALLS
MARLBOROUGH LA
TREADWELLS

PERKERS CL
HIGH ST

93

Rogues' Pit Copse
Holywell Brook
Horse & Jockey (PH)
Manor Farm
Sewage Works
Mill Farm
PARK LA
OAK LA

3

Rosey Copse
Sheepcroft Farm

River Ock

92

Baulking Hill
Oldfield Farm
Stutfield Bridge

2

Green Close Copse
Works
Sheephouse Leaze

91

BAULKING LA
Old Field Meadow
Baulking Grange Farm
Stutfield Brook
Northfield Farm

1

Collier's Farm
Collier's Barn
Hale Farm
Fox Covert

90

32 A 33 B 34 C

D
E
F
River Ock
Gooseywick
Farm
Stanford Park
Island
Moat
Stanford Park
Farm
Little
Wick
Blackacres
Bridge
PARK LA
Blackacres Farm
Stanford Park
Cottages
Blackacres
Cottages
Stutfield Brook
Land Brook
The Pound
(PH)
Millaway
Farm
MILLAWAY LA
Goosey House
Goosey
Green
COW LA
Pound
Farm
Millaway
Bridge
Lane
Farm
GOOSEY LA
Church
Farm
Goosey
CIRCOURT RD
Upper
Circourt Farm
Petwick
Farm
PH
Circourt
Bridge
Childrey Brook
Petwick
Cottage
B4001
NEW RD
Woodhill Brook
Challow Marsh
Farm
A417
93
92
91
90
4
3
2
1
36
37

195
176

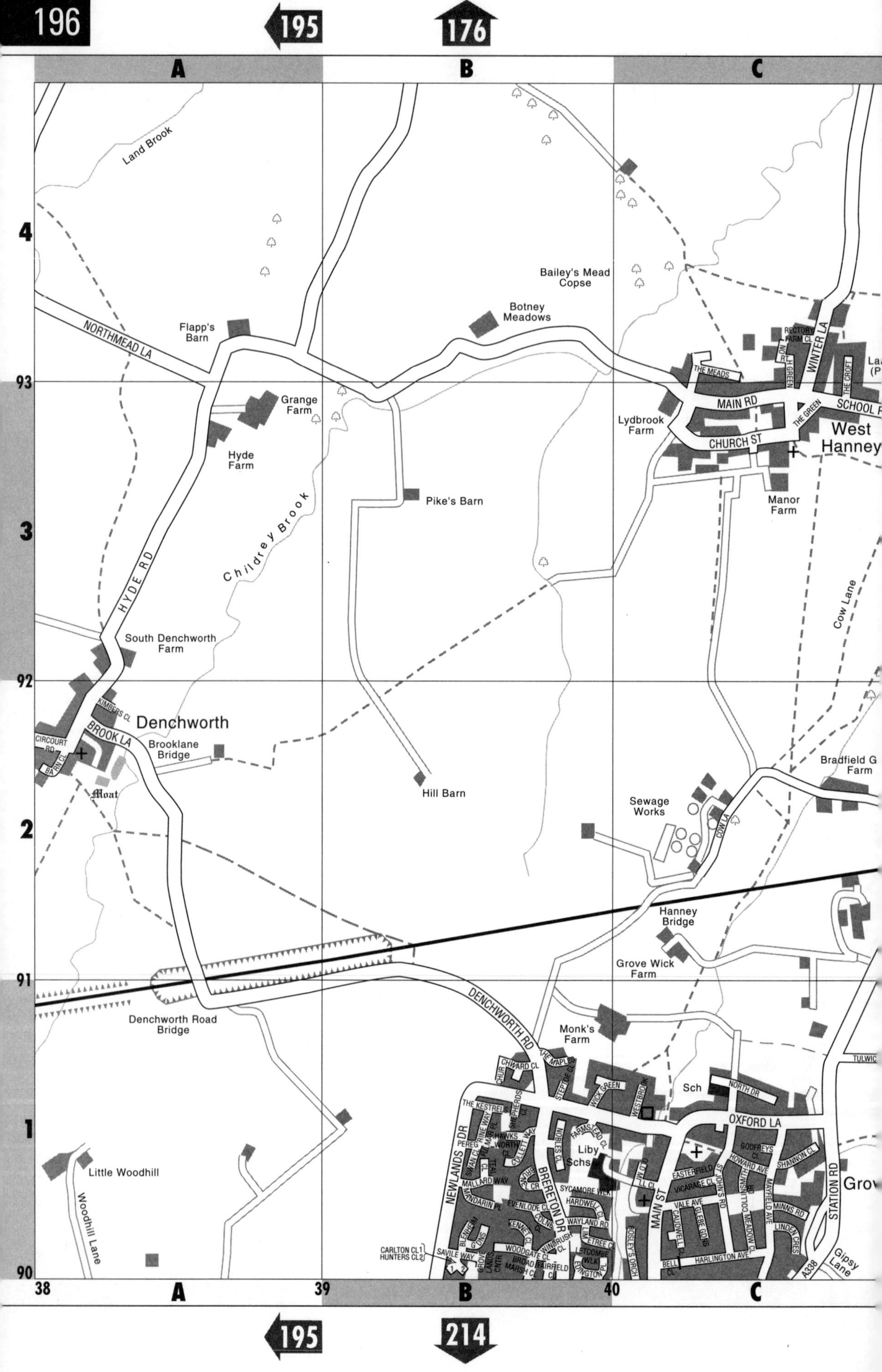
A
B
C
4
3
2
1
93
92
91
90
38
39
40
Land Brook
Bailey's Mead
Copse
Botney
Meadows
Flapp's
Barn
NORTHMEAD LA
Grange
Farm
Hyde
Farm
Pike's Barn
Childrey Brook
HYDE RD
South Denchworth
Farm
KIMBERS CL
Denchworth
CIRCOURT
RD
BROOK LA
Brooklane
Bridge
Moat
Hill Barn
Denchworth Road
Bridge
DENCHWORTH RD
Little Woodhill
Woodhill Lane
RECTORY
FARM CL
NORTH GREEN
WINTER LA
THE MEADS
THE CROFT
MAIN RD
SCHOOL R
THE GREEN
Lydbrook
Farm
CHURCH ST
West
Hanney
Manor
Farm
Cow Lane
Bradfield G
Farm
Sewage
Works
COW LA
Hanney
Bridge
Grove Wick
Farm
Monk's
Farm
TULWIC
CHWARD CL
THE MAPLES
STEP DE CL
WICK GREEN
WESTBROOK
Sch
NORTH DR
OXFORD LA
THE KESTRELS
SHEPHERDS CL
NEWLANDS DR
HAWKS
WORTH
MALLARD WAY
MANDARIN PL
COLLETT WAY
NOBLES CL
BRERETON DR
FARMSTEAD CL
Liby
Schs
SYCAMORE WLK
HARDWELL CL
WAYLAND RD
EVENLODE CL
WOODGATE CL
BROAD
MARSH CL
FAIRFIELD CL
LETCOMBE
WLK
EDINGTON PL
BOSLEY'S ORCH
MAIN ST
EASTERFIELD
VICARAGE CL
VALE AVE
GLEBE GDNS
CAUDWELL CL
BELL CL
HARLINGTON AVE
ST JOHN'S RD
GODFREYS CL
HOWARD AVE
MAYFIELD AVE
MEADOW CL
SHANNON CL
MINNS RD
LINDEN CRES
STATION RD
Grov
A338
Gipsy
Lane
CARLTON CL1
HUNTERS CL2
SAVILE WAY
BLENHEIM
LANDS
CNTR

195
214

D E F

4

93

3

92

2

91

1

90

Letcombe Brook

Poughley Farm

EBBES LA
ASHFIELDS LA
HALL
ASHFIELD
MORLANDS
THE GREEN
Crown Inn (PH)

A338

STEVENTON RD

HANNEY RD

Sch

Hall

THE CAUSEWAY
BROOKSIDE

MEDWAY
MAIN ST
SMUGGS LA
ST JAMES VIEW

Weir Farm

FERRY LA
ORCHARD
BLENHEIM ORCH
MILL ORCH

East Hanney

SUMMERTOWN

Cow Common Brook

Bradfield Barn

Old Man's Lane

Hutchins's Copse

Marsh Copse

The Volunteer (PH)

Grove Park

The Rookery

Portobello Ditch

ARDINGTON LA

Pinmarsh Farm

TULWICK LA

GROVE PARK DR

Tulwick Farm

Neville's Farm

Pill Ditch

A
B
C
4
93
3
92
2
91
1
90
44
45
46
Drayton Copse
Steventon Field
Cow Common
Honeybottom Boarding Kennels
Orchard Farm
Goose Willow
HANNEY RD
Three Elms
The Views
El Sub Sta
Depot
Sewage Works
Steventon
Causeway Farm
Causeway Crossing
Sch
THE CAUSEWAY
STOCKS LA
LC
Little Lane
VICARAGE RD
MILL ST
CASTLE ST
CHURCH LA
Steventon Copse
Ginge Brook
Hill Farm
Hill Barn
East Hendred Brook
Wood's Farm
WOOD'S FARM RD
BARNETT RD
ATLINGS RD
STONEBRIDGE RD
MERE DYKE RD
NORTH WAY
ST MICHAEL'S WAY
SCHOOL CL

D
E
F

4

93

3

92

2

91

1

90

Hall

LOCKWAY
B4017
STEVENTON RD
A34(T)
EAST WAY
HAYWARDS RD

CHIERS DR

Drayton East Way

Sewage Works

Brook Farm

Mill Brook

Hulgrove Farm

B4016
DRAYTON RD
B4016
BROOK ST

THE NURSERY

Drayton Mill

MILL LA
TULLIS CL

Uptown Farm

SOUTH FIELD
HIGH ST

Ginge Brook

Courtfield House

MILTON RD
KATCHSIDE

Frog Hole

BARRET K WAY
BRADSTOCK'S WAY
TYRRELL'S WAY
HARWELL RD

SUTTON RD

Sch

Milton Mill

MILL LA

Milton Manor

PH

HEATHER RD

Cemy

Sch
SCHOOL LA

Milton

HIGH ST
LITTLE

OLD MOOR

Manor Farm

Moor Ditch

SUTTON COURTENAY RD

ABINGDON RD
FIELD GDNS

PH

Butcher's Farm

Milton Lane

THE GREEN

Milton LA
SHEEPWASH LA
KENNET LA

Inn

PUGSDEN LA

EY RD
USEWAY

HIGH ST

Sch

PEMBROKE LA

Recn Gd

MILTON PARK
MILTON PARK
MILTON PARK

MILTON PARK

MILTON PARK

Milton Bridge

Mast

Depot

MILTON RD

Stockslane Farm

A4130

Backhill Lane

New Farm

A4130

A4130

B4017

Steventon Hill

Resr

Midwinters Farm

Steventon House

Milton Hill

SCHOOL LA
MIDWINTER LA
LA
TRENCHARD AVE
DUKE OF YORK AVE
HAVERS AVE

Sch

Milton Heights

Cow Lane

FEATHERBED LA

Research Centre

The Grove Farm

Hungerford Road
A4130

The Pack Horse (Inn)

Milton Hill House

Stert Plantation

A34(T)

199
180

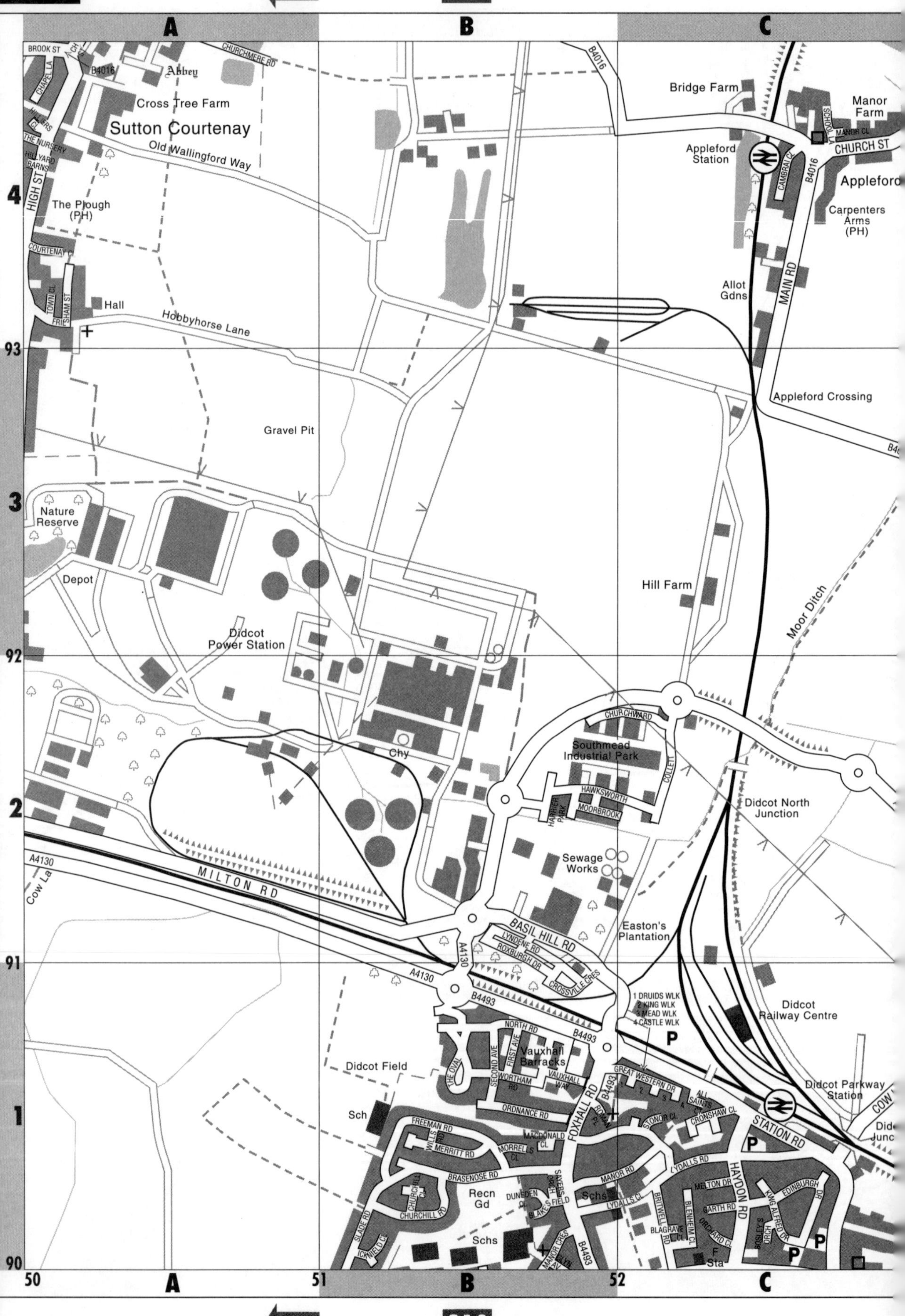
A
B
C
Sutton Courtenay
Cross Tree Farm
Old Wallingford Way
The Plough (PH)
Hall
Hobbyhorse Lane
Gravel Pit
Nature Reserve
Depot
Didcot Power Station
Chy
MILTON RD
A4130
Bridge Farm
Appleford Station
Manor Farm
CHURCH ST
Carpenters Arms (PH)
Allot Gdns
MAIN RD
Appleford Crossing
Hill Farm
Moor Ditch
Southmead Industrial Park
CHURCHWARD
HAWKSWORTH
MOORBROOK
Didcot North Junction
Sewage Works
Easton's Plantation
BASIL HILL RD
Didcot Railway Centre
1 DRUIDS WLK
2 KING WLK
3 MEAD WLK
4 CASTLE WLK
Vauxhall Barracks
Didcot Field
Sch
Didcot Parkway Station
STATION RD
FOXHALL RD
HAYDON RD
Recn Gd
Schs
F Sta
B4493
B4016
50
51
52
90
91
92
93
3
2
1
4

199
218

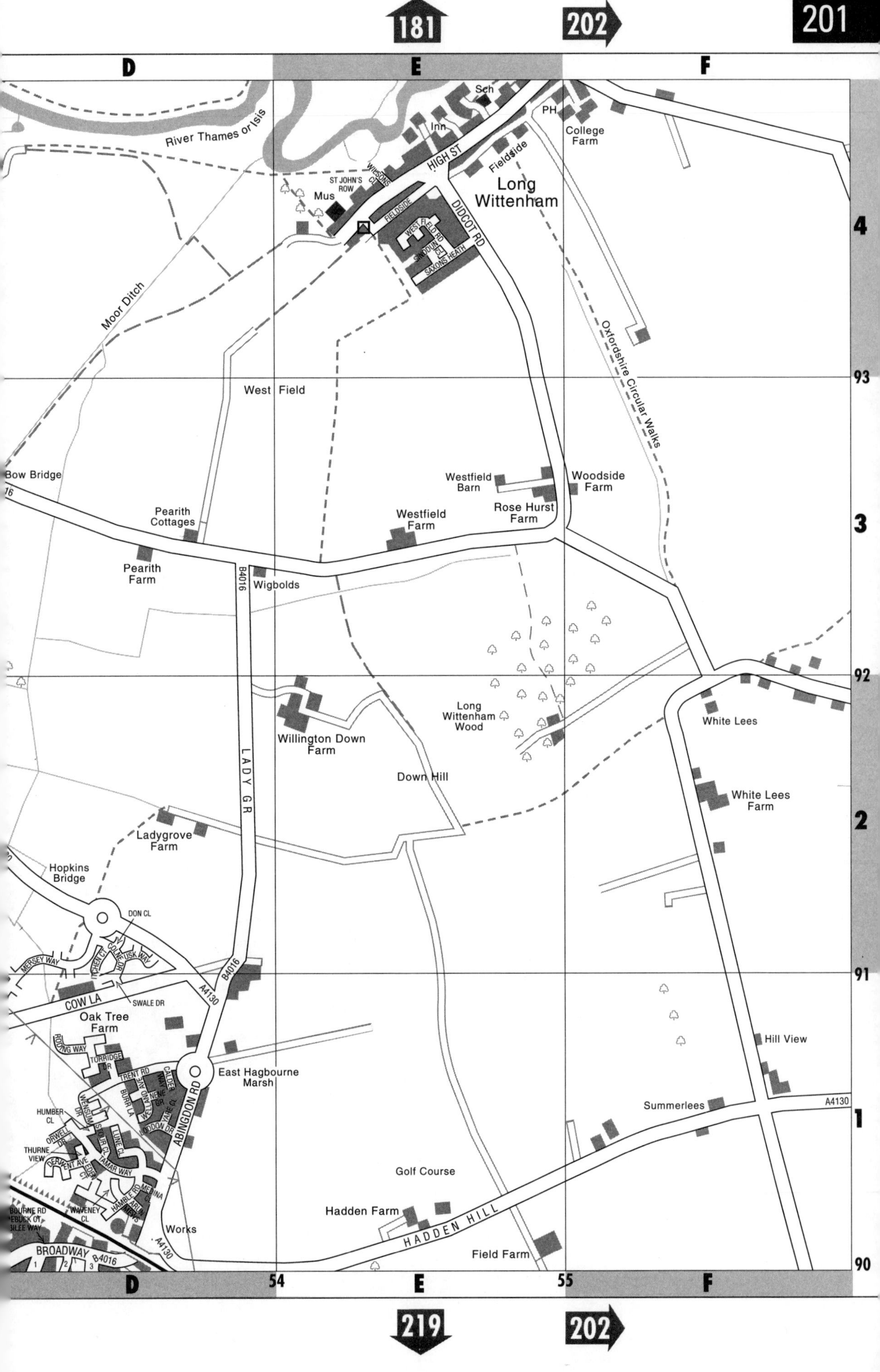

D
E
F

River Thames or Isis

Inn

Sch

PH

College Farm

HIGH ST

Fieldside

St John's Row

WILSON'S CLOSE

Mus

Long Wittenham

4

FIELDSIDE

WEST FIELD RD

SINODUN RD

SAXONS HEATH

DIDCOT RD

Moor Ditch

Oxfordshire Circular Walks

West Field

93

Bow Bridge

Westfield Barn

Woodside Farm

Pearith Cottages

Westfield Farm

Rose Hurst Farm

3

B4016

Pearith Farm

Wigbolds

92

Willington Down Farm

Long Wittenham Wood

White Lees

Down Hill

White Lees Farm

LADY GR

2

Ladygrove Farm

Hopkins Bridge

DON CL

91

MERSEY WAY

LISK WAY

B4016

SWALE DR

COW LA

A4130

Oak Tree Farm

Hill View

RIDING WAY

TORRIDGE DR

TRENT RD

CALDER

East Hagbourne Marsh

ABINGDON RD

HUMBER CL

ORWELL

Summerlees

A4130

THURNE VIEW

TAMAR WAY

MEDINA

HAMBLE

1

BOURNE RD

WAVENEY CL

Golf Course

ROEBUCK CT

JUBILEE WAY

Works

Hadden Farm

HADDEN HILL

Field Farm

BROADWAY

B4016

A4130

90

D
54
E
55
F

201
182

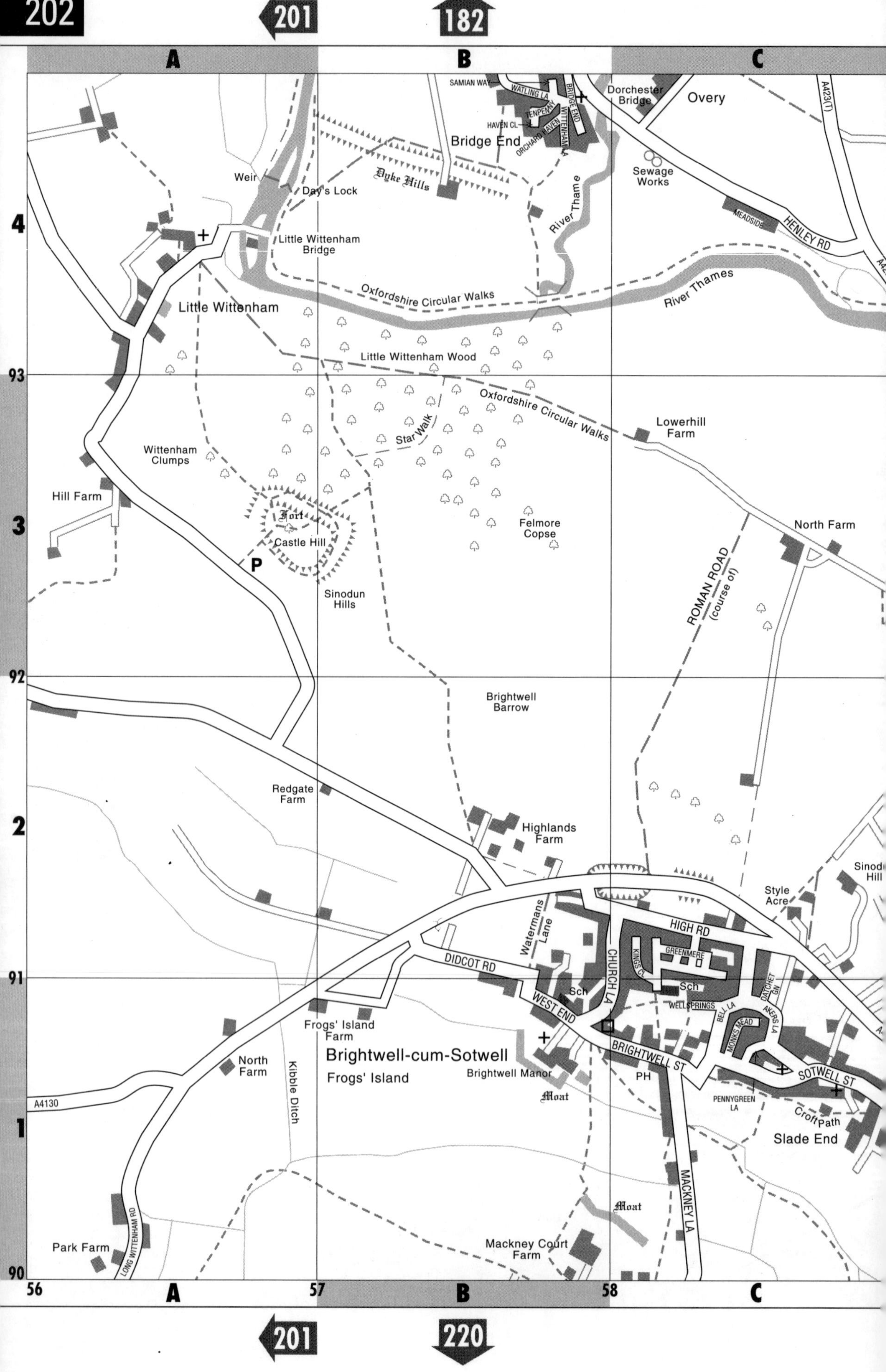
A
B
C
SAMIAN WAY
WATLING LA
TENPENNY
HAVEN CL
ORCHARD HAVEN
BRIDGE END
WITTENHAM LA
Dorchester Bridge
Overy
A423(T)
Bridge End
Sewage Works
Weir
Day's Lock
Dyke Hills
River Thame
MEADSIDE
HENLEY RD
Little Wittenham Bridge
Oxfordshire Circular Walks
River Thames
Little Wittenham
Little Wittenham Wood
Oxfordshire Circular Walks
Lowerhill Farm
Star Walk
Wittenham Clumps
Hill Farm
Fort
Castle Hill
Felmore Copse
North Farm
P
Sinodun Hills
ROMAN ROAD (course of)
Brightwell Barrow
Redgate Farm
Highlands Farm
Style Acre
Watermans Lane
HIGH RD
GREENMERE
KINGS CL
CHURCH LA
DIDCOT RD
Sch
Sch
WEST END
WELLSPRINGS
BELL LA
MONKS MEAD
AKERS LA
DATCHET GN
Frogs' Island Farm
Brightwell-cum-Sotwell
BRIGHTWELL ST
SOTWELL ST
North Farm
Frogs' Island
Brightwell Manor
PH
PENNYGREEN LA
Croft Path
Slade End
A4130
Kibble Ditch
Moat
Moat
MACKNEY LA
LONG WITTENHAM RD
Park Farm
Mackney Court Farm
4
93
3
92
2
91
1
90
56
57
58

201
220

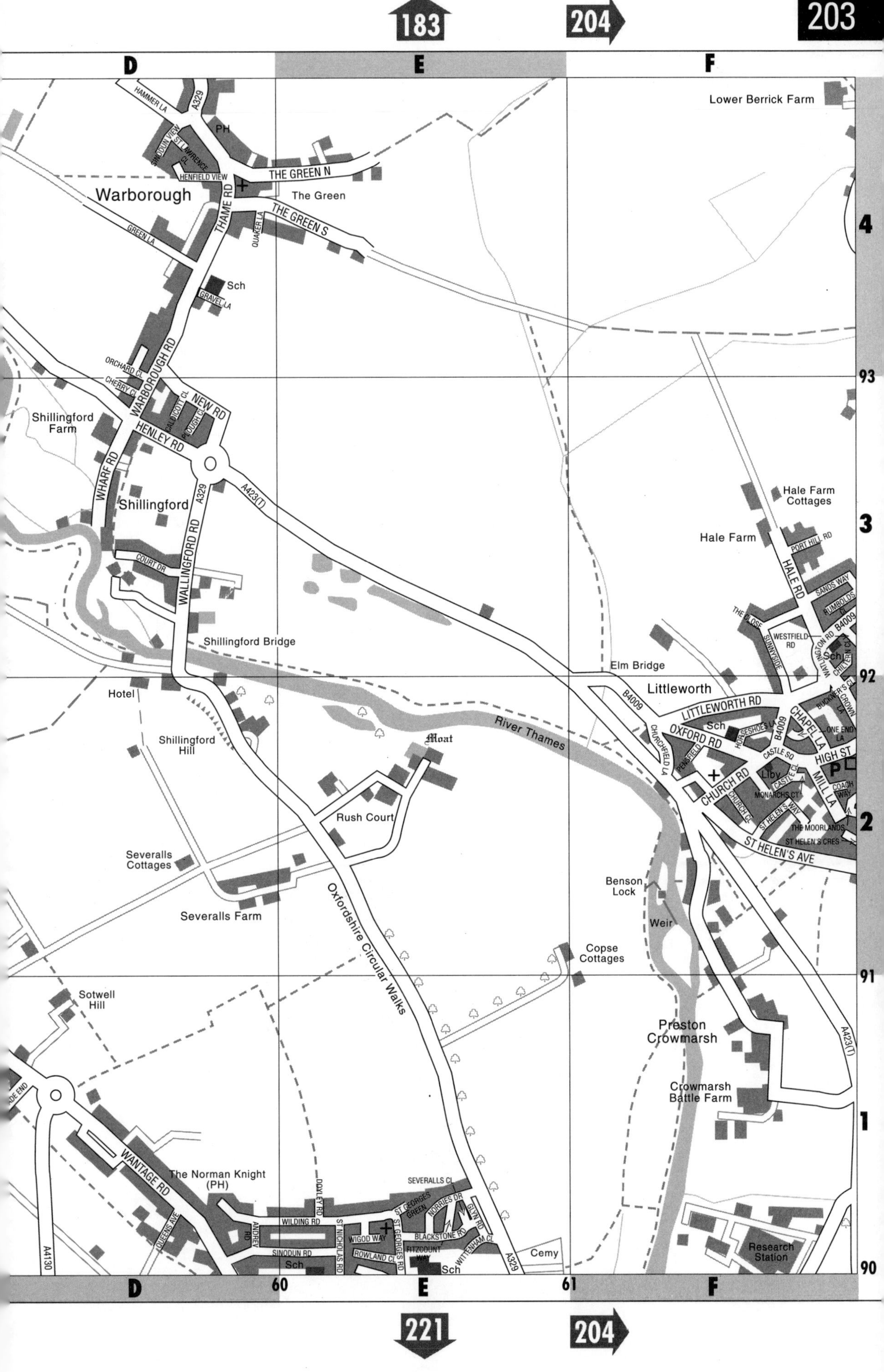
D
E
F
Lower Berrick Farm
Warborough
The Green
THE GREEN N
THE GREEN S
THAME RD
HAMMER LA
A329
PH
Sch
GRAVEL LA
GREEN LA
WARBOROUGH RD
NEW RD
HENLEY RD
Shillingford Farm
Shillingford
WHARF RD
WALLINGFORD RD
COURT DR
A423(T)
Shillingford Bridge
Hotel
Shillingford Hill
Moat
River Thames
Rush Court
Severalls Cottages
Severalls Farm
Oxfordshire Circular Walks
Hale Farm Cottages
Hale Farm
HALE RD
PORT HILL RD
SANDS WAY
Elm Bridge
Littleworth
LITTLEWORTH RD
OXFORD RD
CHURCH RD
CHAPEL LA
HIGH ST
MILL LA
ST HELEN'S AVE
Benson Lock
Weir
Copse Cottages
Preston Crowmarsh
Crowmarsh Battle Farm
Sotwell Hill
WANTAGE RD
The Norman Knight (PH)
A4130
WILDING RD
SINODUN RD
Sch
Cemy
Research Station
4
93
3
92
2
91
1
90
60
61

203
184
203
222

Parson's Farm
Grace's Farm
WELLER CL
Hare Hall
Bunkers
Scald Hill
Home Sweet Home (PH)
CHAPEL LA
Roke
Rumbolds Lane
Roke Farm
Rumbold's Copse
The Horse and Harrow (PH)
Rokemarsh
THE SANDS
GROVE LA B40
Port Hill House
BRAZE LA
Tidmarsh Lane
COTTESMORE LA
Windmill Farm
EYRE'S LA
WATLINGTON RD B4009
THE CEDARS
Fifield Farm
Cottesmore Farm
Hyde Shaw
FIREBRASS
BROOK ST
The Views
Shepherd's Hut (PH)
CAT LA
BRITWELL RD
HAMPDEN WAY
CROWN SQ
OBSERVATORY
PADDOCK
Benson
1 CROWN LA
2 ALDRIDGE CL
3 THE MOORLANDS
Lower Farm
MARTYN'S WAY
CHURCH RD
Ewelme
HIGH ST
OLD LONDON RD
Church Farm
PARSON'S LA
ST HELEN'S AVE
Benson Airfield
GREEN LA
Manor House
The Greyhound (PH)
Sch
Fords Farm
BENSON LA
CLAY LA
DEVON
BELFAST RD
CL
ANDOVER RD
BRAMBER CL
WHITSEY WAY
VIKING RD
SHIPPMINNS
COLWAY RD
ARBOSY RD
LANCASTER AVE
MOSS RD A 4
HAVEN WAY
Rabbits Hill
DAY'S LA
Cow Common
ALISTER TAYLOR DR
GEOFFREY TUTTLE DR
ANTHONY HILL RD
HUDDLESTON AVE
FIELDEN RD
MC KEE SQ
COCKRANE RD
FIELDEN CL
BATTLE RD
BARING WAY
BAKER AVE
BAKER CL
MOSS RD
Swan's W
A423(T)
Sewage Wks
BEGGARSBUSH HILL
The London Road (PH)
Mast
Gravel Pit
Marsh Wood

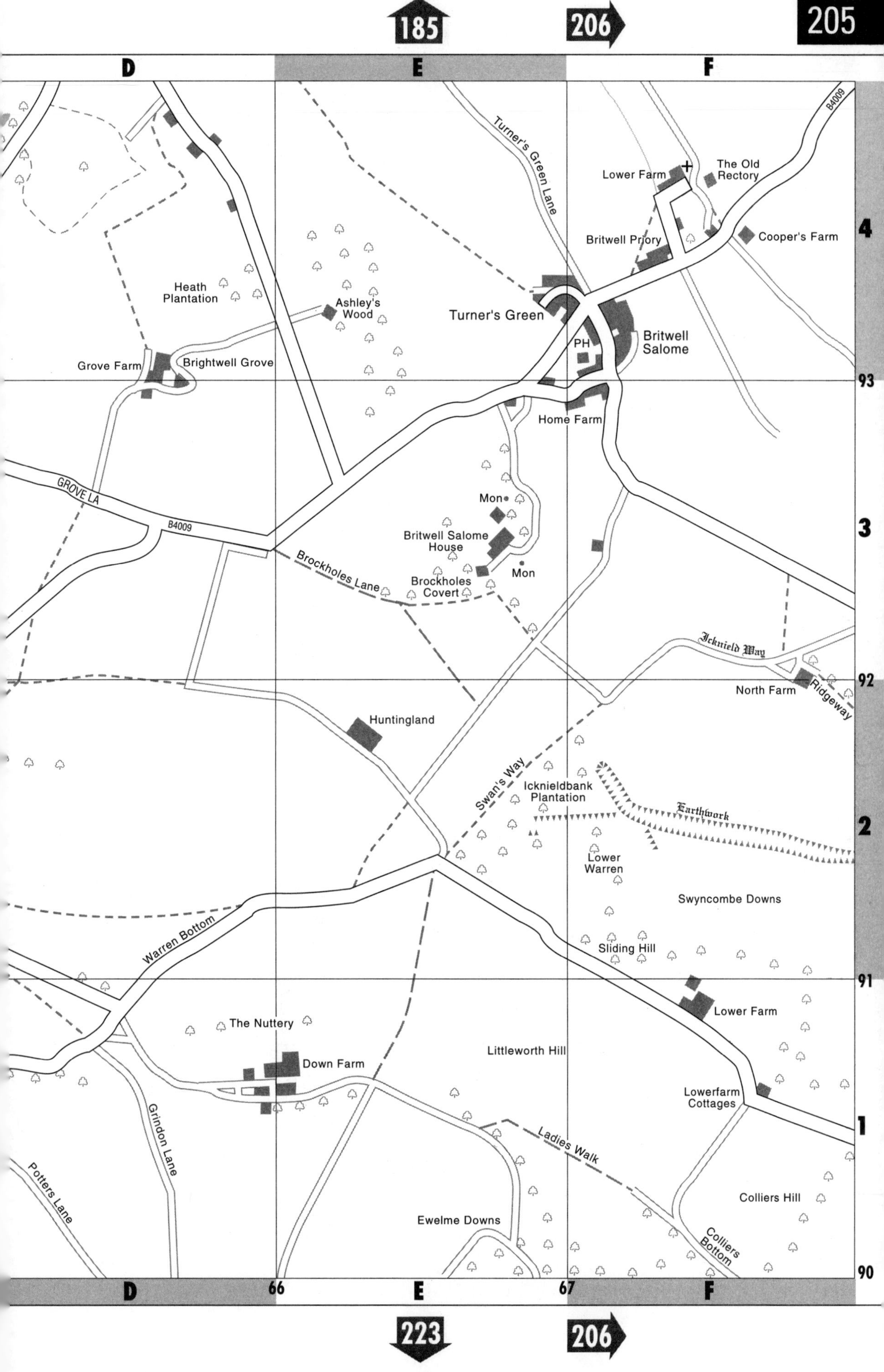

D
E
F

B4009

Lower Farm
The Old
Rectory

Turner's Green Lane

Britwell Priory
Cooper's Farm

4

Heath
Plantation

Ashley's
Wood

Turner's Green

PH

Britwell
Salome

Grove Farm
Brightwell Grove

93

Home Farm

GROVE LA

B4009

Mon

Britwell Salome
House

Brockholes Lane

Brockholes
Covert

Mon

Icknield Way

3

North Farm
Ridgeway

92

Huntingland

Swan's Way

Icknieldbank
Plantation

Earthwork

Lower
Warren

Swyncombe Downs

2

Warren Bottom

Sliding Hill

Lower Farm

91

The Nuttery

Down Farm

Littleworth Hill

Lowerfarm
Cottages

1

Grindon Lane

Ladies Walk

Potters Lane

Colliers Hill

Ewelme Downs

Colliers
Bottom

90

D
66
E
67
F

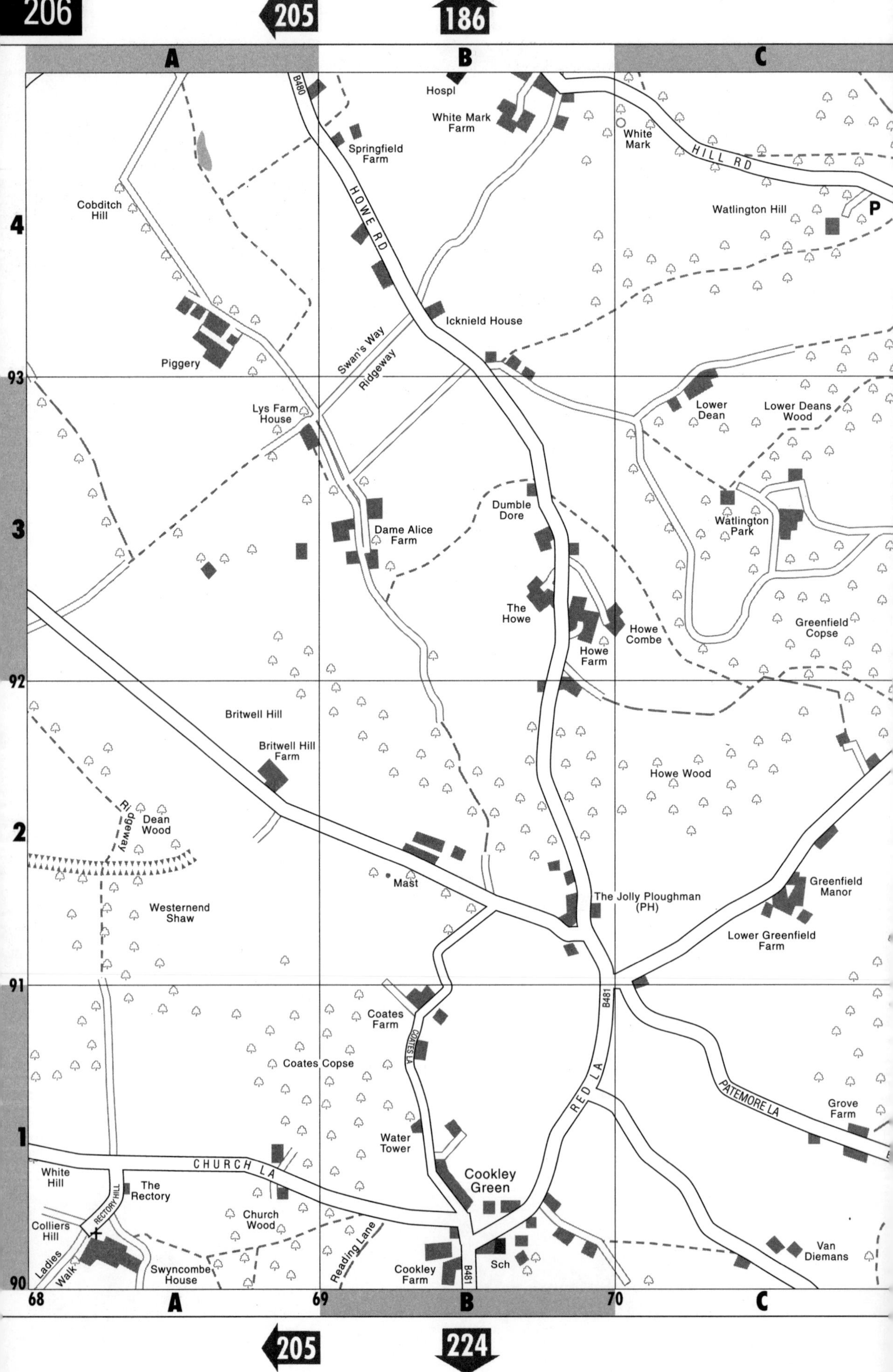

A

B

C

4

93

3

92

2

91

1

90

68

A

69

B

70

C

Hospl

White Mark Farm

White Mark

HILL RD

Watlington Hill

P

Cobditch Hill

Springfield Farm

HOWE RD

Icknield House

Swan's Way

Ridgeway

Piggery

Lys Farm House

Lower Dean

Lower Deans Wood

Dumble Dore

Watlington Park

Dame Alice Farm

Greenfield Copse

The Howe

Howe Combe

Howe Farm

Britwell Hill

Britwell Hill Farm

Howe Wood

Ridgeway

Dean Wood

Mast

The Jolly Ploughman (PH)

Greenfield Manor

Westernend Shaw

Lower Greenfield Farm

B481

Coates Farm

RED LA

PATEMORE LA

Grove Farm

Coates Copse

COATES LA

Water Tower

CHURCH LA

White Hill

The Rectory

Cookley Green

Colliers Hill

Church Wood

Reading Lane

Cookley Farm

Sch

Van Diemans

RECTORY HILL

Ladies Walk

Swyncombe House

B481

D E F

Portways
Oxfordshire Way
Shotridge Wood
Buckingham Bottom
Hungryhill Wood
Barnfield Hanging Wood
Mast
HILL RD
Ibstone
4
Christmas Common
Fox & Hounds (PH)
Mast
Cooper's Wood
Blackmoor Wood
93
Prior's Grove
PH
Northend
Northend Farm
Launder's Farm
Queen Wood
3
HOLLOWAY LA
The White Hart (PH)
Mushroom Farm
Fire Wood
Oxfordshire Way
Swain's Wood
92
HOLLANDRIDGE LA
Greenfield
Longhill Hanging Wood
Blundells
2
Hollandridge Farm
College Wood
Turville Park Farm
Turville Park
91
Roll's Shaw
Greenfield Wood
Whitehill Shaw
Shambridge Wood
1
Pishill Bottom
Whitelands House
Oxfordshire Way
Primrose Cottage
Pishill Bank
B480
B480
90

D 72 E 73 F

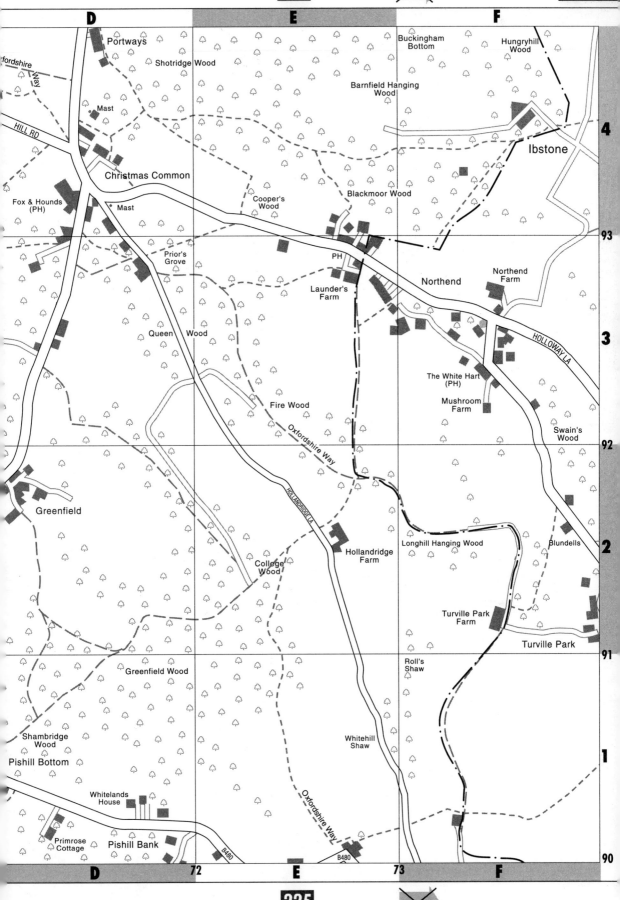

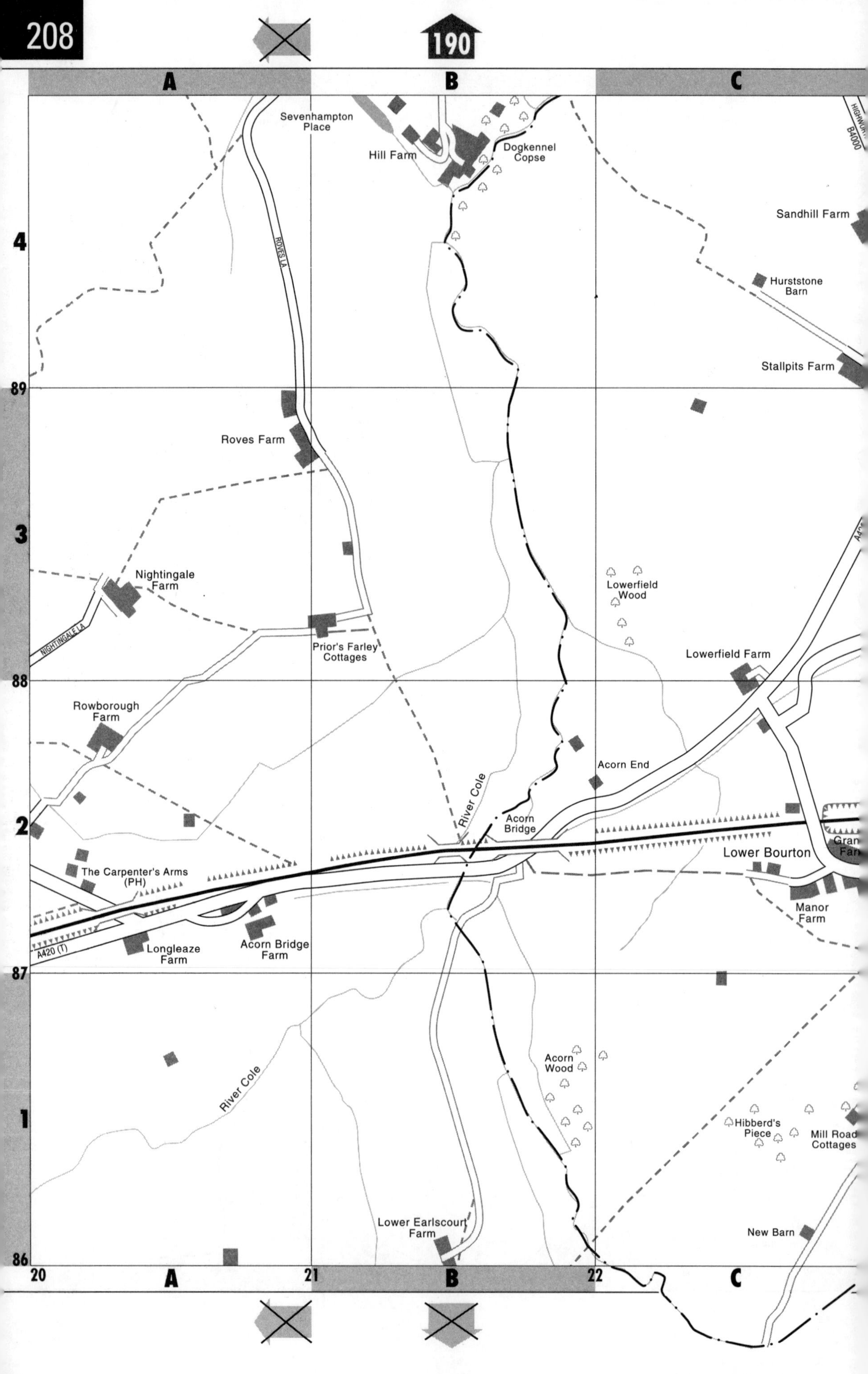

A   **B**   **C**

Sevenhampton Place

Hill Farm

Dogkennel Copse

Sandhill Farm

Hurststone Barn

Stallpits Farm

4

ROVES LA

Roves Farm

89

Lowerfield Wood

Nightingale Farm

3

NIGHTINGALE LA

Prior's Farley Cottages

Lowerfield Farm

88

Rowborough Farm

River Cole

Acorn End

Acorn Bridge

Lower Bourton

Gran Farm

2

The Carpenter's Arms (PH)

Longleaze Farm

Acorn Bridge Farm

A420 (T)

Manor Farm

87

River Cole

Acorn Wood

1

Hibberd's Piece

Mill Road Cottages

Lower Earlscourt Farm

New Barn

HIGHWORTH B4000

A   **B**   **C**

20   21   22

86

191
210
Shrivenham
Royal Military College of Science
Golf Course
Sewage Works
Beckett Stables
Northford Bridge
Broadleaze Farm
Home Farm
Reservoir
Old Canal
Cemy
Rhyme's Cottages
Works
Forty Acre Plantation
Chapelwick Farm
Cowleaze Farm
FB
Ashbury Crossing
The Victoria (PH)
Stainswick Copse
Stainswick Farm
New Road
Bourton
Five Acres Farm
Home Farm
Bourton End
Fern Farm
Zulu Buildings
Bower Brook
Pennyhooks Lane
Steppingstone Lane
HIGHWORTH RD
FARINGDON RD
NORTHFORD HILL
HIGH ST
LONGCOT RD
TOWNSEND RD
STATION RD
STAINSWICK LA
AVENUE RD
THE HILL
B4000
A420(T)
227
210

A
B
C

LONGCOT RD ➤

River Ock

OLD WHARF RD

Talbot
Cottage

Lock's
Cottage

4

89

Cowleaze
Farm

CLAYPIT LA

Galleyherns
Farm

Knighton
Copse

Breaches
Copse

3

Ruffinswick
Farm

88

Odstone
Lands

Hardwell
Farm

Moat

Hardwell Lane

2

New Rd

Compton Marsh
Farm

Odstone
Marsh

Knighton

87

Knighton
Farm

Compton
Beauchamp

Compton
House

Snivelling
Corner

Hardwell
Wood

fort

Memorial

KNIGHTON HILL

1

Knighton
Coombes

Pit
(dis)

Odstone
Farm

Bourton
Gate

B4507

86

26
27
28

A
B
C

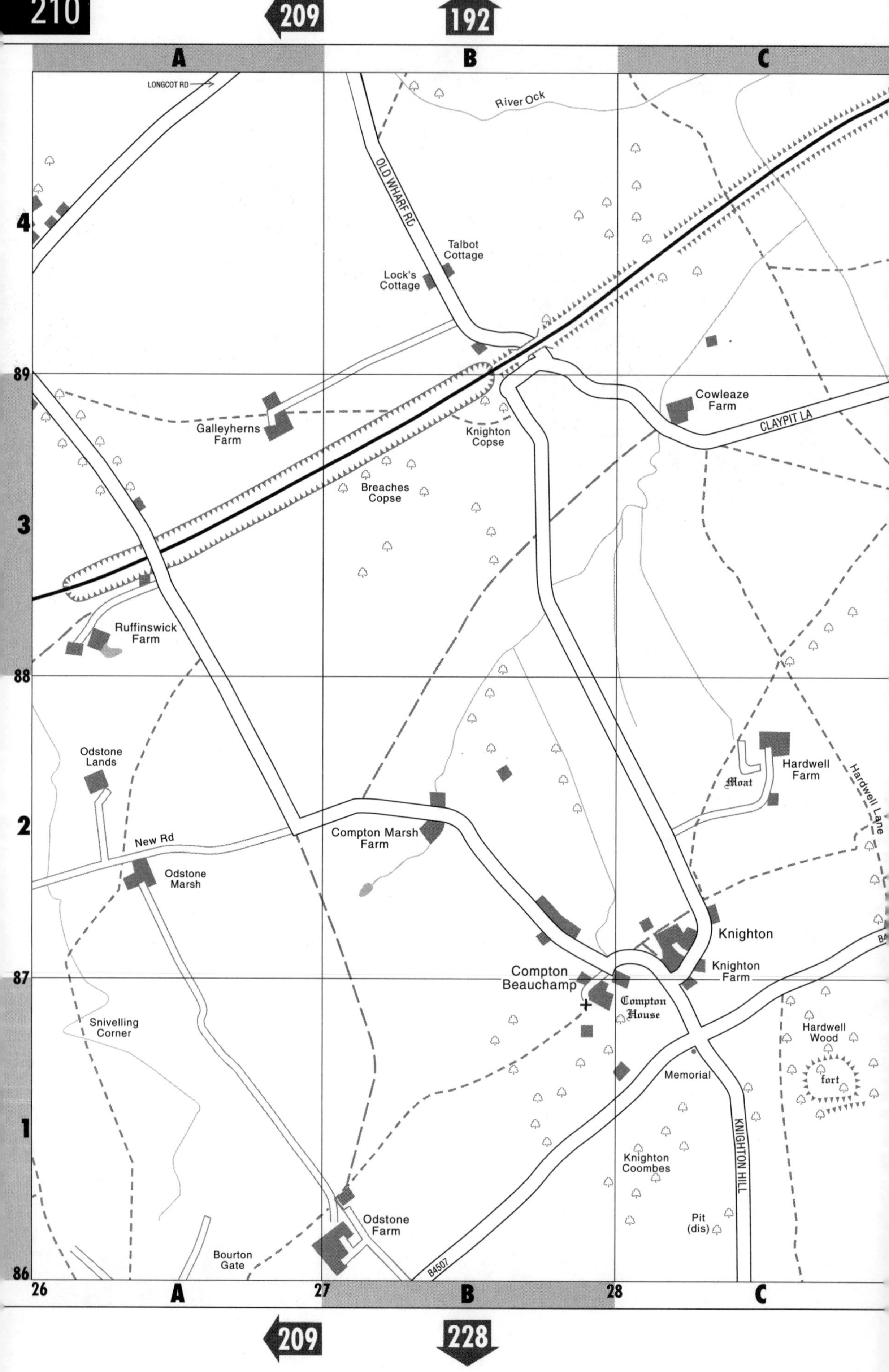

193
212

Common Farm
Uffington Gorse
Wharf Farm
Manor Farm
Little Lane
PH
BAULKING RD
Oxleaze Farm
Sch
BROAD ST
P
Green Lane
HILL VIEW
STATION RD
Uffington
CRAVEN COMM
LADY WLK
CHAPEL LA
UPPER COMM
HIGH ST
PH
CLAYPIT LA
Grounds Farm
Garrard's Farm
PATRICKS ORCH
Chapel Farm
PH
South View Farm
Broadway Farm
FAWLER RD
Stockholm Farm
WOOLSTONE RD
BROAD WAY
MARSH WAY
Lambourn Stud
Woolstone Mill Farm
Fawler Farm
Fawler
Old Mill Pond
Woolstone
Woolstone Lodge
PH
Woolstone Farm
Manor Farm
Sower Hill Farm
Coombes Barn
The Coombes
Woolstone Wells
B4507
Dragon Hill
Britchcombe Farm
B4507
Uffington Wood
The Manger
P
DRAGONHILL RD
White Horse
New Buildings
Uffington Castle fort
White Horse Hill
Oxfordshire Circular Walks
P
Ridgeway
Rams Hill
Uffington Down
Field Barn
D
E
F
4
89
3
88
2
87
1
86
30
31

229
212

◀ 211
▲ 194

A   **B**   **C**

Ladycroft Pond

Church's Copse

Stutfield Brook

4

Long Spinney Copse

Round Spinney Copse

Cross Bargain Farm

Gabbits Copse

Featherbed Lane

Westcot Lane

Fox Covert

South Farm

89

Broadleaze Farm

Kingston Common Farm

3

WESTCOT LA

Fawler Manor

Fawler

Cemy

Tumulus

Drove Way

HILL VIEW

Georgesgreen Farm

Hall Place

WATERY LA

88

Kingston Lisle

Sch

The Plough (PH)

Manor Farm

North Park

Home Farm

WEST ST

Sparsholt

Star (PH)

SPARSHOLT ST

BROADBROOK LA

Kingston Lisle Farm

Westcot Farm

CHURCH WAY

2

Kingston Lisle House

Green Park

Westcot

Sparsholt Park

SWINTON LA

Kingston Lisle Park

B4507

Blowing Stone

87

The Warren

Oakbank Plantations

Seven Acre Hill

BLOWINGSTONE HILL

Oakbank Barn

The Rides

1

Sparsholt Field

Oxfordshire

Ridgeway

Circular Walks

Kingstonhill Barn

Field Barn

Sheephouse Bottom

Clements Cottages

Lodge Farm

86

32   **A**   33   **B**   34   **C**

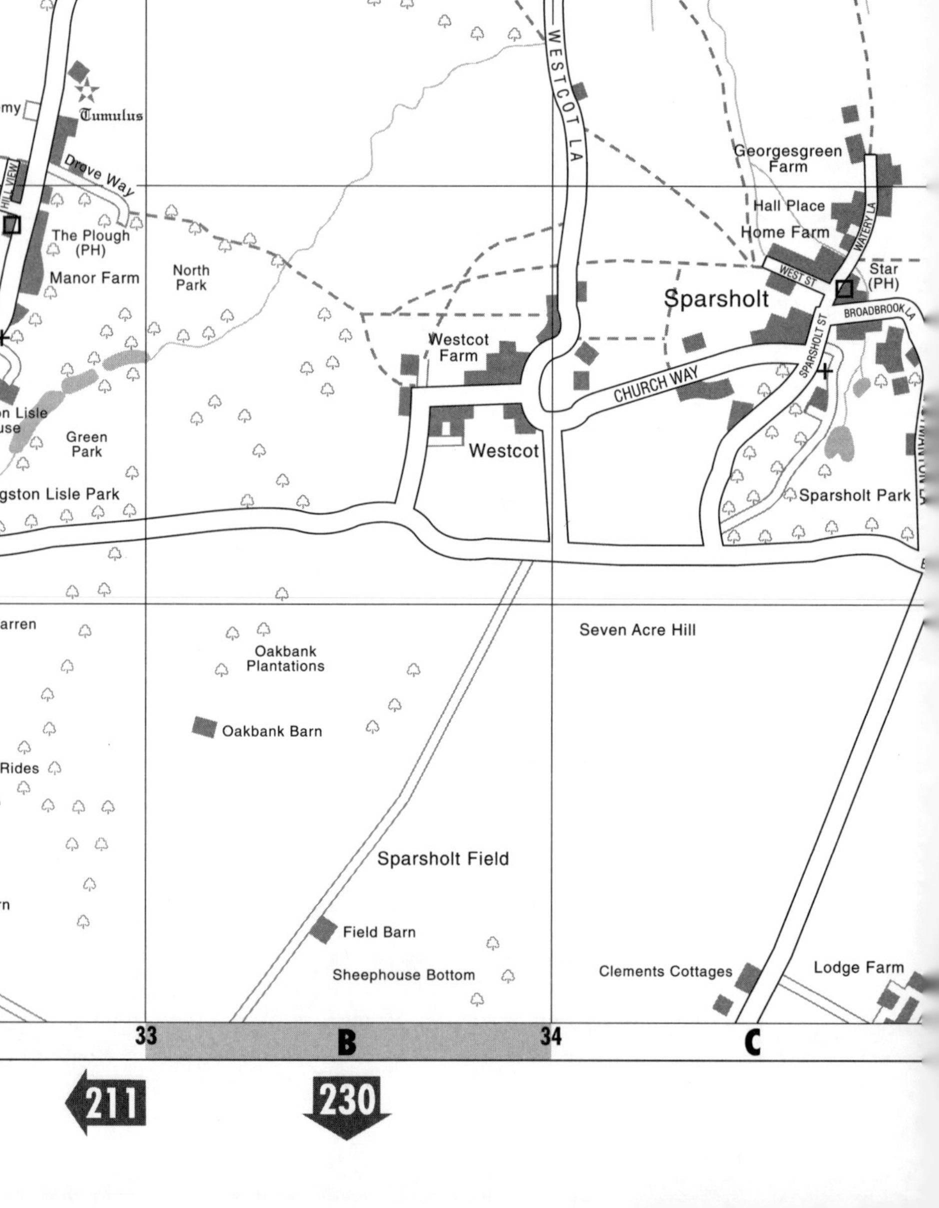

◀ 211
▼ 230

195
214

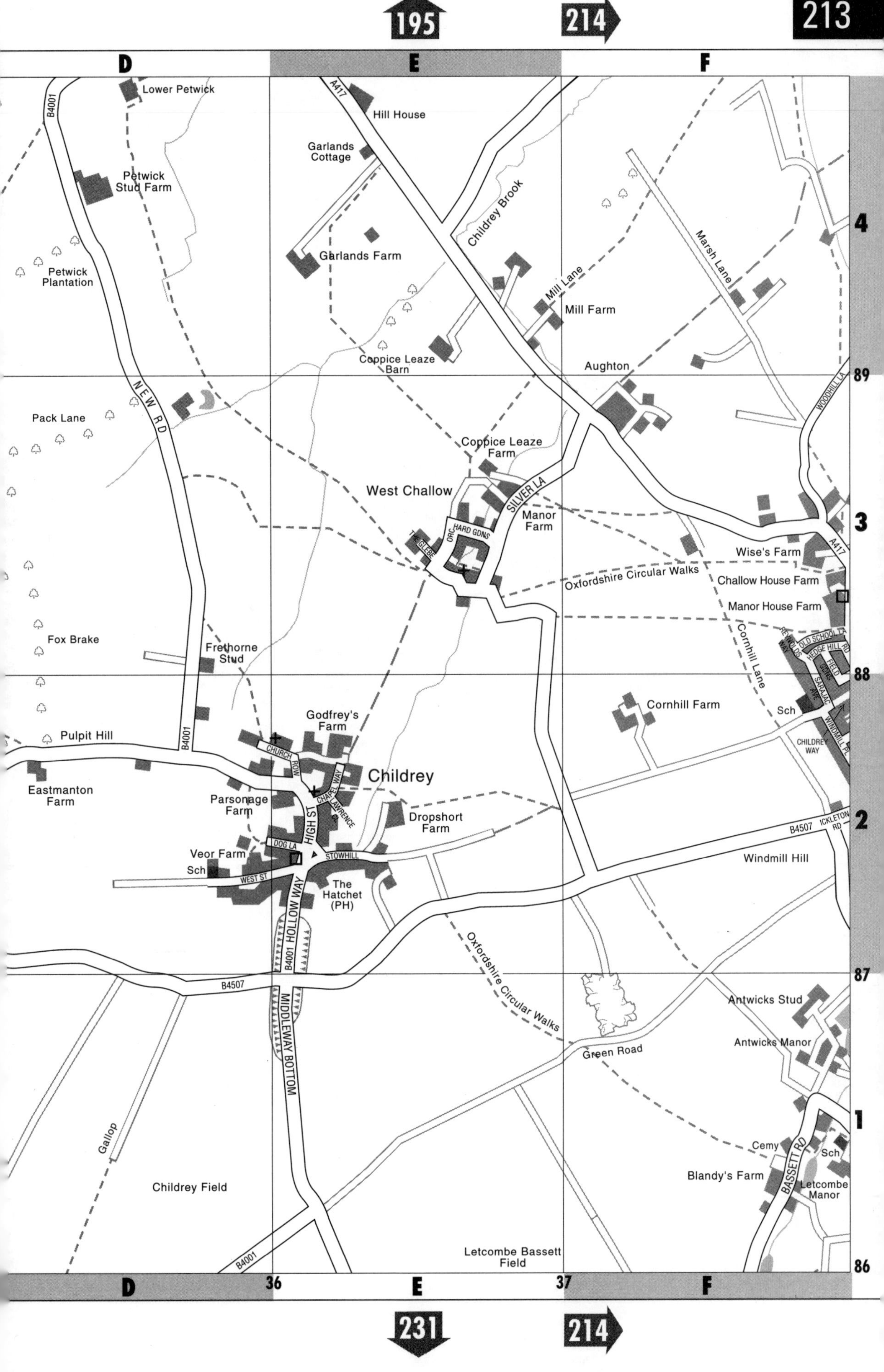
D
E
F
Lower Petwick
Hill House
Garlands Cottage
Petwick Stud Farm
Childrey Brook
Garlands Farm
Petwick Plantation
Mill Lane
Mill Farm
Marsh Lane
Coppice Leaze Barn
Aughton
Pack Lane
NEW RD
Coppice Leaze Farm
West Challow
SILVER LA
Manor Farm
HARD GDNS
THE GLEBE
ORC
Wise's Farm
Oxfordshire Circular Walks
Challow House Farm
Manor House Farm
Fox Brake
Frethorne Stud
Cornhill Lane
Cornhill Farm
Sch
Godfrey's Farm
Pulpit Hill
CHURCH ROW
CHILDREY WAY
Childrey
Eastmanton Farm
Parsonage Farm
CHAPEL WAY
LAWRENCE CL
HIGH ST
Dropshort Farm
B4507
ICKLETON RD
DOG LA
Veor Farm
STOWHILL
Windmill Hill
Sch
WEST ST
The Hatchet (PH)
HOLLOW WAY
B4001
B4507
MIDDLEWAY BOTTOM
Oxfordshire Circular Walks
Antwicks Stud
Antwicks Manor
Green Road
Cemy
Sch
Gallop
BASSETT RD
Blandy's Farm
Letcombe Manor
Childrey Field
Letcombe Bassett Field
B4001
A417
WOODHILL LA
OLD SCHOOL LA
HEDGE HILL RD
REYNOLDS WAY
FIELD GDNS
SARAJAC AVE
WINDMILL PL
4
89
3
88
2
87
1
86
36
37
D
E
F

231
214

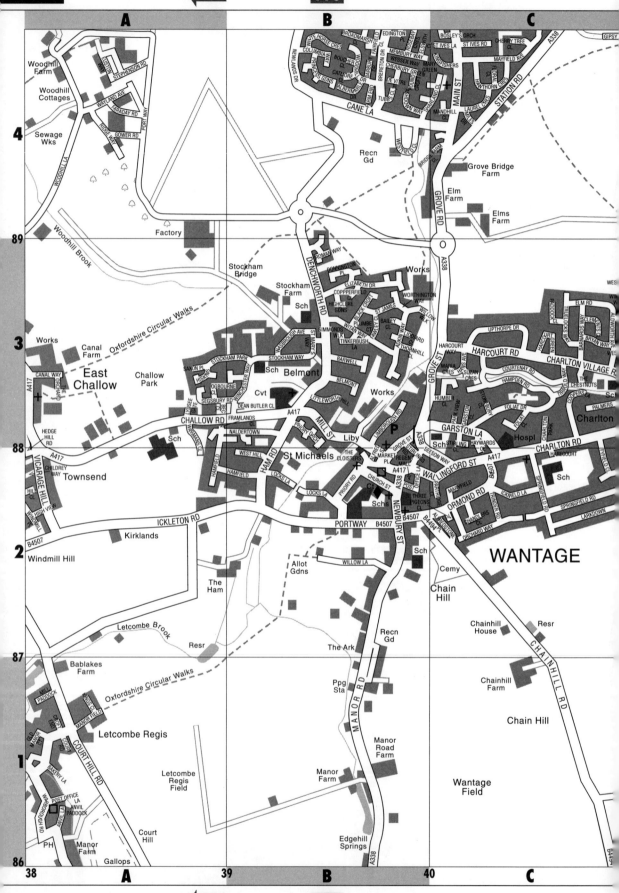

213 196

213 232

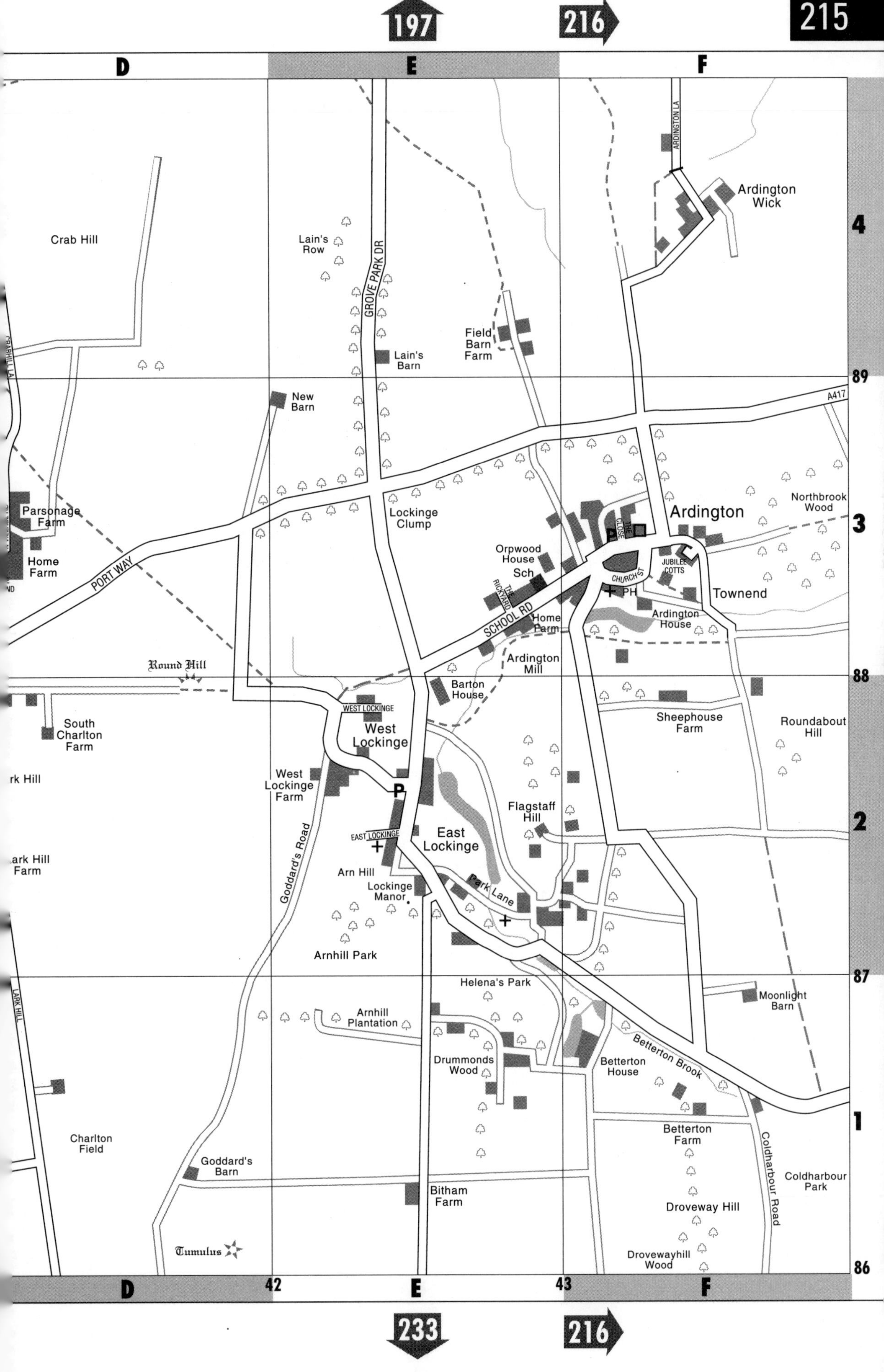

197
216
D
E
F
Crab Hill
Lain's Row
GROVE PARK DR
Lain's Barn
Field Barn Farm
ARDINGTON LA
Ardington Wick
New Barn
A417
Parsonage Farm
Home Farm
PORT WAY
Lockinge Clump
Orpwood House
Sch
THE RICKYARD
SCHOOL RD
Home Farm
THE CLOSE
P
Ardington
Northbrook Wood
JUBILEE COTTS
CHURCH ST
PH
Townend
Ardington House
Ardington Mill
Round Hill
Barton House
WEST LOCKINGE
West Lockinge
South Charlton Farm
Sheephouse Farm
Roundabout Hill
West Lockinge Farm
P
Flagstaff Hill
Goddard's Road
EAST LOCKINGE
East Lockinge
Arn Hill
Lockinge Manor
Park Lane
Arnhill Park
Helena's Park
Moonlight Barn
Arnhill Plantation
Betterton Brook
Drummonds Wood
Betterton House
Charlton Field
Betterton Farm
Coldharbour Road
Coldharbour Park
Goddard's Barn
Bitham Farm
Droveway Hill
Tumulus
Drovewayhill Wood
LARK HILL
4
89
3
88
2
87
1
86
42
43
233
216

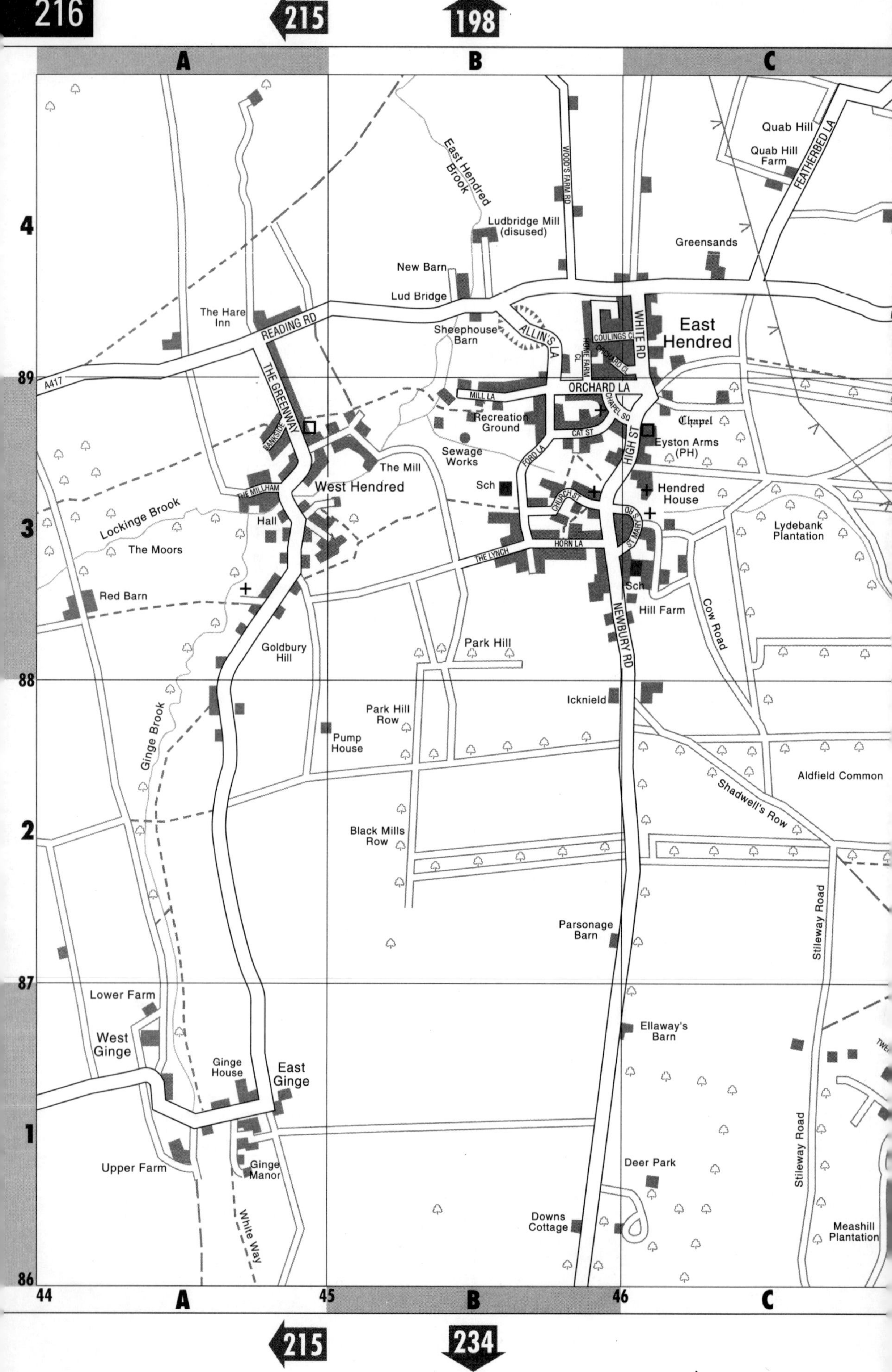

215
198

A
B
C

Quab Hill

Quab Hill
Farm

FEATHERBED LA

4

East Hendred
Brook

WOOD'S FARM RD

Ludbridge Mill
(disused)

Greensands

New Barn

Lud Bridge

WHITE RD

The Hare
Inn

READING RD

Sheephouse
Barn

ALLIN'S LA

HOME FARM
CL

COULINGS CL

ORCHARD LA

East
Hendred

89

A417

THE GREENWAY

BANKSIDE

MILL LA

Recreation
Ground

CAT ST

CHAPEL SQ

Chapel

Eyston Arms
(PH)

89

THE MILLHAM

The Mill

West Hendred

Sewage
Works

FORD LA

HIGH ST

Sch

CHURCH ST

Hendred
House

Lydebank
Plantation

3

Lockinge Brook

Hall

The Moors

HORN LA

THE LYNCH

OLD ST

Sch

Hill Farm

Cow Road

3

Red Barn

Goldbury
Hill

Park Hill

NEWBURY RD

88

Ginge Brook

Park Hill
Row

Icknield

Aldfield Common

88

Pump
House

Shadwell's Row

2

Black Mills
Row

2

Parsonage
Barn

Stileway Road

87

Lower Farm

87

West
Ginge

Ginge
House

East
Ginge

Ellaway's
Barn

Stileway Road

TWE

1

Upper Farm

Ginge
Manor

Deer Park

Meashill
Plantation

1

White Way

Downs
Cottage

86

44

A

45

B

46

C

86

215
234

D
E
F
Cricket Ground
Hungerford Road
Rowstock
CROOM COTTS
A417
A4130
A4185
Rowstock Farm
Horn Down
Hungerford Road
Chimney Corner Plantation
Aldfield Farm
Sewage Works
Padua
GROVE RD
Sch
The Bield
Winaway
Bag's Tree
Harwell Field
Amb & Fire Sta
Harwell Laboratory
Bishop's Manor Farm
Harwell
Cow Lane
Sewage Works
A34(T)
B4493
BLENHEIM HILL
DIDCOT RD
The Driftway
Cemy
Princes Manor Farm
PH
B4493
WANTAGE RD
READING RD
THE HOLLOWAY
East Field Farm
Folly Cottages
Resr
Hagbournehill Farm
Resr
Hagbourne Hill
Tumulus
Limetree Farm
Dismtd Rly
A4185
PERIMETER RD
LIBRARY AVE
FERMI AVE
FROME RD
KENNET RD
CURIE AVE
MAXWELL AVE
THOMSON AVE
RUTHERFORD AVE
FARADAY AVE
BECQUEREL AVE
NORTH DR
SOUTH DR
4
89
3
88
2
87
1
86
48
49

A
B
C

Zulu Farm

DIDCOT RD

B4493

Alma Barn

Down Farm

OXFORD CRES

SLADE RD

WANTAGE RD

B4493

Hospl

DRAKE AVE

COLLINGWOOD AVE

ROBERTS RD

PARK RD

PARK CL

PARK RD

COLBORNE RD

EDMONDS CL

MANOR RD

SHERWOOD

PIXTON CL

FAIRACRES RD

ST ANDREW'S RD

ST ANDREW'S RD

PETERS RD

BROADWAY

WESSEX RD

VICARAGE

A4130

CHURCH

BOURNE

Edmunds Park

CATLAND RD

KYNASTON RD

LYNMOUTH

GLEBE RD

LABURNUM GR

MEREDALE RD

THE CROFT

RICHMERE

RIDGEWAY RD

SINODUN RD

DIDCOT

Cemy

Schs

Swimming Pool

ABBOTT RD

ROYAL BERKSHIRE CTS

SOUTH PARK

QUEENSWAY

HARDINGS STRINGS

GREEN RD

GREEN CL

WARNER CRES

MORSE RD

EDWIN RD

Sch

BARNES CL

MOWBRAY RD

BARNES RD

LOYD RD

COCKCROFT RD

Playing Field

4

89

East Hagbourne

The Driftway

West Hagbourne Field

Coscote

Hall

LAKE RD

WINDSOR CRES

HARWOOD RD

WALCHER CL

UPPER CROSS LA 1
SHOE LA 2

MAIN RD

THE CROFT

NORTH CROFT

Sch

CHURCHLA

Manor Farm

Hakka's Brook

3

Yew Tree Farm

BROOK LA

88

MANOR CL

YORK RD

MAIN ST

FOXGLOVE

Grove Farm

Manor Farm

PH

West Hagbourne

Pumping Station

Pumping Station

Dismantled Railway

Common Barn

Common Lane

2

87

CHILTON RD

STATION RD

BLENHEIM CL

FIELDSIDE

NEWMANS

CHURCH ST

STREAM RD

PROSPECT RD

Owlscote Manor Farm

Frogalley Farm

Sewage Works

PH

ALEXANDER CL

HIGH ST

Upton

1

Lynch Way

Hollow Way

LONDON RD

Upton Lodge

A417

WESTBROOK

Sch

86

50
A
51
B
52
C

D
E
F

A4130

HADDON
HILL
Fulscot
Copse

Fulscot
Bridge

Alders
Farm

North
Moreton

4

LONG WITTENHAM RD

QUEENS CFT

89

Shortlands
Farm

Fulscot
Farm

SANDS RD

3

B4016

Hakka's Brook

CLEMENTS
GREEN

Sch

PH

South
Moreton

CHURCH LA

FIELDSIDE

Tadley

Mound

88

Mill Brook

Brookside

Hagbourne
Mill Farm

BLEWBURY RD

2

West Hagbourne
Moor

Blewbury
Mill

Sheencroft
Farm

87

HAGBOURNE RD

Aston
Upthorpe

MORETON RD

Ham
Cottages

1

The
Old
Mill

Bridus
Way

BESSELS WAY

B4016

Thorpe
Farm

THORPE ST

FULLERS RD

THE CROFT

Upthorpe
Farm

PH

ASTON ST

BERRY LA

MILLBROOK
CL

SOUTH

Winterbrook
Farm

Blewburton
Hill

Fort

SPRING LA

BAKER ST

RECTORY

BESSELS LEA

D
E
F

54
55
86

219
202

A   B   C

4

89

3

88

2

87

1

86

56   A   57   B   58   C

Mackney

Sherwood Farm

MACKNEY LA

ELM RD
LONG WITTENHAM RD
HIGH ST

Kibble Ditch

The Bear
(PH)

DUNSOMER HILL

BEAR LA

Mill Brook

Hithercroft
Farm

Glebe
Cottage

HITHERCROFT

Th e Crown
(PH)

Moat

BROWN LA
PAPER MILL LA

Pumping
Station

Cholsey Hill

Hillgreen
Farm

MILL LA

ANCHOR LA

MORETON RD

Poultry
Farm

The
Manor

Sew
Wo

Manor
Farm

The Lees

CHURCH RD

GOLDFIN

Red Lior
(PH)

Schs

WALLINGFORD
CHEQUER
PL

Lees
Cottages

THE
FORTY

ILGES LA

POUND LA

West
End

STATION RD
DROVESIDE RD

PAVE
COLL

WESTFIELD
SANDY LA
FORD CL

HONEY LA
THORN LA

CRESCENT WAY

NENTWOOD
CL

Pancroft
Farm

The
Elms

WESTFIELD
RD

Cholsey
Station

PAPIST WAY

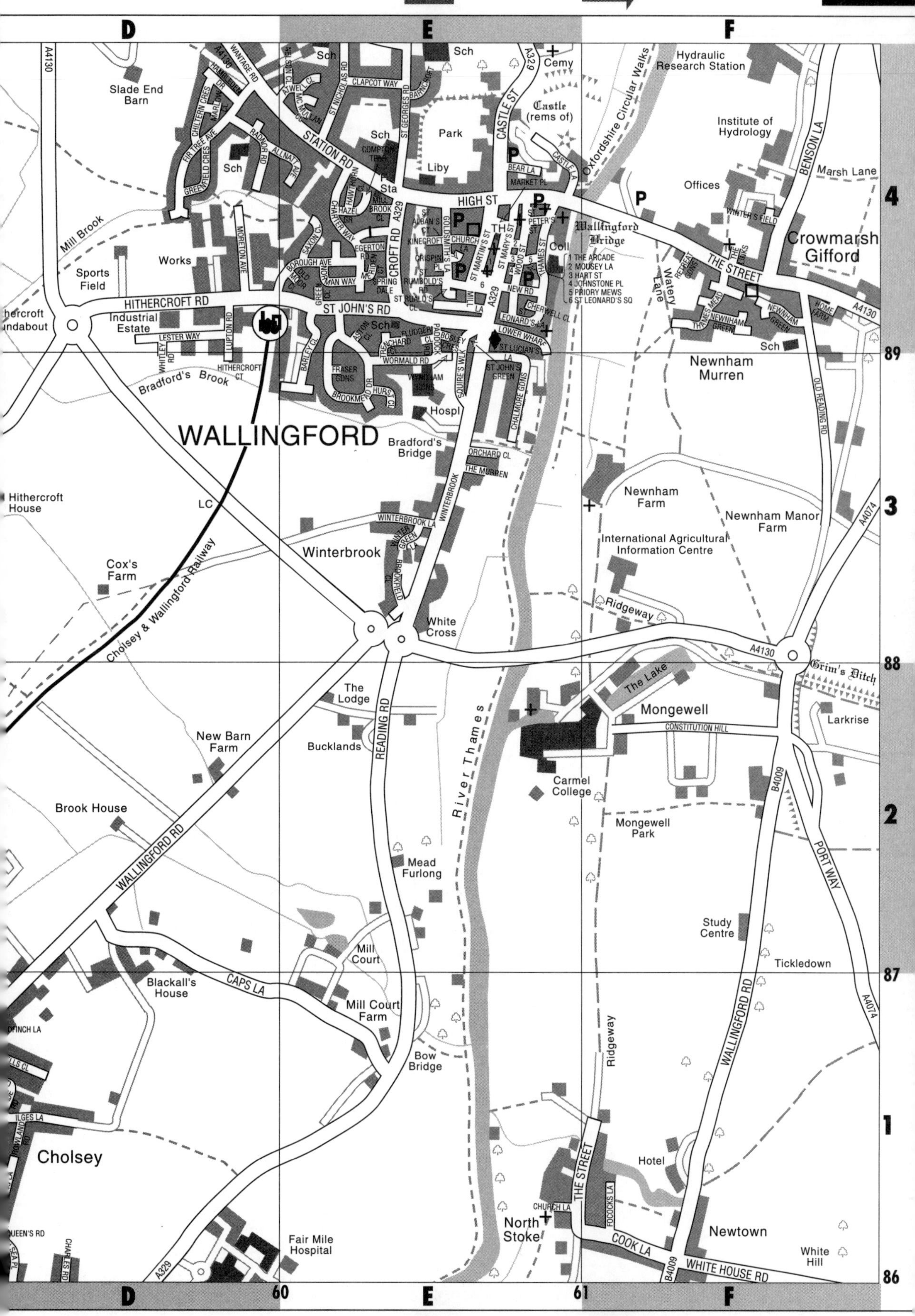
WALLINGFORD
Crowmarsh Gifford
Winterbrook
Newnham Murren
Mongewell
Carmel College
Cholsey
North Stoke
Newtown
River Thames
Wallingford Bridge
Bradford's Bridge
Hydraulic Research Station
Institute of Hydrology
Newnham Farm
Newnham Manor Farm
International Agricultural Information Centre
Fair Mile Hospital
Mill Court Farm
Blackall's House
Cox's Farm
Brook House
New Barn Farm
Slade End Barn
Study Centre
Tickledown
White Hill
Hotel
1 THE ARCADE
2 MOUSEY LA
3 HART ST
4 JOHNSTONE PL
5 PRIORY MEWS
6 ST LEONARD'S SQ

← 221
204 ▲

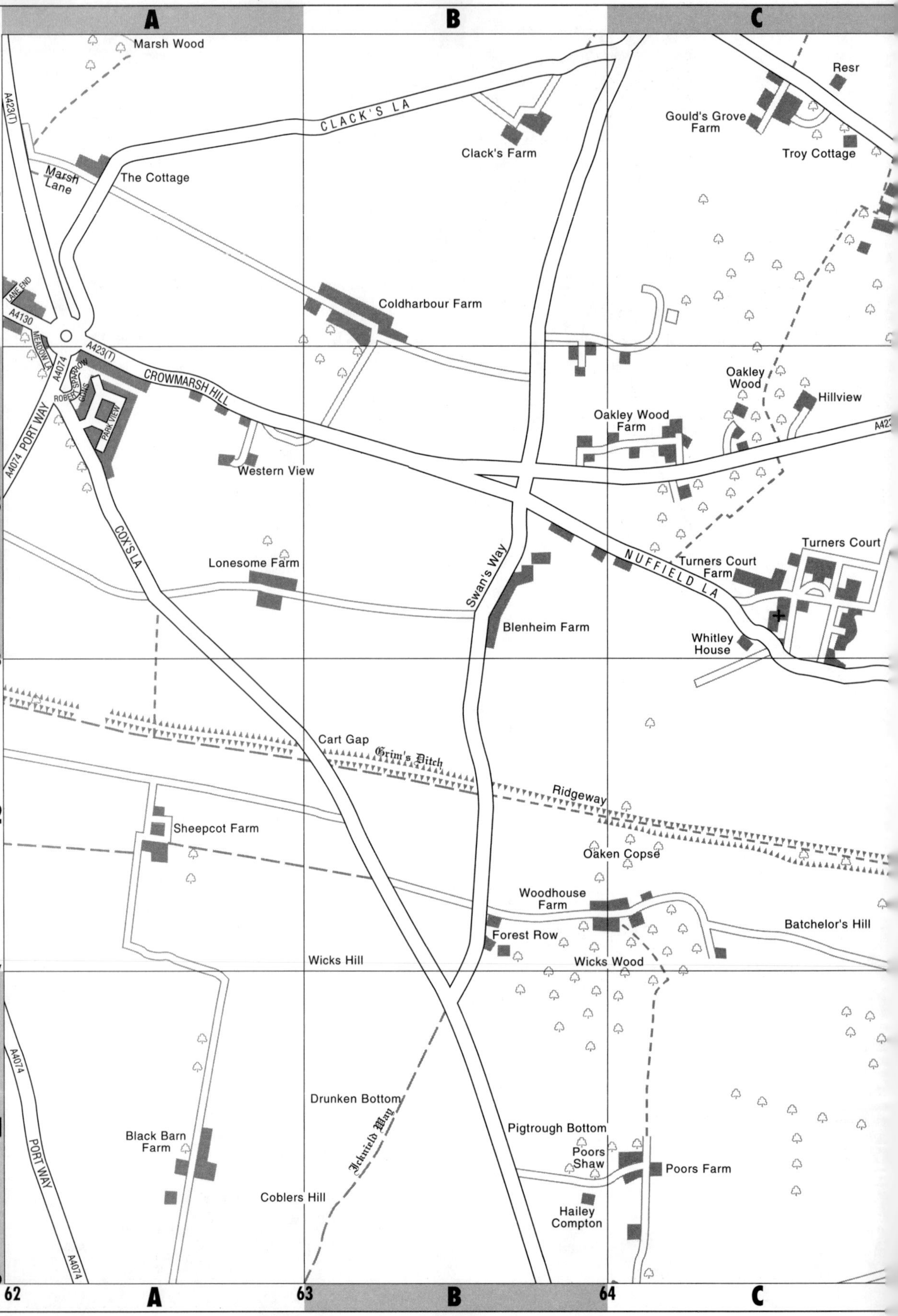

A   **B**   **C**

Marsh Wood

CLACK'S LA

Clack's Farm

Gould's Grove Farm

Resr

Troy Cottage

4

Marsh Lane

The Cottage

A423(T)

A4130

Coldharbour Farm

Oakley Wood

Hillview

89

LANE END

MEADOW LA

A4074

ROBERT SPARROW

CROWMARSH HILL

A423(T)

PARK VIEW

Western View

Oakley Wood Farm

A42

Turners Court

3

COX'S LA

A4074 PORT WAY

Lonesome Farm

Swan's Way

NUFFIELD LA

Turners Court Farm

Blenheim Farm

Whitley House

+

88

Cart Gap

Grim's Ditch

Ridgeway

Oaken Copse

2

Sheepcot Farm

Woodhouse Farm

Forest Row

Batchelor's Hill

Wicks Wood

87

Wicks Hill

A4074

Drunken Bottom

Pigtrough Bottom

1

PORT WAY

Black Barn Farm

Icknield Way

Poors Shaw

Poors Farm

Coblers Hill

Hailey Compton

86

62   **A**   63   **B**   64   **C**

← 221
240 ▼

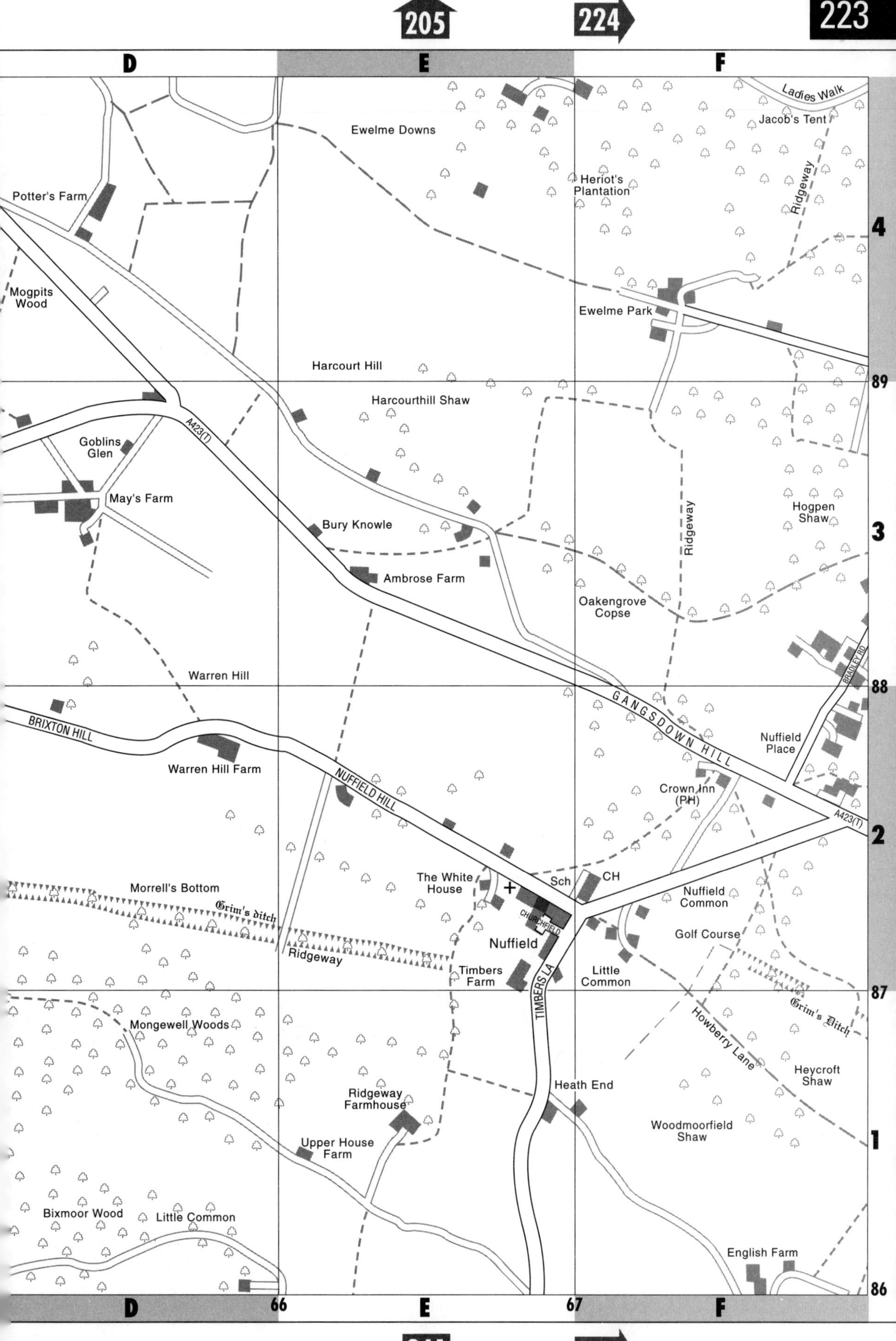

D   E   F

Ladies Walk

Jacob's Tent

Ewelme Downs

Heriot's Plantation

Ridgeway

4

Potter's Farm

Mogpits Wood

Ewelme Park

89

Harcourt Hill

Harcourthill Shaw

A423(T)

Goblins Glen

Ridgeway

Hogpen Shaw

May's Farm

3

Bury Knowle

Ambrose Farm

Oakengrove Copse

Warren Hill

BRADLEY RD

88

BRIXTON HILL

GANGSDOWN HILL

Nuffield Place

Warren Hill Farm

NUFFIELD HILL

Crown Inn (PH)

A423(T)

2

Morrell's Bottom

The White House

Sch

CH

Nuffield Common

Grim's ditch

Ridgeway

CHURCHFIELD

Nuffield

Golf Course

Timbers Farm

Little Common

Grim's Ditch

87

Mongewell Woods

TIMBERS LA

Heath End

Howberry Lane

Heycroft Shaw

Ridgeway Farmhouse

Woodmoorfield Shaw

1

Upper House Farm

Bixmoor Wood

Little Common

English Farm

86

D   66   E   67   F

A   **B**   **C**

B481

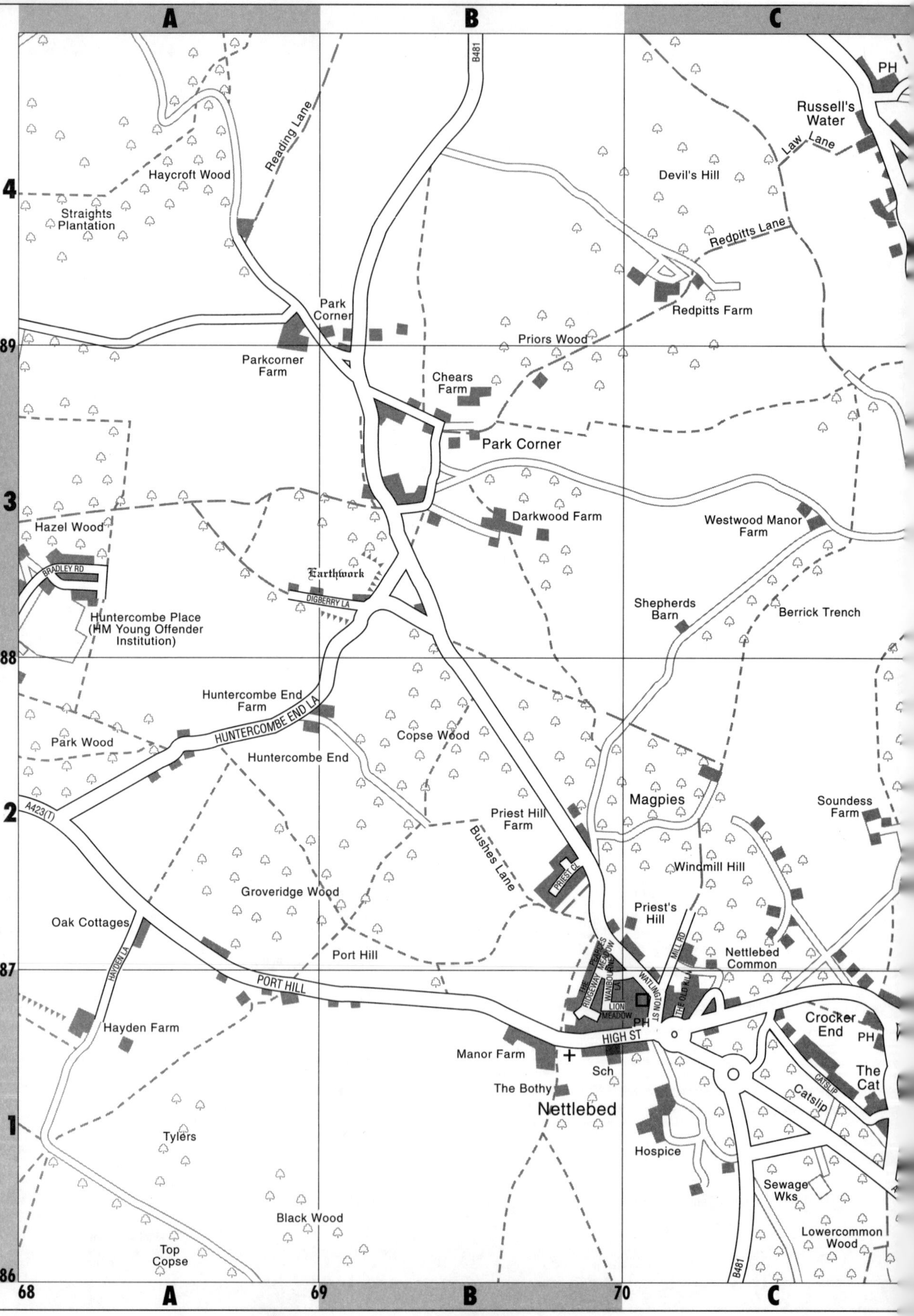

Reading Lane

Russell's
Water

PH

Straights
Plantation

Haycroft Wood

Devil's Hill

Law Lane

4

Redpitts Lane

Park
Corner

Redpitts Farm

89

Priors Wood

Parkcorner
Farm

Chears
Farm

Park Corner

Westwood Manor
Farm

3

Hazel Wood

Darkwood Farm

BRADLEY RD

Earthwork

Shepherds
Barn

Berrick Trench

Hisntercombe Place
(HM Young Offender
Institution)

DIGBERRY LA

88

Huntercombe End
Farm

HUNTERCOMBE END LA

Park Wood

Copse Wood

Magpies

Soundess
Farm

Huntercombe End

A423(T)

2

Priest Hill
Farm

Windmill Hill

Groveridge Wood

Oak Cottages

Busines Lane

Priest's
Hill

Nettlebed
Common

Port Hill

87

Hayden Farm

PORT HILL

Port Hill

MILL RD

Crocker
End

PH

LION
MEADOW

PH

The Cat

Manor Farm

HIGH ST

Sch

Catslip

Tylers

The Bothy

Nettlebed

Hospice

Sewage
Wks

1

Black Wood

Lowercommon
Wood

Top
Copse

B481

86

68   **A**   69   **B**   70   **C**

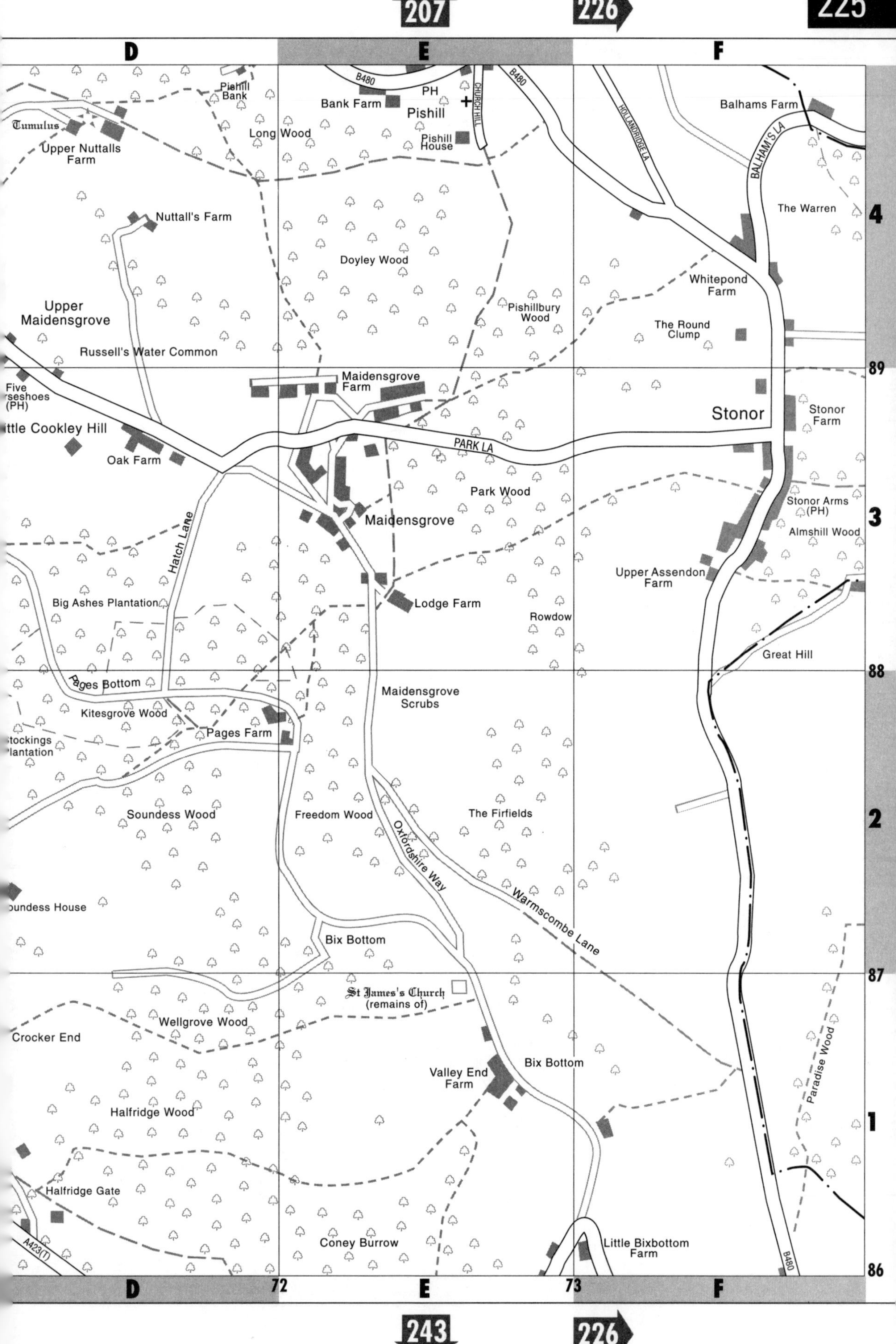
D
E
F
B480
PH
Pishill Bank
Bank Farm
Pishill
CHURCH HILL
Tumulus
Upper Nuttalls Farm
Long Wood
Pishill House
HOLLANDRIDGE LA
Balhams Farm
BALHAM'S LA
The Warren
Nuttall's Farm
Doyley Wood
Whitepond Farm
Upper Maidensgrove
Pishillbury Wood
The Round Clump
Russell's Water Common
Five Horseshoes (PH)
Maidensgrove Farm
Stonor
Stonor Farm
Little Cookley Hill
PARK LA
Oak Farm
Park Wood
Stonor Arms (PH)
Hatch Lane
Maidensgrove
Almshill Wood
Upper Assendon Farm
Big Ashes Plantation
Lodge Farm
Rowdow
Great Hill
Pages Bottom
Maidensgrove Scrubs
Kitesgrove Wood
Pages Farm
Stockings Plantation
Soundess Wood
Freedom Wood
The Firfields
Oxfordshire Way
Warmscombe Lane
Soundess House
Bix Bottom
St James's Church (remains of)
Wellgrove Wood
Crocker End
Paradise Wood
Valley End Farm
Bix Bottom
Halfridge Wood
Halfridge Gate
A423(T)
Coney Burrow
Little Bixbottom Farm
B480
4
89
3
88
2
87
1
86
72
73

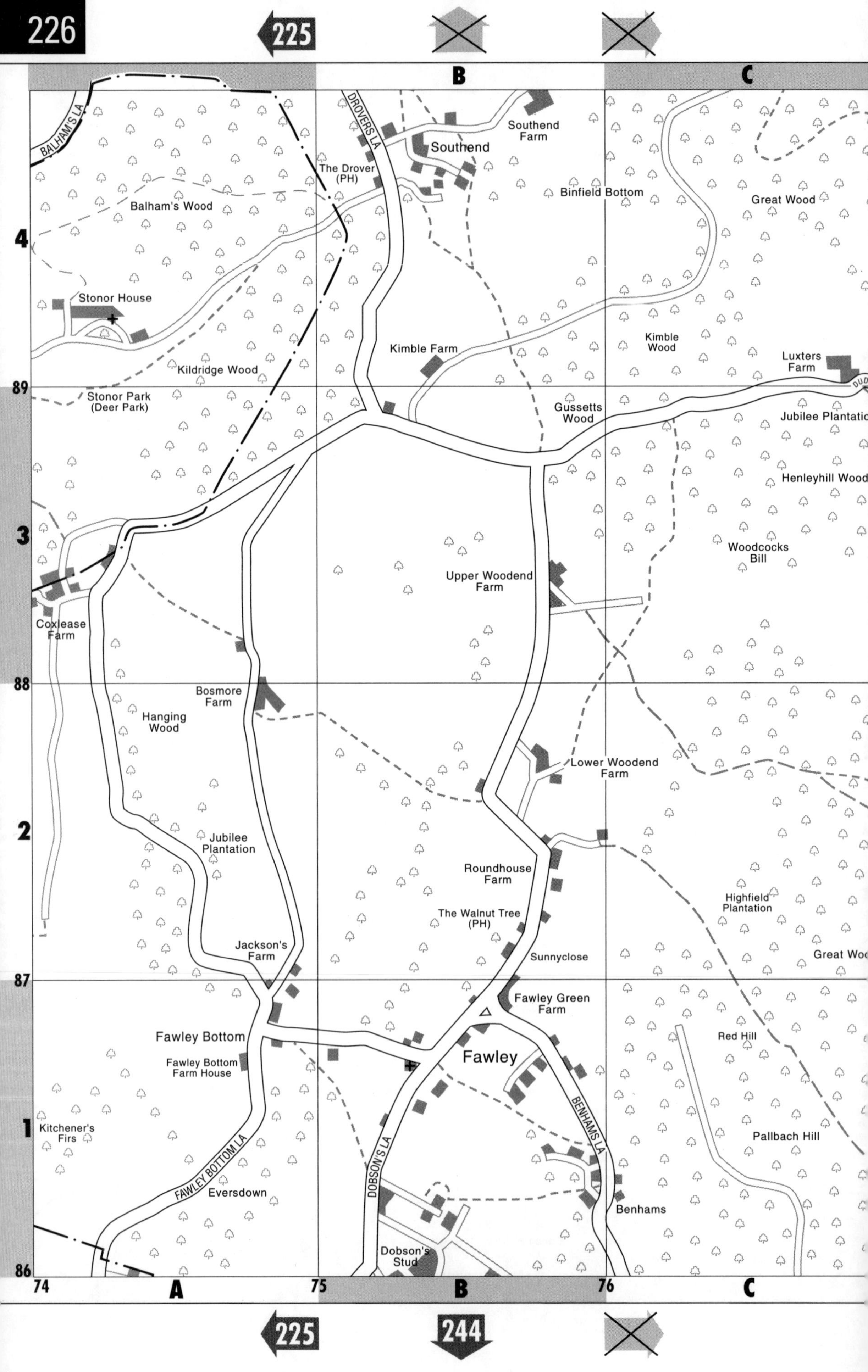

BALHAM'S LA

DROVERS LA

Balham's Wood

The Drover
(PH)

Southend

Southend
Farm

Binfield Bottom

Great Wood

4

Stonor House

Kildridge Wood

Kimble Farm

Kimble
Wood

Luxters
Farm

89

Stonor Park
(Deer Park)

Gussetts
Wood

Jubilee Plantation

DUDL

Henleyhill Wood

3

Upper Woodend
Farm

Woodcocks
Bill

Coxlease
Farm

88

Bosmore
Farm

Hanging
Wood

Lower Woodend
Farm

2

Jubilee
Plantation

Roundhouse
Farm

Highfield
Plantation

Jackson's
Farm

The Walnut Tree
(PH)

Sunnyclose

Great Woo

87

Fawley Green
Farm

Fawley Bottom

Fawley

Red Hill

Fawley Bottom
Farm House

BENHAMS LA

1

Kitchener's
Firs

DOBSON'S LA

Pallbach Hill

FAWLEY BOTTOM LA

Eversdown

Benhams

86

Dobson's
Stud

D E F

4

Lower Dairy

Ham
Copse

85

Sewage
Works

Lower
Farm

Featherbed Lane

3

Botswicky
Copse

Lower Idstone
Farm

Elm Tree
Farm

Idstone

Forty
Farm

NEW TOWN LA

84

Rectory
Farm

THE FORTY

HIGH ST

THE LYNCHES

WEST

PH

HOCKER BENCH

CHURCH LA

Sch

MOUNT PLEASANT

ICKNIELD WAY

WEST END

HAILEY'S OR

CHURCH WAY

2

HINTON SPRINGS

FOXON PL

ICKNIELD WAY

NELL HILL

Little Hinton
Farm

Manor
Farm

Bishopstone

CHURCH ROW

TUCKERS LA

HINTON HILL

Strip
Lynchets

Church
Farm

Bishopstone
Folly

83

Strip
Lynchets

WHITE HILL

HATCHET HILL

Ridge Way

Ridgeway
Farm

Field
System

Ridgeway

1

Charlbury
Hill

ill
nor

82

D 24 E 25 F

B4000

IDSTONE HILL

227
210

A   **B**   **C**

B4507

Odstone Hill

Kingstone Winslow

Winslow
Bank

Odstone
Coombes

Wayland's Smithy
Long Barrow

Kingstone
Farm

4

Knighton
Barn

B4000

Ashbury

STATION RD

POUND PIECE

MALTHOUSE

WALNUT TREES HILL

Kingstone Coombes

Berrycroft

A Sch

HIGH ST

CHAPEL RD

Odstone Barn

85

PH

Kingstone
Barn

Resr

Odstone Circular Walks

IDSTONE RD

ASHBURY HILL

Ashbury
Folly

Down
Folly

3

Comp
Botto

Ridgeway

Idstone
Plantation

IDSTONE HILL

84

Tower Hill

Honeybunch
Corner

2

Red Barn

Odstone Do

83

Hailey Wood

Crowberry
Tump

Kingstone Down

1

Middle Wood

Alfred's Castle

Ashdown House

B4000

82

26   **27**   **28**

A   **B**   **C**

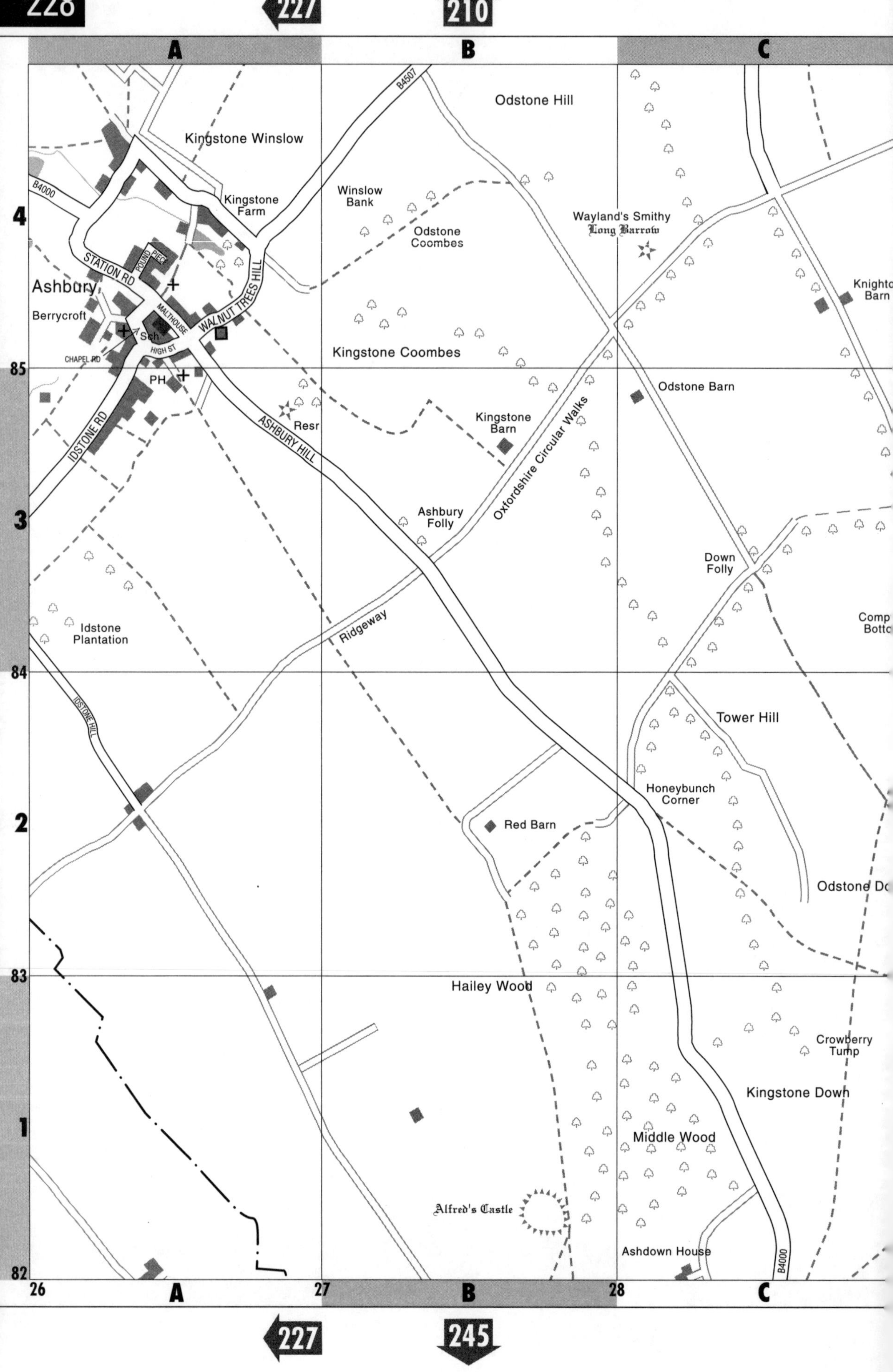

Ridgeway

Uffington
Down

Long
Plantation

4

Woolstone Hill
Barn

Pingoose
Covert

Idlebush
Barrow

Kingston
Warren

85

Gallops

Kingston Warren Down

Gallops

3

Gallops

Woolstone
Down

Compton
Close

84

ghton
wn

Oxfordshire Circular Walks

Gallops

2

Whit
Coombe

Wellbottom
Down

Oxfordshire Circular Walks

Gallops

83

Knighton Bushes
Plantation

Gallops

Lambourn

Baldback
Covert

1

Parkfarm Down

Maddle
Farm

Gallops

Post Down

Weathercock
Hill

Postdown
Border

82

MADDLE RD →

4

Hillbarn
Clump

Oxfordshire Circular Walks

Ridgeway

Rubblepit
Plantation

Pigtrough Bottom

Old
Plantation

Tumulus

Gallops

Hill Barn

Down Barn

Hackpen

85

Mast

Radio Station

Scary Hill

Sparsholt
Firs

3

Gallops

Sparsholt Down

Moss Hill

Green
Down

Faringdon Down Gallop

84

Eastmanton Down

Crog Hill

Tumuli

Boundary
Covert

Oxfordshire Circular Walks

Westcot
Down

2

Long Barrow

Pit Down

Tumuli

Tumulus

Old
Warren

83

Sevenbarrows
House

Gallops

Faringdon Road Down

Gallops

Seven Barrows

Post Down

Long
Covert

Crow Down

1

Sheepdrove Farm

Postdown Farm

Croker's Hole

Wormhill Bottom

82

B4001

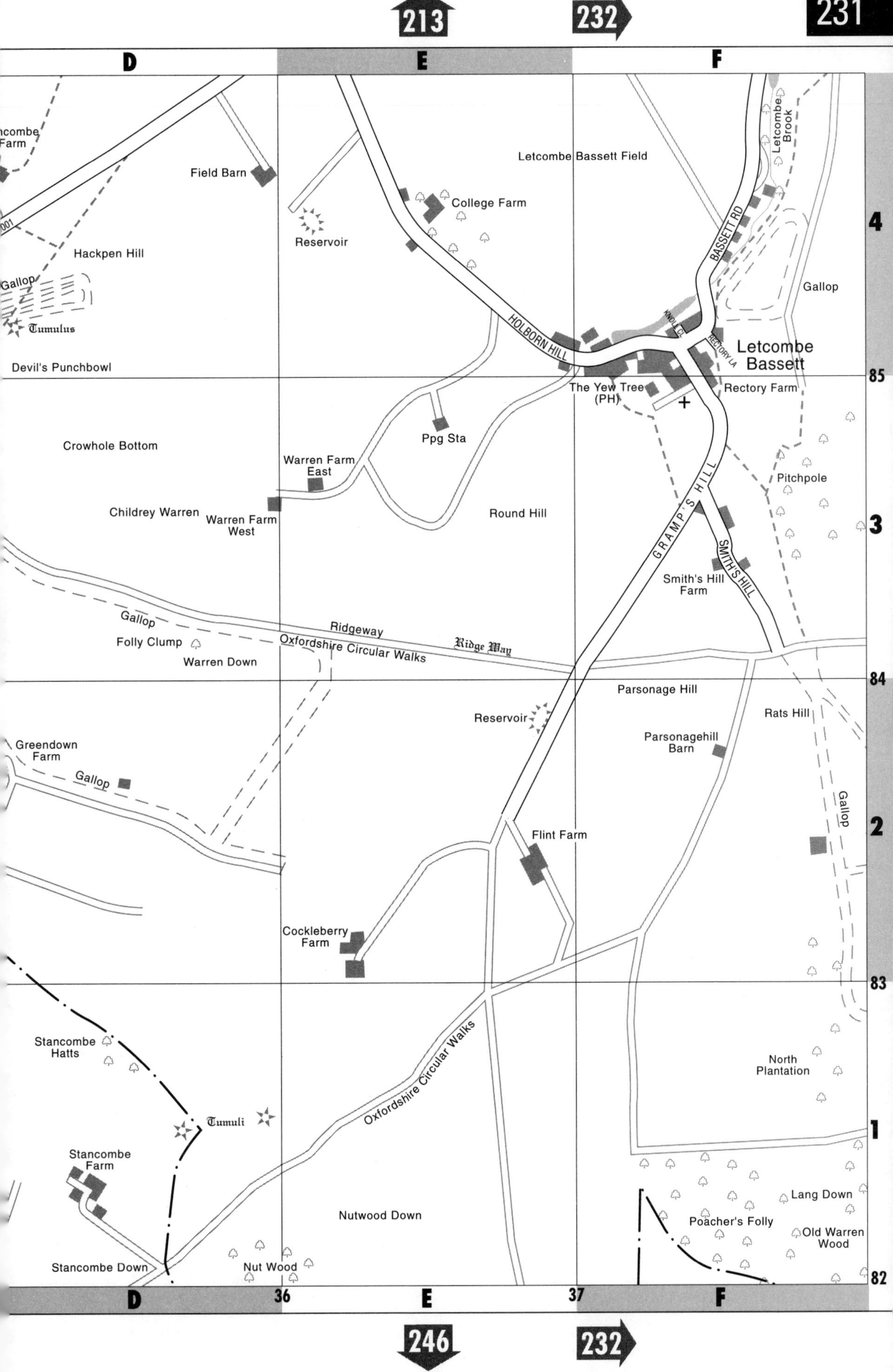

D E F

Field Barn

ncombe
Farm

College Farm

Letcombe Bassett Field

Letcombe
Brook

4

Reservoir

Hackpen Hill

Gallop

Tumulus

Devil's Punchbowl

HOLBORN HILL

Letcombe
Bassett

BASSETT RD

KNOLL CL

RECTORY LA

Gallop

85

Crowhole Bottom

Ppg Sta

The Yew Tree
(PH)

Rectory Farm

Pitchpole

Warren Farm
East

Round Hill

GRAMP'S HILL

SMITH'S HILL

Childrey Warren

Warren Farm
West

Smith's Hill
Farm

3

Gallop

Ridgeway

Ridge Way

Folly Clump

Oxfordshire Circular Walks

Warren Down

Parsonage Hill

84

Greendown
Farm

Reservoir

Parsonagehill
Barn

Rats Hill

Gallop

Gallop

Flint Farm

2

Cockleberry
Farm

North
Plantation

83

Stancombe
Hatts

Oxfordshire Circular Walks

Tumuli

1

Stancombe
Farm

Lang Down

Poacher's Folly

Old Warren
Wood

Stancombe Down

Nutwood Down

Nut Wood

82

D 36 E 37 F

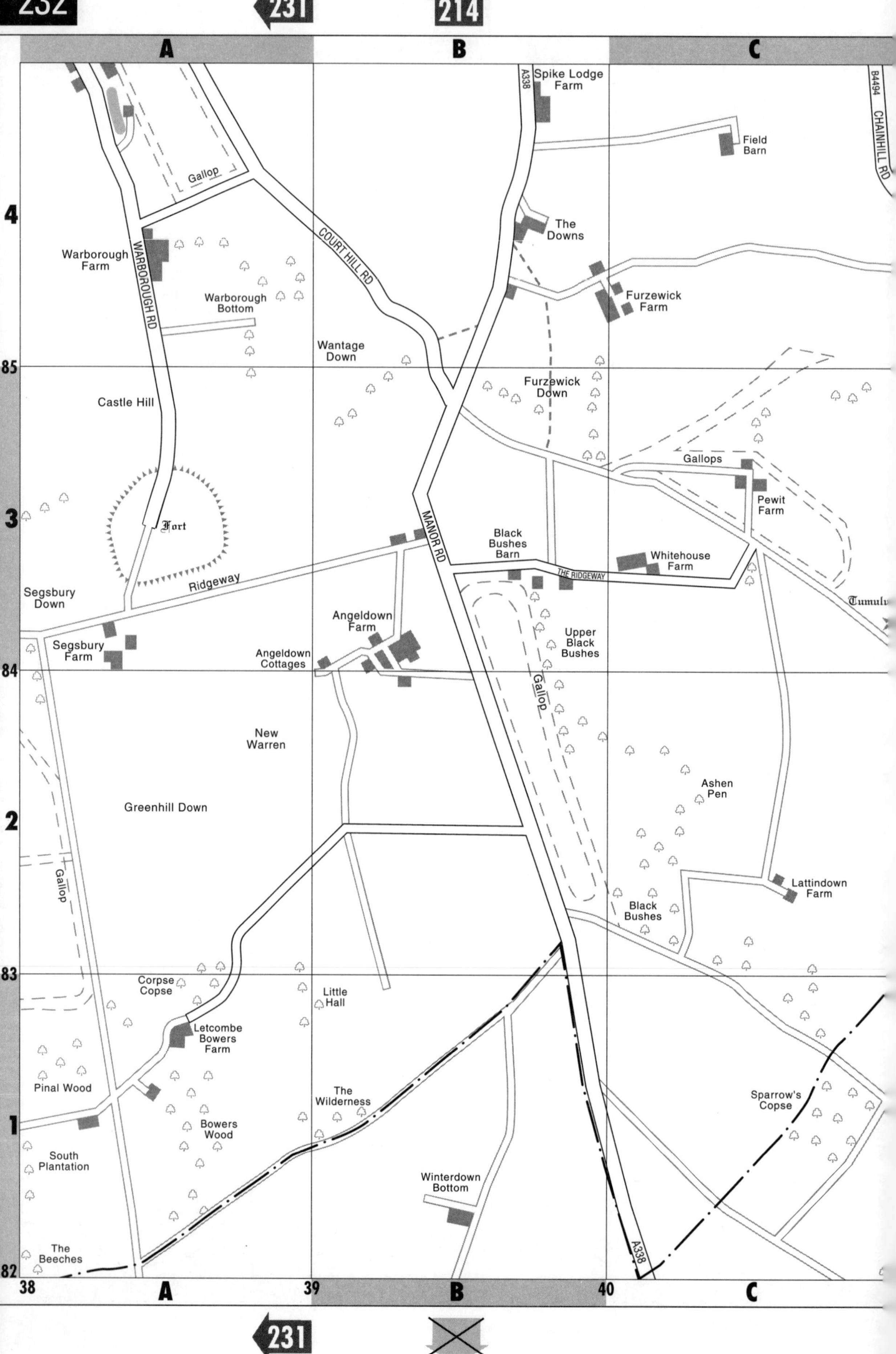
A
B
C
Spike Lodge Farm
A338
B4494
CHAINHILL RD
Field Barn
Gallop
4
The Downs
Warborough Farm
WARBOROUGH RD
COURT HILL RD
Furzewick Farm
Warborough Bottom
Wantage Down
85
Furzewick Down
Castle Hill
Gallops
3
Fort
MANOR RD
Pewit Farm
Black Bushes Barn
Whitehouse Farm
THE RIDGEWAY
Ridgeway
Segsbury Down
Tumulu
Angeldown Farm
Upper Black Bushes
Segsbury Farm
Angeldown Cottages
84
Gallop
New Warren
Ashen Pen
Greenhill Down
2
Gallop
Lattindown Farm
Black Bushes
83
Corpse Copse
Little Hall
Letcombe Bowers Farm
Pinal Wood
The Wilderness
Sparrow's Copse
1
Bowers Wood
South Plantation
Winterdown Bottom
A338
The Beeches
82
38
A
39
B
40
C

D
E
F

Droveway Hill

Coldharbour Road

Chalkhill Barn

Resr

Long Valley Down

4

Goddard's Road

Gallop

CHAINHILL RD

B4494

BURYAM RD

Corsica Pine Wood

Jew's Harp

Ardington Down

The Sycamores

85

Grim's Ditch

Resr

Midsummer Wood

Oxfordshire Circular Walks

Grim's Ditch

Ridgeway

Ridgeway Down

3

Middlehill Down

Monument

Betterton Down

Wether Down

Old Street

Oxfordshire Circular Walks

Yew Down

84

Mead Platt

The Warren

Lattin Down

Betterton Copse

Triangle Wood

Mast

Lockinge Kiln Farm

2

Farnborough Furze Down

Lockinge Down

83

1

Little Coombe Farm

Moonlight Barn

Coombe Down

Farnborough

COPPERAGE RD

Coombe Lodge

B4494

Hall

82

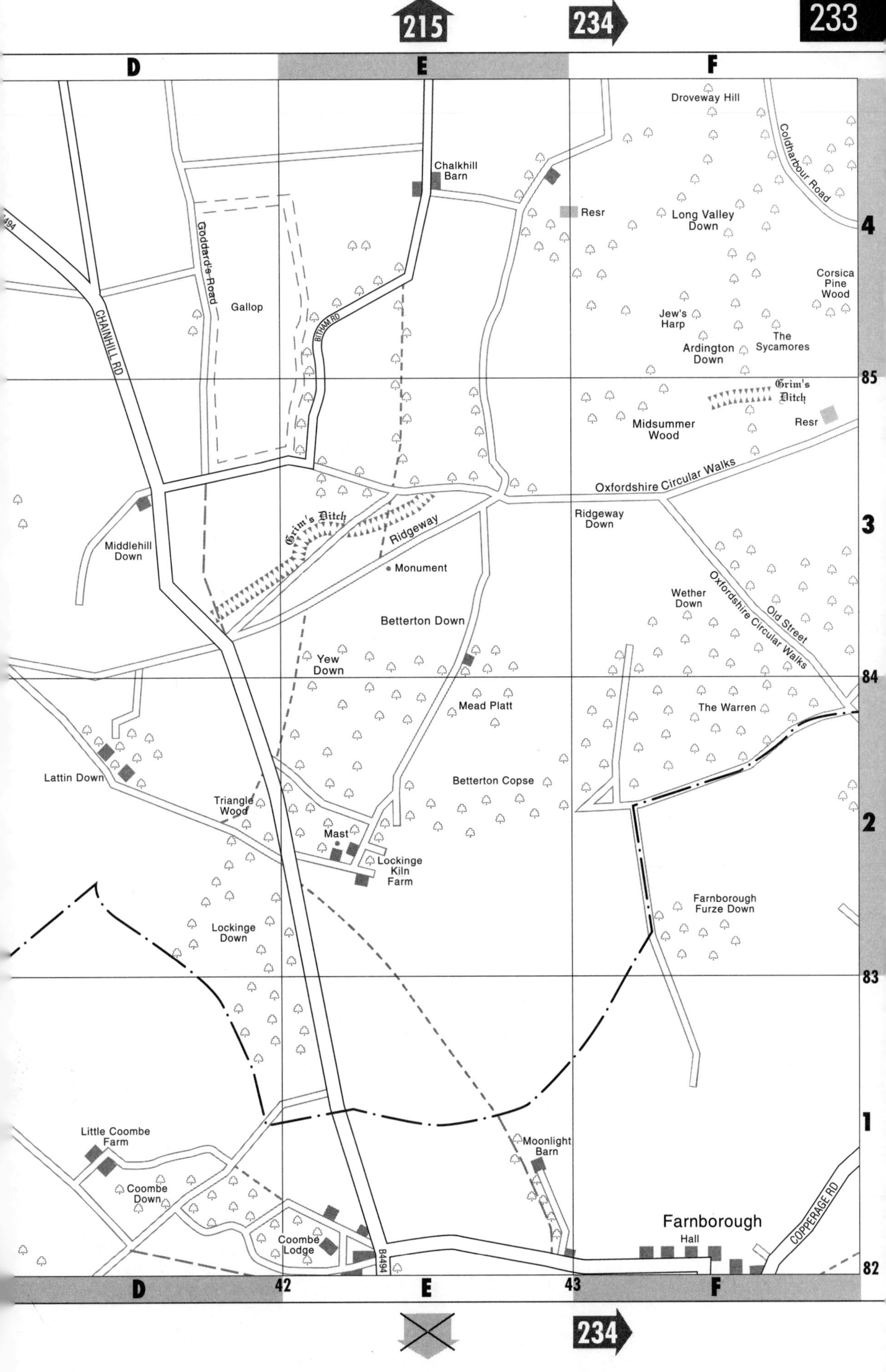

A | **B** | **C**

Diamond
Jubilee
Wood

WhiteWay

Coldharbour
Barn

Tile
Barn

Stileway Road

PLANTATION RD
PITON RD
TEASHILL WAY
LUDD RD
DYER'S WAY
TOWNS WAY
D RD
DYER
STRAITS

Grim's Ditch

4

Coldharbour Road

Grim's Ditch

Resr

East Ginge Down

Knob Down

Fore Down

Foredown
Plantation

Oxfordshire Circular Walks

Ridgeway

Cuckhamsley
Hill

East Hendred
Down

85

Ridgeway
Barn

Scutchamer
Knob

Lew's
Barn

West Ginge
Down

Johnson's
Farm

Upper
Plantation

Gallop

Abbot's
Heath

Sheep Down

3

Down Barn

Kilman
Knoll
Down

Gallops

84

Big
Allens

Little
Allens

Middle
Plantation

Oxfordshire Circular Walk

Gallops

Cow
Down

Curlew

Old Street

Lands
End

Knollend Down

Gallops

2

83

Lower
Barn

COPPERAGE RD

Old Street

Old Down

Starveall
Farm

Harcourt
Farm

1

CATMORE RD

Hernehill Down

82

44 | **A** | 45 | **B** | 46 | **C**

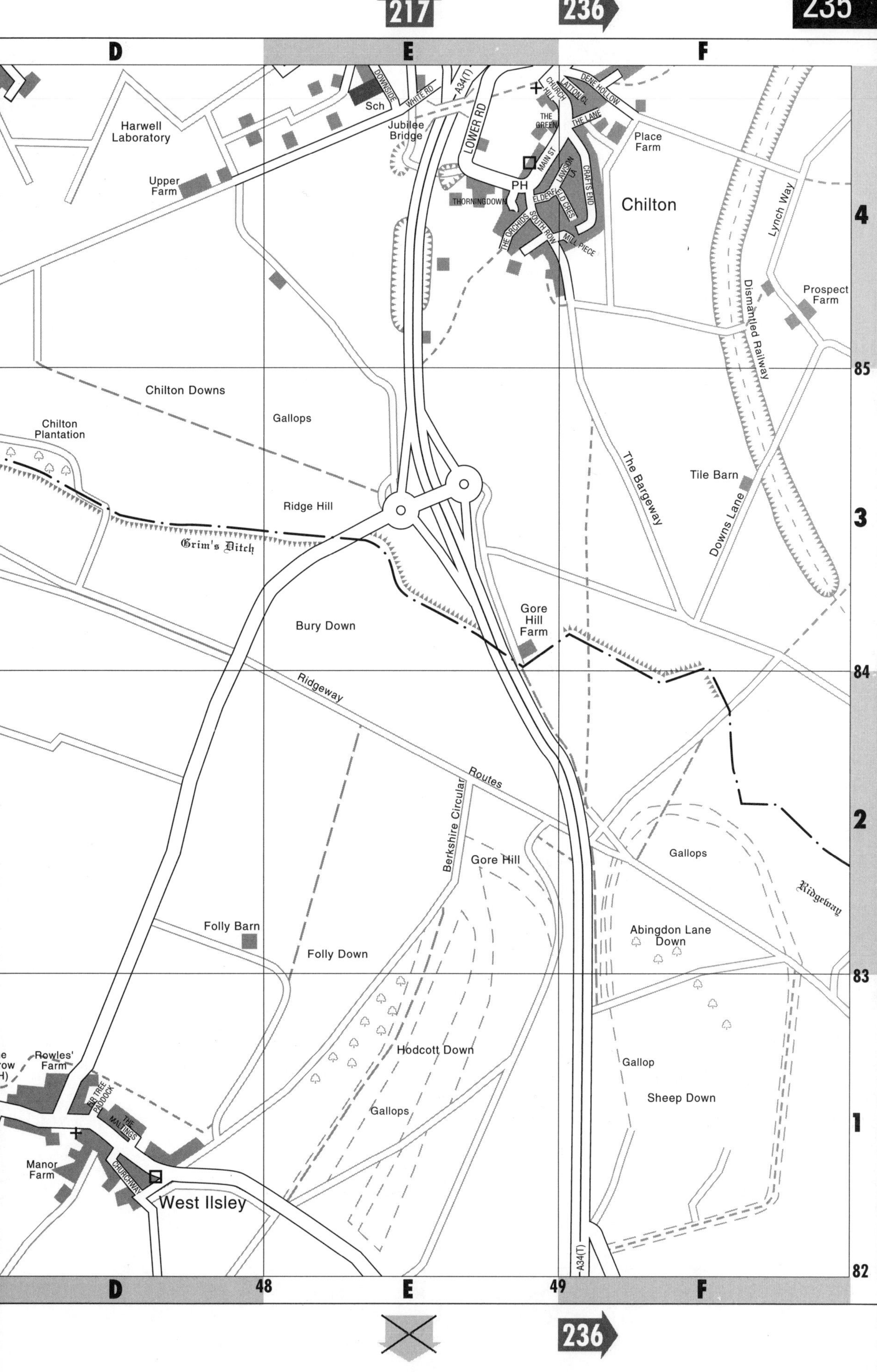

D | E | F

4

85

Harwell Laboratory

Upper Farm

Sch

Jubilee Bridge

DOWNSIDE

WHITE RD

LOWER RD

A34(T)

THORNINGDOWN

PH

MAIN ST

THE ORCHIDS

ELDER LAYS

SOUTH ROW

MILL PIECE

CRAFTS END

THE GREEN

CHURCH HILL

DEAN HOLLOW

ALTON CL

THE LANE

Place Farm

Chilton

Lynch Way

Prospect Farm

Dismantled Railway

Chilton Downs

Gallops

Chilton Plantation

Ridge Hill

Grim's Ditch

The Bargeway

Tile Barn

Downs Lane

3

Bury Down

Gore Hill Farm

84

Ridgeway

Berkshire Circular

Routes

Gore Hill

Gallops

Ridgeway

2

Folly Barn

Folly Down

Abingdon Lane Down

83

Hodcott Down

Gallop

Gallops

Sheep Down

Rowles' Farm

THE MALTINGS

PINE TREE PADDOCK

Manor Farm

CHURCH WAY

West Ilsley

A34(T)

1

82

D | 48 | E | 49 | F

235
218

A   **B**   **C**

A417

WESTBROOK GREEN

LONDON RD

WESTBROOK ST

Wate

4

New Inn
(PH)

New
Buildings

85

Alden
Farm

Churn
Knob

The
Kennels

Churn Knob

Tile
Barn

Saltbox

B O H A M ' S R D

Rose
Cottage

Churn Hill

3

Upper Chanc
Farm

84

Tumulus

Gallops

Old
Butts

Tumuli

Churn
Farm

2

The
Firs

Mounds

Gallops

Gallops

Gallops

Dismantled Railway

83

Several Down

Churn
Rifle Range

Ridgeway

Lower Chance
Farm

Compton
Downs

Gallop

Blewbury
Down

Tumulus

1

Ridgeway

Gallops

Berkshire Circular Routes

Ridgeway

Berkshire
Circular
Routes

82

235

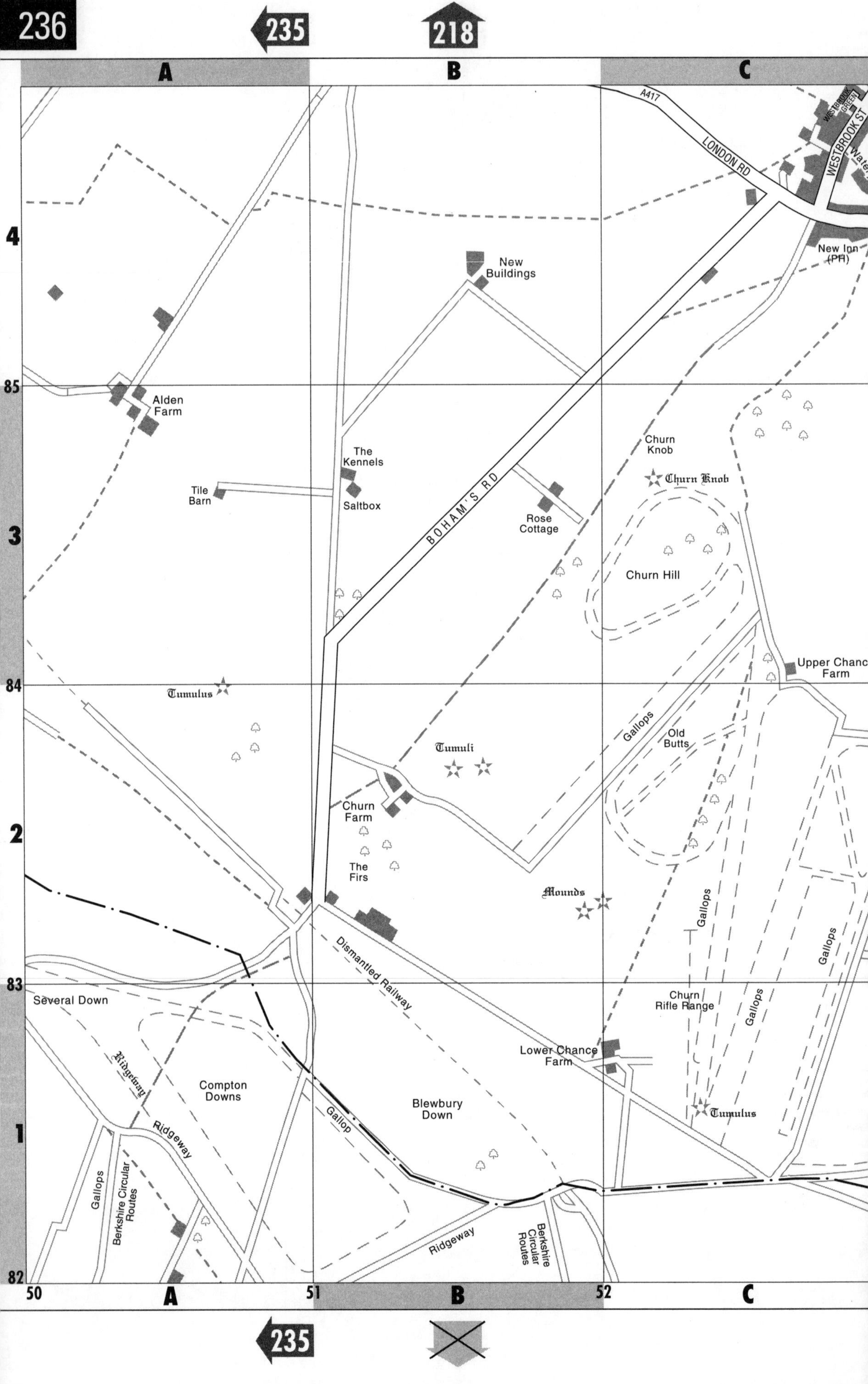

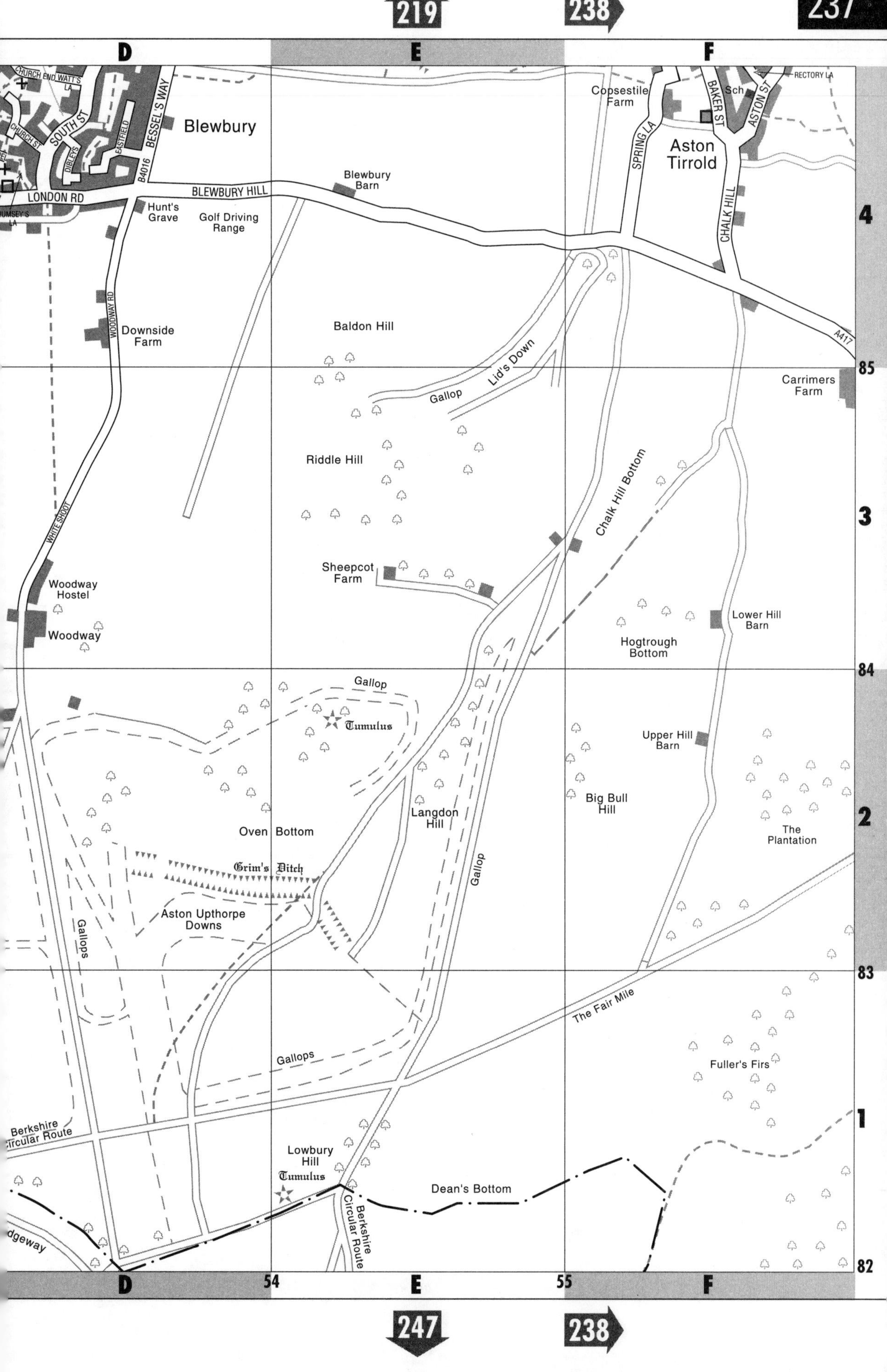

D

Blewbury

CHURCH END WATT'S LA
SOUTH ST
DIBLEYS
EASTFIELD
B4016
CHURCH END
LONDON RD
RUMSEY'S LA

BESSEL'S WAY
WOODWAY RD

BLEWBURY HILL
Hunt's Grave
Golf Driving Range

Blewbury Barn

E

F

Copsestile Farm

Aston Tirrold

SPRING LA
BAKER ST
CHALK HILL
ASTON ST
RECTORY LA
Sch

A417

4

Downside Farm

Baldon Hill

WHITE SHOOT

Lid's Down
Gallop

Carrimers Farm

85

Riddle Hill

Chalk Hill Bottom

3

Woodway Hostel

Woodway

Sheepcot Farm

Lower Hill Barn

Hogtrough Bottom

84

Gallop

Tumulus

Upper Hill Barn

Oven Bottom

Langdon Hill

Gallop

Big Bull Hill

The Plantation

2

Grim's Ditch

Aston Upthorpe Downs

Gallops

The Fair Mile

83

Gallops

Fuller's Firs

Berkshire Circular Route

1

Lowbury Hill
Tumulus

Dean's Bottom

Berkshire Circular Route

Ridgeway

D

54

E

55

F

82

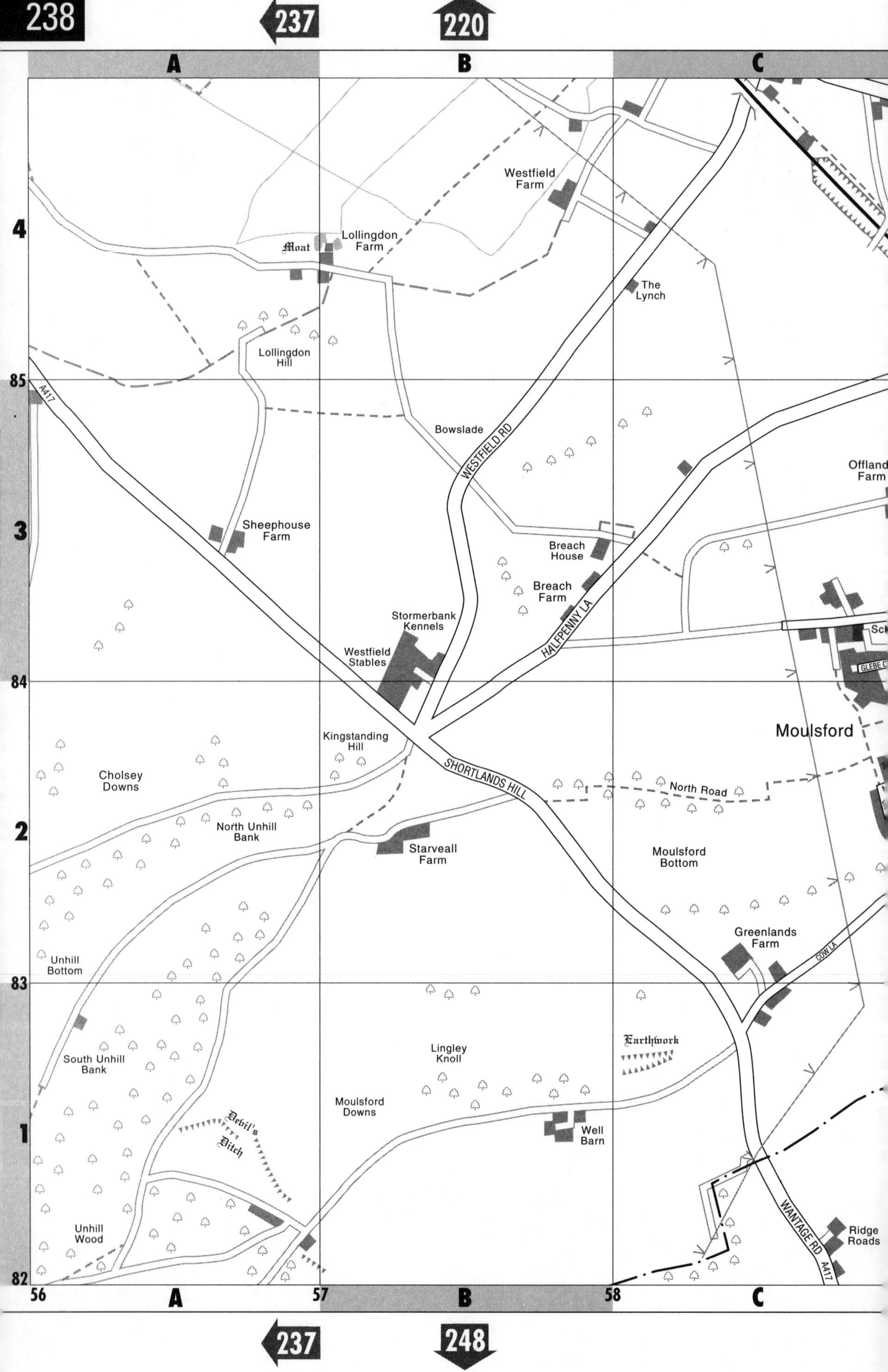
A
B
C
4
85
3
84
2
83
1
82
56
57
58
Westfield Farm
Moat
Lollingdon Farm
The Lynch
Lollingdon Hill
A417
Bowslade
WESTFIELD RD
Offland Farm
Sheephouse Farm
Breach House
Breach Farm
Stormerbank Kennels
HALFPENNY LA
Westfield Stables
GLEBE C
Moulsford
Kingstanding Hill
Cholsey Downs
SHORTLANDS HILL
North Road
North Unhill Bank
Starveall Farm
Moulsford Bottom
Greenlands Farm
Unhill Bottom
COW LA
Lingley Knoll
Earthwork
South Unhill Bank
Moulsford Downs
Devil's Ditch
Well Barn
WANTAGE RD
Unhill Wood
Ridge Roads
A417

D E F

WHITE HOUSE RD

CHARLES RD

PAPIST WAY

A329

ABBOTS MEAD

CHELSEA PL

PH

Hospl

Hospl

Cholsey Marsh
(Nature Reserve)

B4009

4

Barracks
Farm

Inn

The
Gables

Littlestoke
Manor
Farm

Ash
Cottage

85

READING RD

Middle
Barn

Swan's Way

Viaduct

WALLINGFORD RD

The
Oak

Watch
Folly

3

Sch

River Thames

Ridgeway

White Hill

84

Sch

Lower
Farm

Freedom
Cottages

WOODCOTE RD

Ivol
Barn

Hotel

FERRY LA

FERRY RD

Sowberry
Court

FERRY LA

South
Stoke

THE STREET

THE BEECHES RD

CROSS KEYS RD

PH

THE GARDENS

Glebe
Cottages

Lower
Cadley's

2

CHAPEL LA

DEACONFIELD

South
Bank

83

Grove Farm
House

Runsford
Hole

Sewage
Works

Grove
House

Grove
Farm

1

WALLINGFORD RD

PH

Spring
Farm

Icknield Way

BEECH LA

Streatley
Farm

A329

B4009

Spring Farm
Cottages

82

D 60 E 61 F

A   **B**   **C**

White House (PH)

A4074

WHITE HOUSE RD

PORT WAY

The Cottage

Larkstoke Stud

Icknield Way

Swan's Way

Ipsden Farm

THE STREET

Meml

Cross Farm

CRABTREE CORNER

FIR CL

Ipsden

Newtown

Sch

Ipsden House

4

Stone Farm PH

Hailey

Hill Farm

Warren Hill

Warren Hill Farm

Wellplace Farm

Wellplace Zoo

Wellplace

URQU

85

Warrens Chase

GARSONS LA

Swan's Way

Knapps Wichelo

Braziers Park

Garsons Hill

3

Kaffirs

Icknield Farm

BRAZIERS LA

Braziers Cottages

84

Ouseley Barn

Ouseley Barn Cottages

RED LA

Itchen Wood

The Bottom Farm House

Itchen Farm

Strip Lynchets

Hammond Wood

2

Mile End Hill

Catsbrain Hill

83

SOUTH STOKE RD

Upper Cadley's

Dean Farm

Dean Wood

Langtree House

B471 RED LA

Woodcote Fruit Farm

Massey's Pightie

1

Lycroft's Shaw

Broad Street Farm

High Wood

Beech Farm

BEECH LA

Woodcote

BEHOES LA

WAYSIDE GREEN

James Farm

OXFORD RD

TIDMORE LA

Church Farm

Schs

GREENMOOR

GORING RD

B471

P

READING RD

82

62   **A**   **63**   **B**   **64**   **C**

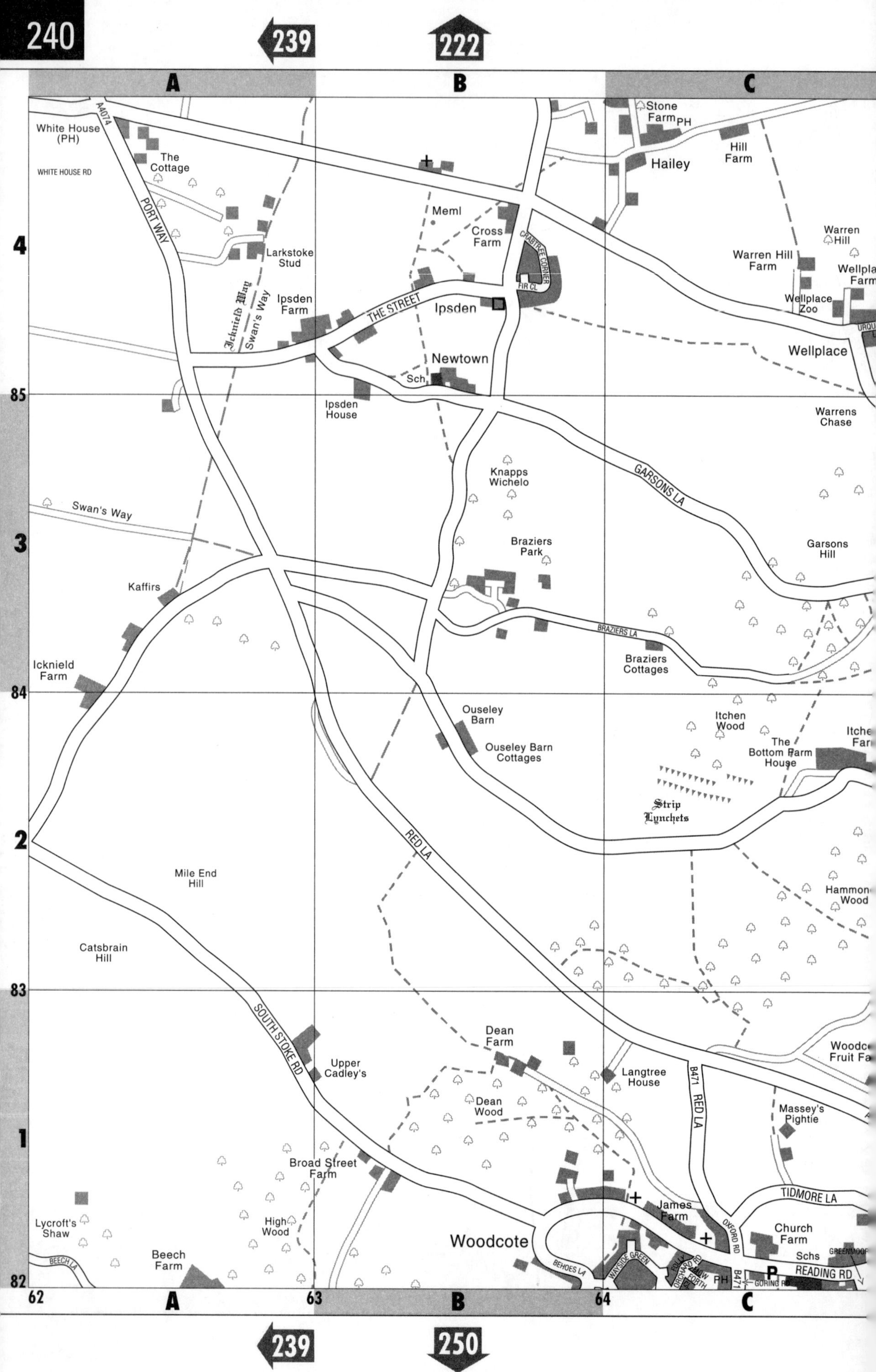

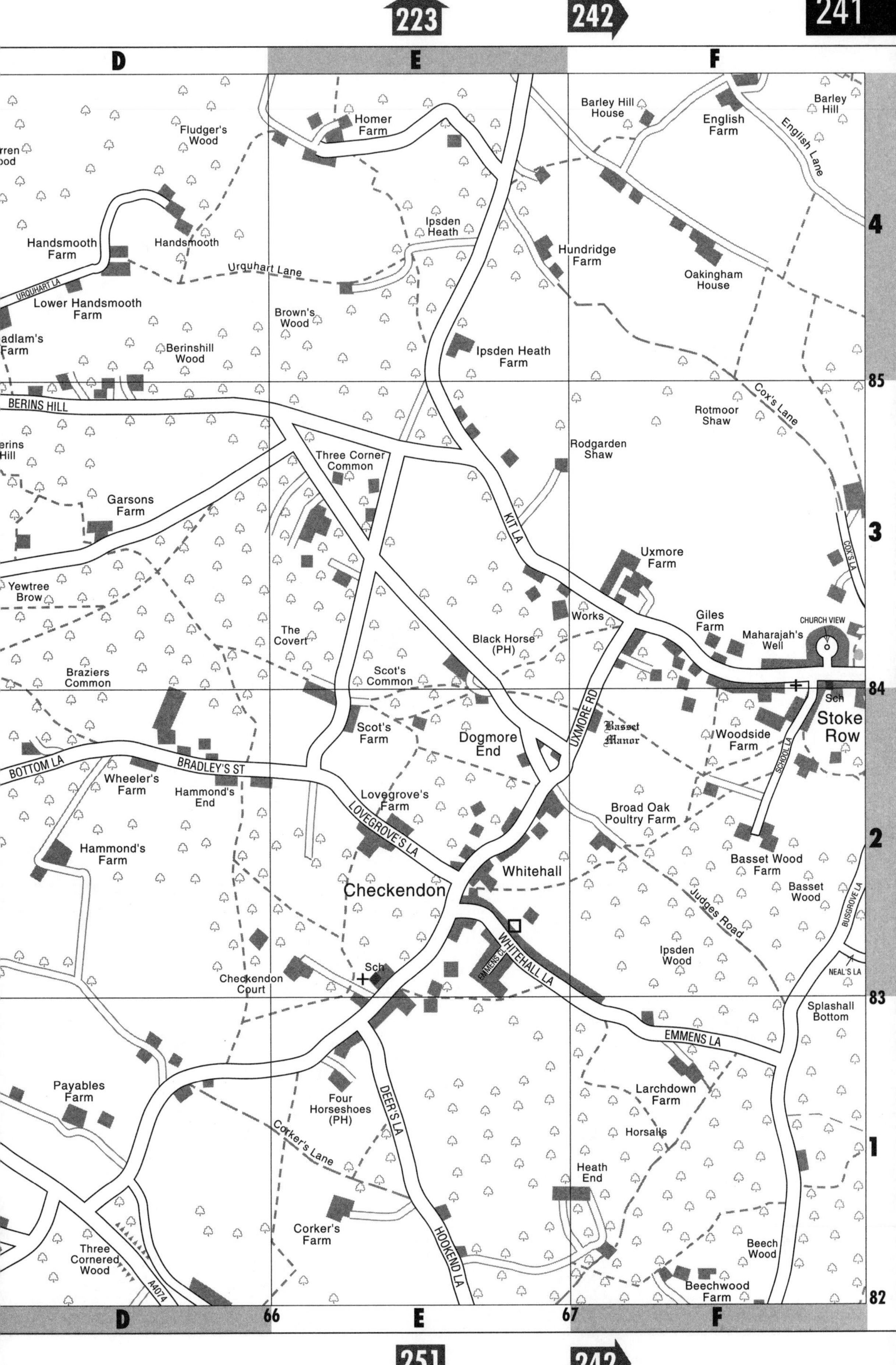

D   E   F

4

85

3

84

2

83

1

82

Fludger's Wood

Homer Farm

Barley Hill House

English Farm

Barley Hill

English Lane

Warren Wood

Handsmooth Farm

Handsmooth

Urquhart Lane

Ipsden Heath

Hundridge Farm

Oakingham House

URQUHART LA

Lower Handsmooth Farm

Brown's Wood

Ipsden Heath Farm

Cox's Lane

Badlam's Farm

Berinshill Wood

Rotmoor Shaw

BERINS HILL

Rodgarden Shaw

Berins Hill

Three Corner Common

KIT LA

Uxmore Farm

Giles Farm

Maharajah's Well

CHURCH VIEW

Garsons Farm

Works

COX'S LA

Yewtree Brow

The Covert

Black Horse (PH)

UXMORE RD

Stoke Row

Sch

Braziers Common

Scot's Common

Basset Manor

Woodside Farm

Scot's Farm

Dogmore End

Bottom La

BOTTOM LA

BRADLEY'S ST

Wheeler's Farm

Hammond's End

Lovegrove's Farm

Broad Oak Poultry Farm

SCHOOL LA

Basset Wood Farm

Basset Wood

BUSGROVE LA

Hammond's Farm

LOVEGROVE'S LA

Whitehall

Judges Road

Checkendon

Ipsden Wood

NEAL'S LA

Checkendon Court

Sch

WHITEHALL LA

Splashall Bottom

EMMENS LA

Payables Farm

DEER'S LA

Four Horseshoes (PH)

Larchdown Farm

Corker's Lane

Horsalls

Heath End

Beech Wood

Corker's Farm

Three Cornered Wood

A4074

HOOKEND LA

Beechwood Farm

241
224

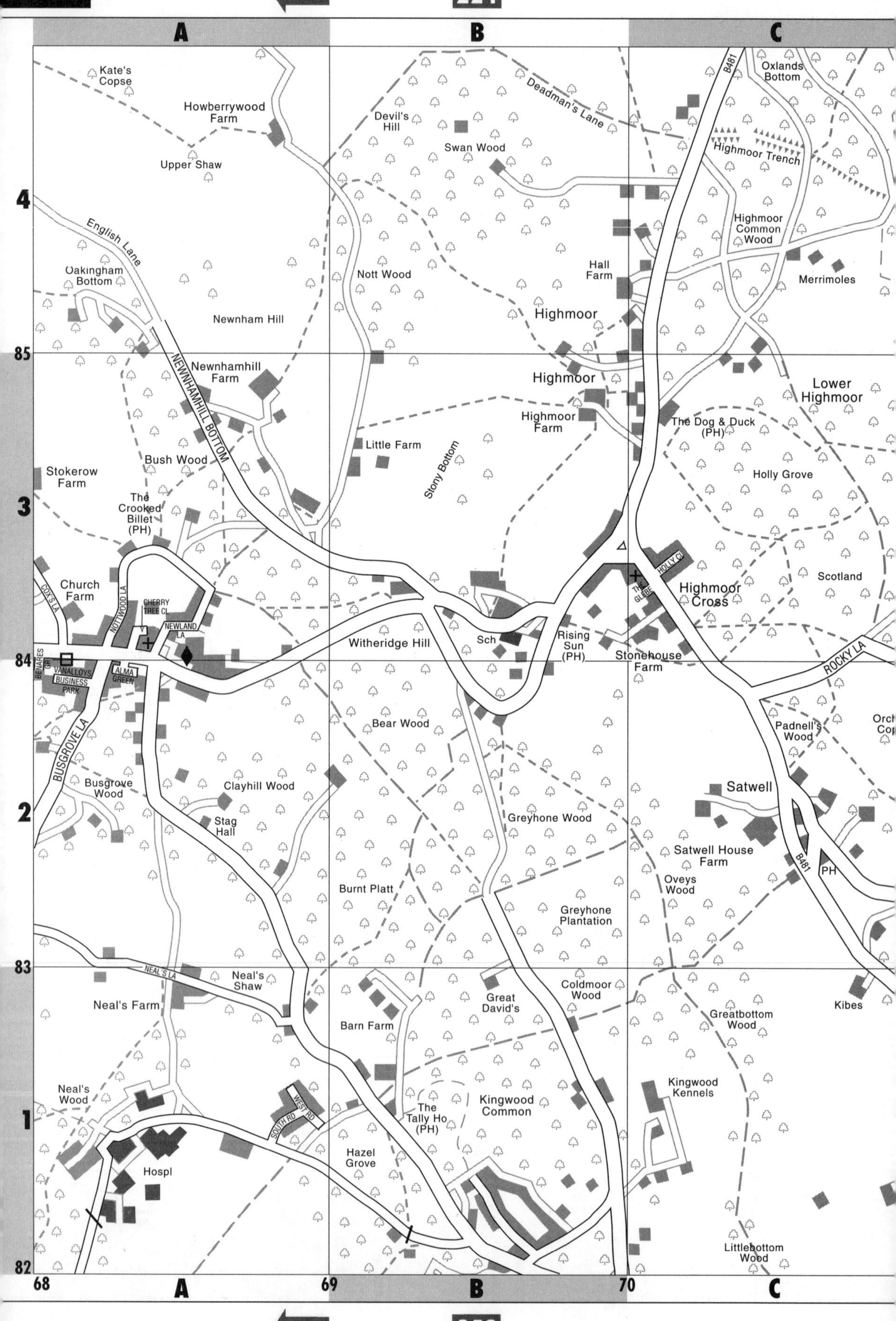
A
B
C
Kate's Copse
Howberrywood Farm
Upper Shaw
Devil's Hill
Swan Wood
Deadman's Lane
Oxlands Bottom
B481
Highmoor Trench
English Lane
Oakingham Bottom
Newnham Hill
Nott Wood
Hall Farm
Highmoor Common Wood
Merrimoles
Highmoor
Highmoor
Lower Highmoor
Newnhamhill Farm
NEWNHAMHILL BOTTOM
Highmoor Farm
The Dog & Duck (PH)
Little Farm
Stony Bottom
Holly Grove
Stokerow Farm
Bush Wood
The Crooked Billet (PH)
Church Farm
COX'S LA
NOTTWOOD LA
CHERRY TREE CL
NEWLAND LA
HOLLY CL
THE GLEBE
Highmoor Cross
Scotland
Witheridge Hill
Sch
Rising Sun (PH)
Stonehouse Farm
ROCKY LA
BENARES GR
VANALLOYS BUSINESS PARK
ALMA GREEN
Bear Wood
Padnell's Wood
Orch Cop
BUSGROVE LA
Busgrove Wood
Clayhill Wood
Stag Hall
Satwell
Greyhone Wood
Satwell House Farm
B481
PH
Burnt Platt
Oveys Wood
Greyhone Plantation
NEAL'S LA
Neal's Shaw
Neal's Farm
Great David's
Coldmoor Wood
Kibes
Barn Farm
Greatbottom Wood
Neal's Wood
The Tally Ho (PH)
Kingwood Common
Kingwood Kennels
WEST RD
SOUTH RD
Hospl
Hazel Grove
Littlebottom Wood
4
85
3
84
2
83
1
82
68
69
70

241
252

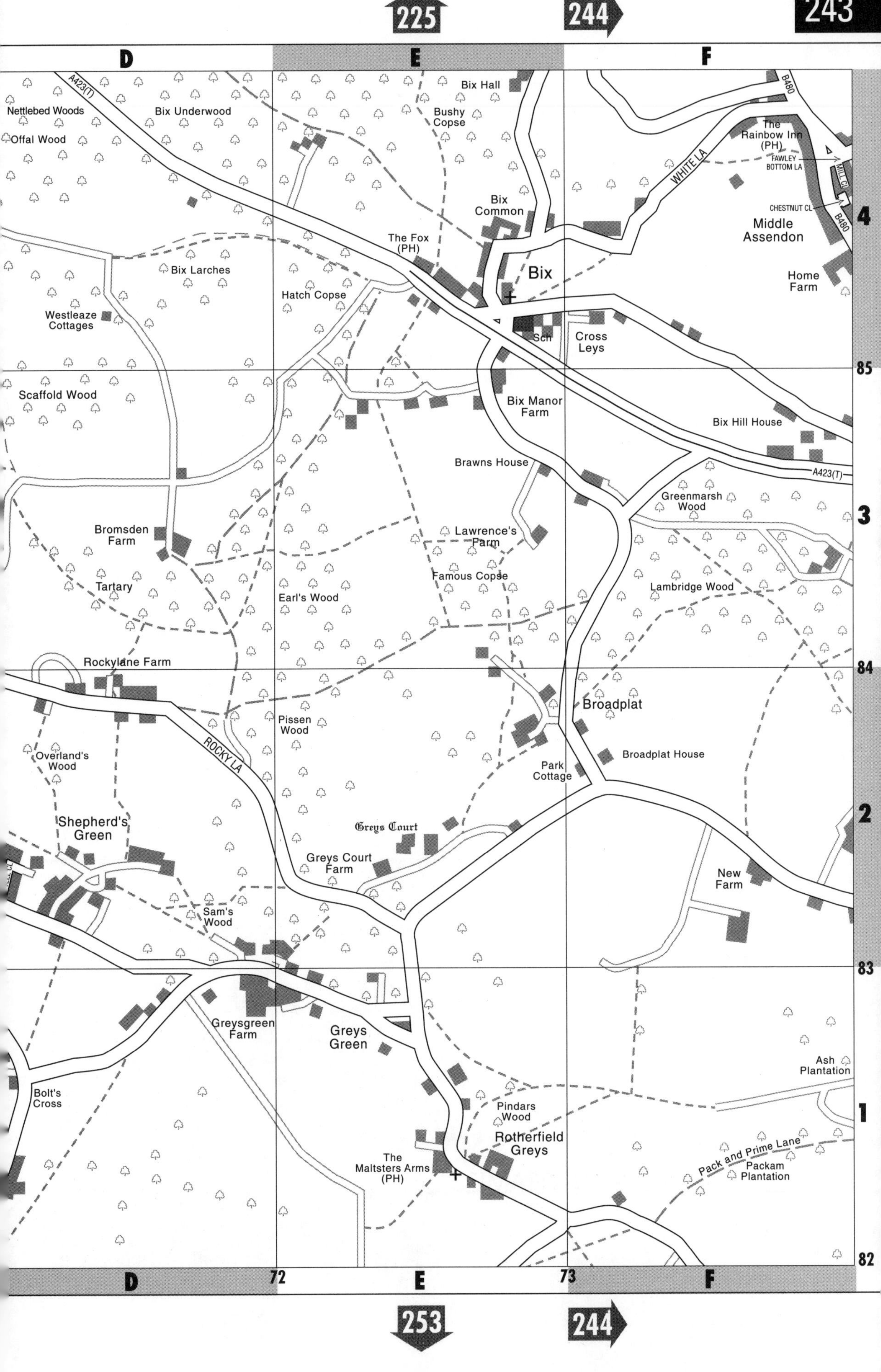

225
244

D   E   F

Nettlebed Woods

Offal Wood

Bix Underwood

Bix Hall

Bushy Copse

The Rainbow Inn (PH)

FAWLEY BOTTOM LA

WHITE LA

B480

CHESTNUT CL

MILL CL

Middle Assendon

4

Bix Larches

Westleaze Cottages

Hatch Copse

Bix Common

The Fox (PH)

Bix

Sch

Cross Leys

Home Farm

85

Scaffold Wood

Bix Manor Farm

Brawns House

Bix Hill House

A423(T)

Greenmarsh Wood

3

Bromsden Farm

Tartary

Earl's Wood

Lawrence's Farm

Famous Copse

Lambridge Wood

Rockylane Farm

84

Overland's Wood

ROCKY LA

Pissen Wood

Broadplat

Park Cottage

Broadplat House

Shepherd's Green

Greys Court

New Farm

2

Sam's Wood

Greys Court Farm

83

Greysgreen Farm

Greys Green

Ash Plantation

1

Bolt's Cross

The Maltsters Arms (PH)

Pindars Wood

Rotherfield Greys

Pack and Prime Lane

Packam Plantation

82

253
244

Middle
Assendon
Farm

Crockmore
Farm

Fawley

Benhams
Wood

Oaken
Grove

BENHAMS LA

4

Round Hill
Farm

Roothouse
Wood

Rowe
Wood

Fawley Court
Farm

Round
Hill

85

The Golden Ball
(PH)
Lower
Assendon

BIX HILL

A423(T)

Great
Hill

Henley
Park

New
Cottages

No Man's
Hill

3

Cemy

Deer Park

Fawley Court

Lambridge
Hill

The Grove

College

Lambridge
Farm

Little
Wood

Wks

84

Lambridge
Wood

FAIR MILE

The
Mount

South
Lodge

LAMBRIDGE WOOD RD

BARN LA

Caravan &
Camping Site

2

Golf Course

Badgemore
End

Swiss
Farm

Court

Badgemore
House

CH

Beechwood

LAMBRIDGE LA

Phyllis
Court

83

Friar
Park

Sch

Lib'y

Wilminster

Sch

Hospl

YORK RD

MARKET
PL

HART ST

PH

1

Parkside

Coll

WHITE HILL

DEANFIELD AVE

Coll

HENLEY-ON-THAMES

College

Henley-on-Thames
Station

Greenfield
Cottages

GREYS RD

Sch

Sch

82

Starveall Farm

Swinley Down

Swinley Copse

Dark Dale

Ashdown Farm

Harley Bushes

Oxfordshire Circular Walks

B4000

Tumuli

Upper Wood

Pumping Station

Whiteshere

Dark Dale

Bishopstone Downs

Idstone Down

Botley Bottom

Dean Bottom

Botley Copse

Russley Park

Bailey Hill

Resr

Bailey Hill Copse

Goorlane Farm

Peaks Down

GOOR LA

Hazelbury Farm

Bailey Hill Farm

Peaks Wood

Gallop

Baydon

Ermin Way

ROMAN ROAD

Westfield Farm

Finche's Farm

East Leaze Farm

BAYDON RD.

DOWNSMEAD

FINCHES LA

Sch

D   27   E   28   F

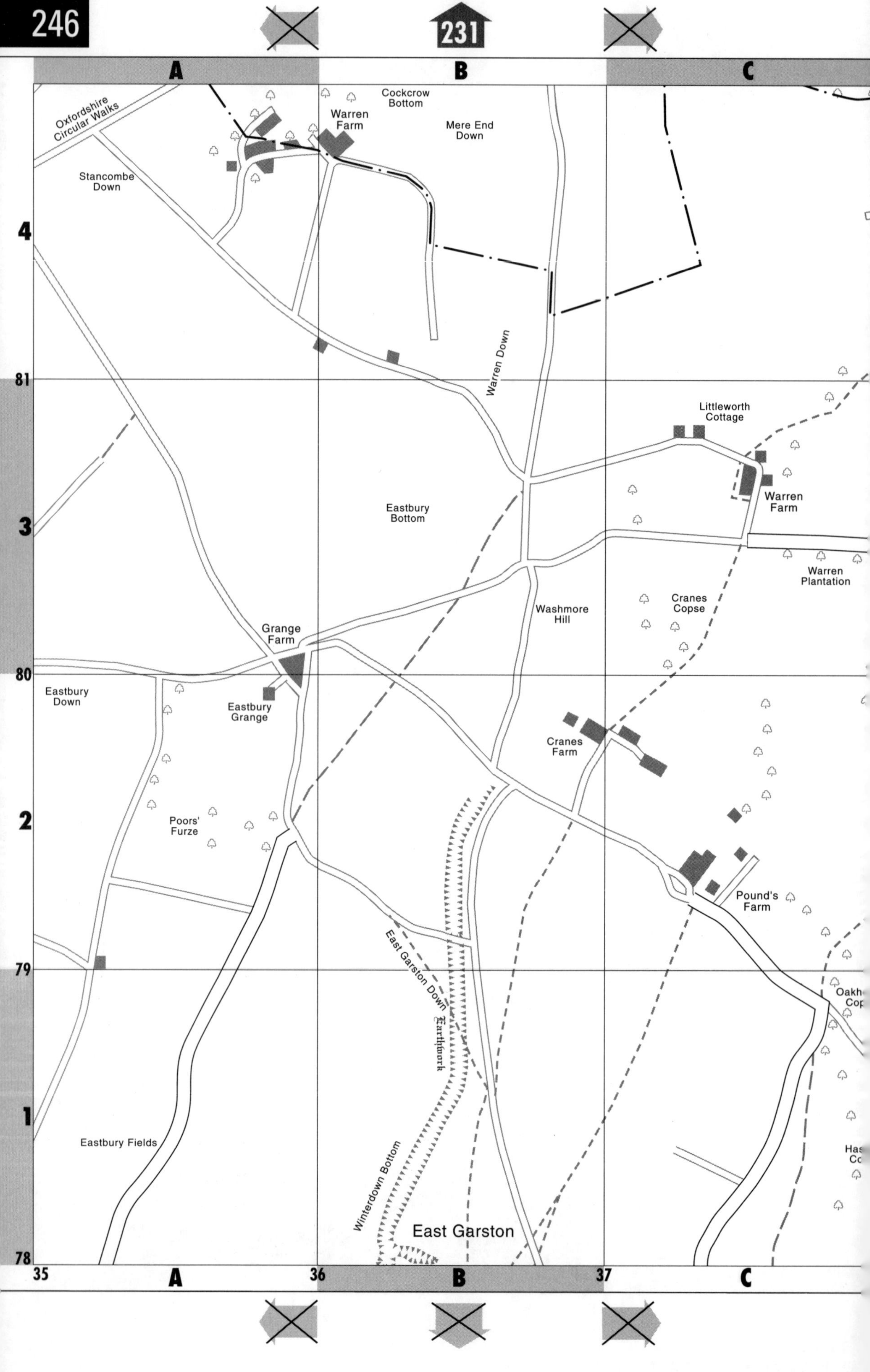

A B C

Oxfordshire
Circular Walks

Cockcrow
Bottom

Warren
Farm

Mere End
Down

Stancombe
Down

4

Warren Down

81

Littleworth
Cottage

3

Eastbury
Bottom

Warren
Farm

Warren
Plantation

Cranes
Copse

Washmore
Hill

Grange
Farm

80

Eastbury
Down

Eastbury
Grange

Cranes
Farm

2

Poors'
Furze

Pound's
Farm

79

East Garston Down

Oakh
Cop

Earthwork

1

Eastbury Fields

Has
Co

Winterdown Bottom

East Garston

78

35 A 36 B 37 C

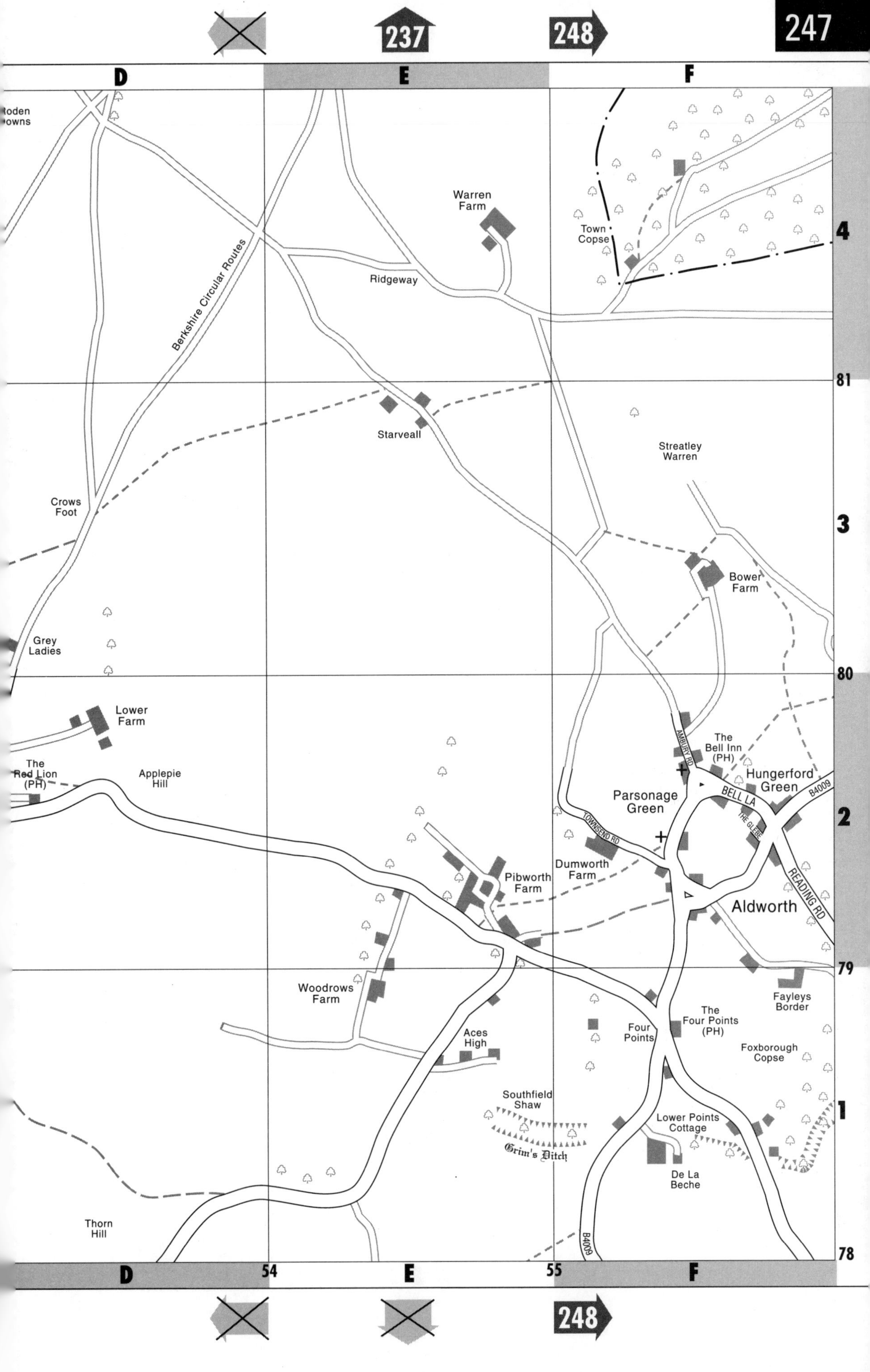
D
E
F
Roden Downs
Warren Farm
Town Copse
Ridgeway
Berkshire Circular Routes
81
Starveall
Streatley Warren
Crows Foot
3
Bower Farm
Grey Ladies
80
Lower Farm
The Bell Inn (PH)
AMBURY RD
The Red Lion (PH)
Applepie Hill
Hungerford Green
Parsonage Green
BELL LA
B4009
THE GLEBE
2
TOWNSEND RD
Dumworth Farm
Pibworth Farm
READING RD
Aldworth
79
Woodrows Farm
Fayleys Border
The Four Points (PH)
Four Points
Aces High
Foxborough Copse
Southfield Shaw
1
Lower Points Cottage
Grim's Ditch
De La Beche
Thorn Hill
B4009
78
54
55
4

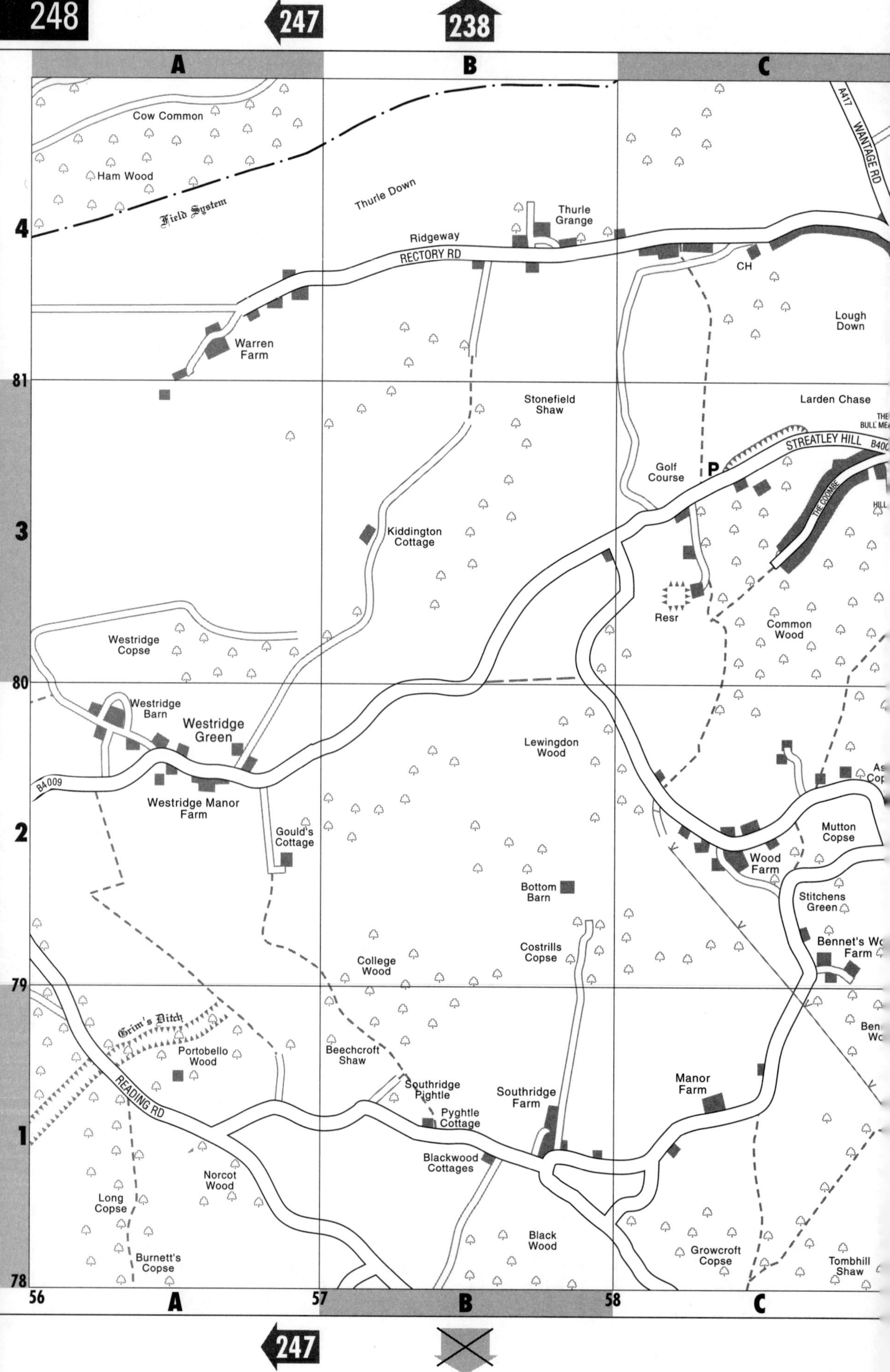

A B C

4

81

3

80

2

79

1

78

Cow Common
Ham Wood
Field System
Thurle Down
Thurle Grange
Ridgeway
RECTORY RD
CH
Lough Down
Warren Farm
Stonefield Shaw
Larden Chase
THE BULL ME
STREATLEY HILL B400
Golf Course
P
Kiddington Cottage
Resr
Common Wood
HILL
Westridge Copse
Westridge Barn
Westridge Green
Lewingdon Wood
As Cop
Mutton Copse
B4009
Westridge Manor Farm
Gould's Cottage
Wood Farm
Stitchens Green
Bottom Barn
Bennet's Wo Farm
College Wood
Costrills Copse
Grim's Ditch
Beechcroft Shaw
Ben Wo
Portobello Wood
Southridge Pightle
Pyghtle Cottage
Southridge Farm
Manor Farm
READING RD
Blackwood Cottages
Norcot Wood
Black Wood
Growcroft Copse
Tombhill Shaw
Long Copse
Burnett's Copse
A417 WANTAGE RD

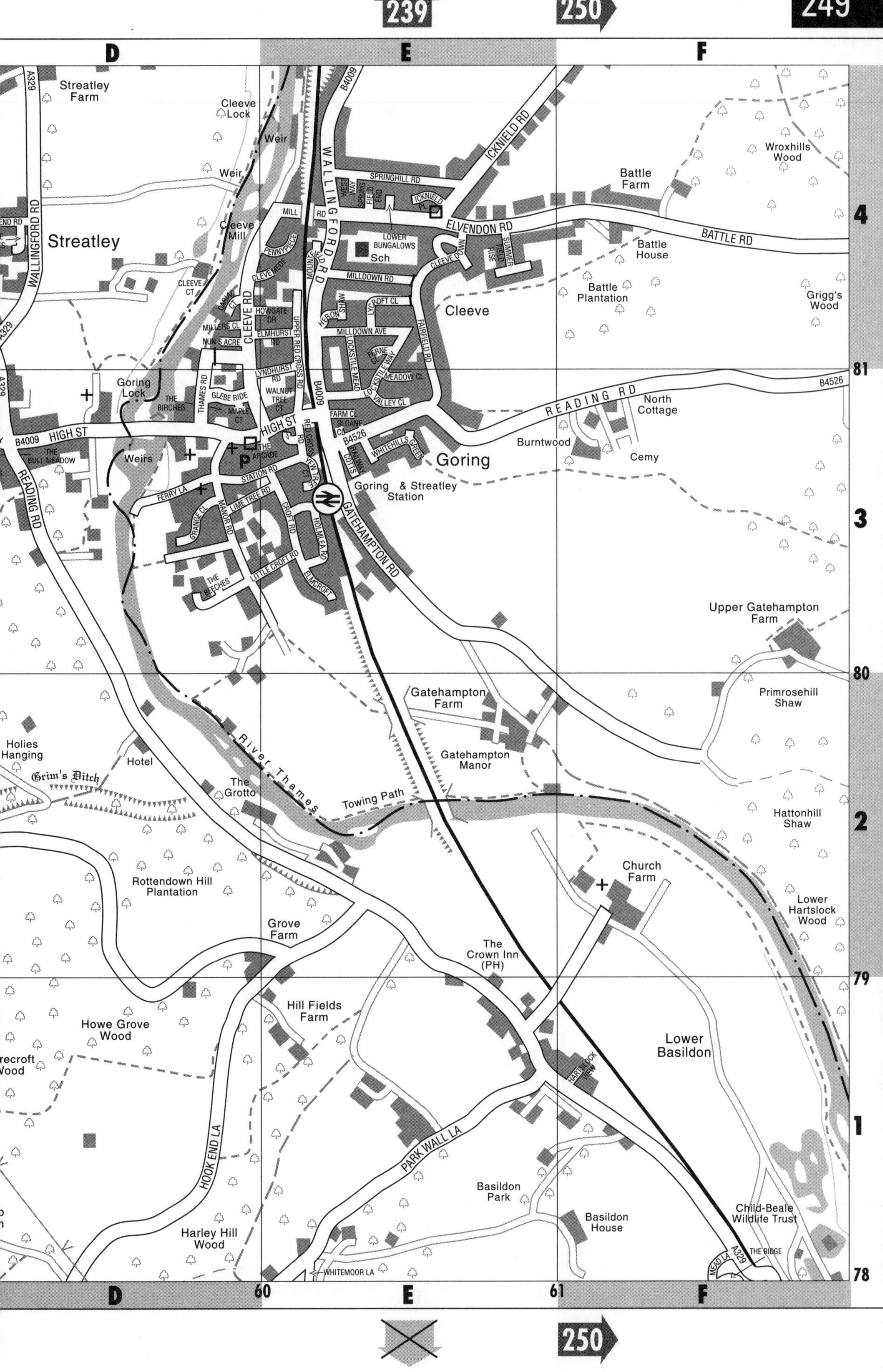
Streatley Farm
Cleeve Lock
Weir
Streatley
Cleeve Mill
Goring Lock
Weirs
Battle Farm
Battle House
Battle Plantation
Wroxhills Wood
Grigg's Wood
Cleeve
Goring
Goring & Streatley Station
North Cottage
Burntwood
Cemy
Upper Gatehampton Farm
Gatehampton Farm
Gatehampton Manor
Primrosehill Shaw
Holies Hanging
Hotel
Grim's Ditch
The Grotto
River Thames
Towing Path
Hattonhill Shaw
Church Farm
Lower Hartslock Wood
Rottendown Hill Plantation
Grove Farm
The Crown Inn (PH)
Hill Fields Farm
Howe Grove Wood
Lower Basildon
Basildon Park
Basildon House
Child-Beale Wildlife Trust
Harley Hill Wood
HOOK END LA
PARK WALL LA
WHITEMOOR LA
HIGH ST
READING RD
WALLINGFORD RD
CLEEVE RD
ICKNIELD RD
ELVENDON RD
BATTLE RD
GATEHAMPTON RD
STATION RD
FERRY LA
B4009
B4526
A329
D
E
F
60
61
4
81
3
80
2
79
1
78

A
B
C

4

BATTLE RD

Woodcroft

BEECH LA

Elmorepark Wood

Fox Covert

ELVENDON LA

Elvendon
Priory

Grigg's
Wood

Old Elvendon Wood

Park Wood

81

B4526

READING RD

Park Farm

Little
Heath

Cray's Pond

SHIRVELL'S HILL

Greenmoor
Farm

Greenmoor
Hill

POTKILN LA

Enclosure

GOING RD

WHITEHOUSE RD

BRIDLE PATH

GREEN LA

LONG

Sch

PH

3

Flint House

Bottom Farm

Blackbird's
Bottom

B471

Little Oaken Wood

Great Chalk
Wood

Stapnall's
Farm

Cold Harbour

Oakwood
Covert

Oaken Wo

80

Coldharbour
Farm

Furzemoor
Plantation

Goff's Clump

Sch

Great Oaks

2

Cockpit
Plantation

Hill Bottom

The Sun (PH)

Paul's Grove

Coombe End
Farm

BRIDLE RD

HILL BOTTOM CL

RIVACRES

Copyhol
Farm

79

Mount Pleasant
Farm

Merricroft's
Wood

Kessells Copse

Beech
Wood

Butler's
Farm

Whitchurch Hill

Hartslock
Wood

Beech Farm

ORCHARD COMBE

1

Wheatley's
Plantation

Fort

Lime Corner

Hartslock
Farm

Coombe Park
Farm

Rivendell
Farm

Stonycroft
Plantation

B471

Bozedown
House

78

62

A

63

B

64

C

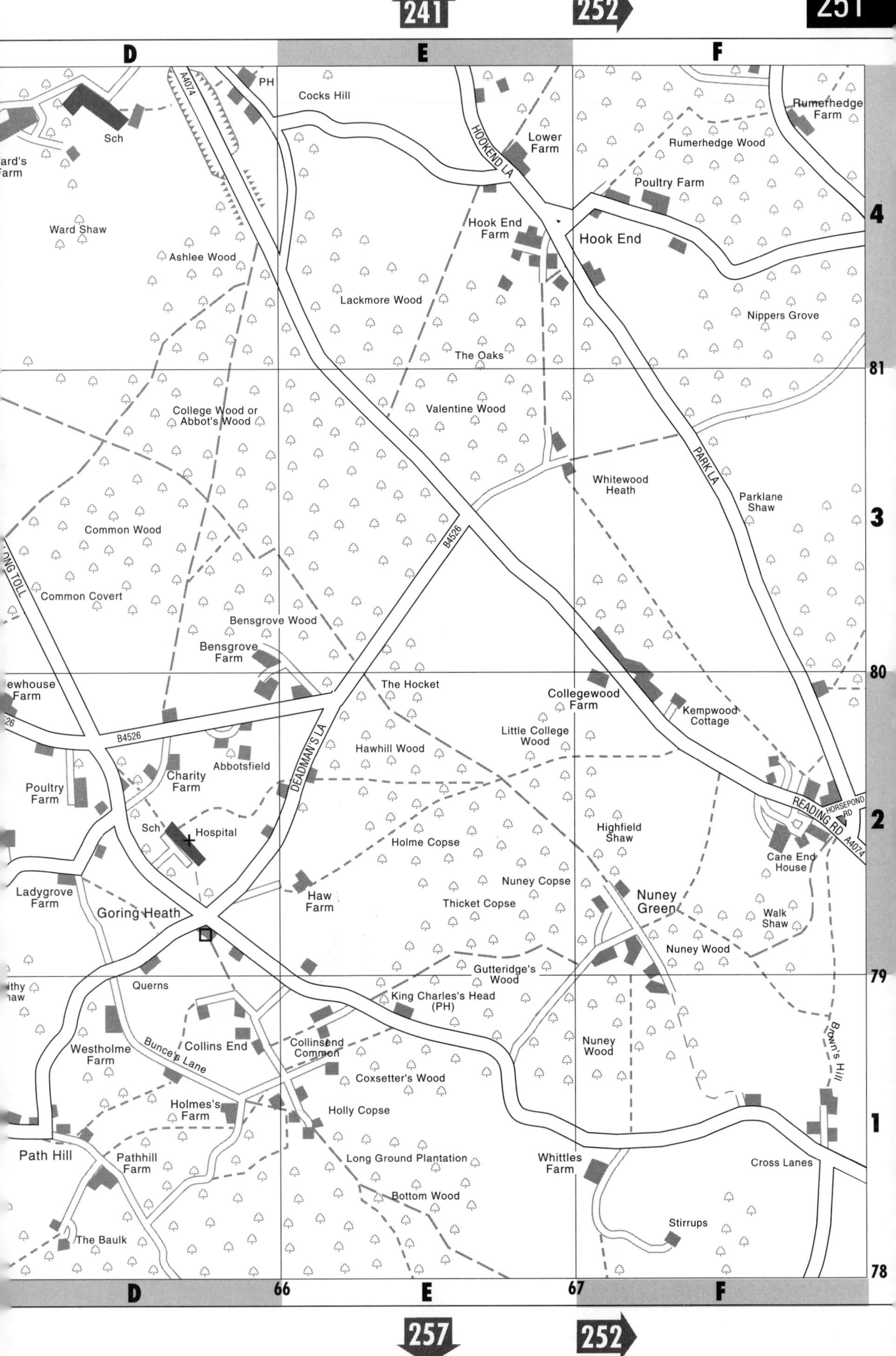

D   E   F

PH
Cocks Hill
ard's Farm
Sch
HOOKEND LA
Lower Farm
Ward Shaw
Ashlee Wood
Hook End Farm
Hook End
Rumerhedge Farm
Rumerhedge Wood
Poultry Farm
Lackmore Wood
Nippers Grove
The Oaks
College Wood or Abbot's Wood
Valentine Wood
PARK LA
Whitewood Heath
Parklane Shaw
Common Wood
B4526
Common Covert
G TOLL
Bensgrove Wood
Bensgrove Farm
The Hocket
Collegewood Farm
Kempwood Cottage
ewhouse Farm
B4526
Abbotsfield
Charity Farm
DEADMAN'S LA
Hawhill Wood
Little College Wood
Poultry Farm
Sch
Hospital
Holme Copse
Highfield Shaw
HORSEPOND RD
READING RD
A4074
Cane End House
Ladygrove Farm
Goring Heath
Haw Farm
Nuney Copse
Thicket Copse
Nuney Green
Walk Shaw
Nuney Wood
ithy aw
Querns
Gutteridge's Wood
79
King Charles's Head (PH)
Westholme Farm
Bunce's Lane
Collins End
Collinsend Common
Coxsetter's Wood
Nuney Wood
Brown's Hill
Holmes's Farm
Holly Copse
Path Hill
Pathhill Farm
Long Ground Plantation
Bottom Wood
Whittles Farm
Cross Lanes
The Baulk
Stirrups

D   66   E   67   F

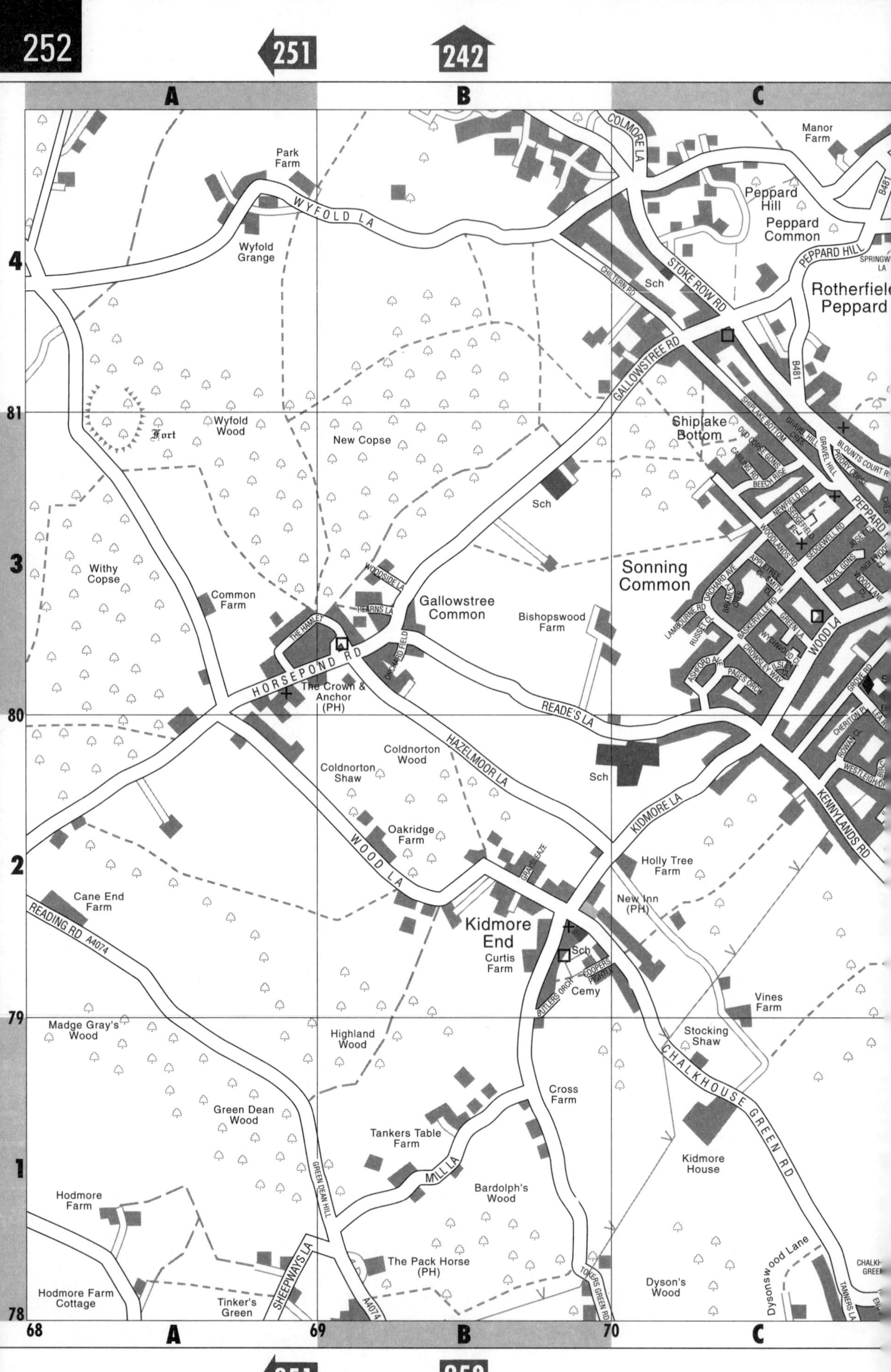

A   B   C

Manor
Farm

COLMORE LA

Park
Farm

WYFOLD LA

Peppard
Hill
Peppard
Common

PEPPARD HILL

SPRINGW
LA

B481

Wyfold
Grange

STOKE ROW RD

Sch

CHILTERN RD

4

Rotherfiel
Peppard

GALLOWSTREE RD

B481

Fort

Wyfold
Wood

New Copse

Shiplake
Bottom

SHIPLAKE BOTTOM LA
GRAVEL HILL
OLD COPSE GDNS

GRAVEL HILL
PRIORY COPSE

BLOUNTS COURT R

81

Sch

Withy
Copse

Common
Farm

WOODSIDE LA

Gallowstree
Common

HEARNS LA

Sonning
Common

NEWFIELD RD
WOODLANDS RD

BEECH LA

HAZEL GDNS

SEDGEWELL RD

PEPPARD

Bishopswood
Farm

3

THE HAMLET

ORCHARD FIELD

RUSSEL CL
LAMBOURNE RD
ORCHARD AVE
GRACE'S
CRES

APPLE TREE
SOUTH
BASKERVILLE LA
GREEN LA
WYRWOOD CL
CROMWELL WAY

WOOD LA

WOOD LANE

HORSEPOND RD

The Crown &
Anchor
(PH)

ASHFORD AV
PAGES ORCH

SILEA

CHERITON PL
ROWAN CL

WESTLEIGH D
GROVE RD

S

80

REALE'S LA

Sch

KIDMORE LA

KENNYLANDS RD

Coldnorton
Wood

HAZELMOOR LA

Coldnorton
Shaw

Oakridge
Farm

GRACE'S LANE

WOOD LA

Holly Tree
Farm

2

Cane End
Farm

New Inn
(PH)

READING RD A4074

Kidmore
End

Curtis
Farm

BUTLER'S ORCH
COOPERS
PIGHTL

Sch

Cemy

Vines
Farm

79

Madge Gray's
Wood

Highland
Wood

Stocking
Shaw

CHALKHOUSE GREEN RD

Green Dean
Wood

Cross
Farm

GREEN DEAN HILL

Tankers Table
Farm

Kidmore
House

1

Hodmore
Farm

MILL LA

Bardolph's
Wood

A4074

Hodmore Farm
Cottage

SHEEPWAYS LA

Tinker's
Green

The Pack Horse
(PH)

TOKERS GREEN LA

Dyson's
Wood

DYSONS WOOD LANE

TANNERS LA

CHALKH
GREEN

78

68   A   69   B   70   C

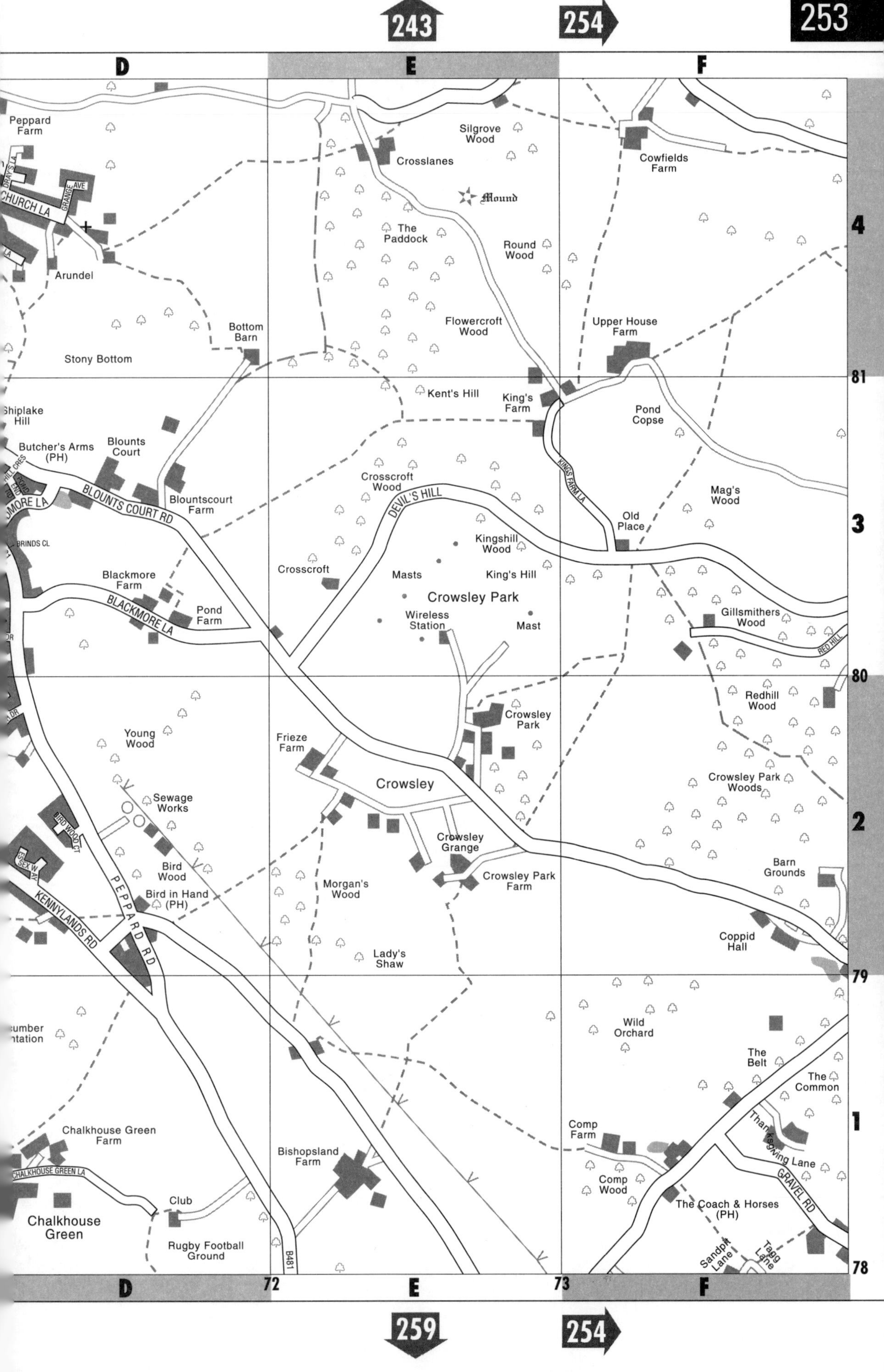

Peppard Farm

CHURCH LA

+

Arundel

Stony Bottom

Bottom Barn

Shiplake Hill

Butcher's Arms (PH)

Blounts Court

BLOUNTS COURT RD

Blountscourt Farm

BLACKMORE LA

Blackmore Farm

Pond Farm

Young Wood

Sewage Works

Bird Wood

Bird in Hand (PH)

KENNYLANDS RD

PEPPARD RD

...umber ...ntation

Chalkhouse Green Farm

CHALKHOUSE GREEN LA

Chalkhouse Green

Club

Rugby Football Ground

Silgrove Wood

Crosslanes

Mound

The Paddock

Round Wood

Flowercroft Wood

Kent's Hill

King's Farm

Crosscroft Wood

DEVIL'S HILL

Crosscroft

Masts

Kingshill Wood

King's Hill

Crowsley Park

Wireless Station

Mast

Frieze Farm

Crowsley

Crowsley Park

Morgan's Wood

Crowsley Grange

Crowsley Park Farm

Lady's Shaw

Bishopsland Farm

B481

Cowfields Farm

Upper House Farm

Pond Copse

KINGS FARM LA

Mag's Wood

Old Place

Gillsmithers Wood

RED HILL

Redhill Wood

Crowsley Park Woods

Barn Grounds

Coppid Hall

Wild Orchard

The Belt

The Common

Comp Farm

Thames...ming Lane

Comp Wood

GRAVEL RD

The Coach & Horses (PH)

Sandpit Lane

Tagg... Lane

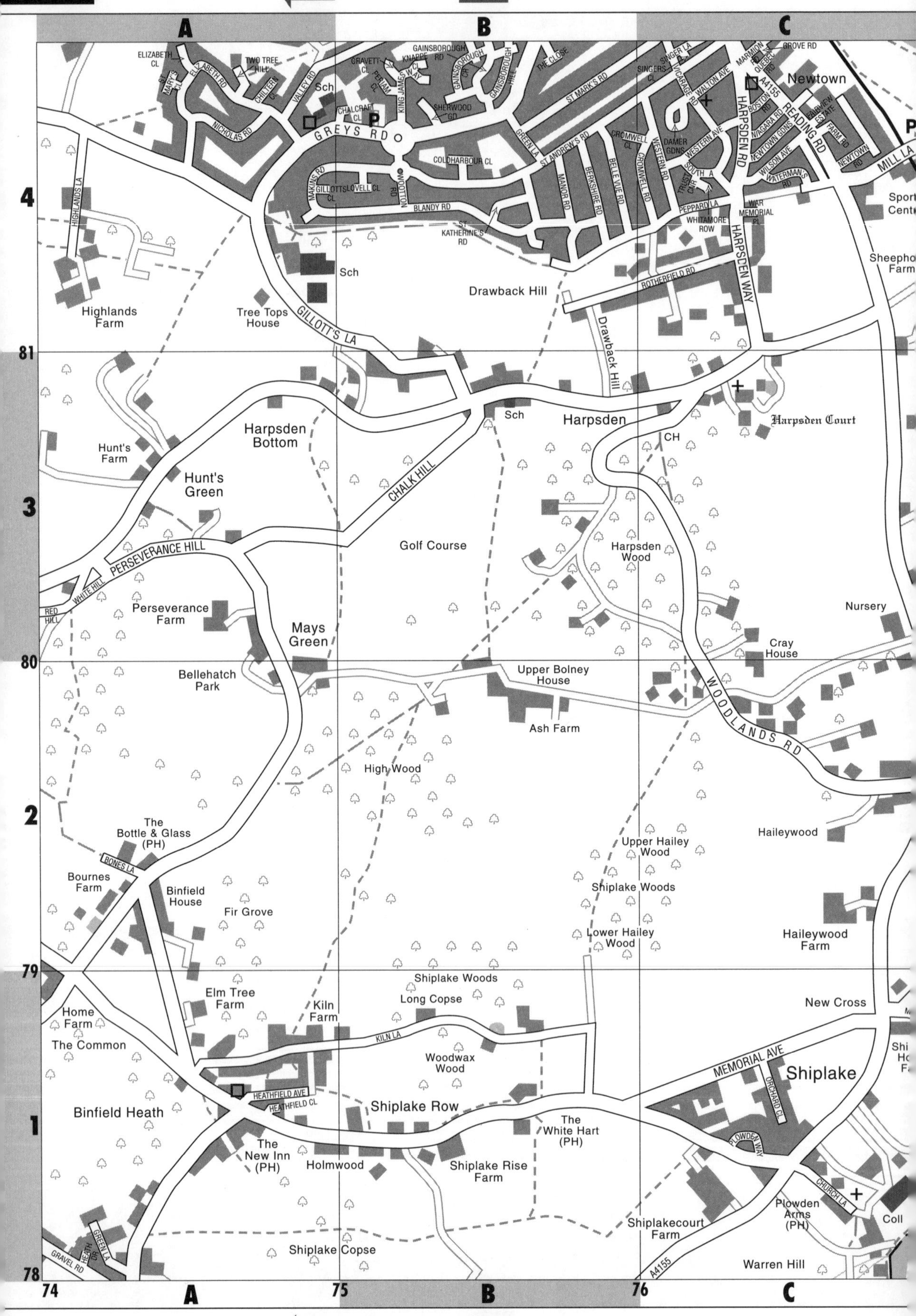

253
244

A   B   C

ELIZABETH CL
MARY'S
ELIZABETH RD
TWO TREE HILL
CHILTERN
VALLEY RD
Sch
GRAVETT CL
KNAPPE
PERLAM
KING JAMES WAY
GREEN LA
GAINSBOROUGH RD
GAINSBOROUGH
THE CLOSE
SINGERS LA
SINGER CL
GROVE RD
NICHOLAS RD
CHALCRAFT CL
SHERWOOD GD
ST MARK'S RD
ST ANDREW'S RD
CROMWELL CL
DAMER GDNS
VICARAGE RD
ORANGE
WALTON AVE
MARMION
QUEEN RD
A4155
READING RD
Newtown

GREYS RD
GILLOTTS
LOVELL CL
MAKINS RD
COLDHARBOUR CL
MANOR RD
BELLE VUE RD
BERKSHIRE RD
CROMWELL RD
WESTERN RD
SOUTH A
PEPPARD LA
WILSON AVE
NEWTOWN GDNS
NEWTOWN AVE
HARPSDEN RD
FAIRVIEW
FARM
GATE
MILL LA
P

4
Highlands Farm
HIGHLANDS LA
BLANDY RD
ST KATHERINE'S RD
Sch
Drawback Hill
ROTHERFIELD RD
WATERMANS
WAR MEMORIAL PL
WHITAMORE ROW
HARPSDEN WAY
Sheepho Farm
Sport Cent

Tree Tops House

GILLOTT'S LA

81
Hunt's Farm
Harpsden Bottom
CHALK HILL
Sch
Harpsden
CH
Harpsden Court
Drawback Hill

3
Hunt's Green
PERSEVERANCE HILL
Golf Course
Harpsden Wood
Nursery

WHITE HILL
RED HILL
Perseverance Farm
Mays Green
Cray House
WOODLANDS RD

80
Bellehatch Park
Upper Bolney House
Ash Farm

High Wood
Haileywood

2
The Bottle & Glass (PH)
BONES LA
Upper Hailey Wood
Shiplake Woods
Lower Hailey Wood
Haileywood Farm

Bournes Farm
Binfield House
Fir Grove

79
Elm Tree Farm
Kiln Farm
Shiplake Woods
Long Copse
New Cross

Home Farm
The Common
KILN LA
Woodwax Wood
MEMORIAL AVE
Shiplake
ORCHARD CL
Shi Ho F

1
Binfield Heath
HEATHFIELD AVE
HEATHFIELD CL
Shiplake Row
The White Hart (PH)
PLOWDEN WAY
CHURCH LA

The New Inn (PH)
Holmwood
Shiplake Rise Farm
Plowden Arms (PH)
Coll

78
GRAVEL RD
GREEN LA
HEWS LA
Shiplake Copse
Shiplakecourt Farm
A4155
Warren Hill

74   A   75   B   76   C

253
260

D   **E**   **F**

Mill Bank

Lock

Weirs

MILL LA

WARGRAVE RD

A321

Happy Valley

Temple Combe

The Druids Temple
Passage Grave

Kenton's Corner
Cottage

Hatchgate
House

White
Cottages

KENTON'S LA

Cockpole
Green

ASHLEY HILL

The Old Hatch
Gate (PH)

WARREN
ROW RD

4

Hatchgate Farm

HATCH GATE
LA

Pit Clump

Worley's Farm

Sch

81

Lower
Bolney
Farm

Bolney
Court

Penny's Lane

Hennerton House

Fairman's
Wood

Crazies Hill

3

Hennerton Backwater

Hennerton
Farm

Gibstroude
Farm

Maple Croft

BOLNEY RD

Kilnpits

River Thames

Wargrave Marsh

Golf
Course

80

MANOR WOOD
GATE

NORTHFIELD AVE

BRAMPTON CHASE

BASMORE
AVE

NORTH DR

LC

LASHBROOK
RD

STATION RD

P

Shiplake
Station

LOWES
CL

Lashbrook

WILLOW LA

Napier Place

2

Lower
Shiplake

THE
CRESCENT

OAKS
RD

BROOK WAY

THE CHESTNUTS

BASKERVILLE LA

BRAMSLEY RD

NEW RD

BADGERS
WLK

WESTFIELD
CREST

MILL RD

MEAD

Lash Brook

Towing Path

Wargrave
Manor

THE
COPSE

THE
SPUR

BLAKES RD

HIGHFIELD PARK

King's
Farm

79

White
Gables

Andrew Duncan
House

Ferry

WARGRAVE HILL

THE BOTLEY

THE
WALLED
GDN

MILL
LANDS

RIDGE WAY

RIVERSIDE

DARK LA

NEWALL
RISE

FANSHAWS WAY

FIDLERS WLK

DUNMOOR
WALK

VICTORIA RD

RECREATION RD

EAST VIEW RD

EAST VIEW
CL

MILL LA

Lock

Weirs

LODDON DR

FISHERMAN'S WAY

HIGH ST

FERRY LA

CHURCH ST

BACKSIDERS LA

P

B477

SCHOOL LA

AUTUMN WLK

MCCRAE'S
WLK

EMMBROOK RD

HAMILTON RD

SILVERDALE RD

SCHOOL HILL

BEVERLEY GDNS

BRAYBROOKE RD

CUTE CN

Upper Wargrave

1

Phillimore's
Island

Wargrave
Station

STATION RD

SPRING
WLK

BAYLISS
RD

Sch

Cemy

Wargrave

MUMBERY HILL B477

78

River Loddon

A321

D   **78**   **E**   **79**   **F**

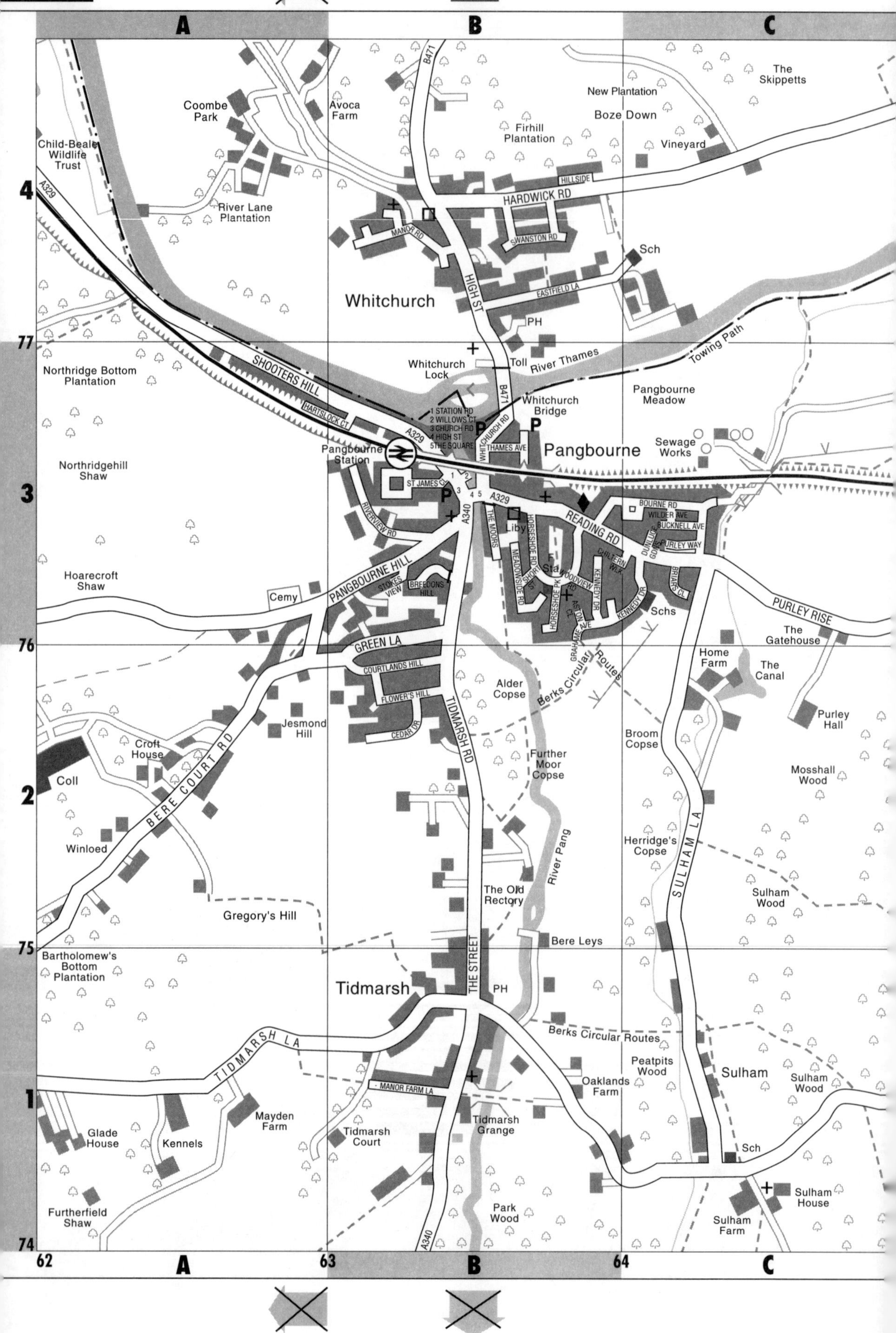

250

A **B** **C**

The Skippetts

Coombe
Park

Avoca
Farm

New Plantation
Boze Down

Child-Beale
Wildlife
Trust

Firhill
Plantation

Vineyard

River Lane
Plantation

HILLSIDE

HARDWICK RD

4

Sch

MANOR RD

SWANSTON RD

EASTFIELD LA

Whitchurch

HIGH ST

PH

Toll
River Thames
Towing Path

77

Northridge Bottom
Plantation

SHOOTERS HILL

Whitchurch
Lock

Whitchurch
Bridge

Pangbourne
Meadow

HARTSLOCK CT

Whitchurch
Rd

1 STATION RD
2 WILLOWS CT
3 CHURCH RD
4 HIGH ST
5 THE SQUARE

B471

Thames Ave

Sewage
Works

Northridgehill
Shaw

A329

Pangbourne
Station

Pangbourne

P

P

St James'

RIVERVIEW RD

P

BOURNE RD
WILDER AVE
BUCKNELL AVE

3

Hoarecroft
Shaw

A340

A329

READING RD

URLEY WAY

THE MOORS

Liby

HORSESHOE RD

F
Sta

MEADOWSIDE RD

GRAHAME AVE

GOODVIEW

KENNEDY DR

KENNEDY DR

DUBLIN

Cemy

PANGBOURNE HILL

STOKES
VIEW

BRECONS
HILL

BRIARS CL

Schs

Berks Circular Routes

The
Gatehouse

76

GREEN LA

COURTLANDS HILL

FLOWER'S HILL

Alder
Copse

Home
Farm

The
Canal

CEDAR DR

Purley
Hall

Jesmond
Hill

TIDMARSH RD

Broom
Copse

PURLEY RISE

BERE COURT RD

Croft
House

Further
Moor
Copse

Mosshall
Wood

2

Coll

River Pang

Herridge's
Copse

SULHAM LA

Winloed

Sulham
Wood

Gregory's Hill

The Old
Rectory

75

Bartholomew's
Bottom
Plantation

Bere Leys

THE STREET

Berks Circular Routes

TIDMARSH LA

Tidmarsh

PH

Peatpits
Wood

Sulham

Sulham
Wood

1

Glade
House

Kennels

Mayden
Farm

MANOR FARM LA

Tidmarsh
Court

Tidmarsh
Grange

Oaklands
Farm

Sch

Sulham
House

Furtherfield
Shaw

A340

Park
Wood

Sulham
Farm

74

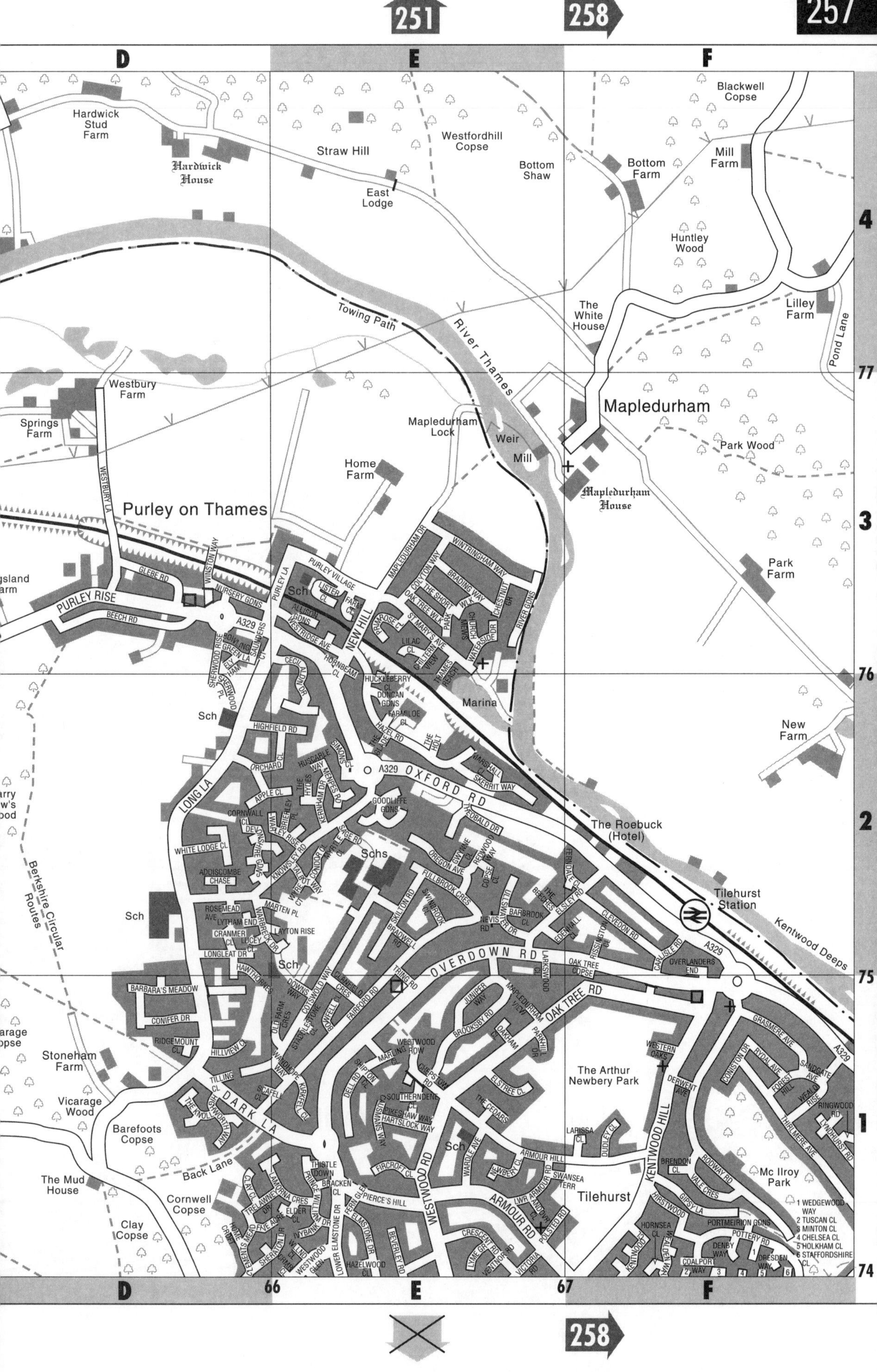

D   E   F

4

77

Mapledurham

3

Purley on Thames

76

2

75

1

74

Hardwick Stud Farm
Hardwick House
Straw Hill
Westfordhill Copse
East Lodge
Bottom Shaw
Bottom Farm
Blackwell Copse
Mill Farm
Huntley Wood
Lilley Farm
Pond Lane
The White House
Towing Path
River Thames
Westbury Farm
Springs Farm
Mapledurham Lock
Weir
Mill
Park Wood
Home Farm
Mapledurham House
Park Farm
Westbury La
Island Farm
Purley Rise
Glebe Rd
Beech Rd
Nursery Gdns
Williston Way
Purley La
Purley Village
A329
New Hill
Mapledurham Dr
Sch
Marina
New Farm
Sherwood Rise
Green La
Sch
Highfield Rd
Orchard
Long La
Apple Cl
Cornwall Cl
White Lodge Cl
Addiscombe Chase
Rosemead Ave
Cranmer Cl
Lytham End
Layton Rise
Longleat Dr
Sch
A329
OXFORD RD
Goodliffe Gdns
The Holt
Skerritt Way
The Roebuck (Hotel)
Copse End
Kentwood Deeps
Tilehurst Station
Overlanders End
Carrisle Rd
Clevedon Rd
Barbara's Meadow
Conifer Dr
Ridgemount Cl
Hillview
Stoneham Farm
Vicarage Wood
Barefoots Copse
Back Lane
DARK LA
Tilling Cl
Berkshire Circular Routes
The Mud House
Cornwell Copse
Clay Copse
Garage Copse
OVERDOWN RD
Juniper Way
Mapledurham View
Oak Tree Copse
OAK TREE RD
Grasmere Ave
Rydal Ave
Sandgate
A329
Ringwood Rd
Weald Rise
The Arthur Newbery Park
Kentwood Hill
Mc Ilroy Park
Tilehurst
Westwood Rd
ARMOUR RD
Armour Hill
Swansea
Vale Cres
Bodway Rd
Portmeirion Gdns
Pottery Rd
Denby Way
Dresden Way
Hornsea Cl
Coalport Way
1 Wedgewood Way
2 Tuscan Cl
3 Minton Cl
4 Chelsea Cl
5 Holkham Cl
6 Staffordshire Cl

257
252

A
B
C
Trench Green
Pithouse Farm
Greendene Farm
Curs Copse
Chazey Heath
Newell's Copse
Golf Course
Tokers Green
Dysons Wood Farm
Tokers Green Farm
Tanners Lane Farm
Fox Hill Farm
Middle Farm
Pack Saddle Inn (PH)
Page's Shaw
Farthingworth Green
Noke End Shaw
Rose Farm
Shipnell's Cottages
Hemdean Bottom
Sandy Hill
Blagrave Farm
Grain Store
Chazey Wood
King's Hill
Gravel Hill
Caversham Heights
Chazey Farm
The Chase
The Fishery
St Mary's Island
River Thames
Poplar Island
Appletree Eyot
Upper Large
Towing Path
Coombe Bank
Thames Side Promenade
Rivermead Leisure Centre
Allot Gdns
READING
Little John's Farm
Reading West Junction
SHEEPWAYS LA
ROKEBY DR
TOKERS GREEN RD
KIDMORE RD
UPPER WOODCOTE RD
WOODCOTE RD
ST PETER'S HILL
The Warren
OXFORD RD
PORTMAN RD
RICHFIELD AVE
4
77
3
76
2
75
1
74
68
69
70

257

253
260

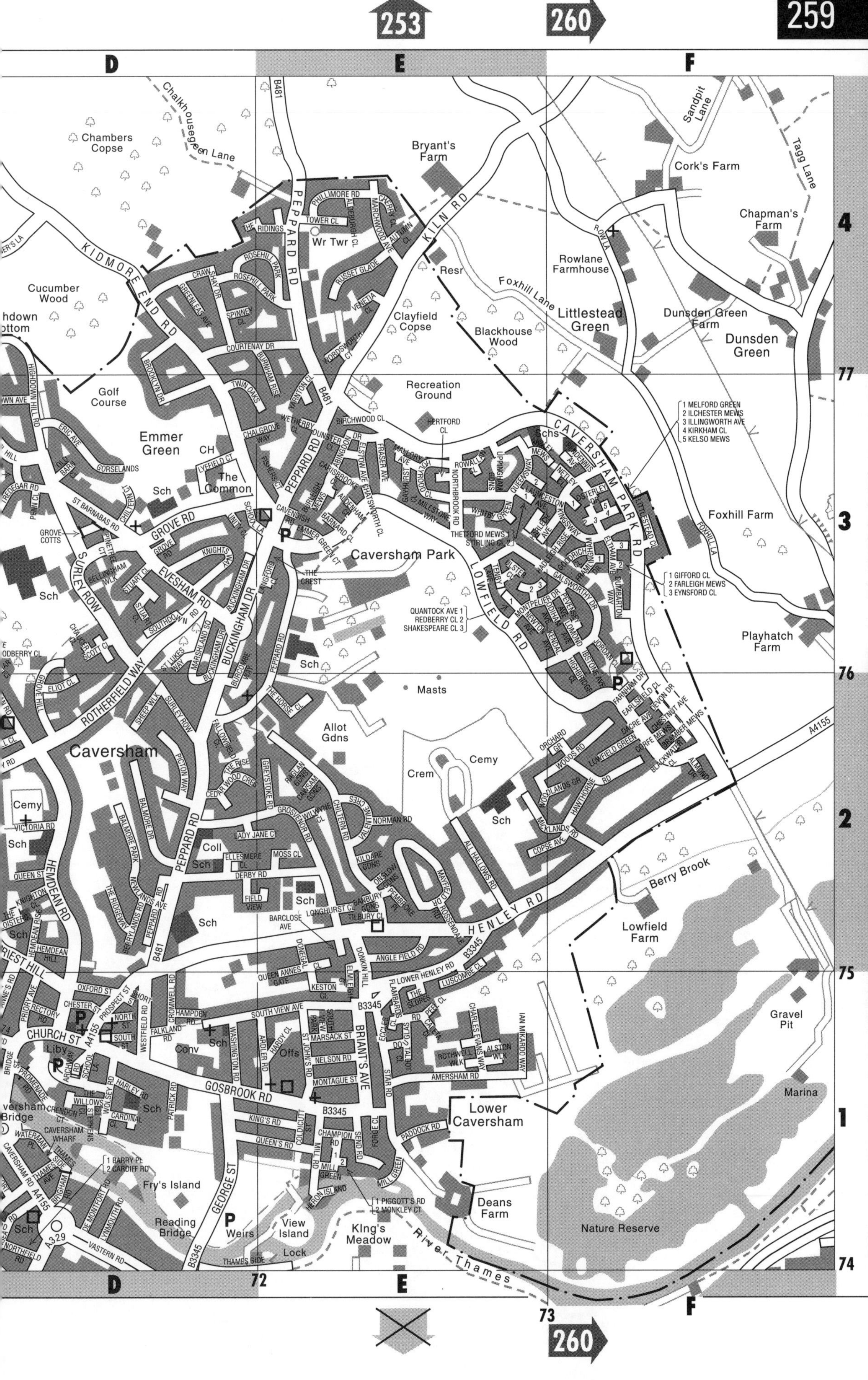
D
E
F
4
77
3
76
2
75
1
74
72
73
Chambers Copse
Chalkhousegreen Lane
Bryant's Farm
Sandpit Lane
Cork's Farm
Tagg Lane
Chapman's Farm
KIDMORE END RD
PEPPARD RD
KILN RD
Wr Twr
Resr
Rowlane Farmhouse
Foxhill Lane
Littlestead Green
Dunsden Green Farm
Dunsden Green
Cucumber Wood
Clayfield Copse
Blackhouse Wood
Golf Course
Recreation Ground
Emmer Green
The Common
CAVERSHAM PARK RD
1 MELFORD GREEN
2 ILCHESTER MEWS
3 ILLINGWORTH AVE
4 KIRKHAM CL
5 KELSO MEWS
Foxhill Farm
Caversham Park
1 GIFFORD CL
2 FARLEIGH MEWS
3 EYNSFORD CL
LOWFIELD RD
QUANTOCK AVE 1
REDBERRY CL 2
SHAKESPEARE CL 3
Playhatch Farm
Masts
Allot Gdns
Cemy
Crem
Caversham
HENLEY RD
Berry Brook
Lowfield Farm
Gravel Pit
Marina
Lower Caversham
Deans Farm
Fry's Island
Reading Bridge
Weirs
View Island
King's Meadow
Lock
River Thames
Nature Reserve
GOSBROOK RD
CHURCH ST
BRIANT'S AVE
GEORGE ST
1 BARRY PL
2 CARDIFF RD
1 PIGGOTT'S RD
2 MONKLEY CT

260

259
254

A
B
C
4
3
2
1
77
76
75
74
74
75
76
Hampstead Farm
Bint's Farm
Round Wood
The Firs
Ash Copse
Dunsden Green
Dunsden Farmhouse
GRAVEL RD
HAMPSTEAD HILL
A4155
HENLEY RD
Hampstead Bottom
Spanhill Copse
The Warren
The Lynch
Hallsmead Ait
Buck Ait
THAMES DR
Berry Brook
SPAN HILL
St Patrick's Bridge
MILESTONE AVE
The Flowing Spring (PH)
Botany Bay
SPRING LA
Towing Path
River Thames
Chalk Pit
Play Hatch
FOXHILL LA
FOXHILL CL
A4155
PLAYHATCH RD
B478
PH
Sonning Eye
Broadmoor Lane
Gravel Works
Marsh Lane
Hotel
Frizers Farm
Sonning Bridge
Aquatic Research Centre
Sonning
Hotel
OLD WELL CT
Mill
THAMES ST
HIGH ST
CHARVIL LA
Weirs
Sonning Lock
B4446 PEARSON RD
Sonning Farm
Holme Park
Sch
LITTLE GLEBE
GARDE RD
GLEBE LA
PADDICK CL
HAWTHORN WAY
BATH RD
Sch
PARKWAY DR
OLD BATH RD
Sonning Golf Course
SONNING LA
HOLMEMOOR DR
POUND LA
Nature Reserve
CH
Duffields Bridge
Holme Park Farm
HOLME PARK FARM LA
BATH RD
WEST DR
MUSTARD LA
COPSE MEAD
THAMES VALLEY BUSINESS PARK
Big Gogs
B4446
SONNING MEADOWS
OLD BATH RD
Buttshill Bridge
ALDERLEY CL
DUFFIELD RD
SOUTH DR
Sch
A4(T)
WESTERN AVE
TIVERTON CL
BUTTS HILL RD
TOWNSIDE
SHEPHERDS HILL
LONDON RD
WARREN RD
RYCROFT CL
FRAMPTON CL
RAVENSBOURNE DR
ROTHWELL GDNS
RADCOT CL
GOODSTOW CL
ROCHESTER AVE
BINGLEY GR
TELFORD CRES
WALMER RD
HANWOOD CL
WYNDHAM CRES
Works

259

USER'S NOTES

EXPLANATION OF THE STREET INDEX REFERENCE SYSTEM

Street names are listed alphabetically and show the locality, the page number and a reference to the square in which the name falls on the map page.

Example: Divinity Rd.   Oxon...142   A4

Divinity Rd   This is the full street name, which may have been abbreviated on the map.

Oxon   This is the abbreviation for the town, village or locality in which the street falls.

142   This is the page number of the map on which the street name appears.

A4   The letter and figure indicate the square on the map in which the centre of the street falls. The square can be found at the junction of the vertical column carrying the appropriate letter and the horizontal row carrying the appropriate figure.

ABBREVIATIONS USED IN THE INDEX
Road Names

Approach	App	Lane	La
Avenue	Ave	North	N
Boulevard	Bvd	Orchard	Orch
Broadway	Bwy	Parade	Par
By-Pass	By-Ps	Passage	Pas
Causeway	Cswy	Place	Pl
Common	Comm	Pleasant	Plea
Corner	Cnr	Precinct	Prec
Cottages	Cotts	Promenade	Prom
Court	Ct	Road	Rd
Crescent	Cres	South	S
Drive	Dri	Square	Sq
Drove	Dro	Street,Saint	St
East	E	Terrace	Terr
Gardens	Gdns	Walk	Wlk
Grove	Gr	West	W
Heights	Hts	Yard	Yd

Key to abbreviations of Town, Village and Rural locality names used in the index of street names.

Locality	Abbreviation	Page	Grid
Abingdon	Abing	180	B4
Adderbury	Adde	23	D2
Adlestrop	Adle	40	B1
Aldworth	Aldw	247	F2
Alvescot	Alve	133	E3
Ambrosden	Ambr	81	E2
Appleton	Apple	158	A4
Ardington	Ard	215	F3
Ascott-under-Wychwood	As u Wy	71	E1
Ashbury	Ashb	228	A4
Aston	Aston	135	F2
Aston Rowant	Ast R	167	E1
Aston Tirrold	Ast T	237	F4
Avon Dassett	Av Da	2	C4
Aynho	Ayn	35	E4
Bampton	Bamp	134	C2
Banbury	Banb	16	B4
Barford St Michael	B St M	32	C3
Barton-on-the-Heath	B on H	26	C3
Baydon	Bayd	245	F1
Beacon's Bottom	B Bot	189	E2
Beckley	Beck	111	D2
Begbroke	Begb	108	A4
Benson	Bens	204	A2
Berinsfield	Berin	182	B3
Berrick Salome	Ber S	184	A1
Bicester	Bice	65	F2
Bishopstone	Bish	227	E2
Bix	Bix	243	E4
Black Bourton	B Bou	133	F3
Blackthorn	Bktn	82	A2
Bladon	Blad	91	E1
Bledington	Bled	54	B1
Bledlow Ridge	Bled R	189	F4
Bletchingdon	Bletch	93	D4
Blewbury	Blew	237	D4
Bloxham	Blox	21	E3
Bodicote	Bod	22	B4
Bourton	Bourt	209	D2
Brackley	Brac	24	A4
Brightwell Baldwin	Br Ba	185	D1
Brightwell-cum-Sotwell	Br-c-S	202	B1
Brill	Bri	98	A1
Brize Norton	Br No	116	B2
Broughton	Brou	15	E1
Buckland	Buckl	154	C1
Bucknell	Buck	65	D4
Burford	Burf	100	C3
Buscot	Busc	171	D4
Carterton	Cart	115	F2
Cassington	Cass	107	E1
Caversham	Caver	259	D2
Chacombe	Chac	10	C2
Chadlington	Chadl	57	D1
Chalgrove	Chalg	184	C3
Charlbury	Charl	73	E2
Charlton-on-Otmoor	Ch-on-O	95	D2
Charney Bassett	Ch Ba	176	A1
Chastleton	Chas	40	B4
Checkendon	Check	241	E2
Chesterton	Chest	79	F4
Childrey	Child	213	E2
Chilson	Chils	71	F2
Chilton	Chil	235	F4
Chinnor	Chin	168	B4
Chipping Norton	Ch No	42	C1
Chipping Warden	Ch Wa	5	F3
Cholsey	Chol	221	D1
Church Westcote	Ch We	68	B3
Churchill	Churc	55	F3
Clanfield	Clan	152	C4
Claydon	Clay	1	B1
Clifton Hampden	Cl Ham	181	E2
Coleshill	Coles	191	D4
Combe	Combe	90	A3
Compton Wynyates	Co Wy	12	B4
Cornwell	Corn	41	E2
Cottisford	Cott	37	F2
Crawley	Crawl	103	F2
Cropredy	Cro	4	C1
Croughton	Crou	36	B4
Crowmarsh Gifford	Cr Gif	221	F4
Cuddesdon	Cudd	144	A2
Culham	Culh	180	A1
Cumnor	Cumn	139	E3
Curbridge	Curb	117	F3
Cutteslowe	Cutte	109	D1
Deddington	Dedd	33	F2
Denchworth	Dench	196	A2
Didcot	Didc	218	C4
Dorchester	Dorch	182	B1
Drayton	Dra	15	E4
Drayton	Dray	179	D1
Drayton St Leonard	D St L	183	D3
Ducklington	Duck	118	A2
Duns Tew	D Tew	47	E3
East Challow	E Cha	214	A3
East Garston	East G	246	B1
East Hagbourne	E Hag	218	C3
East Hanney	E Hann	197	D3
East Hendred	E Hen	216	C4
Eastleach Martin	Ea Mar	131	D4
Elsfield	Elsf	110	B1
Enstone	Enst	58	C3
Epwell	Epw	13	D3
Ewelme	Ewel	204	C2
Eynsham	Eyns	120	C4
Faringdon	Far	172	C2
Farnborough (Warks)	Farn	3	F4
Farnborough (Berks)	Farnb	233	F1
Fawley	Faw	226	B1
Fernham	Fern	193	D2
Fifield	Fif	69	E1
Filkins	Filk	132	B3
Finmere	Fin	39	E4
Finstock	Fins	88	B3
Forest Hill	For H	125	F2
Freeland	Free	106	A4
Fringford	Frin	52	B3
Fritwell	Frit	49	F4
Fulbrook	Fulb	100	C4
Fyfield	Fyf	157	E1
Garford	Garf	177	E3
Garsington	Gars	143	F1
Godington	Gdtn	53	F2
Goring	Gori	249	E3
Great Barrington	Gt Bar	99	E4
Great Bourton	Gt Bo	9	E4
Great Coxwell	Gt Cox	192	B4
Great Haseley	G Has	164	C4
Great Milton	G Mil	145	E1
Great Rollright	Gr Ro	29	D2
Great Tew	Gt Tew	45	E4
Grove	Grove	196	C1
Haddenham	Hadd	130	C3
Hailey	Hail	104	A3
Hampton Poyle	H Poy	93	D2
Hanwell	Hanw	8	C2
Hardwick	Hard	51	E4
Hardwick	Hardw	136	C4
Harwell	Harw	217	F4
Henley-on-Thames	Hen-on-T	244	B1
Hethe	Hethe	52	A4
Highworth	Highw	190	A3
Hinton Waldrist	H Wald	155	F2
Holton	Holt	126	B1
Hook Norton	Ho No	30	A4
Horley	Horl	8	A2
Hornton	Horn	7	E4
Horspath	Hors	143	E3
Horton-cum-Studley	Hor-c-S	111	F3
Ibstone	Ibst	207	F4
Ickford	Ick	128	A2
Idbury	Idb	69	D2
Ilmer	Ilm	149	F4
Islip	Islip	109	F4
Kelmscot	Kelms	151	E2
Kencot	Kenc	132	C3
Kennington	Kenn	141	F1
Kiddington	Kidd	60	A1
Kidlington	Kidl	92	C1
Kidmore End	K End	252	B2
Kingham	King	55	D2
Kings Sutton	K Sut	23	F3
Kingston Bagpuize	K Bag	156	C1
Kingston Lisle	K Lis	212	A2
Kirtlington	Kirt	77	F2
Lambourn	Lamb	229	E1
Langford	Lang	132	B1
Launton	Laun	66	B1
Leafield	Leaf	86	C2
Lechlade	Lech	150	B2
Letcombe Bassett	Let B	231	F4
Lewknor	Lewk	187	D4
Little Compton	Li Co	26	C1
Little Coxwell	Li Cox	192	C4
Little Faringdon	Li Far	150	C4
Little Milton	L Mil	164	A3
Little Tew	Li Tew	45	D3
Littleworth	Little	173	F4
Long Compton	Lo Co	27	F3
Long Crendon	L Cre	129	D3
Long Hanborough	Lo Han	90	B1
Long Wittenham	Lo Wit	201	E4
Longcot	Long	192	B1
Longworth	Longw	156	B2
Lower Heyford	Lo Hey	62	B3
Lower Odington	Lo Od	54	A4
Ludgershall	Lud	98	B4
Lyneham	Lyne	70	C3
Mapledurham	Maple	257	F3
Marcham	March	178	B3
Marsh Gibbon	M Gib	67	F2
Marston	Mars	123	F3
Merton	Mert	95	E4
Middle Barton	Mi Bar	46	C1
Middleton Cheney	Mid Ch	11	D1
Middleton Stoney	Mi Sto	64	A2
Milcombe	Milc	21	D1
Milton (Abingdon)	Mil	199	E3
Milton (Banbury)	Milt	22	B2
Milton under Wychwood	M u Wy	85	D4
Minster Lovell	M Lov	102	C1
Mixbury	Mix	38	B4
Mollington	Moll	4	A2
Moulsford	Moul	238	C2
Murcott	Mur	95	F2
Nettlebed	Nett	224	B1
Newton Purcell	Nwtn P	39	D1
Noke	Noke	110	B4
North Aston	N Ast	48	A3
North Hinksey Village	N Hink	140	C4
North Leigh	N Lei	105	D4
North Moreton	N Mor	219	F4
North Newington	N New	15	D2
Northmoor	Nrthm	138	B1
Nuneham Courtenay	Nu Cou	161	F2
Oddington	Odd	94	C1
Over Norton	O Nor	42	C3
Oxford	Oxon	123	F1
Pangbourne	Pangb	256	B3
Piddington	Pidd	97	F4
Poundon	Pndn	67	F4
Preston Bissett	Pres B	53	F4
Purley on Thames	Purl	257	D3
Radley	Radl	160	C2
Ramsden	Rams	88	A2
Ratley	Rat	2	A2
Reading	Read	258	B1
Rotherfield Peppard	R Pep	252	C4
Salford	Sal	41	F3
Sandford St Martin	S St M	46	B1
Sandford-on-Thames	Sa-on-T	161	D4
Shabbington	Shab	128	B2
Shalstone	Shal	25	F3
Shellingford	Shell	194	A4
Shenington	Shen	6	C1
Shilton	Shilt	115	D3
Shiplake	Shipl	254	C1
Shipton under Wychwood	S u Wy	85	F4
Shipton-on-Cherwell	Sh-on-C	92	A3
Shotteswell	Shot	8	B4
Shrivenham	Shrive	209	D4
Shutford	Shut	14	A3
Sibford Ferris	Si Fe	19	D4
Sibford Gower	Si Go	19	D4
Sonning	Sonn	260	C2
Sonning Common	S Com	252	C3
Souldern	Soul	35	F2
South Hinksey	S Hink	141	E3
South Leigh	S Lei	119	E3
South Moreton	S Mor	219	F3
South Newington	S New	31	F4
South Stoke	S Sto	239	D2
Southrop	Srop	131	D2
Sparsholt	Spars	212	C2
Spelsbury	Spel	72	C4
Stadhampton	Stadh	163	E1
Standlake	Stand	137	E2
Stanford in the Vale	S in V	194	C4
Stanton Harcourt	Sta Ha	137	F4
Stanton St John	St S J	125	F4
Steeple Aston	Ste As	62	A4
Steventon	Steve	198	C2
Stoke Lyne	S Lyn	51	D3
Stoke Row	St Row	241	F2
Stoke Talmage	Sto Ta	165	F2
Stokenchurch	Skch	188	C3
Stonesfield	Stone	89	E4
Stonor	Ston	225	F3
Stratton Audley	S Adly	52	B1
Streatley	Stre	249	D4
Sunningwell	Sunn	159	F3
Sutton Courtenay	Sut C	200	A4
Swalcliffe	Swal	19	F4
Swerford	Swer	30	C2
Swinbrook	Swin	101	F3
Sydenham	Syd	167	E4
Tackley	Tack	77	E3
Tadmarton	Tad	20	B4
Taynton	Tayn	100	A4
Tetsworth	Tet	166	A4
Thame	Tha	147	F4
Tiddington	Tidd	145	F4
Tidmarsh	Tidm	256	B1
Tingewick	Ting	39	F3
Towersey	Tow	148	C4
Turweston	Turw	24	B4
Uffington	Uff	211	E4
Upper Arncott	U Arn	96	C4
Upper Heyford	Up Hey	62	C4
Upton	Upt	218	B1
Wallingford	Wall	221	D3
Wantage	Want	214	C2
Warborough	Warb	203	D4
Wardington	Ward	5	F1
Wargrave	Warg	255	E1
Warkworth	Wark	17	E3
Warmington	Warm	3	D2
Watchfield	Watch	191	F1
Waterperry	Wtpy	127	D1
Watlington	Watl	186	B1
Wendlebury	Wend	80	A2
West Hagbourne	W Hag	218	B2
West Hanney	W Hann	196	C3
West Ilsley	West I	235	D1
Westbury	West	25	D2
Weston-on-the-Green	W-on-G	79	D1
Wheatley	Wheat	144	A4
Whichford	Whi	18	A1
Whitchurch	Whitc	256	B4
Wigginton	Wigg	31	D4
Witney	Witn	104	B1
Woodcote	Woodc	240	B1
Woodstock	Wood	91	D3
Woolstone	Wool	211	D2
Wootton (Kidlington)	Woott	75	F3
Wootton (Oxford)	Woot	159	D4
Worminghall	Worm	127	F3
Wormleighton	Wor	1	A4
Wroxton	Wrox	15	D4
Wytham	Wyth	122	A3
Yarnton	Yarn	108	A3

edford Cl.Banb

Burchester Cl.Banb

Cumberland Rd. Oxon

271

illcraft Rd. St S J

Lammas Cl. Abing

craft Rd. St S J 125 E4
iat Fields. Dray 179 D1
iers Cl. Sut C 200 A4
sborough Cl. Oxon 142 A2
sborough Rd. Oxon 142 A2
side Cl. Banb 16 C2
lside Cl. U Arn 96 C4
lside Rd. Mi Bar 46 C1
'side. Harw 217 D2
side. Whitc 256 B4
top Gdns. Islip 93 F1
top Rd. Caver 258 B3
top. L Cre 129 E3
view Cl. Purl 257 D1
view Rd. Abing 159 F1
view Rd. Oxon 123 D1
werke. Chin 168 B3
y Lawn Ct. Ch No 42 C2
yard Barns. Sut C 200 A4
on Rd. Banb 16 A3
ksey Hill. S Hink 141 D2
ton Hill. Bish 227 D2
ton Rd. H Wald 156 A2
ton Rd. Longw 156 A2
ton Springs. Bish 227 D2
stwood. Read 257 F1
kins. Want 214 A3
hman Dr. Ch No 42 C2
nercroft Ct. Wall 221 D3
nercroft Rd. Wall 221 D4
nercroft. Chol 220 B3
ercroft. S Mor 220 B3
e Mews. Abing 179 F3
et Wood. Charl 73 D2
bbs Cl. Abing 180 A4
son Rd. Cutte 123 D4
cker Bench. Bish 227 E2
ckets Cl. Whitc 250 C2
ckmore St. Oxon 142 B2
garth Pl. Abing 179 F3
g End. Blox 21 F2
g End. Ch Wa 5 F3
born Hill. Let B 231 E4
combe La. Ber S 183 E3
ford Rd. Witn 117 F4
s Cl. Witn 118 B4
kam Cl. Read 257 F1
and Cl. Chin 168 B4
and Pl. Oxon 142 C4
and Rd. Abing 160 A1
andridge La. Ston 207 E2
andridge La. Ston 225 F4
ands Rise. K Sut 23 F2
ey Cres. Oxon 124 C2
iers Cl. Syd 167 E4
iers Cl. Tha 147 F4
iers Cres. Mi Bar 60 C4
ington. L Cre 129 D1
ow Furlong. Cass 107 E1
ow Way. Ayn 35 E4
ow Way. Child 213 E2
ow Way. Oxon 142 B3
oway Hill. Co Wy 12 A1
oway La. Co Wy 12 A1
oway Rd The. Gt Cox 192 A4
oway Rd. Wheat 144 A4
oway The. Harw 217 F3
oway The. Moll 4 A2
y Cl. Bice 65 F3
y Cl. Kidl 108 C4
y Cl. R Pep 242 C3
ybush Rd. Cart 115 E1
ybush Rd. Ho No 30 A4
ybush Row. Oxon 123 D1
n Sq. Bice 65 F3
n Way. Bice 65 F3
ne Park Farm La.
Sonn 260 B1
nemoor Dr. Sonn 260 C1
nlea Rd. Gori 249 E3
way Rd. Witn 118 A4
The. Abing 179 F4
The. Moll 3 F2
The. Purl 257 E2
Weer Cl. Cutte 109 D1
oake Rd. Oxon 124 B2
rood Cl. Caver 259 E3
well Cl. Abing 160 B1
well St. Oxon 123 E1
e Cl. Cart 115 E1
e Cl. Cutte 122 B4
e Cl. Kidl 92 C1
e Cl. Woot 159 D3
e Croft. Read 257 D1
e Farm Cl. Ambr 81 E2
e Farm Cl. E Hen 216 B4
e Farm Cl. S u Wy 85 E4
e Farm Ct. Adde 23 D2
e Farm. Cr Gif 221 F4
efield Cl. Skch 188 C2
eleaze Rd. Watch 209 F4
estall Cl. N Hink 122 A1
estead Cres. Up Hey 63 D4
estead Rd. Banb 16 C1
estead The. Blad 91 E2
estead The. Kidl 108 B4
ey La. Chol 220 C1
ybottom La. Abing 159 D3

Honeyham Cl. Br No 116 B2
Honeysuckle Cl. Bice 65 F3
Honeysuckle Gr. Gars 143 D1
Honor Cl. Kidl 108 C4
Hook End La. Stre 249 D1
Hook Norton Rd. Si Fe 19 D4
Hookend La. Check 251 E4
Hop Gdns. Hen-on-T 244 B1
Hopcraft Cl. U Arn 96 C4
Hopcraft La. Dedd 33 F2
Hopton Rd. Tha 130 A1
Horley Path Rd. Wrox 8 A1
Horley Path Rd. Wrox 15 D4
Horn Hill Rd. Adde 22 C2
Horn Hill. B St M 32 C3
Horn La. Adle 40 A3
Horn La. E Hen 216 B3
Hornbeam Cl. Banb 16 A3
Hornbeam Cl. Purl 257 E3
Hornbeam Dr. Gars 143 D1
Hornbeam Rd. Bice 65 F3
Hornsea Cl. Read 257 F1
Hornton Hollow. Blox 21 E2
Horse Cl The. Caver 259 E2
Horse Close Cotts. G Has 164 B4
Horse Fair. Banb 16 B3
Horse Fair. Ch No 42 C2
Horse Fair. Dedd 33 F2
Horse Shoe La. Chadl 72 A4
Horsecroft. S in V 194 C4
Horseman Cl. Mars 124 A3
Horsemere La. Cass 107 E1
Horsepond Rd. K End 252 A3
Horseshoe La. Woot 75 F2
Horseshoe Pk. Pangb 256 B3
Horseshoe Rd. Bled R 189 E4
Horseshoe Rd. Pangb 256 B3
Horseshoes La. Bens 203 F2
Horsham Cl. Banb 8 C1
Horspath Driftway. Oxon 142 C4
Horspath Rd. Oxon 142 C3
Horton Ave. Tha 148 A4
Horton Cl. Tha 148 A4
Horton La. Milc 21 D1
Horton View. Banb 16 B2
Horwood Cl. Oxon 124 B2
Hosker Cl. Oxon 125 D2
Hound Cl. Abing 160 B1
Howard Ave. Grove 196 C1
Howard Cornish Rd.
March 178 B4
Howard Rd. Banb 16 C3
Howard St. Oxon 142 A3
Howe Cl. Wheat 144 A4
Howe Rd. Watl 206 B4
Howgate Dr. Gori 249 E4
Howland Rd. Tha 148 A3
Hoyle Cl. Witn 104 A2
Huckleberry Cl. Purl 257 E2
Hudleston Ave. Bens 204 B1
Hudson St. Bice 65 E2
Hudson St. Dedd 33 F2
Hugh Allen Cres. Oxon 123 F2
Hughes Cl. Charl 73 E1
Hughes Cres. Long 192 B2
Humber Cl. Didc 201 D1
Humber Cl. Want 214 C3
Humber St. Blox 21 F2
Humber Wlk. Banb 15 F4
Humfrey Rd. Oxon 124 C2
Humphries Cl. Cart 115 F2
Hunsdon Rd. Oxon 142 A2
Hunt Cl. Bice 65 F1
Hunt Rd. Tha 148 A4
Hunt's Cl. Stone 89 E4
Hunter Cl. Abing 160 A2
Hunter Cl. Oxon 142 C3
Huntercombe End La. Nett 224 A2
Hunters Chase. Caver 258 C3
Hunters Cl. Grove 196 B1
Hunters Field. S in V 194 C4
Hunters Piece. Bourt 209 D1
Hunters Point. Chin 168 B3
Hurdeswell. Lo Han 90 A1
Hurdlers Green. Watl 186 A1
Hurst Cl. Wall 221 E3
Hurst La. Cumn 140 A3
Hurst La. Free 106 A4
Hurst Rise Rd. N Hink 140 B4
Hurst St. Oxon 141 F4
Huscarle Way. Purl 257 E2
Hutchcomb Rd. N Hink 140 B4
Huxley Cl. Bice 65 E2
Huxley Cl. Woot 159 D3
Hyde Copse. March 178 B4
Hyde Gr. Blox 21 E2
Hyde Pl. Abing 179 E3
Hyde Rd. Dench 196 A3
Hyde The. Abing 179 E3
Hydes The. Purl 257 E2
Hydrangea Wlk. Banb 9 D1
Hythe Bridge St. Oxon 123 D1

Ian Mikardo Way. Caver 259 E1
Ibstone Ave. Caver 259 F3
Ibstone Rd. Skch 188 B2
Ickford Rd. Shab 128 B1
Ickford Rd. Tidd 145 F4

Ickford Rd. Worm 127 F3
Ickleton Rd. E Cha 214 A2
Ickleton Rd. Want 214 A2
Icknield Cl. Ast R 168 A2
Icknield Cl. Didc 200 B1
Icknield La. Want 214 C2
Icknield Pl. Gori 249 E4
Icknield Rd. Gori 249 E4
Icknield Way. Bish 227 E2
Icknield Way. Bish 227 E2
Idbury Cl. Witn 117 E4
Idstone Hill. Ashb 228 A2
Idstone Rd. Ashb 228 A3
Iffley Rd. Oxon 141 F4
Iffley Turn. Oxon 142 A3
Ilchester Mews. Caver 259 F3
Ilex Cl. S Com 252 C2
Ilges La. Chol 221 D1
Ilkley Rd. Caver 258 C2
Illingworth Ave. Caver 259 F3
Ilsley Cl. S Com 252 C3
Ingham La. Watl 186 A1
Ingle Cl. Oxon 124 A2
Inglewood Cl. S Com 252 C3
Inkerman Cl. Abing 159 E1
Innsworth Rd. Cart 115 F2
Inott Furze. Oxon 142 B4
Ireton Cl. Chalg 184 B3
Ireton Ct. Tha 129 F1
Iron Down Hill. B St M 32 B2
Iron Down Hill. S New 31 F2
Ironstones. Banb 16 A4
Isis Ave. Bice 65 D1
Isis Cl. Abing 160 B1
Isis Cl. Lo Han 106 A4
Islip Rd. Bletch 93 D4
Islip Rd. Cutte 123 D4
Islsley Rd. Oxon 124 C2
Itchen Ct. Didc 201 D2
Ivatt Wlk. Banb 16 C4
Ivy La. Moll 4 A2
Ivy La. Oxon 124 B2
Ivybank. Read 257 E1
Ivydene Rd. Read 258 B1

Jack Straw's La. Oxon 124 A2
Jackdaw La. Oxon 141 F4
Jackies La. Wheat 144 B4
Jackman Cl. Abing 180 A4
Jackson Cl. Cart 115 E1
Jackson Dr. Kenn 141 F1
Jackson Rd. Bled 54 B1
Jackson Rd. Cutte 109 D1
Jacobs Cl. Witn 104 A1
Jacobs Yd. Mi Bar 60 C4
James Ct. Clan 152 C4
James St. Oxon 141 F4
James Wolfe Rd. Oxon 142 C4
Jane Seaman Ct. Sa-on-T 142 C1
Japonica Cl. Bice 65 F3
Japonica Wlk. Banb 9 D1
Jarn Way. Woot 140 B1
Jarvis La. Bice 66 A1
Jasmine Cl. Oxon 142 C2
Javelin Way. Bens 204 B2
Jaynes Cl. Banb 16 B1
Jefferson Way. Tha 148 A4
Jeffersons Piece. Charl 73 E3
Jemmetts Cl. Dorch 182 B1
Jennings La. Harw 217 F4
Jericho St. Oxon 123 D2
Jerome Way. Sh-on-C 92 B3
Jersey Dr. Banb 9 D1
Jersey Rd. Oxon 142 A2
Jervis Cl. Mi Bar 60 C4
Jespers Hill. Far 173 D2
Jesse's La. L Cre 129 E3
Jessops Cl. Mars 123 F3
Jeune St. Oxon 123 F1
Jeune St. Oxon 141 F4
John Buchan Rd. Oxon 124 A3
John Garne Way. Oxon 124 A1
John Lopes Rd. Eyns 120 C4
John Mason Rd. Abing 180 A4
John Morris Rd. Abing 179 F3
John Piers La. S Hink 141 E3
John Snow Pl. Oxon 124 C2
Johnston's Way. Ch No 42 C1
Johnstone Pl. Wall 221 E4
Jordan Cl. Caver 259 F3
Jordan Hill. Cutte 109 D1
Josey Cl. S Com 252 C3
Jourdain Rd. Oxon 142 C2
Jowett Wlk. Oxon 123 E1
Joyce's Rd. S in V 194 B4
Jubilee Cl. Ste As 62 A4
Jubilee Cotts. Ard 215 F3
Jubilee Ct. Banb 16 B3
Jubilee La. M u Wy 85 D4
Jubilee Rd. Skch 188 C2
Jubilee Way. Didc 219 D4
Judd's Cl. Witn 118 B4
Judges Cl. Kidl 108 C4
Junction Rd. Banb 16 C3
Junction Rd. Churc 55 F2
Junction Rd. Oxon 142 B3
Juniper Cl. Banb 9 D1
Juniper Dr. Oxon 142 C1

Juniper Way. Read 257 E1
Juxon St. Oxon 123 D2

Kames Cl. Oxon 142 A3
Katchside. Sut C 199 F3
Katherine's Wlk. Lech 150 B2
Keats Cl. Bice 65 D2
Keats Rd. Banb 16 A2
Keble Cl. Lech 150 B3
Keble Rd. Bice 65 F2
Keble Rd. Oxon 123 E2
Kedleston Rise. Banb 16 C1
Keens La. Chin 168 B3
Keeys Cl. Mi Sto 50 B2
Kelburne Rd. Oxon 142 A2
Kelham Hall Dr. Wheat 144 A4
Kelly's Rd. Wheat 143 F4
Kelmscott Cl. Caver 258 C2
Kelso Mews. Caver 259 F3
Kelvedon Way. Caver 258 C3
Kemps Rd. Adde 23 D3
Kempson Cres. Oxon 142 A1
Kempster Cl. Abing 180 A4
Kendal Ave. Caver 259 F3
Kendal Cres. Cutte 109 D1
Kendal Piece. Charl 73 E2
Kenhill Rd. Shen 6 B1
Kenilworth Ave. Oxon 142 A4
Kenilworth Rd. Cumn 139 F2
Kenilworth Way. Banb 15 F3
Kenley Ave. Cart 115 F2
Kennedy Cl. Oxon 142 C4
Kennedy Cres. Chol 220 C1
Kennedy Dr. Pangb 256 B3
Kennedy Rd. Bice 65 E1
Kennel La. Ch No 42 A1
Kennel La. Steve 199 D3
Kennet Cl. Berin 182 B2
Kennet Cl. Bice 65 E1
Kennet Cl. Grove 196 B1
Kennet Rd. Abing 160 A1
Kennet Rd. Harw 217 E1
Kennett Rd. Oxon 124 B1
Kennington Rd. Kenn 141 F1
Kennington Rd. Kenn 160 C3
Kennington Rd. Radl 160 C3
Kennylands Rd. S Com 253 D2
Kensington Cl. Abing 179 F2
Kensington Cl. K Sut 23 F3
Kent Cl. Abing 180 A4
Kent Cl. Oxon 142 C2
Kenton's La. Warg 255 E4
Kentwood Cl. Chol 220 C1
Kentwood Cl. Read 257 F1
Kentwood Hill. Read 257 F1
Kenville Rd. Kenn 141 F1
Kernham Dr. Purl 257 E2
Kerry Cl. Banb 9 D1
Kersington Cres. Oxon 142 B2
Kerwood Cl. Wood 91 D4
Keston Cl. Caver 259 E1
Kestrel Cl. Cart 115 E2
Kestrel Cres. Oxon 142 B1
Kestrel Croft. Adde 23 D3
Kestrel Pl. Oxon 142 B1
Kestrel Way. Bice 81 D4
Kestrels The. Grove 196 B1
Ketchmere Cl. L Cre 129 E3
Keydale Rd. Wheat 143 F4
Keyser Rd. Bod 22 C4
Keyte's Cl. Adde 23 D2
Kibble Cl. Didc 219 D4
Kiddington Rd. Mi Bar 60 C4
Kidlington Business Park.
Kidl 92 B1
Kidlington Rd. Islip 93 F1
Kidmore End Rd. Caver 259 D4
Kidmore End Rd. Maple 259 D4
Kidmore La. K End 252 C2
Kidmore Rd. Caver 258 C3
Kilbale Cres. Banb 16 B2
Kildare Gdns. Caver 259 E2
Kilkenny La. Br No 115 F3
Kiln Cl. Sa-on-T 161 E4
Kiln La. Gars 143 E1
Kiln La. Oxon 124 C1
Kiln La. Shipl 254 B1
Kiln La. Wheat 144 A4
Kiln Rd. Caver 259 E4
Kiln Rd. Shipl 259 E4
Kimbells Cl. Shab 128 B1
Kimber Cl. Wheat 144 A4
Kimber Rd. Abing 179 E4
Kimbers Cl. Dench 196 A2
Kinecroft. Wall 221 E4
Kineton Rd. Oxon 141 E4
King Alfred Dr. Didc 200 C1
King Edward St. Oxon 123 E1
King James Way.
Hen-on-T 254 B4
King St. Oxon 123 D2
King Wlk. Didc 200 C1
King's Ave. Bice 65 E1
King's Cl. Tha 147 F4
King's Cross Rd. Cutte 123 D4
King's End. Bice 65 E1
King's Head La. Islip 93 F1
King's Head Mews. Ch No 42 C2

King's La. Long 192 A2
King's Mill La. Oxon 123 F1
King's Rd. Banb 16 A3
King's Rd. Caver 259 E1
King's Rd. Tha 148 A4
Kingfisher Cl. Abing 179 F2
Kingfisher Dr. Banb 16 C2
Kingfisher Way. Bice 81 D4
Kingfishers. Grove 214 C4
Kingham Dr. Cart 115 E1
Kingham Rd. Churc 55 F3
Kings Ave. Highw 190 A3
Kings Ave. March 178 B4
Kings Cl. Br-c-S 202 C2
Kings Cl. Hen-on-T 244 B1
Kings Cl. Let B 214 A1
Kings Cl. Worm 127 E3
Kings Farm La. Shipl 253 F3
Kings La. Harw 217 F4
Kings La. Kenc 132 B2
Kings Rd. Blox 21 E2
Kings Rd. Hen-on-T 244 B1
Kings Stile. Mid Ch 10 C1
Kings Way Dr. Kidl 109 D4
Kingsclere Rd. Bice 65 E1
Kingsey Rd. Tha 148 A4
Kingsholme Cl. E Hag 218 C3
Kingsley Rd. Bice 65 D2
Kingsmead. Lech 150 B3
Kingston Cl. Abing 179 F4
Kingston Hts. N Lei 105 D4
Kingston Rd. Oxon 123 D2
Kingstone Hill. Ast R 188 A4
Kingsway. Banb 16 A3
Kingsway. Caver 259 F3
Kingswood La. W Und 98 C3
Kinson Rd. Read 258 A1
Kipling Cl. Bice 65 E2
Kirby Cl. Mi Bar 60 C4
Kirby Rd. Ch We 68 A2
Kirk Cl. Cutte 109 D1
Kirk Cl. Kenn 160 C4
Kirkfell Cl. Read 257 E1
Kirkham Cl. Caver 259 F3
Kirtlington Rd. Up Hey 63 D4
Kit La. St Row 241 E3
Knapp Cl. Abing 179 E4
Knappe Cl. Hen-on-T 254 B4
Knapton's Croft. Lo Hey 62 B3
Knighton Cl. Caver 259 D2
Knighton Hill. Wool 210 C1
Knights Rd. Oxon 142 B1
Knights Way. Caver 259 D3
Knightsbridge La. Sto Ta 186 A3
Knoll Cl. Let B 231 F4
Knoll The. Read 257 D1
Knolles Rd. Oxon 142 B2
Knollys Cl. Abing 160 A2
Knowlands. Highw 190 A4
Knowle Cl. Caver 258 B2
Knowle La. W-on-G 79 D1
Knowsley Rd. Purl 257 E2
Kybald St. Oxon 123 E1
Kynaston Rd. Didc 218 C4
Kysbie Cl. Abing 159 F2

Laburnum Ave. Abing 159 E1
Laburnum Cl. Ambr 81 E2
Laburnum Cres. Kidl 108 C3
Laburnum Gr. Banb 16 B1
Laburnum Gr. Didc 218 C4
Laburnum Rd. N Hink 140 B4
Lacemakers. Chin 168 B3
Lacemakers. L Cre 129 E4
Lacey Dr. Tha 148 A4
Lackmore Gdns. Woodc 250 C4
Ladburn La. Shilt 115 D3
Ladder Hill. Wheat 144 A4
Ladenham Rd. Oxon 142 C2
Lady Gr. Lo Wit 201 D2
Lady Jane Ct. Caver 259 D2
Lady Wlk. Uff 211 E4
Ladygrove Paddock.
Abing 179 E3
Ladywell Cl. N Lei 105 E3
Lake Rd. E Hag 218 C3
Lake Rd. Shriv 209 E4
Lake St. Oxon 141 E3
Lake View. Cott 38 A2
Lakeside Ind Est. Stand 137 F4
Lakeside. Cutte 108 C1
Lamarsh Rd. Oxon 122 C1
Lamb La. Blad 91 D1
Lamb's Cres. Banb 16 C3
Lambe Ave. Mil 199 E2
Lambert Wlk. Tha 129 F1
Lamborough Hill. Woot 159 D3
Lambourn Rd. Oxon 142 A2
Lambourne Cres. Bice 65 F1
Lambourne Rd. S Com 252 C3
Lambrick Way. Abing 179 F2
Lambridge La. Hen-on-T 244 B2
Lambridge La. Hen-on-T 244 B2
Lambridge Wd R.
Hen-on-T 244 A2
Lambs Cl. Kidl 92 C1
Lambton Cl. Oxon 142 C3
Lammas Cl. Abing 159 F1

277

Slade Cl. Oxon

Thames Rd. Harw

lade Cl. Oxon 124 B1
lade End. Br-c-S 203 D1
lade Rd. Chol 221 D1
lade Rd. Didc 200 B1
lade Rd. Skch 188 C2
lade The. Charl 73 E2
lade The. Oxon 142 C4
lave Hill. Hadd 130 C3
laymaker Cl. Oxon 124 C1
loane Cl. Gori 249 E3
lopes The. Caver 259 E1
mith Barry Cres. Ch We 68 A2
mith Barry Rd. Ch We 68 A2
mith Cl. S Com 252 C3
mith's Cl. Aston 135 F1
mith's Hill. Let B 231 F3
mith's La. Wtpy 126 C4
nakehill La. Dedd 33 D2
nipe Rd. Ch We 68 A2
nowdon Mede. Oxon 124 A2
nowswick La. Busc 170 C3
nuff La. Shot 8 B4
nuggs La. E Hann 197 D4
oden Rd. Up Hey 63 E4
olters Cl. Lud 98 B4
omerton Rd. Mi Sto 50 A2
omerton Rd. N Ast 48 A4
omerton Rd. Up Hey 48 C1
omerville Dr. Bice 65 F2
omerville. Didc 219 D4
ongers Cl. N Hink 140 A4
onning La. Sonn 260 B1
onning Meadows. Sonn 260 B1
opwith Rd. Ch We 68 A3
orrel Rd. Oxon 143 D1
otwell St. Br-c-s 202 C1
outh Ave. Abing 159 F1
outh Ave. Hen-on-T 254 C4
outh Ave. Kidl 108 C3
outh Bar St. Banb 16 B3
outh Cl. Kidl 108 C3
outh Dr. Harw 217 E2
outh Dr. Sonn 260 B1
outh End. Gr Ro 29 D2
outh End. Hadd 130 C3
outh Gate Ct. Ch We 68 A2
outh Mere. Br No 116 B2
outh Newington Rd.
B St M 32 B3
outh Newington Rd. Blox 21 D1
outh Par. Cutte 123 D4
outh Park Ave. Didc 218 B4
outh Parks Rd. Oxon 123 E1
outh Rd. St Row 242 A1
outh Row. Chil 235 E4
outh Side. Ste As 62 A4
outh St. Banb 16 C4
outh St. Blew 237 D4
outh St. Caver 259 D1
outh St. Lo Hey 63 D3
outh St. Mi Bar 60 C4
uth St. Oxon 141 D4
outh St. Watch 191 E1
outh Stoke Rd. Woodc 240 A1
outh View Ave. Caver 259 E1
outh View Park. Caver 259 E1
outh View. Gt Bo 9 E4
outham Rd. Banb 9 E2
outham Rd. Cro 4 A2
outham Rd. Gt Bo 9 E2
outham Rd. Moll 4 A2
outhampton St. Far 172 C2
outhby Cl. Apple 158 A4
outhcroft. Mars 123 F3
outhdale Rd. Cutte 123 D4
outhdown Ct. S in V 194 C4
outhdown Rd. Caver 259 D3
outhend. Gars 162 C4
outhern By-pass Rd.
Kenn 141 E2
outhern By-pass Rd.
N Hink 140 C4
outhern By-pass Rd.
Oxon 141 F2
outhern By-pass Rd.
S Hink 141 D2
outhern Rd. Tha 147 F4
outherndene Cl. Read 257 E1
outhfield Dr. Sut C 199 F4
outhfield La. Frit 49 F4
outhfield Park. Oxon 142 A4
outhfield Rd. Oxon 142 A4
outhlands. Aston 135 F1
outhlawn. Witn 117 F4
outhmoor Pl. Oxon 123 D2
outhmoor Rd. Oxon 123 D2
outhmoor Way. Abing 179 F4
outhrop Rd. Ho No 30 A3
outhwold. Bice 65 F3
outhwood Rd. Curb 103 E1
overeign Cl. Didc 219 D4
a Cl. Highw 190 A4
an Hill. Shipl 260 A4
areacre La. Eyns 120 C4
arsey Pl. Cutte 109 D1
arsholt St. Spars 212 C2
ears The. Yarn 108 A3
eedwell St. Oxon 141 E4
Spencer Cl. Bice 65 E2
Spencer Cres. Oxon 142 A2
Spencers Cl. S in V 194 B4
Spenlove Cl. Abing 159 F1
Spenser Ave. Yarn 108 A3
Spey Rd. Abing 159 E2
Spier's La. M Gib 67 F1
Spindleberry Cl. Oxon 142 C1
Spindlers. Kidl 92 C1
Spindleside. Bice 65 F3
Spinney Cl. Caver 259 D4
Spinney Dr. Banb 16 C2
Spinney The. Laun 66 B1
Spinney The. Lech 150 B2
Spinneys Cl. Radl 160 C2
Spinneys The. Enst 58 C3
Spitfire Cl. Bice 66 A2
Sprigs Holly La. Bled R 189 D4
Spring Cl. Witn 118 A4
Spring Copse. S Hink 141 E2
Spring Farm. D Tew 47 E3
Spring Gdns. Abing 179 E4
Spring Hill Rd. Begb 107 F4
Spring Hill. Longw 176 B4
Spring La. Ast T 237 F4
Spring La. Gt Bo 9 E3
Spring La. Hors 143 E4
Spring La. Idb 69 D2
Spring La. Oxon 124 C1
Spring La. Oxon 142 B1
Spring La. Shipl 260 A3
Spring La. Watl 186 B1
Spring Path. Tha 147 F4
Spring Rd. Abing 179 E4
Spring St. Ch No 42 C2
Spring Wlk. Warg 255 E1
Springdale. Wall 221 E4
Springfield Ave. Banb 16 B2
Springfield Cl. Shriv 209 D3
Springfield Cl. Watl 186 B1
Springfield Dr. Abing 179 F4
Springfield End. Gori 249 E4
Springfield Gdns. Chin 168 B4
Springfield Oval. Witn 103 F1
Springfield Park. Witn 103 F1
Springfield Rd. Buck 65 F4
Springfield Rd. Kidl 108 C4
Springfield Rd. N Hink 140 B4
Springfield Rd. Skch 188 C2
Springfield Rd. Want 214 C2
Springhill Rd. Gori 249 E4
Springs The. Witn 118 A4
Springwell Hill. Bletch 78 A1
Springwood La. R Pep 253 D4
Spruce Dr. Bice 65 F3
Spruce Rd. Kidl 108 C4
Spur The. Warg 255 F2
Square Firs. Combe 90 A3
Square The. Abing 179 F4
Square The. Aston 135 F2
Square The. Ayn 35 E4
Square The. Duck 118 A2
Square The. Eyns 120 C4
Square The. K Sut 23 F3
Square The. L Cre 129 E3
Square The. Longw 156 A2
Square The. N Hink 122 B1
Square The. Oxon 142 B2
Square The. Pangb 256 B3
Square The. Swal 19 F4
Squire's Wlk. Wall 221 E3
Squires Cl. Br No 116 B2
Squires Rd. Watch 191 E1
Squitchey La. Cutte 123 D4
Stable Rd. Bice 65 F2
Staddlestone Cl. Read 257 E1
Stadhampton Rd. D St L 183 D3
Stadium Way. Read 258 A1
Staffordshire Cl. Read 257 F1
Stainer Pl. Oxon 123 F2
Stainfield Rd. Oxon 124 A3
Stainswick La. Shriv 209 E2
Stallpits Rd. Shriv 209 D4
Stanbridge Cl. Banb 16 A3
Standlake Rd. Duck 118 B2
Standlake Rd. Hardw 118 B2
Stanford Dr. Abing 179 F4
Stanford Rd. Far 173 D2
Stanier Pl. Banb 16 C4
Stanley Cl. N Hink 140 B4
Stanley Rd. Oxon 141 F4
Stanmore Cres. Cart 115 F2
Stansfeld Pl. Oxon 124 C1
Stansfield Cl. Oxon 124 C1
Stanton Harcourt Rd. Witn 118 B4
Stanton Rd. For H 125 F2
Stanton Rd. N Hink 140 C3
Stanville Rd. N Hink 140 A4
Stanway Cl.Witn 103 E1
Stanway Rd. Oxon 125 D2
Stanwell Cl. Mid Ch 11 D1
Stanwell Dr. Mid Ch 11 D1
Stanwell Lea. Mid Ch 11 D1
Stanwell Rd. Gt Bo 9 E4
Stapleton Rd. Oxon 124 B1
Star La. Watch 191 E1
Star Rd. Caver 259 E1
Starina Croft. Banb 9 D1
Starnham Rd. Duck 118 A2
Starwort Path. Oxon 142 C1
Station App. Bice 65 F1
Station App. Kidl 92 B1
Station Field Ind Est. Kidl 92 B1
Station La. Witn 118 A3
Station Rd. Ashb 228 A4
Station Rd. Ayn 35 D3
Station Rd. B Bou 133 F3
Station Rd. Bamp 134 C3
Station Rd. Bktn 82 A2
Station Rd. Bletch 93 D4
Station Rd. Br No 116 B2
Station Rd. Ch No 42 B1
Station Rd. Chin 168 B3
Station Rd. Chol 220 C1
Station Rd. Churc 54 C2
Station Rd. Cro 4 C1
Station Rd. Culh 180 C2
Station Rd. Didc 200 C1
Station Rd. Eyns 120 C4
Station Rd. Far 172 C2
Station Rd. Gori 249 D3
Station Rd. Grove 214 C4
Station Rd. Hadd 130 C3
Station Rd. Hen-on-T 244 C1
Station Rd. Highw 190 A3
Station Rd. Ho No 30 B4
Station Rd. King 54 C2
Station Rd. Laun 66 C2
Station Rd. Lech 150 B3
Station Rd. Lo Hey 62 B3
Station Rd. M Gib 67 F2
Station Rd. Mi Sto 50 B2
Station Rd. Pangb 256 B3
Station Rd. S Lei 119 E3
Station Rd. S u Wy 70 C1
Station Rd. Shipl 255 D2
Station Rd. Shriv 209 D3
Station Rd. Upt 218 B1
Station Rd. Wall 221 E4
Station Rd. Warg 255 E1
Station Rd. Wheat 144 A4
Station Rd. Wool 211 D4
Station Yard Ind Est. Adde 23 D1
Station Yd. Tha 148 A4
Staunton Rd. Oxon 124 A2
Staverton Rd. Oxon 123 D3
Steady's La. Sta Har 138 A4
Steep Rise. Oxon 124 B3
Steeple Cl. Blox 21 F2
Steepness Hill. B St M 32 C2
Stenton Cl. Abing 179 F3
Stephen Rd. Oxon 124 B2
Stephenson Rd. E Cha 214 A4
Steptoe Cl. Grove 196 B1
Sterling Cl. Bice 66 A2
Sterling Cl. Kidl 108 C4
Sterling Rd. Kidl 108 C4
Sterling Road App. Kidl 92 C1
Sterling Way. Read 258 A1
Stert Rd. Ast R 167 F2
Stert St. Abing 179 F4
Stevenson Cl. Bice 65 E2
Stevenson Dr. Abing 179 E4
Steventon Rd. Dray 199 D4
Steventon Rd. E Hann 197 F4
Stewart St. Oxon 141 E3
Stile Rd. Oxon 124 B2
Stimpsons Cl. N Hink 122 A1
Stirling Cl. Cart 115 E2
Stirling Cl. Caver 259 E3
Stirling Cl. Want 214 C3
Stirling Ct. Banb 15 F3
Stirlings Rd. Want 214 B2
Stockey End. Abing 160 B1
Stockham Park. Want 214 B3
Stockham Way. Want 214 B3
Stocking La. Shen 6 B1
Stockleys Rd. Mars 124 A3
Stockmore St. Oxon 141 F4
Stocks La. Steve 198 C2
Stocks Tree Cl. Yarn 108 A3
Stoke Pl. Oxon 124 B2
Stoke Row Rd. R Pep 252 C4
Stokes View. Pangb 256 B3
Stone Cl. N Hink 122 A1
Stone Croft. Chadl 57 E1
Stone Ct. Gr Ro 29 D2
Stone Hill. Blox 21 E2
Stone House Cl. K Bag 156 C1
Stone Quarry La. Oxon 142 A2
Stone St. Oxon 142 A4
Stone St. Read 258 A1
Stonebridge Rd. Steve 198 C3
Stoneburge Cres. Bice 65 F2
Stonebury Cl. Want 214 C3
Stonefield Dr. Highw 190 A2
Stonefield Way. Shriv 209 E3
Stonefields Riding. Stone 89 E4
Stonehill La. K Bag 176 B4
Stonehill Wlk. Abing 179 F2
Stonehill. Dray 179 E2
Stoneleigh Dr. Cart 115 E3
Stonesfield La. Charl 73 E1
Stonesfield Rd. Combe 90 A3
Stonesfield Riding. Spel 74 B1
Stonesfield. Didc 219 D4
Stoney La. Sto Ta 185 F4
Stonhouse Cres. Abing 160 C1
Stonor Cl. Didc 200 C1
Stonor Pl. Oxon 124 A1
Stour Cl. Didc 201 D1
Stow Rd. Bled 54 B1
Stow Rd. Fif 69 D1
Stowford Rd. Oxon 124 C2
Stowhill. Child 213 E2
Stowood Cl. Oxon 124 C2
Strafford Way. Tha 148 A4
Stratfield Rd. Cutte 123 D3
Stratfield Rd. Kidl 108 C3
Stratford Dr. Eyns 120 B4
Stratford La. Woot 76 A1
Stratford Rd. Dra 15 F4
Stratford Rd. Shen 6 C3
Stratford Rd. Wrox 14 C4
Stratford St. Oxon 141 F4
Strathmore Cl. Cart 115 F3
Stratton Audley Rd. Frin 52 B3
Stratton Audley Rd. S Lyn 51 D3
Stratton Way. Abing 179 F4
Strawberry Hill. Blox 21 F3
Strawberry Path. Oxon 142 C1
Strawberry Terr. Blox 21 F3
Stream Rd. Upt 218 B1
Streatley Hill. Stre 249 D3
Street The. Cr Gif 221 E1
Street The. Cr Gif 221 F4
Street The. Cr Gif 240 B4
Street The. Moul 239 D3
Street The. S Lyn 51 D3
Street The. S Sto 239 D2
Street The. Tidm 256 B1
Stuart Cl. Caver 259 D3
Stuart Way. Tha 130 A1
Stubble Cl. N Hink 140 A4
Stubbs Ave. Oxon 142 C4
Studdridge Ct. Skch 188 B2
Sturges Cl. Oxon 124 C2
Sturt Cl. Charl 73 E1
Sturt Rd. Charl 73 E2
Styles Cl. M Gib 67 F1
Styles The. Harw 217 E4
Sudbury Ct. Far 173 D2
Sudbury La. Longw 156 B2
Suffolk Ct. M Gib 67 F2
Suffolk Way. Abing 179 E3
Sugarswell La. Ratl 6 A3
Sugarswell La. Shen 6 A3
Sugworth Cres. Radl 160 C3
Sugworth La. Radl 160 B3
Sulham La. Pangb 256 C2
Summer Fields. Abing 160 A2
Summer Ley. B St M 32 C3
Summerfield Rd. Cutte 123 D4
Summerfield Rise. Gori 249 E4
Summerfield. Oxon 141 E3
Summerhill Rd. Cutte 123 D4
Summers Cl. Adde 23 D3
Summerside Rd. Buckl 174 C4
Summerton Pl. Ch No 42 C2
Summertown Ct. Cutte 123 D4
Summertown. E Hann 197 D3
Sunderland Ave. Cutte 109 D1
Sunderland Dr. Bice 66 A2
Sundew Cl. Oxon 143 D1
Sunningwell Rd. Oxon 141 E3
Sunningwell Rd. Sunn 159 F2
Sunny Rise. Hors 143 E3
Sunnyside. Bens 203 F3
Sunnyside. Oxon 142 B3
Sunnyside. Wheat 144 B4
Surley Row. Caver 259 D2
Surley Row. Caver 259 D3
Sussex Dr. Banb 9 D1
Sutton Cl. Abing 179 F4
Sutton Courtenay Rd.
Sut C 199 F3
Sutton La. Sta Har 120 A1
Sutton Rd. Mil 199 F3
Sutton Rd. Oxon 124 A3
Sutton Wick La. Dray 179 E1
Suzan Cres. Want 214 C3
Swalcliffe Lea. Swal 14 A1
Swalcliffe Rd. Swal 20 A4
Swalcliffe Rd. Tad 20 A4
Swale Dr. Didc 201 D1
Swallow Cl. Bice 81 D4
Swan Cl. Grove 196 B1
Swan Cl. Lech 150 B2
Swan Cl. Mid Ch 17 F4
Swan Close Rd. Banb 16 B3
Swan Ind Est. Banb 16 B3
Swan La. Burf 100 C3
Swan La. Far 172 C2
Swan La. Gt Bo 9 E4
Swan Lane Cl. Burf 100 C3
Swan St. Eyns 120 C4
Swan St. Oxon 123 D1
Swan Wlk. Tha 147 F4
Swanhall La. Hail 104 A3
Swansea Rd. Read 259 D1
Swansea Terr. Read 257 E1
Swanston Rd. Whitc 256 B4
Sweeps La. Burf 100 C3
Sweet Briar. March 178 B3
Sweetmans Rd. N Hink 140 B4
Swerford Rd. Ho No 30 A3
Swift Cl. Bice 65 E2
Swift Way. Bens 204 B2
Swinbourne Rd. Oxon 142 A1
Swinbrook Cl. Read 257 E2
Swinbrook Rd. Cart 115 E3
Swinbrook Rd. S u Wy 85 F3
Swinburne Rd. Abing 180 A4
Swinburne Rd. Oxon 141 F3
Swindon Rd. Highw 190 A3
Swindon St. Highw 190 A3
Swingburn Pl. Witn 118 A4
Swinstead Ct. Chalg 184 B3
Sworford La. G Mil 144 C3
Sycamore Cl. Abing 159 E1
Sycamore Cl. L Cre 129 E3
Sycamore Cl. Si Go 19 D4
Sycamore Cl. Watl 186 A1
Sycamore Cl. Witn 104 B1
Sycamore Cres. Kenn 160 C4
Sycamore Dr. Banb 16 B1
Sycamore Dr. Cart 115 E2
Sycamore Dr. Tha 147 F4
Sycamore Gdns. Bice 65 F2
Sycamore Rd. Ambr 81 E2
Sycamore Rd. Laun 66 B1
Sycamore Rd. N Hink 140 B4
Sycamore Wlk. Grove 196 B1
Sydenham Gr. Syd 167 F4
Sylvester Cl. Burf 100 C3
Sympson Cl. Abing 179 F3
Syringa Wlk. Banb 9 D1

Tackley Pl. Oxon 123 D2
Tadmarton Rd. Blox 21 D3
Tadmarton Rd. Tad 21 D3
Taggs Gate. Oxon 124 C3
Tait Dr. Up Hey 63 D4
Talbot Cl. Banb 15 F4
Talbot Cl. Caver 259 E1
Talbot Fields. Bamp 135 D2
Talbot Rd. Cutte 109 D1
Talbot Way. Purl 257 E2
Talisman Rd. Bice 80 C4
Tamar Cres. Bice 65 D2
Tamar Way. Didc 201 D1
Tangmere Ave. Cart 115 F2
Tangmere Cl. Bice 66 A2
Tanner's La. Burf 100 B3
Tanners Ct. Charl 73 D2
Tanners La. Adde 22 C2
Tanners La. Eyns 120 C4
Tanners La. Maple 258 C4
Tannery Cl. Burf 100 C3
Taphouse Ave. Witn 104 A1
Tarrant Ave. Witn 104 B1
Taston Rd. Spel 73 D4
Tatham Rd. Abing 159 F1
Tatlings Rd. Steve 198 C3
Taverner Pl. Oxon 123 F2
Tavistock Ave. Didc 218 B4
Tawney St. Oxon 142 A4
Taylor Cl. Bice 65 F2
Tchure The. Dedd 33 F2
Teal Cl. Banb 16 C2
Teal Cl. Grove 196 B1
Teale Cl. U Arn 96 C4
Telford Cres. Sonn 260 C1
Telford Rd. Bice 66 A2
Templar Rd. Cutte 109 D1
Templars Cl. Wheat 144 A4
Temple Rd. Oxon 142 B3
Temple St. Bri 98 A1
Temple St. Oxon 141 F4
Tenby Ave. Caver 259 E3
Tenlands. Mid Ch 17 F4
Tennis The. Cass 107 E1
Tennyson Cl. Banb 16 A2
Tennyson Dr. Abing 179 E3
Tenpenny. Dorch 202 B4
Tenth St. Harw 217 D2
Terrington Cl. Abing 160 A1
Tessa Rd. Read 258 C1
Tew La. Woot 75 F3
Tewer The. Stone 89 E4
Thackley End. Oxon 123 D3
Thame La. Cl Ham 181 D3
Thame La. Culh 180 B2
Thame Park Rd. Tha 148 A3
Thame Rd. Bktn 82 A2
Thame Rd. Chin 168 A4
Thame Rd. G Has 164 C4
Thame Rd. G Mil 145 E1
Thame Rd. Hadd 130 B3
Thame Rd. L Cre 129 E2
Thame Rd. L Mil 164 A4
Thame Rd. Pidd 97 E3
Thame Rd. Tow 148 C4
Thame Rd. Warb 203 D4
Thames Ave. Bice 65 D2
Thames Ave. Pangb 256 B3
Thames Ave. Read 259 D1
Thames Dr. Sonn 260 C4
Thames Gdns. Charl 73 D2
Thames Mead. Cr Gif 221 F4
Thames Rd. Gori 249 D3
Thames Rd. Harw 217 D2

'est St. H-on-T   **Ypres Way. Abing**

OS ORDNANCE SURVEY
STREET ATLASES

The Ordnance Survey / Philip's County Street Atlases provide unique and definitive mapping of entire counties

Counties available

- ◆ **Berkshire**
- ◆ **Buckinghamshire**
- ◆ **East Essex**
- ◆ **West Essex**
- ◆ **North Hampshire**
- ◆ **South Hampshire**
- ◆ **Hertfordshire**
- ◆ **East Kent**
- ◆ **West Kent**
- ◆ **Nottinghamshire**
- ◆ **Oxfordshire**
- ◆ **Surrey**
- ◆ **East Sussex**
- ◆ **West Sussex**
- ◆ **Warwickshire**

The County Street Atlases are revised and updated on a regular basis and new titles are added to the series. Many counties are now available in full-size hardback and softback editions as well as handy pocket-size versions.

The series is available from all good bookshops or by mail order direct from the publisher. However, the order form opposite may not reflect the complete range of titles available so it is advisable to check by telephone before placing your order. Payment can be made by credit card or cheque/postal order in the following ways:

By phone

Phone your order through on our special Credit Card Hotline on 0933 410511. Speak to our customer service team during office hours (9am to 5pm) or leave a message on the answering machine, quoting CSA94, your full credit card number plus expiry date and your full name and address

By post

Simply fill out the order form opposite (you may photocopy it) and send it to:
Cash Sales Department, Reed Book Services, PO Box 5, Rushden, Northants, NN10 6YX

STREET ATLASES

CSA94

	Hardback £12.99		Softback £8.99		Pocket £4.99		Total
	QUANTITY	TOTAL £	QUANTITY	TOTAL £	QUANTITY	TOTAL £	£
Berkshire		ISBN 0-540-05992-7		ISBN 0-540-05993-5		ISBN 0-540-05994-3	
Buckinghamshire		ISBN 0-540-05989-7		ISBN 0-540-05990-0		ISBN 0-540-05991-9	
East Essex		ISBN 0-540-05848-3		ISBN 0-540-05866-1		ISBN 0-540-05850-5	
West Essex		ISBN 0-540-05849-1		ISBN 0-540-05867-X		ISBN 0-540-05851-3	
North Hampshire		ISBN 0-540-05852-1		ISBN 0-540-05853-X		ISBN 0-540-05854-8	
South Hampshire		ISBN 0-540-05855-6		ISBN 0-540-05856-4		ISBN 0-540-05857-2	
Hertfordshire		ISBN 0-540-05995-1		ISBN 0-540-05996-X		ISBN 0-540-05997-8	
East Kent		ISBN 0-540-06026-7		ISBN 0-540-06027-5		ISBN 0-540-06028-3	
West Kent		ISBN 0-540-06029-1		ISBN 0-540-06031-3		ISBN 0-540-06030-5	
Nottinghamshire		ISBN 0-540-05858-0		ISBN 0-540-05859-9		ISBN 0-540-05860-2	
Oxfordshire		ISBN 0-540-05986-2		ISBN 0-540-05987-0		ISBN 0-540-05988-9	
Surrey		ISBN 0-540-05983-8		ISBN 0-540-05984-6		ISBN 0-540-05985-4	
East Sussex		ISBN 0-540-05875-0		ISBN 0-540-05874-2		ISBN 0-540-05873-4	
West Sussex		ISBN 0-540-05876-9		ISBN 0-540-05877-7		ISBN 0-540-05878-5	
Warwickshire	£10.99	ISBN 0-540-05642-1					

Name

Address

Postcode

I enclose a cheque/postal order for £ _____ made payable to **Reed Book Services** or please debit my

◄ *Access*
◄ *American Express*
◄ *Visa*
account by

£ _____

Account number

Expiry date

Signature

Please tick this box if you do not wish your name to be used by other carefully selected organisations that may wish to send you information about other products and services

◆ *Free postage and packing* ◆ *All available titles will normally be dispatched within 5 working days of receipt of order, but please allow up to 28 days for delivery.*